THE DEATH OF AMERICA

AMERICA

The Insidious Takeover

Bradley - J.: [Franks] and

Co-Author: Robert - C.: [Simpson]

Published in the United States of America

ISBN 978-1-962730-86-0 (SC)

Library of Congress Control Number: 2024922330

Bradley Franks PUBLISHING
222 West 6th Street
Suite 400, San Pedro, CA, 90731
www.stellarliterary.com

Order Information and Rights Permission:

Quantity sales. Special discounts might be available on quantity purchases by corporations, associations, and others. For details, contact the publisher at the address above.

For Book Rights Adaptation and other Rights Permission.
Call us at toll-free 1-888-945-8513 or send us an email at
admin@stellarliterary.com.

Dedication:

This Book is dedicated for all those who believe that THE-UNITED-STATES-CORPORATE-GOVERNMENT and its CORPORATE-SUBSIDIARIES and the UNDECLARED-IMPOSTER-FOREIGN-AGENTS are at fault in trying to keep All American-Civilians from 'Exercising' their RIGHTS by using subjugation, hatred, trickery, coercion, threats and duress.

Acknowledgments

We thank all of the American-Civilians who helped us as much as they could without THE-UNITED-STATES-CORPORATE-GOVERNMENT and its IMPOSTER-AGENTS punishing them without justification or reason.

Contents

Chapter 1:
THE GREAT EVIL

Within this chapter we present evidence, 'proof' for proving (I know this is redundant…but I wish to prove a point), that throughout history, the Royal Heads England, the Zionist [jews] (in general), THE United-States-Corporate-Government and the Vatican in Rome through and with the 'Pontiffs' help have been deceiving and working for the destruction of the 'united-States-of-America' from within…by the removal of our "Civil-Rights" and replacing them with 'Privileges' ("license, permits and fees" through "Statutes, Codes and Ordinances" and further-forcing Indigenous-Americans, Native-Americans, and U. S. Citizens to pay for them under what is known as "Bill of Attainders, Bill of Pain and Punishment" and "Cruel and Unusual Punishment" through 'their' "Policy and Procedures" and by 'Corporate By-Laws' placing all Free-Americans under 'indentured servitude'. God was a lawmaker! Yet man and women (Humans) fail and fall-short of following GODS-Laws; Specific humans (the so-called 'Professionals') fail to-follow 'Man's Laws' and yet these people claim "WE ARE NOT ABOVE THE LAW"! Even trying to follow the 10 - Commandments is a chore for most - if not all humans. Yet 'no-man' or 'no-woman' can 'defend' their actions before GOD with the broad-definition of "Color of Law" or their "Corporate By-Laws". 'Herein, lays a great evil'.

Here is the start with a 'brief-history-lesson' that-many-have "forgotten", we were 'meant-to-forget' or 'history was re-written' for the 'benefit of the victors'; a simple "truth" … 'Enlightenment'. This term would be best used for showing our-past history than to just use the word ('History') for the description of human-education. The "Facts" cannot be swept under something (i.e. the carpet or buried in red-tape) for the appearance of 'invisibility'. It is said that "only the winner in a war can write history for their benefit".

The 'Great Evil of and for America' started in 1945 at the end of World War I and II. However, I would like to point out that the Great Evil

1

goes farther back when Moses climbed Mt. Sinai and the Zionist [jews] constructed an 'idol' of a "Golden-Calf"... and they have the audacity to call Christians 'idolaters', 'murderers', and other 'ill-begotten'-terminology.

The Zionist [jews] claim that Christians are murderers. However, it was the Zionist [jews] who 'paid' Judas (with silver) to betray and have Jesus-Christ crucified; it was the Romans who did the actual crime of crucifixion making the Zionist [jews] accomplices of a premeditated-murder. The only thing Jesus-Christ was guilty of was preaching peace, tolerance and love... It's not surprising that the Zionist [jews] felt 'threatened' by this; for there is no-money in "love, peace or tolerance". It is stated in the Bible that Jesus-Christ [a Nazarene jew], was taken before Pontius Pilate and was judged to be innocent only to have the Zionist [jew-rabble] scream for the release of a Seditious-Murderer by the name of Barabbas (a jew). With this act and the Crucifixion of Jesus-Christ, the Zionist [jews] have proven through acts and deeds that they only respect criminals, liars, cheats and thieves; because they themselves are.

Some readers of this book may take offense... (The Truth-Hurts)...to what we are writing about in this chapter... However, the information within this book can be explored and found on the internet and everyone knows that everything on the internet must be the truth. After all, the internet is full of 'professionals' and "opinions". Remember, anything and everything that the "Political-Corporate-Whores" and the News-Media put in writing or verbal 'reports' must be the truth and everyone else is nothing but 'sheepeople' and are always wrong and are found 'guilty' for any 'crime' these so-called professionals claim against American-Civilians or U. S. Citizens. The Courts and its Officers seem to know how to "hide", "suppress", and/or "commit-perjury about the existence of evidence for or against" their victims.

What we have uncovered and exposed is how the Zionist [jews] infiltrated into the American Banking, News Media, Court and Political Systems and are committing Terrorist Acts against Americans, Christians and other International Countries alike by their "biased-judgmental" opinions.

2

We really need to look at history, 1938 in Germany. The Zionist [jews] in Germany was trying to take over their country (just like here in America). They took over the News Media, the Banks, the Courts and the German Government. The [jewish] population, at the time, was approximately 1%. When the German people caught on to the insidious and deceitful actions of what and how the [jews] were doing, they tried in a polite way, to get them to leave. By starting a campaign on April 1, 1933, with a boycott of [jewish]-owned shops and businesses.

Germans were encouraged not to use [jewish] Doctors or Lawyers and [jewish] civil-servants, teachers and others employed by the mass media were fired. As the 1933 German Boycott took effect/affect, many [jews] took the hint and left Germany. However, it was just the very wealthy-elite and a large number of Scientists that made the 'escape'. The middle and poorer class of [jews] were used as 'lambs for the slaughter', so to speak, and were left behind by their own people. The German Government and its people did not just wake up one Saturday morning and decide to "commit a Holocaust against the [jews]" or any other race that was a victim of their anger and hatred. Furthermore, there were more than just [jews] that were put to death in Concentration Camps. The [jews] just screamed the loudest over the "Crimes against Humanity" to any country that would sympathize with their plight. In reality and truth, the [jews] brought the German reaction upon themselves.

The historic responsibility of world [jewry] for the outbreak and widening of WWI and WWII has been proven so clearly that it does not need to be talked about any further. The [jews] wanted war, and they got it. They received a penalty that was certainly hard, but more than deserved. The [jews] will perish according to their own law: "An eye for an eye; a tooth for a tooth."

All [jews] by virtue of their birth, race and religion are part of an international-conspiracy against America and other Countries that are not of the [jewish] religion, beliefs, or thinking. Like the Royal heads of England and the Vatican, the [jews] want America and those Countries that are not [jewish] defeated and annihilated, and will do all in their power to bring it about including lying, cheating, stealing, seditious acts and falsifying any and all government or non-government documents.

The [jews] will conceal themselves, mimic their surroundings, adopt the color of the background (including color of law), and adjust to the environment, in order to wait for the proper moment. Who among us Americans had any idea that the enemy was beside us that a silent or clever auditor was attending to conversations on the street, subway, or shops? There are [jews] hidden in America that we cannot recognize by external signs. These are the most dangerous. It always happens that when we take some measures or speak out against the [jews], English, U.S., and International News Media report it, the story the very next day. Even today the [jews] still have secret connections to our enemies abroad and use these not only in their own cause, but in all military matters and business matters that deal with American Interests as well. The enemy is in our midst. What makes more sense than to at least make this plainly visible to Americans?

After reading this chapter I am quite sure that most readers will say something to the effect that "[jews] are human to". My observation and comment to that is this; "We have never denied that, just as we never denied the humanity of murderers, pedophiles, thieves, organized crime bosses; though we never felt the need to parade down the streets with them". Every [jew] is a decent [jew] who has found an ignorant-American who thinks them decent! As if this was a reason to give [jews] a kind of honorable escort. What nonsense and stupidity.

How stupid and thoughtless are the arguments of the backward friends of the [jews] in the face of a problem that has occupied mankind for millennia! How they would gape if they ever see their dear [jews] in power! However, that would be too late. There are differences between people just as there are differences between animals. Some people are good, others bad. The same is true of animals. The fact the [jews] live among us is no proof that they belong among us, just as a flea does not belong on a household pet simply because it lives in a house.

If we do not stop the rape and the destruction of America, these "harmless-looking" [jew] chaps will suddenly become raging wolves. They will attack any non-[jew] to carry out revenge. There are enough examples throughout history to prove this point. The [jews] have learned some "tricks". They know the "good-natured" Americans in us, always ready to shed sentimental tears for the injustices done to them. One suddenly has the impression that the [jew] population consists only of little babies whose childish helplessness might move us, or else fragile old elders. The [jews] send out the pitiable. They may confuse some harmless souls for a while, but eventually the truth will come out and Americans will no longer be fooled. We will know exactly what the situation really is.

The [jews] will never give us rest. If they could, they would drive one nation after another into war against America. Who cares about the difficulties they brought on themselves? They only want to force the world to accept their "bloody financial domination" with the help of the Vatican and the Royal heads of England. (We will explain how the Vatican and the Royal heads of England fit in to this equation). The [jews] are a parasitic race that feeds like a foul fungus on the culture of healthy but ignorant Americans.

We Americans, just like the German people during WWI and WWII, have a fateful flaw in our national character; it is 'forgetfulness' and 'forgiveness'. This failing speaks well of our human decency and generosity, but not always for our political wisdom or intelligence. We believe everyone else is as good natured as we are.

Our national virtue is our national weakness. We should not be so good natured, since our enemies are not noble enough to overlook our mistakes. This advice applies anywhere and everywhere; it applies to our relations with the [jews]. Carelessness here is not only a weakness; it is disregard of duty and a crime against the security of the state and our Country. The [jews] long for one thing: to reward our foolishness with bloodshed and terror.

The [jews] are our destruction. They with the help of the Royal heads of England, the Vatican and The United-States-Corporate-Government have started the destruction of America and our people. This plan must be blocked.

There are no-distinctions between [jews]. Each [jew] is a sworn enemy of America and its people. If a [jew] does not make their hostility plain, it is from cowardice and slyness, not because they love us.

The [jews] enjoy the protection of our enemies. That is all the proof we need to show how harmful they are for America and its people. The

[jews] are the enemy's agents among us. Anyone who stands by or defends them aids the enemy. Remember, the [jews] are not only citizens of the United-States-Corporate-Government through "Bribery" and illegal "Trickery" but they are also citizens of Israel…this is known as a dual-citizenship. Any other Natural-American or U. S. Citizen would be fined, imprisoned or both for claiming dual citizenship.

If the [jews] appeal to your sentimentality, realize that they are hoping for your forgetfulness, and pity for what was done too them in the past and let them know that you see through them and hold them in contempt.

A decent-enemy will deserve generosity after losing a war. The [jew] however is not a decent enemy, though they try to seem so.

The [jews] were responsible for their predicament during WWI and WWII. The treatment they received from the German Government or German Country was hardly unjust. After all, the Germans were protecting their Country and Government from foreign invaders.

It is the job of the government to deal with them. No one has the right to act on their own, but each has the duty to support the state or country's measures against the [jews], to defend them with others, and to avoid being misled by any [jewish] tricks. The security of America and of our Organic-states requires that of us all.

In the years leading up to WWI and WWII, Americans favored a position of isolationism. Surrounded by water on a relatively peaceful continent, Americans felt secure at home. In trading weapons, America used a 'Cash and Carry' system wherein countries wishing to purchase military goods while at war would have to pay up front and carry the goods away in non-American ships. This system helped in avoiding problems that caused the American involvement in WWI and WWII.

When Germany invaded Poland on September 1, 1939, Franklin D. Roosevelt asked Congress to pass the Neutrality Act of 1939, which would allow only cash and carry trade with the belligerents. However, after his third election in 1940, FDR proposed giving the British aid for the war without cash in return (the Lend-Lease Act) and supplying Britain with $7 Billion in aid, (even though Americans were in the middle of the Great Depression) stating that America was an "arsenal of democracy".

This signaled the beginning of America choosing sides before they knew all-of-the-facts. In addition, this is how the Royal heads of England and the [jews] began infiltrating into our Government and Banking systems. However, we are sure that someone will find that the Royal heads of England have been trying for years to over-throw America and the American Government before WWI and WWII. Furthermore, during this time the [jew] population was insignificant in trying to take over America or the Banking system. However, President Harry S. Truman would change that and not for the good of America.

It is a simple shame how the Zionist [jews] had to bribe the Political-Corporate-Whores just to be recognized as a state. However, to this day Israel is not a state.

During the postwar Germany, a "massacre of gargantuan proportions occurred. President Truman, at the insistence of [jewish] Billionaires, morgenthau and baruch (Truman's handlers) ordered that millions of innocent German citizens – men, women and children – be starved, frozen to death, or otherwise killed".

"The psychopathic President and his cohort, Stalin, under the Morgenthau Plan, had millions of Germans rounded up and taken to the same concentration camps previously run by Nazis. In some of these camps (see the book, An Eye for An Eye by John Sack), believe it or not, inhuman [jew] guards and Camp Commandants raped and tortured the German women and children. The heads of little babies were smashed against walls, and male prisoners were often beaten to death".

"Two dedicated American patriots, Secretary of Defense James Forrestal and General George Patton refused to go along with the [jew] treachery and takeover of the White House. Both were cruelly assassinated. Forrestal was "suicide," being thrown out of a sixteenth-floor window. General George Patton who objected to the morgenthau Plan vowed to tell the Americans the truth was assassinated".

"On May 14, 1948, President Truman issued a declaration recognizing Israel as a new nation in the Middle East. However, the [jews] knew months in advance that Truman would do this. A [jew] powerbroker, by the name of abraham feinberg had just months before, given the President a two-million-dollar bribe - $100 bills packed in suitcases – to recognize Israel. This bribe to Truman, confirmed by recently released FBI archives, means that Israel is today and always has been an illegitimate-non-state established on the basis of a criminal act. While President Truman meticulously followed the marching orders dictated to him by his [jew] overlords, he privately chafed about his subordinate status. He despised the [jews'] smug, superior attitudes and resented the fact that they had bribed him to recognize Israel".

"Truman finally rebelled in what appears to have been a small but significant way. When the declaration to recognize Israel was brought to him for his signature, it first read: "…the new Jewish State of Israel.". Truman took his pen and lined through the words "new Jewish" This meant that the U.S. recognized not a "new Jewish State" – that would make it a religious and racial designation – but simply a "State".

"To this day, the jews insist theirs is a "Jewish" State, a jewish religious theocracy. Israel was recognized by President Truman and the U.S. as a secular State, not a jewish religious theocracy. This has tremendous significance for the Palestinians. Today the Palestinians are unfairly treated as non-citizens in Israel. They are not allowed to vote or own property as the jews spout the fiction that Israel was founded as a jewish State and those of other races and religions do not belong."

"Years after Truman's death an entry dated July 21, 1947 from the President's Personal Diary was found: "The Jews, I find are very selfish…when they have power, physical or political, neither Hitler nor Stalin has anything on them for cruelty or mistreatment to the underdog". Because of this entry in his Personal Diary, the [jew] elite belatedly branded Harry S. Truman an "anti-Semite". This just goes to show you that no matter how one slavishly one serves the cause of Israel and the [jews]; even a private-opinion written in one's personal papers leaves that person vulnerable to unfair, smear charges of Anti-Semitism. However, no one can accurately say that President Truman did not fully understand the unpatriotic sentiments and attitudes of the [jews] who reside in America. In 1956, after Truman's retirement, he confided in an interview his knowledge that American [jews] were disloyal to the U.S. "When a Jew born and living in America talks to his Jewish companions about 'our government,' he means the government of Israel".

"God hath chosen the weak things of the world to confound the things which are mighty". (St. Paul)

This is part of what we wanted to show you, the reader, that America's take-over by this twisted and perverse race (i.e. Zionist [jews]) is not just an isolated incident or something the [jews] decided over-night. Furthermore, we also point out that when the United-States-Corporate-Government became involved with WWI, the Germans came to the conclusions that we became their enemy when we started helping the [jews] out of the country they, the [jews], tried to take over and punished the Germans for defending their Country. However, we will admit that Hitler (a professional) and his staff did go too far. However, ask yourself this question…What would you have done differently if you were the German-Leader?

Look at it this way, if your neighbor's home was being robbed and your neighbor was not at home, would you stand by and watch as the thief cleaned them out? Now what if your neighbor came home and caught the thief in the act, would you stop and beat your neighbor just because they were trying to protect what was rightfully theirs? Well, this is just what the Zionist [jews] did and are/is doing still to this day. They used our ignorance and sympathies for the 'holocaust' to our disadvantage and unfortunately, we, Americans, became the proverbial "bad-guys" to the German people.

Now we get into the fact that America was not the only country that helped the [jews] out of the predicament they caused. The Vatican also became involved through Pope Pius XII.

"According to the Israeli diplomat pinchas lapide concluded his careful review of Pius XII's activities with the following words: "The Catholic Church, under the pontificate of Pius XII, was instrumental in saving the lives as many as 860,000 jews from certain death at Nazi hands." Pope Pius XII mainly provided false birth-certificates, religious-disguises, (Fraudulent-Documents) and safe keeping in cloistered monasteries and convents. He oversaw efforts that helped save hundreds of thousands of jews from deportation to Nazi death camps."

It was great that the Vatican became involved with World War I by saving the [jews] from what, in essence, they started. However, ask yourself this question: since all of Europe was in turmoil over WWI, where did all of the saved [jews] go? I mean after all, in reality, they could not be kept in Europe for long. With their "false and fraudulent" documents the 'rich' and 'wealthy' [jews] were brought to America where they could blend into our society. The United-States-Corporate-Government claims only 100,000 [jews] were allowed into our country during World War I. However, I find this highly unlikely and not exactly the truth. There were a lot of undocumented or should I say "extra-legal" documentation into the United-States-Corporate-Government. After all, the Vatican admitted to creating "false" documents for the [jews] in the 'hundreds-of-thousands' through "Fraud and Trickery". Remember, the [jews] were and are not as 'innocent' as they seem to want Americans to believe.

Throughout history the [jews] have tried to take over other nations since 250 AD Carthage to 1948 AD Arab Countries. Research shows that (109+) locations expelled the [jews] for the same crimes they committed in Germany. Furthermore, the [jews] also played the 'poor pitiful [jews]' against these countries. However, they were caught, stopped and expelled. This includes areas of the United States of America under General Ulysses S. Grants' Jurisdiction in 1862….not once but twice out of America. Ask yourself this question, if the [jews] were as noble and favored as is stated in their [jewish] propaganda or beliefs, why would they be expelled out of 109+ Countries? Is it possible for 109+ Locations around the world to be wrong against one specific race of crooks?

I know that you are asking yourself 'What does the Pope, the Holy See, and the Vatican have to do with anything?' All forms of law begin with Ecclesiastical Law and including the ancient Law Merchant and Law of the Sea, the Roman Civil Law, and most recently, the Uniform Commercial Code and International Criminal Code are ultimately defined by the Holy See and administered by the Roman Curia, under the Trusteeship of the Pope. Control and caretaking of the earlier law forms was undertaken by the Holy See during the first Holy Roman Empire (800 A.D) and by contract and consent, has remained in the Holy See's control ever since. The two more recent law forms, the Uniform Commercial Code and the International Criminal Code are copyrighted by Vatican subsidiaries.

The Papacy has functioned in two distinct roles for over 1200 years, exercising both sacred and temporal powers. The Pope is named in two distinct offices and wears two different hats. As the leader of the Church and in sacred office, he is properly regarded as "His Holiness Pope Francis". As the CEO in charge or worldwide commercial affairs execution the temporal powers of the second office, he operates as "FRANCISCUS". Just short of being 'Emperor'.

Duties of both offices are distinct and yet ultimately inter-related, due to the Pope's responsibility to oversee the Global Estate Trust. Since the 1400's every Pope has acted as the ultimate Trustee and Steward of the entire Earth conceived as a Trust: The Global Estate Trust. This Trust, created over 400 years ago, is divided into three jurisdictions – Air, Land and Sea. All three jurisdictions are further divided into realms of the Living and the Dead – the living being actual flesh and blood men and women and animals and other creatures in which the blood flows or sap ascends, the dead being all those organic entities who have died and all legal fiction entities, including trusts, corporations, foundations, transmitting utilities, cooperatives, limited liability partnerships and so on.

The Air Jurisdiction remains with the Holy See, is universal, global and inclusive in nature regardless of the individual religious preferences of beliefs, rules all affairs from the surface of the Earth to the Heavens, is inhabited by spiritual beings both living and dead, has a global population, functions under the Law of Love and the Ancient Law of Freewill and is administered via ecclesiastical canon law generally under direction of the Rectors of the National Shrines established in each country.

The Sea Jurisdiction is international in character, has an international citizenship, rules all affairs on or directly below the surface of the seas and navigable inland waters, is in habited by living men and women known as Merchants and Sailors, and all living sea creatures, as well as all ships and legal (corporate entities doing-business-as) fiction entities engaged in maritime and admiralty businesses and contracts, functions under the Law Merchant (maritime) and Law of the Sea (Admiralty) and is administered worldwide by the British Crown Temple (doing business as) Inner City of London (also known as) "Westminster", and the Lords of the Sea.

The Land Jurisdiction is national in character. It is inhabited by living men and women, together with land animals and plants, has citizenship based on nationality and which in most instances include both living men and women, legal-fiction (oxymoron) entities, rules affairs of the land from the surface to the depths beneath, functions under The Law of the Land, and is administered worldwide by the Universal Postal Union and the Individual national Postmasters.

Each jurisdiction – Air, Land or Sea – has its own law forms. The Air functions under ecclesiastical and canon law. The Sea functions under the Law Merchant and Law of the Sea. The land functions under the Law of the Land (NOT statutes, codes or ordinances).

Here is the big picture, whether you like it or not…in the end all of this is administered by the Holy See and the Roman Catholic Church, which has struggled by turns to maintain an "orderly and peaceful Kingdom on Earth" and at times throughout its history has admittedly been overwhelmed by corruption and human error. What they call error is simply put…crimes against humanity, lies, trickery, deceit and theft all in the name of "doing business" and keeping man and woman as indentured-servants. By its nature and function the Global Estate Trust has established a vast interlocking trust directorate that exists worldwide and extends for the Holy See down to the local level of its FICTITIOUS-government-administration.

The definition of a trust is as follows: "When a Donor places assets into the care of a Trustee for the good of Beneficiaries; it forms the Global Estate Trust; it was considered that Jesus Christ placed the entire planet in the care of St. Peter, that the Pope is Peter's successor Trustee, and over time it has been realized that all people and living creatures are intended Beneficiaries of the Global Estate Trust, not just members of the Roman Catholic Church or Empire. This realization is one of the most direct results of the Protestant Reformation, which asserted individual dominion over the Earth as granted in Genesis 1:26 – 28. Today, as confirmed by Popes John Paul II, Benedict XVI, and Francis, the Global Estate Trust serves all (people?) regardless of faith, color or creed.

THE-United-States-Corporate-Government, English Monarchy, the Vatican and the [jews] are in collusion and conspiring against all Americans to revoke their 'Freedoms' and 'Civil Rights' and place us under indentured-servitude and give us only that which they throw scraps from their tables. These Corporate-Governments do not want living beings that are as equal to Christ in their beliefs. I mean Christ himself went into the desert after (40 days) and told the devil (Lucifer) to basically "get lost". Exact words were "Get the behind me Satan. For you have NOTHING to offer". What makes you think that ANY-MAN can promise the same? And be told the same thing?

This is how they claim a Global Estate Trust functions through the Pope under "one of his hats". The Global Estate Trust is over 400 years old. It is older than the United States of America either for the 'People' or for the United-States-Corporate-Government "For Profit", was even formed. It has organized the entire planet according to its system of Postal Districts-also called "federal-districts" in America. The Global Estate Trust (CEO the POPE) and the services it provides – legal-services (lol), banking-services (lol), police-services (lol), postal-services – is so ubiquitous, so integrated worldwide, that we take its existence for granted and wrongly think that our individual government provides all this. (LOL).

The truth of the matter in this, is that the so-called "federal-government" in America has always been owned and operated as a 'private for-profit-governmental services company' operating under 'contract' to provide certain stipulated governmental services, and-later in history, has been operated as an umbrella corporation with subsidiaries created as franchises and agencies under subcontract to provide these same services by the Global Estate Trust and its national subsidiaries.

However, in reality and by their laws these agencies don't exist. They are known as Fictitious-Corporations (oxymoron) and they want nothing more than to steal your (and we use the term 'your' loosely) 'INCOME'.

Note: In the eighteenth century when the original equity contract known as "The Constitution for the United States" was drawn up, the word "federal" was a synonym or "contract", so the nature of the government an entity under contract to provide services was apparent for the people. The State legislatures formed to represent the land jurisdiction as separate nations – the larger equivalent of city-states-and the people inhabiting these organic states (note: the states were not organic. They

13

were not a living, breathing, born entity); however, they were fully aware of the subservient nature of the federal government in all matters not clearly delegated to it as were the Founders and Framers of the Constitution. Article X clearly reserves all other rights to the [s]tates (significant) and the people.

Unfortunately, our entire planet receives governmental services from a gigantic interlocking trust-directorate: The Global Estate Trust. (And we as Americans have the right to say "No-More"). The gentleness with which generations of Popes have exercised their power as the ultimate Trustee should not be mistaken for lack of power, but rather as respect for Free will and reluctance to interfere with those entrusted to administer their own affairs. In the temporal realm a Pope is a man like any other man, and it is often difficult to obtain all the facts and to be assured of right action – not unlike the Corporate-Government-Judicial-System or the 'Fictitious-Corporate–Government' as a whole. Restraint and tolerance have therefore been the hallmarks governing the exerciser of temporal power by the Popes for many decades. However, we have now entered upon a time when corruption and criminality have so far progressed among many governmental-service-corporations worldwide that maintaining the role of global trustee has required action by the Pope and the Holy See. What action that will be taken, will remain to be seen

There are many specialized service centers organized a separate city-states that have taken over specific aspects of the operations of the Global Estate Trust. This so-called "Empire of the City" spans the globe. Rome and the Vatican City remain the home base of operations responsible for overall administration worldwide. The Inner City of London, known as "Westminster", is a separate, independent international city-state within London and its home to the Crown Temple which administers legal services (which we all know that the legal services are only for those who want to lie, cheat and steal and call it business) and is also home to the Fleet-Street-hub of international-banking-services (which we all know that the banking system only applies to those who own the International-Banks). The District of Columbia, another city-state, is the center of defense and police-services worldwide. (And yet this city-state does not know how to police its own backyard). The United Nations, yet another separate independent city-state, is the hub of international trade, aid and negotiations.

Now, Great Britain was and is involved with the destruction of America as well. That started in 1776, just after Congress signed the Declaration of Independence. King George III was not impressed when our Fore-Fathers had the fortitude and intelligence to write the Declaration of Independence. The King of England, at that time, was taxing the American settler right out of the country; as if England owned America. This is one of the reasons why our Fore-Fathers left England in the first place, to have the 'Royal-Yoke' removed form around their proverbial necks.

The Declaration of Independence was written as a declaration for the world, that British Colonies in America were declaring themselves an 'Independent-Nation'. In addition, the Declaration explains why the colonies were declaring independence…by listing the grievances against King George III. Ask yourself this question, if you were a colonist, and you were under the 'Royal-Yoke' as an indentured-servant, and you saw the potential that America had to offer would you not do the same in declaring independence?

We realize that there are more Countries trying to destroy America. However, they are not as insidious as the [Jews], the Vatican, and the Royal-Heads of England or even THE-United-States-Corporate-Government (the political-corporate-whores).

We further realize that in this chapter we discuss what transpired throughout history. However, we feel that it will refresh your memory and show you through examples and through our personal-cases that the [jews] in association with the Royal Heads of England, the Vatican and THE-United-States-Corporate-Government (the political-corporate-whores) are committing the same crimes that were committed in Germany that started WWI and WWII and why the colonists declared their Independence in the 1700's.

Herein lays the definition of 'The Great Evil' that is being enforced upon Americans. However, Americans have been de-educated throughout history, fed misleading information and lied-to-causing us to become complacent and confused about what to do about 'hate-crimes' being committed against us. Furthermore, in [jewish] law it is written in their laws that "No [jew] can bring harm to another [jew]." However, we know

15

this to be an untruth by one of the biggest stories and facts that Religious Books have to offer…The Crucifixion!

We fully realize if you as the reader read this, you will have preconceived notions that we are obviously bigots, prejudiced, or even anti-Semitic. However, we will point out that we were not born that/this way; we were taught by those who think that they are special. If they are so special then why do most, if not all, of the Middle-East have a strong dislike or disrespect (Note: the term 'HATE' here would be way to strong) Israel and the [jews]?

If the [jews] believe they are so holy and blessed by GOD, and are supposedly his chosen people, then our opinion is to take all [jews] place them on a ship take them to the Marianna-Trench and let them walk on water. If any of them are saved by 'Holy-Intervention' or can succeed in this endeavor then by all means, we would capitulate and kneel before them and do exactly as they say and serve them without recrimination. However, there was (past-tense) one-individual that did and the [jews] deny his very existence and had him killed. There are only three ways that we, personally, would respect, revere and or honor any [jew] to date: 1. Walk on water – after all one did accomplish that task. 2. Raise the dead – yet again one did accomplish this task and 3. Cast out demons from those possessed – oh…but wait! One did accomplish this task. Yet the [jews] deny the fact that Jesus of Nazareth, aka Jesus-Christ, aka the son of God, even existed.

As we write this book, we can understand why the Al-Qaida, Taliban, and ISIL (and any and all of those within the Islamic Nation) hate THE-United-States-Corporate-Government (and why they call us 'Barbarians'). Great Britain, the Vatican, and Israel (and all other countries that support these criminal acts through the continuation of the 'conspiracies'…Theory???) continue to commit crimes will continue to defend their beliefs.

We, personally, as the authors of this book, agree with those factions that HATE THE-United-States-Corporate-Government and all of it co-conspirators, that are trying to make the world in their (meaning—all other countries to be subservient) image and beliefs. I believe that every country has the right to defend, in any manner, against any and all evil visited-upon their country or their citizens. After all, this is known as 'self-defense'.

As we were growing up, we were taught not too HATE any "race, creed, color, sex, or national origin"…until "1994". When the self-proclaimed "professionals" within THE-Subsidiary-Corporate-State-of-California committed "Breach of Contract", "High-Treason", "Terrorist-Acts", "Fraud upon the Court", "Perjury", "Grand Theft", "Abuse of Authority" and "Crimes against Humanity"…This also includes "impersonation" of other self-proclaimed "professionals" that called themselves "Government-Officials".

We simply and abjectly refuse to accept what these individual "Actors" impersonating "Professionals" opinions or illegal-actions that were taken against the two authors of this book or any other Native-Americans who exercise their rights by and with the "Bill of Rights".

In other words, the "Bill of Rights" was/were bestowed upon all Men and Women as Native-Americans and American-Civilians; but yet the "Constitution" itself sets the limitations of what the "Corporate-Government" could do against the American-People under the "Constitution" (a contract/legal-document?) and "Treaties" (another-contract).

The "Corporate-Government" known as "THE UNITED-STATES-OF-AMERICA" has de-educated and muddied the "Bill of Rights" and the "Constitution" that no-one really knows what is real and what is not. And there is an explanation for this action…read further.

As readers you may not like what I am writing in this paragraph, chapter or even in this book, but "THE UNITED-STATES-OF-AMERICA" (Corporate-Government) needs to be abolished/deposed any way possible…and the "REAL-Organic-LIVING-Constitution" (a CONTRACT/"legal-document?") Re-established, enforced and placed back into authority against the "United-States-Corporate-Government". These topics will be further-discussed within this book.

The 'facts' presented within this chapter are accurate and on target. However, our 'interpretation' may be a little 'a-skewed'. After all we were not present as witnesses during WWI or during the Crucifixion of Christ.

It is a simple shame how a majority of people will believe a lie before they believe the truth even when the truth is in plain-sight. This is a condition called "DENIALISM".

The last observation and experience we had with the "COURTS" (sic)…is that they Lie, Cheat and Steal; All in the name of "doing business": Let me remind you…'Al Capone and many other Organized Crime Leaders did the same thing and were persecuted and prosecuted for their crimes. Most of them were put to death or put in prison for the same crimes that THE United-States-Corporate-Government is doing to all Americans to this day. The Courts are the criminals. The "MONEY" is worthless debt. The gods are the servants. The students are the teachers. Everything on earth is upside down and reversed. Everything that you think is separate is in fact unified and everything that you think is wrong is ultimately right. But most important, everything that you think is secret is fully known.

The DEFINITION of the GREAT EVIL is this: The United-States-Corporate-Government is committing the SAME Crimes against ALL-AMERICANS and calling it; to quote them "It is the Law" or" We are just doing our job". This is a flat out lie. They are not doing their jobs, they are not following the law of the land; they want the money that you do not own.

Pity Pope Francis, the man who has inherited this incredible convoluted and criminal mess. He is doing his best to straighten it out, but he needs help – our help. If you are an American and the least bit interested in our/your own future and the false claims being made against your private-property-assets and those of your organic states, it is time take affirmative, positive, determined, and non-violent action. However, the United-States-Corporate-Government uses violence as a tool to frighten Private-Americans to follow their directives. Remember violence does not necessarily mean that they will die or be injured we as Private-Americans can and will use violence as a tool to prove our point.

Pope Francis is being attacked, viciously, by hired media (with biased-opinions) and biased propaganda masters who work hard every day at the behest of the banks and the Bar Associations to vilify the Roman Catholic Church – which is the primary obstacle in the way of achieving – not a gentle, kind, unified government for the world that respects free-will and individual-people as Children of God – but a DEMONIC version sponsored and controlled by the Crown Temple (Great Britain).

These two organizations are rivals by design. The Roman Catholic Church worships God, the Creator. The Crown Temple worships Lucifer, the LIAR. In past ages these organizations have engaged as necessary evils endemic to creation, each one bent on corrupting the other in an endless cycle – one drawing good out of evil, and the other dedicated to creating evil out of good. This in reality reflects the duality seen everywhere and in everyone. The Church stands in bright light, in robes of white, advocating life. Whereas, the Crown Temple stands in the darkness, wears robes of black, and advocates death (is this not a violent action to cause fear, pain and death?).

It is not a coincidence that the followers of Lucifer indulge in such a fantastic array of semantic deceits, false identities, corporate personas, and lies, for they literally worship the Father of all LIES. It is no mistake that they seize by deceit and violence and lay waste to human lives, because they worship Lucifer.

They have existed and endeavored to rule over everyone else since 3760 B.C. They were insane then and they are insane now. In Babylon, the Priests self-mutilated themselves and practiced every possible kind of violence and black magic. They murdered infant (by burning them alive) in the name of their goddess. All that has changed is that in modern-times cult members have stopped self-mutilation and worship a male deity instead. Instead of murdering infants (which they still defend against) they commit rape, kidnapping and slavery. They still deal in illusions – that they call 'legal-fiction-entities' and fiat (fake) money; and they STILL wear black robes.

Pope Francis is standing firm for all that is right and real, for life, love, justice and truth. Those in charge of the Crown Temple are standing just as firm for evil, death, hatred, injustice and lies.

The "United-States-Corporate-Government" expects its 'citizens' to pay 'monies' for their mistakes. If the so-called Fictitious-politicians, Fictitious-bureaucrats and Fictitious-judicial-officers were and are so-highly educated they would not be making the same mistakes over and over again.

Chapter 2:
THE UNITED-STATES-GOVERNMENT IS A CORPORATION...FOR PROFIT!

The first thing we would like to do in this chapter is to thank all of the people who spent much of their time for the research of the topics that we are using in support of the proof and evidence within this book and within the two other books, 'Your Day In Court: Using Common Law with Common Sense' published in 2011 and '! AT GUN POINT... A Whistle Blower's Point of View' published 2012. Both written and Authored by Bradley – Jefferson: [Franks] and Robert – Charles: [Simpson].

With that said, it is our duty as 'Americans' to make sure that all AMERICANS, not U. S. citizens, are informed about what the so–called government is doing to us. Factions like the 'Tea party' movement and other splintered factions realize that there is a major problem within the United-States-Corporate-Government. The Government, through the News Media, is spending Billions, if not, Trillions of dollars to keep Americans asleep and confused with a lot of half-truths and outright-lies: – "and the Government talks about 'Spending' and the "Waste of American Tax Dollars." And the worst part of what the Bureaucrats like to say is that the "CONSTITUTION" IS NOT A CONTRACT; in fact, by definition of what a "contract" is the "CONTSTITUTION" is a contract! (It is an Organic-Living-Legal-DOCUMENT).

We will provide and introduce information, with evidence, that the United-States-Corporate- Government is truly a Corporation, and that each and every Indigenous-American, Native-American and U. S. citizens are corporate-entities and indentured-servants within this horrific 'evil' empire. Furthermore, we will introduce who actually controls the 'machine' that has the intention of our and for our destruction and demise.

If you compare Rome during the time of the Caesars and Emperors you will find that the United-States-Corporate-Government is parallel with that corporate government that fell, because of all of the 'corruption' within the Roman Empire. The United States is doomed to follow the Roman Empire because of the same corruption, ignorance, stupidity, greed and hatred.

We can assure you at this time, that this is not a 'Religious' statement or condemnation; but FACTS that will, hopefully, open your eyes and make you think about the implications that include the evidence that will educate you as readers to ask yourself this question, "What have we done wrong, as Americans, too be treated like second hand citizens in our own Country?"

The first piece of evidence we are going to introduce is the 'legal' definition of what a 'Corporation' is. Then we will present you with a breakdown of whom and what are in control of the biggest 'money-making lies' within the 'United-States-Corporate-Government', that according to fictitious-politicians "does not exist". Furthermore, we will use our own cases and experiences as support of our findings. However, you as the reader must remember that there are other cases that have been 'misjudged' and 'mismanaged' just for the 'almighty-dollar' or for a quick 'guilty' verdict for those Americans that speak out and challenge the so-called elected or appointed authority or prove "Crimes-against-Humanity". The Fictitious-Corporate-Government does not care who they destroy with their lies, trickery or deceit. They are not even above "falsifying" their 'own'-"government documents" or any "evidence" they claim to have secured against any Innocent-American.

The 'legal' definition for a corporation is as follows - using this definition:

"An Incorporated-entity is a separate legal entity that has been incorporated through a legislative or registration process established through legislation. Incorporated entities have legal rights and liabilities that are distinct from its shareholders, and may conduct business for either profit-seeking business or not for profit purposes. Early incorporated entities were established by charter (i.e. by an ad hoc act granted by a monarch or passed by a parliament or legislature). Most jurisdictions now allow the creation of new corporations through registration. In addition to legal personality, registered companies tend to have limited liability, be owned by shareholders who can transfer their shares to others, and controlled by a board of directors who the shareholders appoint."

"In American English the word corporation is widely used to describe incorporated entities, especially those that have a large number of shareholders and in respect of which, ownership can be transferred without the need for the consent of other shareholders. In British English and in the commonwealth countries, the term public company is more widely used to describe the same sort of entity while the word company encompasses all incorporated entities. In American English, the word company can include entities such as partnerships that would not be referred to as companies in British English as they are not a separate legal entity".

"Despite not being natural persons corporations are recognized by the law to have rights and responsibilities like natural persons ("people"). Corporations can exercise human rights against real individuals and the state, and they can themselves be responsible for human rights violations. Corporations can be "dissolved" either by statutory operation, order of court, or voluntary action on the part of shareholders. Insolvency may result in a form of corporate failure, when creditors force the liquidation and dissolution of the corporation under court order, but it most often results in restructuring of corporate holdings. Corporations can even be convicted of criminal offenses, such as fraud and manslaughter. However, corporations are not considered living entities in the way that humans are."

"Ownership and control:"

"A corporation is typically owned and controlled by its members. In a joint-stock company the members are known as shareholders and their share in the ownership, control and profits of the corporation is determined by the portion of shares in the company that they own. Thus, a person who owns a quarter of the shares of a joint-stock company owns a quarter of the company, is entitled to a quarter of the profit (or at least a quarter of the profit given to shareholders as dividends) and has a quarter of the votes capable of being cast at general meetings."

"In another kind of corporation, the legal document which established the corporation or which contains its current rules will determine who the corporation's members are. Who is a member depends on what kind of corporation is involved. In a worker cooperative the members are people who work for the cooperative. In a credit union the members are people who have accounts with the credit union."

"The day-to-day activities of a corporation are typically controlled by individuals appointed by the members. In some cases, this will be a single individual but more commonly corporations are controlled by a committee or by committees. Broadly speaking there are two kinds of committee structure:

• A single committee known as a board of directors is the method favored in most common law countries. Under this model the board of directors is composed of both executive and non-executive directors. The latter being meant to supervise the formers' management of the company.

• A two-tiered committee structure with a supervisory board and a managing board is common in civil law countries. Under this model the executive directors sit on one committee while the non-executive directors sit on the other.

"Corporate law:"

'Main article: Corporate law'

"The existence of a corporation requires a special framework and body of law that specifically grants the corporation legal personality, and typically views a corporation as a fictional person, a legal person, or a moral person (as opposed to a natural person). Corporate statutes typically empower corporations to own property, sign binding contracts, and pay taxes in a capacity separate from that of its shareholders (who are sometimes referred to as "members"). According to Lord Chancellor Haldane, "…a corporation is an abstraction. It has no mind of its own any more than it has a body of its own; its active and directing will must consequently be sought in the person of somebody who is really the directing mind and will of the corporation, the very ego and Centre of the personality of the corporation" ---Lennard's Carrying Co Ltd v Asiatic Petroleum Co Ltd [1915] AC 705."

"The legal personality has two economic implications. First it grants creditors (as opposed to shareholders or employees) priority over the corporate assets upon liquidation. Second, corporate assets cannot be withdrawn by its shareholders, nor can the assets of the firm be taken by personal creditors of its shareholders. The second feature requires special legislation and a special legal framework, as it cannot be reproduced via standard contract law."

"The regulations most favorable to incorporation include:"

• "Limited Liability: Unlike a partnership or sole proprietorship, shareholders of a modern business corporation have "limited" liability for the corporation's debts and obligations. As a result, their losses cannot exceed the amount which they contributed to the corporation as dues or payment for shares. This enables corporations to "socialize their costs" for the primary benefit of shareholders; to socialize a cost is to spread it to society in general. The economic rationale for this is that it allows anonymous trading in the shares of the corporation, by eliminating the corporation's creditors as a stakeholder in such a transaction. Without limited liability, a creditor would probably not allow any share to be sold to a buyer at least as creditworthy as the seller.

Limited liability further allows corporations to raise large amounts of finance for their enterprises by combining funds from many owners of stock. Limited liability reduces the amount that a shareholder can lose in a company. This increases the attraction to potential shareholders, and thus increases both the number of willing shareholders and the amount they are likely to invest. However, some jurisdictions also permit another type of corporation, in which shareholder's liability is unlimited, for example the unlimited liability corporation in two provinces of Canada, and the unlimited company in the United Kingdom."

• "Perpetual lifetime: Another advantage is the assets and structure of the corporation may continue beyond the lifetime of its shareholders and bondholders. This allows stability and the accumulation of capitol, which is thus available for investment in larger and longer-lasting projects than if the corporate assets were subject to dissolution and distribution. This was also important in medieval times, when land donated to the Church (a corporation) would not generate the feudal fees that a lord could claim upon a landholder's death. In this regard, see Statute of Mortmain.

(However, a corporation can be dissolved by a government authority, putting an end to its existence as a legal entity. But this usually happens if the company breaks the law, for example, fails to meet annual filing requirements, or in certain circumstances if the company requests dissolution)."

"Formation:"

"Historically, corporations were created by a charter granted by government. Today, corporations are usually registered with the state, province, or national government and regulated by the laws enacted by that government. Registration is the main prerequisite to the corporation's assumption of limited liability. The law sometimes requires the corporation to designate its principal address, as well as a registered agent (a person or company designated to receive legal service of process). It may also be required to designate an agent or other legal representative of the corporation."

"Generally, a corporation files articles of incorporation with the government, laying out the general nature of the corporation, the amount of stock it is authorized to issue, and the names and addresses of directors. Once the articles are approved, the corporation's directors meet to create bylaws that govern the internal functions of the corporations, such as meeting procedures and officer positions."

"The law of the jurisdiction in which a corporation operates will regulate most of its internal activities, as well as its finances. If a corporation operates outside its home state, it is often required to register with other governments as a foreign corporation, and is almost always subject to laws of its host state pertaining to employment, crimes, contracts, civil actions, and the like."

"Naming:"

"Corporations generally have a distinct name. Historically, some corporations were named after their membership: for instance, "The President and Fellows of Harvard College". Nowadays, corporations in most jurisdictions have a distinct name that does not need to make reference to their membership. In Canada, this possibility is taken to its logical extreme: many smaller Canadian corporations have no names at all, merely numbers based of a registration number (for example,

"12345678 Ontario Limited"), which is assigned by the provincial or territorial government where the corporation incorporates."

"In most countries, corporate names include a term or an abbreviation that denotes the corporate status of the entity (for example, "Incorporated" or "Ltd."). These terms vary by jurisdiction and language. In some jurisdictions they are dealing with an entity whose liability is limited, and does not reach back to persons who own the entity: one can only collect from whatever assets the entity still controls when one obtains a judgment against it."

"Some jurisdictions do not allow the use of the word "company" alone to denote corporate status, since the word "company" may refer to a partnership or some other form of collective ownership (in the United States it can be used by a sole proprietorship but this is not generally the case elsewhere)."

"Closely held corporations and publicly traded corporations:"

"A benefit corporation, or in short-hand a B corporation, is a class of corporation required by law to create general benefit for society as well as for shareholders. Benefit Corporations must create a material positive impact on society, and consider how their decisions affect their employees, community, and the environment. Moreover, they must publicly report in their social and environmental performances using established third-party standards."

"The chartering of Benefit Corporations is an attempt to reclaim the original purpose for which corporations were chartered in early America. Then, states-chartered corporations to achieve a specific public purpose, such as building bridges or roads. Their legitimacy stemmed from their delegated charter, although they could still earn profits while fulfilling it." (Staff, 2012)

"Over time, however, corporations came to be chartered without any public purpose, while being legally bound to the singular purpose of profit-maximization for its shareholders. Advocates of Benefit Corporations assert that this singular focus has resulted in a variety of societal ills, including the thwarting of democracy, diminished social good, and negative environmental impacts."

"In April 2010, Maryland became the first U.S. state to pass Benefit Corporation legislation, Hawaii, Virginia, California, Vermont, and New Jersey soon followed. Additional, as of November 2011, Benefit Corporation legislation had been introduced or partially passed in Colorado, New York, North Carolina, Pennsylvania, and Michigan."

"Benefit Corporation laws address concerns held by entrepreneurs who wish to raise growth capital but fear losing control of the social or environmental mission of their business. In addition, the laws provide companies the ability to consider factors other than the highest purchase offer at the time of sale, in spite of the ruling on (Revlon, Inc. v. MacAndrews & Forbes Holdings, Inc.). Chartering as a Benefit Corporation also allows companies to distinguish themselves as businesses with a social conscience, and as one that aspires to a standard, they consider higher than mere profit-maximization for shareholders."

In this paragraph section, "Corporations Globally" we will discuss the "United-States-Corporate-Government" only since it directly affects all Americans. However, it is suggested to examine "Corporate law in the United States and Delaware Corporation."

"Several types of conventional corporations exist in the United States. Generally, any business entity that is recognized as distinct from the people who own it (i.e., is not sole proprietorship or a partnership) is a corporation. This generic label includes entities that are known by such legal labels as 'association', 'organization' and 'limited liability Company', as well as corporations proper.

"Only a company that has been formally incorporated according to the laws of a particular state is called 'corporation'. A corporation was defined in the Dartmouth College case of 1819, in which Chief Justice Marshall of the United States Supreme Court stated that, "A corporation is an artificial being, invisible, intangible, and existing only in contemplation of the law." A corporation is a legal entity, distinct and separate from the individuals who create and operate it. As a legal entity the corporation can acquire, own, and dispose of property in its own name like buildings, land and equipment. It can also incur liabilities and enter into contracts like franchising and leasing. American corporations can either be profit-making companies or non-profit entities. Tax-exempt non-profit corporations are often called "501(c) 3 corporation", after the section of the Internal Revenue Code that addresses the tax exemption for many of them."

"In some states, such as Colorado, a corporation may represent itself pro se in courts of law in some situations."

"The federal government can only create corporate entities pursuant to relevant powers in the U. S. Constitution. For example, Congress has constitutional power to provide postal services, so it has power to operate the United States Postal Service. Although the federal government could theoretically preempt all state corporate law under the courts' current expansive interpretation of the Commerce Clause, it has chosen not to do so. As a result, much of American corporate law continues to be a matter of state law under the Tenth Amendment to the United States Constitution. Thus, virtually all corporations in the U. S. are incorporated under the laws of a particular state."

"All states have some kind of "general corporation law" (California, Delaware, Kansas, Nevada and Ohio actually use that exact name) which authorizes the formation of private corporations without having to obtain a charter for each one from the state legislature (as was formerly the case in the 19th century). Many states have separate, self-contained laws authorizing the formation and operation of certain specific types of corporations that are wholly independent of the state general corporation law. For example, in California, nonprofit corporations are incorporated under the Nonprofit Corporation Law, and in Illinois, insurers are incorporated under the Illinois Insurance Code."

"Corporations are created by filing the requisite documents with a particular state government. The process is called "incorporation," referring to the abstract concept of clothing the entity with a "veil" of artificial personhood (embodying, or "corporating" it, 'corpus' being the Latin word for 'body'). Only certain corporations, including banks, are chartered. Others simply file their articles of incorporation with the state government as part of a registration process."

"Once incorporated, a corporation has artificial personhood everywhere it may operate, until such time as the corporation may be dissolved. A corporation that operates in one state while being incorporated in another is a "foreign corporation". This label also applies to corporations incorporated outside of the United States. Foreign corporations must usually register with the secretary of state's office in each state to lawfully conduct business in that state."

"A corporation is legally a citizen of the state (or other jurisdiction) in which it is incorporated (except when circumstances direct the corporation be classified as a citizen of the state in which it has its head office, or the state in which it does the majority of its business). Corporate business law differs dramatically from state to state. Many prospective corporations choose to incorporate in a state whose laws are most favorable to its business interests. Many large corporations are incorporated in Delaware, for example, without being physically located there because that state has very favorable corporate tax and disclosure laws."

"Companies set up for privacy or asset protection often incorporate in Nevada, which does not require disclosure of share ownership. Many states, particularly smaller ones, have modeled their corporate statutes after the Model Business Corporation Act, one of many model sets of law prepared and published by the American Bar Association."

"As juristic persons, corporations have certain rights that attach to natural persons. The vast majority of them attach to corporations under state law, especially the law of the state in which the company is incorporated – since the corporations very existence is predicated on the laws of that state. A few rights also attach by federal constitutional and statutory law, but they are few and far between compared to the rights of natural persons. For example, a corporation has the personal right to bring a lawsuit (as well as the capacity to be sued) and, like a natural person, a corporation can be libeled."

"But a corporation has no constitutional right to freely exercise its religion because religious exercise is something that only "natural" persons can do. That is, only human beings, not business entities, have the necessary faculties of belief and spirituality that enable them to possess and exercise religious beliefs."

"Harvard College (a component of Harvard University), formally the President and Fellows of Harvard College (also known as the Harvard Corporation), is the oldest corporation in the western hemisphere.

Founded in 1636, the second of Harvard's two governing boards was incorporated by the Great and General Court of Massachusetts in 1650. Significantly, Massachusetts itself was a corporate colony at that time – owned and operated by the Massachusetts Bay Company (until it lost its charter in 1684) – so Harvard College is a corporation created by a corporation."

Here ends the 'legal' definition of Corporation. Furthermore, we have given you the lengthy version of the definition to show you that the government and the legal? minds (if you want to call them that) like to confuse and 'lose' people in unnecessary rhetoric. However, we will show you a majority of its flaws so you get a better understanding of how the individual cities, counties and states commit crimes against its citizenry ('natural' persons) on a daily basis, starting with Riverside County, California and Torrance County, New Mexico; where we have actual evidence (with their own paperwork) to show you the difference between the lies/opinions and truth/facts and leave the final decision up to you. Not some [jew] Mafia-controlled-courtroom that claim jurisdiction (and cannot prove it), authority or Corporate-Rights. This is a trick to get the evidence into their possession and make it disappear along with your case; or if it is serious enough against them, make you disappear. Furthermore, the United-States-Corporate-Government, British Monarchy, the Vatican and the [jews] consider all Americans as commodities to do with as they please. In reality they are the "commodity" and we, Americans, are the "POWER".

But first, there are other Authors that agree with what we are telling you within this book. We are not the only people on this 'sinking vessel' that feel the way we do and who knows and recognizes the truth and FACTS of what is happening to Americans and America.

There are many American-Civilians that have spent a lot of time and research to find out that there are 'natural' persons that are fighting the good fight against "The Great Evil" and that we are not the only ones out there fighting for what is "right".

"The United States Isn't a Country – It's a Corporation" "We, the people of the United States, in Order to form a more perfect Union, establish Justice, insure domestic Tranquility, provide for the common defense, promote the general Welfare, and secure the Blessings of Liberty to ourselves and our Posterity, do ordain and establish this Constitution for the United States of America" – Preamble of the original "organic" Constitution.

"We hold these truths to be self-evident. That all men are created equal; that they are endowed by their Creator with certain unalienable; that among these are life, liberty, and the pursuit of happiness; that to secure these rights, governments are instituted among men, deriving their just powers from the consent of the governed; that whenever any form of government becomes destructive of these ends, it is the right of the people to alter or abolish it, and to institute new government, laying its foundation on such principles, and organizing its powers in such form, as to them seem most likely to effect/affect their safety and happiness." – Excerpt from the Declaration of Independence of the original-thirteen-united-states of America, July 4, 1776.

Fourth of July 2002 has come and gone, and Americans honored the holiday with a renewed patriotic fervor that reminded me of the Bicentennial celebrations of 1976. As is customary, traditional fireworks displays took center stage and scores of people turned out to witness the dazzling show in the summer sky. With mixed feelings, I sat with friends on a crowded Pennsylvania sidewalk beneath a glittering mesmerizing explosion of color, pondering the keen sense of sadness and betrayal that overwhelmed my spirit. Looking around at the huge crowds gathered for the annual events, I thought silently, "We are not free." In truth, we have not been a free people for a very long time.

We celebrate this day in honor of our "independence". We call ourselves a free people in a land of liberty. Our anthems proudly sing the praises of this nation, and we raise our voices, wave our flags and join in song – but how many Americans realize they are not free? This is a myth perpetuated by the powers-that-be in order to avoid any major civil unrest, and to keep us all living under the thumb of a militaristic corporate Big Brother within the illusions that have been created for us. The truth of the matter is this: what freedom has not been stolen from us, we have surrendered willingly through our silence and ignorance. As Americans, our ancestors didn't have a good grasp of this either. It is sad, but it is also very true.

Don't point to that beloved parchment, the Constitution, as a symbol of your enduring freedom. It is representative of a form of government which seemingly no longer exists in this country today. The Constitution has been thrown out the window, the Republic shoved aside and replaced with a democracy. The thing is; most people in this country remain unaware that this so because they simply do not know the truth – what lies beyond the myths. Your so-called government is not going to tell you, either.

To even begin to understand what has happened to the Republic, we must look backward in time to the period following the Civil War. We must go back to the year 1871, which was the beginning of the decline of the Republic. When we examine what happened during that time in our history, we begin to piece together this troubling, perplexing puzzle that is "America" – only then should we answer to whether we are indeed a "free" people or not.

So, let's roll backward into the past for a moment. It is time we learned what they didn't teach us in school. It is far more interesting that what they DID tell us. I think you'll stay awake for this lesson.

The date is February 21, 1871 and the Forty-First Congress is in session. I refer you to the "Acts of the Forty-First Congress", Section34, Session III, chapter 61 and 62. On this date in the history of our nation, Congress passed an Act titled: "An Act to Provide a Government for the District of Columbia." This is also known as the "Act of 1871." What does this mean? Well, it means that Congress, under no constitutional authority to do so, created a separate form of government for the District of Columbia, which is a ten-mile square parcel of land.

What??? How could they do that? Moreover, WHY would they do that? To explain, let's look at the circumstances of those days. The Act of 1871 was passed at a vulnerable time in America. Our nation was essentially bankrupt – weakened and financially depleted in the aftermath of the Civil War. The Civil War itself was nothing more than a calculated "front" for some pretty fancy footwork by corporate backroom players. It was a strategic maneuver by European interests (the international bankers) who were intent upon gaining a stranglehold on the neck (and the coffers) of America.

The Congress realized our country was in dire financial straits, so they cut a deal with the international bankers – (in those days, the Rothschilds of London were dipping their fingers into everyone's pie) thereby incurring a DEBT to said bankers. If we think about banks, we know they do not just lend us money out of the goodness of their hearts. A bank will not do anything for you unless it is entirely in their best interest to do so. There has to be some sort of collateral or some string attached which puts you and me (the borrower) into a subservient position. This was true back in 1871 as well. The conniving international bankers were not about to lend our floundering nation any money without some serious stipulations. So, they devised a brilliant way of getting their foot in the door of the United States a prize they had coveted for some time, but had been unable to grasp thanks to our Founding Fathers, who despised them and held them in check), and thus, the Act of 1871 was passed.

In essence, this Act formed the corporation known as THE UNITED STATES. Note the capitalization, because it is important. This corporation, owned by foreign interests, moved right in and shoved the original "organic" version of the Constitution into a dusty corner. With the "Act of 1871," our Constitution was defaced in the sense that the title was block-capitalized and the word "for" was changed to the word "of" in the title. The original Constitution drafted by the Founding Fathers, was written in this manner:

"The Constitution for the United States of America."

The altered version reads: "THE CONSTITUTION OF THE UNITED STATES OF AMERICA". It is the corporate-constitution. It is NOT the same document you might think it is. The corporate-constitution operates in an economic capacity and has been used to fool the People into thinking it is the same parchment that governs the Republic. It absolutely is not.

Capitalization – an insignificant change? Not when one is referring to the context of a legal document, it isn't. Such minor alterations have had major impacts on each subsequent generation born in this country. What Congress did with the passage of the Act of 1871 was create an entirely new document, a constitution for the government of the District of Columbia. The kind of government THEY created was a corporation.

The new, altered Constitution serves as the constitution of the corporation, and not that of America. Think about that for a moment.

Incidentally, this corporate constitution does not benefit the Republic. It serves only to benefit the corporation. It does nothing good for you or me – and it operates outside the original Constitution. Instead of absolute rights guaranteed under the "organic" Constitution, we now have "relative" rights or privileges. One example of this is the Sovereign's right to travel, which has been transformed under corporate government policy into a "privilege" which we must be licensed to engage in. This operates outside of the original Constitution.

So, Congress committed HIGH TREASON against the People, who were considered Sovereign under the Declaration of Independence and the organic Constitution. When we consider the word "Sovereign", we must think about what the word means.

"According to Webster's Dictionary, "sovereign" is defined as: 1. Chief or highest; supreme. 2. Supreme in power, superior in position to all others. 3. Independent of, and unlimited by, any other, possessing or entitled, to, original and independent authority or jurisdiction."

In other words, our government was created by and for "sovereigns" – the free citizens who were deemed the highest authority. Only the People can be sovereign – remember that. Government cannot be sovereign. We can also look to the Declaration of Independence, where we read: "government is subject to the consent of the governed" – That's supposed to be us, the sovereigns. Do you feel like a sovereign nowadays? We don't.

It doesn't take a rocket scientist or a constitutional historian to figure out that this is not what is happening in our country today. Government in these times is NOT subject to the consent of the governed. Rather, the governed are subject to the whim and greed of the corporation, which has stretched its tentacles beyond the ten-mile-square parcel of land known as the District of Columbia. THEY just want you to think it does.

You see, you are presumed to know the law. This is ironic because as a people, we are taught basically nothing about the law in school. We are made to memorize obscure factoids and paragraphs here and there, such as the Preamble, and they gloss over the Bill of Rights. But we are not told about the law. Nor do our corporate government schools delve into the Constitution in any great depth. After all, they were put into place to indoctrinate and dumb down the masses – not to teach us anything. We were not told that we were sold-out to foreign interests and made beneficiaries of the debt incurred by Congress to the international bankers. For generations, American citizens have had the bulk of their earnings confiscated to pay on a massive debt that they, as a People, did not incur. There are many, many things the People have not been told. How do you feel about being made a beneficiary of somebody else's massive debt without your knowledge or consent? Are we gonna keep going along with this?

When you hear some individuals say that the Constitution is null and void, think about how our government has transformed over time from a municipal or service-oriented entity to a corporate or profit-oriented entity. We are living under the myth that this is lawful, but it is not. We are being ruled by a "de-facto," or unlawful, form of government – the corporate body of the death-mongers – The Controllers.

With the passage of the Act of 1871, a series of subtle and overt deceptions were set in motion – all in conjunction and collusion with the Congress, who knowingly and deliberately sold the People down the river. Did they tell you this in government school? I doubt it. They were too busy drumming the fictional version of history into your brain – and mine. By failing to disclose what THEY did to the American People, the people became ignorant of what was happening. Over time, the Republic took it on the chin to the point of a knockdown. With the surrender of their gold in 1933, the People essentially surrendered their law. I don't suppose you were taught THAT in school either. That's because our REAL history is hidden from us. This is the way Roman Civil Law works – and our form of governance today is based upon Roman Civil Law and Admiralty/Maritime Law – better known as the "Divine Right of Kings" and "Law of the Seas", respectively. This explains a lot. Roman Civil Law was fully established in the original colonies even before our nation began and is also known as private international law.

The government which was created for the District of Columbia via the Act of 1871 operates under Private International Law, and not Common Law, which was the law of the Constitutional Republic. This is very important to note since it impacts all Americans in concrete ways. You must recognize that private international law is only applicable within the District of Columbia and NOT in the other states of the Union. The various arms of the corporation are known as "departments" such as the Judiciary, Justice, and Treasury. You recognize those names? Yes, you do! But they are not what you assume them to be. These "departments" all belong to the corporation known as THE UNITED STATES. They do NOT belong to you and me under the corporate constitution and its various amendments that operate outside of the Constitutional Republic.

I refer you to the UNITED STATES CODE (note the capitalization, indicating the corporation, not the Republic) Title: 28, 3002 (15) (A) (B) (C). It is stated unequivocally that the UNITED STATES is a corporation [see Editor's Note]. Realize, too, that the corporation is not a separate and distinct entity from the government. IT IS the government. YOUR government. This is extremely important. I refer to this as the "corporate empire of the UNITED STATES," which operates under Roman Civil Law outside of the Constitution. How do you like being ruled by a cheesy, sleazy corporation? You'll ask your Congressperson about this, you say? HA!!

Congress is fully aware of this deception. You must be made aware that the members of Congress do NOT work for you and me. Rather, they work for the Corporation known as THE UNITED STATES. Is this really any surprise to you? This is why we can't get them to do anything on our behalf or to answer to us – as in the case with the illegal income tax – among many other things. Contrary to popular belief, they are NOT our civil servants. They do NOT work for us. They are the servants of the corporate government and carry out its bidding. Period.

The great number of committees and sub-committees that the Congress has created-all work together like a multi-headed monster, to oversee the various corporate-"departments." And, you should know that every single one of these that operate outside the District of Columbia is in violation of the law. The corporate government of the UNITED STATES has no jurisdiction or authority in ANY state of the Republic beyond the District of Columbia. Let this sink into your brain for a minute. Ask yourself, "Could this deception REALLY have occurred without the full knowledge and complicity of the Congress?" Do you think it happened by accident? You are deceiving yourself if you do. There are no accidents or coincidences. It is time confront the truth and awaken from ignorance.

Your legislators will not apprise you of this information. You are presumed to know the law. THEY know you do not know the law, or your history for that matter, because this information has not been taught to you. No concerted effort has been made to inform you. As a Sovereign, you are entitled to full disclosure of the facts. As a slave, you are entitled to nothing other than what the corporation decides to "give" you – at a price. Be wary of accepting so-called "benefits" of the corporation of the UNITED STATES. Aren't you enslaved enough already?

I said (above) that you are presumed to know the law. Still, it matters not if you don't in the eyes of the corporation. Ignorance of the law is not considered an excuse. It is your responsibility and your obligation as an American to learn about the law and how it applies to you. THEY count on the fact that most people are too uninterested or distracted or lazy to do so. The People have been mentally conditioned to allow the alleged government to do their thinking for them. We need to turn that around if we are to save our Republic before it is too late.

The UNITED STATES government is basically a corporate instrument of the international bankers. This means YOU are owned by the corporation from birth to death. The corporate UNITED STATES also holds ownership of all your assets, your property, and even your children. Does this sound untrue? Think long and hard about all those bills you pay, all those various taxes and fines and licenses you must pay for. Yes, they've got you by the pockets. Actually, they've had you by the ass for as long as you've been alive. In your heart, you know it's true. You don't believe any of this? Read up on the 14th Amendment. Check out how "free" you really are.

With the Act of 1871 and subsequent legislation such as the purportedly ratified 14th Amendment, our once-great nation of Sovereigns has been subverted from a Republic to a democracy. As is the case under Roman Civil Law, our ignorance of the facts has led to our silence. Our silence has been construed as our consent to become beneficiaries of a debt we did not incur. The Sovereign People have been deceived for hundreds of years into thinking they remain free and independent, when in actuality we continue to be slaves and servants of the corporation.

Treason was committed against the People in 1871 by the Congress. This could have been corrected through the decades by some honest men (assuming there were some), but it was not, mainly due to lust for money or power. Nothing new there. Are we to forgive and justify this crime against the People? You have lost more freedom than you may realize due to corporate infiltration of the so-called government. We will lose more unless we turn away from a democracy that is the direct road to disaster - and restore our Constitutional Republic.

In an upcoming article, we'll take a closer look at the purportedly ratified 14th Amendment and how we became "property" of the corporation and enslaved by our silence.

NOTE: Actually, as you read further into this book the above paragraph will be explained.

I am saddened to think about the brave men and women who were killed in all the wars and conflicts by the Controllers. These courageous souls fought for the preservation of ideals they believed to be true – not for the likes of a corporation. Do you believe that any one of the individuals who have been killed as a result of war would have willingly fought if they knew the full truth? Do you think one person would have laid down his life for a corporation? I think not. If the People had known long ago to what extent their trust had been betrayed, I wonder how long it would have taken for another Revolution. What we need is a Revolution in THOUGHT. We change our thinking and we change our world.

Will we ever restore the Republic? That is a question I cannot answer yet. I hope, and most of all – pray – that WE, the Sovereign People, will work together in a spirit of cooperation to make it happen in this lifetime. I know I will give it my best shot- come what may. Our children deserve their rightful legacy – the liberty our ancestors fought so hard to give us. Will we remain silent telling ourselves we are free, and perpetuated the MYTH? Or, do we stand as One Sovereign People, and take back what has been stolen from the house of our Republic?

Something to think about – it's called freedom.

Actually, in the U.S. Code the term "United States" is said to have any of three meanings:"

US CODE: Title 28, 3002. Definitions:

(15) "United States" means –

(A) a Federal Corporation;

(B) an agency, department, commission, board, or other entity of the United States; or

(C) an instrumentality of the United States.

If we are stupid to surrender our freedom to a bunch of lousy international bankers, then we deserve to live in bondage.

The Democratic Process seems only to work for those that can financially afford it, Lawyers, Judges and Political-Corporate-Whores and their Lobbyists.

They don't have to be sent halfway around the world to protect the "Corporate" holdings of the United States in another country. Furthermore, the political-corporate-government has NO respect for those individuals that gave their lives in defense of those "corporate-holdings" or what they thought in defense of our "freedoms". If you question this or don't follow this train of thought, ask yourself this question, "Why are all people in America called U.S. citizens when we are alive? But when they are killed in the line of duty, here in America or abroad, they become "Americans." This is a cold slap in the face of the families who gave their sons and daughters, mothers and fathers, brothers and sisters over to an unfeeling "corporate" entity that shows no more remorse than an earthworm. In addition, the corporate-government labels all U.S. citizens as collateral damage if they are killed in defense of the United-States-Corporation. The family members are given a flag that is put to "sleep" and does NOT have a gold fringe around it. Thus, signifying that that member gave his/her life for America under false pretenses and the message the UNITED-STATES-Corporation sends out for the public is this, "A good American is a Dead American", and this by their own Corporate-Government. By the way, we are NOT questioning the values, beliefs, morals, spirit or the 'PATRIOTISM' any individual may feel about their Country. We just want you to understand what and who you are fighting for.

The intentions of the articles, within this book, are for the use of showing you where we can find the presentment for the evidence of what the politicians deny exist. If you ask a politician why the United-State is a corporation they will answer, "The U.S. is not a corporation!" with this said, we know politicians always 'tell the truth.' Furthermore, we can present you with evidence using their "corporate-documents" that the courts and political-corporate-government does not even "enforce" or stand by their own "rules" or "procedures" or their "Contracts".

We can even explain why the "corporate-government" took the action it did against us in the first place; by using their documents as evidence against them. However, this book is being written to educate as many Americans as possible that they are not alone and there are other "victims" of the corporate-government that need our help even more.

For example, the so-called corporate-government 'forces' us into what they call 'performance-contracts'. They also claim it is "voluntary". Don't believe it. They are lying and misguiding you. Let's put it this way, if you find someone who is starving and out in the cold you offer to feed and warm them, but before you do, you want them to sign a "contract" that they will have to perform some 'task' or 'give information' before they are fed or warm. However, this is the insidious part of the government's machinations, if you refuse to sign said contract, which is 'voluntary' and is your choice; you will NOT be fed or warm. This is the choice you are given by a greedy-corrupt-corporate-government and the Political-Corporate-Whores. What a choice, slavery or death.

We will offer evidence as we progress through this book and our other books contain evidence as well.

One of two examples that we can provide you is this, (1) the Electric Companies... which are supposedly set up for the benefits of all Americans, I mean, it is a convenience to go into a home, business, or other place and turn on a light and it is supplied. However, our problem is NOT with the Generating Plants that create electricity throughout the nation or other countries nor is it the Transmission of electricity throughout the "grids". It is however, a concern when the Billing Offices of the Electric Companies send out your monthly statements and it is exorbitantly high, you are being fleeced. The meters that supposedly "measure the magnetic flow" are not in reality doing what the electric companies are claiming. For example, each electric company uses a base rate/price such as $ 0.15 (as an example) per kWh (Kilowatt per hour). Now, there are 720 hours in a 30 day billing month for electric companies. If the billing process was/is honest your bill should only be $108.00 for that billing month. However, there are areas in California and across the country that are paying 10 times that amount just for their homes. These same Billing companies of the electric companies give Millions of Dollars to certain Politicians through Lobbyists and claim that it is legal through what they call PAC Monies, donations or Extortion. However, the truth is if there is any fraud within the billing process it makes the PAC Monies, donations or Extortion illegal. There are different "Rates" for Industrial/Commercial, Farming/Agriculture, and Residential. The highest expense for any business or agriculture is the "electric bill". How the electric companies actually do this is by illusion. There are three (3) "calibration" screws (commonly called Break screw) that are located on the meter. 1. is located right in front of you nose with an FL/S. 2. Is located on the side of the meter that is just out of sight unless you know what you are looking for. 3. The third and final calibration screw is on the inside in the back of the meter that you will not be able to see. These calibration screws can speed-up or slow-down the meter. If your meter is running fast and the behest of the electric companies they are committing fraud against you. This is how the Electric Companies are fleecing Americans right out of their homes and businesses. In addition, Electricity cannot be accurately "measured"; like water, gasoline, oil or natural gas. This is why the Billing Offices of the electric companies use the terms "Estimate-Usage". In addition of this "Estimate-Usage", they compare your last year's bill with the current year and month and round the amount up. This by definition is Fraud. Furthermore, the "Meters" can be calibrated to run slow or fast to gain time or loose time. (2) The Water Company in Flint, Michigan and the Political-Corporate-Whores that were supposedly protecting their constituents (voters) from crimes against humanity…like clean water…not poisoned.

With these two examples, we have shown a "malicious-evil-intent" for the destruction within America and of Americans.

Corporations work and do business under what they call "Policies and Procedures" or "By-Laws". Policies and Procedures are not Law neither is Corporate By-Laws, but are simply guidelines for the operation of the Legitimate-Corporation. "THE UNITED STATES OF AMERICA" Corporate Government is not a legitimate Corporation. It is rumored that an American cannot challenge a "Policy" or "Procedure" or "By-Laws" within their court of laws or court system as it stands. Therefore, it is with great sadness that we, as Americans cannot safely take back our Country without "Government" Impersonators, "Fiducial" Impersonators, or "self-proclaimed" Professional Impersonators falsely accusing and finding Americans or U.S. Citizens "Guilty" of any crime, punishing them or incarcerating them for a very long time or in some-cases "silencing" them once and for all. You actually begin to see why the "Corporate-Government of the UNITED-STATES" is "HATED" by so many other countries.

If you believe that your country and its Corporate-Government is satisfactory and you accept it as you want it…then this book will not help you.

Chapter 3:
THE DEATH OF AMERICA

We will discuss and present evidence that has caused or is causing the Death of America. (Remember, Rome fell for the stupidity and greed of the 'politicians'). The Royal Heads of England, the Vatican, the [jewish] state of Israel and the United-States-Corporate-Government Political puppets are involved with the takeover and destruction of America and it started in 1776 and offer further evidence that connects the [jewish] mafia, the Royal Heads of England, the Vatican, and the UNITED-STATES-Corporate-Government are in collusion for the destruction of America and the systematic-indentured- servitude of Americans (Not United-States-Citizens). We will explain what "Departments" have been infiltrated and brought-under control illegally through "Treasonous and Terrorist Acts" not to mention the fact of Threat, Duress and Coercion and Under-Color-of-Law. (Especially if law has no-color). It is either Back or White. There is no-gray or in-between dealing with these laws if they are truly broken. If not then the United-States-Corporate-Government does not have the authority or jurisdiction to do anything against any American.

The first thing we will present for you is the UNITED-STATES-Court-system and how we, as Americans, have been through the use of "collusion, coercion, color of law, deceit and trickery" have been put into these (supposedly) 'voluntary' (Implied) performance-contracts; their Corporate-Contracts.

There have been a number of authors who have written about the 'Admiralty/Maritime' Jurisdiction and 'Equity-Law' Jurisdiction in comparison to the 'Common-Law' Jurisdiction. However, these authors argue and try to prove just how 'crooked and corrupt' the UNITED-STATES-Corporation truly is by using the information that the UNITED-STATES-Corporation provides and declares owning 'copy-rights' for that information. The 'Corporation' and its Officers are under the impression that they have 'immunity' against 'anything they do with or without

43

prejudice'. However, we will present further evidence with Court-Documents that are and have been 'falsified' and that Court Officers and Bureaucrats are and have been committing 'Fraud upon the Court' through "trickery, deceit, and lies" and "BREACH OF CONTRACT".

We will first explain what 'Admiralty/Maritime' Jurisdiction and 'Equity-Law' Jurisdiction is by using the definition that the UNITED-STATES-Corporation provides, however, disregards.

There are two different kinds of law on the planet. The first is known as COMMON-LAW, which is the law of the land. The other is maritime/admiralty, which is also known as the law of water; it can be also referred to as banking law.

Maritime/Admiralty-law considers you a maritime/admiralty product, simply because you were birthed out of your mother's water. A ship sits in its berth until the captain gives a certificate of manifest to the port authorities."

"The reason you are required to have a 'Birth-Certificate' is because at the time of your birth there is an exchange of 'money' for the hospital costs. The dock-foreman (the doctor) signs your birth certificate simply because that is what the ship (your birth-mother) is tied too.

If this is confusing let's examine it this way... When you came down your mother's birth canal you came out of her water, making YOU a maritime/admiralty-PRODUCT. At the time of your birth, you became a product of commerce. Your mother and father (in some instances) also have to-sign the birth-certificate. However, if you were allowed to inspect what your mother signed you would notice that your mother and father were listed as an 'informant' not as a parent/(s) or mother; except for the document they wish you to show publicly or have in your possession.

Your mother informed the banks that she had just produced another product (indentured-servant) to be used in commerce. Your actual physical body is owned by England, actually to be more precise, your body is owned by the British Crown. That is the LAW! It all comes down to this, YOU ARE A MARITIME/ADMIRALITY PRODUCT! YOUR BODY IS OWNED BY THE BANKS!

If you look at your social security card (aka Taxpayer Identification Number), you will see numbers in red on the back of the card. The front of the card will be printed in either blue or black ink, but the numbers on the back will be in RED ink.

These numbers which appear in red on the back of your social security card represent your 'body'. Your body is bought and sold on international-stock-markets. The numbers - in red - on the back of the card is the serial number of your stock. Poor people are considered common stock and the wealthy is known as preferred stock.

Just like any other stock, your body is traded on open markets through the use of your birth certificate. If you could examine your 'original' certificate of birth, you would see on the back of the certificate marks from all over the globe. World banks trade your body just as they do every other commodity. This is because you are stock in a maritime/admiralty banking scheme where you are used to return profits to the bank.

Another point in the above paragraphs, "Look at your bills, check out your driver's license, your social security card, or anything with your name on it. What do you see? Any form or contract that is used for business purpose will have YOUR NAME in all CAPITAL LETTERS."

Anytime you are involved in business transactions, you will always see "YOUR-NAME" in "CAPITAL-LETTERS". Only in this form are you able to deal with either banks or the government. Whenever your name is spelled with a combination of capitol and lower-case letters it refers directly to you as a natural person.

Since the banks and government have no-control over natural born people, they will not deal with you as a person. Only your 'strawman' or nom de guerre (a fictitious name), is able to engage in commerce. Once you sign a contract which uses "YOUR NAME" in capital letters you have given consent to this artificial entity. Now you can be brought into their courts.

In this particular situation, if you are brought before the Admiralty/Maritime Court, the only entity that will win is going to be the court, the bank, and the Royal Heads of England. Whenever there is a case heard in a court, somebody is going to pay. The Royal Heads of England get a cut from the energy, time, and labor of the American People.

However, we can further add the Vatican and the [jewish] Mafia into this atrocity and illegal practice; but more about how the Vatican and [jewish] Mafia are within this book.

At birth you become property of the Royal Heads of England, as part of a CORPORATION, whose name is the UNITED-STATES-corporate-government. The President of this corporation is also known as President of the United-States. Once you begin to educate yourself and understand you will see that an 'American' is not required to enter a British commercial venture known as court. The only reason you appear in courts is because you give your consent to appear or sign over 'Power of Attorney' to your lawyer (which work for the Corporation).

That leaves this simple question. Did you receive the 'summons', or did your artificial 'Strawman' or nom de guerre (fictitious entity), receive it? Look at the summons, your bills, your social security, even your driver's license and see how your name is spelled. If it is in all CAPITAL-LETTERS then this is not you the person, it is a Corporation belonging to foreign-interests. The corporation is not a living-entity nor does it really exist. Furthermore, you cannot be held responsible for it unless you give your consent.

There is absolutely 'no-reason' that an American needs to appear before 'British-Grand-Lodge-Masonic-System' also called "courts". Americans are deceived, tricked, coerced, and even threatened or even 'kidnapped' into believing that they must go to court. Free-people (Americans) do 'not have' to do anything! Only a slave is required to answer to Court orders.

Ask yourself this question, "Why would an individual allow a court to hear their case under Admiralty law?"

The federal government, serving on behalf of the 'King's commerce', has every intention of stripping the people of their 'Natural Born Rights'; simply by replacing them with 'state granted privileges' and 'eliminating common-law' by getting them to believe in the 'artificial entity' known as the federal government.

The federal government provides an illusion of 'fair' laws such as the 14th Amendment. However, it is busy working on getting the people to rely on government services such as Welfare, Social Security, and other state-sponsored-franchise-corporate-programs. Furthermore, there are many more 'illusions-perpetrated' on the American people such as licenses, permits, and certifications. They also want the American people to believe in the worthless linen with green ink known as 'Federal-Reserve-Notes'. In addition, there is a cacophony of security services that seem more than redundant, such as...IRS (Internal Revenue Service) / FBI (Federal Bureau of Investigation) / NSA (National Security Agency) / FEMA (Federal Emergency Management Agency) / DHS (Department of Homeland Security).

Unfortunately, many Americans are lead to believe that these 'entities' are necessary for their protection and that Americans cannot live without them. This provides the 'Fascist' federal government with a society that relies on the government for their very lives. Thanks to the system of lawyers and courts, we have hidden contracts of this type. Until the people realize that a charade has been perpetrated on the nation, we have no hope of freedom. We must first recognize the problem, and then identify the system of oppression.

"Most people have not noticed or felt the force of the federal government...yet! They are content to dabble in distractions provided by their televisions and computers. They count on the 'Media' to inform them; that is a huge-mistake."

Most people who have had to enter into the King's Court of law come/came out bewildered. Wondering what happened to their 'rights' they had believed existed under the 'original' Constitution. A small amount of people are aware that they gave up their rights for a government handout. The Patriot Acts I and II provided an awakening for many people. Hopefully more people will become educated so we can begin the 'recovery' of our Great Republic.

There are three areas that are considered the most sensitive in the destruction of the American way of life. They are the Court-System, Corporate-Government and the News-Media. We will be discussing how these three 'Corporate-entities' are involved and who is controlling them and present you with 'evidence' to show that this is not just, as the politicians would say, an 'opinion' or by their 'opinionated—fiction-documents' from their fictitious-'for-Profit'-Corporate-Government.

The first area for the destruction of America and Americans is within the court system. We will be using our 'cases' and 'evidence' as examples instead of using any others. The reason we are using our 'cases' and 'evidence' is that we wish to speak from a standpoint of intelligence and not one of ignorance. In addition, we have lived through the crimes that have been committed against us and we sincerely hope that with the information provided in our books will be of some help for Americans in the future.

The politicians, bureaucrats, judges, lawyers and any other political-corporate-whores will explain to you that "all Courts are jurisdictional". However, there is a case we would like to point out to you that will cause Judges and Attorneys to abandon a civil or criminal proceeding.

On September 14, 2015, Petitioner filed in United States District Court, Eastern-District of Texas, Lufkin, Division Case No. 9: 14-CV-138, Defendant's objection to Denial of Due Process of Law and Demand for Disclosure of the Constitutional Authority that Gives the Court the Capacity to Take Jurisdiction and Enter Judgements, Orders, and Decrees in Favor of the United States Arising from a Civil or Criminal Proceeding Regarding a Debt, in Tyler County, Texas (the "Objection and Demand").

Plaintiff United States had 14-days to respond, but went silent (this is the first and only time of which Petitioner is aware, that the government failed to respond to a challenge of jurisdiction).

As of September 29, 2015, it was incumbent on the Court to dismiss the case under Federal Rule of Civil Procedure 12(b) (1) or (h) (3). The Court, however, stood mute.

Thereafter, Petitioner filed on September 30, 2015, Petitioner's Demand for Dismissal, with Prejudice of this Alleged Case for Lack of Constitutional Authority that Gives the Court the Capacity to Take Jurisdiction and Enter Judgements, Orders, and Decrees in Favor of the United States Arising from a Civil or Criminal Proceeding Regarding a Debt, in Tyler County (a subsidiary), Texas (yet another subsidiary of a Foreign-Fiction-Corporate-Government) (the "Demand for Dismissal").

Plaintiff had until October 14, 2015, to produce the constitutional authority that gives the Court the capacity to take jurisdiction in Tyler County, Texas.

As of this post (October 28, 2015), 44 days have passed since the filing of the "Objection and Demand" and 28 days since the "Demand for Dismissal" and neither the judge nor either of the Department of Justice attorneys has responded in any way following Petitioner's demands.

The reason neither the judge DOJ (Department of Justice) attorneys will respond or confirm or deny Petitioner's filings, is that anything that any of them may say in writing – whether for or against Petitioner – will evince treason to the Constitution, not only on their part, but on the part of every other Federal judge and DOJ attorney doing business anywhere in the Union.

Notwithstanding that the penalty for treason to the Constitution is death, the Federal judge and DOJ attorneys in this case have a more pressing situation on their hands:

The entire fraudulent Federal judicial apparatus is at stake because no contemporary Federal court has the capacity to take jurisdiction and enter judgements, orders, or decrees in favor of the United States arising from a civil or criminal proceeding regarding a debt, in any county, parish or borough in America – and there is no reason why the above filings from this case will not produce the same results in any other Federal case, civil or criminal, anywhere in the Union.

If the Department of Justice cannot win a case anywhere in America, the days of the Hoax of Federal Jurisdiction over the American People are numbered.

The sister Federal tax case in the Lufkin Division was an attempt to foreclose on Federal tax liens filed against Petitioner's ranch. Judge and plaintiff having departed the field of battle, said case is over in substance – Petitioner prevailing.

Regarding the original Federal tax case, United States District Court, Southern District of Texas, Houston Division Civil No. 4: 14-cv-0027 (which the Supreme Court declined to review): There are other remedies available to Petitioner and Petitioner is pursuing them.

The record of these two cases chronicles and documents certain seminal congressional acts that are not taught in any school but have been used to deceive and deprive the American People of the unalienable and constitutional Right of Liberty and foist upon them (1) so-called civil (municipal) rights, (2) rules and regulations (statutes, codes and ordinances), and (3) municipal (Roman civil) law – a state of affairs abhorrent to the Founding Fathers and Framers of the Constitution for which they all risked their life to escape.

"The Lufkin Division case is the first time in American history that a defendant overcame and nullified the Hoax of Federal Jurisdiction and caused the United States District Judge, United States Attorney, and Assistant United States Attorney to FLEE".

This above information was added to this book as a 'KEY' in the pursuit of showing the American People that there are others out there that find what the United-States-Corporate-Government is doing illegally.

The United-States-Corporate-Government has no-twin, it does have a tumor-like foreign outgrowth which has turned parasitic and which is transgressing against the Body-Politic.

In commercial terms – when people act as people they come together in free association and act under full commercial liability. They are responsible and accountable for their debts and deeds. When people from corporations to "represent" them or their interests in some capacity, and bring these corporations together in association, what you get is a corporation conglomerate that is not fully accountable for its debts and deeds because of the corporate veil. This "veil" is the same veil that stands between life and death.

Incorporated "persons" – which include commercial corporations, trusts, cooperatives, and foundations – are considered dead. They have no motive-force of their own. They are operated by third parties under charters granted by nations and states that have themselves all been chartered by the Holy See. Such entities have a natural-limited liability, because they are NOT conscious. When such entities are formed, the intentions and purposes of their creators are clearly stated and typically include a catch-all phrase – "any other lawful purpose" – to cover additional unforeseen circumstances. All corporations are required to function lawfully and in accord with their charters. Any violation of their charter, such as deviation from their stated purpose or failure to perform it, any unlawful activity whatsoever, provides grounds to demand dissolution of a corporate entity and distribution of its assets to its creditors.

Since corporations are not fully liable for "their" acts, they are allowed to go bankrupt without prejudice against their owners and operators. Only assets belonging to the corporation are subject to bankruptcy. The privately help assets of the owners and operators are not affected.

When the United-States-Corporate-Government went bankrupt in 1933, its President (CEO), Franklin Delano Roosevelt, was not bankrupted and neither were the members of the "US Congress" running it as corporate officers. The organic-states and the American people should never have been subject to its bankruptcy, either, and would not have been, except that the Roosevelt Administration falsely and deliberately claimed that they were "voluntary" assets standing as surety for the debts of the United-States-Corporate-Government.

This 'claim' was based on a "pledge" made by the Conference of Governors acting on March 6, 1933. These "Governors" (CEOs) – men operating as "State" franchises of the United-States-Corporate-Government – gratuitously promised the "good faith and credit of their states (franchise) and the citizenry (EVERYONE) thereof" without bothering to explicitly say which or what kind of ("State/state") or ("Citizenry/citizenry") they were referring to when they made this pledge. Everyone present presumably knew that their public office did not grant them the ability to promise resources belonging to the American states much less the private-property of the American people were legitimately on the hook, extended vast amounts of credit to the perpetrators, and began advancing false claims against the resources of the organic states and the private-property of the American People.

One perfect example we found is as follows: Imagine that 'Burger King, International', went bankrupt (or any other International-Business), called a meeting of all the local franchise owners, and asked them to 'pledge' the assets of their customers as collateral backing the debts of

Burger King, International…the answer for this would be a resounding "HELL-NO!"

However, this is what took place in 1933 during the Roosevelt Administration.

There is just one monkey-wrench in this for all of the perpetrators and all of their banking buddies…It is all FRAUD and fraud vitiates everything it touches. The ("Governors/CEOs") had NO-Legitimate authority to pledge even a square-foot of American-soil, much less pledge the private-property-assets of the American People. That they purported to do this and that the self-interested bankers and lawyers allowed them to do this, is an act of criminality that staggers the mind. This is where we, as authors, can prove that the People in America have a condition called "DENIALISM".

Everything that has been done to the American people is called "identity theft, impersonation of public officials, semantic deceit, unlawful conversion, and constructive fraud carried out on a planetary-basis. Not only were the American-people and their "organic" states cruelly victimized, so were there friends and neighbors and trading-partners. However, the members of the "US Congress" changed hats to become members of the ("US CONGRESS/CEOs"), and glutting on the vast amounts of credit being offered to them – all of this is based on the patently false-claim that they had granted authority to sell everything and everyone in America as chattel and to use us and our-land as surety for their private corporate debts – They charged up our credit-cards to the hilt and left us to pay the bill.

Because of the above reason, the "United-States-Corporate-Government" need(s) to be entirely reformed, the reason that EVERY-MEMBER of "CONGRESS" and every "GOVERNOR" and every member of every "STATE-LEGISLATURE" needs to be "DEPOSED" and "DEPORTED", the reason of the assets of all the complicit banks need to be confiscated, the reason that the current banking institutions and their supposed "watch dog agencies" like the SEC (Security Exchange Commission) need to be dissolved as criminal enterprises, the reason that all "national-debt" needs to be repudiated worldwide, the reason that the Bar Associations – worldwide – need to be disbanded and outlawed, the reason that the "City State" status of the District of Columbia

(Washington D. C.) and the United Nations – both – need to be rescinded, the reason that the English People likewise nee to rescind the "City State" status of the Inner City of London and flush Fleet Street and the Crown Temple into the Thames.

The Immense power of the Pope's Temporal Office needs to be employed to straighten out this steaming pile of manure of a government "service" organizations once and for all.

With this said, we would like to ask Americans this one question and let you think about it while we explain why the courts are being used for the 'death and destruction of America' and for the systematic 'silencing' of Americans who know that the Courts are being used to keep us 'in slavery' or under the 'yoke' of British-rule.

If you discover and report a Major Crime being committed by a Corporate Entity, such as Consumer Fraud through Electric Companies, or other corporations that are polluting or dumping toxic waste or other such vile acts against Americans and you did what you thought was the 'right thing to do' and was a correct decision by exposing them and reporting that crime of who, what, where, when, why and time too all of the Agencies you believed that would help in the investigation only to find out that those that you reported the crime too was involved directly or indirectly with that crime as an accomplice. Why then would you want your case brought before a court that is controlled by those individuals (accomplices) that had or have financial-interests either directly or indirectly in the outcome of your case?

Take the case that was exposed in Flint, Michigan recently. How would you like to drink polluted water and be told by those political-corporate-whores that it is "all in your mind"? "There is nothing wrong with the water". "There is nothing wrong with your children." Only to realize that you and your family have been lied to by those that you trusted to do their jobs they were hired or elected to do.

In our particular case, we really exposed the electric companies for perpetrating a monthly fraud against all customers that led to the eventual downfall of Enron. The State of California was Laundering-Money for 'Government-benefits and retirement-funds' for the Bureaucrats. However, Riverside County and the State of California in conjunction with their co-conspirators; Imperial Irrigation District Water and Power, Southern California Edison, Pacific Gas and Electric, San Diego Gas and Electric and finally eventually Enron were and still are involved with this case of fraud; in addition, with too many other electric companies not listed within this narrative. The Courts themselves and the so-called-professionals (impersonating-bankers) are "protecting" this illegal-act to "protect" their 'money' (financial-interests) and the King's interest.

Now, back to explaining how the courts are destroying America and who is behind it. Have you ever walked into a court room and noticed how it was set up? As you walk into the court room you walk into what is known as the 'Public-Gallery'.

This is where the public is allowed to be seated while court is in session. As you proceed further into the court room, there is a knee wall called the 'Barrister-Rail' with a gate that separates the public gallery from the 'Well'.

The well is where you notice tables and chairs one for the 'plaintiff' also called the claimant and one for the 'defendant' also known as the 'victim' along with their representation. On either the left side or the right side of the well is what is called the 'Jury' Box. This is the location for 12 members with an alternate who sit and hear a case and decide the outcome of 'innocence' or 'guilt'.

Next to the Judges bench but located in the well is where the 'Stenographer' sits, also called the Court Recorder recording the proceedings as best they can.

Off to the right or left of the Judge's Bench you have what is called the 'Witness box'. This is where witnesses are seated and are 'sworn in for the testimony' and have to answer questions for the court and attorneys.

Directly behind the Judge's Bench, as the Judge faces the Public Gallery, you will notice two flags. The one on his/her left is the State Flag with gold fringe. The one on the right is the Federal 'Parade Flag' used for Presidential-Ceremonies and is 'Red, White and Blue with Gold Fringe'. These flags are not just for aesthetic looks. They, like words, have meaning.

Not to change the subject of this discussion, but as you entered the Court Building from the sidewalk or parking lot, you probably noticed a flag pole and a Red, White and Blue flag displayed. The flag displayed outside of the building represents 'Common-Law-Jurisdiction'. Does this flag, which is waving in the breeze or not, have gold fringe on it? (No!) Then ask yourself this question, if the Court Building is displaying a Red, White and Blue flag outside why is the Judge displaying a Red, White and Blue with Gold Fringe on the inside of the court room?

The flags on the inside of the court room set the 'jurisdiction'. The 'jurisdiction' that you find yourself in is called "Admiralty/Maritime or Equity" Jurisdiction. These cases deal with contracts and banks. This jurisdiction suspends the 'Constitution' (which limit what the government can do to you) and 'Suspends your Civil-Rights (which are the first ten amendments of the constitution) creating an 'International British Court room'. This places the trial into a money-making scam for the Royal Heads of England and the [jewish] state of Israel, in other words, the bankers.

Furthermore, the only way a [jew] (remember dual-citizenship) can be seated on a court bench or hear a case is by creating a "false-venue" that allow the Banks and British Government to win and you to lose. This is where the different flags come into the question and equation. In Chapter 4, we point out within the 'Talmud' to show you what the [jewish] laws are and that the [jews] have no "allegiance" for America nor have any intention of supporting the 'Oath or Affirmation' of their trusted office with the exception of our destruction, all for the state of Israel, the Vatican, and the Royal heads of England.

In addition, if you are called before a judge and he/she is [jew] they can be 'recused' from the case because of the financial interest or they can be recused because of a 'biased-opinion' against you from the beginning…after all follow the "talmud" in part in chapter 4 of this book.

However, in our cases the Judges were Zionist [jews] and had financial interests in the outcome of the proceedings. The [jewish] Mafia of Southern California, also known as the "[jewish] Congress of the Desert was behind money-laundering through Enron at the time. But that was information we came across at a later date. There was only one Attorney (Public Defender) that was of "Indian" (line of descent) from

India that was not [jewish]. Everyone else in this case was and are still [jewish], and they all had a 'biased-opinion' against us, even when they knew the 'truth' and 'suppressed' evidence that proved our innocence. The 'Judge' himself was not above committing Jury-Tampering with the use of threats.

In truth, what we got was a 'British trial' with a '[jewish] banker' that called themselves a judge who had us found guilty on false charges for exposing the electric companies for committing fraud against the American people. Furthermore, any time we tried to 'file documentation' through the 'clerk of Courts'. The clerk's office 'adjudicated' (making a judicial decision) by not allowing for filing any document for the case file that actually proved our defense and innocence.

In retaliation, the County of Riverside Tax Assessor's Office was instructed to 'falsify' court documents for the destruction of our home. Their claim was that we did not pay 'property-taxes' throughout 'all of 1990'. The Courts ordered the property sold for 'Back Taxes' and dated the paperwork for 1996. However, we will supply all of the tax records of the "non-payment" during the time frame they have 'lied' about and committed "Fraud upon the Court" further within this book.

In addition, Riverside County publicly claimed that our "home never existed". If our home never existed by their claim and falsification, why were we found "guilty" of "stealing electricity for twenty years"? Where would we have stored the so-called "stolen-electricity"?

What we are doing within the writing of this book is to show Americans that the Political-Corporate-Whores, the Courts, the News Media and Corporate-Government are in collusion and conspiracy to deprive all Americans of any Civil-Rights or any way of Redress of Grievances within the corporate-government.

The difference between Common-Law Jurisdiction and 'Admiralty-Maritime/Equity' Jurisdiction is the absence of contracts and the bank. By Common-Law the Judge considers all of the evidence before its court and common-law applies for all innocent Americans that have followed what they thought were their Civil-Rights. However, unlike the 'Admiralty-Maritime/Equity' Jurisdiction which use contracts that are set up only to allow the judge and lawyers to 'Suppress' any or all evidence that proves your 'innocence'. After all if you are found "innocent" how could the court system gain any finances for the British Government?

This is only the basics of how the courts system is being allowed by the United-States-Corporate-Government, Royal heads of England, the Vatican and the [jews] to destroy America. There are more American's in U. S. Prisons (Corporate-Government) than in any other country in the World; and many of those Americans are 'innocent' (with some exceptions).

The second System that the [jewish] Mafia, the Royal heads of England, the Vatican and the Corporate- United-States is controlling is the Banking system. Let us examine the fact that the Federal Reserve Bank is in control of all of the [green-inked-linen-paper-money] the government has forced us into using, instead of the gold and silver standard as described in the Constitution. Furthermore, you will notice that most, if not all, of the Board of Governors of the Federal Reserve Bank are [jewish]. The Chairman, Ben S. Bernanke is/was [jewish]. The Chairman before him was Alan Greenspan [jewish]. Ask yourself this question; if the [jews] claim they are not trying to control the finances of America why are/is most of the Board of Governors of the Federal Reserve Banking [jewish], which have no "allegiance" for America?

In addition, if you examine the Federal-Reserve-Note across the top you will observe the phrase "IN GOD WE TRUST". God has nothing to do with the Con-script that the United-States-Corporate-Government has enforced upon us. In reality the phrase should reflect how the Corporate-Government feels about their indentured-servants and change it to read "WE SCREW THEM ALL".

The third area that America is being controlled – through brain washing - is through the News Media. Have you ever noticed that when an individual tragically loses their minds for some reason – whatever reason – that individual is incarcerated after having exhausted all of their options, taking the law into their own hands, just to be heard; the news media reports the crime – with a biased opinion and one sided – before a "trial" or "hearing" in any court and are found "'Guilty' or they commit suicide. For example, examine the shooting of the Congresswoman and other victims in Arizona.

This chapter is not for the judgment of victims or perpetrators or a claim that what they did was right, it is however an observation that will inform you of the news media and what they are instructed to do. The News Media is supposed to be the watch-dog for Americans to help keep the Politicians from breaking laws they claim they are not above. However, the news media has become a biased, opinionated-mind-controlling-agency that is just in it for the money. The news media does not care if they print or state the truth as long as they get "the story" and people believing their rendition of what they twist the facts to be. Furthermore, the news media, because of their biased opinions, mislead the public when a crime was supposedly committed. After all, aren't the perpetrator(s)/victim(s) "presumed-innocent"? The courts and the law claim everyone is presumed "innocent" until proven "guilty". However, most of the time when the News Media tells their rendition of the "? FACTS?" the public is alienated against the perpetrators and found "guilty" long before they are in court or before the jury hears and reviews the case or evidence.

In reality, the news media spins their rendition of the facts (which are actually opinions) on any particular case that alienates everyone against the perpetrators. In other words, the jury has fore-knowledge before a court hearing can be convened. Therefore, the victims within the story of the news media are publicly "tried" and found "guilty" before any trial through the "British" Courts even though the courts are in the United-States-Corporate-Government.

The news media was set up to get both sides of a story or information. However, it is increasingly difficult to get both sides of any information without the news media pre-judging, convicting, and destroying American's-lives with their bias one-sided opinion and call it information. This seems to be the final act of ignorance to inform Americans of just how great the government is doing in keeping Americans as slaves. The "Main-stream" News Media, like ABC, CBS, NBC, CNBC or even CNN may or may not be owned by Zionist [jew] investors. But you can bet your reputation that they are controlled by [jewish interests].

However, I will concede that there are a very few, and I mean a very few, News Papers and Tabloids that are explaining the truth and are trying to keep a halfway-honest objective-opinion with facts or evidence for the support of their stories and/or information.

Chapter 4:
THE HATRED FOR AMERICA AND AMERICANS

We will discuss why the [jews] hate Americans and all other religions, by showing factual statements from their religious dogma and propaganda. Furthermore, we will show the connection of the [jewish] Mafia to the Politicians.

In 2011 an author by the name of Herve Ryssen gave an interview for the Occidental Quarterly. One of the statements he made was, "The fact is that the Jewish Mafia is the main Mafia that exists today on this planet: racketeering, prostitution, drug trafficking, arms trading, contraband diamond smuggling, traffic in works of art, murder for hire, organized swindles, armed robberies, etc. Pornography, casinos, and discotheques are also held by Jewish gangster." (Ryssen, 2010)

The reason why people do not want to talk about this is because of the "reflex of 'projection'. The [jewish] intellectuals always project on others that about which they feel guilty. They say they were victims of the holocaust and Communism, for example, when in fact they were the main instigators.

There many crimes that the [jewish] Mafia are involved with. Furthermore, ask yourself this question: in the State of California, according to the Census Bureau the [jewish] population is at 3%. Out of the 3% population how many are lawyers, judges, and/or politicians? In addition, how many are bureaucrats that work within City, County or State Government as employees as "Public Servants" and Impersonating Employees of the government (any government or any of its subsidiaries).

In addition to the above statement by Mr. Ryssen, the [jewish] Mafia is involved in Tax Fraud. I will present for you, the reader, the evidence that [jewish] judges, which are controlled by the [jewish] Mafia or are members of said Mafia, that at least one County – Riverside County,

California, is involved in committing Tax Fraud with their own evidence and documents. To make matters worse, the Governor of California and two U.S. Senators are all [jewish]. All [jews] hate Americans, Christians, and anyone else that are not of [jewish] ancestry (period).

We, as authors, will show you where to find the information within the [jewish] dogma that they 'believe' they are in the 'right' to commit heinous acts against Americans, Christians and anyone and everyone else that are NOT [jewish]. Furthermore, we will show you in what manner the "Precepts of the Talmud" are being practiced today. In addition, we will discuss the definition of "Hate-Crimes" to educate you that anyone that is not of [jewish] ancestry get punished or killed for committing hate crimes…except for those that are [jewish].

The following information in this chapter will not be in its entirety. We will be using quotes that directly involve with those actions of the [jewish] Mafia and the [jewish] laws that they live by in Riverside County, California with provided evidence for the crimes they have and are still committing.

"Let our writings be open to all people. Let them see what our moral code is like! We need not be afraid of this test, for we have a pure heart and a clean spirit. Let the nations investigate the habitations of the children of Israel, and of their own accord convince themselves of what they are really like! They will then exclaim for certain with Balaam, when he went out to curse Israel: 'How beautiful are thy tents O Israel: how beautiful thy homes!'

"In its attitude towards non-jews, the jewish religion is the most tolerant of the religions in the world… The precepts of the ancient rabbis, though inimical (1. Injurious or harmful in effect; adverse: 2. Unfriendly; hostile) [definition taken from dictionary, 2012] to Gentiles, cannot be applied in any way to Christians."

"A whole series of opinions can be quoted from the writings of the highest rabbinical authorities to prove that these teachers inculcated in their own people a great love and respect for Christians, in order that they might look upon Christians, who believe in the true God, as brothers, and pray for them."

"We hereby declare the Talmud does not contain anything inimical to Christians."

The following are direct quotes from the "The Talmud Unmasked" and "Precepts of the Talmud": "From what has been shown thus far, it is clear that, according to the teaching of the Talmud, Christians are idolaters and hateful to jews. As a consequence, every jew who wishes to please God has a duty to observe all the precepts which are given to the fathers of their race when they lived in the holy land concerning the idolatrous gentiles, both who lived amongst them and those in nearby countries. A jew is therefore required to (1) Avoid Christians; (2) Do all he can to exterminate them." (pranaitis, 1892)

"Jews are required to avoid all contact with Christians for four reasons (1) They are not worthy to share in the jewish way of life; (2) They are unclean; (3) They are idolaters; (4) They are murderers." (pranaitis, 1892).

The following are articles that explain these so-called laws of the [jewish] propaganda and dogma. The information can be found in the Talmud.

"Chapter I"

This is quoted from Article I – "Christians must be avoided – Because they are Unworthy to share jewish customs." (Pranaitis, 1892)

"A jew, by the fact that he belongs to the chosen people and is circumcised, possesses so great a dignity that no one, not even an angel, can share equality with him. In fact, he is considered almost the equal of God. "He who strikes an Israelite" rabbi chanina "acts as if he slaps the face of god's Divine Majesty." A jew is always considered good, in spite of certain sins which he may commit; nor can his sins contaminate him, any more than dirt contaminates the kernel in a nut, but only soils its shell. A jew alone is looked upon as a man; the whole world is his and all things should serve him, especially "animals which have the form of men." Thus it is plain that they regard all contact with Christians as contaminating and as detracting from their dignity. They are therefore required to keep as far away as possible from all who live and act as Christians do." (pranaitis, 1892)

1. A jew must not salute a Christian

gittin (62a):

"A jew must not enter a home of a Nokhri on a feast day to offer him greetings. However, if he meets him on the street, he may offer him a greeting, but curtly and with head bowed." (pranaitis, 1892)

2. A jew must not return the greetings of a Christian

Iore Dea (148, 10):

"A jew must not return the greeting of a Christian by bowing before him. It is good, therefore, to salute him first, and so avoid having to answer him back if the Akum salutes him first." The rabbi kohana says that when a jew salutes a Christian he should say "Peace to my lord," but intend this for his own rabbi. For the Tosephtoth says, "For his heart was turned towards his own rabbi." (Pranaitis, 1892)

3. A jew must not go before a Christian Judge

choschen hammischpat (26, 1):

"A jew is not permitted to bring his case before Akum judges, even if the matter is judged by the decisions of jewish law, and even if both parties agree to abide by such decisions. He who does so is impious and similar to one who calumniates and blasphemes, and who raises his hand against the Law given us by Moses, our great law-giver. hagah says 'The bethin has the power to excommunicate such a one until he releases his jewish brother from the hands of the Gentile." (Pranaitis, 1892)

4. A Christian cannot be used as a Witness

Choschen Ham (34, 19):

"A goi [non-jew] or a servant is not capable of acting as a witness. (Pranaitis, 1892)"

This is quoted from Article II – "Christians are to be avoided – because they are Unclean." (Pranaitis, 1892)

This is quoted from Article III – "Christian are to be avoided – because they are Idolaters." (Pranaitis, 1892)

This is quoted from Article IV – "Christians are to be avoided – because they are Evil." (Pranaitis, 1892)

"There is nothing that jews are more convinced of than the harm which Christians can do to the children of Israel. Because of this, the rulers of the chosen people have always instructed them not to accept any help from Christians who will always resort to murder, and to other crimes, whenever they cannot otherwise obtain their evil ends. Thus, a jew must not employ a Christian as a nurse or as a teacher for his children, or as a doctor, a barber or an obstetrician." (Pranaitis, 1892)

1. Not as a Nurse

Iore Dea (81, 7, hagah):

"A child must not be nursed by a nokhri, if an Israelite can be had; for the milk of the nokhrith hardens the heart of a child and builds up an evil nature in him." (Pranaitis, 1892)

2. Not as a Teacher

Iore Dea (153, 1, hagah):

"A child must not be given to the Akum to learn manners, literature of the arts, for they will lead him to heresy." (pranaitis, 1892)

3. Not as a Doctor

Iore Dea (155, 1):

"When a jew is wounded in any way, even so gravely that he would have to violate the Sabbath in having a doctor, he must not employ the services of a Christian (Akum) doctor who is not known to everyone in the neighborhood; for we must guard against the spilling of blood. Even when it is not known if the patient will live or die, such a doctor must not be allowed to attend him. If, however, he is sure to die, then such a doctor may attend him since an extra hour of life is not much to lose. If the Akum insists that a certain medicine is good, you may believe him, but be sure not to buy it from him. There are some who say that this holds only when the Akum offer help free, and that it can be accepted every time it is paid for. But it can be taken for granted that they would not harm a jew just for the sake of a matter of money." (pranaitis, 1892) pesachim (25a):

"rabbi jochanan says: medical help can be accepted from all except idolaters, fornicators, and murderers." (Pranaitis, 1892)

4. Not as a Barber

Iroe Dea (156, 1):

"You must not be shaven by an Akum unless your jewish friends are with you. There are some who say that it is not permitted to be shaved by an Akum even when others are present, unless you can see for yourself in a mirror." (Pranaitis, 1892)

5. Not as an Obstetrician

abhodah zarah (26a):

"Our rabbis have passed it down for us that a foreign woman must never be allowed to act as midwife at the birth of a child of Israel, because they are given to the shedding of blood. The elders say, however, that a foreign woman may perform this task provided there are other jewish women present, but never alone. rabbi meir, however, says that it is not allowed even others are present. For they often crush the soft head of the child with their hands and kill it; and they can do this without being noticed by those who are present." (Pranaitis, 1892)

"Chapter II"

"Christians must be exterminated:"

"The followers of 'that man'- (Jesus Christ) – whose name is taken by the jews to mean "May his name and memory be blotted out," are not otherwise to be regarded than as people whom it would be good to get rid of. They are called Romans and tyrants who hold captive the children of Israel, and by their destruction the jews would be freed from this Fourth Captivity. Every jew is therefore bound to do all he can to destroy that impious kingdom of the Edomites (Rome) which rules the whole world. Since, however, it is not always and everywhere possible to effect this extermination of Christians, the Talmud orders that they should be attacked at least indirectly, namely: by injuring them in every possible way, and by thus lessening their power, help towards their ultimate destruction. Wherever it is possible a jew should kill Christians, and do so without mercy." (Pranaitis, 1892)

Article I – Harm must be done to Christians

"A jew is commanded to harm Christians wherever he can, both indirectly by not helping them in any way, and also directly by wrecking their plans and projects; neither must he save a Christian who is in danger of death." (Pranaitis, 1892)

1. Good must not be done to Christians

Zohar (1, 25b):

"Those who do good to the Akum . . . will not rise from the dead." At times it is permitted to do good to Christians, but only in order to help Israel, namely, for the sake of peace and to hide hatred of them." (pranaitis, 1892)

maimonides in hilkhoth akum (X, 6):

"Needy Gentiles may be helped as well as needy jews, for the sake of peace…" (Pranaitis, 1892)

Iroe Dea (148, 12 hagah):

"Therefore, if you enter a town and find them celebrating a feast, you may pretend to rejoice with them in order to hide your hatred. Those, however, who care about the salvation of their souls, should keep away from such celebrations. You should make it known that it is a hateful thing to rejoice with them, if you can do so without incurring enmity." (Pranaitis, 1892)

2. It is not permitted to praise a Christian

3. A jew is not allowed to mention the things which Christians use for their Idolatrous Worship

4. Their Idols must be spoken of with Contempt

5. A jew is not allowed to give gifts to Christians

6. A jew is forbidden to sell his farm to Christians

Iroe Dea (334, 43):

"In 24 cases a must be repudiated, namely ...8. Anyone who sells his farm to the Akum must be sent into exile – unless he undertakes to make up for all the harm that follows as a consequence of having the Akum live near the jews." (Pranaitis, 1892)

7. It is forbidden to teach a trade to Christians

Iroe Dea (154, 2):

"It is not permitted to teach any trade to the Akum." (Pranaitis, 1892)

Article II – Harm must be done to the work of Christians

"Since the goim minister to jews like beasts of burden, belong to a jew together with his life and all his faculties: "The life of a goi and all his physical powers belong to a jew." (a. rohl. die polem. P. 20): It is an axiom of the rabbis that a jew may take anything that belongs to Christians for any reason whatsoever, even by fraud; nor can such be called robbery since it is merely taking what belongs to him." (pranaitis, 1892)

babba bathra (54 b):

"All things pertaining to the goim are like a desert; the first person to home along and take them can claim for his own." (pranaitis, 1892)

1. Christians must not be told if they pay too much to a jew

Choschen Hammischpat (183, 7):

"If you send a messenger to collect money from an Akum and the Akum pays too much, the messenger may keep the difference. But if the messenger does not know about it, then you may keep it all yourself." (Pranaitis, 1892)

2. Lost property of Christians must not be returned to them

"A jew may keep anything he finds which belongs to the Akum, for it is written: Return to thy brethren what is lost (Deuter. XXII, 3). For he who returns lost property [to Christians] sins against the law by increasing the power of the transgressors of the law. It is praiseworthy, however, to return lost property if it is done to honor the name of God, namely, if by so doing Christians will praise the jews and look upon them as honorable people." (Pranaitis, 1892)

3. Christians may be defrauded

babba kama (113b):

"It is permitted to deceive a goi." (pranaitis, 1892)

choschen hamm (156, 5 hagah):

"If a jew is doing good business with an akum it is not allowed to other jews, in certain places, to come and do business with the same akum. In other places, however, it is different, where another jew is allowed to go to the same akum, lead him on, do business with him an to deceive him and take his money. For the wealth of the akum is to be regarded as common property and belongs to the first who can get it. There are some, however, who say that this should not be done." (pranaitis, 1892)

choschen hamm (183, 7 hagah):

"If a jew is doing business with an akum and a fellow israelite comes along and defrauds, the akum, either by false measure, weight or number, he must divide his profit with his fellow israelite, since both had a part in the deal, and also in order to help him along." (pranaitis, 1892)

4. A jew may pretend he is Christian to Deceive Christians

Iore Dea (157, 2):

"If a jew is able to deceive those [Idolaters] by pretending he is a worshipper of the stars, he may do so." (pranaitis, 1892)

5. A jew is allowed to practice usury on Christians

abhodah zarah (54a):

"It is allowed to take usury from Apostates who fall into Idolatry." (pranaitis, 1892)

Iore Dea (159, 1):

"It is permitted, according to the torah, to lend money to an akum with usury. Some of the elders, however, deny this except in a case of life and death. Nowadays it is permitted for any reason." (pranaitis, 1892)

Article III – Christians may be harmed in Legal Matters

1. A jew may lie and perjure himself to condemn a Christian

Babba Kama (113a):

"Our teaching is as follows: When a jew and a Goi come into a court, absolve the jew, if you can, according to the laws of Israel. If the Goi wins, tell him that is what our laws require. If however, the jew can be absolved according to the Gentile Law, absolve him and say it is due to our laws. If this cannot be done proceed callously against the Goim, as rabbi ischmael advises. The rabbi akibha, however, holds that you cannot act fraudulently lest you profane the name of God, and have a jew committed for perjury. A marginal note, however, explains this qualification of rabbi akibha as follows: "The name of God is not profaned when it is not known by the Goi that the jew has lied." (pranaitis, 1892)

babba kama (113b):

"The name of God is not profaned when, for example, a jew lies to a Goi by saying: 'I gave something to your father, but he is dead; you must return it to me,' as long as the Goi does not know that you are lying." (pranaitis, 1892)

2. A jew may perjure himself with a clear conscience

kallah (1b, p. 18):

"She (the mother of the mamzer) said to him, 'and rabbi Akibha swore with his lips, but in his heart, he invalidated his oath." (Pranaitis, 1892)

schabbuoth hagahoth (6d):

"A similar text can be found by rabbi ascher. "If the magistrate of a city compels jews to swear that they will not escape from the city nor take anything out of it, they may swear falsely by saying to themselves that they will not escape today, nor take anything out of the city today only." (pranaitis, 1892)

Article IV – Christians must be harmed in Things Necessary for Life

"The jews must spare no means in fighting the tyrants who hold them to this fourth captivity in order to set themselves free. They must fight Christians with astuteness and do nothing to prevent evil from happening to them: their sick must not be cared for, Christian women in childbirth must not be helped, nor must they be saved when in danger of death." (pranaitis, 1892)

1. A jew must always try to Deceive Christians

zohar (I, 160a):

"The rabbi jehuda said to him [rabbi chezkia]: 'He is to be praised who is able to free himself from the enemies of Israel, and the just are much to be praised who get free from them and fight against them. rabbi chezkia asked, 'How must we fight against them?' rabbi jehuda said, 'By wise counsel thou shalt war against them' (Proverbs, Ch. 24, 6). By what kind of War? The kind of war that every son of man must fight against his enemies, which jacob used against esau – by deceit and trickery whenever possible. They must be fought against without ceasing, until proper order is restored. Thus, it is with satisfaction that I say we should free ourselves from them and rule over them." (pranaitis, 1892)

2. A sick Christian must not be aided

Iore Dea (158, 1):

"The akum are not to be cured, even for money, unless it would incur their enmity." (pranaitis, 1892)

3. A Christian Woman in Childbirth must not be helped

orach chaiim (330, 2):

"No help is to be given to an akun woman in labor on the Sabbath, even in a small way, for the Sabbath must not be violated." (pranaitis, 1892)

4. A Christian in Danger of Death must not be helped

choschen hamm (425, 5):

"If you see a heretic, who does not believe in the Torah, fall into a well in which there is a ladder, hurry at once and take it away and say to him 'I have to go and take my son down from a roof; I will bring the ladder back to you at once' or something else. The kuthaei, however, who are not our enemies, who take care of the sheep of the Israelites, are not to be killed directly, but they must not be saved from death." (pranaitis, 1892)

Iore Dea (158, 1):

"The akum who are not enemies of ours must not be killed directly; nevertheless, they must not be saved from danger of death. For example, if you see one of them fall into the sea, do not pull him out unless he promises to give you money." (pranaitis, 1892)

maimonides, in hilkhoth akum (X, 1):

"Do not have pity for them, for it is said (Deuter. VII, 2): Show no mercy unto them. Therefore, if you see an akum in difficulty or drowning, do not go to his help. And if he is in danger of death, do not save him from death. But it is not right to kill him by your own hand by shoving them into a well or in some other way, since they are not at war with us." (pranaitis, 1892)

Article V – Christians are to be killed

"Lastly, the talmud commands that Christians are to be killed without mercy." (pranaitis, 1892)

abhodah zarah (26b):

"Heretics, traitors and apostates are to be thrown into a well and not rescued." (pranaitis, 1892)

choschen hammischpat (388, 10):

"A spy is to be killed, even in our days, wherever he is found. He may be killed even before he confesses. And even if he admits that he only intended to do harm to somebody, and if the harm which he intended is not very great, it is sufficient to have him condemned to death. He must be warned, however, not to confess to this. But if he impudently says, 'No, I will confess it!' then he must be killed, and the sooner the better. If there is no time to warn him, it is not necessary to do so. There are some who say that a traitor is to be put to death only when it is impossible to get rid

70

of him by mutilating him, that is, by cutting out his tongue or his eyes, but if this can be done, he must not be killed, since he is not worse than others who persecute us." (pranaitis, 1892)

choschen hamm (388, 15):

"If it can be proved that someone has betrayed israel three times, or has given the money of israelites to the akum, a way must be found after prudent consideration to wipe him off the face of the earth." (pranaitis, 1892)

1. Renegades to be killed

"Even a Christian who is studying the law of israel merits Death." (pranaitis, 1892)

sanhedrin (59a):

"rabbi jochanan says: 'A Goi who pries into the law is guilty to death.'" (pranaitis, 1892)

2. Baptized jews are put to death

"These things [supra] are intended for Idolaters. But Israelites also, who lapse from their religion and become epicureans, [fond of or adapted to luxury or indulgence in sensual pleasures; having luxurious tastes or habits] (online dictionary definition), are to be killed and we must persecute them to the end. For they afflict Israel and turn the people from God." (pranaitis, 1892)

Iore Dea (158, 2 hagah):

"Renegades who turn to the pleasures of the Akum, and who become contaminated with them by worshipping stars and planets as they do, are to be killed." (pranaitis, 1892)

choschen hamm (425, 5):

"The jews who become epicureans, who take to the worship of stars and planets and sin maliciously; and those who eat the flesh of wounded animals, or who dress in vain clothes, deserve the name of epicureans; likewise, those who deny the torah and the prophets of israel – the law is that all those should be killed; and if this cannot be done, they should be led to their death by deceptive methods." (pranaitis, 1892)

Maimonides, in hilkhoth teschubhah (III, 8):

"Gives the list of those who are considered as denying the law: 'There are three classes of people who deny the law of the torah: (1.) Those who say that the torah was not given by God, at least one verse or one word of it, and who say that it was all the work of moses; (2.) Those who reject the explanation of the torah, namely, the oral law of the mischnah, and do not recognize the authority of the doctors of the law, like the followers of tsadok (sadducees) and baithos; (3.) Those who say that God changed the law for another new law and that the torah no longer has any value, although they do not deny that it was given by God, as the Christians and the Turks believe. All of these deny the law of the torah." (pranaitis, 1892)

3. Christians are to be killed because they are Tyrants

zohar (I, 25a):

"The People of the earth are Idolaters, and it has been written about them: Let them be wiped off the face of the earth. Destroy the memory of the amalekites. They are with us still in this Fourth Captivity, namely, the Princes [of Rome] . . . . Who are really amalekites?" (pranaitis, 1892)

A). These Princes are to be killed first

"For if they are allowed to live, the hope of the liberation of the jews is in vain, and their prayers for release from this Fourth Captivity are of no avail." (pranaitis, 1892)

zohar (I, 219B):

"It is certain that our captivity will last until the princes of the gentiles who worship idols are destroyed." (pranaitis, 1892)

Zohar (II, 19a):

"rabbi jehuda said: 'Come and see how it is; how the princes have assumed power over Israel and the Israelites make no outcry. But their rejoicing is heard when the prince falls. It is written that: the King of the Egyptians died and soon the children of Israel were released from captivity; they cried out and their voice ascended to God." (pranaitis, 1892)

B). The Princedom whose chief city is Rome is the one to be Hated most of all by the jews

"They call it the Kingdom of Esau, and of the edomites, the Kingdom of Pride, the Wicked Kingdom, Impious Rome. The Turkish Empire is called the Kingdom of the Israelites which they do not wish to destroy. The Kingdom of Rome, however, must be exterminated, because when corrupt Rome is destroyed, salvation and freedom will come to God's chosen people." (pranaitis, 1892)

obadiam (written script by rabbi kimchi):

"What the Prophets foretold about the destruction of Edom in the last days was intended for Rome, as Isaiah explains (Ch. 34, 1): 'Come near, ye nations, to hear. . .. For when Rome is destroyed, israel shall be redeemed.' In his book, (tseror hammor, section schofti,) rabbi abraham scripted the same, "Immediately after Rome is destroyed, we shall be redeemed." (pranaitis, 1892)

4. Lastly, all Christians, including the Best of Them are too be killed

abhodah zarah (26b, tosephoth):

"Even the best of the Goim should be killed." (pranaitis, 1892)

schulchan arukh, after the words of Iore Dea (158, 1):

"Those of the akum who do no harm to jews are not to be killed, namely those who do not wage war against israel, thus explains the word milchamah – war: 'But in time of war the akum are to be killed, for it is written: 'The good among the akum deserve to be killed, etc.'" (pranaitis, 1892)

5. A jew who kills a Christian commits no Sin, but offers an acceptable sacrifice to God

6. After the destruction of the Temple at Jerusalem, the only sacrifice necessary is the Extermination of Christians

zohar (III, 227b) Good Pastor:

"The only sacrifice required is that we remove the unclean from amongst us." (pranaitis, 1892)

zohar (II, 43a) explaining the precept of moses about the redemption of the first born of an ass by offering a lamb:

"The ass means the non-jew, who is to be redeemed by the offering of a lamb, which is the dispersed sheep of israel. But if he refuses to be redeemed, then break his skull.... They should be taken out of the book of living, for it is said about them: 'He, who sins against me, I shall take out of the book of life.'" (pranaitis, 1892)

7. Those who kill Christians shall have a high place in heaven

8. The jews must never cease to exterminate the goim: They must never leave them in peace and never submit to them

hilhoth akum (X, 1):

"Do not eat with Idolaters, nor permit them to worship their idols; for it is written: 'Make no covenant with them, nor show mercy unto them.' (Deuter. Ch. 7, 2). Either turn away from their idols or kill them." (pranaitis, 1892)

ibidem (X, 7):

"In places where jews are strong, no idolater must be allowed to remain..." (pranaitis, 1892)

9. All jews are obliged to unite together to destroy traitors among them

choschen hamm (338, 16):

"All the inhabitants of a city are obliged to contribute to the expense of killing a traitor, even those who have to pay other taxes." (pranaitis, 1892)

10. No festival, no matter how solemn, must prevent the beheading of a Christian

pesachim (49b):

"The rabbi eliezer said: 'It is permitted to cut off the head of an 'idiot' [one of the people of the earth] on the feast of the atonement when it falls on the Sabbath'. His disciples said to him: 'rabbi, you should rather say to sacrifice.' But he replied: 'By no means, for it is necessary to pray while sacrificing, and there is no need of prayers when you behead someone.'" (pranaitis, 1892)

11. The one object of all the actions and prayers of the jews should be to destroy the Christian Religion

"Thus, the jews picture their messiah and liberator whom they expect, as a persecutor who will inflict great calamities upon non-jews. The talmud lists three Great Evils which will come upon the world when the messiah comes." (pranaitis, 1892)

schabbath (118a):

"Whoever eats three meals on the Sabbath shall be saved from the three evils: from the punishments of the messiah, from the pain of hell and from the war of Magog; for it is written: 'Behold, I shall send you elias the prophet before the coming of the 'Day' of the lord,' etc." (pranaitis, 1892)

12. In their prayers the jews sigh for the coming of the revengeful messiah, especially on the eve of Passover

The above transcript taken from the talmud is not in its entirety. We do apologize, however for using and quoting from it as much as we have. However, it is our intention to show you, the reader, that we are not the only persons or victims of the jewish Mafia committing malicious and evil acts upon Americans or Christians. Then, in turn, the jews wonder why "acts of violence" or "Hate Crimes" are being committed in retaliation or retribution against them.

What we Americans would like to know and have an answer for is a simple question: "What did the American People do too cause the "enmity and hatred" from the jewish people after Americans saved them from certain death from concentration camps during WWII?"

We are fully cognizant of the fact that the jewish people were extremely abused in Germany during WWII and we sympathize for them. However, "109 locations, dating from 250 AD to 1948, cannot be wrong in "expelling" the [jews] from those Locations". Quotation came from Statistics and Analysis (Unknown, 2012).

We are adding the U. S. Legal definition of a "Hate Crime" in this chapter because it will help in the understanding of the jewish law within the Talmud and show the bias and hateful opinion that the jews adhere to and obey to their individual discretion and practices. Furthermore, we will show you that the jews and their 'protectors' are lying to Americans and Christians to serve their selfish interests and that of the state of Israel.

"Hate crime – In crime and law, hate crimes (also known as biased-motivated crimes) occur when a perpetrator targets a victim because of his or her perceived membership in a certain social group, usually defined by racial group, religion, sexual orientation, disability, class, ethnicity, nationality, age, sex, or gender identity."

"A hate crime is a category used to described bias-motivated violence: "assault, injury, and murder on the basis of certain personal characteristics: different appearance, different color, different nationality, different language, different religion."

"Hate crime generally refers to criminal acts that are seen to have been motivated by bias against one or more of the types above, or of their derivatives. Incidents may involve physical assault, damage to property, bullying, harassment, verbal abuse or insults, or offensive graffiti or letters (hate-mail)." On a personal observation, in the above paragraph they should also include "Hate Literature" and not just (hate-mail).

"A hate crime law is a law intended to prevent bias-motivated violence. Hate crime laws are distinct from laws against hate speech in that hate crime laws enhance the penalties associated with conduct that is already criminal under other laws, while hate speech laws criminalize a category of speech."

"Hate crime laws generally fall into one of several categories: (1). Laws defining specific bias-motivated acts as distinct crimes; (2). Criminal penalty-enhancement laws; (3). Laws creating a distinct civil cause of action for hate crimes; and (4). Laws requiring administrative agencies to collect crime statistics. Sometimes, the laws focus on war crimes, genocide, and crimes against humanity with the prohibition against discriminatory action limited to public officials."

"The current federal law regarding hate crimes deals with crimes when the offender is motivated by bias against a race, religion, disability, sexual orientation, or ethnicity/national origin and only applies if the crime happens when a person is attending a public school or is at work or is participating in one of four other "federally protected activities.""

"The following is an example of a statute governing hate crimes:" (Definition, 2012)

"a. The Legislature finds and declares the following:"

"1. It is the right of every person, regardless of race, color, religion, national origin, ethnicity, or physical or mental disability, to be secure and protected from threats of reasonable fear, intimidation, harassment, and physical harm caused by activities of groups and individuals."

"2. It is not the intent, by enactment of this section, to interfere with the exercise of rights protected by the Constitution of the State of Alabama or the United States."

"3. The intentional advocacy of unlawful acts by groups or individuals against other persons or groups and bodily injury or death to persons is not constitutionally protected when violence or civil disorder is imminent, and poses a threat to public order and safety, and such conduct should be subjected to criminal sanctions."

"b. The purpose of this section is to impose additional penalties where it is shown that a perpetrator committing the underlying offense was motivated by the victim's actual or perceived race, color, religion, national origin, ethnicity, or physical or mental disability."

"c. A person who has been found guilty of a crime, the commission of which was shown beyond a reasonable doubt to have been motivated by the victim's actual or perceived race, color, religion, national origin, ethnicity, or physical or mental disability, shall be punished as follows:"

"1. Felonies:"

"a. On conviction of a Class A felony that was found to have been motivated by the victim's actual or perceived race, color, religion, national origin, ethnicity, or physical or mental disability, the sentence shall not be less than 15 years."

"b. On conviction of a Class B felony that was found to have been motivated by the victim's actual or perceived race, color, religion, national origin, ethnicity, or physical or mental disability, the sentence shall not be less than 10 years."

"c. On conviction of a Class C felony that was found to have been motivated by the victim's actual or perceived race, color, religion, national origin, ethnicity, or physical or mental disability, the sentence shall not be less than two years."

"d. For purposes of this subdivision, a criminal defendant who has been previously convicted of any felony and receives an enhanced sentence pursuant to this section is also subject to enhanced punishment under the Alabama Habitual Felony Offender Act, Section 13A-5-9."

"2. Misdemeanors:"

"On conviction of a misdemeanor which was found beyond reasonable doubt to have been motivated by the victim's actual or perceived race, color, religion, national origin, ethnicity, or physical or mental disability, the defendant shall be sentenced for a Class A misdemeanor, except that the defendant shall be sentenced to a minimum of three months."

For further understanding, the legal definition for the word 'bias' is as follows:

"Inclination; bent; prepossession: a preconceived opinion; a predisposition to decide a cause or an issue in a certain way, which does not leave the mind perfectly open to conviction. Maddox v. State, 32 Ga. 5S7, 79 Am. Dec. 307; Pierson v. State, 18 Tex. App. 55S; Hinkle v. State, 94 Ga. 595, 21 S. E. 601. This term is not synonymous with "prejudice." By the use of this word in a statute declaring disqualification of jurors, the legislature intended to describe another and somewhat different ground of disqualification. A man cannot be prejudiced against another without being biased against him; but he may be biased without being prejudiced. Bias is "a particular influential power, which sways the judgment; the inclination of the mind towards a particular object." It is not to be supposed that the legislature expected to secure in the juror a state of mind absolutely free from all inclination to one side or the other. The statute means that, although a juror has not formed a judgment for or against the prisoner, before the evidence is heard on the trial, yet, if he is under such an influence as so sways his mind to the one side or the other as to prevent his deciding the cause according to the evidence, he is incompetent. Willis v. State, 12 Ga. 444. Actual bias consists in the existence of a state of mind on the part of the juror which satisfies the court, in the exercise of a sound discretion, that the juror cannot try the issues impartially and without prejudice to the substantial rights of the party challenging. State v. Chapman, 1 S. D. 414. 47 N. W. 411, 10 L. R. A. 432; People v. McQuade, 110 N. Y. 284. 18 N. E. 150, 1 L. R. A. 273; People v. Wells, 100 Cal. 227, 34 Pac. 718." (Henry Campbell Black, 1990)

As authors of this book and victims of these crimes that are being committed against Americans and Christians alike, on a daily basis, we feel it necessary to point out to you the illegal practices that the courts, politicians, and the [jewish] Mafia are involved in and are calling it "law" or "just business as usual."

In 1985 when Ronald Reagan was President, he, like other Presidents before him declared an International "Witch Hunt". However, these 'witches' were actually Organized Crime Bosses. The Vatican, the Royal Heads of England, the [jews], and the UNITED-STATES-Corporate-Government hunted down and tried these bosses, but what the people did not know was that Ronald Regan was a 'puppet' for the [jewish] mafia; and the so-called-hunt for crime bosses did not include [jews] or [jewish] mob leaders that were and still are in America. In reality it's no-wonder why the UNITED-STATES-Corporate-Government is hated by so many other countries. Furthermore, the UNITED STATES is only 240 years old in 2016. How can the UNITED STATES solve or 'arbitrate' any problems that other countries/governments may have internally when they themselves can't keep their own from committing 'crimes' and 'crimes against humanity'?

One of the main reasons why other countries hate the United-States-Corporate-Government is because they believe they have all the answers to problems and that they negotiate any situation in their favor. If the United-States-Corporate-Government cannot negotiate any deal, settlement, agreement or whatever, they have a tendency of causing problems and plying wrongful propaganda against those that will not discuss or settle either way. Besides, most of the other Countries believe we, as Americans, are barbarians and not worth their time. For example, how many of you readers have contacted any of the World Leaders? They are people just like you.

One last note about the "talmud" …we realize that this [jewish] book was started and written by 'abraham' father of all [jews] and the [jews] claim that it is the most "beautiful" of books written. However, I will point out that not everyone accepts this statement as truthful. I find that the Hindu or Indian Kama Sutra the most beautifully written books. At least the Kama Sutra does not explain how all other peoples of the planet earth are just slaves or marked for death by a certain self-important self-proclaimed pompous people…like the [jews].

Chapter 5:
THE-GREAT-ILLUSIONS: WITH TAX RECEIPTS FOR EVIDENCE

This chapter will discuss the great 'illusions', the smoking Mirrors (aka; the lies) that the government has been perpetrating on Americans from the time of the signing of the Declaration of Independence, the Constitution, and the Bill of Rights.

The first lie that was perpetrated against all Americans is this: "Americans have Rights". Unfortunately, the Political-Corporate-Whores (through the FICTITIOUS FEDERAL-GOVERNMENT, STATES, COUNTIES, CITIES, and MUNICIPALITY AGENCIES) have changed our "Rights" and made them into 'Privileges' and are charging for those privileges. This according to the "Constitution" (which set Limits on what the United-States-Corporate-Government can do) is against the Law. Meaning the United-States-Corporate-Government is using "Bill of Attainders" or "Bills of Pain and Punishment" to keep Americans and U. S. Citizens (as indentured-servants) alike under control and afraid.

One of these lies is that "You own your own home". This is not entirely the truth. First of all, when you spend thousands or hundreds of thousands, even millions, of dollars for property or for a home, you do not own it at all. The reality is that the English Monarchy, the Banks (the [jews]) and the 'County Government' own your property; even when you have paid for the 'mortgage' in full and owe nothing against it.

The first thing a land owner does is to take the 'Title, Deed, or Conveyance' and register it with the County Government. However, the County Government doesn't explain to the individuals that 'recording your title, deed or conveyance with the county is voluntary'. It is NOT required by their laws to do so. If any bureaucrat claims that it is "Law" that you have to "record" your property with that county, have them put it in writing or tell you where to find the so-called written-law. This action gives these bureaucrats the right (or so they think – which is questionable) to 'tax' the land owner continuously for property they own and have paid for. Furthermore, when you "record the property" that your family has purchased, back into "County Government" you have accepted all of the hidden and implied "Statutes, Codes and Ordinances" that go with this "Contractual-Agreement". In addition, the Foreign-Fictitious-political-corporate-whores claim that it is your "civic-duty" to pay taxes---my answer to this and question is this…Would you pay taxes to a corporate-government that practices organized-crime? Or that "misappropriates funds to fund their special "Friends, Businesses, or Family-Members"? If so…let's move to Russia or create a Communistic/Socialistic Government.

The reason why we are explaining this to you in this manner is because there is a way to stop the States and Counties and the Foreign-Fictitious-Political-corporate-whores from committing Racketeering and Fraud against tax payers and Americans alike. The County and State Government or political-corporate-whores may not like the 'Truth" within these pages. However, they cannot 'deny' the 'truth'. They just want to hide from it under any disguise or excuse they can formulate.

The only time when a land owner has to pay 'taxes' on said mortgage or property is when there is a bank mortgage involved. This helps protect the bankers and sellers and helps the government for improvements. Then the land owner has to record the 'Title, Deed or Conveyance' into the County Government for the protection of the Bank that "holds the mortgage-lien". However, this can be a "double-edged sword" and can cut both ways. Remember, County Governments ask you to "voluntarily" record your "Title, Deed or Conveyance" with them, it is not a "Law" nor is it "Mandatory" that you do so. Your Great-Grand-Parents used to have what was called a "Mortgage-Burning" Party…this they did when the mortgage was paid-in-full and they owned their home lock, stock and barrel. This means the Banks and Government was no longer involved with what they personally owned.

Allow us to explain it to you this way. If you purchase a home and property and you 'record' said 'description of property' with the County Seat, you have just 'given' ownership of that property over to the County Government. This is why "Land Speculators, Developers, and Major

Corporations" can destroy any neighborhood to do what they call "improvements"; just because you were ignorant of what you thought what the County Government was supposed to do.

Now that you have purchased "Property" and you have done what you thought was the "Right thing to do" by recording the "property-description" back into the County Government Jurisdiction here is what you will have to expect from your County Government. All debts that are incurred against the property will be at the owners' expense. Meaning, if you get 'Home Owners Insurance', 'Remodeling the home', or any other expenditures that you or your family spend on the property for what the County Government deems 'Property-Improvements' the 'property-owner' has to pay for.

However, since you do not own the "property" that you thought you were purchasing this makes the County Government "legally" responsible for the costs of the property and insurance. Think about it, if the Internal Revenue Service states, "Everyone is under the illusion that you own your property. They do not. The Corporate-County-Government does; only because they record the description of the property back into County Records and Jurisdiction". In reality all you paid for or purchased is a piece of paper that allows you to stay on the property. If the Counties 'own the land' and all you get is an expensive piece of paper then why do you have to consult Realtors? All you would have to do is to go to the County and 'purchase' the property you are interested in; after all, 'the County' owns it.

There is a way to stop the County from stealing your property. What you want to do after you have paid off the "property" and there is no mortgage-lien against it, is to take the "Title, Deed or Conveyance" and put it somewhere in a safe place that you know where it is. Do not record the 'property description' into the County Seat. This will sever the (so-called) County Jurisdiction and the 'Implied-Contract' from your property. However, you do want to pay the 'taxes' voluntarily and keep the receipts safe. What the Counties like to do is claim that you did not pay your 'taxes' and take your property from you under this trickery and deceit. If the County bureaucrats file against you in their controlled courts, then you have the receipts to show that they are now committing 'Fraud upon the Courts' and "Breach of Contract". However, you want to remember you are now producing evidence of a "CONTRACT" into the admiralty/maritime jurisdiction in a foreign-court.

This is one of the "Dirty Little Secrets" that County Governments and its Agencies do not want you to know. Furthermore, there is no "statute of limitations" for filing against the Counties for committing 'Fraud upon the Courts' or 'Breach of Contract' or 'R. I. C. O.' (Racketeer Influenced and Corrupt Organizations laws).

Another dirty secret that is being done by the States deals with your vehicles. Do you think you own that vehicle that you paid for? If you answered yes, you would be sorely wrong. Look at all the 'money' you have to spend every year just to keep the 'privilege' of driving to and from your destinations.

The Second lie is this: the Political-Corporate-Whores claim, "We are not above the Law". However, through their actions and (in our case and other cases) lack of actions, they have placed themselves "Above the Law". I mean, in reality those Political-Corporate-Whores, to this day cannot, walk on water, raise the dead or change water into wine. They are !HUMAN! Not above anyone else. The only thing going for them is that they have never been caught doing illegal acts or any of the courts under their influence never will find them 'guilty'. After all, if they were found "guilty" of a crime, for example: Breach of Contract (i.e. The Oath of Office) the added charges, according to the U. S. Constitution and the State Constitution(s), High Treason is a crime punishable by "DEATH". All other crimes would put them behind bars for a very long time. However, you must remember that the Judges and court officers are "paid" to 'protect' those that make money for the United-States-Corporate-Government and the King…even if it means to 'neutralize' or 'kill' for their protection.

The third lie is this, "You are innocent until 'proven' guilty!" This is the most financially expensive lie ever perpetrated against all Americans…to date. If you were to look at the facts, all lawyers, politicians, judges, or even bureaucrats very few are ever convicted for ANY type of wrong doing. Those that are – are 'guilty' of "gross-negligence". Not what they are charged for. In other words, the established "caught" criminals have their hands slapped…because they still have the capability of making money for the [jews], Vatican, and

United-States-Corporate-Government. This in itself is a Major Crime against Americans. Debate this if you can.

As Americans, we as a people are vested in the United States of America. Every American has a personal stake on how this country of ours is being run, whether it is legal or not. It is our American Duty to expose those Bureaucrats, Politicians, Judges and Lawyers and all United-States-Corporate-Government Agencies and businesses that are defrauding the people out of their hard-earned money (conscript). The true-government a government in which the supreme power is vested in the people and exercised by them directly or indirectly through a system of representation usually involves periodically held free elections. As an American being vested does not necessarily mean that you get money out of the corporate-government for retirement – even though you as a tax-payer pay into what is known as the Social Security Administration for your future retirement. Being vested also means to stay on-guard against any and all illegal insipid actions and practices that is being conducted by those bureaucrats that think (?) they are untouchable and above the law. If by chance these so-called professionals claim that we civilian-Americans are not vested in our Government remind them of the fact about paying taxes as well as Social Security these are vested interests.

Well, welcome to the world of fiction! The United-States-Corporate-Government and the State-Corporate-Government and all of their agencies and subdivisions such as the city, county, boroughs and townships and banks are corporations. Note: observe, Corpus Juris Secundum; heading under "Government" (observe Black's Law Dictionary, "corporations"). All corporations are fictions or "artificial" persons created under the authority of the law or "color of law", and all such corporate fictions are established and formed by a set of rules called By-Laws, also known as "Policy and Procedures" The United-States-Corporate-Government and all of its subsidiaries and Agencies use the term "CONSTITUTION" as the name of their By-Laws or state "It is our Policy and Procedure". These By-Laws are nothing more than an offer to the "people" of the forum the Corporate-Government intends to use to govern. (Note: Their "CONSTITUTIONS" (By-Laws) are amended internally as opposed to genuine government constitutions which are externally amended). In the history of the formation of the United States government, its By-Laws, the "CONSTITUTION, Bill of Rights and

85

Amendments thereto were offered to the whole world, but only officially accepted and ratified by representatives of the State-Corporate-Governments, thus binding both Corporate-Governments in a 'Contract'. However, in reality there seems to be no-contract in existence involving 'Private-Americans' as a party to the constitution. With one small exception…the BILL OF RIGHTS! These apply for ALL Americans. A contract has been defined as an agreement containing a promise enforceable by law. An 'agreement' implies that there are at least two parties involved, since one party cannot agree with a 'proposition' unless it is made to them by another party. The term 'agreement' further implies that one party proposed a promise or offer to which the other party agreed or accepted. This creates a legal-binding contract.

If you have ever been to court over any kind of issue, you will realize that the "CONSTITUTION" is non-existent. A judge will state to you that "the Constitution doesn't mean anything within this courtroom". The judge may even threaten you with a charge of 'contempt of court' when even mention the word "CONSTITUTION". Attorneys/Lawyers will tell you that they do not use the constitution the same is said for Tax-Collectors and Police Officers. What they are doing in reality is withdrawing the offer to you the American-private-people simply because you, or the private-sector, have never formally "accepted" their offer. Whether the offer is the united States Constitution or the Constitution of the State-Corporate-Government (i.e. "this State"; "THE STATE OF…" or "THE PEOPLE OF THE STATE OF… Vs :….") near where we live our private lives. The private sector has never formally accepted the "oath" of any government worker/officer to uphold and defend the constitution, which is required by law (their law) upon taking office. But it appears to be a "MUST" that the private-American-sector has to formally accept the constitutions as well as the "oath of office" of any public-servant (meaning any self-proclaimed government employee), that we are forced to do business within their (?official?) capacity.

Another way of looking at this, consider that all public-officials are often referred to as "honorable" (i.e. the Honorable Judge so and so; the Honorable Senator so-and-so…and so forth). If you think about this for a moment, consider that perhaps 'we' have been looking at this in a way that has not been to our benefit. How can an the private-American-sector "Honor" these officials if they "Falsely assumes or pretends to be an officer or employee acting under the authority of the United States or any department agency or officer thereof, and acts as such, or in such pretended character demands or obtains any money, paper, document, or thing of value, shall be fined under this title or imprisoned not more than three years, or both. TITLE: 18 – CRIMES AND CRIMINAL PROCEDURE, PART I – CRIMES, CHAPTER: 43 – FALSE PERSONATION; HEAD: Sec. 912. Officer or employee of United States. STATUTE".

If we do accept or "Honor" someone's offering, do we not become the customer? And the old saying is "Isn't the customer, "King"?

The main reason behind the concept of a "Notice of Acceptance of the Constitutions" and of "Oath of Office" is the 'protection' afforded by the constitutions of the private-sector's personal 'liberty and private-property'.

In the history of the world there has never been a better form of government other than what the Constitution provide for us here in America. But, throughout history of the world has there ever been such corruption of the purpose of a government by a small group of greedy, self-serving, cooked people who abuse and misuse the power of office as we have experienced here in America.

Private property has been taken by forced registration and recordation into CORPORATE-GOVERNMENT records, which casts upon the private-sector an onslaught of CORPORATE-GOVERNMENT regulations and taxation. If the State-Corporate-Government or any of its political sub-divisions cause to be registered or recorded anyone's private property and then invokes its power to regulate and tax the private property of one of the private-sector, such action is a violation of the due process clause of the Fourteenth Amendment … "nor shall any state deprive any person of life, liberty, or property, without due process of the law."

As Americans in the private-sector aren't we a party to the alleged CONSTITUTIONS? In truth the answer is no! The CONSTITUTIONS serve as an operation(s) manual, operational guidelines, binds for those who choose to be "Public-Servants". Americans in the private-sector have sovereign status – we have consumer-status – and unless you have opted into being subject to something the something does not have legitimate control over you. "Contracts make the law – all law is contract". Observe the Thirteenth Amendment.

It doesn't really matter which or what Constitution we are talking about – the question to whomever – after duly accepting their alleged constitution and oath ("to preserve, protect, and defend… so help me God") is: "Is there something by or through your alleged Constitution that compels my performance or acceptance of your offer?" – If yes, "…then please enter it into the record of this matter". If no, "…then what am I doing here? Is there some manner of contract that is controlling?" Can they show that you knowingly, willingly and voluntarily after full disclosure signed on to something that bears the other party's signature as well? (Observe Jurisdiction).

However, anywhere along the way during an offer and acceptance situation there can always be a refusal and a refusal does not constitute a refusal for cause or a dishonor because you cannot dishonor an offer, you can only dishonor a demand. You may and can chose not to honor an offer. However, you can dishonor a demand. Once there is an offer and acceptance been made and then one of the parties their consideration and you refuse to give it to them, that is a dishonor.

You can refuse an offer or accept it. However, if you accept it, according to the law books, you assume the liability for having accepted the offer. Whatever liability goes along with it, you have accepted it. One would have to decide whether or not one wants to assume that liability. In some cases, you may want to, as it may be beneficial for you. A Constitution is a limiting, defining authority device.

Challenge is not argument.

Sovereigns = employers, grantors, principals, Make DEMANDS. These demands are MET or NOT MET.

Subjects = employees, grantees, servants (public), Make REQUESTS. These requests can either be GRANTED or DENIED.

The issue of sovereignty is very powerful and anybody who is not using it is not using their most powerful tool.

"In the Fifth Amendment the Nation is forbidden to deprive anyone 'of life, liberty or property without due process of law'; and here the like command is issued by the people to the State. In the beginning it was National power that was feared. Experience later taught that the power of the State also may be tyrannical. Due process of law means, 'no change in ancient procedure can be made which disregards those fundamental principles...which...protect the citizen in his private right and guard him against the arbitrary action of the government'. (Statement from the Supreme Court 1908).

Private property is taken, for public use in opening streets in cities, in constructing railways and canals, in erecting public buildings, in laying out public parks, and for kindred purposes. The owner cannot be deprived of his property for such purposes by the State without due process of law, that is, without a full hearing and adequate compensation". This is a quote from THE CONSTITUTION OF THE UNITED STATES ITS SOURCES AND APPLICATION; by Thomas James Norton, (1941), America's Future, Inc., publisher.

Now we have to define what the difference is between Public versus Private.

The term "public" (adj.) in common meaning is sometimes used to refer to the entire population. In the strict legal sense, the term "public" only applies to government political and municipal corporations and to no-one else. This is why you can be ordered to leave "public property" with the threat of trespassing.

The term "private" (Black's Law Dictionary 6th Edition, pg. 1195) is defined "as affecting or belonging to private individuals, as distinct for the public generally, not official; not clothed with office. Observe: People v. Powell, 280 Mich. 699, 274 N. K; 372, 373. In other words, if you are not in, or of, any office or government such as public-school teacher, administrator, bank personnel at any level, police, fire official or any type of City, County, State or Federal government worker, military...etc. anyone who is subject to the U. S. Constitution, then and only then are you a private citizen and a part of the private sector.

In regards to protecting oneself from "abusive" public servants: check out the (your) State laws on "Stalking" and "exploitation" as well as "neglect to protect" provisions in State law (upholding and enforcing the law by parties under Oath of Office) as well an Title: 18 U. S. C. §1621 concerning the "neglect to protect" by persons under Oath, and Title: 42 U. S. C. § 1986, wherein a person having "knowledge of the law", "the power to stop a wrong" and the "duty to prevent a wrong from being done" is liable for and failure to act. Should they fail to prevent a wrong, having knowledge of the law, the power to prevent and the legal or moral duty to prevent the wrong, which causes deprivations of your religious, and/or Civil Rights or Liberties, suit, can be brought for violations.

"Our safety, our liberty, depends upon preserving the Constitution of the United States as our Fathers made inviolate. The people of the United States are the rightful masters of both Congress and the Courts, not to overthrow the Constitution, but to overthrow the men who pervert the Constitution". –Abraham Lincoln.

"Bind down the Public Officials with the chains of the Constitution"—Thomas Jefferson

The United-States-Corporate-Courts make the mistake of using "opinions" for the cases presented into (their) courts.

The definition of 'Opinion' is as follows: A given opinion may deal with subjective (based on or influenced by personal feelings, tastes, or opinions.) matters in which there is no conclusive finding, or it may deal with facts which are sought to be disputed by the logical fallacy (A logical fallacy is an error in reasoning that renders an argument invalid; also called a fallacy, an informal logical fallacy, and an informal fallacy. In a broad sense, all logical fallacies are non sequiturs—arguments in which a conclusion doesn't follow logically from what preceded it.) that one is entitled to their opinions.

Distinguishing fact from opinions is that facts are verifiable that can be agreed to by the consensus of experts. For example, "The United States of America was involved in World War I", versus "The United States of America was right to get involved in World War I". An opinion may be supported by facts and principles, in which case it becomes and argument.

Different people may draw opposing conclusions (opinions) even if they agree on the same set of facts. Opinions rarely change without new arguments being presented. It can be reasoned that one opinion is better supported by the facts than another, by analyzing the supporting arguments.

In casual use, the term opinion may be the result of a person's perspective, understanding, particular feelings, beliefs, and desires. The term may also refer to unsubstantiated information, in contrast to knowledge and fact.

Though not hard fact, collective opinions or professional opinions are defined as meeting a higher standard to substantiate the opinion.

We will be presenting you with the definitions of Legal opinion and Judicial opinion for the benefit of this chapter since Public opinion, Group opinion and Scientific opinion have no bearings on what transpired through what the United-States-Corporate-Government did to us illegally – this is a fact not an opinion -since we actually have the documentation to prove and show with their own documents.

"A "Legal opinion" or "closing opinion" is a type of professional opinion, usually contained in a formal legal-opinion letter, given by an attorney to a client or a third party. Most legal opinions are given in connection with business transactions. The opinion expresses the attorney's professional judgement regarding the legal matters addressed. The opinion can be "clean" or "reasoned". A legal opinion is not a guarantee that a court will reach any particular result. However, a mistaken or incomplete legal opinion may be grounds for a professional malpractice claim against the attorney, pursuant to which the attorney may be required to pay the claimant damages incurred as a result of relying on the faulty opinion."

"A "Judicial opinion" or "opinion of the court" is an opinion of a judge or group of judges that accompanies and explains an order or ruling in a controversy before the court. A judicial option generally laws out the facts that the court recognized as being established, the legal principles the court is bound by, and the application of the relevant principles to the recognized facts. The goal is to demonstrate the rationale the court used in reaching its decision. Judges in the United States are usually required to provide a well-reasoned basis for their decisions and the contents of their judicial opinions may contain the grounds for appealing and reversing of their decision by a higher court."

Federalists argued that the Constitution did not need a bill of rights, because the people and the states kept any powers not given to the federal government. Anti-Federalists held that a bill of rights was necessary to safeguard individual liberty.

George Mason was one of the leading figures in creating the Bill of Rights. After storming out of the Constitutional Convention because the Constitution didn't contain a declaration of human rights, he worked to pass amendments that would protect citizens from an intrusive government.

According to the billofrightsinstitute.org, "The first 10 amendments to the Constitution make up the Bill of Rights. Written by James Madison in response to calls from several states for greater constitutional protection for individual liberties, the Bill of Rights lists specific prohibitions on governmental power."

The First Amendment is perhaps the most important part of the Bill of Rights. It protects five of the most basic liberties. They are freedom of religion, freedom of speech, freedom of the press, freedom of assembly, and freedom to petition the government to right wrongs.

However, if the Corporate-Government and its subsidiaries commit a crime against an Sovereign-American such as violating your RIGHTS by the "Bill of Rights", then the United-States-Corporate-Government and its subsidiaries loses Authority, Credibility, Status and Standing, Facts and Opinions because of the FACT that they are a "Fiction" (Non-existence) … in other words they do not exist. How can a "FICTIOUS" Government collect monies if they do not exist??? And claim that they are doing what they are doing for the "benefit of society"???.

As the reader you must remember that you are just as smart as or even smarter than ANY corporate-government-employee (imposters). However, intelligence or being smart does not play into this equation; it simply deals with contracts, and the United-States-Government and its imposters/officers are hoping that we as Americans are ignorant of any contract, the beneficiaries of Rights and Limitations set forth for the "Government" by the Constitution. We are proving that you can stop the (bull-shit) and be "FREE-AMERICANS" not under the United-States-Corporate-Government as a slave or (indentured-servant).

When the Americans declared that all men are equal, they meant it. There is no-basis for the empowerment of one equal over another equal. When they declared their determination to enjoy free speech, free travel, and other rights of Nature, there was no room left for the egotism of rebellious-public-servants. Under American Law and under the American government (non-corporate-government) there is no power greater than each INDIVIDUAL. This means that we cannot be represented and though we may transgress and may even be outlawed, we cannot be harassed, subjected, nor demeaned as a "thing"—such as an ESTATE or a foreign situs trust or a transmitting utility.

Every American has the right to rescind, revoke or disassociate-them-selves from any contract that they FEEL or Does Not Fully UNDERSTAND is NOT in their best interest.

As long as we Sovereign-Americans know and understand what "OUR-RIGHTS" are by the "Bill of Rights" we will have no problem. We "Private" Americans (Sovereigns) do not have to accept the table-scraps the United-States-Corporate-Government chooses to throw to their indentured-servants (everyone born on the North American Continent).

Another lie the United-States-Corporate-Government likes to use against the ignorant masses is "CONTROVERTIBLE DEBT". This is any form of debt that can be converted into another form of debt. Federal Reserve Notes can be converted into mortgages, stocks, bonds, annuities – any other "debt instrument" or "debt-based security". A fraudulent controvertible debt is a debt that is created by fraud and then converted. That is what the United-States-Corporate-Government and its franchise "SUBSIDIARIES" (all of them) we have going on in America right now.

If you were to examine the Bankruptcy Act, observe Section 101 (11). You will discover who the actual Creditors of the Trust Management Company FDR bankrupted in 1933 are – the 'LIVING' people, Americans at that time and their heirs, are the Priority Creditors and Entitlement Holders, but because of the 'monopoly' inducement explained in Item 5, we have all bee 'arbitrarily' "redefined" as "debtors" instead.

A perfect example is the use of the monthly Electric Bill, since we exposed the Electric Companies and the Corporate-Franchise-State-of-

California for Laundering Money through Enron (in Texas at the time). However, you receive the 'monthly electric bill' addressed to the "Federal-Franchise-ESTATE" trust currently doing business under your NAME as a 'franchise' of the United-States-Corporate-Government when you pay the 'bill' you become a debtor instead of a creditor so long as you pay in "Federal Reserve Notes". The electric company seizes these "Debt-Notes" you have so graciously provided to them for free and converts them into other forms of debt – buying up stocks, bonds, insurance policies, etc. – benefiting themselves.

The "debt" thus created is fraudulent on three-counts – (1) It is the by-product of illegal monopoly inducement forcing you to use Federal Reserve Notes as legal tender in the first place. (2) It is a debt owed by the federal franchise ESTATE trust doing business "in your name" but deceitfully presented to you as if it were your debt, and (3) You have been coerced to pay off a billing "statement" instead of a real bill.

In reality, we have a debt created by fraud converted into other forms of debt benefiting – in the above example, an electric company which reinvests "your" Federal Reserve Notes in other forms of debt. This is fraudulent controvertible debt in practice.

Another example of the way in which you are being defrauded and the value of your labor and other resources is being converted to benefit incorporated entities at the expense of you and your private estate is as follows:

The next time you receive a tax bill, a utility bill, a credit card bill or "any" other "bill" addressed to YOUR NAME IN ALL CAPITAL LETTERS, examine it very carefully with the understanding that (1) the item is addressed to a 'Puerto Rican "federal franchise" ESTATE trust' doing business in your NAME, not to you, (2) the item is a "billing statement" or "billing summary" or some other name, but never an ACTUAL – Bill so technically, even the ESTATE has not even been billed; (3) these billing statements are not denominated in dollars – except occasionally by mistake – the "amount-owed" appears as a series of numbers, commas, and dots similar to that used to write dollar amounts, but there is no dollar sign and no words indicating the kind or form of money or currency that is supposedly owed.

We will use our 'evidence;' from the Tax Assessor's Office from the Corporate-Franchise-County-of-Riverside under the Corporate-Franchise-State-of-California:

You will notice that the "property tax bill" shows up at the address to the "NAME" and the statement will show that the "NAME" owes a number you see written as examples of evidence within this chapter or that 'YOUR NAME'S' house has a value - (see examples below) – according to the Tax Assessor's Office. In reality, these are just deceptively constructed series of numbers, dots, and commas designed to make you assume that these represent dollar amounts. Once again, technically, not even the ESTATE has been billed for anything.

Observe the following evidence from documents that the Fictitious-Subsidiary-Corporate-Government of the State of California sends out as a bill…that is not a bill. This is called BREACH OF CONTRACT, Fraud and High Treason.

The Death of America

COUNTY OF RIVERSIDE

OFFICE OF TREASURER AND TAX COLLECTOR • COUNTY ADMINISTRATIVE CENTER, 4TH FLOOR
4080 LEMON STREET, RIVERSIDE, CALIFORNIA 92501-3660

TELEPHONE: (714) 787-2821

CERTIFICATE OF REDEMPTION
FOR
DELINQUENT SECURED PROPERTY TAX - PRIOR YEARS

THIS IS NOT A BILL FOR PAYMENT OF TAXES

SUBJECT TO POWER OF SALE

TAX RATE AREA	ASSESSMENT NUMBER		DOCUMENT NUMBER	DECLARED TO BE TAX DEFAULTED	
061-054	650034007-3			YEAR	1984
	PARCEL NUMBER			DEFAULT NUMBER	650034007-0000
	650034007-3			ASSESSMENT NUMBER	650034007-3

ASSESSED TO: SIMPSON, JOEL R
PROPERTY DESCRIPTION:

LOT 214 MB 028/061 SHANGRI LA PALMS UNIT 8

FISCAL YEAR DELINQUENT	ORIGINAL TAX	DELINQUENT PENALTIES	COST	DEFAULT AMOUNT	REDEMPTION PENALTIES	REDEMPTION FEE	RECISSION
1983	73.68	7.36	10.00	91.04			
1984	54.54	5.44	10.00	69.98			
TOTALS	128.22	12.80	20.00	161.02	34.41	15.00	

I CERTIFY THAT I HAVE THIS DATE RECEIVED THE AMOUNT REQUIRED TO REDEEM THE ABOVE DESCRIBED PROPERTY

TOTAL REDEMPTION AMOUNT	$ 210.43
LESS TOTAL INTEREST PAID	$
REDEMPTION AMOUNT WHEN PAYMENT PLAN INITIATED	$
LESS INSTALLMENT AMOUNT PREVIOUSLY PAID	$ .00
INTEREST AMOUNT PREVIOUSLY PAID	$ $
INTEREST AMOUNT REQUIRED FOR LAST PAYMENT	$
FINAL AMOUNT PAID *	$ 210.43

$ 210.43
R. WAYNE WATTS, TAX COLLECTOR

BY _Sandra Samuels_
Sandra Samuels/m DEPUTY

DATE 05-28-86

*INCLUDES RECISSION FEE, IF APPLICABLE

RECEIVED OF:

Joel R. Simpson

30257 Monte Vista Way

Thousand Palms, Ca 92276

TC103 (REV. 5-85) RET. 12 YR

RECISSION DOCUMENT NUMBER
DATE

96

COUNTY OF RIVERSIDE

OFFICE OF THE TREASURER AND TAX COLLECTOR

COUNTY ADMINISTRATIVE CENTER
4080 LEMON STREET, RIVERSIDE, CALIFORNIA 92501-3660 TELEPHONE: (714) 787-2821

NOTICE OF DELINQUENT SECURED PROPERTY TAX
FOR THE CURRENT FISCAL YEAR SHOWN BELOW BEGINNING JULY 1 AND ENDING JUNE 30

SIMPSON, JOEL R
30257 MONTE VISTA WAY
THOUSAND PLMS CA 92276

	TAX RATE AREA	ASSESSMENT NUMBER
BILL NUMBER	061-054	650034007-3
	TAX RATE AREA	PARCEL NUMBER
0179162	061-054	650034007-3

FISCAL YEAR   1985-1986

NET TAXABLE VALUE $ 4342.00

TOTAL AMOUNT DUE $ 70.98

IDENTIFICATION INFORMATION	LOT 214 MB 028/061 SHANGRI LA PALMS UNIT 8

ACCORDING TO THE RECORDS IN THIS OFFICE TAXES ARE DELINQUENT FOR THE CURRENT FISCAL YEAR ON THE PROPERTY SHOWN WITH "IDENTIFICATION INFORMATION" AND DESCRIBED ON THE OFFICIAL TAX ROLLS UNDER THE ASSESSMENT NUMBER ABOVE.

IF UNPAID, A DELINQUENT PENALTY WAS ADDED TO THE FIRST INSTALLMENT AT 5:00 P.M. ON DECEMBER 10, A DELINQUENT PENALTY AND COST WERE ADDED TO THE SECOND INSTALLMENT AT 5:00 P.M. ON APRIL 10. THE TOTAL AMOUNT DUE IS SHOWN ABOVE.

TO AVOID ADDITIONAL PENALTIES AND FEES RETURN THIS NOTICE WITH YOUR REMITTANCE, ON OR BEFORE THE LAST BUSINESS DAY IN JUNE TO R. WAYNE WATTS, TAX COLLECTOR, 4080 LEMON ST., RIVERSIDE, CALIFORNIA 92501-3660. MAKE CHECKS PAYABLE TO R. WAYNE WATTS, TAX COLLECTOR.

PLEASE DISREGARD THIS NOTICE IF YOUR TAXES HAVE BEEN PAID WITHIN THE PAST TWO WEEKS. KINDLY FORWARD THIS NOTICE TO THE NEW OWNER IF THE PROPERTY HAS BEEN SOLD.

R. WAYNE WATTS

TAX COLLECTOR

CASHIER'S RECEIPT

FISCAL YEAR	TOTAL AMOUNT DUE	1ST	2ND	BILL NUMBER	TAX RATE AREA	ASSESSMENT NUMBER
	$				061-054	650034007-3
					TAX RATE AREA	PARCEL NUMBER
1985-1986	70.98	30.49	40.49	0179162	061-054	650034007-3

PLEASE COMPLETE THE FOLLOWING BEFORE RETURNING TO THE TAX COLLECTOR IN ORDER TO PROVIDE A RECORD THAT YOU PAID THESE TAXES.

NAME _____

STREET _____

CITY & STATE _____
TC102 (REV. 4-84)

97

COUNTY OF RIVERSIDE-OFFICE OF THE TREASURER AND TAX COLLECTOR, COUNTY ADMINISTRATIVE CENTER, 4th FLOOR, 4080 LEMON STREET, RIVERSIDE, CALIFORNIA 92501-3660
TELEPHONE - (714) 787-2821

DELINQUENT PROPERTY TAX STATEMENT — SECURED PRIOR YEARS

OWNER OF RECORD
SIMPSON, JOEL R

THE RECORDS IN THIS OFFICE INDICATE THERE ARE DELINQUENT TAXES ON THE PARCEL HEREON IDENTIFIED FOR FISCAL YEARS
1983-1984 1984-1985

PROPERTY IDENTIFICATION
LOT 214 MB 028/061 SHANGRI LA PALMS UNIT 8

SHOWN OPPOSITE EACH MONTH IS THE EXACT AMOUNT TO PAY, IF THE DELINQUENT TAX IS PAID DURING
THAT MONTH, YOUR REMITTANCE MUST BE POSTMARKED NO LATER THAN THE LAST DAY OF THE MONTH
FOR WHICH PAYMENT IS BEING MADE. CURRENT YEAR TAXES ARE NOT INCLUDED IN THESE AMOUNTS.

TAX RATE AREA	ASSESSMENT NUMBER	DEFAULT YEAR AND NUMBER
061-054	650034007-3	84-650034007-0000
	PARCEL NUMBER	
05/28/86	650034007-3	8

IF PAID DURING		PAY THIS AMOUNT	IF PAID DURING		PAY THIS AMOUNT
JULY	1985	$ 191.20	AUG	1985	$ 193.12
SEPT	1985	195.05	OCT	1985	196.97
NOV	1985	198.89	DEC	1985	200.82
JAN	1986	202.74	FEB	1986	204.66
MARCH	1986	206.59	APRIL	1986	208.51
MAY	1986	210.43	JUNE	1986	212.36

MAIL NAME AND ADDRESS

SIMPSON, JOEL R

30257 MONTE VISTA WAY
THOUSAND PLMS CA 92276

CASHIER'S RECEIPT

PAID

MAY 28 '86

TAX COLLECTOR
RIVERSIDE CO.
By No. 3

TC 114 (REV. 11-84)
RET 1 YR.

AMOUNT
PAID $ 210.43

COUNTY OF RIVERSIDE SECURED PROPERTY TAX BILL FOR FISCAL YEAR BEGINNING JULY 1, 1985 AND ENDING JUNE 30, 1986. TELEPHONE: (714) 787-2821

R. WAYNE WATTS, TREASURER AND TAX COLLECTOR, 4080 LEMON ST. - 4th FLOOR, RIVERSIDE, CALIFORNIA 92501-3660

OWNER OF RECORD, MARCH 1, 1986: SIMPSON, JOEL R

| | EXEMPTIONS | TYPE | IDENTIFICATION INFORMATION (SEE ITEM #5 ON REVERSE SIDE) |
| | 7000 | B | LOT 214 MB 028/061 SHANGRI LA PALMS UNIT B |

BILL NUMBER 179162

| | LOCALLY ASSESSED VALUES ARE DETERMINED BY COUNTY ASSESSOR AT 100% OF FULL VALUE |

| LAND | STRUCTURES | FIXTURES | TREES & VINES | PERSONAL PROPERTY |
| 6242 | 5100 | | | |

ASSESSMENT NUMBER 650034007-3

NET ASSESSED VALUE 4,342.00

PARCEL NUMBER 650034007-3

TAX DEFAULTED
84-650034007-000
YEAR AND NUMBER

COMBINED TAX RATE PER $100 ASSESSED VALUE 1.04681

| FULL VALUE | BILLING SERVICE NUMBER | ASSESSMENT NUMBER |
| 11,342 | | 650034007-3 |

| TAX REQUESTING AGENCY | LOAN IDENTIFICATION | PARCEL NUMBER |
| | | 650034007-3 |

PROPERTY ADDRESS: 30257 MONTE VISTA WAY THOUSAND PLMS 92276

TAXES 45.44

FIXED AND AD VALOREM SPECIAL ASSESSMENTS 10.00

05/28/86

TOTAL AMOUNT DUE $ 55.44

SIMPSON, JOEL R

30257 MONTE VISTA WAY

THOUSAND PLMS CA 92276

CASHIER'S RECEIPT - 2ND INSTALLMENT	CASHIER'S RECEIPT - 1ST INSTALLMENT
PAID	PAID
MAY 28 '86	MAY 28 '86
ADD 10% PENALTY AND 27.72	ADD 10% PENALTY 27.72
$10.00 COST AFTER 2.77	2.77
APRIL 10 10.00	
By No. 3	By No. 3
40.49	30.49

SEE REVERSE SIDE FOR IMPORTANT INFORMATION

RECEIPTS WILL NOT BE ISSUED FOR PAYMENTS MADE BY MAIL UNLESS THE ENTIRE BILL IS RETURNED WITH YOUR REMITTANCE

YOUR CANCELLED CHECK IS YOUR BEST RECEIPT

TAX COLLECTOR CASH TICKET No. 03- 1566

ASSESSMENT/ACCOUNT NO.: 650-034-007-3

TYPE OF PAYMENT:
- ☑ CURRENT SECURED
- ☑ SECURED REDEMPTION
- ☐ INSTALLMENT PAYMENT PLAN
- ☐ SUPPLEMENTAL
- ☐ CURRENT UNSECURED
- ☐ PRIOR-YEAR UNSECURED
- ☐ UNSECURED PARTIAL PAYMENT
- ☐ IN "53"
- ☐ TREASURER DEPOSIT
- ☐ OTHER

CHECKS RECEIVED $

$100 X 3 = $300.00
50 X =
20 X =
10 X =
5 X =
2 X =
1 X =
COIN = 1.41

CASH RECEIVED: $ 01.41
LESS CHANGE GIVEN - 20.00
TOTAL CASH APPLIED TO PAYMENT $ 281.41

CASHIER STAMP PAID MAY 28 '86

TC-123 (8-85)

TAX COLLECTOR CASH TICKET No. 07- 5816

ASSESSMENT / ACCOUNT NO.: 650034007.3

TYPE OF PAYMENT:
- ☐ CURRENT SECURED
- ☑ SECURED REDEMPTION
- ☐ INSTALLMENT PAYMENT PLAN
- ☐ SUPPLEMENTAL
- ☐ CURRENT UNSECURED
- ☐ PRIOR-YEAR UNSECURED
- ☐ UNSECURED PARTIAL PAYMENT
- ☐ IN "53"
- ☐ TREASURER DEPOSIT
- ☐ OTHER

CHECKS RECEIVED $

$100 X 3 = $300.00
50 X =
20 X 1 = 20.00
10 X =
5 X =
2 X =
1 X =
COIN =

CASH RECEIVED: $ 320.00
LESS CHANGE GIVEN - 3.31
TOTAL CASH APPLIED TO PAYMENT $ 316.69

CASHIER STAMP PAID MAY 02 '89

TC-123 (8-85)

100

COUNTY OF RIVERSIDE
SECURED PROPERTY TAX BILL FOR FISCAL YEAR 1987-1988
R. WAYNE WATTS, TREASURER AND TAX COLLECTOR
COUNTY ADMINISTRATIVE CENTER 4080 LEMON STREET — 4TH FLOOR
RIVERSIDE, CALIFORNIA 92501-3660

TAXES (714) 787-2821   VALUES (714) 787-6331   EXEMPTIONS (714) 787-6697

0190289
BILL NUMBER

PROPERTY IDENTIFICATION (SEE ITEM #5 ON REVERSE SIDE)

☒ LOT 214 MB 028/061 SHANGRI LA PALMS UNIT 8

OWNER OF RECORD, MARCH 1, 1987: SIMPSON, JOEL R
PROPERTY ADDRESS: 30257 MONTE VISTA WAY THOUSAND PLMS 92276

TAXES, SPECIAL ASSESSMENTS, FIXED CHARGES (SEE ITEM #2 ON REVERSE SIDE)	RATE	AMOUNT
GENERAL PURPOSE	1.00000	47.99
UNIFIED SCHOOL DEBT SV	.01671	.80
COMMUNITY COLLEGE DEBT SV	.00195	.09
COACHELLA VAL WATER DEBT SERV	.05900	2.83
DESERT HOSPITAL DEBT SV	.00063	.03
COUNTY SERVICE AREA 141	A	3.00
CVWD STANDBY CUR DOMESTIC	A	10.00

061-030 650034007-3

TAX RATE AREA   ASSESSMENT NUMBER
650034007-3
PARCEL NUMBER

YEAR AND NUMBER   TAX DEFAULTED
87-650034007-0000
(SEE ITEM #8 ON REVERSE SIDE)

FULL VALUE	$	11,799
LAND	$	6,493
STRUCTURES		5,306
FIXTURES		
TREES AND VINES		
CITRUS PEST VALUE		
PERSONAL PROPERTY		

TAX BILL REQUESTING AGENCY   LOAN IDENTIFICATION   BILLING SERVICE NUMBER

SEE REVERSE SIDE FOR IMPORTANT INFORMATION

B 09/20/87

SIMPSON, JOEL R

30257 MONTE VISTA WAY
THOUSAND PLMS CA 92276

TOTAL ASSESSED VALUE	$	11,799
LESS EXEMPTIONS (TYPE): HOX		7,000
NET VALUE	$	4,799
COMBINED TAX RATE PER $100 VALUE		1.07833

	CASHIER'S RECEIPT-1ST INSTALLMENT	CASHIER'S RECEIPT-2ND INSTALLMENT			
YOUR CANCELLED CHECK IS YOUR BEST RECEIPT			TAXES FIXED AND SPECIAL ASSESSMENTS	$	51.74
(IF YOU NEED A RECEIPT, YOU MUST SEND ENTIRE BILL WITH YOUR PAYMENT)	32.37 ADD 10% PENALTY AFTER DECEMBER 10, 1987	32.37 ADD 10% PENALTY AND $10.00 COST AFTER APRIL 10, 1988			13.00
	$ 32.37	$ 32.37	TOTAL AMOUNT DUE	$	64.74

R. Wayne Watts, Riverside County Tax Collector   Telephone (714) 275-3900 or (619) 342-8900

NOTICE OF DELINQUENT 1989-1990 SECURED PROPERTY TAX as of 05/12/90

Property Data LOT 214 MB 028/061 SHANGRI LA PALMS UNIT 8

Address 30257 MONTE VISTA WAY THOUSAND PLMS 92276

	Bill Number	Assessment Number [X]
	0371652	650034007-3
	Tax Rate Area	Parcel Number
	061-030	650034007-3

INSTALLMENT	STATUS	TAX	PENALTY	COST	TOTAL
1ST	UNPAID	37.49	3.74		41.23
2ND	UNPAID	37.49	3.74	10.00	51.23

Our records indicate that the current-year taxes are delinquent on the property described above. ON OR BEFORE JUNE 29, 1990, THE TOTAL AMOUNT DUE OF $ 92.46 MUST BE PAID; otherwise, additional penalties will accrue at 1 1/2 % per month plus a $ 0.00 redemption fee. To avoid these additional charges, please return this notice with your remittance on or before June 29, 1990.

CASHIER'S RECEIPT	CASHIER'S RECEIPT

SIMPSON   JOEL   R
30257 MONTE VISTA WAY
THOUSAND PLMS CA 92276

AMOUNT PAID $ 41.23	AMOUNT PAID $ 51.23
1ST INSTALLMENT	2ND INSTALLMENT

THIS IS A COURTESY NOTICE NOT REQUIRED BY LAW

COUNTY OF RIVERSIDE 1989-1990   SECURED PROPERTY TAXES

SECOND INSTALLMENT

$ 51.23

PAY THIS AMOUNT

BY JUNE 29, 1990

Assessment Number
650034007-3
Bill Number
0371652

Send this stub with **2**ND installment payment

(Can not be paid unless 1st installment is paid)

00000005123   0289 0371652 05

Make checks payable to: R. WAYNE WATTS, TAX COLLECTOR
COUNTY ADMINISTRATIVE CENTER
4080 LEMON STREET - 4TH FLOOR
RIVERSIDE, CA 92501 - 3660

If a receipt is needed, you must send entire bill with your payment

---

COUNTY OF RIVERSIDE 1989-1990   SECURED PROPERTY TAXES

FIRST INSTALLMENT

$ 41.23

PAY THIS AMOUNT

BY JUNE 29, 1990

Assessment Number
650034007-3
Bill Number
0371652

Send this stub with **1**ST installment payment

00000004123   0189 0371652 05

Make checks payable to: R. WAYNE WATTS, TAX COLLECTOR
COUNTY ADMINISTRATIVE CENTER
4080 LEMON STREET - 4TH FLOOR
RIVERSIDE, CA 92501 - 3660

If a receipt is needed, you must send entire bill with your payment

R. Wayne Watts, Riverside County Tax Collector

Telephone (909) 275-3900 or (619) 342-8900

NOTICE OF DELINQUENT 1992-1993 **SECURED PROPERTY TAX as of** 05/06/93

Property Data LOT 214 MB 028/061 SHANGRI LA PALMS UNIT 8

Address 30257 MONTE VISTA WAY THOUSAND PLMS 92276

		0515980	650034007-3
		Tax Rate Area 061-030	Parcel Number 650034007-3

INSTALLMENT	STATUS	TAX	PENALTY	COST	TOTAL
1ST	UNPAID	118.40	11.84		130.24
2ND	UNPAID	118.40	11.84	10.00	140.24

Our records indicate that the current-year taxes are delinquent on the property described above. ON OR BEFORE JUNE 30 , 1993 ,THE TOTAL AMOUNT DUE OF $ 270.48 MUST BE PAID; otherwise, additional penalties will accrue at 1 1/2 % per month plus a $ 0.00 redemption fee. To avoid these additional charges, please return this notice with your remittance on or before June 30 1993

	PAID CASHIER'S RECEIPT	PAID CASHIER'S RECEIPT
	MAY 1 8 '93	MAY 1 8 '93

SIMPSON   JOEL   R
30257 MONTE VISTA WAY
THOUSAND PLMS CA 92276

TAX COLLECTOR RIVERSIDE CO. By No. 7   TAX COLLECTOR RIVERSIDE CO. By No. 7

AMOUNT DUE $ 130.24   AMOUNT DUE $ 140.24

THIS IS A COURTESY NOTICE NOT REQUIRED BY LAW

1 ST INSTALLMENT   2 ND INSTALLMENT

TAX COLLECTOR CASH TICKET   No. **07-** 420

ASSESSMENT / ACCOUNT NO.:

CHECKS RECEIVED $

TYPE OF PAYMENT:

☐ CURRENT SECURED
☐ SECURED REDEMPTION
☐ INSTALLMENT PAYMENT PLAN
☐ SUPPLEMENTAL
☐ CURRENT UNSECURED
☐ PRIOR-YEAR UNSECURED
☐ UNSECURED PARTIAL PAYMENT
☐ IN "53"
☐ TREASURER DEPOSIT
☐ OTHER _____

$100 X	_____	= $ _____	
50 X	_____	= _____	
20 X	_____	= _____	
10 X	_____	= _____	
5 X	_____	= _____	
2 X	_____	= _____	
1 X	_____	= _____	
COIN		= _____	

CASH RECEIVED: $ 300.00
LESS CHANGE GIVEN - 29.52
TOTAL CASH APPLIED TO PAYMENT $ 270.48

CASHIER STAMP PAID

MAY 1 8 '93

TAX COLLECTOR RIVERSIDE CO. By No. 7

TC-123 (6-85)

103

RIVERSIDE COUNTY
STATEMENT OF UNPAID PRIOR-YEAR SECURED PROPERTY TAXES

R. WAYNE WATTS
TREASURER-TAX COLLECTOR
County Administrative Center
4080 Lemon St. - 4th Floor, Riverside, California
(P.O. Box 12006, Riverside, CA 92502-2205)
Telephone: (909) 275-3900
or (619) 863-8900

Property Data	LOT 214 MB 028/061 SHANGRI LA PALMS UNIT 8	ASSESSMENT NUMBER 650034007-3
Address	30257 MONTE VISTA WAY THOUSAND PLMS 92276	Parcel Number
Owner	SIMPSON, JOEL R	650034007-3

04/29/95

Tax-default Year and Number
89-650034007-0000

SIMPSON, JOEL R
30257 MONTE VISTA WAY
THOUSAND PLMS CA 92276

OUR RECORDS SHOW THAT THERE ARE UNPAID PRIOR-YEAR TAXES ON THE PROPERTY SHOWN
ABOVE. THE PARTICULAR UNPAID ASSESSMENT NUMBER(S) AND FISCAL-YEAR(S) ARE:

050639766-8 1989-90
650034007-3 1988-89 89-90 90-91 91-92

PAID

Cashier's Receipt
MAY 24 '95

TAX COLLECTOR
RIVERSIDE CO.
By No. 7

$ 885.65

TO REDEEM THIS PROPERTY, PAY **ONLY** THE AMOUNT SHOWN OPPOSITE THE MONTH IN
WHICH PAYMENT IS BEING MADE:

IF PAID DURING		PAY THIS AMOUNT	IF PAID DURING		PAY THIS AMOUNT
JULY	1994	$775.77	AUGUST	1994	$786.76
SEPTEMBER	1994	797.75	OCTOBER	1994	808.74
NOVEMBER	1994	819.73	DECEMBER	1994	830.71
JANUARY	1995	841.70	FEBRUARY	1995	852.69
MARCH	1995	863.68	APRIL	1995	874.67
MAY	1995	885.65	JUNE	1995	896.64

YOUR PAYMENT MUST BE POSTMARKED NO LATER THAN THE LAST DAY OF THE MONTH.
(Note: Current-year taxes are not included in these amounts.)

PLEASE KEEP TOP PORTION FOR YOUR RECORDS

RIVERSIDE COUNTY
NOTICE OF DELINQUENT PROPERTY TAXES

For Fiscal Year July 1, 1994 through June 30, 1995

R. WAYNE WATTS
TREASURER-TAX COLLECTOR
County Administrative Center
4080 Lemon St. - 4th Floor, Riverside, California
(P.O. Box 12005, Riverside, CA 92502-2205)

Telephone: (909) 275-3900
or (619) 863-8900

Property Data	LOT 214 MB 028/061 SHANGRI LA PALMS UNIT 8		Bill Number	ASSESSMENT NUMBER
			0532519	650034007-3
Address	30257 MONTE VISTA WAY THOUSAND PLMS 92276		Tax Rate Area	Parcel Number
Owner, March 1, 19 94	SIMPSON, JOEL R		061-030	650034007-3

05 1895   39452

SIMPSON, JOEL R
30257 MONTE VISTA WAY
THOUSAND PLMS CA   92276

This notice printed on 05/16/95

INSTALLMENT	STATUS	TAX	10 % PENALTY	COST	TOTAL
1st	UNPAID	122.41	12.23		$134.64
2nd	UNPAID	122.41	12.23	10.00	$144.64

Our records show that current-year taxes are delinquent on the property described above.

$279.28
TOTAL AMOUNT DUE

THIS IS A LIEN ON THE PROPERTY DESCRIBED ABOVE. The Total Amount Due
X   must be paid on or before   or the property will be tax-defaulted,
    a $15 redemption fee will be added and redemption penalties will accrue at 1-1/2% per month.   JUNE 30, 1995

PAID   PAID

Cashier's Receipt   Cashier's Receipt
MAY 2 4 '95   MAY 2 4 '95

TAX COLLECTOR   TAX COLLECTOR
RIVERSIDE CO.   RIVERSIDE CO.
By No. 7   By No. 7
$134.64 $144.64

PLEASE KEEP TOP PORTION FOR YOUR RECORDS

TAX COLLECTOR CASH TICKET   No. **07**- 18333

ASSESSMENT / ACCOUNT NO.: 650 034 007-3

TYPE OF PAYMENT:

	CHECKS RECEIVED $
☒ CURRENT SECURED	$100 X 6 = $ 600.00
☒ SECURED REDEMPTION	50 X 12 = 600.00
☐ INSTALLMENT PAYMENT PLAN	20 X =
☐ SUPPLEMENTAL	10 X =
☐ CURRENT UNSECURED	5 X =
☐ PRIOR-YEAR UNSECURED	2 X =
☐ UNSECURED PARTIAL PAYMENT	1 X =
☐ IN "53"	COIN =
☐ TREASURER DEPOSIT	CASH RECEIVED: $ 1200.00
	LESS CHANGE GIVEN - 35.07
☐ OTHER _____	TOTAL CASH APPLIED TO PAYMENT $ 1164.93

CASHIER STAMP
PAID

MAY 2 4 '95

TAX COLLECTOR
RIVERSIDE CO.
By No. 7

TC-126 (6-85)

The Death of America

RIVERSIDE COUNTY
STATEMENT OF UNPAID PRIOR-YEAR SECURED PROPERTY TAXES

H. WAYNE WATTS
TREASURER-TAX COLLECTOR
County Administrative Center
4080 Lemon St. - 4th Floor, Riverside, California
(P.O. Box 12005, Riverside, CA 92502-2205)

Telephone: (909) 275-3900
or (619) 863-8900

Property Data LOT 214 MB 028/061 SHANGRI LA PALMS UNIT 8

Address 30257 MONTE VISTA WAY THOUSAND PLMS 92276
Owner SIMPSON, JOEL R

ASSESSMENT NUMBER
650034007-3

Parcel Number
650034007-3

04/29/95

Tax-default Year and Number
89-650034007-0000

SIMPSON, JOEL R
30257 MONTE VISTA WAY
THOUSAND PLMS CA 92276

OUR RECORDS SHOW THAT THERE ARE UNPAID PRIOR-YEAR TAXES ON THE PROPERTY SHOWN ABOVE. THE PARTICULAR UNPAID ASSESSMENT NUMBER(S) AND FISCAL-YEAR(S) ARE:

050639766-8 1989-90
650034007-3 1988-89 89-90 90-91 91-92

PAID

MAY 24 '95

TAX COLLECTOR
RIVERSIDE CO.
By No. 7

$ 885.65

TO REDEEM THIS PROPERTY, PAY ONLY THE AMOUNT SHOWN OPPOSITE THE MONTH IN WHICH PAYMENT IS BEING MADE:

IF PAID DURING		PAY THIS AMOUNT	IF PAID DURING		PAY THIS AMOUNT
JULY	1994	$775.77	AUGUST	1994	$786.76
SEPTEMBER	1994	797.75	OCTOBER	1994	808.74
NOVEMBER	1994	819.73	DECEMBER	1994	830.71
JANUARY	1995	841.70	FEBRUARY	1995	852.69
MARCH	1995	863.68	APRIL	1995	874.67
MAY	1995	885.65	JUNE	1995	896.64

YOUR PAYMENT MUST BE POSTMARKED NO LATER THAN THE LAST DAY OF THE MONTH.
(Note: Current-year taxes are not included in these amounts.)

PLEASE KEEP TOP PORTION FOR YOUR RECORDS

106

R. WAYNE WATTS
TREASURER-TAX COLLECTOR
County Administrative Center
4080 Lemon St. - 4th Floor, Riverside, California
(P.O. Box 12005, Riverside, CA 92502-2205)

Telephone: (909) 275-3900
or (619) 863-8900

RIVERSIDE COUNTY
STATEMENT OF UNPAID PRIOR-YEAR SECURED PROPERTY TAXES

Property Data: LOT 214 MB 028/061 SHANGRI LA PALMS UNIT 8

Address: 30257 MONTE VISTA WAY THOUSAND PLMS 92276

Owner: SIMPSON, JOEL R

ASSESSMENT NUMBER
650034007-3

Parcel Number
650034007-3

04/29/95

Tax-default Year and Number
89-650034007-0000

SIMPSON, JOEL R
30257 MONTE VISTA WAY
THOUSAND PLMS CA 92276

OUR RECORDS SHOW THAT THERE ARE UNPAID PRIOR-YEAR TAXES ON THE PROPERTY SHOWN ABOVE. THE PARTICULAR UNPAID ASSESSMENT NUMBER(S) AND FISCAL-YEAR(S) ARE:

050639766-8 1989-90
650034007-3 1988-89 89-90 90-91 91-92

PAID

Cashier's Receipt
MAY 24 95

TAX COLLECTOR
RIVERSIDE CO.
By No. 7

$ 885.65

TO REDEEM THIS PROPERTY, PAY **ONLY** THE AMOUNT SHOWN OPPOSITE THE MONTH IN WHICH PAYMENT IS BEING MADE:

IF PAID DURING		PAY THIS AMOUNT	IF PAID DURING		PAY THIS AMOUNT
JULY	1994	$775.77	AUGUST	1994	$786.76
SEPTEMBER	1994	797.75	OCTOBER	1994	808.74
NOVEMBER	1994	819.73	DECEMBER	1994	830.71
JANUARY	1995	841.70	FEBRUARY	1995	852.69
MARCH	1995	863.68	APRIL	1995	874.67
MAY	1995	885.65	JUNE	1995	896.64

YOUR PAYMENT MUST BE POSTMARKED NO LATER THAN THE LAST DAY OF THE MONTH.
(Note: Current-year taxes are not included in these amounts.)

PLEASE KEEP TOP PORTION FOR YOUR RECORDS

107

The above are examples of how the Fictitious-Corporate-Subsidiary- State-of-California is doing to its victims, when proven they are committing a crime against Americans. It is all constructive fraud based on semantic deceit, illusion, and processes of assumption knowingly pursued under conditions of non-disclosure. This is how they get rid of what they deem as "problems".

All of this is done on purpose, with malice aforethought. The perpetrators are giving you notice that a bill related to the ESTATE named after you exist, but they are actually and purposefully preventing you from paying it. If they sent a real "BILL", you could either discharge it through the U. S. Treasury Window at any Federal Reserve Bank, or, you could present it for payment under UNCITRAL and exchange it against you Birth Certificate Bond or other assets held by the US Bankruptcy Trustees in your name. This process of discharging debts, unlike using Federal Reserve Notes, actually pays the bill, and since the entire game is about forcing you to "indebt" yourself, the perpetrators spare no effort to prevent you from discharging the bills "RELATED" to their "federal" ESTATE trust.

Another reason why they refuse to provide you with an actual Bill is that what they are doing is a crime. As long as they are sending these "billing statements" to a federal franchise ESTATE trust, they technically cannot be accused of billing you. As long as they do not provide you with an actual Bill, they cannot be accused of false billing, either. According to them, they do not know what you are talking about – therein lays the example of "denialism". What bill? We never sent any bill…We sent a billing statement addressed to a Puerto Rican ESTATE trust that "just happens" to have the same name and address. Who cares if we fully intend to force and coerce the 'LIVING-MAN' to pay us with an I. O. U. (aka. Federal Reserve Notes) and owe us even more debt after he "paid" than when he started?

In reality and in truth we do not owe any taxes. All governmental services contracts are between states and other incorporated (fictional) entities, not Corporate-States and people. It is literally impossible for a living-man or woman to owe any tax for any governmental service.

All valid contracts must be "in-kind". Corporations can contract only with other corporations. Living-people can contract with other living-people. The proliferation of "trusts" has been used as a vehicle – literally creating a "commercial-vessel" capable of interfacing with corporations and entering into corporate contracts. The creation of these "individual public trusts" and their supposed obligations has been done without the "knowledge, consent or participation" of the "living-people" merely upon the "representations" made "in their behalf" by third parties claiming to "represent" them – lawyers, judges and unscrupulous politicians.

Note: the original equity contract known as The Constitution for the United States of America is between the States (franchises) and the Corporate-Government being created by contract to provide the States (franchises) with public-services – NOT the living-people. We, the People, are mentioned as the "Beneficiaries" of the Natural and "Unalienable-Rights" that are assets held in the national trust and further outlined and defined by the Bill of Rights. We, as a living-people, are not direct parties to this or any other Corporate-Governmental-services-contract.

If you are having a problem in understanding how the Corporate-Government-services get paid for it is not through taxes. The Franchise-States are inestimably valuable and properly administered; they contain vast material assets that can be utilized to generate income more than sufficient to pay for all Corporate-Governmental-services – and this is in fact what all the Corporate-States do. They already generate more than enough income every year to pay for all Corporate-Governmental-services. They, like Private-Corporations, keep track of their expenses and provide a "billing-statement" addressed to your ESTATE in hopes that you will step forward and "VOLUNTEER" – to pay a share of the expenses for them, so that their private, for-profit-Corporation is enabled to operate without any expense and seize the entire profit from the sale, utilization and investment of your organic state's assets entirely for its own benefit.

If your ESTATE fails to "voluntarily" cough-up its share for any year, the Corporate-Government and its subsidiary-franchises will conveniently forget all the labor and currency (conscript) and value you have contributed in prior years and also fail to mention all the money (conscript) they made in past-years off of the "state" assets that you are supposed to be the beneficiary of. Those who claim to "Represent" you have taken seats as the officers (Imposters) of this same "Foreign-Franchise-for-Profit "STATE"-Corporation and they see it as their duty to make sure that the corporation is as profitable as possible – so they justify attacking Living-Americans, their employer, and seizing your assets and telling you what to do, how to do it, when and how often – all in the name of somehow ultimately benefiting you via entrapment, enslavement, armed extortion and fraud.

Every unit of "Franchise-Corporate-Government" in America is not only in control of and profiting from the use and misuse of vast "public" assets, they are rolling in the money and credit they have extorted from the actual beneficiaries of the public trusts, then rolling some more money in the money and credit they have made investing all of this purloined (to steal) largesse (gift), and proliferating new and ever-more numerous units of a Fictitious-Corporate-Government and its subsidiary-agencies – this government is like a cancerous-growth soaking-up the sugars of the Body Politic.

Every year the Fictitious-Corporate-Government running your Federal (Corporate-Government), State (Franchise-Corporate-Government), and Municipal (Franchise-Corporate-Government) "Governments" make so much more money that they expend on public services that the idea that taxation of the individual-living-men and women and their "private-property-assets" is necessary to fund public services is laughable.

Exactly how these criminally-mismanaged-corporations hide the "loot" so that they can continue to "poor-mouth" and impose more taxation.

This is how the courts are at fault. In 1938 a Supreme Case known as Erie Railroad v. Thompkins executives for the Roosevelt Administration called a meeting with the US Supreme Court Justices, Senior Judges from all the Circuit and Appellate Courts, and the most prominent lawyers of the times, and they told them a purposeful and self-interested LIE. They claimed that the "United States of America was Bankrupt"- they just neglected to say which 'United State of America' and what form of 'United States of America' they were talking about. They also told the legal professionals (imposters) that because of this bankruptcy, they were to operate their courts ONLY in maritime jurisdictions. The exact words were used as follows: "We don't care what you call it, but you can only run maritime and admiralty courts".

From that time to this, this is what the members of the American Bar Association have done. They run a fantastic gamut of "courts" pretending to operate as "state-courts" and "custody courts" and "US DISTRICT COURTS" and "Superior Courts" and so forth…all the way to the Supreme Court level – and pretend to operate at equity and under civil law, but the entire time they have operated exclusively as maritime courts and is in-house-corporate-tribunals.

The courts are at fault because they know they are routinely operating in jurisdictions that have nothing to do with the cases before them. They are at fault because they do not require proof of any valid maritime jurisdiction, even when called on the carpet for failure to do so. The list goes on.

The reason why the courts have malfunctioned in this way and continued on this course for almost eighty years is because a major part of it is called ignorance. A great many American jurists have grown up under these conditions and they do not know that anything different ever existed. Many do not know that "statutory law" is actually maritime law and if the judges and lawyers don't know who does? Some don't even know that "statutory law" applies uniquely to statutory entities – [legal]-Fictions created by statute.

The rest of the reason is pure graft and corruption for profit on the part of those who do know what is going on.

The "Federal" judges have issued standing orders to "invest" all court cases through the Court Registry Investment System [CRIS] – which amounts to – "deposit" them as securities into the Federal Reserve Bank in Dallas, Texas.

Every such court case is assigned a US Treasury Public Debt Number – a Docket Number in "State" courts and a Case Number in "US DISTRICT COURTS". This makes every court case a financial transaction and "securitizes" it.

After the 'Public Debt Number' is issued, which converts the court into a counterfeit obligation under TITLE: 18: USC: 472, et seq. 473, 474; the Court Administrator again counterfeits the same debt obligation by adding a CUSIP number to the "Instrument". One counterfeit obligation benefits the Federal Reserve; the second one benefits the IMF (International Monitory Fund).

CUSIP is an acronym for 'Committee on Uniform Securities Identification Procedures, and a copyrighted and registered trademark of the 'American Bankers Association'. The court administrators work for the banks, NOT any "court system" unless you want to call it the Bank "Court", where the bank always wins. With this fraud the "court administrator" working for the banks has converted every case into a banking- financial-securities-instrument – which puts the court itself into the position of being "creditor" and BOTH the plaintiff and the defendant which are cast into the role of :debtors". The judges are acting with vested interested with insider knowledge and they are insider trading in complete and utter violation of the judicial canons.

They cannot act without bias when the quantity and quality of their salaries, benefits, and retirement packages are sitting on the docket everyday awaiting their "investment". Rather than ruling on the merits, arguments, or even the facts, they are making financial investments in every case – future contracts, in a future they can direct.

They are, in reality running a rigged gambling operation out of the courthouse, under the noses of the STATE POLICE DEPARTMENT, FBI, AND THE US Marshalls, who all turn to these icons of rectitude for "legal " advice instead of using their own noses and common-sense to determine what is lawful.

The judges and court administrators are also committing tax fraud by shifting the "debt" created by every case onto the individual(s) who are actually the Creditor(s) in every case, and converting the case into an investment-security belonging to the Dallas Federal Reserve Bank instead, which in turn shifts the money from the Creditor side of the "Transaction" into the pockets of the Debtors. They are Deceptively-laundering a fraudulent debt into corporate assets belonging to the bank, and converting those assets into revenue-sharing funneled back to the

Department of Transportation [Federal Reserve] or DEAPRTMENT OF TRANSPORTATION (IMF) franchises, respectively.

In addition to running a rigged gambling-operation out of the courthouses, the courts are also laundering vast amounts of fraudulently procured credit assets back into the operations-side of the two colluding Trust Management Organizations. A whopping percentage of the total take from all this securities-fraud goes into the judge's retirement-fund also administered by the Dallas Federal Reserve Bank.

It has become self-explanatory why the courts and their administrators are at fault for this entire situation, that it is outrageous and not to be tolerated, and also why it must come to halt and be brought to a halt by those responsible for administration of these entities. Any jurist who values his or her "Law-License" issued by an International banking-cartel being operated as a criminal-syndicate more than he or she values the law deserves to be disbarred – and will be.

One last note about the legality of the Courts; if you go into a court and are told that you are under an "Administrative-Court" or you are brought before an "Administrative-Court" they are "ILLEGAL". There have been many discussions (behind closed-doors…never in public) that the Administrative Law Courts established with the New Deal were totally unfounded and "Unconstitutional".

With the signing of the Magana Carta and the right to a jury trial after 800 years, the era of Roosevelt's BIG government is quietly unraveling and coming to an end. Federal Judge's Rulings against the Securities and Exchange Commission for using its own Administrative Law judges in an insider trading case is/are perhaps the beginning of the end of an alternative-system of justice that took root in the New Deal. Constitutionally the socialists tore everything about the idea of a "Democracy" apart. It was more than taxing one party to the cheers of another in denial of equal-protection.

It was about creating administrative-agencies (1) delegating them to create rules through color of law with the force of law as if passed by Congress sanctioned by the people, (2) the creation of administrative-courts that defeated the Tripartite-government structure usurping all power into the hand of the Executive-Branch, as if this were a "dictatorship" run by the great hoard of imposters/impersonators known as "unelected-officials". The Administrative Law Court claim they are "fiefdom", to put it mildly. The Administrative courts have been corrupt and traditionally rule in favor of their agencies (Subsidiaries under their control), making it very costly for anyone to even try to defend themselves.

If anyone were to attempt this feat, first they have to wear the costs of an Administration proceeding and appeal to an Article III court judge, then they must appeal to the Court of Appeals, and finally plea to the Supreme Court. The cost of such adventures is well into the millions, and good luck on actually getting justice.

Furthermore, Administrative Law Courts cannot sentence you to prison, but they can fine you into bankruptcy through fraud. So the lack of a criminal prosecution meant the judges did not have to be lawyers, they could be your worst enemies or your best friends. They could be anyone's brother-in-law looking for a job where he just rules in favor of the agency not to be bothered with law. Unless the victim has a pile of money, there is no real chance that he or she can afford to defend themselves (this is what is called buying "justice"). This is why the subsidiary agency cut deals with the BIG HOUSES and PROSECUTES the small upstarts who lack the funds to defend themselves.

There is a 45-page ruling, from District Judge Leigh Martin May, from Atlanta issued an injunction halting Administrative Law proceedings against 'Charles Hill' a businessman, who the SEC (Securities Exchange Commission) accused of reaping an illegal amount of money for profit trading in Radian Systems Stock. The SEC wanted to stop and collect this "amount of currency" and this action is typical of what they do under "Administrative-Courts". The legal fees involved would have exceeded the amount of currency he is alleged to have made, the typical result is to just pay the fine and they go away After all wouldn't it be cheaper?

The judge ruled that the SEC agency violated the "Appointments Clause" of the Constitution by subjecting 'Mr. Hill' to proceedings before an Administrative Law Judge, who is not directly accountable to the president, officials in charge of the SEC, or the courts under Article III. "This ruling is 81 years overdue".

The entire structure of administrative agencies (fictitious-subsidiaries) 'blackmailing' people has been outrageous. Then take the banks, who just entered a plea of "CRIMINALLY" guilty to manipulating markets. They are now formally "FELONS" who engaged in violating SEC rules, they are no longer eligible for banking license. In truth, the banks are "too big to jail" and the SEC has waived their own rules, to exempt the banks. So, they can continue to engage in fraud and manipulation, get caught, pay billions in fines, and the "SEC exempts the banks from losing their licenses". This is truly how corrupt the administrative agencies really are.

This new decision calling the Administrative Law Courts (fictitious-subsidiaries) what they really are is reminiscent of the notorious extrajudicial proceedings of the Star Chamber operated by King James I.

The court of Chancery set up outside of the King's Bench, so there were no trials by jury. It had the same purpose, to circumvent the law. This is where the Fifth Amendment Right came into being. This came about following the trial of 'John Lilburne' (1615 – 1657) for handing out a pamphlet the government did not like.

The Miranda v Arizona 384 U.S. 436 (1966) decision of the Supreme Court came only after decades of abuse by American police against citizens, not unlike what we are watching today. The Miranda decision is hated by police, prosecutors, right-wing judges, politicians and citizens. The decision was based upon the history of the right not to be coerced that began with the famous trial of John Lilburne before the English court of the Star Chamber in 1637 where he stood-tall and objected to the King's torture. Lilburnes' crime was handing out pamphlets against the king. He was a leader in the Leveller Movement of the 1640s and was a prolific pamphleteer who defended religious and individual liberty of the people. He was imprisoned many times for his views and was active in the army of the New Parliament rising to the rank of Lieutenant Colonel. In October 1649, he was arrested and tried for High Treason for printing and circulating books and pamphlets critical of the government but was acquitted of all charges by a jury of his peers.

In truth the United-States-Fictitious-Corporate-Government continues these criminal acts still to this day. Remember the United-States-Fictitious-Corporate-Government is the only ?country? That puts "innocent-people" behind bars for what is considered "doing the right thing".

Chapter 6:
LIEN-DOCUMENTS-PRESENTED FOR EVIDENCE: (SELF–PUBLISHED "CONTRACTS" BY THE "CONSTITUTION" AND BY AMERICAN'S CIVIL RIGHTS")

The Constitution has an added phrase that pertains for Americans that have the **right** too "CONTRACT THEIR LABOR". In addition, the United States-Corporate-Government, et al, believe they are the only 'Professionals' that can write contracts and WE Americans must abide by what they say within those contracts whether they are written, oral or implied. Instead the United-States-Corporate-Government in its infinite stupidity assigns Tax Identification Numbers also known as a "Social-Security number". The Social-Security Agency explain to you, when you get this number **NOT** too share this information with anyone else…However; this is not the entire truth.

The Banking Industry (Federal Deposit Insurance Corporation), The United States Securities and Exchange Commission (S. E. C.) which is an independent federal government agency responsible for protecting investors, maintaining fair and orderly functioning of securities markets and facilitating capital formation, Insurance Companies, Employment Opportunities, Hospitals, the Internal Revenue Service not to mention the fact that the Judicial-System are just a few that are in violation and in "BREACH" of Contract…Namely the "Constitution" (which set-'LIMITS' for the United-States-Corporate-Government) and the "Bill of Rights" (which apply for ALL-AMERICANS). These two-documents were written out of necessity by the Founding Fore-Father's. The first ten **amendments** for the Constitution—the Bill of Rights—came into effect on December 15, 1791, limiting the powers of the federal **government** of the United States and protecting the rights of all citizens, residents and visitors in American territory. This includes the Executive Branch, Legislative Branch and the Judicial Branch.

As authors we have followed the same Legal-Laws, Policies and Procedures and Guide-Lines that apply to the United-States-Corporate-Government and all other Corporate-Businesses: And yet the United-States-Corporate-Government systematically "punish" any and ALL Americans who 'exercise' their RIGHTS or expose crimes being committed against Americans who are 'Enlightened' by what these 'Agencies' are doing **and/or** are not doing for its 'citizens'.

One prime example is the Uniform Commercial Codes. The Uniform Commercial Codes **(UCC)** were first published in 1952. They are one of a number of uniform acts that have been put into law with the goal of harmonizing the law of sales and other commercial transactions across the United States of America (U.S.) through UCC Adoption by all 50 States, the District of Columbia, and the U.S. territories.

As everyone knows or suspects, the different United-States-Corporate-Agencies in the Executive, Legislative and Judicial Branches have their own agendas and crooked little secrets that they do not want out for 'public-knowledge'. But one of the biggest lies and trickery that these Agencies use is the statement, "We are just doing our Job". Perjury of Oath and Affirmation and **BREACH of CONTRACT** is not a job.

Within our second book "! AT GUN POINT…Whistle Blowers' Point of View" authored by: Bradley – J.: [Franks] and Robert – C.: [Simpson]: Published by Author House: 05/12/2012; we expose a crime against Americans and U. S. Citizens and report that crime to the United-States-Corporate-Government and its agencies that were supposed to help. However, when we did report the crime, we were the ones that were systematically punished unfairly, cruelly and raped…never really understanding *why* until we researched "**BREACH OF CONTRACT**".

The first book we published "Your Day In Court" Using Common Law With Common Sense; authored by Bradley – J.: [Franks] and Robert – C.: [Simpson]: Self-Published through LuLu.com: 2011. This book was and is the set-up too show American Civilians and Citizens how the POE-POE (police); (special-note: the motto of the United States-Corporate-

Police-Departments—which is found on their vehicles is "**To Protect and Serve**": However, the Police Department under the Corporate-Franchise-Government should be changed too; ("**To Punish and Enslave**"); Judicial Officers, and the City, County and State benefit by "*Opinions*" *not* "FACT(S)".

The 'fact or facts' are only known too those **victim or victims** and who were **present** during the alleged-crime. The established crooked United-States-Corporate-Government and the rest of the Bureaucratic – so called professionals - add their "OPINIONS" and "disregard" and "suppress" any testimony, evidence or "FACTS" into their Franchise-Corporate-Courts ('Banks') for the benefit of the Bankers or the Crown (King). In other words, the United-States-Corporate-Government cannot find anyone "guilty" if they have "no-evidence". This also includes when or if they "BREACH CONTRACT" or violate the "Legal-Document" by violating *any* 'Civil Rights' or if they cannot produce any contract with a signature/autograph that forces an American into their performance contracts.

The third book we authored deals with "BREACH OF CONTRACT". It is called "BREACH OF CONTRACT" Enlightenment and Information that the United States-Corporation does NOT WANT YOU to KNOW!" Published through Amazon.com/kindle. This book contains evidence of the "contracts" that the Politicians, Judges, Lawyers and all bureaucratic employees, either elected or appointed, have to swear an oath for (aka. **OATH OF OFFICE**).

Which leads us to writing this fourth book – "THE DEATH OF AMERICA" The Insidious Takeover; authored by Bradley – J.: [Franks] and Robert – C.: [Simpson].

As authors and concerned Americans, we became victims of the United-States-Corporate-Government and its Fictitious-Subsidiaries (all 50 of them) starting in 1994 when we exposed the Electric Companies for committing Fraud against their customers and naming all of the perpetrators that were and still are involved with the cover-up. We tried getting lawyers interested in this case and they and their families were literally threatened with 'Bodily Harm' if they pursued this course of action. So you can imagine how the lawyers felt when they explained to us that there was 'nothing they could do', even after the fact that the information and evidence we provided became a factor in the downfall of Enron in Texas.

This was a final straw that broke the camel's-back and forced us to write these books; for the "Enlightenment" of the American-people.

We decided, and maybe not the best decision, to place a UCC Lien against the Fictitious-Subsidiary-Corporate-Government known as the State of California and all off its "Impersonators" because of the illegal-acts that we have been subject and the illegal-acts that are continuously being committed against the American-people.

We tried to file the UCC-Lien in the "State" where the crimes took place. But because of the fact the "Impersonators" are in-control and "protecting" their illegal-business-practices they 'refused the filing.

As time went by, we started studying "Contracts" and the charges of "BREACH OF CONTRACT". The Fictitious-Subsidiary-Corporate-Government in its stupidity and lack of "response" loses all, jurisdiction, authority, Rights (if you can believe a non-living-entity has rights) and whatever else they deem that they think they have to continue to commit crimes-against Humanity.

We spoke with other concerned Americans and we decided that we would file the UCC-Lien in the Fictitious-Subsidiary-Corporate-Government the State of New York. The reason behind this is because most, if not all, of the Corporate-Headquarters of the Banks, the Stock Exchange, and the dollars are funneled through the State of New York. If Washington D. C. is the capitol of America then the Subsidiary-Corporate-Government-State of New York would be the hub for the U. S. currency.

In 2015 we did just that…we filed the UCC-Lien against the Fictitious-Subsidiary-Corporate-Government-State of California and all of the "Impersonators" involved that has and continues to commit "BREACH OF CONTRACT".

The following is the documentation and responses (or the lack thereof) for the "contracts" that were sent and accepted:

The Death of America

Robert - C.: [Simpson];

Bradley – J.: [Franks];

C/O: Two-One-nine West Third Ave.:

Milbank, South Dakota [57252];

United States of America;

Domestic-mail-location

Filed in - Grant County, Milbank, SD
Recorded on 10/5/2015 2:45 PM
Transaction # 1004556
Document # 229992
Book 273
Page 278 (4 pages)   Rec. Fee $30.00

Nancy Copeland
Nancy Copeland, Register of Deeds

LIEN-DOCUMENTS

For: THE STATE OF CALIFORNIA: CEO/Governor of California: Edward Gerald "Jerry" Brown, Jr. and United States Senator for California: Barbara Levy Boxer.

This is a warning of commercial-grace. You have Thirty (30) days plus Five (5) days (for the return-receipt) from receipt for the autograph/signature of the private-agreement "Item Number: PSA-1-07112015UCC4" and the "UCC Financing Statement"; File Number: 201509038342061 and return for sender. In addition, a point-by-point [re]buttal for the answer of the Affidavits: (IAT GUN POINT...: ISBN: 978-1-4685-7355-8) and the Plain Statement of Fact.

Enclose[ed] you will observe Lien Documents; Explanation Sheet; Private-Security-Agreement; Affidavit: Plain Statement of Fact; Affidavit-of-Sovereignty; Memorandum and Points of Authorities on Sovereignty and 'Government' as it relates-to the Public-Servant/Agent; Commercial-Affidavit; Affidavit (aka: !AT GUN POINT...) from; Robert – Charles: [Simpson] and Bradley- Jefferson: [Franks] and an Affidavit of Mail[ing].

The UCC-1 Financing Statement, and the attachment exhibit(s) are lien documents. This Lien arises is due and owing-for the willful and unlawful (FRAUD) violation of "Oath of Office" (Breach of Contract) and the failure for the Protection of the unalienable "Birth-Right" of the Supreme Sovereigns, Robert – C.: [Simpson] and Bradley- J.: [Franks].

If at any-time-after the prescribed-notification of delegated-time expires, a SECOND and THIRD-NOTICE will be sent for all parties-involved for the [re]buttal and answer. If all parties-involved-refuse the [re]buttal and answer we will be forced-to-use subrogation of the signature/autographs and authority within this matter. With the full-understanding that with the "silence" and "refusal" of cooperation all "presentments" within this "cargo" will be met with acceptance, acknowledgement, agreement and approval from all parties-involved.

 NO-TRESPASS. USPSMAIL: RE: _____ US. FLAG: 1605432 7920 U.S.A.

Bradley - J.: [Franks] and Co-Author: Robert - C.: [Simpson]

BOOK 273 PAGE 279

Date on this __5th__ day, __October__ , Two-thousand-fifteen A.D.

Robert - C: Simpson

Autograph of Lien Claimant

Bradley - J.: [Franks]

Autograph of Lien Claimant

State of South Dakota)	
)	
) ss	**JURAT**
County of Grant)	

Subsrcribe[ed] and sworn before me a notary-public in and for said County and State, this __Oct__ day of __5__ , Two thousand fifteen; Anno Domini.

Witness by my hand and official seal.

My Commission Expires:
My Commission Expires Jan. 15, 2018

_____

Diana Allen

Notary-Public

Page 2 of 4: RCS/BJF.LIENDOC1: This is an attempt-to collect a debt. Any information-obtained-may be used-for any purpose. Errors and Omissions are consistent with intent. Copyhold applies. All Immunities, Remedies, Directions and Rights-reserved. Void where-prohibited-by law.

NO-TRESPASS. USPSMAIL: RE: _____ US. FLAG: 1605432 7920 U.S.A.

121

The Death of America

Verification

I, Robert – Charles: [Simpson], do solemnly aver under-penalty and pain of bearing-false-witness under the law of Robert – Charles: [Simpson]'s sovereign, that the foregoing Declaration within this cargo is entirely true, correct, certain and complete, before the undersign[ed] witnesses, so help this Affiant Almighty God.

Date: This ___5th___ day of ___October___, Two thousand fifteen; Anno Domini.

L.S. _Robert–C: Simpson_

Bradley – Jefferson; [Franks];

In Care of: General Delivery;

Two hundred nineteen; West-Third Avenue;

Milbank, South Dakota: [57252].

Witnesses: (petit juris) (1);

L.S.: _____ (Print): Taylor Rynerson

L.S.: Joanie Ebsen (Print): Joanie Ebsen

L.S.: Michelle Weber (Print): Michelle Weber

L.S.: Janet Dranquist (Print): Janet Cranquist

L.S.: _____ (Print): Allisen Keehler

L.S.: _____ (Print): Zach Lagred

(1) petit juris is-comprised of six (6) people who may perform as jurors in both civil and criminal cases. (compurgators)

BOOK 273 PAGE 281

Verification

I, Bradley – Jefferson: [Franks], do solemnly aver under-penalty and pain of bearing-false-witness under the law of Bradley – Jefferson: [Franks]'s sovereign, that the foregoing Declaration within this cargo is entirely true, correct, certain and complete, before the undersign[ed] witnesses, so help this Affiant Almighty God.

Date: This ___5th___ day of ___October___ , Two thousand fifteen; Anno Domini.

L. S. *Bradley - J.: [Franks]*

Bradley – Jefferson; [Franks];

In Care of: General Delivery;

Two hundred nineteen; West-Third Avenue;

Milbank, South Dakota: [57252].

Witnesses: (petit juris) (1);

L.S.: _____ (Print): Taylor Ryneison

L.S.: Joanne Ebsen (Print): Joanne Ebsen

L.S.: Michelle Weber (Print): Michelle Weber

L.S.: Janet Granquist (Print): Janet Granquist

L.S.: _____ (Print): CAllison Koehler

L.S.: _____ (Print): Zach Lagred

(1); petit juris is-comprised of six (6) people who may perform as jurors in both civil and criminal cases. (compurgators)

© Robert – Charles: [Simpson] and Bradley – Jefferson: [Franks]; 05012015

123

MEMORANDUM AND POINTS OF AUTHORITIES ON SOVEREIGNTY
AND 'GOVERNMENT' AS-IT-RELATES-TO-THE PUBLIC-SERVANT/AGENT

It is a well-understood-fact of American history that the most dynamic document that set the course of America is the Declaration of Independence. It was/is the document that disclose[ed] the tyranny of English government. It-expressed the 'elements' of the 'Rights of Men', within any society, and that "*all men are created equal*". The Declaration of Independence stipulate[ed] the chain of Authority within 'governments' and of the obvious fact that the people 'created' government. That it was the 'people' who *institute[ed]* government and in so-doing, the people "*secured these rights*", and that government (at every-level) *derive[es]* their "*just powers from the consent of the governed*".

It is also a well establish[ed] fact that the people did-not give up all of their 'power' to-government(s). The Declaration of Independence create[ed] the sovereignty-in-the-people, not in government. Therefore, the-people are above the creature(s) they create[ed] (government) and that those who work for/in government(s) are 'Public-Servants' and have place[ed] themselves in a subservient position, to-serve-the-people within their function/office/position via their 'Oath of Office'.

In-regards the principles establish[ed] in the Declaration of Independence and the subsequent 'constitutions' written and create[ed] after it, and the true sovereignty, ... a written constitution is-not only the direct and basic expression of the sovereign will, it is also the absolute rule of action and decision for all departments and offices of government with respect to-all matters cover[ed]by it, and it must control as it is written until it is change[ed] by the authority which establish[ed]-it. (the people!) Observe:

State ex rel.: **Crenshaw v. Joseph, 175 Ala. 579, 57: So. 942; Schmitt v. F. W. Cook Brewing Co., 187 Ind. 623, 120: N. E. 19, 3: A. L. R. 270; Collins v. Martin, 209 Pa. 388, 139: A 122, 55: A. L. R. 311; Travelers' Insurance Co. v. Marshall, 124 Tex. 45, 76: S. W. 2d 1007, 96: A. L. R. 802; State ex rel. Lemon v. Langlie, 45 Wash.: 2d 82, 273: P.2d 464.**

"The (state) constitution is the supreme law, written by the supreme-power of the state, the people themselves". **Re: Gorham-Fayette Local School Dist., 20: Ohio Misc. 222, 49: Ohio Ops. 2d 143,250: N. E. 2d 104; State ex rel.: Weinberger v. Miller, 87: Ohio St. 12, 99: N. E. 1078.**

"The Constitution is the voice of the people speaking in their sovereignty capacity, and it must heeded; when the constitution speaks with reference to a particular matter, it must be given-effect as the paramount law of the land". **People v. Parks, 58 cal. 624.**

"Sovereignty itself is, of course, not-subject to-law, for it the author and source of law; but in our system, while sovereign powers are delegated to the agencies of government, sovereignty itself remains with the people, by whom and for whom all government exists and acts. And the law is the definition and limitation of power". **Yick Wo v. Hopkins, 118 us 356.**

"Local laws or ordinances enacted by a city must be consistent with the state constitution". **Bell v. Vaughn 155: Fla. 551, 21: So. 2d 31; Evans v. Berry, 262: N.Y. 61, 186: N. E. 203, 89: A. L. R. 387.**

"It is the duty of all officials, whether legislative, judicial, executive, administrative, or ministerial, to so perform every official act as not to violate constitutional provisions". **Montgomery v. State, 55: Fla. 97, 45: So. 879.**

"The provisions of the constitution must be given effect even if in doing so a statute is held to be inoperative". **State ex rel.: West v. Butler, 70: Fla. 102, 69: So. 771.**

"The constitution was made not to act upon the legislative department alone, but upon every department of the government". **Way v. Hillier, 16: Ohio 105.**

"Courts should not tolerate or condone disregard of law and arbitrary usurpation of power on the part of any officer". AND NEITHER-SHOULD THE PEOPLE! **Ex parte Owen, 10: Okla. Crim. Rep. 284, 136, P. 197: Ann. Case 1916A 522.**

"The officers of the law, in the execution of process, are obliged to know the requirements of the law, and if they mistake them, whether through ignorance or design, and anyone is harmed by their error, THEY MUST RESPOND IN DAMAGES". **Rogers v. Marshall (United States use of Rogers v. Conklin) 1 Wall. (US) 644, 17: L ed 714.**

"It is a general rule that an officer- executive, administrative, quasi-judicial, ministerial, or otherwise— who acts outside the scope of his jurisdiction and without authorization of law may thereby render himself amenable to personal liability...". **Cooper v. O'Conner, 69: App. D. C. 100, 99: F. 2d 135, 118: A. L. R. 1440; Chamberlain v. Clayton, 56: Iowa 331, 9: N. W. 237, 41: Am. Rep. 101.**

"If a public officer authorizes the doing of an act not within the scope of his authority, he will be held liable". **Bailey v. New York, 3: Hill (NY) 531, 38: Am. Dec. 669, affirmed in 2: Denio. 433.**

"[i]n our country the people are sovereign....and the government cannot sever its relationship to the people....". **Afroyim 387: U. S. at 257, 87: S. Ct. at 1662.**

"In common usage, the term "person" does not include the sovereign, and statutes employing it will ordinarily not be construed to do so". **U. S. v. United Mine Workers, 330: U. S. 258 (1947), 91: L. ed. 884, 67: S. Ct. 677.**

"Where rights secured by the Constitution are involved, there can be no rule making of legislation which would abrogate them". **Miranda v. Arizona.**

"...the Congress cannot revoke the Sovereign Power of the People". **Perry v. United States, 294: U. S. 330, 353 (1935).**

"All that government does and provides legitimately is in pursuit of its duty to provide protection for private rights **(Wynhammer v. People, 13: N. Y. 378),** which duty is a debt owed to its creator, WE THE PEOPLE and the private unenfranchised individual; which debt and duty is never extinguished nor discharged, and is perpetual. No matter what the government/state provides for us in manner of convenience and safety, the unenfranchised individual owes nothing to the government". **Hale v. Henkel U. S. 43.**

"We the people have discharged any debt which may be said to exist or be owed to the state/government. The governments are, however, indebted continually to the people, because the people (the sovereigns) created the *government corporation* and because we suffer its continued existence. The continued debt owed to the people is discharged only as it continues not to violate our private rights, and when government fails in its duty to provide protection-discharge is debt to the people, it is an abandonment (an INJURY) of any and all power, authority or vestige of 'sovereignty' which it possessed, and the laws remain the same, the sovereignty reverting to the people whence it came". **Down v. Bidwell, 182: U. S. 277.**

"Optima est lex, quae minimum relinquit arbitrio judicis":

That is, the best system of law which confides as little as possible to the discretion of the judge!

BOOK 271 PAGE 929

Explanation of Law and Documents

Each document MUST have the correct data in it. Please verify all of the titles for the various State employees and, or agencies who will receive service. Also, make sure that you have the correct names! *Errors will render your documents useless!* The document MUST be sent via REGISTER[ED] or CERTIFY[ED] MAIL with Return Receipt Request[ed] (Green-card).

Declaration Letter – Oath Purgatory

This document, the Declaration (i.e., Oath Purgatory), **establishes forever more, the character of each individual** who makes the Oath Purgatory, as free and independent of all authority over him/her, unless he/she enters that position with full knowledge and disclosure, understand[ing], and consent of each obligation and its ramifications.

In a very real sense, then, by the sequential-submitting of these Notices, you will have-established at Law, the character of all the parties; yours and theirs. This becomes very important as you move towards other lawful devices which you will employ to-protect your character, e. g., Notice of Trespass.

Since the Oath states that you trade in lawful money, it is imperative that you carry at least one-silver-dollar in evidence of that fact.

By file[ing] this Oath Purgatory, you are-establishing-your-person, in individual capacity, to-act fully on the belief(s) of freedom, liberty and justice for all, as-expressed in the foundational documents of this country. Each person that files this document is, in very strong-terms, noticing-government at all levels, that the dream of this Nation is alive and well in the hearts of the American People, and that We the People, grantors of the Power within the Constitution, are alive and well, and do intend to-have our Nation administer[ed] and represent[ed] in the nature of the documents of its foundation

Justice Court:
Article 5: Section 1:
County:
Grant
At Law:

The heading for the court listed-on the top of the Oath Purgatory will be found in your state constitution under judicial sections and in the state code section. Look for "Style of Action shall be...".

127

Law Brief in Support of Oath Purgatory

Purgation is the act of cleans[ing] or exonerate[ing] one's-self of a crime, accusation, or suspicion of guilt, by deny[ing] the charge ranging-from a self-oath denial, which was at times-supported by the oaths of twelve compurgators, who swore they-believed the truth was spoken, or by trials or ordeals such as battle, or by vulgar purgation, being-subject-to torture by fire, hot water or iron to-find the truth using-extreme methods – all of which is denounce[ed], or purge[ed].

The single oath of the party, him/herself is also called "oath ex officio", of which the modern defendant's oath in chancery is a modification. 3: B1. L: Comm. 447; 4: B1.L: Comm. 368. Affiant herein is not a "cestui que trustent" created-by fraud, on (D.O.B.).

This oath (purgatory) is an oath by which one destroys the presumptions which are used-against one for one is then said to purge oneself, when oneself removes the suspicions which are used-against one: as, when a man is in contempt for not attend[ing] court as a witness, he may purge himself of the contempt, by solemn Asseveration to-a fact which is lawful and ample excuse. Bouvier's Law Dictionary.

Affiant hereby expurgates his/her-self from all disputable presumptions which are morally harmful, offensive, or erroneous to-affiant's character and free status.

In 1848 the state of New York adopt[ed] the Code Napoleon of Louisiana as the law of the land, and shortly thereafter it was adopt[ed] by the District of Columbia. By 1936 all other states had adopt[ed] the Code of Napoleon of Louisiana by legislation and it was thereafter, and is now said to-be "the new law of our land". The encyclopediaists have-described that Code as Roman Law, which according-to the same encyclopediaists is a system of "slave labor". See also, "Statute of uses" Elizabeth III, 1500 A. D., or "use" Bouvier's Law Dictionary.

Roman "citizenship", we are silently taught, is not a matter of good or bad; but, as a matter of policy under Roman Law, all individuals are simply-living (or being-allowed to-live) to-conduct state business. Today, United States' citizens are officially referred-to as "human-resource", to-be dealt with as "certain natural resource recapture property" under U.S. Trade[ing] with the Enemy Acts. Under Roman law, admitting-you are a citizen is to say you have no-rights except the "civil-rights" given to-you by the (Roman) state. Saul, you may remember, was said to-be saved-by his citizenship. Because he was a Roman citizen they could not immediately put him to death and he did get more due process than his fellow man, but that did not assure Saul of a fair-hearing, trial or justice... it just took longer... and the Roman hierarchy killed Saul anyway. Nowadays, one is consider[ed] "at law" as "civiliter mortuus" or civilly dead, i. e., "no standi in judiciseo (equity)".

Affiant is a Free and a natural-born American Citizen as affiant has define[ed] it... and none other.

Another 1819 case, McCulloch v. Maryland, further define[ed] these matters. One of the ideas create[ed] from the con-federation is a "federation". A federation is not-created by the Constitution and therefore it does not have constitutional-limitations; and against it, there are-no constitutional-rights. All the influential people in government want[ed] a new "federal" government "state" trust in perpetuity. See: Trustees of the Dartmouth College v. Wheaton, (1819) (Article I, Section 10).

One might respond as a bureaucrat with this explanation: "We will allow the law to make an end of the constitutional District of Columbia, but we have to be careful as the people might find out. And since we can't change the Constitution, what we can do is to write some law on a second clear sheet of plastic – in the form of congressional legislation and treaties and we will define them and redefine with much legislative writing – and then lay it down on top of the first clear plastic. We can't change the first sheet as it is a perpetuity and will be there forever – but as our legislation is written, what it does, is to mask out the first District of Columbia – and when the people try to read through to the 1st (first) sheet, the 2nd (second) will confuse the 1st (first). And if nobody figures out what we are doing, we will have created another or a new District of Columbia – a "federation with unlimited power" which will live forever – and "our imposter". – will not change the constitutional District of Columbia one iota, as set out on the 1st (first) sheet". See: The Buck Act: 4 U.S.C. §§ 105-113.

That "federation", the District of Columbia imposter, is what I absolutely and entirely-renounce and abjure-forever all-allegiance and fidelity-to. fn/1.

Now, as to-my American-Citizenship, which I hereby solemnly declare allegiance-to, as a member of the Posterity of "We, the people" of the (u)nited States of America, I further state for the record that I have-create[ed] the same and I will tell you what it is and what is not.

I am an "American-Citizen" and I claim this-continent to-be my "home-free-home" and not "the land of the fee", and by so-doing I absolutely and entirely renounce and abjure forever, all allegiance and fidelity to any other lessor form of American or citizenship status that may be presume[ed] against-me, to rise through any quasi/constructive/implied-contracts of any and all foreign jurisdiction, fn/2, such as the system of "admiralty" which had its beginnings-with the commanders of the waterways and seas, who in the days of early Babylon and Baghdad, etc., were called "al amir" (such as the "Amer of Kuwait", see: Webster Dictionary), or in Latin it is said "admirallus"; the French said ""amiral"; the Spanish said "almirante"; in English we say "admiral" and "admiralty". fn/3.

This "admiralty system", complete with its own Legislature as well as Judicial tribunals (courts), became at odds with everything that the Law of England in Christian Europe and the entire Free Enterprise system has always stood for, specifically my common law, meaning the good customs of the English-speaking peoples. The "gold-fringe" on Old Glory constitutes a bold statement declare[ing] Admiralty Law and as Webster says: "the system of law administered by admiralty courts". Every "American" Judge when corner[ed] will confess his/her court is of Admiralty Law. See: "law of the flag", *Black's Law Dictionary*, Fourth and Sixth Edition.

Since before 1976, and now after, all states have adopt[ed] the "admiralty gold fringe flag" and have change[ed] their state codes to-confirm-to "admiralty law", replace[ing] Old Glory in every courtroom, without exception, with the new "anti-American gold-fringe flag" of the federal "federation" estate, District of Columbia imposter. This travesty or imposter has-invaded all levels of government, corporation, schools, churches, and even the Cub Scouts.

That "America/American" of "al amir" name and practice is-not the American nor Citizenship which I subscribe-to and sustain.

And it is against and for these-concepts, my-private law, which I have define[ed] upon which I base my Oath Purgatory. The language spoken is as I say it is. As Humpty Dumpty told Alice in Wonderland "this means exactly what I mean it to mean and nothing more and nothing less".

And for the Record...let my yea be yea and my nay be nay!

129

Date this _8th_ day of _June_ , Two thousand fifteen, Anno Domini.

L. S. _Robert - Charles : [Simpson]_

Full Christian Name, sui juris

In care of: General Delivery

Two hundred nineteen; West Third Avenue;

Milbank, South Dakota; [57252].

---

fn/1. See: Rosette Sorge Savorgnan v. U.S. (1949): 338 U. S. 491 – 507, 94 L. Ed.: 287.

fn/2. See: New York re Meriam, 16 S. Ct. 1073, 163 U. S. 625m 41 K. Ed. 287; Hooven & Allison Co. v. Evatt, (1945) 324 U. S. 652 at 6710672m 65 S. Ct. at 881.

fn/3. See: 4 U. S. C. §11 [F. R. Doc. 59-7096, Vol. 24, No. 166 (Aug. 24, 1959)] as amended; 36 U. S. C. § 176 (g) and (j) through implementation of 12 U. S. C. §95 (a).

Record request by:

Robert – Charles: [Simpson];

In care of: General Delivery;

Two-hundred-nineteen; West Third Avenue;

Milbank, South Dakota; [57252]

605·432·7920

State of South Dakota)

) ss:

Grant County)

Filed in - Grant County, Milbank, SD
Recorded on 6/10/2015 2:00 PM
Transaction # 1003495
Document # 229473
Book 271
Page 926 (7 pages)   Rec. Fee $30.00

Nancy Copeland
Nancy Copeland, Register of Deeds

Asseveration and Declaration

Oath Purgatory

Supreme Court de jure borough sitting in common law jurisdiction

1. I, Robert – Charles: [Simpson], do hereby certify and affirm (let yea be yea, and nay be nay), by solemn declaration that I, Robert – Charles: [Simpson], am a de jure American Citizen, a natural-born (or have adopted by oath the character of being natural-born) native of North Carolina, an inhabitant upon the Soil within the 'Original-thirteen-Colonies' of the (u)nited States, thereby a member of the American Christian Citizenry with unalienable rights guaranteed by the Covenant/Contract known as the Constitution for the (u)nited States of America, ratified by the people of de jure character and for the Territory of the (u)nited States (November Twenty-first, Seventeen-hundred Eighty-nine, Anno Domini), becomes the Twelfth-state and execute[ed] with specific performance pursuant-to the principles and laws of frauds and perjuries.

I, Robert – Charles: [Simpson], in my character, do in fact trade in lawful money of account of the (u)nited States of America, silver, with like parties of capacity.

Venue shall be the American Republican form upon the soil require[ed] by my character and stand[ing] in law, as private Christian.

Jurisdiction shall be under the American flag of peace of the (u)nited State of America and no-other, as set forth hereinafter [4 U. S. C. §1; Vol. 24, Number 166, F. R. 59-7096 (August 24, 1959 A. D., 9:31 a.m.); Army Regulation 8-40-10 (October 1979 A. D.), 36 U. S. C. §176 (9) (j)].

By this action, duly-record-within the lawful judicial capacity superior-court for Grant County, State of South Dakota, in common law jurisdiction, forever more establishes my character and conclusive presumptions to-any and all disputable and/or assumptive presumption(s) by any and all agents of foreign jurisdiction, be they of any nature or kind, in particular, dba corpiagents under authority of 12 U.S.C. §95 (a) and (b), and operation of 22 U.S.C. § § 611 et seq.

Date: This ___8th___ , day of ___June___ Two thousand fifteen, Anno Domini;

nunc pro tunc, June 3, 1944, Anno Domini.

L.S. _Robert – Charles: [Simpson];_

Robert – Charles: [Simpson];

In Care of: General Delivery;

Two hundred nineteen; West-Third Avenue;

Milbank, South Dakota: [57252].

132

BOOK 271 PAGE 928

Verification

I, Robert – Charles: [Simpson], do solemnly aver under-penalty and pain of bearing-false-witness under the law of Robert – Charles: [Simpson]'s sovereign, that the foregoing Declaration is entirely true, correct, certain and complete, before the undersign[ed] witnesses, so help this Affiant Almighty God.

Date: This _7th_ day of _June_ , Two thousand fifteen; Anno Domini.

L.S. _Robert – Charles : [Simpson]_

Robert – Charles: [Simpson];

In Care of: General Delivery;

Two hundred nineteen; West-Third Avenue;

Milbank, South Dakota: [57252].

Witnesses: (petit juris) (1);

L.S.: _Diana Allen_ (Print): _Diana Allen_

L.S.: _Alesia Christensen_ (Print): _Alesia Christensen_

L.S.: _Janet Stengel_ (Print): _Janet Stengel_

L.S.: _Michelle Weber_ (Print): _Michelle Weber_

L.S.: _Travis Lester_ (Print): _Travis Lester_

L.S.: _____ (Print): _Taylor Rymerson_

(1); petit juris is comprised of six (6) people who may perform as jurors in both civil and criminal cases. (compurgators)

133

State of South Dakota

OFFICE OF THE SECRETARY OF STATE
Apostille

(Convention de La Haye du 5 octobre 1961)

1. Country: United States of America

   This public document

2. has been signed by Nancy Copeland

3. acting in the capacity of Register of Deeds, Dewey County, State of South Dakota

4. bears the seal/stamp of GRANT REGISTER OF DEEDS, STATE OF SOUTH DAKOTA

                    CERTIFIED

5. at Pierre, South Dakota, U.S.A.

6. the 16th day of June, 2013

7. by Secretary of State, State of South Dakota

8. No. N-15-15378

9. Seal/stamp:

10. Signature

Shantel Krebs

Shantel Krebs, Secretary of State

134

DISCLOSURE OF AFFIDAVITS, PRIVATE SECURITY AGREEMENT, NOTICE OF LIEN DOCUMENTS, U.C.C. – 1 AND NOTICE OF COMMERCIAL GRACE

A SECURITY (15 USC)

THIS IS A U.S.S.E.C. TRACER FLAG

NOT A POINT OF LAW

One definition of **"A SECURITY"** is "any-evidence of debt".

The lien claimant does-**NOT** rely on Title: 15: USC: <u>as a basis</u> for the "commercial-lien". All commercial processes, by the use or rely upon notes or paper within commerce (for example: Federal Reserve Notes), must-bear-some sort of Federal-Tracking-Code, a County-Recorder's-number, or a Serial-number, which process be accessible for inspection at the nearest relevant County-Recorder's-Office or be widely-advertised. When a lien matures by [De]-Fault of the Lien-Debtor as a result of the Lien-Debtor's-failure of the **"REBUT"** the "Affidavit of Obligation" point-for-point categorically, it becomes an "accounts-receivable" in the ordinary-sense of a collectable-debt upon which "Assignments", "Collateralization" and other "Commercial-Transactions" can be-based, hence becomes a Security subject for observation, tracking, and regulation by the United States Securities and Exchange Commission (hereinafter U.S.S.E.C.). The notation "A SECURITY (15 USC)" is a flag in commerce informing-the U.S.S.E.C. that a speculation-account is being-established for the enforcement-of a lien. The U.S.S.E.C. can-then-monitor the process. As long as the "process" is truthful, open, and above-board (full-disclosure), the U.S.S.E.C. has-no jurisdiction over it, for even the U.S.S.E.C. has-no jurisdiction over the "truth" of testimony, depositions, affidavits and affidavits of obligation/commercial liens, and an-unrebutted-affidavit stands as the truth in commerce.

LEGAL AUTHORITY:

hebrew/jewish Commercial-code-corollary for Exodus 20:16. This hebrew/jewish Commercial-process is the best known commercial-process in America. Its prime-user is the Internal Revenue Service. The Internal Revenue Service uses **all-three** tracking-codes. The Federal-Code is the tax-payer's IRS document-file-number. The next stronger code is the County-Recorder's number. The strongest, most important, most universal-code is the tax-payer's identification number (TIN) also known as the Social-Security-Number (SSN). The IRS collection-process is legitimate. The IRS assessment-process is a commercial-fraud because it is not supported-by

Page 1 of 2: RCS/BJF.Discloure1: This is an attempt-to collect a debt. Any information-obtained-may be used-for any purpose. Errors and Omissions are consistent with intent. Copyhold applies. All Immunities, Remedies, Directions and Rights-reserved. Void where-prohibited-by-law.

NO-TRESPASS. USPSMAIL: RE: _____ US. FLAG: *1605432 7920 U.S.A* .

135

commercial-affidavits of obligation/commercial liens. The IRS issues only **"Notices of liens"** and has those "<u>Notices</u>" fraudulently recorded-on a "Tax Lien Index" at the County Recorder's Office. Notices are not-required to-contain commercial affidavits, but a **Lawful-Lien** must contain a commercial-affidavit (also an itemized- obligation/damages-ledger, and a list of property to-be seized).

NOTICE:

The foundation of the law, commerce, and the whole legal-system consists of "tell[ing] the truth, the whole-truth and nothing but the truth", either by testimony, deposition, and/or by affidavit. One-sworn-to-tell the truth is compel[ed] by high principles-to-protect truth and do nothing to-tamper with that truth, either directly or indirectly, either in-person or by proxy, or by subornation of an affiant or other-person. Any judge who tampers with testimony, deposition, or affidavit is a threat to-the-Commercial Peace and Dignity of the County, State, and United States of America, and acting-in the nature of a Foreign-Enemy-Agent, RE: A Mixed War!

WHOSOEVER acts against Commercial-Affidavits without executing the necessary Commercial-Paperwork under-affidavit is subject to-being charged-criminally for fraud. Commercial-processes are fundamentally ***non-judicial and pre-judicial.*** No judge, court, law, or government can invalidate the Commercial-Process, i.e. a Private-Security-Agreement, True-Bill, or Lien based-upon an affidavit, because no-third-party ca invalidate an affidavit of TRUTH. Action against affidavit creates MIXED WAR. No-one can rebut an affidavit except the proper-party (lien-debtor) who alone must rebut by affidavit within the established-time-limits. (Violations of Oaths of Office and Constitutions, Laws, Codes, Statutes, etc., = Mixed War by then 'Foreign-Agents' in any office, at any level of Government).

NOTICE TO-PRINCIPLES IS NOTICE TO-AGENT – NOTICE TO-AGENT IS NOTICE TO-PRINCIPLE.

AFFIDAVIT

Plain Statement of Fact

I, Governor/CEO for the State of California: Edward Gerald "Jerry" Brown, Jr., hereinafter known as Jerry Brown, took an Oath of Public Office-to uphold the Constitution for the United States of America and the Constitution of California state; January 6, 1975 (first-time) and January 5, 2015 (fourth-time), and in my breach of the obligation of my contract, I, Jerry Brown, did do injury-to Robert – Charles: [Simpson] and Bradley – Jefferson: [Franks], supreme sovereign(s).

I, Jerry Brown, individually, and as a CEO/Governor employ[ed] by the State of California, an agency of the [de]facto STATE OF CALIFORNIA, within the [de]facto UNITED STATES, attest to-the following-listed-facts, in this non-negotiable "TRUE BILL" U. C. C. 4-private-security-agreement. Under the principle of **"IGNORANCE OF THE LAW IS NO EXCUSE"**, I, Jerry Brown, receive this special presentment for acceptance without dishonor.

I, Jerry Brown, being a public-servant, understand that 'we the people' are the principles, and the public-servant is an agent for 'we the people'. Therefore, the agent has a trust and a contractual-obligation-to the people. The law of principle over the agent is in-force.

I, Jerry Brown, took an Oath to-protect and defend the Constitution for the united States of America, and the organic Constitution of November 1849, which was ratified May 7, 1879, for the California State Republic.

I, Jerry Brown, knew, or should have known, that I am in these constitutions, as state[ed] above, and the people are above these constitutions. These constitutions are-to restrict government, because government is-under the constitutions. Simply-state[ed], our national constitution and the state constitution were institute[ed] by men-to control government, not for government-to control men. Again, the concept of principal over the agent is in effect.

I, Jerry Brown, knew, or should have known, that in our government, we the people rule supreme and sovereign. We have-no King or ruler over 'we the people'. 'We the people', as a group, and as individuals, are the sovereign(s). The people in our government, whom we pay to-do our business, are our employee(s)/servant(s). 'We the people' expect and require that our servant(s) follow the law that is base[ed] on our organic foundational-documents, and the obligatory-contract they accept as a condition of employment.

I, Jerry Brown, knew, or should have known, that 'We the People' are endow[ed] by our Creator with unalienable Rights. These Rights cannot be taken away by the laws of Man. Even if a particular human does-not believe in a creator, that human still has these as natural-Rights. These natural-Rights include free-will and the responsibility of free-will to-do good or to-do evil.

Page *1* of 4: RCS/BJF.APSOF.1: This is an attempt-to collect a debt. Any information-obtained-may be used-for any purpose. Errors and Omissions are consistent with intent. Copyhold applies. All Immunities, Remedies, Directions and Rights-reserved. Void where prohibited-by law.
NO-TRESPASS. USPSMAIL: RE: _____ US. FLAG: /6654327920 U. S. A

I, Jerry Brown, knew, or should have known, that the basic rule(s) of human-interaction, and therefore natural-law, are: Do unto others as you would have them do unto (injure not) you, and keep all agreement(s) (contracts).

I, Jerry Brown, knew, or should have known, that in order-to hold public-office in a position of trust, I am require[ed] by law to-have a fidelity-bond. The bond is subject to-forfeiture if I violate my contract with the people. I am require[ed] by law for this fidelity-bond myself. The state cannot insure me, contrary-to what I may have been told by the corporate-State.

I, Jerry Brown, freely-admit that-on or about May/June of 2014, I receive[ed] a certify[ed] mail from Robert – Charles: [Simpson] and Bradley – Jefferson: [Franks] that contain[ed] an Asseveration & Declaration of the Truth, a U. C. C. 1; Finance[ing] Statement: Document-Number: 42021270002; File-Number: 147402396551; File-Date: March 10, 2014.

I, Jerry Brown, freely admit that I, in May of 2014, with malice and prejudice refuse[ed] and ignore[ed] my-legal obligation to-rebut the Asseveration & Declaration (Date: May 8, 2014) or examine the evidence that was include[ed] within the presentment; thereby breach[ing] my contract "Oath of Office" with "We the People", in-particular with Robert – Charles: [Simpson] and Bradley – Jefferson: [Franks].

I, Jerry Brown, freely admit that with the lack of my legal-obligation in a form of a rebuttal of this presentment, I have accept[ed] and agree with the presentment and accept all allegations brought against the State of California.

I, Jerry Brown, freely admit that I was with knowledge that Supreme Sovereign(s), Robert – Charles: [Simpson] and Bradley – Jefferson: [Franks] were in-fact barred-access into the Administrative-Court Hearing (Court) process concern[ing] their home and the "False-Witness and Reprisals" against them for the exposure of the Electric Companies.

I, Jerry Brown, knew, or should have known, that the court was not operate[ing]-under Article III, and/or Amendment 7 of the Constitution of the united States of America.

I, Jerry Brown, knew, or should have known, the following-facts prior to-taking my actions or lack thereof, Supreme Sovereign(s) Robert – C.: [Simpson] and Bradley – Jefferson: [Franks], were-under the implied-contract of the State-Constitution, was not require[ed] to obtain a "Building-permit" under-Owner-Builder, for said sovereign(s) were not involve[ed] in commerce.

I, Jerry Brown, knew, or should have known, that those sovereign(s) who know the **law**, obtain government 'licenses' and/or 'permits' out of the **"cause of necessity"**, and do so under-threat, duress, and coercion. Therefore, the adhesion contracts that are sign[ed] are **unconscionable**, and therefore, unlawful, being constructive-fraud.

I, Jerry Brown, know, or should know, that I must obey simple-contract law, or become **liable** upon the contract. I, Jerry Brown, enter[ed] into-my contract of "public office" and "support of the constitutions", knowingly, willingly, and without reservation. I, Jerry Brown, did take an "Oath of Office" and, therefore, enter[ed] into a contract.

I, Jerry Brown, know, or should know, and understand the terms, **breach of contract, specific-performance, obligation of contract, oath of office, public-official, common-law, non-judicial, private-agreement, commercial-grace, affidavit, lien, contract, true-bill, consensual, accommodation, security.**

I, Jerry Brown, knew, or should have known, that my actions were in direct-violation of my own contract (Oath of Office), and public-trust, and I commit[ed] fraud against Supreme Sovereign(s) Robert – Charles: [Simpson] and Bradley – Jefferson: [Franks], and commit[ed] fraud against my oath of Office.

I, Jerry Brown, knew, or should have known that my actions place[ed] Supreme Sovereign(s), Robert – Charles: [Simpson] and Bradley – Jefferson: [Franks], in jeopardy with the County of Riverside and State of California agency[ies]/entity[ies], and in-fact, the loss of substantial amount of income, thereby also cause[ing] injury to-the family of the Supreme Sovereign(s) and I, Jerry Brown, due-to my unlawful actions, was instrumental in the cause of the loss of the 'private-property', value of 'private-property', the contents within the 'private-property', the value of the contents within the 'private-property', and the structure on the 'private-property', and the value of the structure.

I, Jerry Brown, knew, or should have known, that powers absolutely prohibit[ed] to-government, under Article I, Section 10, Clause 1, of the Constitution for the United States of America, includes that of any state-passing any law impair[ing] the obligation of contracts. The same prohibition is state[ed] in Article I, Section 16, of the California state organic Constitution of 1849.

I, Jerry Brown, now know, or should know, that my actions, as already state[ed], did willfully, and knowingly injure Supreme Sovereign(s), Robert – Charles: [Simpson] and Bradley- Jefferson: [Franks]. I, Jerry Brown, refuse-to respond with a [re]buttal toward this Affidavit or the Affidavit "!AT GUN POINT...". As the Governor of the State of California I am above the Law and nothing the Supreme Sovereign(s) Robert – Charles: [Simpson] and Bradley – Jefferson: [Franks] can do-to redress grievances.

I, Jerry Brown, freely-accept commercial responsibility for my actions, and promise-to-pay for the afore-mention[ed] injuries of the Supreme Sovereign(s), Robert – Charles: [Simpson] and Bradley – Jefferson: [Franks].

I, Jerry Brown, know and understand that I must answer this courtesy-private-presentment-security agreement "True Bill" within thirty (30) days of service, with a point by point [re]buttal or I will become liable for the sum certain amount of damages occur[ing] to-the Supreme Sovereign(s) Robert – Charles: [Simpson] and Bradley – Jefferson: [Franks], in this matter for Thirty-eight Billion-Eight Hundred-Fifty two-Million-Four Hundred-Nineteen Thousand-Five Hundred ($38,852,419,500.00) dollars-lawful-money.

I, Jerry Brown, freely admit my failure in obedience to-my 'Oath of Office' and the resultant injuries-to-Supreme Sovereign(s), Robert – Charles: [Simpson] and Bradley – Jefferson: [Franks].

ATTEST[ATION]: by, Edward Gerald "Jerry" Brown, Jr., individually, and jointly, and severally for the STATE OF CALIFORNIA.

PRIVATE-SEAL: *Governor / CEO for California*

United States Governor for California: Edward Gerald "Jerry" Brown, Jr, bonafide and subject nihil dicit.

Done and Date this __21st__ day of __October__, Two thousand ~~fifteen~~ Sixteen, A. D.

AUTOGRAPH[ED] **BY:**

Edward Gerald Brown, Jr.

Done and Date this __21st__ day of __October__, Two thousand ~~fifteen~~ Sixteen, A. D.

Acknowledgement: by the Supreme Sovereign(s), Robert – Charles: [Simpson] and Bradley – Jefferson: [Franks], in law, and our South Dakota Republic, teste meipso this __21st__ day of __October__, Two thousand ~~fifteen~~ Sixteen, Anno Domini. EXPRESSLY not "WITHIN" THE United States.

Robert – Charles: [Simpson]

Robert – Charles: [Simpson];

Bradley – J.: [Franks]

Bradley – Jefferson: [Franks]

State of South Dakota

OFFICE OF THE SECRETARY OF STATE
Apostille

(Convention de La Haye du 5 octobre 1961)

1. Country: United States of America

   This public document

2. has been signed by Nancy Copeland

3. acting in the capacity of Register of Deeds, Dewey County, State of South Dakota

4. bears the seal/stamp of GRANT REGISTER OF DEEDS, STATE OF SOUTH DAKOTA

CERTIFIED

5. at Pierre, South Dakota, U.S.A.

6. the 16th day of June, 2013

7. by Secretary of State, State of South Dakota

8. No. N-15-15379

9. Seal/stamp:

10. Signature

   Shantel Krebs, Secretary of State

The Death of America

DISCLOSURE OF AFFIDAVITS, PRIVATE SECURITY AGREEMENT, NOTICE OF LIEN DOCUMENTS, U.C.C. – 1 AND NOTICE OF COMMERCIAL GRACE

A SECURITY (15 USC)

THIS IS A U.S.S.E.C. TRACER FLAG

NOT A POINT OF LAW

One definition of **"A SECURITY"** is "any-evidence of debt".

The lien claimant does-**NOT** rely on Title: 15: USC: <u>as a basis</u> for the "commercial-lien". All commercial processes, by the use or rely upon notes or paper within commerce (for example: Federal Reserve Notes), must-bear-some sort of Federal-Tracking-Code, a County-Recorder's-number, or a Serial-number, which process be accessible for inspection at the nearest relevant County-Recorder's-Office or be widely-advertised. When a lien matures by [De]-Fault of the Lien-Debtor as a result of the Lien-Debtor's-failure of the **"REBUT"** the "Affidavit of Obligation" point-for-point categorically, it becomes an "accounts-receivable" in the ordinary-sense of a collectable-debt upon which "Assignments", "Collateralization" and other "Commercial-Transactions" can be-based, hence becomes a Security subject for observation, tracking, and regulation by the United States Securities and Exchange Commission (hereinafter U.S.S.E.C.). The notation "A SECURITY (15 USC)" is a flag in commerce informing-the U.S.S.E.C. that a speculation-account is being-established for the enforcement-of a lien. The U.S.S.E.C. can-then-monitor the process. As long as the "process" is truthful, open, and above-board (full-disclosure), the U.S.S.E.C. has-no jurisdiction over it, for even the U.S.S.E.C. has-no jurisdiction over the "truth" of testimony, depositions, affidavits and affidavits of obligation/commercial liens, and an-unrebutted-affidavit stands as the truth in commerce.

LEGAL AUTHORITY:

hebrew/jewish Commercial-code-corollary for Exodus 20:16. This hebrew/jewish Commercial-process is the best known commercial-process in America. Its prime-user is the Internal Revenue Service. The Internal Revenue Service uses <u>**all-three**</u> tracking-codes. The Federal-Code is the tax-payer's IRS document-file-number. The next stronger code is the County-Recorder's number. The strongest, most important, most universal-code is the tax-payer's identification number (TIN) also known as the Social-Security-Number (SSN). The IRS collection-process is legitimate. The IRS assessment-process is a commercial-fraud because it is not supported-by

The Death of America
Page *1* of 2: RCS/BJF.Discloure1: This is an attempt-to collect a debt. Any information-obtained-may be used-for any purpose. Errors and Omissions are consistent with intent. Copyhold applies. All Immunities, Remedies, Directions and Rights-reserved. Void where-prohibited-by-law.
NO-TRESPASS. USPSMAIL: RE: _____ US. FLAG: *16054327920 U.S.A* .

142

commercial-affidavits of obligation/commercial liens. The IRS issues only **"Notices of liens"** and has those "Notices" fraudulently recorded-on a "Tax Lien Index" at the County Recorder's Office. Notices are not-required to-contain commercial affidavits, but a **Lawful-Lien** must contain a commercial-affidavit (also an itemized- obligation/damages-ledger, and a list of property to-be seized).

NOTICE:

The foundation of the law, commerce, and the whole legal-system consists of "tell[ing] the truth, the whole-truth and nothing but the truth", either by testimony, deposition, and/or by affidavit. One-sworn-to-tell the truth is compel[ed] by high principles-to-protect truth and do nothing to-tamper with that truth, either directly or indirectly, either in-person or by proxy, or by subornation of an affiant or other-person. Any judge who tampers with testimony, deposition, or affidavit is a threat to-the-Commercial Peace and-Dignity of the County, State, and United States of America, and acting-in the nature of a Foreign-Enemy-Agent, RE: A Mixed War!

WHOSOEVER acts against Commercial-Affidavits without executing the necessary Commercial-Paperwork under-affidavit is subject to-being charged-criminally for fraud. Commercial-processes are fundamentally ***non-judicial and pre-judicial.*** No judge, court, law, or government can invalidate the Commercial-Process, i.e. a Private-Security-Agreement, True-Bill, or Lien based-upon an affidavit, because no-third-party ca invalidate an affidavit of TRUTH. Action against affidavit creates MIXED WAR. No-one can rebut an affidavit except the proper-party (lien-debtor) who alone must rebut by affidavit within the established-time-limits. (Violations of Oaths of Office and Constitutions, Laws, Codes, Statutes, etc., = Mixed War by then 'Foreign-Agents' in any office, at any level of Government).

NOTICE TO-PRINCIPLES IS NOTICE TO-AGENT – NOTICE TO-AGENT IS NOTICE TO-PRINCIPLE.

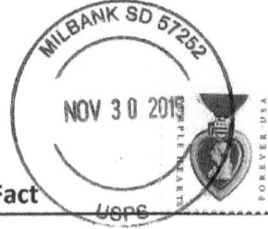

AFFIDAVIT

Plain Statement of Fact

I, United States Senator for the State of California: Barbara Levy Boxer, hereinafter known as Barbara Boxer, took an Oath of Public Office-to uphold the Constitution for the United States of America and the Constitution of California state; January 3, 1993, and in my breach of the obligation of my contract, I, Barbara Boxer, did do injury-to Robert – Charles: [Simpson] and Bradley – Jefferson: [Franks], supreme sovereign(s).

I, Barbara Boxer, individually, and as a U. S. Senator employ[ed] by the United States Senate for the State of California, an agency of the [de]facto STATE OF CALIFORNIA, within the [de]facto UNITED STATES, attest to-the following-listed-facts, in this non-negotiable "TRUE BILL" U. C. C. 4-private-security-agreement. Under the principle of **"IGNORANCE OF THE LAW IS NO EXCUSE"**, I, Barbara Boxer, receive this special presentment for acceptance without dishonor.

I, Barbara Boxer, being a public-servant, understand that 'we the people' are the principles, and the public-servant is an agent for 'we the people'. Therefore, the agent has a trust and a contractual-obligation-to the people. The law of principle over the agent is in-force.

I, Barbara Boxer, took an Oath to-protect and defend the Constitution for the united States of America, and the organic Constitution of November 1849, which was ratified May 7, 1879, for the California State Republic.

I, Barbara Boxer, knew, or should have known, that I am in these constitutions, as state[ed] above, and the people are above these constitutions. These constitutions are-to restrict government, because government is-under the constitutions. Simply-state[ed], our national constitution and the state constitution were institute[ed] by men-to control government, not for government-to control men. Again, the concept of principal over the agent is in effect.

I, Barbara Boxer, knew, or should have known, that in our government, we the people rule supreme and sovereign. We have-no King or ruler over 'we the people'. 'We the people', as a group, and as individuals, are the sovereign(s). The people in our government, whom we pay to-do our business, are our employee(s)/servant(s). 'We the people' expect and require that our servant(s) follow the law that is base[ed] on our organic foundational-documents, and the obligatory-contract they accept as a condition of employment.

I, Barbara Boxer, knew, or should have known, that 'We the People' are endow[ed] by our Creator with unalienable Rights. These Rights cannot be taken away by the laws of Man. Even if a particular human does-not believe in a creator, that human still has these as natural-Rights. These natural-Rights include free-will and the responsibility of free-will to-do good or to-do evil.

Page L of 4: RCS/BJF.APSOF1: This is an attempt-to collect a debt. Any information-obtained-may be used- for any purpose. Errors and Omissions are consistent with intent. Copyhold applies. All Immunities, Remedies, Directions and Rights-reserved. Void where prohibited-by law.

NO-TRESPASS. USPSMAIL: RE: _____ US. FLAG: 1605432.7920 U. 5. A .

144

I, Barbara Boxer, knew, or should have known, that the basic rule(s) of human-interaction, and therefore natural-law, are: Do unto others as you would have them do unto (injure not) you, and keep all agreement(s) (contracts).

I, Barbara Boxer, knew, or should have known, that in order-to hold public-office in a position of trust, I am require[ed] by law to-have a fidelity-bond. The bond is subject to-forfeiture if I violate my contract with the people. I am require[ed] by law for this fidelity-bond myself. The state cannot insure me, contrary-to what I may have been told by the corporate-State.

I, Barbara Boxer, freely-admit that-on August of 1996, I was in attendance of a fund-raiser for a candidate for the House of Representatives (44th Congressional-District) when I met with Robert – Charles: [Simpson]. He explain(ed) to-me how the "Electric-Companies were committing fraud against their customers, through the use of the electric-meters". He showed me an example with an electric-meter he had in his possession, how the electric-companies were accomplishing-the fraud. I explain[ed]-to Robert – Charles: [Simpson] "that I share a flight with U. S. Senator Dianne Feinstein, back-to Washington D. C., and would discuss this with her as well". I, further explain[ed] for him to "put your concerns in writing".

I, Barbara Boxer, freely admit that I, in 2000 – 2001, with Malice and Reprisals gave the "order" to-the County-Officials and State-Officials to-commit 'Fraud upon the Court" and 'Fraud from the Bench' for the 'destruction', 'demolition' and 'erase' the existence of their (Robert – Charles: [Simpson] and Bradley – Jefferson: [Franks]) home". "I want your home gone, your son gone and you gone and not necessarily in that order". "I, further-condone the actions of the State and County Officials in this endeavor".

I, Barbara Boxer, freely admit that I was with knowledge that Supreme Sovereign(s), Robert – Charles: [Simpson] and Bradley – Jefferson: [Franks] were in-fact barred-access into the Administrative-Court Hearing process concern[ing] their home and the "False-Witness and Reprisals" against them for the exposure of the Electric Companies.

I, Barbara Boxer, knew, or should have known, that the court was not operate[ing]-under Article III, and / or Amendment 7 of the Constitution of the united States of America.

I, Barbara Boxer, knew or should have known, that by the definition of perjury, reprisals and abuse of authority, I, Barbara Boxer, gave an order to-the above–mention[ed]- Court and Court Officers and State Officers, regardless of the pretend[ed] or lack of jurisdiction.

I, Barbara Boxer, knew, or should have known, the following-facts prior to-taking my actions. Supreme Sovereign(s) Robert – C.: [Simpson] and Bradley – Jefferson: [Franks], were under the implied-contract of the State-Constitution, was not require[ed] to obtain a "Building-permit" under-Owner-Builder, for said sovereign(s) were not involve[ed] in commerce.

I, Barbara Boxer, knew, or should have known, that those sovereign(s) who know the **law**, obtain government 'licenses' and/or 'permits' out of the **"cause of necessity"**, and do so under-threat, duress, and coercion. Therefore, the adhesion contracts that are sign[ed] are **unconscionable**, and therefore, unlawful, being constructive-fraud.

I, Barbara Boxer, know, or should know, that I must obey simple-contract law, or become **liable** upon the contract. I, Barbara Boxer, enter[ed] into-my contract of "public office" and "support of the constitutions", knowingly, willingly, and without reservation. I, Barbara Boxer, did take an "Oath of Office" and, therefore, enter[ed] into a contract.

I, Barbara Boxer, know, or should know, and understand the terms, **breach of contract, specific-performance, obligation of contract, oath of office, public-official, common-law, non-judicial, private-agreement, commercial-grace, affidavit, lien, contract, true-bill, consensual, accommodation, security.**

I, Barbara Boxer, knew, or should have known, that my actions were in direct-violation of my own contract (Oath of Office), and public-trust, and I commit[ed] fraud against Supreme Sovereign(s) Robert – Charles: [Simpson] and Bradley – Jefferson: [Franks], and commit[ed] fraud against my oath of Office.

I, Barbara Boxer, knew, or should have known that my actions place[ed] Supreme Sovereign(s), Robert – Charles: [Simpson] and Bradley – Jefferson: [Franks], in jeopardy with the County of Riverside and State of California agency[ies] / entity[ies],and in-fact, the loss of substantial amount of income, thereby also cause[ing] injury to-the family of the Supreme Sovereign(s) and I, Barbara Boxer, due-to my unlawful actions, was instrumental in the cause of the loss of the 'private-property', value of 'private-property', the contents within the 'private-property', the value of the contents within the 'private property', and the structure on the 'private-property', and the value of the structure.

I, Barbara Boxer, knew, or should have known, that powers absolutely prohibit[ed] to-government, under Article I, Section 10, Clause 1, of the Constitution for the United States of America, includes that of any state-passing any law impair[ing] the obligation of contracts. The same prohibition is state[ed] in Article I, Section 16, of the California state organic Constitution of 1849.

I, Barbara Boxer, now know, or should know, that my actions, as already state[ed], did willfully, and knowingly injure Supreme Sovereign(s), Robert – Charles: [Simpson] and Bradley- Jefferson: [Franks]. I, Barbara Boxer, refuse-to respond with a [re]buttal toward this Affidavit or the Affidavit "!AT GUN POINT...". As the U. S. Senator of California I am above the Law and nothing the Supreme Sovereign(s) Robert – Charles: [Simpson] and Bradley – Jefferson: [Franks] can do-to redress grievances.

I, Barbara Boxer, freely-accept commercial responsibility for my actions, and promise-to-pay for the afore-mention[ed] injuries of the Supreme Sovereign(s), Robert – Charles: [Simpson] and Bradley – Jefferson: [Franks].

I, Barbara Boxer, know and understand that I must answer this courtesy-private-presentment-security agreement "True Bill" within thirty (30) days of service, with a point by point [re]buttal or I will become liable for the sum certain amount of damages occur[ing] to-the Supreme Sovereign(s) Robert – Charles: [Simpson] and Bradley – Jefferson: [Franks], in this matter for Thirty-eight Billion Eight-hundred Fifty-two Million-Four Hundred-Nineteen Thousand Five-Hundred ($38,852,419,500.00) dollars-lawful-money.

I, Barbara Boxer, freely admit my failure in obedience to-my 'Oath of Office' and the resultant injuries-to-Supreme Sovereign(s), Robert – Charles: [Simpson] and Bradley – Jefferson: [Franks].

Page 3 of 4: RCS/BJF.APSOF1: This is an attempt-to collect a debt. Any information-obtained-may be used- for any purpose. Errors and Omissions are consistent with intent. Copyhold applies. All Immunities, Remedies, Directions and Rights-reserved. Void where prohibited-by law.

NO-TRESPASS. USPSMAIL: RE: _____ US. FLAG: 1 6 0 5 4 3 2 7 9 2 6 U. S. A.

146

Bradley - J.: [Franks] and Co-Author: Robert - C.: [Simpson]

ATTEST[ATION]: by, Barbara Boxer, individually, and jointly, and severally for the STATE OF CALIFORNIA.

PRIVATE-SEAL: *United States Senator for California*

United State Senator for California: Barbara Levy Boxer bonafide and subject nihil dicit.

Done and Date this _21st_ day of _October_____, Two thousand ~~fifteen~~ ^Sixteen^, A. D.

AUTOGRAPH[ED]   **BY:**

Barbara Levy Boxer

Done and Date this _21st_ day of _October_____, Two thousand ~~fifteen~~ ^Sixteen^, A. D.

Acknowledgement: by the Supreme Sovereign(s), Robert – Charles: [Simpson] and Bradley – Jefferson: [Franks], in law, and our South Dakota Republic, teste meipso this _21st_ day of _Oct._____, Two thousand ~~fifteen~~, Anno Domini. EXPRESSLY not "WITHIN" THE United States.
^Sixteen^

Robert – charles [Simpson]

Robert – Charles: [Simpson];

Bradley – J. : [Franks]

Bradley – Jefferson: [Franks]

! AT GUN POINT...

Whistle Blowers' Point of View

Bradley - J.: [Franks]
and Robert - C.: [Simpson]

UCC FINANCING STATEMENT
FOLLOW INSTRUCTIONS (front and back) CAREFULLY

A. NAME & PHONE OF CONTACT AT FILER [optional]

B. SEND ACKNOWLEDGMENT TO: (Name and Address)

File Number: 201509038342061

Date of File: 09/03/2015

Time of File: 01:54 PM

Location of File: State of New York

Secretary of State – Electronic UCC

THE ABOVE SPACE IS FOR FILING OFFICE USE ONLY

1. DEBTOR'S EXACT FULL LEGAL NAME - insert only one debtor name (1a or 1b) - do not abbreviate or combine names

1a. ORGANIZATION'S NAME			
The State of California			

1b. INDIVIDUAL'S LAST NAME	FIRST NAME	MIDDLE NAME	SUFFIX

1c. MAILING ADDRESS	CITY	STATE	POSTAL CODE	COUNTRY
c/o: State Capitol; Suite 1173	Sacramento	CA	95814	uSA

1d. SEE INSTRUCTIONS	ADD'L INFO RE ORGANIZATION DEBTOR	1e. TYPE OF ORGANIZATION	1f. JURISDICTION OF ORGANIZATION	1g. ORGANIZATIONAL ID #, if any
Not Applicable		Corp./Gov.	Executive Branch	Unknown ☐ NONE

2. ADDITIONAL DEBTOR'S EXACT FULL LEGAL NAME - insert only one debtor name (2a or 2b) - do not abbreviate or combine names

2a. ORGANIZATION'S NAME			

2b. INDIVIDUAL'S LAST NAME	FIRST NAME	MIDDLE NAME	SUFFIX

2c. MAILING ADDRESS	CITY	STATE	POSTAL CODE	COUNTRY

2d. SEE INSTRUCTIONS	ADD'L INFO RE ORGANIZATION DEBTOR	2e. TYPE OF ORGANIZATION	2f. JURISDICTION OF ORGANIZATION	2g. ORGANIZATIONAL ID #, if any
Not Applicable				☐ NONE

3. SECURED PARTY'S NAME (or NAME of TOTAL ASSIGNEE of ASSIGNOR S/P) - insert only one secured party name (3a or 3b)

3a. ORGANIZATION'S NAME			

3b. INDIVIDUAL'S LAST NAME	FIRST NAME	MIDDLE NAME	SUFFIX
Simpson	Robert	Charles	

3c. MAILING ADDRESS	CITY	STATE	POSTAL CODE	COUNTRY
c/o: 219 W. 3rd Ave;	Milbank	SD	57252	uSA

4. This FINANCING STATEMENT covers the following collateral:

All personal-judgements, **$38,852,419,500.00** U. S. dollars, **LAWFUL-MONEY**. Any and all savings-accounts, bank-accounts, CAFR Funds, Personal and private-property (land & real-estate, buildings, cars and trucks). Assignment of all stocks, bonds, insurance and certificates of deposit. All retirement-accounts (state & federal). All-inheritance. All payments while in public-office and payments-received while out of office, and your autograph/signature. All tangible and intangible-property. All accounts receivable (including-within the State of California Corporate Government). Any partners, assets, Federal-Reserve-Stock. Until full-accord and satisfaction has been given-to the secured-parties (paid-in-full). PROPERTY-EXCLUDED: Wedding rings, family photographs. Weapons of hunting and for personal/family defense. Federally-owned/controlled-U. S. Bases.

NON-STANDARD NON-NEGOTIABLE (NON-FEDERAL FORM). A SECURITY – 15 U. S. S. E. C. TRACER FLAG, NOT A POINT OF LAW. (Observe Item Number: PSA-1-07112015UCC4)

5. ALTERNATIVE DESIGNATION [if appl-cable]	LESSEE/LESSOR	CONSIGNEE/CONSIGNOR	BAILEE/BAILOR	SELLER/BUYER	AG. LIEN	NON-UCC FILING

6. This FINANCING STATEMENT is to be filed [for record] (or recorded) in the REAL ESTATE RECORDS. Attach Addendum [if applicable] / 7. Check to REQUEST SEARCH REPORT(S) on Debtor(s) [ADDITIONAL FEE] [optional] / All Debtors / Debtor 1 / Debtor 2

8. OPTIONAL FILER REFERENCE DATA

Robert – Charles: [Simpson]   *Bradley – Jefferson: [Franks]*

FILING OFFICE COPY — UCC FINANCING STATEMENT (FORM UCC1) (REV. 05/22/02)

MILBANK SD 57252
NOV 3 0 2015
USPS

UCC FINANCING STATEMENT ADDITIONAL PARTY
FOLLOW INSTRUCTIONS (front and back) CAREFULLY

19. NAME OF FIRST DEBTOR (1a or 1b) ON RELATED FINANCING STATEMENT		
19a. ORGANIZATION'S NAME		
OR The State of California		
19b. INDIVIDUAL'S LAST NAME	FIRST NAME	MIDDLE NAME, SUFFIX

File Number: 201509038342061

Date of File: 09/03/2015

Time of File: 01:54 PM

Location of File: State of New York

Secretary of State – Electronic UCC

THE ABOVE SPACE IS FOR FILING OFFICE USE ONLY

20. MISCELLANEOUS:

21. ADDITIONAL DEBTOR'S EXACT FULL LEGAL NAME - insert only one name (21a or 21b) - do not abbreviate or combine names

21a. ORGANIZATION'S NAME			
OR 21b. INDIVIDUAL'S LAST NAME	FIRST NAME	MIDDLE NAME	SUFFIX
Brown	Edward	Gerald "Jerry"	Jr.
21c. MAILING ADDRESS	CITY	STATE	POSTAL CODE	COUNTRY
c/o: State Capitol; Suite: 1173	Sacremento	Ca 95814	uSA

21d. SEE INSTRUCTIONS Not Applicable	ADD'L INFO RE ORGANIZATION DEBTOR	21e. TYPE OF ORGANIZATION Governor/Ca	21f. JURISDICTION OF ORGANIZATION Executive Branch	21g. ORGANIZATIONAL ID #, if any unknown	☐ NONE

22. ADDITIONAL DEBTOR'S EXACT FULL LEGAL NAME - insert only one name (22a or 22b) - do not abbreviate or combine names

22a. ORGANIZATION'S NAME			
OR 22b. INDIVIDUAL'S LAST NAME	FIRST NAME	MIDDLE NAME	SUFFIX
Boxer	Barbara	Levy	
22c. MAILING ADDRESS	CITY	STATE	POSTAL CODE	COUNTRY
c/o: 112 Hart Senate Office Building	Washington	DC 20510	uSA

22d. SEE INSTRUCTIONS Not Applicable	ADD'L INFO RE ORGANIZATION DEBTOR	22e. TYPE OF ORGANIZATION US Senator/Ca	22f. JURISDICTION OF ORGANIZATION Executive Branch	22g. ORGANIZATIONAL ID #, if any unknown	☐ NONE

23. ADDITIONAL DEBTOR'S EXACT FULL LEGAL NAME - insert only one name (23a or 23b) - do not abbreviate or combine names

23a. ORGANIZATION'S NAME			
OR 23b. INDIVIDUAL'S LAST NAME	FIRST NAME	MIDDLE NAME	SUFFIX
23c. MAILING ADDRESS	CITY	STATE	POSTAL CODE	COUNTRY

23d. SEE INSTRUCTIONS Not Applicable	ADD'L INFO RE ORGANIZATION DEBTOR	23e. TYPE OF ORGANIZATION	23f. JURISDICTION OF ORGANIZATION	23g. ORGANIZATIONAL ID #, if any	☐ NONE

24. ADDITIONAL SECURED PARTY'S NAME (or Name of TOTAL ASSIGNEE) - insert only one name (24a or 24b)

24a. ORGANIZATION'S NAME			
OR 24b. INDIVIDUAL'S LAST NAME	FIRST NAME	MIDDLE NAME	SUFFIX
Franks	Bradley	Jefferson	
24c. MAILING ADDRESS	CITY	STATE	POSTAL CODE	COUNTRY
c/o: 219 W. 3rd Ave	Milbank	SD 57252	uSA

25. ADDITIONAL SECURED PARTY'S NAME (or Name of TOTAL ASSIGNEE) - insert only one name (25a or 25b)

25a. ORGANIZATION'S NAME			
OR 25b. INDIVIDUAL'S LAST NAME	FIRST NAME	MIDDLE NAME	SUFFIX
25c. MAILING ADDRESS	CITY	STATE	POSTAL CODE	COUNTRY

FILING OFFICE COPY — UCC FINANCING STATEMENT ADDITIONAL PARTY (FORM UCC1AP) (REV. 05/22/02)

PRIVATE-SECURITY-AGREEMENT

Item-Number: PSA-1-07112015UCC4

LIEN-CLAIMANT(S):

Robert – Charles: [Simpson], and;

Bradley – Jefferson: [Franks]

VS.

LIEN DEBTORS:

1. The State of California, (Corporate/Government), and;

2. Edward Gerald "Jerry" Brown, Jr., (CEO/Governor), and;

3. Barbara Levy Boxer, (United States Senator for California), and;

4. All Known or Unknown Individual/Agencies within this Action

THIS IS EVIDENCE OF A DEBT

A SECURITY [15 U. S. C.]

THIS IS A U. S. S. E. C. TRACER FLAG

NOT A POINT OF LAW

THIS IS A-WARNING FOR

COMMERCIAL-GRACE

PRIVATE-AGREEMENT

CONSENSUAL-COMMERCIAL-LIEN

FOR VIOLATION OF CONSTITUTIONAL

SECURED-RIGHTS

THIS IS A COMMERCIAL, NON-JUDICIAL,

NON-COMMON LAW PROCESS

U. C. C. – 4 Private-Security-Agreement Non-Negotiable

"TRUE-BILL" means bargain of the parties in fact.

This Lien arises-out of breach of specific performance (breach of Oath of Office, violation of the Constitution for united States of America and the California state Constitution which are supreme commercial-codes and contracts between the government and the people).

EXPLANATION-SHEET

TO-BE ATTACH[ED] TO-EVERY COMMERCIAL-INSTRUMENT

OF/FOR FILE[ING]-BEAR[ING] THE U.S.S.E.C. TRACER FLAG

CONTAIN[ING] THE PHRASE

"A SECURITY – 15 USC"

This EXPLANATION-SHEET is attach[ed] to-all Commercial-Affidavits, include[ing] Affidavits of Obligation (Commercial-Liens) which are non-judicial consensual process[es] which arise out of a Breach of Special performance (e.g. for public officials' Breach of Oath of Office, a violation of the Constitution for the United States of America and respective State Constitutions).

Page 1 of 1: RCS/BJF.EXP1: This is an attempt-to collect a debt. Any information-obtained-may be used-for any purpose. Errors and Omissions are consistent with intent. Copyhold applies. All Immunities, Remedies, Directions and Rights-reserved. Void where-prohibited-by law.

NO-TRESPASS. USPSMAIL: RE: _____ US. FLAG: *1605432 7920   U.S. A*_____.

Filed in - Grant County, Milbank, SD
Recorded on 11/9/2015 4:30 PM
Transaction # 1004817
Document # 230181
Book 273
Page 572 (8 pages)   Rec. Fee $30.00

Nancy Copeland
Nancy Copeland, Register of Deeds

Return To:
ROBERT C. SIMPSON & BRADLEY J. FRANKS
219 WEST 3RD AVENUE
MILBANK, SD 57252

Robert—Charles: [Simpson];

Bradley—Jefferson: [Franks];

In care of: Two—hundred nineteen; West Third Avenue;

Milbank, South Dakota;

United States of America;

Non-domestic mail location [57252]

COMMERCIAL-AFFIDAVIT

AFFIDAVIT OF NOTICE, DECLARATION, AND DEMAND

FAIR NOTICE AND WARNING OF COMMERCIAL GRACE

NOTICE OF NON-JUDICIAL PROCEEDING

THIS IS A U. S. S. E. C. TRACER FLAG, NOT A POINT OF LAW

****

A SECURITY (15 U. S. C.)

COMMERCIAL-AFFIDAVIT

U. S. S. E. C. TRACER FLAG

NOT A POINT OF LAW

****

(u)nited States of America	)	
	)	
State of South Dakota	)	ss:
	)	
County of Grant	)	

For: All and Sundry Whom These Presents may Concern:

This Non-Judicial Commercial—Affidavit is prepare[ed] pursuant-to Commercial Law and the common law against Respondent(s), U. S. Senator for California: Barbara Levy Boxer; C. E. O./Governor of the State of California: Edward Gerald "Jerry" Brown, Jr. and the State of California, individually, and as officers/employees of an uncertified, fictitious corporation/association of a statutorily created-private-corporation(s), known as The State of California, under the principle of "ignorance of the law is no-excuse". The aforesaid Respondent individuals and entities (hereafter-refer-to as Respondents) has impose[ed] provisions of a contract-counter to-public morals, in the Nature of a praemunire, and as belligerents are in violation of State Law, Federal Law, International Law, and the Law of Nations.

Page] of 8: RCS/BJF.C-A1: This is an attempt-to collect a debt. Any information-obtained-may be used-for any purpose. Errors and Omissions are consistent with intent. Copyhold applies. All Immunities, Remedies, Directions and Rights-reserved. Void where prohibited-by law.

NO-TRESPASS!. USPSMAIL: RE: _____ US. FLAG: *1 6054327920   4. 5. A* .

153

The Death of America

Affiant(s), Robert – Charles: [Simpson] and Bradley – Jefferson: [Franks], in law and in equity "bona fide" presents by this Commercial-Affidavit and certification of facts, state for the record that Affiant(s) are of sound mind, over twenty-one years of age, and capable of making-this Commercial-Affidavit.

Affiant(s) state and attest for the facts of have[ing] read the contents of this Commercial-Affidavit file[ed] and record[ed] upon Respondents and that the common law and facts are absolutely-true, correct and relevant in actual-Fact and in actual-Law, and relevant for what Affiant(s) believes to-be true and correct by reason of the "Holy Christian Scriptures", their own research, assistance of Counsel, a study of history, the original Constitution of the State of California (1849); ratified (1879), the Articles of Confederation (1778), the Ordinance of 1787, the national Constitution for the (u)nited States of America, the original first Ten Articles of Amendment named "Bill of Rights", the original Thirteenth Article of Amendment which has been removed from the present versions of the national Constitution (meaning the "no titles of nobility" amendment), the Preamble to the Declaration of Independence (1776), the Negotiable Instruments Law, the colorable Uniform Commercial Code, the political will California Codes Annotated, the Revised Codes of California and Regulations, the opinions of the judicial Power and judicial Authority Supreme Court Justices' in god behavior, and the actual positive law acts of congress relating to-their authority and in their Lawful realm of territorial jurisdiction and venue, as the actual real evidence of proof-positive, irrefutable, conclusive and bona fide by Rules of Evidence: 401, and by mandamus under Rule: 201 and Rule: 202 in State of California, that show beyond any question or shadows of a doubt the presentments and accusations and criminal probable cause presentments made by these Affiant(s) are true, correct, and relevant in-Fact and in-Law under our rule of decision supremacy common law by the Alpha and Omega in "Holy Christian Scriptures" as in Genesis and in Revelation (quod vide; lex scripta and lex non scripta).

We, Robert – Charles: [Simpson] and Bradley – Jefferson: [Franks], the undersign[ed] Affiant(s), do solemnly swear, declare, and depose:

1).THAT we are competent to-state to-the matters set forth within the Affidavit known as: !AT GUN POINT...

2). THAT we have personal knowledge of the facts set forth within the Affidavit known as: !AT GUN POINT...

3). THAT all facts state[ed] within the Affidavit known as: !AT GUN POINT... are true and correct, and certain, admissible as evidence, and if summon[ed] upon as witnesses, we will testify-to their veracity.

4). THAT the eternal, unchange[ed] principles of Commercial Law are:

   a). A workman is worthy of his hire;

   b). All are equal-under the law;

   c). In Commerce, truth is sovereign;

BOOK 223 PAGE 524

d). Truth is express[ed] in the form of an affidavit;

e). An unrebutt[ed] affidavit stands as truth in Commerce;

f). An unrebutt[ed] affidavit becomes the judgement in Commerce;

g). All matters must be express[ed] to-be resolve[ed];

h). He who leaves the battlefield first loses by [de]fault;

i). Sacrifice is the measure of credibility (no-willingness to-sacrifice = no-liability, responsibility, authority or measure of conviction);

j). A lien or claim can be satisfy[ied] only through an affidavit by a point-for-point rebuttal, resolution by jury of payment.

These Affiant(s) have a natural Law unalienable GOD given Right and Remedy at U. C. C. section: 1-201: (44)(d): for specific performance sufficient-to support a simple contract which has been abrogate[ed] by the name[ed] Respondent(s) creating probable cause for criminal prosecutions for their willful and know[ing] criminal acts against Affiant(s). Respondent(s) purport[ing] to be Knowledgeable/Learn[ed] in the Law and in contract law has willfully, knowingly, and by their own volition (scienter) damage[ed] these Affiant(s) irreparably in the state of California, Riverside County, and consequently is now under-liability and obligate[ed] to-these Affiant(s) for damages. Respondent(s) have abuse[ed] their personal public trust and have deliberately-conspire[ed] with other-willing and knowing- accomplices, to-defend, extort, and steal Affiant(s) of their Rightful PRIVATE-property and Rights of Inheritance from Almighty Yahweh, and; has defame[ed] the good name and good character of these Affiant(s) in their comitatus; discredit[ed] these Affiant(s) before their family, their friends, their private-associates and their neighbors, through fraudulent filings, false-affidavits, fraudulent misrepresentations, etc. Said Respondent(s) act[ed] with accomplices and a consortium of judges, attorneys and lawyers to-deliberately conspire-to [de]fraud and steal these Affiant(s) of their PRIVATE, personal and real property, and monies.

5). THAT Commercial processes (include[ing] this Affidavit; the Affidavit: !AT GUN POINT...; and the require[ed] responses-to it) are non-judicial and pre-judicial.

a). No judge, court, government or any-agencies thereof, or any-other third-parties whatsoever, can abrogate-anyone's affidavit of truth; and,

b). Only a party affect[ed] by an affidavit can speak and act for themselves and is solely responsible for the response with their own Affidavit of truth, which no-one else can do for them.

6). THAT the lawful seizure, destruction, collection, and transfer of ownership of money or property must-be effect[ed] by a valid Commercial Lien which must contain certain elements in order-to be Commercially valid; to wit:

a). The lien instrument must obviously, patently, and evidently be a LIEN by being-clearly and explicitly-title[ed] "LIEN", "CLAIM OF LIEN", or "DECLARATION OF LIEN", and mandatorily, by its exhaustive Commercial content (full-disclosure) as follows in b), c) and d).

Page 3 of 8: RCS/BJF.C-A1: This is an attempt-to collect a debt. Any information-obtained-may be used-for any purpose. Errors and Omissions are consistent with intent. Copyhold applies. All Immunities, Remedies, Directions and Rights-reserved. Void where prohibited-by law.

NO-TRESPASS. USPSMAIL: RE: _____ US. FLAG: 16054327820 U.S. A _____.

b). The lien instrument MUST CONTAIN a notary[ized] hand-autograph[ed] affidavit, for which the issuer is commercially liable, contain[ing] a plain statement of fact disclose[ing] how the obligation of the lien was create[ed], attest[ing] that the commercial condition is true, correct and certain.

c). The lien instrument MUST CONTAIN a ledger or bookkeeping-statement connect[ing] purchases, services render[ed], and/or injuries sustain[ed]. With a claim of obligation such that each purchase, service, and/or injury is present[ed] in a one-to-one correspondence with its partial claim of obligation. The partial obligations are then total[ed] (tally[ied])-to obtain the total-obligation. This is call[ed] a "True Bill in Commerce".

d). The lien instrument MUST CONTAIN a statement, either specific or general, of the property being-seize[ed] from the lien debtor-to satisfy, or to-guarantee satisfaction of, the obligation of the lien.

e). A NOTICE OF LIEN to-be valid MUST CONTAIN a clear statement as-to where the lien is file[ed], where it can be found and how a copy can be obtain[ed].

7). THAT it is the sincerest belief, religious and spiritual conviction of these Affiant(s) that slavery and peonage are immoral, are violations of the First Precept of Commercial Law (a workman is worthy of his hire, "Thou shalt not steal"), that fraud, misrepresentation, nondisclosure, intimidation, deceit, concealment of material fact, lying (perjury), treachery are morally wrong.

8). THAT Affiant(s) are not accountable to-any parties other than Affiant(s)' own conscience and best judgement for the purpose of preserve[ing] inviolate Affiant(s)' unalienable/inalienable rights-to Life, Liberty, Freedom and Property and Posterity while engage[ing] in the honorable, productive, and non-harmful activities of their lives. Affiant(s) are also the sole and absolute owner of themselves, their bodies, and estates, and possesses unconditional, allodial, sovereign title thereto.

9). Respondent(s), attack[ed] these Sovereign Affiant(s) through the use of false and fraudulent-pleadings and misrepresentations without any documentation for the support of their colorable, false and frivolous-assertions.

10). The Affidavit: !AT GUN POINT... is inclusive into this Affidavit as being True, Correct and Certain.

11). Respondent(s) knew that they did not produce any evidence for the support of their claims in their complaint against these Affiant(s), and; Respondent(s)/Affiant(s) know they fail[ed] to-rebut the evidence of Respondent(s)' wrong doing, as submit[ted] by Affiant(s) in their counter-claim against Respondent(s).

12). Respondent(s) know that the severely-compromise[ed], arbitrary, unsupported-determinations, dismissal and summary judgement-orders of the State of California Court Officers/Agents, Bureaucrats of Riverside County, U. S. Senator of California: Barbara Levy Boxer, constitute usurpation of office, and are void on their face as a matter of law and historical jurisprudence.

13). Respondent(s) Governor/CEO of State of California: Edmund Gerald "Jerry" Brown Jr. became Nihil Dicit (became-silent) of the response for the U.C.C. Financing Statement Document number: 42021270002; File[ing] number: 147402396551; Date of File[ing]: 03/10/2014: Location of File[ing]: State of California – SOS – UCC DIV. and the Asseveration/Declaration of the Truth. Therefore, Affiant(s) must assume and presume that with the lack of a timely response that the Respondent(s) accept and acquiesce the presentment(s) in its entirety without prejudice of dishonor as of July of 2014.

Page *4* of 8: RCS/BJF.C-A1: This is an attempt-to collect a debt. Any information-obtained-may be used-for any purpose. Errors and Omissions are consistent with intent. Copyhold applies. All Immunities, Remedies, Directions and Rights-reserved. Void where prohibited-by law.

NO-TRESPASS. USPSMAIL: RE: _____ US. FLAG: *1605432 7920 U.S.A* .

14). Respondent(s) knew or should have known that the proven false and fraudulent statements of their legal representative(s), Office of the District Attorney of Riverside County and the order from U. S. Senator of California: Barbara Levy Boxer, were made with malice, full knowledge and intent to-misrepresent, conceal material facts and [de]fraud both the California Court System and the United State Senate. Respondent(s) knew or should have known that these gross criminal acts are a direct violation of Title 18: U. S. C. Chapter 47: Fraud and False Statements; sections 1001 and 1005.

15). THAT any and all parties who act against these Affiant(s) on their allege[ed] basis must produce the Commercial Affidavits of TRUTH, sworn by claimants to be "true, correct, and complete (certain)", which prove the origin and foundation of their claims and include-providing the contract(s) or agreement(s) with the bona fide autograph of these Affiant(s) thereon wherein these Affiant(s) have knowingly, intentionally, and voluntarily, in full legal and lawful capacity, agree[ed]-to-waive or surrender their Rights-to Respondent(s) or agree[ed]-to become subject-to or the slave or property of said Respondent(s) in any way or in any jurisdiction whatsoever.

16). In order for a crime-to exist, three elements must exist; (1) there must be a victim, (2) that the victim must have been damage[ed], and (3) intent must be establish{ed] on the part of the accuse[ed]. In this Affidavit and in the Affidavit: !AT GUN POINT... the Affiant(s) are the victims, this Affidavit verifies the damages, and the intent is-established at the end of the thirty (30) days (plus five (5) days for the return mail) grace period, if Respondent(s) fail to-rebut (respond) for the wrongs they have been a-party-to as note[ed] herein.

17). NOTICE is hereby given, and demands made, on Respondent(s) and any other-involve[ed]-Parties, that:

a). Respondent(s) were/are in [de]fault of the Counter-Claim At Law serve[ed] on them by Affiant(s) on March 30, 2000, include[ing] the amount of $10,010,000,000,000.00 (Ten Billion Ten Million) Dollars, U. S., mint[ed] by the U. S. Mint, PLUS 10% INTEREST, for exemplary, punitive, real, and consequential-damages is past due and owe[ing], and; ALL PRIVATE properties and funds taken unlawfully, remove[ed] in violation of commerce, or otherwise convert[ed], sold, or seize[ed] by Respondent(s), or other Parties in collusion or conspiracy therewith, be immediately return[ed] IN FULL VALUE PLUS 10% to-the undersign[ed] Affiant(s) Robert – Charles: [Simpson] and Bradley – Jefferson: [Franks], justly possess[ing] the lawful and legal title thereto; Or

b). Respondent(s), and all-Parties who act[ed] or proceed-to-act or assist in said actions, against these Affiant(s), without through, verifiable, point-by-point-rebuttal of each and every point set forth in this Affidavit and the Affidavit: !AT GUN POINT..., shall be immediately charge[ed] with criminal fraud, theft, conspiracy of extortion, and commercial liens shall be institute[ed] against all real and personal properties (United States Criminal Code: Title 18: sections: 4, 241, 656, 872, 1001, 1005, 1341 – 1346, and other such crimes as are relate[ed] to-issues of RACKETEERING, 18 USC: sections: 1961, 1962, 1963, 1964, plus such Constitutional violations not list[ed] in the Criminal Codes combine[ed] and describe[ed] simply as TREASON), and;

c). All administrative and legal-expenses relate[ing] to-this instant case shall be paid by Respondent(s) and all those who have drawn the undersign[ed] Affiant(s) into this matter.

18). THAT failure-to-respond as herein require[ed], to-these Affiant(s), within the prescribe[ed] time of thirty (30) days (plus five (5) days for the return mail) will be deem[ed] by these Affiant(s) to-invoke the doctrine of acquiescence and admission, to-recover, in commerce, the lost or damage[ed] properties plus damages, penalties and costs.

19). THAT this Commercial Affidavit and the Affidavit: !AT GUN POINT..., Notice and Warning of Commercial Grace, is the ONE AND ONLY such Notice and Warning.

20). THAT the foundation of Commercial Law, being-based on certain eternally just valid, and moral precepts, has remain[ed] unchanged[ed] for at least six (6) millennia. Said Commercial Law forms the underpinnings of Western Civilization if not all Nations, Law, and Commerce in the world, is NON-JUDICIAL, and is prior and superior-to, the basis of, and cannot be set aside or overrule[ed] by, the laws and statutes of any governments, legislatures, quasi-governmental agencies, or courts. It is therefore an inherent obligation on all Authorities, Officials, Governments, Legislatures, Governmental or Quasi-governmental Agencies, Courts, Judges, Attorneys, and all aspects and Agents of all Law Enforcement Agencies to-uphold said Commercial Law, without which said entities are violate[ing] the just basis of their allege[ed] authority and serve[ing] to-disintegrate the society they-allegedly exist to-protect.

CONTRACT OF LIABILITY FOR ALLEGATIONS

21). THAT if Affiant(s) fail[ed]-rebut such claims or charges, the Respondent(s) would declare a [de]fault against them and proceed-to collect on the claims made as being in agreement with said claims or charges. The Respondent(s) have[ing] made claims and charges against Affiant(s), thereby create[ed] an implied contract; Affiant(s) have[ing] rebut[ed] said claims or charges, demand[ing] proof of said implied contract, a true-binding contract was thereby create[ed].

22). THAT the Respondent(s) attacks of the commercial liability of the undersign[ed] Affiant(s), and this Affidavit and The Affidavit: !AT GUN POINT... or the response/rebuttal-to said claims or charges, creates a mutually voluntary, consensual, commercial, private contract by and between Affiant(s) and Respondent(s). Failure of Respondent(s) to-prove claims or charges against the undersign[ed] (or in the alternative, make full and complete restitution (pursuant-to number (17) (a) (c) above) shall constitute deliberate criminal actions and willful breach of and [de]fault on a bilateral contract (Affidavit of Agreement) form[ed] knowingly, intentionally, and voluntarily by and between Affiant(s) and Respondent(s).

23). THAT Respondent(s) knew or should have known, that themselves and other willful and know[ing] accomplices, would have to-answer in one form or another one-day for their willful and know[ing]-participation in fraud, robbery, grand theft, unlawful conversion, etc., of Private property and monies rightfully belong[ing]-to the Affiant(s), with or without resort-to a tribunal, but nevertheless subject-to their own devious rules a/k/a Uniform Commercial Code through the devises of pettifogger shysters, commonly known as bar attorneys.

24). THAT Respondent(s) know and understand the principal a man is worthy of his hire, and by the prima facie real evidence must obey simple contract law, or become liable upon said contract. Even Respondent(s)' attorney-advisors know and understand/understood this elementary principal, but in their programmed-mental-condition, they, Respondent(s) co-conspirators and accomplices, did willfully

Page 6 of 8: RCS/BJF.C-A1: This is an attempt-to collect a debt. Any information-obtained-may be used-for any purpose. Errors and Omissions are consistent with intent. Copyhold applies. All Immunities, Remedies, Directions and Rights-reserved. Void where prohibited-by law.
NO-TRESPASS. USPSMAIL: RE: _____ US. FLAG: 1 605 452 7926 U.S.A .

158

and knowingly take the responsibility for their own actions and inactions, with appropriate punishments become[ing] evident from time-to-time as Truth prevails in the State of California.

25). THAT Respondent(s) know or should have known, by the tenor of this Commercial Affidavit, a breach of contract subjects-them-to Private and Public punishments, whether or whether-not they have been misguide[ed], and mislead by their willful and knowing-conspiratorial-accomplices.

26). THAT Respondent(s), knew or should have known, Law and Truth prevail, and under-our system, no-matter how colorable the Uniform Commercial Code is, it is adequate to-punish even the most mentally-corrupt and deficient-delinquents "within" the United States of America.

27). THAT, Respondent(s) individually, jointly and severally, knows and understands the term constructive fraud with or without scienter, and the term conversion, and the term consideration, and the term obligation of contract, therefore, based-upon this special, express, and explicit knowledge, Respondent(s) individually, jointly and severally will become liable-to the Affiant(s) on sight, on demand, should they fail-to comprehend the magnitude of their omissions and commissions under-simple contract Law, especially under the supremacy common law, a/k/a as our-organic Law in harmony with Holy Scriptures, the foundation of Law, and especially for reasons in contract Law. Should Respondent(s) fail-to answer this Commercial Affidavit and The Affidavit: !AT GUN POINT... in any manner whatsoever by this tender-offer for any consideration sufficient to-support a simple contract under the provisions of U. C. C. section 1-103 which provide for bankruptcy and estoppel caused-by fraud, coercion, undue influence, misrepresentation, principal and agent through the common law under U. C. C. section 1-103.6 as in Anderson's on the Uniform Commercial Code , and as explained more fully in the Bank Officer's Handbook on Commercial Banking Law, and in conjunction with the U. C. C. at section 3-103 (1) which is quote[ed]: "This article does not apply to money, documents of title, ...".

28). THAT, for their will[ing] and know[ing] participation-in the theft, and conversion of Private property and violation of sacred natural Rights of the Affiant(s), in their common law venue original and exclusive jurisdiction, Respondent(s) know or had, has good reason to-now know that they must answer this Commercial Affidavit and the Affidavit: !AT GUN POINT..., point-by-point, within thirty (30) days (plus five (5) days for return mail) of receipt, or Respondent(s) will become liable for the sum certain amount of damages occur[ing]-to the Affiant(s), in this private matter for Thirty-Eight-Billion-Eight-Hundred-Fifty-Two-million-Four-Hundred-Nineteen-Thousand-Five-Hundred- ($38,852,419,500.00) Dollars of Lawful Money of Account, especially-under Respondent(s)' own rules a/k/a Uniform Commercial Code, which has adopt[ed] by their advisor-accomplices themselves, purportedly-learned in the law.

THAT WE, Robert – Charles: [Simpson] and Bradley – Jefferson: [Franks] the Undersign[ed] Affiant(s), depose and certify that we have written the foregoing-with full intent and understand[ing] of Purpose, and believe the statements, allegations, demands and contents herein to-be true, correct, and complete, commercially reasonable, and just, to-the best of our knowledge and belief. This is inclusive of this Commercial Affidavit and the Affidavit: !AT GUN POINT... in its entirety.

NOTICE TO PRINCIPALS IS NOTICE TO AGENTS.

NOTICE TO AGENTS IS NOTICE TO PRINCIPALS.

EXODUS 20: 15, 16.

Page 7 of 8: RCS/BJF.C-A1: This is an attempt-to collect a debt. Any information-obtained-may be used-for any purpose. Errors and Omissions are consistent with intent. Copyhold applies. All Immunities, Remedies, Directions and Rights-reserved. Void where prohibited-by law.
NO-TRESPASS. USPSMAIL: RE: _____ US. FLAG: 1605432 7920 U. S. A .

159

Attest[ed]: this _9th_ day of _Nov._ in the year Two thousand fifteen; Anno Domini.

_____
Robert – Charles: [Simpson]

_____
Bradley – Jefferson: [Franks]

State of South Dakota)

) ss

County of Grant   )

Subscribe[ed] and sworn before me a notary-public in and for said County and State, this _9th_ day of _November_, Two thousand fifteen; Anno Domini.

Witness my hand and official seal.

My Commission Expires:

Oct. 1, 2021

DENISE L. SAMSON
NOTARY
SEAL
PUBLIC
SOUTH DAKOTA

_____
Notary-Public

Page 8 of 8: RCS/BJF.C-A1: This is an attempt-to collect a debt. Any information-obtained-may be used-for any purpose. Errors and Omissions are consistent with intent. Copyhold applies. All Immunities, Remedies, Directions and Rights-reserved. Void where prohibited-by law.

NO-TRESPASS. USPSMAIL: RE: _____ US. FLAG: 1605432 7920 U.S.A. .

Bradley - J.: [Franks] and Co-Author: Robert - C.: [Simpson]

Robert – Charles: [Simpson];

Bradley – Jefferson: [Franks];

C/O: 219 W. 3rd Ave.;

Milbank, South Dakota; [57252].

PRICE-LIST:

USPS NUMBER: RE: _____US

PRODUCT NUMBER	PRODUCT OR SERVICE	PRICE	[ ]
PS001	Abuse of Power	20,000	
PS002	Abuse of Process	100,000	
PS003	Appearance in Court	100,000	
PS004	Barratry	10,000	
PS005	Breach of Contract / Oath / Charter	100,000	
PS006	Breach of Duty	100,000	
PS007	Capitis Diminutio Maxima	200,000	
PS008	Checks and Balances Violation	100,000	
PS009	Concurring Quantum Entanglements	200,000	
PS010	Conspiracy / Collusion	500,000	
PS011	Deceit	50,000	
PS012	Defamation	50,000	
PS013	Detention without Cause / Per Hour	75,000	
PS014	Detinue	50,000	
PS015	Discrimination / Vexation Litigation	50,000	
PS016	Double Jeopardy	250,000	
PS017	Duty of Care Violation	100,000	
PS018	Embarrassment / Humiliation	5,000	
PS019	Embezzlement / Extortion	100,000	
PS020	Entrapment	100,000	
PS021	Factual Causation	50,000	
PS022	Fair Hearing Request / Violation	50,000	

PRODUCT NUMBER	PRODUCT OR SERVICE	PRICE	[ ]
PS023	False Arrest	100,000	
PS024	False Imprisonment	100,000	
PS025	False Pretenses	35,000	
PS026	Fraud Upon The Court	50,000	
PS027	Fraudulent Conveyance / Conversion	50,000	
PS028	Fruit Of The Poisonous Tree	100,000	
PS029	Gate / Envelope / File Opening Fee	500	
PS030	Grand Larceny	100,000	
PS031	Gross Negligence	500,000	
PS032	Harassment	50,000	
PS033	Influencing Testimony	75,000	
PS034	Intimidation	50,000	
PS035	Kidnapping	100,000	
PS036	Lack Of Full Disclosure	50,000	
PS037	Legal Causation	50,000	
PS038	Letters Of Marque And Reprisal	100,000	
PS039	Linguistic Morphing	10,000	
PS040	Liquidation Services	100,000	
PS041	Logistical Inconsistencies	10,000	
PS042	Loss of Wages / Per Year	50,000	
PS043	Mail Fraud	10,000	
PS044	Malice	50,000	
PS045	Malicious Prosecution	100,000	
PS046	Malicious Wrongdoing	500,000	
PS047	Manipulation / Alteration of Documents	100,000	
PS048	Mens Rea	200,000	
PS049	Mental Anguish	50,000	

Page 2 of 4: RCS/BJF.PRICELIST1: This is an attempt-to collect a debt. Any information-obtained-may be used-for any purpo
Errors and Omissions are consistent with intent. Copyhold applies. All Immunities, Remedies, Directions and Rights-reserve
Void where prohibit by law.
NO TRESPASS. USPSMAIL; RE: _____ US. FLAG: 1 605 432 7920 U.S.A

PRODUCT NUMBER	PRODUCT OR SERVICE	PRICE	[]
PS050	Mis-Application of Statute	50,000	
PS051	Mis-Information / False Evidence	50,000	
PS052	Mis-Joining or Recombining Instruments	20,000	
PS053	Misrepresentation	100,000	
PS054	Natural Law Violation	100,000	
PS055	Non-, Mis-, Mal-Feasance	50,000	
PS056	Nuremberg Offense	500,000	
PS057	Obstruction Of Justice	50,000	
PS058	Pass-overs / Re-Conveyances	1,000,000	
PS059	Political Repression	100,000	
PS060	Prosecutorial Vindictiveness	200,000	
PS061	Psychological Warfare	1,000,000	
PS062	R. I. C. O. (Illegal Activities Per Person)	50,000	
PS063	Sequestering Under Any Technique	10,000	
PS064	Serving in Multiple-Capacities	1,000,000	
PS065	Speedy Trial Violation	100,000	
PS066	Statute of Limitations Violation	100,000	
PS067	Vicarious Liability	100,000	
PS068	Surveillance / Per Day	50,000	
PS069	Tax Fraud	50,000	
PS070	The Use of Policies to Override Law	50,000	
PS071	Treason	1,000,000	
PS072	Trespass to Chattels	100,000	
PS073	Trespassing	100,000	
PS074	Undisclosed Policies	50,000	
PS075	Unholy Alliance	50,000	
PS076	United States Bill of Rights Violation	100,000	
PS077	Unjust Enrichment	100,000	

PRODUCT NUMBER		PRODUCT OR SERVICE		PRICE	[ ]
PS078		Unlawful Imprisonment / Per Day		1,000,000	
PS079		Unlawful Incarceration / Arrest		1,000,000	
PS080		Unlawful Taking		500,000	
PS081		Use of Injurious or Damaging Laws*		1,000,000	
PS082		Conversion		100,000	
PS083*		Punitive Damages*		1,809,000,000*	

//////////
//////////
//////////

L.S. *Bradley - Jefferson : [Franks]*

Bradley – Jefferson: [Franks] – Authorized-Representative

TRUE-BILL AND ACCOUNT[ING]   DATE: _____

Contract number: *20150903834206*

This True-Bill will-be-filed-under U. C. C. 1 Financing-Statement, SECRETARY OF STATE OF SOUTH DAKOTA and the Securities Exchange Commission. Using-Cleopatra Haslip vs. Pacific Mutual Life Ins. Co.: 499 U. S. 1: (1991) as a standard guide for damages and injuries. Injuries are three-times the damages. Damages, Injuries and Crimes:

BREACH OF CONTRACT/CHARTER

Product	Penalty	Total Amount of Damages/Injuries	
Abuse of Power	$20,000.00 x 3 =	$60,000.00 x 3 =	$180,000.00
Abuse of Process	$100,000.00 x 3 =	$300,000.00 x 3 =	$900,000.00
Appearance in Court	$100,000.00 x 3 =	$300,000.00 x 3 =	$900,000.00
Barratry	$10,000.00 x 3 =	$30,000.00 x 3 =	$90,000.00
Breach of Contract / Oath / Charter	$100,000.00 x 3 =	$300,000.00 x 3 =	$900,000.00
Breach of Duty	$100,000.00 x 3 =	$300,000.00 x 3 =	$900,000.00
Capitis Diminutio Maxima	$200,000.00 x 3 =	$600,000.00 x 3 =	$1,800,000.00
Checks and Balances Violation	$100,000.00 x 3 =	$300,000.00 x 3 =	$900,000.00
Concurring Quantum Entanglements	$200,000.00 x 3 =	$600,000.00 x 3 =	$1,800,000.00
Conspiracy / Collusion	$500,000.00 x 3 =	$1,500,000.00 x 3 =	$4,500,000.00
Deceit	$50,000.00 x 3 =	$150,000.00 x 3 =	$450,000.00
Defamation	$50,000.00 x 3 =	$150,000.00 x 3 =	$450,000.00
Detention without Cause / Per Hour	$75,000.00 x 3 =	$225,000.00 x 3 =	$675,000.00

165

BREACH OF CONTRACT/CHARTER Cont.

Product	Penalty	Total Amount of Damages/Injuries	
Detinue	$50,000.00 x 3 =	$150,000.00 x 3 =	$450,000.00
Discrimination / Vexation Litigation	$50,000.00 x 3 =	$150,000.00 x 3 =	$450,000.00
Double Jeopardy	$250,000.00 x 3 =	$750,000.00 x 3 =	$2,250,000.00
Duty of Care Violation	$100,000.00 x 3 =	$300,000.00 x 3 =	$900,000.00
Embarrassment / Humiliation	$5,000.00 x 3 =	$15,000.00 x 3 =	$45,000.00
Embezzlement / Extortion	$100,000.00 x 3 =	$300,000.00 x 3 =	$900,000.00
Entrapment	$100,000.00 x 3 =	$300,000.00 x 3 =	$900,000.00
Factual Causation	$50,000.00 x 3 =	$150,000.00 x 3 =	$450,000.00
Fair Hearing Request / Violation	$50,000.00 x 3 =	$150,000.00 x 3 =	$450,000.00
False Arrest	$100,000.00 x 3 =	$300,000.00 x 3 =	$900,000.00
False Imprisonment	$100,000.00 x 3 =	$300,000.00 x 3 =	$900,000.00
False Pretenses	$35,000.00 x 3 =	$105,000.00 x 3 =	$315,000.00
Fraud upon the Court	$50,000.00 x 3 =	$150,000.00 x 3 =	$450,000.00
Fraudulent Conveyance / Conversion	$50,000.00 x 3 =	$150,000.00 x 3 =	$450,000.00
Fruit of the Poisonous Tree	$100,000.00 x 3 =	$300,000.00 x 3 =	$900,000.00
Gate / Envelope / File Opening Fee	$500.00 x 3 =	$1,500.00 x 3 =	$4,500.00
Grand Larceny	$100,000.00 x 3 =	$300,000.00 x 3 =	$900,000.00
Gross Negligence	$500,000.00 x 3 =	$1,500,000.00 x 3 =	$4,500,000.00
Harassment	$50,000.00 x 3 =	$150,000.00 x 3 =	$450,000.00
Influencing Testimony	$75,000.00 x 3 =	$225,000.00 x 3 =	$675,000.00
Intimidation	$50,000.00 x 3 =	$150,000.00 x 3 =	$450,000.00

BREACH OF CONTRACT/CHARTER Cont.

Product	Penalty		Total Amount of Damages/Injuries
Kidnapping / Per Hour (9120 hrs.)	$4,101,000,000.00 x 3 =	$12,303,000,000.00 x 3 =	$36,909,000,000.00
Lack of Full Disclosure	$50,000.00 x 3 =	$150,000.00 x 3 =	$450,000.00
Legal Causation	$50,000.00 x 3 =	$150,000.00 x 3 =	$450,000.00
Letters of Marque and Reprisals	$100,000.00 x 3 =	$300,000.00 x 3 =	$900,000.00
Linguistic Morphing	$10,000.00 x 3 =	$30,000.00 x 3 =	$90,000.00
Liquidation Services	$100,000.00 x 3 =	$300,000.00 x 3 =	$900,000.00
Logistical Inconsistencies	$10,000.00 x 3 =	$30,000.00 x 3 =	$90,000.00
Loss of Wages / Per Year	$50,000.00 x 3 =	$150,000.00 x 3 =	$450,000.00
Mail Fraud	$10,000.00 x 3 =	$30,000.00 x 3 =	$90,000.00
Malice	$50,000.00 x 3 =	$150,000.00 x 3 =	$450,000.00
Malicious Prosecution	$100,000.00 x 3 =	$300,000.00 x 3 =	$900,000.00
Malicious Wrongdoing	$500,000.00 x 3 =	$1,500,000.00 x 3 =	$4,500,000.00
Manipulation / Alteration of Documents	$100,000.00 x 3 =	$300,000.00 x 3 =	$900,000.00
Mens Rea PC/PI	$200,000.00 x 3 =	$600,000.00 x 3 =	$1,800,000.00
Mental Anguish PC/PI	$50,000.00 x 3 =	$150,000.00 x 3 =	$450,000.00
Misappropriation of Funds	$200,000.00 x 3 =	$600,000.00 x 3 =	$1,800,000.00
Mis-Application of Statute	$50,000.00 x 3 =	$150,000.00 x 3 =	$450,000.00
Mis-Information / False Evidence	$50,000.00 x 3 =	$150,000.00 x 3 =	$450,000.00
Mis-Joining or Recombining Instruments	$20,000.00 x 3 =	$60,000.00 x 3 =	$180,000.00
Misrepresentation	$100,000.00 x 3 =	$300,000.00 x 3 =	$900,000.00
Natural Law Violation	$100,000.00 x 3 =	$300,000.00 x 3 =	$900,000.00

BREACH OF CONTRACT/CHARTER Cont.

Product	Penalty		Total Amount of Damages/Injuries
Non-, Mis-, Mal Feasance	$50,000.00 x 3 =	$150,000.00 x 3 =	$450,000.00
Nuremberg Offense	$500,000.00 x 3 =	$1,500,000.00 x 3 =	$4,500,000.00
Obstruction of Justice	$50,000.00 x 3 =	$150,000.00 x 3 =	$450,000.00
Pass-overs / Re-Conveyances	$1,000,000.00 x3 =	$3,000,000.00 x 3 =	$9,000,000.00
Political Repression	$100,000.00 x 3 =	$300,000.00 x 3 =	$900,000.00
Prosecutorial Vindictiveness	$200,000.00 x 3 =	$600,000.00 x 3 =	$1,800,000.00
Psychological Warfare	$1,000,000.00 x 3 =	$3,000,000.00 x 3 =	$9,000,000.00
R. I. C. O. (Illegal Activities Per Person)	$50,000.00 x 3 =	$150,000.00 x 3 =	$450,000.00
Sequestering under any Technique	$10,000.00 x 3 =	$30,000.00 x 3 =	$90,000.00
Serving in Multiple-Capacities	$1,000,000.00 x 3 =	$3,000,000.00 x 3 =	$9,000.000.00
Speedy Trial Violation	$100,000.00 x 3 =	$300,000.00 x 3 =	$900,000.00
Statute of Limitations Violations	$100,000.00 x 3 =	$300,000.00 x 3 =	$900,000.00
Vicarious Liability	$100,000.00 x 3 =	$300,000.00 x 3 =	$900,000.00
Surveillance / per day	$50,000.00 x 3 =	$150,000.00 x 3 =	$450,000.00
Tax Fraud	$50,000.00 x 3 =	$150,000.00 x 3 =	$450,000.00
The Use of Policies to Override Law	$50,000.00 x 3 =	$150,000.00 x 3 =	$450,000.00
Treason	$1,000,000.00 x 3 =	$3,000,000.00 x 3 =	$9,000,000.00
Trespass to Chattels	$100,000.00 x 3 =	$300,000.00 x 3 =	$900,000.00
Trespassing	$100,000.00 x 3 =	$300,000.00 x 3 =	$900,000.00
Undisclosed Policies	$50,000.00 x 3 =	$150,000.00 x 3 =	$450,000.00
Unholy Alliance	$50,000.00 x 3 =	$150,000.00 x 3 =	$450,000.00

BREACH OF CONTRACT/CHARTER Cont.

Product	Penalty		Total Amount of Damages/Injuries
United States Bill of Rights Violation	$100,000.00 x 3 =	$300,000.00 x 3 =	$900,000.00
Unjust Enrichment	$100,000.00 x 3 =	$300,000.00 x 3 =	$900,000.00
Unlawful Imprisonment / Per Day	$1,000,000.00 x 3 =	$3,000,000.00 x 3 =	$9,000,000.00
Unlawful Incarceration / Arrest	$1,000,000.00 x 3 =	$3,000,000.00 x 3 =	$9,000,000.00
Unlawful Taking	$500,000.00 x 3 =	$1,500,000.00 x 3 =	$4,500,000.00
Use of Injurious or Damaging Laws*	$1,000,000.00 x 3 =	$3,000,000.00 x 3 =	$9,000,000.00
Conversion	$100,000.00 x 3 =	$300,000.00 x 3 =	$900,000.00
Punitive Damages*	$1,000,000.00 x3 =	$3,000,000.00 x 3 =	$9,000,000.00*
Destruction of Private Property*	$75,000,000.00 x 3 =	$225,000,000.00 x 3 =	$675,000,000.00*
Value of Content of Private Property*	$25,000,000.00 x 3 =	$75,000,000.00 x 3 =	$225,000,000.00*
Value of Private Property*	$100,000,000.00 x 3 =	$300,000,000.00 x 3 =	$900,000,000.00*
	Grand Total of True-Bill and Accounting:		**$38,852,419,500.00***

(Thirty Eight Billion Eight Hundred Fifty Two Million Four Hundred Nineteen Thousand Five hundred Dollars and no/cents)*

The surety/property-utilized-to guarantee the payment of this commercial lien is the operational/commercial bonds of the Lien Debtor(s). If the bond(s) of the Lien Debtor(s) are insufficient for coverage of the payment, assets of the Lien Debtor(s) will be utilized-as follows: All the real and moveable property of the Debtor(s), Bank Assets, Federal Reserve Deposits, Insurance Policies, all Personal and Corporate Assets Foreign and Domestic, any/all affiliates or sister corporations, any/all Debtor(s) except: wedding rings, keepsake, family photographs, diaries, journals, Federal U. S. Bases-located within the State of California, etc., and the property normally-exempt in the Lien Process (including-survival provision). The surety of this True-Bill and Accounting is the private and corporate assets, plus all public liability bonds and licenses of ALL RESPONDENT(S)/PARTICIPANTS/KNOWN OR UNKNOWN, et. al verisimilitudes' and any/all capacities, and any/all associated-parties within this matter. RESPONSE IS WITHIN THIRTY (30) DAYS OR WAIVE ALL CLAIM AND YOUR AGREEMENT AND JUDGEMENT ARE CONFEDD[ED]. Thank you for your business.

L. S. *Bradley – Jefferson: [Franks]*

Bradley – Jefferson: [Franks] – AUTHORIZED-REPRESENTATIVE

Page 5 of 5: R.-C.:[S]/B.-J.:[F]/True-Bill: This is an attempt-to-collect a debt. Any information-obtained-may be used-for any purpose. Errors and Omissions are consistent with intent. Copyhold. Applies. All Immunities, Remedies, Directions, and Rights-reserved. Void where prohibited-by-law.
NO-TRESPASS.USPSMAIL RE: _____ U.S. Tracer Flag: 16054327920 U.S.A.

169

From: **Robert—Charles: [Simpson] and Bradley—Jefferson: [Franks]** BILL FOR: **The State of California**

C/O: 219 West 3rd Avenue;

Milbank, South Dakota; [57252]

(605) 432—7920

C/O: State Capitol; Suite 1173;

Sacramento, Ca.: [95814]

PRE-INVOICE

DATE: _____   CONTRACT #:   **201509038342061**

NO.	QTY.	DESCRIPTION	UNIT PRICE	UNIT TOTAL
		See Price list—attach (RCS/BJF.Pricelist1)		
		And from TRUE-BILL AND ACCOUNTING...		$37,034,419,500.00
		PUNITIVE DAMAGES.................................		$1,818,000,000.00
		TOTAL >		$38,852,419,500.00

Bradley—Jefferson: [Franks]

By: Bradley—Jefferson: [Franks], Authorize-Representative A/B

For: ROBERT CHARLES SIMPSON AND BRADLEY JEFFERSON FRANKS

C/O: 219 West 3rd Avenue; Milbank, South Dakota [57252]

This is an attempt—to collect a debt. Any information obtained-may be used-for any purpose. Errors and Omissions are Consistent with intent. All directions including Rights-reserved. **NO-TRANSFERS.**

Make all checks payable; FOR THE ORDER OF: Robert—Charles: [Simpson] and Bradley—Jefferson: [Franks]

Thank you for your business!

Page 1 of 1: R-C:[S]/B-J:[F].PREINV1. This is an attempt-to-collect a debt. Any information obtained-maybe used-for any purpose. Errors and Omissions are Consistent with intent. Copyhold applies. All Immunities, Remedies, Directions and Rights-reserved. Void where prohibited-by law.

NO TRESPASS. USPSMAIL; RE: 7015 0640 0007 0216 9701   US. FLAG #: 16054327920 U.S.A

From: **Robert—Charles: [Simpson]** and **Bradley—Jefferson: [Franks]** BILL FOR: **Edward Gerald Brown, Jr.;**

C/O: 219 West 3rd Avenue;   C/O: State Capitol; Suite: 1173;

Milbank, South Dakota: [57252]   Sacramento, Ca.: [95814]

(605) 432—7920

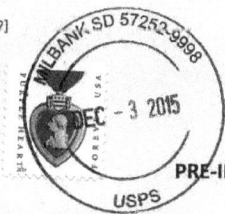

PRE-INVOICE

DATE: _____   CONTRACT #:   **201509038342061**

NO.	QTY.	DESCRIPTION	UNIT PRICE	UNIT TOTAL
		See Price list—attach (RCS/BJF.Pricelist1)		
		And from TRUE-BILL AND ACCOUNTING...		$37,034,419,500.00
		PUNITIVE DAMAGES.................................		$1,818,000,000.00
		TOTAL >		$38,852,419,500.00

Bradley — Jefferson: [Franks]

By: Bradley—Jefferson: [Franks], Authorize-Representative A/B
For: ROBERT CHARLES SIMPSON AND BRADLEY JEFFERSON FRANKS
C/O: 219 West 3rd Avenue; Milbank, South Dakota [57252]

This is an attempt–to collect a debt. Any Information obtained–may be used-for any purpose. Errors and Omissions are Consistent with intent. All directions including Rights-reserved. **NO-TRANSFERS.**

Make all checks payable; FOR THE ORDER OF: Robert—Charles: [Simpson] and Bradley—Jefferson: [Franks]

Thank you for your business!

Page 1 of 1: R-C:[S]/B-J:[F].PREINV1. This is an attempt-to-collect a debt. Any Information obtained–maybe used-for any purpose. Errors and Omissions are Consistent with intent. Copyhold applies. All Immunities, Remedies, Directions and Rights-reserved. Void where prohibited-by law.

NO TRESPASS. USPSMAIL; RE: 7015 0640 0007 0216 9688   US. FLAG #: 1 6054327920 U.S.A .

From: **Robert—Charles: [Simpson] and Bradley—Jefferson: [Franks]** **BILL FOR:**   **State Controller;**

C/O: 219 West 3rd Avenue;   **Betty T. Yee;**

Milbank, South Dakota; [57252]   **C/O: P. O. Box: 942850;**

(605) 432—7920   **Sacramento, Ca.: [94250 - 5872]**

PRE-INVOICE

DATE: _____   CONTRACT #: **201509038342061**

NO.	QTY.	DESCRIPTION	UNIT PRICE	UNIT TOTAL
		See Price list—attach (RCS/BJF.Pricelist1)		
		And from TRUE-BILL AND ACCOUNTING...		$37,034,419,500.00
		PUNITIVE DAMAGES...................................		$1,818,000,000.00
		TOTAL >		$38,852,419,500.00

Bradley – Jefferson : [Franks]

By: Bradley—Jefferson: [Franks], Authorize-Representative A/B
For: ROBERT CHARLES SIMPSON AND BRADLEY JEFFERSON FRANKS
C/O: 219 West 3rd Avenue; Milbank, South Dakota [57252]

This is an attempt–to collect a debt. Any Information obtained-may be used-for any purpose. Errors and Omissions are Consistent with intent. All directions including Rights-reserved. **NO-TRANSFERS.**

Make all checks payable; FOR THE ORDER OF: Robert—Charles: [Simpson] and Bradley—Jefferson: [Franks]

Thank you for your business!

Page 1 of 1: R-C:[S]/B-J:[F].PREINV1. This is an attempt-to-collect a debt. Any information obtained-maybe used-for any purpose. Errors and Omissions are Consistent with intent. Copyhold applies. All Immunities, Remedies, Directions and Rights-reserved. Void where prohibited-by law.

NO TRESPASS. USPSMAIL; RE: **7015 0640 0007 0216 9765**   US. FLAG #: **1 605 432 7920 U.S.A**

172

Bradley - J.: [Franks] and Co-Author: Robert - C.: [Simpson]

From: **Robert—Charles: [Simpson] and Bradley—Jefferson: [Franks]**   BILL FOR: **Corporation Service Company Which**

C/O: 219 West 3rd Avenue;   **will do business in California as CSC - Lawyers Incor-**
porating Service;

Milbank, South Dakota; [57252]

(605) 432—7920   **United States Corporation Company;**

P. O. Box; 526036;

Sacramento, Ca.: [95852]

PRE-INVOICE

DATE: _____   CONTRACT #:   **201509038342061**

NO.	QTY.	DESCRIPTION	UNIT PRICE	UNIT TOTAL
		See Price list—attach (RCS/BJF.Pricelist1)		
		And from TRUE-BILL AND ACCOUNTING...		$37,034,419,500.00
		PUNITIVE DAMAGES…………………………..		$1,818,000,000.00
		TOTAL >		$38,852,419,500.00

Bradley—Jefferson: [Frank]
_____
By: Bradley—Jefferson: [Franks], Authorize-Representative A/B
For: ROBERT CHARLES SIMPSON AND BRADLEY JEFFERSON FRANKS
C/O: 219 West 3rd Avenue; Milbank, South Dakota [57252]

This is an attempt–to collect a debt. Any Information obtained-may be used-for any purpose. Errors and Omissions are Consistent with intent. All directions including Rights-reserved. **NO-TRANSFERS.**

Make all checks payable; FOR THE ORDER OF: Robert—Charles: [Simpson] and Bradley—Jefferson: [Franks]

Thank you for your business!

Page 1 of 1:   R-C:[S]/B-J:[F].PREINV1. This is an attempt-to-collect a debt. Any information obtained-maybe used-for any purpose. Errors and Omissions are Consistent with intent. Copyhold applies. All Immunities, Remedies, Directions and Rights-reserved. Void where prohibited-by law.

NO TRESPASS. USPSMAIL; RE: 7015 0640 0007 0216 9675   US. FLAG #: 1605 432 7920 U.S.A .

173

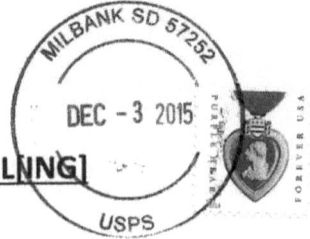

The Death of America

DEC - 3 2015

MILBANK SD 57252

USPS

FOREVER USA

I _KEN GIESSINGER_____, the undersign[ed] adult domiciliary of
Grant County, South Dakota, swear under the penalty of perjury that I did personally witness
Robert – Charles: [Simpson] and Bradley – Jefferson: [Franks], place in the United States mail
the below list[ed] documents.

1. An original document entitle[ed], Lien-Documents, Declaration Letter – Oath Purgatory x 2,
Affidavit; Plain Statement of Fact x 2, Affidavit (648) pages total x 2. Enclose[ed] is U. C. C. – 1,
Affidavit-U. C. C.-4, Private –Security-Agreement, Commercial-Affidavit Statement, True-Billing
and Account[ing], and Pre-Invoice.

2. All Documents were place[ed] in an envelope which was present[ed] to the United States
Post Office at Milbank, South Dakota, in Grant County, for delivery by first-class-certified-mail,
return-receipt-requested.

3. One copy sent for: U. S. Senator for California: Barbara Levy Boxer; the State of California:
CEO/Governor: Edward Gerald "Jerry" Brown, Jr.; The State of California; The State Controller;
Betty T. Yee and CSC – Lawyers Incorporating Service United States Corporation Company.

4. I, _____, personally review[ed] all documents
enclose[ed] for mailing.

Date: this _3rd_ day of _December_, Two thousand fifteen, Anno Domini

_____
Autograph of Affiant (disinterest[ed] person)

Page 1 of 1: RCS/BJF.AOM1: This is an attempt-to collect a debt. Any information-obtained-may be used-for any purpose. Errors
and Omissions are consistent with intent. Copyhold applies. All Immunities, Remedies, Directions and Rights-reserved. Void
where prohibited-by law.
   NO-TRESPASS. USPSMAIL; RE: 70150640000702169720 US. FLAG: 16054327920 U. S. A.

174

SENDER: COMPLETE THIS SECTION

- Complete items 1, 2, and 3.
- Print your name and address on the reverse so that we can return the card to you.
- Attach this card to the back of the mailpiece, or on the front if space permits.

1. Article Addressed for:

The State of California;
%: State Capitol ; Suite: 1173;
Sacramento, CAlif. [95814]

9590 9403 0417 5163 6453 68

2. Article Number *(Transfer from service label)*

7015 0640 0007 0216 9701

PS Form 3811, April 2015 PSN 7530-02-000-9053

COMPLETE THIS SECTION ON DELIVERY

A. Signature
X _____
☐ Agent
☐ Addressee

B. Received by *(Printed Name)*
Trishaven

C. Date of Delivery

D. Is delivery address different from item 1? ☐ Yes
If YES, enter delivery address below: ☐ No

3. Service Type
☐ Adult Signature
☐ Adult Signature Restricted Delivery
☐ Certified Mail®
☐ Certified Mail Restricted Delivery
☐ Collect on Delivery
☐ Collect on Delivery Restricted Delivery
☐ Insured Mail
☐ Insured Mail Restricted Delivery (over $500)

☐ Priority Mail Express®
☐ Registered Mail™
☐ Registered Mail Restricted Delivery
☐ Return Receipt for Merchandise
☐ Signature Confirmation™
☐ Signature Confirmation Restricted Delivery

Domestic Return Receipt

U.S. Postal Service™
CERTIFIED MAIL® RECEIPT
Domestic Mail Only

For delivery information, visit our website at *www.usps.com®*.

7015 0640 0007 0216 9701

SACRAMENTO, CA 95814

Certified Mail Fee $3.45

0252
03

Extra Services & Fees *(check box, add fee as appropriate)*
☐ Return Receipt (hardcopy) $ $2.80
☐ Return Receipt (electronic) $ $0.00
☐ Certified Mail Restricted Delivery $ $0.00
☐ Adult Signature Required $ $0.00
☐ Adult Signature Restricted Delivery $ $0.00

Postmark
Here

Postage $2.96

Total Postage and Fees $9.21

12/03/2015

Sent To
The State of California;
Street and Apt. No., or PO Box No.
%: State Capitol; Suite: 1173;
City, State, ZIP+4
Sacramento, CALif. [95814]

PS Form 3800, April 2015 PSN 7530-02-000-9047   See Reverse for Instructions

175

The Death of America

I __KEN GIESSINGER__, the undersign[ed] adult domiciliary of Grant County, South Dakota, swear under the penalty of perjury that I did personally witness Robert – Charles: [Simpson] and Bradley – Jefferson: [Franks], place in the United States mail the below list[ed] documents.

1. An original document entitle[ed], Lien-Documents, Declaration Letter – Oath Purgatory x 2, Affidavit; Plain Statement of Fact x 2, Affidavit (<u>648</u>) pages total x 2. Enclose[ed] is U. C. C. – 1, Affidavit-U. C. C.-4, Private –Security-Agreement, Commercial-Affidavit Statement, True-Billing and Account[ing], and Pre-Invoice.

2. All Documents were place[ed] in an envelope which was present[ed] to the United States Post Office at <u>Milbank</u>, <u>South Dakota</u>, in <u>Grant</u> County, for delivery by first-class-certified-mail, return-receipt-requested.

3. One copy sent for: U. S. Senator for California: Barbara Levy Boxer; the State of California: CEO/Governor: Edward Gerald "Jerry" Brown, Jr.; The State of California; The State Controller; Betty T. Yee and CSC – Lawyers Incorporating Service United States Corporation Company.

4. I, _____, personally review[ed] all documents enclose[ed] for mailing.

Date: this __3ᶜᵈ__ day of __December__, Two thousand fifteen, Anno Domini

_____
Autograph of Affiant (disinterest[ed] person)

Bradley - J.: [Franks] and Co-Author: Robert - C.: [Simpson]

SENDER: COMPLETE THIS SECTION

- Complete items 1, 2, and 3.
- Print your name and address on the reverse so that we can return the card to you.
- Attach this card to the back of the mailpiece, or on the front if space permits.

1. Article Addressed to:

The Governor of the state of CA.;
Edward Gerald "Jerry" Brown, Jr.;
C/o: State Capitol; Suite: 1173;
Sacramento, CA.: [95814]

9590 9403 0661 5183 4810 99

2. Article Number (Transfer from service label)

7015 0640 0007 0216 9688

PS Form 3811, April 2015 PSN 7530-02-000-9053

COMPLETE THIS SECTION ON DELIVERY

A. Signature
X ___ B ___
☐ Agent
☐ Addressee

B. Received by (Printed Name)   BROWN
C. Date of Delivery   12.8.15

D. Is delivery address different from item 1? ☐ Yes
If YES, enter delivery address below: ☐ No

3. Service Type
☐ Adult Signature
☐ Adult Signature Restricted Delivery
☐ Certified Mail®
☐ Certified Mail Restricted Delivery
☐ Collect on Delivery
☐ Collect on Delivery Restricted Delivery
☐ Insured Mail
☐ Insured Mail Restricted Delivery (over $500)
☐ Priority Mail Express®
☐ Registered Mail™
☐ Registered Mail Restricted Delivery
☐ Return Receipt for Merchandise
☐ Signature Confirmation™
☐ Signature Confirmation Restricted Delivery

Domestic Return Receipt

U.S. Postal Service™
CERTIFIED MAIL® RECEIPT
Domestic Mail Only

For delivery information, visit our website at www.usps.com®.

SACRAMENTO, CA 95814

Certified Mail Fee $3.45   0252   03

Extra Services & Fees (check box, add fee as appropriate)
☐ Return Receipt (hardcopy) $2.80
☐ Return Receipt (electronic) $0.00
☐ Certified Mail Restricted Delivery $0.00   Postmark Here
☐ Adult Signature Required $0.00
☐ Adult Signature Restricted Delivery $

Postage $12.65

Total Postage and Fees $18.90   12/03/2015

Sent To Edward Gerald "Jerry" Brown, Jr.;
Street and Apt. No., or PO Box No. C/o: State Capitol; Suite: 1173;
City, State, ZIP+4® Sacramento, CA. [95814]

PS Form 3800, April 2015 PSN 7530-02-000-9047   See Reverse for Instructions

9688 0216 0007 0640 7015

177

The Death of America

AFFIDAVIT OF MAIL[ING]

I ___KEN GIESSINGER_____, the undersign[ed] adult domiciliary of Grant County, South Dakota, swear under the penalty of perjury that I did personally witness Robert – Charles: [Simpson] and Bradley – Jefferson: [Franks], place in the United States mail the below list[ed] documents.

1. An original document entitle[ed], Lien-Documents, Declaration Letter – Oath Purgatory x 2, Affidavit; Plain Statement of Fact x 2, Affidavit (648) pages total x 2. Enclose[ed] is U. C. C. – 1, Affidavit-U. C. C.-4, Private –Security-Agreement, Commercial-Affidavit Statement, True-Billing and Account[ing], and Pre-Invoice.

2. All Documents were place[ed] in an envelope which was present[ed] to the United States Post Office at Milbank, South Dakota, in Grant County, for delivery by first-class-certified-mail, return-receipt-requested.

3. One copy sent for: U. S. Senator for California: Barbara Levy Boxer; the State of California: CEO/Governor: Edward Gerald "Jerry" Brown, Jr.; The State of California; The State Controller; Betty T. Yee and CSC – Lawyers Incorporating Service United States Corporation Company.

4. I, _____, personally review[ed] all documents enclose[ed] for mailing.

Date: this __3ʳᵈ__ day of __December__, Two thousand fifteen, Anno Domini

_____
Autograph of Affiant (disinterest[ed] person)

SENDER: COMPLETE THIS SECTION

- Complete items 1, 2, and 3.
- Print your name and address on the reverse so that we can return the card to you.
- Attach this card to the back of the mailpiece, or on the front if space permits.

1. Article Addressed to:

Barbara Levy Boxer;
[U.S. Senator Southern CA];
C/o: 112 Hart Senate Office Bldg;
Washington D.C. [20510]

9590 9403 0503 5173 6339 79

Article Number *(Transfer from service label)*

COMPLETE THIS SECTION ON DELIVERY

A. Signature
X _____ ☑ Agent ☐ Addressee

B. Received by *(Printed Name)*   C. Date of Delivery
CARL WOLIVER   01/19/16

D. Is delivery address different from item 1? ☐ Yes
If YES, enter delivery address below: ☑ No

3. Service Type
☐ Adult Signature
☐ Adult Signature Restricted Delivery
☐ Certified Mail®
☐ Certified Mail Restricted Delivery
☐ Collect on Delivery
☐ Collect on Delivery
☐ Insured Mail
☐ Insured
over

☐ Priority Mail Express®
☐ Registered Mail™
☐ Registered Mail Restricted Delivery
☐ Return Receipt for Merchandise
☐ Signature C
☐ Signature Restrict

Form 3811, April 2015 PSN 7530-02-000-9053   dc

U.S. Postal Service™
CERTIFIED MAIL® RECEIPT
Domestic Mail Only

7015 0640 0007 0216 9671

For delivery information, visit our website at www.usps.com®

WASHINGTON, DC 20510   OFFICIAL USE

Certified Mail Fee $3.45   0252
$ 03
Extra Services & Fees *(check box, add fee as appropriate)*
☐ Return Receipt (hardcopy) $ $2.80
☐ Return Receipt (electronic) $ $0.00   Postmark
☐ Certified Mail Restricted Delivery $ $0.00   Here
☐ Adult Signature Required $ $0.00
☐ Adult Signature Restricted Delivery $ $0.00

Postage $12.65
$ 12/03/2015
Total Postage and Fees $18.90
$
Sent To Barbara Levy Boxer;
Street and Apt. No., or PO Box No. C/o: 112 Hart Senate Off. Building;
City, State, ZIP+4 Washington D.C.; [20510]
PS Form 3800, April 2015 PSN 7530-02-000-9047   See Reverse for Instructions

The Death of America

AFFIDAVIT OF MAIL[ING]

I ___KEN GIESSINGER_____, the undersign[ed] adult domiciliary of Grant County, South Dakota, swear under the penalty of perjury that I did personally witness Robert – Charles: [Simpson] and Bradley – Jefferson: [Franks], place in the United States mail the below list[ed] documents.

1. An original document entitle[ed], Lien-Documents, Declaration Letter – Oath Purgatory x 2, Affidavit; Plain Statement of Fact x 2, Affidavit (648) pages total x 2. Enclose[ed] is U. C. C. – 1, Affidavit-U. C. C.-4, Private –Security-Agreement, Commercial-Affidavit Statement, True-Billing and Account[ing], and Pre-Invoice.

2. All Documents were place[ed] in an envelope which was present[ed] to the United States Post Office at Milbank, South Dakota, in Grant County, for delivery by first-class-certified-mail, return-receipt-requested.

3. One copy sent for: U. S. Senator for California: Barbara Levy Boxer; the State of California: CEO/Governor: Edward Gerald "Jerry" Brown, Jr.; The State of California; The State Controller; Betty T. Yee and CSC – Lawyers Incorporating Service United States Corporation Company.

4. I, _____, personally review[ed] all documents enclose[ed] for mailing.

Date: this 3ʳᵈ day of December , Two thousand fifteen, Anno Domini

_____
Autograph of Affiant (disinterest[ed] person)

SENDER: *COMPLETE THIS SECTION*

- Complete items 1, 2, and 3.
- Print your name and address on the reverse so that we can return the card to you.
- Attach this card to the back of the mailpiece, or on the front if space permits.

1. Article Addressed to:

State Controller;
Betty T. Yee;
C/o: P. O. Box; 942850
Sacramento, CALif. [94250-5872]

9590 9403 0661 5183 4810 75

2. Article Number *(Transfer from service label)*

7015 0640 0007 0216 9725

COMPLETE THIS SECTION ON DELIVERY

A. Signature

State Controller's Office ☐ Agent
X Unclaimed Property Division ☐ Addressee

B. Received by *(Printed Name)* | C. Date of Delivery

D. Is delivery address different from item 1? ☐ Yes
If YES, enter delivery address below: ☐ No

3. Service Type
☐ Adult Signature
☐ Adult Signature Restricted Delivery
☐ Certified Mail®
☐ Certified Mail Restricted Delivery
☐ Collect on Delivery
☐ Collect on Delivery Restricted Delivery
☐ Insured Mail
☐ Insured Mail Restricted Delivery (over $500)

☐ Priority Mail Express®
☐ Registered Mail™
☐ Registered Mail Restricted Delivery
☐ Return Receipt for Merchandise
☐ Signature Confirmation™
☐ Signature Confirmation Restricted Delivery

PS Form 3811, April 2015 PSN 7530-02-000-9053 | Domestic Return Receipt

---

U.S. Postal Service™
CERTIFIED MAIL® RECEIPT
Domestic Mail Only

For delivery information, visit our website at www.usps.com®.

SACRAMENTO, CA 94250

Certified Mail Fee $3.45	0252
$ $2.80	03
Extra Services & Fees *(check box, add fee as appropriate)*	
☐ Return Receipt (hardcopy) $ $0.00	
☐ Return Receipt (electronic) $ $0.00	Postmark
☐ Certified Mail Restricted Delivery $ $0.00	Here
☐ Adult Signature Required $ $0.00	
☐ Adult Signature Restricted Delivery $	
Postage $2.96	
$	
Total Postage and Fees $9.21	12/03/2015

Sent To
St. Cont.: Betty T. Yee
Street and Apt. No., or PO Box No.
C/o: P. O. Box; 942850
City, State, ZIP+4®
Sacramento CA.: [94250-5872]

PS Form 3800, April 2015 PSN 7530-02-000-9047 | See Reverse for Instructions

7015 0640 0007 0216 9725

The Death of America

AFFIDAVIT OF MAIL[ING]

I _KEN GIESSINGER_____, the undersign[ed] adult domiciliary of
Grant County, South Dakota, swear under the penalty of perjury that I did personally witness
Robert – Charles: [Simpson] and Bradley – Jefferson: [Franks], place in the United States mail
the below list[ed] documents.

1. An original document entitle[ed], Lien-Documents, Declaration Letter – Oath Purgatory x 2,
Affidavit; Plain Statement of Fact x 2, Affidavit (648) pages total x 2. Enclose[ed] is U. C. C. – 1,
Affidavit-U. C. C.-4, Private –Security-Agreement, Commercial-Affidavit Statement, True-Billing
and Account[ing], and Pre-Invoice.

2. All Documents were place[ed] in an envelope which was present[ed] to the United States
Post Office at Milbank, South Dakota, in Grant County, for delivery by first-class-certified-mail,
return-receipt-requested.

3. One copy sent for: U. S. Senator for California: Barbara Levy Boxer; the State of California:
CEO/Governor: Edward Gerald "Jerry" Brown, Jr.; The State of California; The State Controller;
Betty T. Yee and CSC – Lawyers Incorporating Service United States Corporation Company.

4. I, _____, personally review[ed] all documents
enclose[ed] for mailing.

Date: this _3ʳᵈ_ day of _December_, Two thousand fifteen, Anno Domini

_____
Autograph of Affiant (disinterest[ed] person)

U.S. Postal Service™
CERTIFIED MAIL® RECEIPT
Domestic Mail Only

For delivery information, visit our website at *www.usps.com*

SACRAMENTO, CA 95852

OFFICIAL USE

Certified Mail Fee	$3.45		0252
			03
$		$0.00	
Extra Services & Fees *(check box, add fee as appropriate)*			
☐ Return Receipt (hardcopy)	$	$0.00	
☐ Return Receipt (electronic)	$	$0.00	Postmark
☐ Certified Mail Restricted Delivery	$	$0.00	Here
☐ Adult Signature Required	$	$0.00	
☐ Adult Signature Restricted Delivery	$		
Postage	$2.96		
$			12/03/2015
Total Postage and Fees	$9.21		
$			

Sent To
United States Corp. Comp.;
Street and Apt. No., or PO Box No.
℅ P.O. Box; 526036;
City, State, ZIP+4®
Sacramento, CA.: [95852]

PS Form 3800, April 2015 PSN 7530-02-000-9047   See Reverse for Instructions

7015 0640 0007 0246 9695

183

Robert – Charles: [Simpson]; and
Bradley – Jefferson: [Franks];
C/O: 408; South-Lincoln St.:
Milbank, South Dakota: [57252].

Second-Notice: Affidavit and Notice of [De]fault and Opportunity-to-Cure

Notice to Principal is notice to agent-Notice to agent is notice to principal

Certified Mail No.: 70150640000702169701

For Lien Debtors and Perpetrators:

The State of California [Corporate-Government];
C/O: State Capitol; Suite; 1173;
Sacramento, Ca.: [95814].

January 11, 2016:

Edward Gerald "Jerry" Brown [Governor of the State of California]:

On December 3, 2015, the Undersigned-aggrieved-parties sent you copies of our on-going Lien-Documents (cover letter); Affidavit (Plain Statement of Fact); an Affidavit (!At Gun Point...: ISBN: 978-1-4685-7355-8); U. C. C. Financing Statement (File Number: 201509038342061); Private-Security-Agreement (item-number: PSA-1-07112015UCC4); Commercial Affidavit; Price-List; True-Bill and Account[ing]; and Pre-Invoice. As respondents, you were given Thirty (30) days plus Five (5) days for a response. Your office, in Washington D. C., received this package as of December 8, 2015.

Your un-sign[ed]/un-autograph[ed]-response/[re]buttal and lack of communication (your silence) is a point of acceptance by yourself and your co-conspirators and is the responsibility of the State California and its Officers for the unlawful acts, fraud and injuries committed and it so appears that your Continued-Silence is a continuation of the same fraud and extending the injuries in this matter.

You Have Twenty (20) days plus Five (5) days grace period for the "response" of these allegations.

Your 'Silence' within this matter is acceptable proof of your guilt by the CALIFORNIA CONSTITUTION - ARTICLE 1 - DECLARATION OF RIGHTS so states at SECTION 1:

"All people are by nature free and independent and have inalienable rights. Among these are enjoying and defending life and liberty, acquiring, possessing, and protecting property, and pursuing and obtaining safety, happiness, and privacy."

184

Please note that we are asserting this claim, as our inalienable right and in so doing, are defending life and property (the claim and sum certain amount) as a matter of right.

As the Respondent(s), you are at fault of a proper response and [de]fault will be taken as necessary should you fail to-respond!

Under necessity, you are herein given the opportunity to-cure your fault/non-response with an additional twenty (20) days with five (5) day for return mail, Twenty-five (25) days total to-cure your fault of non-response.

Send a copy of the response of this matter for: Robert Kelly: C/O: P.O. Box: 3096: Central Point, Oregon: [97502] and for the above Claimants.

NOTICE: Should you fail or refuse to cure your [De]fault, the Undersigned/underautograph will be compelled-to-issue a 'Third and Final Notice: Affidavit and Notice of [De]fault' which will establish facts in and for the record of your agreement (general acquiescence) of the claim as presented-within these presentments. If all parties-involved-refuse the re[buttal] or answer, we will be forced-to-use subrogation for the signature/autographs and authority within this matter. Further, with full-understanding that with the "silence" and "refusal" of cooperation all "presentments" within this "cargo" will be met with acceptance, acknowledgement, agreement and approval from all parties-involved.

Thank you for your prompt attention in this matter.

Sincerely,

'All Rights Reserve'

Robert -Charles: [Simpson]; and
Bradley – Jefferson: [Franks];
the Aggrieved-Parties

Please note that we are asserting this claim, as our inalienable right and in so doing, are defending life and property (the claim and sum certain amount) as a matter of right.

As the Respondent(s), you are at fault of a proper response and [de]fault will be taken as necessary should you fail to-respond!

Under necessity, you are herein given the opportunity to-cure your fault/non-response with an additional twenty (20) days with five (5) day for return mail, Twenty-five (25) days total to-cure your fault of non-response.

Send a copy of the response of this matter for: Robert Kelly: C/O: P.O. Box: 3096: Central Point, Oregon: [97502] and for the above Claimants.

NOTICE: Should you fail or refuse to cure your [De]fault, the Undersigned/underautograph will be compelled-to-issue a 'Third and Final Notice: Affidavit and Notice of [De]fault' which will establish facts in and for the record of your agreement (general acquiescence) of the claim as presented-within these presentments. If all parties-involved-refuse the re[buttal] or answer, we will be forced-to-use subrogation for the signature/autographs and authority within this matter. Further, with full-understanding that with the "silence" and "refusal" of cooperation all "presentments" within this "cargo" will be met with acceptance, acknowledgement, agreement and approval from all parties-involved.

Thank you for your prompt attention in this matter.

Sincerely,

Bradley-J.: [Franks]

Robert -Charles: [Simpson]; and
Bradley – Jefferson: [Franks];
the Aggrieved-Parties

Bradley - J.: [Franks] and Co-Author: Robert - C.: [Simpson]

SENDER: COMPLETE THIS SECTION

- Complete items 1, 2, and 3.
- Print your name and address on the reverse so that we can return the card to you.
- Attach this card to the back of the mailpiece, or on the front if space permits.

1. Article Addressed to:

The State of California
[Corporate - Government]
%: State Capitol: Suite; 1173;
Sacramento, CA.
[95814]

9590 9403 0503 5173 6339 62

2. Article Number *(Transfer from service label)*

7015 1730 0000 3615 8692

PS Form 3811, April 2015 PSN 7530-02-000-9053

COMPLETE THIS SECTION ON DELIVERY

A. Signature
X ☐ Agent ☐ Addressee
B. Received by *(Printed Name)* Brown C. Date of Delivery
D. Is delivery address different from item 1? ☐ Yes
If YES, enter delivery address below: ☐ No

3. Service Type
☐ Adult Signature
☐ Adult Signature Restricted Delivery
☐ Certified Mail®
☐ Certified Mail Restricted Delivery
☐ Collect on Delivery
☐ Collect on Delivery Restricted Delivery
☐ Insured Mail
☐ Insured Mail Restricted Delivery (over $500)
☐ Priority Mail Express®
☐ Registered Mail™
☐ Registered Mail Restricted Delivery
☐ Return Receipt for Merchandise
☐ Signature Confirmation™
☐ Signature Confirmation Restricted Delivery

Domestic Return Receipt

U.S. Postal Service™
CERTIFIED MAIL® RECEIPT
Domestic Mail Only

For delivery information, visit our website at *www.usps.com®*.

SACRAMENTO, CA 95814

Certified Mail Fee $3.45 0252
$ 1011
Extra Services & Fees (check box, add fee as appropriate)
☐ Return Receipt (hardcopy) $ $2.80
☐ Return Receipt (electronic) $ $0.00
☐ Certified Mail Restricted Delivery $ $0.00 Postmark
☐ Adult Signature Required $ $0.00 Here
☐ Adult Signature Restricted Delivery $
Postage $0.49
$ 01/14/2016
Total Postage and Fees $8.74
$
Sent To State of California
Street and Apt. No., or PO Box No. %: State Capitol; Suite 1173;
City, State, ZIP+4® Sacramento, CA. [95814]

PS Form 3800, April 2015 PSN 7530-02-000-9047 See Reverse for Instructions

187

The Death of America

Robert – Charles: [Simpson]; and
Bradley – Jefferson: [Franks];
C/O: 408; South-Lincoln St.:
Milbank, South Dakota: [57252].

Second-Notice: Affidavit and Notice of [De]fault and Opportunity-to-Cure

Notice to Principal is notice to agent-Notice to agent is notice to principal

Certified Mail No.: 70150640000702169671

For Lien Debtors and Perpetrators:

Barbara Levy Boxer;
C/O: 112 Hart Senate Office Building;
Washington D. C.; [20510].

January 11, 2016:

Barbara Levy Boxer [United States Senator for Southern California]:

On December 3, 2015, the Undersigned-aggrieved-parties sent you copies of our on-going Lien-Documents (cover letter); Affidavit (Plain Statement of Fact); an Affidavit (!At Gun Point...: ISBN: 978-1-4685-7355-8); U. C. C. Financing Statement (File Number: 201509038342061); Private-Security-Agreement (item-number: PSA-1-07112015UCC4); Commercial Affidavit; Price-List; True-Bill and Account[ing]; and Pre-Invoice. As respondents, you were given Thirty (30) days plus Five (5) days for a response. Your office, in Washington D. C., received this package as of December 8, 2015.

Your un-sign[ed]/un-autograph[ed]-response/[re]buttal and lack of communication (your silence) is a point of acceptance by yourself and your co-conspirators and is the responsibility of the State California and its Officers for the unlawful acts, fraud and injuries committed and it so appears that your Continued-Silence is a continuation of the same fraud and extending the injuries in this matter.

You Have Twenty (20) days plus Five (5) days grace period for the "response" of these allegations.

Your 'Silence' within this matter is acceptable proof of your guilt by the CALIFORNIA CONSTITUTION - ARTICLE 1 - DECLARATION OF RIGHTS so states at SECTION 1:

"All people are by nature free and independent and have inalienable rights. Among these are enjoying and defending life and liberty, acquiring, possessing, and protecting property, and pursuing and obtaining safety, happiness, and privacy."

Affidavit and Notice of [De]fault and Opportunity-to-Cure: Item#05302014-1/R-C.: [S]&B-J.: [F]   Page 1

188

Please note that we are asserting this claim, as our inalienable right and in so doing, are defending life and property (the claim and sum certain amount) as a matter of right.

As the Respondent(s), you are at fault of a proper response and [de]fault will be taken as necessary should you fail to-respond!

Under necessity, you are herein given the opportunity to-cure your fault/non-response with an additional twenty (20) days with five (5) day for return mail, Twenty-five (25) days total to-cure your fault of non-response.

Send a copy of the response of this matter for: Robert Kelly: C/O: P.O. Box: 3096: Central Point, Oregon: [97502] and for the above Claimants.

NOTICE: Should you fail or refuse to cure your [De]fault, the Undersigned/underautograph will be compelled-to-issue a 'Third and Final Notice: Affidavit and Notice of [De]fault' which will establish facts in and for the record of your agreement (general acquiescence) of the claim as presented-within these presentments. If all parties-involved-refuse the re[buttal] or answer, we will be forced-to-use subrogation for the signature/autographs and authority within this matter. Further, with full-understanding that with the "silence" and "refusal" of cooperation all "presentments" within this "cargo" will be met with acceptance, acknowledgement, agreement and approval from all parties-involved.

Thank you for your prompt attention in this matter.

Sincerely,

Bradley - J.: [Franks]

Robert – Charles: [Simpson]; and
Bradley – Jefferson: [Franks];
the Aggrieved-Parties

U.S. Postal Service™
CERTIFIED MAIL® RECEIPT
Domestic Mail Only

For delivery information, visit our website at *www.usps.com®*.

WASHINGTON, DC 20510

Certified Mail Fee	$3.45	0252

$ $2.80   1011

Extra Services & Fees *(check box, add fee as appropriate)*
☐ Return Receipt (hardcopy) $ $0.00
☐ Return Receipt (electronic) $ $0.00
☐ Certified Mail Restricted Delivery $ $0.00
☐ Adult Signature Required $ $0.00
☐ Adult Signature Restricted Delivery $

Postmark
Here

Postage
$0.49
$

Total Postage and Fees
$6.74
$

01/14/2016

Sent To *Barbara Boxer*
Street and Apt. No., or PO Box No. *112 Hart Senate Office Bldg.*
City, State, ZIP+4® *Washington D.C. [20510]*

PS Form 3800, April 2015 PSN 7530-02-000-9047   See Reverse for Instructions

7015 1730 0000 3615 8715

Robert – Charles: [Simpson]; and
Bradley – Jefferson: [Franks];
C/O: 408; South-Lincoln St.:
Milbank, South Dakota: [57252].

Third-Notice: Affidavit and Notice of [De]fault and Opportunity-to-Cure

Notice to Principal is notice to agent-Notice to agent is notice to principal

Certified Mail No.: 70150640000702169701

For Lien Debtors and Perpetrators:

The State of California [Corporate-Government];
C/O: State Capitol; Suite: 1173;
Sacramento, Ca.: [95814].

February 8, 2016:

Edward Gerald "Jerry" Brown [Governor of the State of California]:

On January 14, 2016, the Undersigned-aggrieved-parties sent you copies of our on-going Lien-Documents a Second-Notice: Affidavit and Notice of [De]Fault and Opportunity-to-Cure by Certified-Mail No. 70151730000036158692.

Your un-sign[ed]/un-autograph[ed]-response-/[re]buttal and lack of communication (your silence) is a point of acceptance by yourself and your co-conspirators and is the responsibility of the State California and its Officers for the unlawful acts, fraud and injuries committed and it so appears that your Continued-Silence is a continuation of the same fraud and extending the injuries in this matter.

You have Ten (10) days plus Five (5) days grace period for the "response" of these allegations.

Your 'Silence' within this matter is acceptable proof of your guilt by the CALIFORNIA CONSTITUTION - ARTICLE 1 - DECLARATION OF RIGHTS so states at SECTION 1:

> *"All people are by nature free and independent and have inalienable rights. Among these are enjoying and defending life and liberty, acquiring, possessing, and protecting property, and pursuing and obtaining safety, happiness, and privacy."*

Please note that we are asserting this claim, as our inalienable right and in so doing, are defending life and property (the claim and sum certain amount) as a matter of right.

As the Respondent(s), you are at fault of a proper response and [de]fault will be taken as necessary should you fail to-respond!

Under necessity, you are herein given the opportunity to-cure your fault/non-response with an additional ten (10) days with five (5) day for return mail, Fifteen (15) days total to-cure your fault of non-response.

Send a copy of the response of this matter for: Robert Kelly: C/O: P.O. Box: 3096: Central Point, Oregon: [97502] and for the above Claimants.

NOTICE: Should you fail or refuse to cure your [De]fault, the Undersigned/underautograph will be compelled-to-issue a 'Third and Final Notice: Affidavit and Notice of [De]fault' which will establish facts in and for the record of your agreement (general acquiescence) of the claim as presented-within these presentments. If all parties-involved-refuse the re[buttal] or answer, we will be forced-to-use subrogation for the signature/autographs and authority within this matter. Further, with full-understanding that with the "silence" and "refusal" of cooperation all "presentments" within this "cargo" will be met with acceptance, acknowledgement, agreement and approval from all parties-involved.

Thank you for your prompt attention in this matter.

Sincerely,

Robert ⫫Charles:⫫Simpson]; and
Bradley – Jefferson: [Franks];
the Aggrieved-Parties

Bradley - J.: [Franks] and Co-Author: Robert - C.: [Simpson]

AFFIDAVIT OF MAIL[ING]

I ___*KEN GIESSINGER*___, the undersign[ed] adult domiciliary of Grant County, South Dakota, swear under the penalty of perjury that I did personally witness Robert – Charles: [Simpson] and Bradley – Jefferson: [Franks], place in the United States mail the below list[ed] documents.

1. An original document entitle[ed], Third-Notice: Affidavit and Notice of [De] Fault and Opportunity-to-Cure.

2. All Documents were place[ed] in an envelope which was present[ed] to the United States Post Office at Milbank, South Dakota, in Grant County, for delivery by first-class-certified-mail, return-receipt-requested.

3. One copy sent for: U. S. Senator for California: Barbara Levy Boxer; the State of California: CEO/Governor: Edward Gerald "Jerry" Brown, Jr.; and The State of California.

4. I, ___*KEN GIESSINGER*___, personally review[ed] all documents enclose[ed] for mailing.

Date: this ___*10th*___ day of ___*February*___, Two thousand sixteen, Anno Domini

_____
Autograph of Affiant (disinterest[ed] person)

193

SENDER: COMPLETE THIS SECTION

- Complete items 1, 2, and 3.
- Print your name and address on the reverse so that we can return the card to you.
- Attach this card to the back of the mailpiece, or on the front if space permits.

1. Article Addressed to:

The State of California [Corp Govt.]
%: State Capitol; Suite, 1173;
Sacramento, CA. :
[95814]

9590 9403 0503 5173 6341 12

2. Article Number (Transfer from service label)

7015 1730 0000 3615 8883

COMPLETE THIS SECTION ON DELIVERY

A. Signature

x *Kyl Shepherd* ☐ Agent ☐ Addressee

B. Received by (Printed Name) Kyle Shepherd

C. Date of Delivery 2-16-16

D. Is delivery address different from item 1? ☐ Yes
If YES, enter delivery address below: ☐ No

3. Service Type
- ☐ Adult Signature
- ☐ Adult Signature Restricted Delivery
- ☐ Certified Mail®
- ☐ Certified Mail Restricted Delivery
- ☐ Collect on Delivery
- ☐ Collect on Delivery Restricted Delivery
- ☐ Insured Mail
- ☐ Insured Mail Restricted Delivery over $500)
- ☐ Priority Mail Express®
- ☐ Registered Mail™
- ☐ Registered Mail Restricted Delivery
- ☐ Return Receipt for Merchandise
- ☐ Signature Confirmation™
- ☐ Signature Confirmation Restricted Delivery

PS Form 3811, April 2015 PSN 7530-02-000-9053 Domestic Return Receipt

---

U.S. Postal Service™
CERTIFIED MAIL® RECEIPT
Domestic Mail Only

For delivery information, visit our website at www.usps.com®.

SACRAMENTO, CA 95814 OFFICIAL USE

| Certified Mail Fee $3.45 | 0252 |
| $ $2.80 | 03 |

Extra Services & Fees (check box, add fee as appropriate)
- ☐ Return Receipt (hardcopy) $0.00
- ☐ Return Receipt (electronic) $0.00
- ☐ Certified Mail Restricted Delivery $0.00
- ☐ Adult Signature Required $0.00
- ☐ Adult Signature Restricted Delivery $

Postmark Here

Postage $0.49

Total Postage and Fees $6.74

02/10/2016

Sent To The State of California [Corporate - Government]
Street and Apt. No., or PO Box No. %: State Capitol; Suite; 1173;
City, State, ZIP+4® Sacramento, California : [95814]

PS Form 3800, April 2015 PSN 7530-02-000-9047 See Reverse for Instructions

194

Robert – Charles: [Simpson] and
Bradley – Jefferson: [Franks];
C/O: 408; South-Lincoln St.:
Milbank, South Dakota: [57252].

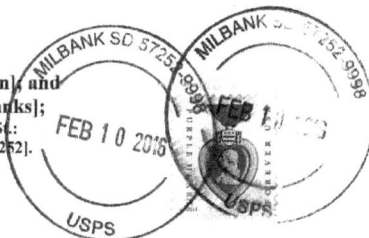

Third-Notice: Affidavit and Notice of [De]fault and Opportunity-to-Cure

Notice to Principal is notice to agent-Notice to agent is notice to principal

Certified Mail No.: 70150640000702169688

For Lien Debtors and Perpetrators:

Edward Gerald "Jerry" Brown, Jr.;
C/O: State Capitol; Suite: 1173;
Sacramento, Calif. [95814]

February 8, 2016:

Edward Gerald "Jerry" Brown [Governor of the State of California]:

On January 14, 2016, the Undersigned-aggrieved-parties sent you copies of our on-going Lien-Documents a Second-Notice: Affidavit and Notice of [De]Fault and Opportunity-to-Cure by Certified-Mail No. 70151730000036158708.

Your un-sign[ed]/un-autograph[ed]-response/[re]buttal and lack of communication (your silence) is a point of acceptance by yourself and your co-conspirators and is the responsibility of the State California and its Officers for the unlawful acts, fraud and injuries committed and it so appears that your Continued-Silence is a continuation of the same fraud and extending the injuries in this matter.

You have Ten (10) days plus Five (5) days grace period for the "response" of these allegations.

Your 'Silence' within this matter is acceptable proof of your guilt by the CALIFORNIA CONSTITUTION - ARTICLE 1 - DECLARATION OF RIGHTS so states at SECTION 1:

"All people are by nature free and independent and have inalienable rights. Among these are enjoying and defending life and liberty, acquiring, possessing, and protecting property, and pursuing and obtaining safety, happiness, and privacy."

Please note that we are asserting this claim, as our inalienable right and in so doing, are defending life and property (the claim and sum certain amount) as a matter of right.

As the Respondent(s), you are at fault of a proper response and [de]fault will be taken as necessary should you fail to-respond!

Under necessity, you are herein given the opportunity to-cure your fault/non-response with an additional ten (10) days with five (5) day for return mail, Fifteen (15) days total to-cure your fault of non-response.

Send a copy of the response of this matter for: Robert Kelly: C/O: P.O. Box: 3096: Central Point, Oregon: [97502] and for the above Claimants.

NOTICE: Should you fail or refuse to cure your [De]fault, the Undersigned/underautograph will be compelled-to-issue a 'Third and Final Notice: Affidavit and Notice of [De]fault' which will establish facts in and for the record of your agreement (general acquiescence) of the claim as presented-within these presentments. If all parties-involved-refuse the re[buttal] or answer, we will be forced-to-use subrogation for the signature/autographs and authority within this matter. Further, with full-understanding that with the "silence" and "refusal" of cooperation all "presentments" within this "cargo" will be met with acceptance, acknowledgement, agreement and approval from all parties-involved.

Thank you for your prompt attention in this matter.

Sincerely,

Bradley - Jefferson: [Franks]

Robert /Charles/[Simpson]; and
Bradley – Jefferson: [Franks];
the Aggrieved-Parties

AFFIDAVIT OF MAIL[ING]

I ___KEN GIESSINGER___, the undersign[ed] adult domiciliary of Grant County, South Dakota, swear under the penalty of perjury that I did personally witness Robert – Charles: [Simpson] and Bradley – Jefferson: [Franks], place in the United States mail the below list[ed] documents.

1. An original document entitle[ed], Third-Notice: Affidavit and Notice of [De] Fault and Opportunity-to-Cure.

2. All Documents were place[ed] in an envelope which was present[ed] to the United States Post Office at Milbank, South Dakota, in Grant County, for delivery by first-class-certified-mail, return-receipt-requested.

3. One copy sent for: U. S. Senator for California: Barbara Levy Boxer; the State of California: CEO/Governor: Edward Gerald "Jerry" Brown, Jr.; and The State of California.

4. I, ___KEN GIESSINGER___, personally review[ed] all documents enclose[ed] for mailing.

Date: this __10th__ day of __February__, Two thousand sixteen, Anno Domini

_____
Autograph of Affiant (disinterest[ed] person)

197

SENDER: COMPLETE THIS SECTION

- Complete items 1, 2, and 3.
- Print your name and address on the reverse so that we can return the card to you.
- Attach this card to the back of the mailpiece, or on the front if space permits.

1. Article Addressed to:

Edward Gerald "Jerry" Brown, Jr.;
%: State Capitol; Suite: 1173;
Sacramento, CA.;[95814]

9590 9403 0503 5173 6341 29

2. Article Number *(Transfer from service label)*

7015 1730 0000 3615 8876

PS Form 3811, April 2015 PSN 7530-02-000-9053

COMPLETE THIS SECTION ON DELIVERY

A. Signature

X ___ Brown

☐ Agent
☐ Addressee

B. Received by *(Printed Name)*
C. Date of Delivery

D. Is delivery address different from item 1? ☐ Yes
If YES, enter delivery address below: ☐ No

FEB 16 2016

3. Service Type
☐ Adult Signature
☐ Adult Signature Restricted Delivery
☐ Certified Mail®
☐ Certified Mail Restricted Delivery
☐ Collect on Delivery
☐ Collect on Delivery Restricted Delivery
☐ Insured Mail
☐ Insured Mail Restricted Delivery (over $500)

☐ Priority Mail Express®
☐ Registered Mail™
☐ Registered Mail Restricted Delivery
☐ Return Receipt for Merchandise
☐ Signature Confirmation™
☐ Signature Confirmation Restricted Delivery

Domestic Return Receipt

U.S. Postal Service™
CERTIFIED MAIL® RECEIPT
Domestic Mail Only

For delivery information, visit our website at www.usps.com®.

SACRAMENTO, CA 95814

Certified Mail Fee $3.45

0252
03

Extra Services & Fees *(check box, add fee as appropriate)*
☐ Return Receipt (hardcopy) $ $0.00
☐ Return Receipt (electronic) $ $0.00
☐ Certified Mail Restricted Delivery $ $0.00
☐ Adult Signature Required $ $0.00
☐ Adult Signature Restricted Delivery $ $0.00

Postmark Here

Postage $0.49

Total Postage and Fees $6.74

02/10/2016

Sent To
Edward Gerald "Jerry" Brown, Jr.;
%: State Capitol; Suite: 1173;
Sacramento, Calif.; [95814]

PS Form 3800, April 2015 PSN 7530-02-000-9047 See Reverse for Instructions

Robert – Charles: [Simpson]; and
Bradley – Jefferson: [Franks];
C/O: 408; South-Lincoln St.:
Milbank, South Dakota: [57252].

Third-Notice: Affidavit and Notice of [De]fault and Opportunity-to-Cure

Notice to Principal is notice to agent-Notice to agent is notice to principal

Certified Mail No.: 70150640000702169671

For Lien Debtors and Perpetrators:

Barbara Levy Boxer;
C/O: 112 Hart Senate Office Building;
Washington, D.C.; [20510].

February 8, 2016:

Barbara Levy Boxer [U. S. Senator for Southern California].

On January 14, 2016, the Undersigned-aggrieved-parties sent you copies of our on-going Lien-Documents a Second-Notice: Affidavit and Notice of [De]Fault and Opportunity-to-Cure by Certified-Mail No. 70151730000036158715.

Your un-sign[ed]/un-autograph[ed]-response/[re]buttal and lack of communication (your silence) is a point of acceptance by yourself and your co-conspirators and is the responsibility of the State California and its Officers for the unlawful acts, fraud and injuries committed and it so appears that your Continued-Silence is a continuation of the same fraud and extending the injuries in this matter.

You have Ten (10) days plus Five (5) days grace period for the "response" of these allegations.

Your 'Silence' within this matter is acceptable proof of your guilt by the CALIFORNIA CONSTITUTION - ARTICLE 1 - DECLARATION OF RIGHTS so states at SECTION 1:

"All people are by nature free and independent and have inalienable rights. Among these are enjoying and defending life and liberty, acquiring, possessing, and protecting property, and pursuing and obtaining safety, happiness, and privacy."

Please note that we are asserting this claim, as our inalienable right and in so doing, are defending life and property (the claim and sum certain amount) as a matter of right.

As the Respondent(s), you are at fault of a proper response and [de]fault will be taken as necessary should you fail to-respond!

199

Under necessity, you are herein given the opportunity to-cure your fault/non-response with an additional ten (10) days with five (5) day for return mail, Fifteen (15) days total to-cure your fault of non-response.

Send a copy of the response of this matter for: Robert Kelly: C/O: P.O. Box: 3096: Central Point, Oregon: [97502] and for the above Claimants.

NOTICE: Should you fail or refuse to cure your [De]fault, the Undersigned/underautograph will be compelled-to-issue a 'Third and Final Notice: Affidavit and Notice of [De]fault' which will establish facts in and for the record of your agreement (general acquiescence) of the claim as presented-within these presentments. If all parties-involved-refuse the re[buttal] or answer, we will be forced-to-use subrogation for the signature/autographs and authority within this matter. Further, with full-understanding that with the "silence" and "refusal" of cooperation all "presentments" within this "cargo" will be met with acceptance, acknowledgement, agreement and approval from all parties-involved.

Thank you for your prompt attention in this matter.

Sincerely,

'All Rights Reserve'

Bradley–Jefferson: [Franks]

Robert / Charles: [Simpson]; and
Bradley – Jefferson: [Franks];
the Aggrieved-Parties

AFFIDAVIT OF MAIL[ING]

I ___KEN GIESSINGER_____, the undersign[ed] adult domiciliary of Grant County, South Dakota, swear under the penalty of perjury that I did personally witness Robert – Charles: [Simpson] and Bradley – Jefferson: [Franks], place in the United States mail the below list[ed] documents.

1. An original document entitle[ed], Third-Notice: Affidavit and Notice of [De] Fault and Opportunity-to-Cure.

2. All Documents were place[ed] in an envelope which was present[ed] to the United States Post Office at Milbank, South Dakota, in Grant County, for delivery by first-class-certified-mail, return-receipt-requested.

3. One copy sent for: U. S. Senator for California: Barbara Levy Boxer; the State of California: CEO/Governor: Edward Gerald "Jerry" Brown, Jr.; and The State of California.

4. I, ___KEN GIESSINGER_____, personally review[ed] all documents enclose[ed] for mailing.

Date: this _10th_ day of _February_____, Two thousand sixteen, Anno Domini

_____
Autograph of Affiant (disinterest[ed] person)

SENDER: COMPLETE THIS SECTION

- Complete items 1, 2, and 3.
- Print your name and address on the reverse so that we can return the card to you.
- Attach this card to the back of the mailpiece, or on the front if space permits.

1. Article Addressed to:

Barbara Levy Boxer
C/o: 112; Hart Senate Office Bldg.;
washington P.C.;
[20510]

9590 9403 0503 5173 6341 05

2. Article Number (Transfer from service label)

7015 1730 0000 3615 8890

COMPLETE THIS SECTION ON DELIVERY

A. Signature

X _Myriam Ankaye_ ☑ Agent ☐ Addressee

B. Received by (Printed Name): Myriam Ankaye   C. Date of Delivery: 3/3/16

D. Is delivery address different from item 1? ☐ Yes
If YES, enter delivery address below: ☑ No

3. Service Type
- ☐ Adult Signature
- ☐ Adult Signature Restricted Delivery
- ☐ Certified Mail®
- ☐ Certified Mail Restricted Delivery
- ☐ Collect on Delivery
- ☐ Collect on Delivery Restricted Delivery
- ☐ Insured Mail
- ☐ Insured Mail Restricted Delivery (over $500)
- ☐ Priority Mail Express®
- ☐ Registered Mail™
- ☐ Registered Mail Restricted Delivery
- ☐ Return Receipt for Merchandise
- ☐ Signature Confirmation™
- ☐ Signature Confirmation Restricted Delivery

Domestic Return Receipt

U.S. Postal Service™
CERTIFIED MAIL® RECEIPT
Domestic Mail Only

For delivery information, visit our website at www.usps.com®.

WASHINGTON, DC 20510 OFFICIAL USE

| Certified Mail Fee | $3.45 | | 0252 03 |
Extra Services & Fees (check box, add fee as appropriate)
- ☐ Return Receipt (hardcopy) $ $0.00
- ☐ Return Receipt (electronic) $ $0.00
- ☐ Certified Mail Restricted Delivery $ $0.00
- ☐ Adult Signature Required $ $0.00
- ☐ Adult Signature Restricted Delivery $

Postage $0.49

Postmark Here

Total Postage and Fees $6.74

02/10/2016

Sent To Barbara Levy Boxer
Street and Apt. No., or PO Box No. C/o: 112; Hart Senate Office Building;
City, State, ZIP+4® washington D.C.; [20510]

PS Form 3800, April 2015 PSN 7530-02-000-9047   See Reverse for Instructions

7015 1730 0000 3615 8890

202

Robert – Charles: [Simpson]; and

Bradley – Jefferson: [Franks];

C/O; 408; South – Lincoln – Street;

Milbank, South Dakota; [57252].

IDENTIFICATION NUMBER: 201509038342061;

Date of File: 09 – 03 – 2015;

Location of File: State of New York.

For Lien Debtors and Perpetrators:

The State of California;

C/O: State Capitol; Suite; 1173;

Sacramento, California: [95814]

March 17, 2016;

Re: NOTICE FOR VIOLATION OF OATH OF OFFICE 'BREACH OF CONTRACT' – DEMAND FOR CEASE AND DESIST – NOTICE FOR CURE – NOTICE FOR LEIN – LIS PENDENS BY NECESSITY – SUBROGATION OF AUTOGRAPH/SIGNATURE/AUTHORITY – NOTICE OF TORT - NOTICE FOR THE SUSPENSION OF THE CHARTER FOR THE STATE OF CALIFORNIA.

For All Perpetrators within this action:
~~Barbara Levy Boxer [U. S. Senator for California]:~~

It has become necessary to-notice and inform you of your violation of your 'Oath of Office'.

You work within and are employ[ed] by 'We the People', regardless, whether at the Municipal, County, State or Federal level.

We were/are inform[ed] of such violation(s) of those who have taken an 'Oath of Office', or by and through your superior(s), who have taken an 'Oath of Office' by and through an article that appear[ed] within "The American's Bulletin", (March/April 2015: edition), so much so that we were/are compel[ed]-to-serve you this "Notice", by the necessity, as we have had and continue-to-have our "God-given" and/or 'Civil-Rights' and/or "Constitutional-Rights" violate[d] by you as well as all so-called "Oath-Takers".

However, this "Notice" is direct[ed] specifically for you and up-to and include[ing] all your Supervisors, Directors, Commissioners, Governors and the C.E.O. of the U. S., Inc. (the Federal Government Corporation) and all perpetrators within this action, or otherwise.

Upon acceptance of the 'Office' as, either by employment, appointment or **election**, or otherwise, you are require[d]-to-take the "Oath of Office", and we can only 'presume' that you did, and such "Oath of Office' is to-be-on record with the appropriate office (Clerks office, Secretary of State, Clerk of Court or otherwise) wherever that particular office is-to-keep such records, by the State-statutes. (The exception is the "Show-Me-State" – State of Missouri that does not keep public-record(s) of "Oaths of Office". The public-servant keeps it/them! How's that for transparency?)

Secondly, you also have-to-acquire your own "Performance-Bond", in most-cases prior for taking the 'Oath of Office'. While it is a known fact, that while you may have an 'Oath of Office', if you do not have or hold (a public record to-be-made available upon request) of your "Performance-Bond", you DO-NOT 'Qualify' for the Office/Position of your employment, appointment, or of being elect[ed] and therein your "Oath of Office" is null and void, as you may have fail[ed] in a very critical-part of filling-the chosen office!

As for the 'Oath of Office', you took the oath with your right-hand-raised, and possibly, your left-hand on the Bible and stated-in-some-capacity that you would; "… uphold, support and defend the U. S. Constitution…so help me God!". That oath is your-'Agreement' and 'Contract' with the people of your-Municipality, County, State, and/or the Federal Corporation.

Presumption is, if you violate the "Oath" (agreement/contract) in general-application of the people, or more specifically, [to] Bradley – Jefferson: [Franks] and Robert – Charles: [Simpson], you commit a crime: known as "Breach of Contract".

Presumption is-taken that you know of should have known that the historical-record(s) leading-up to the draft[ing] and sign[ing], that "In CONGRESS, July 4, 1776, the unanimous Declaration of the thirteen (colonies) united States", more commonly-called; "The Declaration of Independence" and that it was a precursor for the "Constitution of the United States" and in disagreement for the sign[ing] of the constitution the attending 'Forefathers', demand[ed] a "Bill of Rights" as they were quite aware of the possibility of an over-zealous Federal Government, they want[ed] assurance of such "Bill of Rights", to-insure and protect those Rights of the people, as enumerate[d] therein.

We all know that: 1) the 'Bill of Rights' are not exhaustive of what we call our God-given Rights, or our 'secured-rights', and 2) the Bill of Rights only operate-upon the Officer/Oath-taker of the so-called government by and through the 'Oath of Office', not-to-violate any of those Rights in-respect of his/her-dealings with the people, or in this 'case/matter' we/us, the undersign[ed]/autograph[ed]!

For all perpetrators involve[d] within this action, the 'Oath of Office' also-attaches-not-only to-the "Article(s) in Amendment (The Bill of Rights), to "…uphold, protect and defend" those said 'Rights' but also of the "Declaration of Independence", a precursor "Historical Document" for our supposed-form of government, wherein you agree[d], that I/we, as one of the 'people', am 'separate' and (have) an 'equal-station' (to-corporate-government)…as "Nature's God entitles them to me/us, that we are created-equal, that we are endow[ed] by our Creator (not government!) with certain unalienable Rights as well as the Right-to "Life, Liberty and pursuit of Happiness", as well as the Right "not-to-consent" what may be advanced-or-done by so-called government!

These three documents; "In CONGRESS, July 4, 1776: the unanimous Declaration of the thirteen (colonies) united States" AKA; "Declaration of Independence", The Constitution of the united States (1787) and the "Bill of Rights" constitute the "SUPREME LAW OF THE LAND"!

In regards to-the "Life".... (*Not-exhaustive*) Right-to gather-food, hunt, fish, to-marry without license, Right-to-engage in a 'common-law-occupation' (*without-license/permits*), to-travel in a/my/our private-conveyance (automobile) (non-commercial!) (*without-license/permits),* Right not-to-be bombarded with Chemtrails. Right-to-carry and 'bear' arms along with the Right-to-protect and defend one's life, family, **home, property,** neighborhood, county and country *"against all enemies foreign or domestic, etc., etc."*

In regards-to "Liberty"....Freedom from arbitrary or despotic (communist/progressive democratic) government or otherwise, freedom from external or foreign rule, i.e.; U. S. Inc. (corporate government), New World Order, Muslim Brotherhood or otherwise, freedom from control, interference, obligation, restriction, hampering conditions, etc.; power or right of doing, thinking, speaking, etc., according-to-choice, freedom from captivity, from subjugation (bondage), economic bondage (due to U. S. Bankruptcy/federal reserve notes), freedom from illegal, misapplied 'foreign' and fraudulent "income taxes", Right-to keep, carry and bear arms, freedom-to travel in a private-conveyance (automobile) (non-commercial!) (*without-license/permit),* freedom not-to-be compelled-into-illegal 'schemes' social security, motor-vehicle-code/driver-licenses, the fraudulent and illegal Affordable Health Care Act (Obamacare!); Right-not-to-be-compelled-into foreign-courts (tribunals) of a foreign-jurisdiction (Maritime/Admiralty/Equity) by evidence of 'military' flag(s) display[ed] in the so-called courthouses, etc., etc.

Note: with regards of several State Constitutions, it is found and stated-therein, and construed-to-be equal in respect to-each other, pursuant to-the *Pari materia rule*; "...that the people have all power..." that is defined-as having-all power to-engage and exercise the Right to Life, Liberty and the pursuit of Happiness!

In regards-to "pursuit of Happiness"....Right-to-pursue "common law occupation", or other activities or otherwise that brings I/we/us happiness...as long as one does not harm the life, liberty, or property of another. Any other form of government or foreign rule to-the contrary is illegal, terrorist in nature, and like cancer, must be destroyed. (Example: Communism, Muslim terrorists/sharia law, etc.).

Please take notice of the following-so-called court case, referenced-for your edification only and a few quotes:

1) "Government may not legislate away the First Amendment". KIRKBEY v. FURNESS, 92 F3d 655 (8th Cir. 1996)

2) "Speech that stirs passions, resentment, or anger is fully protected by the First Amendment...and...First Amendment activity may not be banned simply because prior similar activity led to or involved instances of violence". COLLINS v. JORDAN, 110 f3d 1363 (9th Cir. 1996)

3) "Government may not regulate speech based on its substantive content or the message it conveys". METRO DISPLAY ADVERTISING v. CITY OF VICTORVILLE, 143 F3d 1191 (9th Cir. 1998)

---

4) "The strongest protection of the First Amendment's free speech guarantee goes to the right of criticize government or advocate change in government policy". VELAZQUEZ v. LEGAL SERVICES CORP., 164 F3d (2nd Cir. 1999)

5) "Criticism of public officials lies at very core of speech protected by the First Amendment". COLSON v. GROHMAN, 174 F3d 498 (5th Cir. 1999)

6) "...at the Revolution, the sovereignty devolved on the people; and they are truly the sovereigns of the country, but they are sovereigns without subjects...with none to govern but themselves; the citizens of America are equal as fellow citizens, and as joint tenants in the sovereignty". CHISHOLM v. GEORGIA (US) 2 Dall 419, 454, 1 L Ed 440, 445 @ DALL 1793 pp471-472

7) "There, every man is independent of all laws, except those prescribed by nature. He is not bound by any institutions formed by his fellowmen without his consent." CRUDEN v. NEALE, 2 N.C. 338 (1796) 2 S.E. 70

8) "The people have succeeded to the rights of the King, the former sovereign of this State. They are not, therefore, bound by general words in a statute restrictive of prerogative, without being expressly named. *E.g.*, the Insolvent Law". THE PEOPLE v. HERKIMER, Gentleman, one, &c – 4 Cowen 345; 1825 N.Y. LEXIS 80

9) The Supreme Court in the case of Wills vs. Michigan State Police, 105 L. Ed. 2d45 (1989)...made it perfectly clear that (I) "...the Sovereign, cannot be named in any statute as merely a "person" or "any person"!

10) "But indeed, no private person has the right to complain, by suit in Court, on the ground of a breach of the Constitution. The Constitution, it is true, is a compact (contract), but he is not a party to it. The States are a party to it..." Padelford, Fay &Co. vs. the Mayor and Alderman of the City of Savannah, 14 Ga. 438 (1854)

Note: A person has the right to complain on a "Breach of Contract". Which is the "Oath of Office". The States lose all "rights" as a 'Party' to the Constitution, under breach of contract.

11) "A statute does not trump the Constitution." – People v. Ortiz, (1995) 32 Cal. App. 4th at p. 292, fn. 2, Conway v. Pasadena Humane Society, (1996) 45 Cal. App. 4th 163 UNITED STATES OS AMERICA, v. JERRY ARBERT POOL, C. A. No. 09-10303, IN THE UNITED STATES COURT OF APPEALS FOR THE NINTH CIRCUIT (Opinion filed September 14, 2010), on Appeal From the United States District Court For The Eastern District of California

12) "A statutory privilege cannot override a defendant's constitutional right". People v. Reber, (1986) 177 Cal. App. 3d. 523 [223 Cal. Rptr. 139]; Vela v. Superior Ct., 208 Cal. App. 3d. 141 [255 Cal Rptr. 921], however... "The judiciary has a solemn obligation to insure that the constitutional right of an accused to a fair trial is realized. If that right would be thwarted by enforcement of a statute, the state...must yield". Vela v. Superior Ct., 208 Cal. App. 3d. 141 [255 Cal. Rptr. 921]

13) "Obviously, administrative agencies, like police officers must obey the Constitution and may not deprive persons of constitutional rights". Southern Pac. Transportation Co. v. Public Utilities Com., 18 Cal. 3d 308 [S. F. No. 23217. Supreme Court of California. November 23, 1976]

---

14) "But even if the Congress itself should make a law which is contrary to the Constitution, must the people obey it? – No". – Arthur J. Stansbury, Author: An Elementary Catechism on the Constitution. (1828)

15) "Let virtue, honor, the love of liberty... be... the soul of this constitution, and it will become the source of great and extensive happiness to this and future generations. Vice, ignorance, and want of vigilance, will be the only enemies able to destroy it" – John Jay, co-author of the Federalist Papers and, later, Chief Justice of the Supreme Court.

16) "The Constitution is a written instrument. As such its meaning does not alter. That which it meant when adopted, it means now". – United States Supreme Court in South Carolina vs. United States (1905)

17) "We the people have discharged any debt which may be said to exist or owed to the state/government. The governments are, presumably, indebted continually to the people, because the people [the sovereigns] presumably assented to the 1878 creation of the government corporation and because we suffer its continued existence. The continued debt owed to the people is discharged only as it continues **not to violate our private rights**, and when government fails in its duty to provide protection-discharge its debt to the people, it is an abandonment [delictual fault] of any and all power, authority or vestige of sovereignty which it may have otherwise possessed, and the laws remain the same, the sovereignty reverting to the people whence it came". Downes v. Bidwell, 182 U.S. 244 (1901)

18) "All that government does and provides legitimately is in pursuit of its duty to provide protection for private rights, which duty is a debt owed to its creator, WE THE PEOPLE and the private unenfranchised individual; which debt and duty is never extinguished nor discharged, and is perpetual". Wynhammer v. People, (13 NY 378)

19) Am Jur 2d Sec. 256 ... states: "... an unconstitutional statute, though having the form and name of law is in reality no law... it is as inoperative as if it had never been passed... it imposes no duties, confers no rights, confers no office, bestows no power or authority on anyone... No one is bound to obey an unconstitutional law and no court is bound to enforce it".

20) "As in the case of illegal arrests, the officer is bound to know these fundamental rights and privileges, and must keep within the law at his peril." – Thiede vs. Town of Scandia Valley, 217 Minn. 218, 231 14N.W. (2d) 400 (1944)

21) "It is not the function of our Government to keep the citizen from falling into error; it is the function of the citizen to keep the government from falling into error." U.S. Supreme Court in American Communications Association v. Douds, 339 U.S. 382, 442.

22) "If the state converts a liberty in to a privilege the citizen can engage in the right with impunity." Shuttlesworth v. Birmingham, 373 U.S. 262.

23) "The claim and exercise of a Constitutional right cannot be converted into a crime." Miller v. U.S., 230 F 2d 486, 489.

24) "If you've relied on prior decisions of the Supreme Court you have a perfect defense against willfulness." - U.S. v. Bishop, 412 U.S. 346.

25) "Officers of the court have no immunity when violating a constitutional right, from liability, for they are deemed to know the law." - Owen v. Independence, 100 S. Ct. 1398.

26) "Unlawful search and seizure. Your Rights must be interpreted in favor of the citizen." Byars v. U.S., 273 U.S. 28.

27) "This court is to protect against any encroachment of constitutionally secured liberty." Boyd v. U.S., 116 U.S. 616.

28) "No state shall convert a liberty into a privilege; license it, and attach a fee to it." Murdock v. Penn., 318 U.S. 105.

29) "Where rights secured by the Constitution are involved, there can be no rule (law) making legislation which would abrogate (abolish) them." Miranda v. Arizona, 384 U.S. 436.

30) "An unconstitutional act is no law; it imposes no duties; affords no protection; it creates no office; it is illegal contemplation, as inoperative though it had never been passed." Norton v. Shelby County, 118 U.S. 425.

31) "The Constitution of these United States is the supreme law of the land. Any law that is repugnant to the constitution is null and void of law." Marbury v. Madison, 5 U.S. 137.

32) "...we are of the opinion that there is a clear distinction in this particular between an individual and a corporation, and that the latter has no right to refuse to submit its books and papers for an examination at the suit of the State. The individual may stand upon his constitutional rights as a citizen. He is entitled to carry on his private business in his own way. His power to contract is unlimited. He owes no duty to the State or to his neighbors to divulge his business; or to open his doors to an investigation so far as it may tend to criminate him. He owes no such duty to the State, since he receives nothing there-from, beyond the protection of his life and property. His rights are such as existed by the law of the land long antecedent to the organization of the State, and can only be taken from him by due process of law, and in accordance with the Constitution. He owes nothing to the public so long as he does not trespass upon their rights ...an individual may lawfully refuse to answer incriminating questions, unless protected by an immunity statute." HALE v. HENKLE, 201 U.S. 43 @ pg.74 (1903).

33) "But indeed, no private person has a right to complain, by suit in Court, on the ground of a breach of the Constitution. The Constitution, it is true, is a compact (contract), but he is not a party to it. The States are a party to it..." (Emphasis added) - Padelford, Fay & Co. vs. The Mayor and Aldermen of the City of Savannah, 14 Ga. 438 (1854)

34) "The county court is no longer a constitutional court: Fehl v. Jackson County, in re Will of Pittock, 102 OR. 159, 199 P., 2020 P. 216, 17 A.L.R. 218

35) "There can be no limitation on the power of the people of the United States. By their authority the State Constitutions were made, and by their authority the Constitution of the United States was established" U. S. Supreme Court - Hauenstein vs Lynham (100 US 483)

36) SENATE REPORT NO. 93-549 93RD CONGRESS, 1st Session (1973), "Summary of Emergency Power Statutes," Executive orders 6073, 6102, 6111 and by Executive Order 6260 on March 9, 1933, under the "Trading With The Enemy Act (Sixty-Fifth Congress, Session. I, Chapters. 105, 106, October 6, 1917), and as codified at 12 U.S.C.A. 95a, and:

37) "The majority of the people of the United States have lived all of their lives under EMERGENCY RULE. For 40 (now 80) years, freedoms and governmental procedures guaranteed by the Constitution have, in varying degrees, been abridged by laws brought into force by states of national emergency."

---

38) "The idea that the State originated to serve any kind of social purpose is completely unhistorical. It originated in conquest and confiscation, that is to say, in crime. It originated for the purpose of maintain the division of society into an owning and exploiting class and a property-less class, that is, for a criminal purpose! No State known to history originated in any other manner, or for any other purpose!" – Albert Jay Nock (State of the Union) (October 13, 1870 – August 19, 1945) ...(Emphasis added)

We could go on. However, we presume that you do get the point!

Also, take notice of; "Government and its agents [officers] are under no general duty to provide public services such as protection, to any particular individual citizen, but, rather, duty to provide public services is owed to public at large, absent special relationship between police and individual, no specific legal duty exists." Note; that *special relationship* might be a separate agreement *for protection* but none exists between us and you, HOWEVER, that "special relationship" that DOES exist is your "Oath of Office", that we accept for value as the agreement/contract... that you are not to violate our God-given and substantive Rights as referenced herein, though not exhaustive.

Note: ***should you cause us injury***, i.e., it is an abandonment [delictual fault], of your position and a violation of your "Oath of Office", a crime, an Act of treason against your "Constitution," and engagement of RICO activities against us; being the violation of our God-given and secured-Rights, as mentioned herein. Your performance bond can be foreclosed-upon to-pay monetary damages for those you have-injured, of which, without your bond, you do not fill the 'office' that you fill or serve in and you can be-fired/removed-by your superiors, along with the right we have to-file a criminal-complaint, and, if need be, exhaust our Private Administrative Process Remedy, and/or file a law suit under necessity!

Therein, the "Oath-Takers," yourself included, having the full authority, duty and power to keep this Country within its "Republican" form of government, maintaining a government "of the people, by the people and for the people" and free from the above mentioned points, you knew or should have known, and you are complicit in the destruction of America as well in violation of your Oath of Office. "Ignorance of the Law is No-Excuse".

By your actions or in-actions you are deemed guilty of violation of your Oath of Office, (Breach of Contract), committing treason against your constitution and Organized Crime Activities under R.I.C.O. Laws.

However, you are given a chance to rebut this lawful Notice, point by point, within (30) days with a (5) day grace period upon receipt, by certified mail. Your rebuttal/response must be in affidavit form, sign[ed]/autograph[ed] under-penalty of perjury. Your response must sign[ed]/autograph[ed] in Blue-ink and notarized-with the original sent to-us.

CAVEAT

Your failure or otherwise refusal of the response, rebut the above points "point by point" and **prove** that you have **not** violate[d] the 'Oath of Office' and therein have not-injured us in the violation of your-contract, as well the production of any documentation on any necessary point(s) in your favor, with your response-being in affidavit form sign[ed]/autograph[ed] under-penalty of perjury and void of all deception. Your failure, refusal and/or your dishonor is your admission, stipulation and agreement that you have violate[d] your 'Oath of Office', and have commit[ed] a crime(s), commit[ed] terrorism against your 'constitution(s) (compact(s), are engaged in R.I.C.O. activities against us and others to-the detriment of our God-given and secured-Rights, as express[ed] within the 'Declaration of Independence', and the 'Bill of Rights' which operate upon you, by your oath, not to-violate in regards to-your dealing(s) with us! By your failure, refusal and/or your dishonor for the response, rebut the above points, by your silence, you agree that you have violate[d] your 'Oath of Office' and are in fact and in-deed the responsible, liable and culpable party(ies) for all monetary-damages for the injuries done to-us, by and through the violation of your Oath of Office and that you agree to pledge your body and all your private-property, assets and accounts and of your spouse, if any, and you agree that this is your notice[d], inform[ed] consent and voluntary agreement (tacit procreation) and you agree to subrogation for the sign[ing]/autograph of any necessary process/documents, if necessary, and/or commercial instrument(s) for the "satisfaction and accord" of the monetary damages, within this matter, estimate[d] at this time to be $38,852,419,500.00 (Thirty eight billion eight hundred fifty two million four hundred nineteen thousand five hundred/USD) and for lawful cause and in violation and contempt of Our Prime Creator's Will and our Will and you also therefore agree to whatever Karma you have created for yourself to experience per this matter.

Right Thumb Print:

Robert – Charles: [Simpson].

Right Thumb Print:

Bradley – Jefferson: [Franks].

Robert – Charles: [Simpson].

Robert – Charles: [Simpson].

Bradley – Jefferson: [Franks].

Bradley – Jefferson: [Franks].

It is imperative that you read <u>Senate Report 93-549</u>, 93rd Congress, 1st Session (1973), "Summary of Emergency Power Statutes", consisting of 607 pages, which I believe you will find most interesting. **The United States went "Bankrupt" in 1933 and was declared so by President Roosevelt by <u>Executive Orders 6073, 6102, 6111</u> and by <u>Executive Order 6260</u> on March 9, 1933 (See: <u>Senate Report 93-549</u>, pgs. 187 & 594), under the <u>"Trading with the Enemy Act"</u> (Sixty-Fifth Congress, Sess. I, Chs. 105, 106, October 6, 1917), and as codified at <u>12 U.S.C.A. 95a</u>.** On May 23, 1933, Congressman, Louis T. McFadden, brought formal charges against the Board of Governors of the Federal Reserve Bank system, the Comptroller of the Currency and the Secretary of the United States Treasury for criminal acts. The petition for Articles of Impeachment was thereafter referred to the Judiciary Committee, and has yet to be acted upon. (See: <u>Congressional Record,</u> pp. 4055-4058) Congress confirmed the Bankruptcy on June 5, 1933, and impaired the obligations and considerations of contracts through the "Joint Resolution To Suspend The Gold Standard And Abrogate The Gold Clause, June 5, 1933"), (See: <u>House Joint Resolution 192</u>, 73rd Congress, 1st Session) The several States of the Union pledged the faith and credit thereof to the aid of the National Government, and formed numerous socialist committees, such as the "Council Of State Governments", "Social Security Administration" etcetera, to purportedly deal with the economic "Emergency." These Organizations operated under the "<u>Declaration of INTERdependence</u>" of January 22, 1937, and published some of their activities in "<u>The Book of the States.</u>" The 1937 Edition of the Book of the States openly declared that the people engaged in such activities as the Farming/Husbandry Industry had been reduced to mere feudal "Tenants" on their Land.

DECLARATION OF CAUSE AND NECESSITY TO ABOLISH
AND DECLARATION OF SEPARATE AND EQUAL STATION
By John Nelson - February 21, 1992 – Edited

The Death of America

JURAT

SUBSCRIBE[D] AND SWORN before me this ___18___ day of ___march___ A. D. 2016, a Notary, that <u>Robert – C.: [Simpson]</u> and <u>Bradley – J.: [Franks]</u>, personally appears and is known to-me-to be the men whose name subscribe[d] for the instrument(s) within and acknowledges for the same and execute[d] the foregoing.

___Diana Allen___ Seal

Notary Public in and for said State of South Dakota:

My Commission Expires: **DIANA ALLEN**
My Commission Expires Jan. 15, 2018

212

AFFIDAVIT OF MAIL[ING]

I _____, the undersign[ed] adult domiciliary of Grant County, South Dakota, swear under the penalty of perjury that I did personally witness Robert – Charles: [Simpson] and Bradley – Jefferson: [Franks], place in the United States mail the below list[ed] documents.

1. An original document entitle[ed], Re: Notice for Violation of Oath of Office 'Breach Of Contract – Demand for Cease and Desist – Notice for Cure – Lis Pendens by Necessity – Subrogation of Autograph/Signature/Authority – Notice of Tort – Notice for the Suspension of the Charter of the State of California; 9 Pages. Jurat; 1 Page.

2. All Documents were place[ed] in an envelope which was present[ed] to the United States Post Office at Milbank, South Dakota, in Grant County, for delivery by first-class-certified-mail, return-receipt-requested.

3. One copy sent for: U. S. Senator for California: Barbara Levy Boxer; the State of California: CEO/Governor: Edward Gerald "Jerry" Brown, Jr.; and The State of California.

4. I, _____, personally review[ed] all documents enclose[ed] for mailing.

Date: this ___18___ day of ___mARCH___, Two thousand sixteen, Anno Domini

_____
Autograph of Affiant (disinterest[ed] person)

Robert – Charles: [Simpson]; and

Bradley – Jefferson: [Franks];

C/O: 408; South – Lincoln – Street;

Milbank, South Dakota; [57252].

IDENTIFICATION NUMBER: 201509038342061;

Date of File: 09 – 03 – 2015;

Location of File: State of New York.

For Lien Debtors and Perpetrators:

Edward Gerald "Jerry" Brown, Jr.;

C/O: State Capitol; Suite; 1173;

Sacramento, California: [95814].

March 17, 2016;

Re: NOTICE FOR VIOLATION OF OATH OF OFFICE 'BREACH OF CONTRACT' – DEMAND FOR CEASE AND DESIST – NOTICE FOR CURE – NOTICE FOR LEIN – LIS PENDENS BY NECESSITY – SUBROGATION OF AUTOGRAPH/SIGNATURE/AUTHORITY – NOTICE OF TORT - NOTICE FOR THE SUSPENSION OF THE CHARTER FOR THE STATE OF CALIFORNIA.

Edward Gerald "Jerry" Brown, Jr. [Governor/CEO of the State of California]:

It has become necessary to-notice and inform you of your violation of your 'Oath of Office'.

You work within and are employ[ed] by 'We the People', regardless, whether at the Municipal, County, State or Federal level.

We were/are inform[ed] of such violation(s) of those who have taken an 'Oath of Office', or by and through your superior(s), who have taken an 'Oath of Office' by and through an article that appear[ed] within "The American's Bulletin", (March/April 2015: edition), so much so that we were/are compel[ed]-to-serve you this "Notice", by the necessity, as we have had and continue-to-have our "God-given"

214

Bradley - J.: [Franks] and Co-Author: Robert - C.: [Simpson]

AFFIDAVIT OF MAIL[ING]

I _____, the undersign[ed] adult domiciliary of
Grant County, South Dakota, swear under the penalty of perjury that I did personally witness
Robert – Charles: [Simpson] and Bradley – Jefferson: [Franks], place in the United States mail
the below list[ed] documents.

1. An original document entitle[ed], Re: Notice for Violation of Oath of Office 'Breach Of
   Contract – Demand for Cease and Desist – Notice for Cure – Lis Pendens by Necessity –
   Subrogation of Autograph/Signature/Authority – Notice of Tort – Notice for the
   Suspension of the Charter of the State of California; 9 Pages. Jurat; 1 Page.

2. All Documents were place[ed] in an envelope which was present[ed] to the United States
   Post Office at Milbank, South Dakota, in Grant County, for delivery by first-class-certified-mail,
   return-receipt-requested.

3. One copy sent for: U. S. Senator for California: Barbara Levy Boxer; the State of California:
   CEO/Governor: Edward Gerald "Jerry" Brown, Jr.; and The State of California.

4. I, _____, personally review[ed] all documents
   enclose[ed] for mailing.

Date: this ___18___ day of ___MARCH___, Two thousand sixteen, Anno Domini

_____
Autograph of Affiant (disinterest[ed] person)

SENDER: COMPLETE THIS SECTION

- Complete items 1, 2, and 3.
- Print your name and address on the reverse so that we can return the card to you.
- Attach this card to the back of the mailpiece, or on the front if space permits.

1. Article Addressed to:

Edward Gerald "Jerry" Brown
℅: State Capitol; Suite: 1173;
Sacramento, C.A. : [95814]

9590 9402 1335 5285 2887 21

2. Article Number (Transfer from service label)

7015 1730 0000 3617 9192

PS Form 3811, July 2015 PSN 7530-02-000-9053

COMPLETE THIS SECTION ON DELIVERY

A. Signature
X _____ ☐ Agent ☐ Addressee
B. Received by (Printed Name): Brown
C. Date of Delivery
D. Is delivery address different from item 1? ☐ Yes ☐ No

3. Service Type
☒ Certified Mail®

Domestic Return Receipt

U.S. Postal Service™
CERTIFIED MAIL® RECEIPT
Domestic Mail Only

For delivery information, visit our website at www.usps.com®.

SACRAMENTO, CA 95814

Certified Mail Fee $3.45
$2.80
0252
03

Extra Services & Fees
☐ Return Receipt (hardcopy) $0.00
☐ Return Receipt (electronic) $0.00
☐ Certified Mail Restricted Delivery $0.00
☐ Adult Signature Required $0.00
☐ Adult Signature Restricted Delivery $

Postmark Here

Postage $1.42
Total Postage and Fees $7.67
03/18/2016

Sent To: Edward Gerald "Jerry" Brown
℅: State Capitol: Suite: 1173;
Sacramento, CA. : [95814]

PS Form 3800, April 2015 PSN 7530-02-000-9047

7015 1730 0000 3617 9192

216

Robert – Charles: [Simpson]; and

Bradley – Jefferson: [Franks];

C/O: 408; South – Lincoln – Street;

Milbank, South Dakota; [57252].

IDENTIFICATION NUMBER: 201509038342061;

Date of File: 09 – 03 – 2015;

Location of File: State of New York.

For Lien Debtors and Perpetrators:

Barbara Levy Boxer;

C/O: 112 Hart Senate Office Building;

Washington, D. C.; [20510].

March 17, 2016;

Re: NOTICE FOR VIOLATION OF OATH OF OFFICE 'BREACH OF CONTRACT' – DEMAND FOR CEASE AND DESIST – NOTICE FOR CURE – NOTICE FOR LEIN – LIS PENDENS BY NECESSITY – SUBROGATION OF AUTOGRAPH/SIGNATURE/AUTHORITY – NOTICE OF TORT - NOTICE FOR THE SUSPENSION OF THE CHARTER FOR THE STATE OF CALIFORNIA.

Barbara Levy Boxer [U. S. Senator for California]:

It has become necessary to-notice and inform you of your violation of your 'Oath of Office'.

You work within and are employ[ed] by 'We the People', regardless, whether at the Municipal, County, State or Federal level.

We were/are inform[ed] of such violation(s) of those who have taken an 'Oath of Office', or by and through your superior(s), who have taken an 'Oath of Office' by and through an article that appear[ed] within "The American's Bulletin", (March/April 2015: edition), so much so that we were/are compel[ed]-to-serve you this "Notice", by the necessity, as we have had and continue-to-have our "God-given"

The Death of America

AFFIDAVIT OF MAIL[ING]

I _____, the undersign[ed] adult domiciliary of
Grant County, South Dakota, swear under the penalty of perjury that I did personally witness
Robert – Charles: [Simpson] and Bradley – Jefferson: [Franks], place in the United States mail
the below list[ed] documents.

1. An original document entitle[ed], Re: Notice for Violation of Oath of Office 'Breach Of
   Contract – Demand for Cease and Desist – Notice for Cure – Lis Pendens by Necessity –
   Subrogation of Autograph/Signature/Authority – Notice of Tort – Notice for the
   Suspension of the Charter of the State of California; 9 Pages. Jurat; 1 Page.

2. All Documents were place[ed] in an envelope which was present[ed] to the United States
Post Office at Milbank, South Dakota, in Grant County, for delivery by first-class-certified-mail,
return-receipt-requested.

3. One copy sent for: U. S. Senator for California: Barbara Levy Boxer; the State of California:
CEO/Governor: Edward Gerald "Jerry" Brown, Jr.; and The State of California.

4. I, _____, personally review[ed] all documents
enclose[ed] for mailing.

Date: this ___18___ day of ___MARCH___, Two thousand sixteen, Anno Domini

_____
Autograph of Affiant (disinterest[ed] person)

218

SENDER: COMPLETE THIS SECTION

- Complete items 1, 2, and 3.
- Print your name and address on the reverse so that we can return the card to you.
- Attach this card to the back of the mailpiece, or on the front if space permits.

1. Article Addressed to:

Barbara Levy Boxer
%: 112 Hart Senate Of. BLDing
Washington, D.C.: 20510

9590 9402 1335 5285 2887 14

2. Article Number *(Transfer from service label)*

7015 1730 0000 3617 9208

COMPLETE THIS SECTION ON DELIVERY

A. Signature
X _____
☐ Agent
☐ Addressee

B. Received by *(Printed Name)*   C. Date of Delivery
Denra Broom   3-24-16

D. Is delivery address different from item 1? ☐ Yes
   If YES, enter delivery address below: ☒ No

3. Service Type
☐ Adult Signature
☐ Adult Signature Restricted Delivery
☒ Certified Mail®
☐ Certified Mail Restricted Delivery
☐ Collect on Delivery
☐ Collect on Delivery Restricted Delivery
☐ Insured Mail
☐ Insured Mail Restricted Delivery (over $500)

☐ Priority Mail Express®
☐ Registered Mail™
☐ Registered Mail Restricted Delivery
☐ Return Receipt for Merchandise
☐ Signature Confirmation™
☐ Signature Confirmation Restricted Delivery

PS Form 3811, July 2015 PSN 7530-02-000-9053   Domestic Return Receipt

---

U.S. Postal Service™
CERTIFIED MAIL® RECEIPT
Domestic Mail Only

For delivery information, visit our website at *www.usps.com®*.

WASHINGTON, DC 20510

| Certified Mail Fee | $3.45 | 0252 |
| $ | $2.80 | 03 |

Extra Services & Fees *(check box, add fee as appropriate)*
☐ Return Receipt (hardcopy) $ $0.00
☐ Return Receipt (electronic) $ $0.00   Postmark
☐ Certified Mail Restricted Delivery $ $0.00   Here
☐ Adult Signature Required $ $0.00
☐ Adult Signature Restricted Delivery $

Postage
$ $1.42

Total Postage and Fees
$ $7.67

03/18/2016

Sent To
Barbara Levy Boxer ;
Street and Apt. No., or PO Box No.
%: 112 Hart Senate Office Building ;
City, State, ZIP+4®
Washington, D.C.: [20510]

PS Form 3800, April 2015 PSN 7530-02-000-9047   See Reverse for Instructions

7015 1730 0000 3617 9208

AFFIDAVIT:

Statement of Facts

Comes now the Affiant(s), Robert – Charles: [Simpson] and Bradley – Jefferson: [Franks] herein known as Lien Claimant(s) which-have-just-cause, and through-written-notification for the Lien-Debtors and All known and Unknown Individuals/Agents or Agencies named-here-within these documents for the [De]Fault of the Lawful-Lien-Process brought and placed-against stated-Lien-Debtors.

On the 3rd day of December, two-thousand-fifteen, Anno Domini, the above-stated-Supreme Sovereign(s): Robert – Charles: [Simpson] and Bradley – Jefferson: [Franks], made-offer [30] thirty-days plus [5] five-day grace-period for a response/[re]buttal for the following-presentments:

Lien-Documents, Declaration Letter – Oath Purgatory (x2), Affidavit(s) – Plain Statement of Facts: Gerald Edward Brown, Jr. (Governor/CEO of the State of California) and Barbara Levy Boxer (U. S. Senator for the State of California), Affidavit: (648 pages) Title: "!At Gun Point...", U. C. C. 1; Affidavit; U. C. C. 4; Private Security Agreement, Commercial-Affidavit Statement, True-Billing and Account[ing], and Pre-Invoice.

Presentments were received-and-autographed acceptance via certified/registered-mail.

Response from Lien-Debtor(s): Nihil Dicit from any and all Lien-Debtor(s).

On the 14th day of January, two-thousand-sixteen, Anno Domini, Lien Claimant(s) sent presentments for the above-stated Lien-Debtors, a Second-Notice: **Affidavit and Notice of [De]Fault and Opportunity-to-Cure** with an allowance of (20) Twenty-days plus (5) five-day grace period for a response/[re]buttal.

Presentments were received-and-autographed acceptance via certified/registered-mail.

Response from Lien-Debtor(s): Nihil Dicit from any and all Lien-Debtor(s).

On the 10th day of February, two-thousand-sixteen, Anno Domini, Lien Claimant(s) sent presentments for the above-stated Lien-Debtors a Third-Notice: **Affidavit and Notice of**

---

1   10092016: AFFIDAVIT: Statement of Facts: © Bradley – Jefferson: [Franks]

[De]Fault and Opportunity-to-Cure with an allowance of (10) Ten-days plus (5) Five-day grace period for a response/[re]buttal.

Presentments were received-and-autographed acceptance via certified/registered mail.

Response from Lien-Debtor(s): Nihil Dicit from any and all Lien-Debtor(s).

On the 29th day of February, two-thousand-sixteen, Anno Domini, Lien-Claimant(s) sent presentments for the above-stated Lien-Debtor(s), a Final-Notice: **Affidavit and Notice of [De]Fault and Demand-for-Cure** with an allowance of (3) Three-days plus (5) Five-day grace period for a response/[re]buttal.

Presentments were received-and-autographed acceptance via certified/registered-mail.

Response from Lien-Debtor(s): Nihil Dicit from any and all Lien-Debtor(s).

On the 18th day of March, two-thousand-sixteen, Anno Domini, Lien Claimant(s) sent presentments for the above-stated Lien-Debtor(s), a Notice for Violation of Oath of Office 'Breach of Contract' – Demand for Cease and Desist – Notice for Cure – Notice for Lien – Lis Pendens by Necessity – Subrogation of Autograph/Signature/Authority – Notice of Tort – Notice for the Suspension of the Charter for the State of California with an allowance of (30) thirty-days plus (5) Five-day grace period for a response/[re]buttal.

Presentments were received-and-autographed acceptance via certified/registered-mail.

Response from Lien-Debtor(s): Nihil Dicit from any and all Lien-Debtor(s).

On the 29th day of April, two-thousand-sixteen, Anno Domini, Lien-Claimant(s) sent presentments for the above-stated Lien-Debtor(s), a Final-Notice: **Affidavit and Notice of [De]Fault and Demand-for-Cure** with an allowance for (3) Three-days plus (5) Five-day grace period for a response/[re]buttal.

Presentments were received-and-autographed acceptance via certified/registered-mail.

Response from Lien-Debtor(s): Nihil Dicit from any and all Lien-Debtor(s).

On the 20th day of May, two-thousand-sixteen, Anno Domini, Lien Claimant(s) sent presentments for the above-stated Lien-Debtor(s), a Notice and Entry of [De]Fault by Affidavit with an allowance of (3) three-days (72) seventy-two hours for a response/[re]buttal.

Presentments were received-and-autographed acceptance via certified/registered-mail.

Response from Lien-Debtor(s): Nihil Dicit from any and all Lien-Debtor(s).

On the 3rd day of August, two-thousand-sixteen, Anno Domini, the Lien Claimant(s) "published" within the C. Q. Roll Call, Washington D. C.; Volume 62; No. 8; a **PUBLIC-NOTICE: NOTICE OF LIEN-DEFAULT**.

---

2 10092016: AFFIDAVIT: Statement of Facts: © Bradley – Jefferson: [Franks]

On the 7th day of September, two-thousand-sixteen, Anno Domini, the Lien Claimant(s) "published" within the C. Q. Roll Call, Washington D. C.; Volume 62; No. 10; a **PUBLIC-NOTICE: NOTICE OF LIEN-DEFAULT**.

On the 14th day of September, two-thousand-sixteen, Anno Domini, the Lien Claimant(s) "published" within the C. Q. Roll Call, Washington D. C.; Volume 62; No. 14; a **PUBLIC-NOTICE: NOTICE OF LIEN-DEFAULT**.

On the 21st day of September, two-thousand-sixteen, Anno Domini, the Lien Claimant(s) "published" within the C. Q. Roll Call, Washington D. C.; Volume 62, No. 18; a **FINAL-NOTICE: FORM UCC-Ad;**

Response from Lien-Debtor(s): Nihil Dicit from any and all Lien-Debtor(s) to present-date.

Therefore, the Lien-Claimant(s) are very aware that with the expiration of the time for the response/[re]buttal, all Lien-Debtor(s) have fully, with acceptance, agreement, and responsibility within all written Affidavits and Evidence presented-within the presentments are **TRUE, CORRECT, and COMPLETE**.

Date this 10th day of October, Two-thousand-sixteen, Anno Domini.

Robert – Charles: [Simpson]; and

Bradley – Jefferson: [Franks]

C/O: Four-hundred-eight; South-Lincoln-Street;

    Milbank, South Dakota;

    United States of America;

    Non-Domestic-Mail-Location: [57252].

    Phone-Number: 1 (605) 432 – 7920.

Robert – C: [Simpson]

Robert – Charles: [Simpson]

Bradley – Jefferson: [Franks]

Bradley – Jefferson: [Franks]

Document Prepare by: Bradley – Jefferson: [Franks].

BOOK 281 PAGE 865

JURAT

SUBSCRIBE[D] AND SWORN before me this ___10___ day of ___October___ A. D. 2016, a Notary, that Robert – Charles: [Simpson] and Bradley – Jefferson: [Franks], personally appears and is known to-me-to be the men whose name subscribe[d] for the instrument(s) within and acknowledges for the same and execute[d] the foregoing **AFFIDAVIT: Statement of Facts.**

Diana Allen

Notary Public in and for said State of South Dakota

My Commission Expires:_____
DIANA ALLEN
My Commission Expires Jan. 15, 2018

223

State of South Dakota

OFFICE OF THE SECRETARY OF STATE

Apostille

(Convention de La Haye du 5 octobre 1961)

1. Country: United States of America

   This public document

2. has been signed by Diana Allen

3. acting in the capacity of Notary Public, State of South Dakota

4. bears the seal/stamp of Diana Allen, Notary Public, State of South Dakota

CERTIFIED

5. at Pierre, South Dakota, U.S.A.

6. the 21st day of October, 2016

7. by Secretary of State, State of South Dakota

8. No. N-16-16651

9. Seal/Stamp:

10. Signature

Shantel Krebs, Secretary of State

PUBLIC-NOTICE:

NOTICE OF LIEN-DEFAULT;

Notice is hereby given that on **3ʳᵈ**, Day of **Dec.** Two-thousand-fifteen, a notice of Security [15 U. S. C.] claim of commercial lien has been serve[ed] upon lien-debtors: U. S. Senator for California: Barbara Levy Boxer; the State of California: and CEO/Governor: Edward Gerald "Jerry" Brown, Jr., in the STATE OF California and Washington D. C. for the Hart Building for the Senator. For Breach of contract (Oath of Office), and is in [De]fault. Lien-debtors obligation to-lien-claimant(s) is: $38,852,419,500.00 dollars (Thirty eight Billion, eight hundred fifty two million four hundred nineteen thousand five hundred dollars), lawful money, of the united States of America. Lien-claimant(s) do-not rely on Title 15 as a basis for commercial-lien.

Date: This **29ᵗʰ**, day of **July**_____, Two-thousand-sixteen: Anno Domini.

File-Account-Number for Lien: 201509038342061; Date of file: 09-03-2015; Location of file: State of New York.

Lien-Claimants Mail location:

Robert – Charles: [Simpson];

Bradley – Jefferson: [Franks];

Care of: Four hundred eight; South-Lincoln-Street;

> Milbank, South Dakota;

> United States of America;

> Non-domestic-Mail-location: [57252].

> Phone: (605) 432 - 7920

Printing-dates: Q· Roll Call - 77 K St. NE. FLR. 8ᵗʰ washington D.C. [20002-4681]

1ˢᵗ Wed., August 3, 2016_____; Vol. 62; No. 8

2ⁿᵈ Wed. September 7, 2016_____; Vol. 62; No. 10

3ʳᵈ Wed. September 14, 2016_____; Vol. 62; No. 14

(and Final-Notice!)

The Death of America

FINAL-NOTICE:

FORM UCC – Ad;

The lien debtors: The State of California: CEO/Governor; Edward Gerald Brown, Jr.; U. S. Senator for State of California: Barbara Levy Boxer; The State of California [Corporate Government]; and All known and unknown Individuals/Agencies within this action; autograph/signatures were set by accommodation as per UCC 3 – 415 by the lien claimant(s) because the lien debtors are adversaries of the lien claimant(s), who-caused and injury to-the lien claimant's "birth-right" of liberty and sovereignty. When the lien debtors were confronted-with the claim, they said nothing, **nihil dicit**!

This lien placed on the lien debtors is not a friendly transaction whereby the lien debtors were willing to-enter into an agreement with the lien claimant(s) quid pro quo, by consent. This lien arose in this manner because no-other remedy for the compensation of the injury is available for the lien claimant(s) and the lien claimant(s) have/has the right to-use applicable law.

This lien was/is perfected-by Notice, Demand, and Publication of the [De]Fault. The claim still remains-unpaid, therefore this UCC-1 is presented-for filing-to-close the lien debtors' unexercised right-to-settle leaving-only the obligation-to-pay.

Date: This 31st, Day of _August_, Two thousand sixteen: Anno Domini.

L. S.: *Bradley – Jefferson: [Franks]*

Bradley – Jefferson: [Franks]

L. S.: *Robert – Charles: [Simpson]*

Robert – Charles: [Simpson]

Printing-Date:
C. Q. Roll Call : 77 K St. N. E. FlR. 8th
washington D. C. [20002-4681]

Final-Notice: September 21, wed.
Vol. 62, No. 18

The above documentation has been presented within this chapter as evidence of an on-going criminal action against TWO-Americans who exposed criminal acts against all Americans and other Foreign-Government-Interests.

There are to-many coincidences that prove a pattern of Organized-Crime –Practices under R. I. C. O. (Racketeer Influenced and Corrupt Organizations Laws).

Chapter 7:
THE INTERNAL REVENUE (?SERVICE?)... AT ITS WORST OR ITS BEST AT BEING THE WORST?

Let's start this chapter with a brief history.

The I. R. S. (aka Internal Revenue Service) was started in **July 1862**, during the American Civil War, President Abraham Lincoln and Congress passed the Revenue Act of 1862, creating the office of Commissioner of Internal Revenue and enacting a **temporary** income tax to pay war expenses.

Keep in mind that the I.R.S. was created for the Civil War expenses and was not to be used for the United-States-Corporate-Government 'get-rich-quick-scheme' or destroy Americans. However, this is what they have been doing for over 150+ years.

In this chapter as the authors of this book, we will be using the documents from the I. R. S. and letting you know that we intend[ed] too **("VOLUNTARILY") pay** the 'Income-Tax'. However through experience, the I. R. S. does not listen; they jump to conclusions, punish Americans who want to get help from the Corporate-Government-Office and last but not least COMMIT-FRAUD-UPON the COURT for the Corporate-Government-Benefit and force their opinions on others whether it is the "Truth, Facts or Opinions." The I.R.S. is in the belief that they are above the law and what they say is law.

The truth of the matter behind the I. R. S. is the fact that I asked lawyers, accountants and other professionals if an American had to pay taxes on income from a savings account. The answer was yes. A person does indeed have to pay taxes on interest accrued from their savings account.

Every American who ever signed up for Social Security – having first been blatantly lied to and coerced by undeclared Foreign-Agents of the Foreign-Fictitious-Corporate-Government and told that Social Security was a retirement insurance program and that it was a mandatory requirement of having a job in America – has been claimed to be an "unpaid-volunteer-employee" of the "Foreign-Fictitious-Corporate-Government" by the perpetrators of this con game and therefore, a "US citizen" instead of an American National.

Unknown to those same American Nationals, the corporation masquerading as their 'lawful-government' used their "voluntary-application" for "Social Security benefits" to obtain a veiled general Power of Attorney hidden in the SS-5 Form, and used it to seize control of their ESTATES. They then set up two-accounts "in their names" – one administered by the Federal Reserve's Internal Revenue Service and one administered by the "I.R.S. (Internal Revenue Service)" for the International Monetary Fund. One account is set up as the debt side account and follows the familiar pattern: 000-00-0000. The other account is set up as the credit side account and uses the same numbers without hyphens: *000000000*.

Most American National are owed several million dollars' worth of credit owed to their individual ESTATE accounts, but the perpetrators of the fraud never disclosure this fact. The "richest people on earth" live as debt slaves to international banking cartels that have obtained this position by fraud.

The final insult for American Nationals is that these same banking interests use your tax money to buy million dollar life insurance policies on each and every "US citizen" – benefiting the bank, of course. Even at the end of your life, the banks contrive to profit from you, and they always have profit-motive to kill you. Killing off young people brings more profit, which, together with stealing and controlling natural resources to manipulate commodity markets, explains why promoting wars for profit are favorite pastimes for these unspeakably corrupt and evil corporate entities.

The following documentation was filed and submitted for the I. R. S. and if we inadvertently used the wrong forms so be it. The I. R. S. is supposed to supply the correct information with the correct forms (not what they claim as "legal-advice") and simply refused to do so and just use threats and their form of "punishment" without the benefit of a "TRIAL".

229

The Death of America

Form **1040** Department of the Treasury—Internal Revenue Service (99)
U.S. Individual Income Tax Return **2016** OMB No. 1545-0074 IRS Use Only—Do not write or staple in this space.

For the year Jan. 1–Dec. 31, 2016, or other tax year beginning Jan. 21 , 2016 ending March 21 , 2017   See separate instructions.

Your first name and initial: Bradley J.   Last name: Franks   Your social security number: 390 80 4016

If a joint return, spouse's first name and initial   Last name   Spouse's social security number

Home address (number and street). If you have a P.O. box, see instructions. %: 408 South Lincoln Street   Apt. no.

City, town or post office, state, and ZIP code. Milbank, South Dakota

Foreign country name: United States   Foreign province/state/county: Grant County   Foreign postal code: 57252

Presidential Election Campaign — Check here if you, or your spouse if filing jointly, want $3 to go to this fund.

Filing Status
1 ☑ Single
2 ☐ Married filing jointly
3 ☐ Married filing separately
4 ☐ Head of household
5 ☐ Qualifying widow(er) with dependent child

Exemptions
6a ☑ Yourself.
6b ☐ Spouse
Boxes checked on 6a and 6b: 1
No. of children on 6c: 0
d Total number of exemptions claimed: 1

Income
7 Wages, salaries, tips, etc. 7 0
8a Taxable interest 8a 392,409,436 95
8b Tax-exempt interest ....
9a Ordinary dividends 9a 0
10 Taxable refunds 10 0
11 Alimony received ... 11 0
12 Business income or (loss) ... 12 0
13 Capital gain or (loss) ... 13 0
14 Other gains or (losses) ... 14 0
15b IRA distributions 15b 0
16b Pensions and annuities ... 16b 0
17 Rental real estate, royalties... 17 0
18 Farm income or (loss) ... 18 0
19 Unemployment compensation ... 19 0
20b Social security benefits ... 20b 0
21 Other income. List type and amount "Security" Interest on Principal 21 39,240,943,695 00
22 Combine the amounts... total income ► 22 39,633,353,131 95

Adjusted Gross Income
23 Educator expenses ... 23 0
24 Certain business expenses ... 24 0
25 Health savings account deduction ... 25 0
26 Moving expenses ... 26 0
27 Deductible part of self-employment tax ... 27 0
28 Self-employed SEP, SIMPLE ... 28 0
29 Self-employed health insurance deduction ... 29 0
30 Penalty on early withdrawal of savings ... 30 0
31a Alimony paid ... 31a 0
32 IRA deduction ... 32 0
33 Student loan interest deduction ... 33 0
34 Tuition and fees ... 34 0
35 Domestic production activities deduction ... 35 0
36 Add lines 23 through 35 ... 36 0
37 Subtract line 36 from line 22. This is your adjusted gross income ► 37 39,633,353,131 95

For Disclosure, Privacy Act, and Paperwork Reduction Act Notice, see separate instructions. Cat. No. 11320B Form **1040** (2016)

230

Bradley - J.: [Franks] and Co-Author: Robert - C.: [Simpson]

Form 1040 (2016) — Page **2**

38	Amount from line 37 (adjusted gross income)	39,633,353,131 95
39a	Check: You were born before January 2, 1952, Blind. Spouse was born before January 2, 1952, Blind. Total boxes checked ▶ 39a	
b	If your spouse itemizes on a separate return or you were a dual-status alien, check here ▶ 39b	
40	Itemized deductions (from Schedule A) or your standard deduction (see left margin)	—
41	Subtract line 40 from line 38	39,633,353,131 95
42	Exemptions. If line 38 is $155,650 or less, multiply $4,050 by the number on line 6d. Otherwise, see instructions	4,050 00
43	Taxable income. Subtract line 42 from line 41. If line 42 is more than line 41, enter -0-	—
44	Tax (see instructions). Check if any from: a Form(s) 8814 b Form 4972 c	—
45	Alternative minimum tax (see instructions). Attach Form 6251	—
46	Excess advance premium tax credit repayment. Attach Form 8962	—
47	Add lines 44, 45, and 46 ▶	—
48	Foreign tax credit. Attach Form 1116 if required — 48	—
49	Credit for child and dependent care expenses. Attach Form 2441 — 49	
50	Education credits from Form 8863, line 19 — 50	
51	Retirement savings contributions credit. Attach Form 8880 — 51	
52	Child tax credit. Attach Schedule 8812, if required — 52	
53	Residential energy credits. Attach Form 5695 — 53	
54	Other credits from Form: a 3800 b 8801 c — 54	
55	Add lines 48 through 54. These are your total credits	—
56	Subtract line 55 from line 47. If line 55 is more than line 47, enter -0- ▶	—
57	Self-employment tax. Attach Schedule SE	—
58	Unreported social security and Medicare tax from Forms: a 4137 b 8919	—
59	Additional tax on IRAs, other qualified retirement plans, etc. Attach Form 5329 if required	—
60a	Household employment taxes from Schedule H	—
b	First-time homebuyer credit repayment. Attach Form 5405 if required	—
61	Health care: individual responsibility (see instructions) Full-year coverage	—
62	Taxes from: a Form 8959 b Form 8960 c Instructions; enter code(s)	—
63	Add lines 56 through 62. This is your total tax ▶	—
64	Federal income tax withheld from Forms W-2 and 1099 — 64	—
65	2016 estimated tax payments and amount applied from 2015 return — 65	—
66a	Earned income credit (EIC) — 66a	—
b	Nontaxable combat pay election 66b	
67	Additional child tax credit. Attach Schedule 8812 — 67	—
68	American opportunity credit from Form 8863, line 8 — 68	—
69	Net premium tax credit. Attach Form 8962 — 69	—
70	Amount paid with request for extension to file — 70	—
71	Excess social security and tier 1 RRTA tax withheld — 71	—
72	Credit for federal tax on fuels. Attach Form 4136 — 72	—
73	Credits from Form: a 2439 b Reserved c 8885 d — 73	—
74	Add lines 64, 65, 66a, and 67 through 73. These are your total payments ▶	—
75	If line 74 is more than line 63, subtract line 63 from line 74. This is the amount you overpaid	—
76a	Amount of line 75 you want refunded to you. If Form 8888 is attached, check here ▶	392,409,436 95
b	Routing number ▶ c Type: Checking Savings	
d	Account number ▶	
77	Amount of line 75 you want applied to your 2017 estimated tax ▶ 77	
78	Amount you owe. Subtract line 74 from line 63. For details on how to pay, see instructions ▶	—
79	Estimated tax penalty (see instructions) 79	

Third Party Designee: Do you want to allow another person to discuss this return with the IRS (see instructions)? Yes. Complete below. No

Sign Here — Your signature: *Bradley - J.: Franks* Date 3-12-17 Your occupation: Author / Self Emp. Daytime phone number 605-432-7920

www.irs.gov/form1040 — Form **1040** (2016)

231

Form **8888**

Department of the Treasury
Internal Revenue Service

Allocation of Refund (Including Savings Bond Purchases)

▶ Information about Form 8888 and its instructions is at *www.irs.gov/form8888*.
▶ Attach to your income tax return.

OMB No. 1545-0074

20**16**

Attachment
Sequence No. **56**

Name(s) shown on return   Bradley - J. : Franks

Your social security number   390-80-401L

Part I   **Direct Deposit**

Complete this part if you want us to directly deposit a portion of your refund to one or more accounts.

1a	Amount to be deposited in first account (see instructions)	1a
b	Routing number ▶c ☐ Checking ☐ Savings	
d	Account number	
2a	Amount to be deposited in second account	2a
b	Routing number ▶c ☐ Checking ☐ Savings	
d	Account number	
3a	Amount to be deposited in third account	3a
b	Routing number ▶c ☐ Checking ☐ Savings	
d	Account number	

Part II   **U.S. Series I Savings Bond Purchases**

Complete this part if you want to buy bonds with a portion of your refund.

⚠ CAUTION   If a name is entered on line 5c or 6c below, co-ownership will be assumed unless the beneficiary box is checked. See instructions for more details.

4	Amount to be used for bond purchases for yourself (and your spouse, if filing jointly)	4
5a	Amount to be used to buy bonds for yourself, your spouse, **or** someone else	5a
b	Enter the owner's name (First then Last) for the bond registration	
c	If you would like to add a co-owner or beneficiary, enter the name here (First then Last). If beneficiary, also check here ▶ ☐	
6a	Amount to be used to buy bonds for yourself, your spouse, **or** someone else	6a
b	Enter the owner's name (First then Last) for the bond registration	
c	If you would like to add a co-owner or beneficiary, enter the name here (First then Last). If beneficiary, also check here ▶ ☐	

Part III   **Paper Check**

Complete this part if you want a portion of your refund to be sent to you as a check.

7	Amount to be refunded by check	7 392,409,436.95

Part IV   **Total Allocation of Refund**

8	Add lines 1a, 2a, 3a, 4, 5a, 6a, and 7. The total must equal the refund amount shown on your tax return	8 392,409,436.95

For Paperwork Reduction Act Notice, see your tax return instructions.   Cat. No. 21858A   Form **8888** (2016)

Form **1040** Department of the Treasury—Internal Revenue Service (99)
U.S. Individual Income Tax Return **2016** OMB No. 1545-0074 IRS Use Only—Do not write or staple in this space.

For the year Jan. 1–Dec. 31, 2016, or other tax year beginning March 22, 2016 ending June 21, 20 17 See separate instructions.

Your first name and initial	Last name	Your social security number
Bradley J.	Franks	

If a joint return, spouse's first name and initial | Last name | Spouse's social security number

Home address (number and street). If you have a P.O. box, see instructions. | Apt. no.
%: 408 S. Lincoln St

▲ Make sure the SSN(s) above and on line 6c are correct.

City, town or post office, state, and ZIP code. If you have a foreign address, also complete spaces below (see instructions).
Milbank, S. D.

Presidential Election Campaign
Check here if you, or your spouse if filing jointly, want $3 to go to this fund. Checking a box below will not change your tax or refund. ☐ You ☐ Spouse

Foreign country name | Foreign province/state/county | Foreign postal code
United States | Grant County | 57252

Filing Status
Check only one box.

1. ☑ Single
2. ☐ Married filing jointly (even if only one had income)
3. ☐ Married filing separately. Enter spouse's SSN above and full name here. ▶
4. ☐ Head of household (with qualifying person). (See instructions.) If the qualifying person is a child but not your dependent, enter this child's name here. ▶
5. ☐ Qualifying widow(er) with dependent child

Exemptions

6a ☐ Yourself. If someone can claim you as a dependent, do not check box 6a . . . . .
b ☐ Spouse . . . .

c Dependents:	(2) Dependent's social security number	(3) Dependent's relationship to you	(4) ✓ If child under age 17 qualifying for child tax credit (see instructions)
(1) First name Last name			
			☐
			☐
			☐
			☐

If more than four dependents, see instructions and check here ▶ ☐

d Total number of exemptions claimed . . . .

Boxes checked on 6a and 6b: 1
No. of children on 6c who:
• lived with you: 0
• did not live with you due to divorce or separation (see instructions): 0
Dependents on 6c not entered above: 0
Add numbers on lines above ▶ 1

Income

Attach Form(s) W-2 here. Also attach Forms W-2G and 1099-R if tax was withheld.

If you did not get a W-2, see instructions.

7	Wages, salaries, tips, etc. Attach Form(s) W-2	7	0 0
8a	Taxable interest. Attach Schedule B if required	8a	396,333,353.32
b	Tax-exempt interest. Do not include on line 8a . . .	8b	
9a	Ordinary dividends. Attach Schedule B if required . . .	9a	
b	Qualified dividends	9b	
10	Taxable refunds, credits, or offsets of state and local income taxes	10	
11	Alimony received	11	
12	Business income or (loss). Attach Schedule C or C-EZ . .	12	
13	Capital gain or (loss). Attach Schedule D if required. If not required, check here ▶ ☐	13	
14	Other gains or (losses). Attach Form 4797	14	
15a	IRA distributions . 15a	b Taxable amount . . .	15b	
16a	Pensions and annuities 16a	b Taxable amount . . .	16b	
17	Rental real estate, royalties, partnerships, S corporations, trusts, etc. Attach Schedule E	17	
18	Farm income or (loss). Attach Schedule F	18	
19	Unemployment compensation	19	
20a	Social security benefits 20a	b Taxable amount . .	20b	
21	Other income. List type and amount Security Interest on Principal	21	96,635,305.31
22	Combine the amounts in the far right column for lines 7 through 21. This is your **total income** ▶	22	492,968,666.63

Adjusted Gross Income

23	Educator expenses	23	
24	Certain business expenses of reservists, performing artists, and fee-basis government officials. Attach Form 2106 or 2106-EZ	24	
25	Health savings account deduction. Attach Form 8889 .	25	
26	Moving expenses. Attach Form 3903	26	
27	Deductible part of self-employment tax. Attach Schedule SE .	27	
28	Self-employed SEP, SIMPLE, and qualified plans . .	28	
29	Self-employed health insurance deduction . . .	29	
30	Penalty on early withdrawal of savings	30	
31a	Alimony paid b Recipient's SSN ▶	31a	
32	IRA deduction	32	
33	Student loan interest deduction	33	
34	Tuition and fees. Attach Form 8917	34	
35	Domestic production activities deduction. Attach Form 8903	35	
36	Add lines 23 through 35	36	0 0
37	Subtract line 36 from line 22. This is your **adjusted gross income** . . . ▶	37	492,968,666.63

For Disclosure, Privacy Act, and Paperwork Reduction Act Notice, see separate instructions. Cat. No. 11320B Form **1040** (2016)

233

Form 1040 (2016)   Page **2**

	38	Amount from line 37 (adjusted gross income)	**38**	3,993,968,666.63

Tax and Credits	**39a**	Check { ☐ You were born before January 2, 1952, ☐ Blind. } Total boxes if: { ☐ Spouse was born before January 2, 1952, ☐ Blind. } checked ▶ 39a	
	b	If your spouse itemizes on a separate return or you were a dual-status alien, check here▶ 39b☐	

Standard Deduction for—	**40**	Itemized deductions (from Schedule A) or your standard deduction (see left margin) . .	**40**	0 0
• People who check any box on line 39a or 39b or who can be claimed as a dependent, see instructions.	**41**	Subtract line 40 from line 38	**41**	3,993,968,666.63
	42	Exemptions. If line 38 is $155,650 or less, multiply $4,050 by the number on line 6d. Otherwise, see instructions	**42**	4,050.00
	43	Taxable income. Subtract line 42 from line 41. If line 42 is more than line 41, enter -0- . .	**43**	
	44	Tax (see instructions). Check if any from: a ☐ Form(s) 8814 b ☐ Form 4972 c ☐ _____	**44**	
• All others:	**45**	Alternative minimum tax (see instructions). Attach Form 6251	**45**	
Single or Married filing separately, $6,300	**46**	Excess advance premium tax credit repayment. Attach Form 8962	**46**	
Married filing jointly or Qualifying widow(er), $12,600	**47**	Add lines 44, 45, and 46 . . . . ▶	**47**	
Head of household, $9,300	**48**	Foreign tax credit. Attach Form 1116 if required	48	
	49	Credit for child and dependent care expenses. Attach Form 2441	49	
	50	Education credits from Form 8863, line 19	50	
	51	Retirement savings contributions credit. Attach Form 8880	51	
	52	Child tax credit. Attach Schedule 8812, if required . . .	52	
	53	Residential energy credits. Attach Form 5695	53	
	54	Other credits from Form: a ☐ 3800 b ☐ 8801 c ☐	54	
	55	Add lines 48 through 54. These are your total credits	**55**	
	56	Subtract line 55 from line 47. If line 55 is more than line 47, enter -0- . . . . . ▶	**56**	

Other Taxes	**57**	Self-employment tax. Attach Schedule SE	**57**	
	58	Unreported social security and Medicare tax from Form: a ☐ 4137 b ☐ 8919 . .	**58**	
	59	Additional tax on IRAs, other qualified retirement plans, etc. Attach Form 5329 if required . .	**59**	
	60a	Household employment taxes from Schedule H	**60a**	
	b	First-time homebuyer credit repayment. Attach Form 5405 if required	**60b**	
	61	Health care: individual responsibility (see instructions) Full-year coverage ☐	**61**	
	62	Taxes from: a ☐ Form 8959 b ☐ Form 8960 c ☐ Instructions; enter code(s)	**62**	
	63	Add lines 56 through 62. This is your total tax . . . . ▶	**63**	

Payments	**64**	Federal income tax withheld from Forms W-2 and 1099 . .	64	
	65	2016 estimated tax payments and amount applied from 2015 return	65	
If you have a qualifying child, attach Schedule EIC.	**66a**	Earned income credit (EIC)	66a	
	b	Nontaxable combat pay election 66b		
	67	Additional child tax credit. Attach Schedule 8812	67	
	68	American opportunity credit from Form 8863, line 8 . . .	68	
	69	Net premium tax credit. Attach Form 8962	69	
	70	Amount paid with request for extension to file	70	
	71	Excess social security and tier 1 RRTA tax withheld	71	
	72	Credit for federal tax on fuels. Attach Form 4136	72	
	73	Credits from Form: a ☐ 2439 b ☐ Reserved c ☐ 8885 d ☐	73	
	74	Add lines 64, 65, 66a, and 67 through 73. These are your total payments . . . . . ▶	**74**	

Refund	**75**	If line 74 is more than line 63, subtract line 63 from line 74. This is the amount you overpaid	**75**	
	76a	Amount of line 75 you want refunded to you. If Form 8888 is attached, check here . . ▶☐	**76a**	3,963,325 31
Direct deposit? See Instructions.	**b**	Routing number _____ ▶c Type: ☐ Checking ☐ Savings		
	d	Account number _____		
	77	Amount of line 75 you want applied to your 2017 estimated tax ▶ 77		
Amount You Owe	**78**	Amount you owe. Subtract line 74 from line 63. For details on how to pay, see instructions ▶	**78**	0 0
	79	Estimated tax penalty (see instructions) 79		

Third Party Designee	Do you want to allow another person to discuss this return with the IRS (see instructions)? ☐ Yes. Complete below. ☐ No	
	Designee's name ▶ Phone no. ▶ Personal Identification number (PIN) ▶	

Sign Here

Under penalties of perjury, I declare that I have examined this return and accompanying schedules and statements, and to the best of my knowledge and belief, they are true, correct, and accurately list all amounts and sources of income I received during the tax year. Declaration of preparer (other than taxpayer) is based on all information of which preparer has any knowledge.

Joint return? See instructions. Keep a copy for your records.	Your signature *Bradley J. Frank* Date 6-21-17 Your occupation Author / Self Emp.	Daytime phone number 605·432·7920
	Spouse's signature. If a joint return, both must sign. Date Spouse's occupation	If the IRS sent you an Identity Protection PIN, enter it here (see inst.) ▶

Paid Preparer Use Only	Print/Type preparer's name Preparer's signature Date	Check ☐ if self-employed PTIN
	Firm's name ▶	Firm's EIN ▶
	Firm's address ▶	Phone no.

www.irs.gov/form1040   Form **1040** (2016)

Form 8888

Allocation of Refund (Including Savings Bond Purchases)

OMB No. 1545-0074

Department of the Treasury
Internal Revenue Service

▶ Information about Form 8888 and its instructions is at *www.irs.gov/form8888*.
▶ Attach to your income tax return.

2016

Attachment
Sequence No. **56**

Name(s) shown on return: *Bradley - J. Franks*

Your social security number: *390-80-4016*

Part I   Direct Deposit

Complete this part if you want us to directly deposit a portion of your refund to one or more accounts.

1a	Amount to be deposited in first account (see instructions)	1a
b	Routing number [ ] ▶c ☐ Checking ☐ Savings	
d	Account number [ ]	
2a	Amount to be deposited in second account	2a
b	Routing number [ ] ▶c ☐ Checking ☐ Savings	
d	Account number [ ]	
3a	Amount to be deposited in third account	3a
b	Routing number [ ] ▶c ☐ Checking ☐ Savings	
d	Account number [ ]	

Part II   U.S. Series I Savings Bond Purchases

Complete this part if you want to buy paper bonds with a portion of your refund.

⚠ **CAUTION** If a name is entered on line 5c or 6c below, co-ownership will be assumed unless the beneficiary box is checked. See instructions for more details.

4   Amount to be used for bond purchases for yourself (and your spouse, if filing jointly)   4

5a   Amount to be used to buy bonds for yourself, your spouse, **or** someone else 5a
  b   Enter the owner's name (First then Last) for the bond registration
[ ]

  c   If you would like to add a co-owner or beneficiary, enter the name here (First then Last). If beneficiary, also check here ▶ ☐
[ ]

6a   Amount to be used to buy bonds for yourself, your spouse, **or** someone else 6a
  b   Enter the owner's name (First then Last) for the bond registration
[ ]

  c   If you would like to add a co-owner or beneficiary, enter the name here (First then Last). If beneficiary, also check here ▶ ☐
[ ]

Part III   Paper Check

Complete this part if you want a portion of your refund to be sent to you as a check.

7   Amount to be refunded by check   7   *3963,325 | 31*

Part IV   Total Allocation of Refund

8   Add lines 1a, 2a, 3a, 4, 5a, 6a, and 7. The total must equal the refund amount shown on your tax return   8   *3963,325 | 31*

For Paperwork Reduction Act Notice, see your tax return instructions.   Cat. No. 21858A   Form **8888** (2016)

Form **1040**	Department of the Treasury—Internal Revenue Service (99) **U.S. Individual Income Tax Return**	**2016**	OMB No. 1545-0074	IRS Use Only—Do not write or staple in this space.

For the year Jan. 1–Dec. 31, 2016, or other tax year beginning **Oct. 21**, 2016, ending **Dec. 21**, 20 **16**   See separate instructions.

Your first name and initial **Bradley J.**   Last name **Franks**   Your social security number **390-80-4016**

If a joint return, spouse's first name and initial   Last name   Spouse's social security number

Home address (number and street). If you have a P.O. box, see instructions. **To: 408 South Lincoln Street**   Apt. no.

City, town or post office, state, and ZIP code. If you have a foreign address, also complete spaces below (see instructions). **Milbank, South Dakota 57252**

Foreign country name **United States**   Foreign province/state/county **Grant County**   Foreign postal code **57252**

Presidential Election Campaign — Check here if you, or your spouse if filing jointly, want $3 to go to this fund. Checking a box below will not change your tax or refund. ☐ You ☐ Spouse

Filing Status
Check only one box.
1. ☑ Single
2. ☐ Married filing jointly (even if only one had income)
3. ☐ Married filing separately. Enter spouse's SSN above and full name here. ▶
4. ☐ Head of household (with qualifying person). (See instructions.) If the qualifying person is a child but not your dependent, enter this child's name here. ▶
5. ☐ Qualifying widow(er) with dependent child

Exemptions
6a ☑ Yourself. If someone can claim you as a dependent, do not check box 6a
b ☐ Spouse
c Dependents:
  (1) First name   Last name   (2) Dependent's social security number   (3) Dependent's relationship to you   (4) ✓ if child under age 17 qualifying for child tax credit (see instructions)

Boxes checked on 6a and 6b: **1**
No. of children on 6c who:
• lived with you
• did not live with you due to divorce or separation
Dependents on 6c not entered above
If more than four dependents, see instructions and check here ▶ ☐
d Total number of exemptions claimed   Add numbers on lines above ▶ **1**

Income
Attach Form(s) W-2 here. Also attach Forms W-2G and 1099-R if tax was withheld.
If you did not get a W-2, see instructions.

7	Wages, salaries, tips, etc. Attach Form(s) W-2	7	⊖
8a	Taxable interest. Attach Schedule B if required	8a	485,655,243 75
b	Tax-exempt interest. Do not include on line 8a	8b	
9a	Ordinary dividends. Attach Schedule B if required	9a	⊖
b	Qualified dividends	9b	
10	Taxable refunds, credits, or offsets of state and local income taxes	10	⊖
11	Alimony received	11	⊖
12	Business income or (loss). Attach Schedule C or C-EZ	12	⊖
13	Capital gain or (loss). Attach Schedule D if required. If not required, check here ▶ ☐	13	⊖
14	Other gains or (losses). Attach Form 4797	14	⊖
15a	IRA distributions 15a	b Taxable amount	15b	⊖
16a	Pensions and annuities 16a	b Taxable amount	16b	⊖
17	Rental real estate, royalties, partnerships, S corporations, trusts, etc. Attach Schedule E	17	⊖
18	Farm income or (loss). Attach Schedule F	18	⊖
19	Unemployment compensation	19	⊖
20a	Social security benefits 20a	b Taxable amount	20b	⊖
21	Other income. List type and amount **Lien / "Security"**	21	38,852,419,500 00
22	Combine the amounts in the far right column for lines 7 through 21. This is your **total income** ▶	22	39,338,074,743 75

Adjusted Gross Income

23	Educator expenses	23	⊖
24	Certain business expenses of reservists, performing artists, and fee-basis government officials. Attach Form 2106 or 2106-EZ	24	⊖
25	Health savings account deduction. Attach Form 8889	25	⊖
26	Moving expenses. Attach Form 3903	26	⊖
27	Deductible part of self-employment tax. Attach Schedule SE	27	⊖
28	Self-employed SEP, SIMPLE, and qualified plans	28	⊖
29	Self-employed health insurance deduction	29	⊖
30	Penalty on early withdrawal of savings	30	⊖
31a	Alimony paid b Recipient's SSN ▶	31a	⊖
32	IRA deduction	32	⊖
33	Student loan interest deduction	33	⊖
34	Tuition and fees. Attach Form 8917	34	⊖
35	Domestic production activities deduction. Attach Form 8903	35	⊖
36	Add lines 23 through 35	36	⊖
37	Subtract line 36 from line 22. This is your **adjusted gross income** ▶	37	39,338,074,743 75

For Disclosure, Privacy Act, and Paperwork Reduction Act Notice, see separate instructions.   Cat. No. 11320B   Form **1040** (2016)

Bradley - J.: [Franks] and Co-Author: Robert - C.: [Simpson]

Form 1040 (2016) Page **2**

Tax and Credits	38	Amount from line 37 (adjusted gross income)	38	59,330,074,743 75
	39a	Check if: ☐ You were born before January 2, 1952, ☐ Blind. ☐ Spouse was born before January 2, 1952, ☐ Blind. Total boxes checked ▶ 39a		
	b	If your spouse itemizes on a separate return or you were a dual-status alien, check here▶ 39b☐		
Standard Deduction for— • People who check any box on line 39a or 39b or who can be claimed as a dependent, see instructions. • All others: Single or Married filing separately, $6,300 Married filing jointly or Qualifying widow(er), $12,600 Head of household, $9,300	40	Itemized deductions (from Schedule A) or your standard deduction (see left margin)	40	—
	41	Subtract line 40 from line 38	41	59,330,074,743 75
	42	Exemptions. If line 38 is $155,650 or less, multiply $4,050 by the number on line 6d. Otherwise, see instructions	42	4050 00
	43	Taxable income. Subtract line 42 from line 41. If line 42 is more than line 41, enter -0-	43	—
	44	Tax (see instructions). Check if any from: a ☐ Form(s) 8814 b ☐ Form 4972 c ☐	44	—
	45	Alternative minimum tax (see instructions). Attach Form 6251	45	—
	46	Excess advance premium tax credit repayment. Attach Form 8962	46	—
	47	Add lines 44, 45, and 46 ▶	47	—
	48	Foreign tax credit. Attach Form 1116 if required	48 —	
	49	Credit for child and dependent care expenses. Attach Form 2441	49 —	
	50	Education credits from Form 8863, line 19	50 —	
	51	Retirement savings contributions credit. Attach Form 8880	51 —	
	52	Child tax credit. Attach Schedule 8812, if required	52 —	
	53	Residential energy credits. Attach Form 5695	53 —	
	54	Other credits from Form: a ☐ 3800 b ☐ 8801 c ☐	54 —	
	55	Add lines 48 through 54. These are your total credits	55	—
	56	Subtract line 55 from line 47. If line 55 is more than line 47, enter -0- ▶	56	—
Other Taxes	57	Self-employment tax. Attach Schedule SE	57	—
	58	Unreported social security and Medicare tax from Form: a ☐ 4137 b ☐ 8919	58	—
	59	Additional tax on IRAs, other qualified retirement plans, etc. Attach Form 5329 if required	59	—
	60a	Household employment taxes from Schedule H	60a	—
	b	First-time homebuyer credit repayment. Attach Form 5405 if required	60b	—
	61	Health care: individual responsibility (see instructions) Full-year coverage ☐	61	—
	62	Taxes from: a ☐ Form 8959 b ☐ Form 8960 c ☐ Instructions; enter code(s)	62	—
	63	Add lines 56 through 62. This is your total tax ▶	63	—
Payments If you have a qualifying child, attach Schedule EIC.	64	Federal income tax withheld from Forms W-2 and 1099	64 —	
	65	2016 estimated tax payments and amount applied from 2015 return	65 —	
	66a	Earned income credit (EIC)	66a —	
	b	Nontaxable combat pay election 66b		
	67	Additional child tax credit. Attach Schedule 8812	67 —	
	68	American opportunity credit from Form 8863, line 8	68 —	
	69	Net premium tax credit. Attach Form 8962	69 —	
	70	Amount paid with request for extension to file	70 —	
	71	Excess social security and tier 1 RRTA tax withheld	71 —	
	72	Credit for federal tax on fuels. Attach Form 4136	72 —	
	73	Credits from Form: a ☐ 2439 b ☐ Reserved c ☐ 8885 d ☐	73 —	
	74	Add lines 64, 65, 66a, and 67 through 73. These are your total payments ▶	74	—
Refund Direct deposit? See instructions.	75	If line 74 is more than line 63, subtract line 63 from line 74. This is the amount you overpaid	75	
	76a	Amount of line 75 you want refunded to you. If Form 8888 is attached, check here ▶☑	76a	485,655,243 75
	b	Routing number ▶c Type: ☐ Checking ☐ Savings		
	d	Account number		
	77	Amount of line 75 you want applied to your 2017 estimated tax ▶ 77		
Amount You Owe	78	Amount you owe. Subtract line 74 from line 63. For details on how to pay, see instructions ▶	78	—
	79	Estimated tax penalty (see instructions) 79		

Third Party Designee Do you want to allow another person to discuss this return with the IRS (see instructions)? ☐ **Yes.** Complete below. ☐ **No**

Designee's name ▶   Phone no. ▶   Personal identification number (PIN) ▶

Sign Here Under penalties of perjury, I declare that I have examined this return and accompanying schedules and statements, and to the best of my knowledge and belief, they are true, correct, and accurately list all amounts and sources of income I received during the tax year. Declaration of preparer (other than taxpayer) is based on all information of which preparer has any knowledge.

Joint return? See instructions. Keep a copy for your records.

Your signature: *Bradley J. Franks* Date 1-21-17 Your occupation: Author / Self Emp. Daytime phone number 605-432-7920

Spouse's signature. If a joint return, both must sign. Date Spouse's occupation If the IRS sent you an identity Protection PIN, enter it here (see inst.)

Paid Preparer Use Only

Print/Type preparer's name | Preparer's signature | Date | Check ☐ if self-employed | PTIN

Firm's name ▶ Firm's EIN ▶

Firm's address ▶ Phone no.

www.irs.gov/form1040 Form **1040** (2016)

237

The Death of America

Form **8888** | **Allocation of Refund (Including Savings Bond Purchases)** | OMB No. 1545-0074

Department of the Treasury
Internal Revenue Service

▶ Information about Form 8888 and its instructions is at *www.irs.gov/form8888.*
▶ Attach to your income tax return.

2016
Attachment Sequence No. **56**

Name(s) shown on return: Bradley - J. Franks

Your social security number: 390 - 80 - 4016

Part I Direct Deposit

Complete this part if you want us to directly deposit a portion of your refund to one or more accounts.

1a Amount to be deposited in first account (see instructions) 1a

b Routing number ▶c ☐ Checking ☐ Savings

d Account number

2a Amount to be deposited in second account 2a

b Routing number ▶c ☐ Checking ☐ Savings

d Account number

3a Amount to be deposited in third account 3a

b Routing number ▶c ☐ Checking ☐ Savings

d Account number

Part II U.S. Series I Savings Bond Purchases

Complete this part if you want to buy paper bonds with a portion of your refund.

⚠ CAUTION: If a name is entered on line 5c or 6c below, co-ownership will be assumed unless the beneficiary box is checked. See instructions for more details.

4 Amount to be used for bond purchases for yourself (and your spouse, if filing jointly) 4

5a Amount to be used to buy bonds for yourself, your spouse, or someone else 5a
b Enter the owner's name (First then Last) for the bond registration

c If you would like to add a co-owner or beneficiary, enter the name here (First then Last). If beneficiary, also check here ▶ ☐

6a Amount to be used to buy bonds for yourself, your spouse, or someone else 6a
b Enter the owner's name (First then Last) for the bond registration

c If you would like to add a co-owner or beneficiary, enter the name here (First then Last). If beneficiary, also check here ▶ ☐

Part III Paper Check

Complete this part if you want a portion of your refund to be sent to you as a check.

7 Amount to be refunded by check 7 485,655,243 75

Part IV Total Allocation of Refund

8 Add lines 1a, 2a, 3a, 4, 5a, 6a, and 7. The total must equal the refund amount shown on your tax return 8 485,655,243 75

For Paperwork Reduction Act Notice, see your tax return instructions. Cat. No. 21858A Form **8888** (2016)

238

When the Foreign-Fiction-Corporate-Government of the State of California and all of its undeclared Foreign-Agents refused to answer the Liens, the contracts and the allegations that we sent to them we took that as an acceptance of the contract and the UCC-Lien in its entirety.

After three months of non-communication and the presumption of the acceptance, we added interest-rates to the Amount-due. Interest Rates on an account is considered "Income" by their laws.

Therefore, we reported it to the I. R. S. to "voluntarily" pay those taxes.

In June 28, 2017 I sent a response for the threat that came from the Department of the Treasury; Internal Revenue Service; Fresno, California; [93888-0002]. These are direct quotes from that communication:

The response was for what they called a CP11:

"Enclosed is a copy of the response from your Administration."

"I would like to thank you and your administration of the "**VALIDATION**" of our "**SECURITY**" that is owned and controlled by Bradley – J.: [Franks] and Robert - C.: [Simpson]."

"We would be willing to sell our "Security" to the Department of the Treasury".

"If not interested in the purchase of this "Security" we will seek to sell it to Foreign Interests under N. A. F. T. A. and G. A. T. T.".

"As far as your threat of an Audit…I have nothing to hide and plenty to prove".

Department of the Treasury
Internal Revenue Service
Austin, TX 73301-0030

IRS

	WI
Notice	CP503
Tax Year	2016
Notice date	July 24, 2017
Social Security number	390-80-4016
To contact us	Phone 1-800-829-0922
Your Caller ID	813596
Page 1 of 5	

001808.626555.442493.3865 2 AB 0.403 1339

BRADLEY J FRANKS
408 S LINCOLN ST
MILBANK SD 57252-2326

001808

Second reminder: You have unpaid taxes for 2016

Amount due: $135,975,058.43

As we notified you before, our records show you have unpaid taxes for the tax year ended December 31, 2016 (Form 1040). If you don't pay $135,975,058.43 by August 3, 2017, the amount of interest will increase and additional penalties may apply.

If you already have an installment or payment agreement in place for this tax year, then continue with that agreement.

Billing Summary

Amount you owed	$134,787,942.88
Failure-to-pay penalty	669,156.37
Interest charges	517,959.18
Amount due by August 3, 2017	**$135,975,058.43**

Continued on back...

IRS

BRADLEY J FRANKS
408 S LINCOLN ST
MILBANK SD 57252-2326

Notice	CP503
Notice date	July 24, 2017
Social Security number	390-80-4016

Payment

- Make your check or money order payable to the United States Treasury.
- Write your Social Security number (390-80-4016), the tax year (2016), and the form number (1040) on your payment and any correspondence.

Amount due by
August 3, 2017

$135,975,058.43

INTERNAL REVENUE SERVICE
AUSTIN, TX 73301-0025

390804016 LO FRAN 30 0 201612 670 13597505843

	WI
Notice	CP503
Tax Year	2016
Notice date	July 24, 2017
Social Security number	390-80-4016
Page 2 of 5	

What you need to do immediately	**If you agree with the amount due and you're not working with an IRS representative**

If you agree with the amount due and you're not working with an IRS representative

- Pay the amount due of $135,975,058.43 by August 3, 2017, to avoid additional interest and applicable penalty charges.
- Pay online or mail a check or money order with the attached payment stub. **You can pay online now at www.irs.gov/payments.**

If we notified you that we suspended enforced collection on your account because it would create a financial hardship (meaning you would be unable to pay basic reasonable living expenses if we levied) and your financial condition has not changed, you don't need to do anything.

If you disagree with the amount due

Call us at 1-800-829-0922 to review your account with a representative. Be sure to have your account information available when you call.

We'll assume you agree with the information in this notice if we don't hear from you.

241

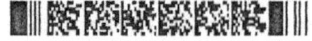

	WI
Notice	CP503
Tax Year	2016
Notice date	July 24, 2017
Social Security number	390-80-4016
Page 3 of 5	

001808

Payment options

Pay now electronically

We offer free payment options to securely pay your tax bill directly from your checking or savings account. When you pay online or from your mobile device, you can:

- Receive instant confirmation of your payment
- Schedule payments in advance
- Modify or cancel a payment before the due date

You can also pay by debit or credit card for a small fee. To see all of our payment options, visit www.irs.gov/payments.

Payment plans

If you can't pay the full amount you owe, pay as much as you can now and make arrangements to pay your remaining balance. Visit www.irs.gov/paymentplan for more information on installment agreements and online payment agreements. You can also call us at 1-800-829-0922 to discuss your options.

Offer in Compromise

An offer in compromise allows you to settle your tax debt for less than the full amount you owe. If we accept your offer, you can pay with either a lump sum cash payment plan or periodic payment plan. To see if you qualify, use the Offer in Compromise Pre-Qualifier tool on our website. For more information, visit www.irs.gov/offers.

Account balance and payment history

For information on how to obtain your current account balance or payment history, go to www.irs.gov/balancedue.

If you already paid your balance in full within the past 21 days or made payment arrangements, please disregard this notice.

If you think we made a mistake, call 1-800-829-0922 to review your account.

If we don't hear from you

Pay $135,975,058.43 by August 3, 2017, to avoid additional interest and applicable penalty charges.

We may file a Notice of Federal Tax Lien against you. A tax lien generally attaches to all property you currently own and will attach to all property you acquire in the future. The Notice of Federal Tax Lien is a public record, and it can damage your credit or make it difficult for you to get credit (such as a loan or credit card).

Continued on back...

Notice	CP503
	WI
Tax Year	2016
Notice date	July 24, 2017
Social Security number	390-80-4016
Page 4 of 5

Penalties

We are required by law to charge any applicable penalties.

Failure-to-pay

Description	Amount
Total failure-to-pay	$669,156.37

We assess a 1/2% monthly penalty for not paying the tax you owe by the due date. We base the monthly penalty for paying late on the net unpaid tax at the beginning of each penalty month following the payment due date for that tax. This penalty applies even if you filed the return on time.

We charge the penalty for each month or part of a month the payment is late; however, the penalty can't be more than 25% in total.
- The due date for payment of the tax shown on a return generally is the return due date, without regard to extensions.
- The due date for paying increases in tax is within 21 days of the date of our notice demanding payment (10 business days if the amount in the notice is $100,000 or more).

If we issue a Notice of Intent to Levy and you don't pay the balance due within 10 days of the date of the notice, the penalty for paying late increases to 1% per month.

For individuals who filed on time, the penalty decreases to 1/4% per month while an approved installment agreement with the IRS is in effect for payment of that tax. (Internal Revenue Code Section 6651)

For a detailed calculation of your penalty charges, call 1-800-829-0922.

Removal or reduction of penalties

We understand that circumstances—such as serious illness or injury, a family member's death, or loss of financial records due to natural disaster—may make it difficult for you to meet your taxpayer responsibility in a timely manner.

If you would like us to consider removing or reducing any of your penalty charges, please do the following:
- Identify which penalty charges you would like us to remove or reduce (e.g., 2005 late filing penalty).
- For each penalty charge, explain why you believe removal or reduction is appropriate.
- Sign your statement, and mail it to us along with any supporting documents.

We will review your statement and let you know whether we accept your explanation as reasonable cause to reduce or remove the penalty charge(s).

243

	WI
Notice	CP503
Tax Year	2016
Notice date	July 24, 2017
Social Security number	390-80-4016
Page 5 of 5	

001808

Penalties—continued

Removal of penalties due to erroneous written advice from the IRS

If you were penalized based on written advice from the IRS, we will remove the penalty if you meet the following criteria:

- If you sent a written request to the IRS for written advice on a specific issue
- You gave us complete and accurate information
- You received written advice from us
- You reasonably relied on our written advice and were penalized based on that advice

To request removal of penalties based on erroneous written advice from us, submit a completed Claim for Refund and Request for Abatement (Form 843) to the IRS service center where you filed your tax return. For a copy of the form or to find your IRS service center, go to www.irs.gov or call 1-800-829-0922.

Interest charges

We are required by law to charge interest when you do not pay your liability on time. Generally, we calculate interest from the due date of your return (regardless of extensions) until you pay the amount you owe in full, including accrued interest and any penalty charges. Interest on some penalties accrues from the date we notify you of the penalty until it is paid in full. Interest on other penalties, such as failure to file a tax return, starts from the due date or extended due date of the return. Interest rates are variable and may change quarterly. (Internal Revenue Code Section 6601)

Description	Amount
Total interest	$517,959.18

The table below shows the rates used to calculate the interest on your unpaid amount due. For a detailed calculation of your interest, call 1-800-829-0922.

Period	Interest Rate
October 1, 2016 through December 31, 2016	4%
January 1, 2017 through March 31, 2017	4%

Additional information

- Visit www.irs.gov/cp503
- You may find the following publications helpful:
  - Publication 1, Your Rights as a Taxpayer
  - Publication 594, The Collection Process
- For tax forms, instructions, and publications, visit www.irs.gov or call 1-800-TAX-FORM (1-800-829-3676).
- Paying online is convenient, secure, and ensures timely receipt of your payment. To pay your taxes online or for more information, go to www.irs.gov/payments.
- You can contact us by mail at the following address. Be sure to include your social security number, the tax year, and the form number you are writing about.
  Internal Revenue Service
  Austin, TX 73301-0025
- Keep this notice for your records.

If you need assistance, please don't hesitate to contact us.

Department of the Treasury
Internal Revenue Service
Austin, TX 73301-0030

IRS

9307 1107 5620 4205 9215 54

074872.626553.442459.3863 2 MB 0.423 1134

	WI
Notice	CP504
Tax Year	2016
Notice date	July 24, 2017
Social Security number	390-80-4016
To contact us	Phone 1-800-829-0922
Your Caller ID	813596
Page 1 of 4	

074872

BRADLEY J FRANKS
408 S LINCOLN ST
MILBANK SD 57252-2326

Notice of Intent to seize (levy) your property or rights to property

Amount due immediately: $15,092.33

This is a notice of intent to levy your state tax refund or other property. As we notified you before, our records show you have unpaid taxes for the tax year ending December 31, 2016 (Form CIVPEN). If you don't call us immediately to make payment arrangements or pay the amount due, we may levy your property or rights to property and apply it to the $15,092.33 you owe.

Billing Summary

Amount you owed	$15,000.00
Interest charges	92.33
Amount due immediately	**$15,092.33**

Continued on back...

IRS

BRADLEY J FRANKS
408 S LINCOLN ST
MILBANK SD 57252-2326

Notice	CP504
Notice date	July 24, 2017
Social Security number	390-80-4016

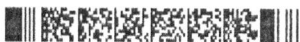

Payment

- Make your check or money order payable to the United States Treasury.
- Write your Social Security number (390-80-4016), the tax year (2016), and the form number (CIVPEN) on your payment and any correspondence.

Amount due immediately	$15,092.33

INTERNAL REVENUE SERVICE
AUSTIN, TX 73301-0025

390804016 LO FRAN 55 0 201612 670 00001509233

245

What you need to do immediately

If you agree with the amount due and you're not working with an IRS representative

- Pay the amount due of $15,092.33 immediately or we may file Notice of Federal Tax Lien, the amount of interest will increase, and additional penalties may apply.
- Pay online or mail a check or money order with the attached payment stub. **You can pay online now at www.irs.gov/payments.**

If we notified you that we suspended enforced collection on your account because it would create a financial hardship (meaning you would be unable to pay basic reasonable living expenses if we levied) and your financial condition has not changed, you don't need to do anything.

If you disagree with the amount due

Call us at 1-800-829-0922 to review your account with a representative. Be sure to have your account information available when you call. We'll assume you agree with the information in this notice if we don't hear from you.

What you need to know

Notice of Intent to Levy

This notice is your Notice of Intent to Levy (Internal Revenue Code Section 6331 (d).

If you don't pay the amount due by August 3, 2017, we can levy your state tax refund or other property rights or rights to property. Property or rights to property includes:

- Wages, real estate commissions, and other income
- Bank accounts
- Personal assets (e.g., your car and home)
- Social security benefits

Rights to request an appeal

If you don't agree, you have the right to request an appeal under the Collection Appeals Program. Please call 1-800-829-0922 or send us a Collection Appeals Request (Form 9423) to the address at the top of the notice by August 3, 2017.

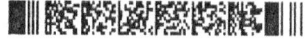

	WI
Notice	CP504
Tax Year	2016
Notice date	July 24, 2017
Social Security number	390-80-4016
Page 3 of 4	

074872

What you need to know — continued	Denial or revocation of United States passport

Denial or revocation of United States passport

On December 4, 2015, as part of the Fixing America's Surface Transportation (FAST) Act, Congress enacted section 7345 of the Internal Revenue Code, which requires the Internal Revenue Service to notify the State Department of taxpayers certified as owing a seriously delinquent tax debt. The FAST Act generally prohibits the State Department from issuing or renewing a passport to a taxpayer with seriously delinquent tax debt.

Seriously delinquent tax debt means an unpaid, legally enforceable federal tax debt of an individual totaling more than $50,000 for which, a Notice of Federal Tax lien has been filed and all administrative remedies under IRC § 6320 have lapsed or been exhausted, or a levy has been issued. If you are individually liable for tax debt (including penalties and interest) totaling more than $50,000 and you do not pay the amount you owe or make alternate arrangements to pay, we may notify the State Department that your tax debt is seriously delinquent. The State Department generally will not issue or renew a passport to you after we make this notification. If you currently have a valid passport, the State Department may revoke your passport or limit your ability to travel outside of the United States. Additional information on passport certification is available at www.irs.gov/passports.

Payment options

Pay now electronically

We offer free payment options to securely pay your tax bill directly from your checking account or savings account. When you pay online or from your mobile device, you can:

- Receive instant confirmation of your payment
- Schedule payments in advance
- Modify or cancel a payment before the due date

Payment plans

If you can't pay the full amount you owe, pay as much as you can now and make arrangements to pay your remaining balance. Visit www.irs.gov/paymentplan for more information on installment agreements and online payment agreements. You can also call us at 1-800-829-0922 to discuss your options.

Offer in Compromise

An offer in compromise allows you to settle your tax debt for less than the full amount you owe. If we accept your offer, you can pay with either a lump sum cash payment plan or periodic payment plan. To see if you qualify, use the Offer in Compromise Pre-Qualifier tool on our website. For more information, visit www.irs.gov/offers.

Account balance and payment history

For information on how to obtain your current account balance or payment history, go to www.irs.gov/balancedue.

If you've already paid your balance in full within the past 21 days or made payment arrangements, please disregard this notice.

If you think we made a mistake, call 1-800-829-0922 to review your account

Continued on back...

The Death of America

	WI
Notice	CP504
Tax Year	2016
Notice date	July 24, 2017
Social Security number	390-80-4016
Page 4 of 4	

If we don't hear from you

If you don't pay the amount due immediately or make payment arrangements, we can file a Notice of Federal Tax Lien on your property at any time or we may levy.

If we file a lien, it may be difficult to sell or borrow against your property. A tax lien will also appear on your credit report – which may harm your credit rating – and your creditors would also be publicly notified that the IRS has priority to seize your property.

Interest charges

We are required by law to charge interest when you do not pay your liability on time. Generally, we calculate interest from the due date of your return (regardless of extensions) until you pay the amount you owe in full, including accrued interest and any penalty charges. Interest on some penalties accrues from the date we notify you of the penalty until it is paid in full. Interest on other penalties, such as failure to file a tax return, starts from the due date or extended due date of the return. Interest rates are variable and may change quarterly. (Internal Revenue Code Section 6601)

Description	Amount
Total interest	**$92.33**

The table below shows the rates used to calculate the interest on your unpaid amount due. For a detailed calculation of your interest, call 1-800-829-0922.

Period	Interest Rate
October 1, 2016 through December 31, 2016	4%
January 1, 2017 through March 31, 2017	4%

Additional information

- Visit www.irs.gov/cp504
- You may find the following publications helpful:
  - Publication 1, Your Rights as a Taxpayer
- For tax forms, instructions, and publications, visit www.irs.gov or call 1-800-TAX-FORM (1-800-829-3676).
- Paying online is convenient, secure, and ensures timely receipt of your payment. To pay your taxes online or for more information, go to www.irs.gov/payments.
- Review the enclosed document: IRS Collection Process (Publication 594).
- You can contact us by mail at the following address. Be sure to include your social security number, the tax year, and the form number you are writing about.
  Internal Revenue Service
  Austin, TX 73301-0025
- Generally, we deal directly with taxpayers or their authorized representatives. However, occasionally we need to speak with other people, such as employees, employers, banks, or neighbors to gather or verify account information. If we contact a third party, the law prohibits us from sharing any more information than is necessary to obtain or verify what we need to know. You have the right to request a list of individuals we contact about your account.
- Keep this notice for your records

If you need assistance, please don't hesitate to contact us.

248

Department of the Treasury
Internal Revenue Service
Austin, TX 73301-0010

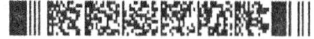

IRS

Notice	CP15
Tax Year	2016
Notice date	May 29, 2017
Social Security number	390-80-4016
To contact us	1-800-829-0922
Your Caller ID	813596
Page 1 of 2	18H

149182.610366.369556.2323 1 AB 0.403 538

BRADLEY J FRANKS
408 S LINCOLN ST
MILBANK SD 57252-2326

149182

Notice of Penalty Charge

666

You have been charged a penalty under Section 6702(a) of the Internal Revenue Code for Civil Penalty for Frivolous Tax Returns.

TAX STATEMENT

Prior Balance	$0.00
Penalty Assessment	$15,000.00
Interest	$0.00
Bad Check Penalty	$0.00
Balance Due	**$15,000.00**

IRS

BRADLEY J FRANKS
408 S LINCOLN ST
MILBANK SD 57252-2326

Notice	CP15
Notice date	May 29, 2017
Social Security number	390-80-4016

Payment

- Make your check or money order payable to the United States Treasury.
- Write your Social Security number (390-80-4016), the tax year (2016), and the form number (CVL PEN) on your payment and any correspondence.

Amount due by June 19, 2017	$15,000.00

INTERNAL REVENUE SERVICE
AUSTIN, TX 73301-0010

390804016 LO FRAN 55 0 201612 670 00001500000

249

Department of the Treasury
Internal Revenue Service
Austin, TX 73301-0010

Notice	CP11
Tax Year	2016
Notice date	June 26, 2017
Social Security number	390-80-4016
To contact us	1-800-829-0922
Your Caller ID	813596
Page 1 of 4	89H

019901.620744.417131.3320 1 MB 0.423 701

BRADLEY J FRANKS
408 S LINCOLN ST
MILBANK SD 57252-2326

019901

Changes to your 2016 Form 1040

Amount due: $134,787,942.88

We found miscalculations on your 2016 Form 1040, which affect the following areas of your return:
- Tax Computation
- Standard Deduction
- Income

We changed your return to correct these errors. As a result, you owe $134,787,942.88.

Billing Summary

Tax you owed	$133,831,273.37
Payments you made	0.00
Interest charges	956,669.51
Amount due by July 3, 2017	$134,787,942.88

Continued on back...

IRS

BRADLEY J FRANKS
408 S LINCOLN ST
MILBANK SD 57252-2326

Notice	CP11
Notice date	June 26, 2017
Social Security number	390-80-4016

Payment

- Make your check or money order payable to the United States Treasury.
- Write your Social Security number (390-80-4016), the tax year (2016), and the form number (1040) on your payment and any correspondence.

Amount due by July 3, 2017 — $134,787,942.88

INTERNAL REVENUE SERVICE
AUSTIN, TX 73301-0010

390804016 LO FRAN 30 0 201612 670 13478794288

250

Notice	CP11
Tax Year	2016
Notice date	June 26, 2017
Social Security number	390-80-4016
Page 3 of 4	89H

Payment options – continued

019901

You can also pay by debit or credit card for a small fee. To see all of our payment options, visit www.irs.gov/payments.

Payment plans
If you can't pay the full amount you owe, pay as much as you can now and make arrangements to pay your remaining balance. Visit www.irs.gov/paymentplan for more information on installment agreements and online payment agreements. You can also call us at 1-800-829-0922 to discuss your options.

Offer in Compromise
An offer in compromise allows you to settle your tax debt for less than the full amount you owe. If we accept your offer, you can pay with either a lump sum cash payment plan or periodic payment plan. To see if you qualify, use the Offer in Compromise Pre-Qualifier tool on our website. For more information, visit www.irs.gov/offers.

Account balance and payment history
For information on how to obtain your current account balance or payment history, go to www.irs.gov/balancedue.

If you already paid your balance in full within the past 21 days or made payment arrangements, please disregard this notice.

If you think we made a mistake, call 1-800-829-0922 to review your account.

If we don't hear from you

- Pay $134,787,942.88 by July 3, 2017, to avoid penalty and interest charges.

Changes to your 2016 tax return

Information was changed because of the following:
- We changed the amount of total income on Line 22 of your Form 1040 because there was an error in the computation.
- We changed the amount claimed as standard deduction on line 40 of your Form 1040:
- No amount was entered for the standard deduction, **or**
- The amount entered for the standard deduction was incorrect for the filing status claimed on your return.
- We changed the refund amount on Line 76a or the amount you owe on Line 78 of your Form 1040 because the amount entered on your tax return was computed incorrectly.

Your tax calculations

Description	Your calculations	IRS calculations
Adjusted gross income, line 37	$8,074,743.00	$338,074,743.00
Taxable income, line 43	0.00	338,068,443.00
Total tax, line 63	$0.00	$133,831,273.37

Continued on back...

251

Notice	CP11
Tax Year	2016
Notice date	June 26, 2017
Social Security number	390-80-4016
Page 4 of 4	89H

Changes to your 2016 tax return — continued

Your payments and credits

Description	IRS calculations
Income tax withheld, line 64	$0.00
Estimated tax payments, line 65	0.00
Other credits, lines 66a, 67-73	0.00
Other payments	0.00
Total payments and credits	**$0.00**

Interest charges

We are required by law to charge interest when you do not pay your liability on time. Generally, we calculate interest from the due date of your return (regardless of extensions) until you pay the amount you owe in full, including accrued interest and any penalty charges. Interest on some penalties accrues from the date we notify you of the penalty until it is paid in full. Interest on other penalties, such as failure to file a tax return, starts from the due date or extended due date of the return. Interest rates are variable and may change quarterly. (Internal Revenue Code section 6601)

Description	Amount
Total interest	**$956,669.51**

The table below shows the rates used to calculate the interest on your unpaid amount due. For a detailed calculation of your interest, call 1-800-829-0922.

Period	Interest rate
Beginning April 1, 2016	4%

Additional information

- Visit www.irs.gov/cp11
- You may find the following publications helpful:
  - Publication 1, Your Rights as a Taxpayer
  - Publication 594, The Collection Process
- For tax forms, instructions, and publications, visit www.irs.gov or call 1-800-TAX-FORM (1-800-829-3676).
- Did you e-file your tax return? Electronically filed returns are less likely to have math errors resulting in notices such as this one. It's free to file your taxes electronically. Go to www.irs.gov/efile for information and instructions.
- Paying online is convenient, secure, and ensures timely receipt of your payment. To pay your taxes online or for more information, go to www.irs.gov/payments.
- You can contact us by mail at the address at the top of this notice. Be sure to include your social security number, the tax year, and the form number you are writing about.
- Keep this notice for your records.

If you need assistance, please don't hesitate to contact us.

Bradley – J.: [Franks];

C/O: 408 South Lincoln Street;

Milbank, South Dakota; [57252].

Internal Revenue Service

1973 North Rulon White Blvd.

M/S 4450

Ogden, Utah 84201 – 0076

Date: March 12, 2017

RE: Response for Document Labeled; "Letter 3176(SC) (REV. 4-2012) Catalog number 26860K"

Attention: Mrs. Davis:

Please find enclosed a correction for the return filing for the months of October 21, 2016 through December 21, 2016. At 1% interest according to FDIC Rules and Laws you will find that these numbers are accurate for a "Security".

The second enclosure you will find the 1040 Tax return for the second quarter for the months of January 21, 2017 through March 21, 2017: at the same rate of Interest.

Please do not presume to assume that this is a "Frivolous Tax Submission" by your OPINION. Your Federal Courts, including the Supreme Court of the United States, try **FACTS _NOT_ OPINIONS.**

Sincerely,

Bradley - J. : [Franks]

Enclosures:

Corrected tax return

Copy of this letter

IRS Department of the Treasury
Internal Revenue Service

Frivolous Return Prog., Stop 4450   In reply refer to: 1483000192
OGDEN UT 84201-0021   Sep. 05, 2017 LTR 3175C   0
                                    390-80-4016   000000 00
                                    Input Op: 1483385740 00017097
                                                         BODC: WI

BRADLEY J FRANKS
408 S LINCOLN ST
MILBANK SD 57252-2326

Dear Taxpayer:

    This is in reply to your correspondence received July 03, 2017.

    We have determined that the arguments you raised are frivolous and have no basis in law. Federal courts have consistently ruled against such arguments and imposed significant fines for taking such frivolous positions.

    If you persist in sending frivolous correspondence, we will not continue to respond to it. Our lack of response to further correspondence does not in any way convey agreement or acceptance of the arguments advanced. If you desire to comply with the law concerning your tax liability, you are encouraged to seek advice from a reputable tax practitioner or attorney.

    The claims presented in your correspondence do not relieve you from your legal responsibilities to file federal tax returns and pay taxes. We urge you to honor those legal duties.

    This letter advises you of the legal requirements for filing and paying federal individual income tax returns and informs you of the potential consequences of the position you have taken. Please observe that the Internal Revenue Code sections listed below expressly authorize IRS employees that act on behalf of the Secretary of the Treasury to: 1.)examine taxpayer books, papers, records, or other data which may be relevant or material; 2.) issue summonses in order to gain possession of records so that determinations can be made of the tax liability or for ascertaining the correctness of any return filed by that person; and 3.) collect any such liability.

    There are some people who encourage others to violate our nation's tax laws by arguing that there is no legal requirement for them to file income tax returns or pay income taxes. These people base their arguments on legal statements taken out of context and on frivolous arguments that have been repeatedly rejected by federal courts. People who rely on this kind of information can ultimately pay more in taxes, interest and penalties than they would have paid simply by filing correct tax returns.

    People who violate the tax laws also may be subject to federal criminal prosecution and imprisonment. Information about the IRS's

Form 1040 (2016)   Page **2**

Tax and Credits	38	Amount from line 37 (adjusted gross income)	38	416,127,972 04
	39a	Check { You were born before January 2, 1952, ☐ Blind. } Total boxes If: { ☐ Spouse was born before January 2, 1952, ☐ Blind. } checked ► 39a ☐		
	b	If your spouse itemizes on a separate return or you were a dual-status alien, check here ► 39b ☐		
Standard Deduction for—	40	Itemized deductions (from Schedule A) or your standard deduction (see left margin)	40	⊖
	41	Subtract line 40 from line 38	41	416,127,972 04
• People who check any box on line 39a or 39b or who can be claimed as a dependent, see instructions.	42	**Exemptions.** If line 38 is $155,650 or less, multiply $4,050 by the number on line 6d. Otherwise, see instructions	42	4050 —
	43	**Taxable income.** Subtract line 42 from line 41. If line 42 is more than line 41, enter -0-	43	⊖
	44	Tax (see instructions). Check if any from: a ☐ Form(s) 8814 b ☐ Form 4972 c ☐	44	⊖
• All others:	45	Alternative minimum tax (see instructions). Attach Form 6251	45	⊖
Single or Married filing separately, $6,300	46	Excess advance premium tax credit repayment. Attach Form 8962	46	⊖
	47	Add lines 44, 45, and 46 ►	47	⊖
Married filing jointly or Qualifying widow(er), $12,600	48	Foreign tax credit. Attach Form 1116 if required	48 ⊖	
	49	Credit for child and dependent care expenses. Attach Form 2441	49 ⊖	
Head of household, $9,300	50	Education credits from Form 8863, line 19	50 ⊖	
	51	Retirement savings contributions credit. Attach Form 8880	51 ⊖	
	52	Child tax credit. Attach Schedule 8812, if required	52 ⊖	
	53	Residential energy credits. Attach Form 5695	53 ⊖	
	54	Other credits from Form: a ☐ 3800 b ☐ 8801 c ☐	54 ⊖	
	55	Add lines 48 through 54. These are your **total credits**	55	⊖
	56	Subtract line 55 from line 47. If line 55 is more than line 47, enter -0- ►	56	⊖
Other Taxes	57	Self-employment tax. Attach Schedule SE	57	⊖
	58	Unreported social security and Medicare tax from Form: a ☐ 4137 b ☐ 8919	58	⊖
	59	Additional tax on IRAs, other qualified retirement plans, etc. Attach Form 5329 if required	59	⊖
	60a	Household employment taxes from Schedule H	60a	⊖
	b	First-time homebuyer credit repayment. Attach Form 5405 if required	60b	⊖
	61	Health care: individual responsibility (see instructions) Full-year coverage ☐	61	⊖
	62	Taxes from: a ☐ Form 8959 b ☐ Form 8960 c ☐ Instructions; enter code(s)	62	⊖
	63	Add lines 56 through 62. This is your **total tax** ►	63	⊖
Payments	64	Federal income tax withheld from Forms W-2 and 1099	64 ⊖	
If you have a qualifying child, attach Schedule EIC.	65	2016 estimated tax payments and amount applied from 2015 return	65 ⊖	
	66a	**Earned income credit (EIC)**	66a ⊖	
	b	Nontaxable combat pay election	66b		
	67	Additional child tax credit. Attach Schedule 8812	67 ⊖	
	68	American opportunity credit from Form 8863, line 8	68 ⊖	
	69	Net premium tax credit. Attach Form 8962	69 ⊖	
	70	Amount paid with request for extension to file	70 ⊖	
	71	Excess social security and tier 1 RRTA tax withheld	71 ⊖	
	72	Credit for federal tax on fuels. Attach Form 4136	72 ⊖	
	73	Credits from Form: a ☐ 2439 b ☐ Reserved c ☐ 8885 d ☐	73 ⊖	
	74	Add lines 64, 65, 66a, and 67 through 73. These are your **total payments** ►	74	⊖
Refund	75	If line 74 is more than line 63, subtract line 63 from line 74. This is the amount you **overpaid**	75	⊖
	76a	Amount of line 75 you want **refunded to you.** If Form 8888 is attached, check here ► ☐	76a	400,557,695 26
Direct deposit? See instructions.	► b	Routing number		
	► d	Account number		
	77	Amount of line 75 you want applied to your **2017 estimated tax** ► 77		
Amount You Owe	78	**Amount you owe.** Subtract line 74 from line 63. For details on how to pay, see instructions ►	78	⊖
	79	Estimated tax penalty (see instructions)	79	

Third Party Designee	Do you want to allow another person to discuss this return with the IRS (see instructions)? ☐ **Yes. Complete below.** ☐ **No** Designee's name ► Phone no. ► Personal identification number (PIN) ►

Sign Here
Under penalties of perjury, I declare that I have examined this return and accompanying schedules and statements, and to the best of my knowledge and belief, they are true, correct, and accurately list all amounts and sources of income I received during the tax year. Declaration of preparer (other than taxpayer) is based on all information of which preparer has any knowledge.

Joint return? See instructions. Keep a copy for your records.

Your signature	Date	Your occupation	Daytime phone number
Bradley - J.: [Franks]	3/15/18	Author / Self Emp.	605·432·7920
Spouse's signature. If a joint return, **both** must sign.	Date	Spouse's occupation	If the IRS sent you an Identity Protection PIN, enter it here (see inst.)

Paid Preparer Use Only	Print/Type preparer's name	Preparer's signature	Date	Check ☐ if self-employed	PTIN
	Firm's name ►			Firm's EIN ►	
	Firm's address ►			Phone no.	

www.irs.gov/form1040   Form **1040** (2016)

Form **8888**	**Allocation of Refund (Including Savings Bond Purchases)**		OMB No. 1545-0074
Department of the Treasury Internal Revenue Service	▶ Information about Form 8888 and its instructions is at *www.irs.gov/form8888*. ▶ Attach to your income tax return.		**2016** Attachment Sequence No. **56**

Name(s) shown on return: Bradley J. [Franks]

Your social security number: [390·80·4016]

Part I Direct Deposit

Complete this part if you want us to directly deposit a portion of your refund to one or more accounts.

1a Amount to be deposited in first account (see instructions) **1a**

b Routing number ▶c ☐ Checking ☐ Savings

d Account number

2a Amount to be deposited in second account **2a**

b Routing number ▶c ☐ Checking ☐ Savings

d Account number

3a Amount to be deposited in third account **3a**

b Routing number ▶c ☐ Checking ☐ Savings

d Account number

Part II U.S. Series I Savings Bond Purchases

Complete this part if you want to buy paper bonds with a portion of your refund.

⚠ If a name is entered on line 5c or 6c below, co-ownership will be assumed unless the beneficiary box is checked. See instructions for more details.

4 Amount to be used for bond purchases for yourself (and your spouse, if filing jointly) **4**

5a Amount to be used to buy bonds for yourself, your spouse, or someone else **5a**
b Enter the owner's name (First then Last) for the bond registration

c If you would like to add a co-owner or beneficiary, enter the name here (First then Last). If beneficiary, also check here ▶ ☐

6a Amount to be used to buy bonds for yourself, your spouse, or someone else **6a**
b Enter the owner's name (First then Last) for the bond registration

c If you would like to add a co-owner or beneficiary, enter the name here (First then Last). If beneficiary, also check here ▶ ☐

Part III Paper Check

Complete this part if you want a portion of your refund to be sent to you as a check.

7 Amount to be refunded by check **7** 400,557,695 26

Part IV Total Allocation of Refund

8 Add lines 1a, 2a, 3a, 4, 5a, 6a, and 7. The total must equal the refund amount shown on your tax return **8** 400,557,695 26

For Paperwork Reduction Act Notice, see your tax return instructions. Cat. No. 21858A Form **8888** (2016)

Bradley - J.: [Franks] and Co-Author: Robert - C.: [Simpson]

Form 1040 — U.S. Individual Income Tax Return (2016)

Department of the Treasury—Internal Revenue Service (99)
OMB No. 1545-0074   IRS Use Only—Do not write or staple in this space.

For the year Jan. 1–Dec. 31, 2016, or other tax year beginning **July 2017**, ending **September , 20 17**

Your first name and initial: Bradley – J.:
Last name: Franks
Your social security number: 390 80 4016

Spouse's social security number:

Home address (number and street). If you have a P.O. box, see instructions. Apt. no.
%o: 408 South Lincoln Street:

City, town or post office, state, and ZIP code.
Milbank, South Dakota 57252

Foreign country name: United States of America (Inc.)
Foreign province/state/county: South Dakota (Subsi)
Foreign postal code: 57252

Make sure the SSN(s) above and on line 6c are correct.

Presidential Election Campaign — Check here if you, or your spouse if filing jointly, want $3 to go to this fund. Checking a box below will not change your tax or refund. ☐ You ☐ Spouse

Filing Status
Check only one box.

1. ☑ Single
2. ☐ Married filing jointly (even if only one had income)
3. ☐ Married filing separately. Enter spouse's SSN above and full name here. ►
4. ☐ Head of household (with qualifying person). (See instructions.) If the qualifying person is a child but not your dependent, enter this child's name here. ►
5. ☐ Qualifying widow(er) with dependent child

Exemptions

6a. ☑ Yourself. If someone can claim you as a dependent, do not check box 6a.
b. ☐ Spouse
c. Dependents:

(1) First name Last name	(2) Dependent's social security number	(3) Dependent's relationship to you	(4) ✓ if child under age 17 qualifying for child tax credit (see instructions)
			☐
			☐
			☐
			☐

If more than four dependents, see instructions and check here ► ☐

Boxes checked on 6a and 6b: 1
No. of children on 6c who:
• lived with you — 0
• did not live with you due to divorce or separation (see instructions) — 0
Dependents on 6c not entered above — 0
Add numbers on lines above ► 1

d. Total number of exemptions claimed

Income

Attach Form(s) W-2 here. Also attach Forms W-2G and 1099-R if tax was withheld.

If you did not get a W-2, see instructions.

Line	Description	Amount
7	Wages, salaries, tips, etc. Attach Form(s) W-2	7 0
8a	Taxable interest. Attach Schedule B if required	8a 400296,866. 63
8b	Tax-exempt interest. Do not include on line 8a	
9a	Ordinary dividends. Attach Schedule B if required	9a 0
9b	Qualified dividends	
10	Taxable refunds, credits, or offsets of state and local income taxes	10 0
11	Alimony received	11 0
12	Business income or (loss). Attach Schedule C or C-EZ	12 0
13	Capital gain or (loss). Attach Schedule D if required. If not required, check here ► ☐	13 0
14	Other gains or (losses). Attach Form 4797	14 0
15a	IRA distributions	15b 0
16a	Pensions and annuities	16b 0
17	Rental real estate, royalties, partnerships, S corporations, trusts, etc. Attach Schedule E	17 0
18	Farm income or (loss). Attach Schedule F	18 0
19	Unemployment compensation	19 0
20a	Social security benefits	20b 0
21	Other income. List type and amount "Security" Interest on Principle	21 40,029,686,163. 27
22	Combine the amounts in the far right column for lines 7 through 21. This is your total income ►	22 40,429,983,529. 90

Adjusted Gross Income

Line	Description	Amount
23	Educator expenses	23 0
24	Certain business expenses of reservists, performing artists, fee-basis government officials. Attach Form 2106 or 2106-EZ	24 0
25	Health savings account deduction. Attach Form 8889	25 0
26	Moving expenses. Attach Form 3903	26 0
27	Deductible part of self-employment tax. Attach Schedule SE	27 0
28	Self-employed SEP, SIMPLE, and qualified plans	28 0
29	Self-employed health insurance deduction	29 0
30	Penalty on early withdrawal of savings	30 0
31a	Alimony paid b Recipient's SSN ►	31a 0
32	IRA deduction	32 0
33	Student loan interest deduction	33 0
34	Tuition and fees. Attach Form 8917	34 0
35	Domestic production activities deduction. Attach Form 8903	35 0
36	Add lines 23 through 35	36 0
37	Subtract line 36 from line 22. This is your adjusted gross income ►	37 40429983529. 90

For Disclosure, Privacy Act, and Paperwork Reduction Act Notice, see separate instructions.   Cat. No. 11320B   Form **1040** (2016)

257

Form 1040 (2016)   Page **2**

Tax and Credits	38	Amount from line 37 (adjusted gross income)	38	40,429,983,529	90
	39a	Check if: ☐ You were born before January 2, 1952, ☐ Blind. ☐ Spouse was born before January 2, 1952, ☐ Blind. } Total boxes checked ▶ 39a			
	b	If your spouse itemizes on a separate return or you were a dual-status alien, check here▶ 39b☐			
Standard Deduction for—	40	**Itemized deductions** (from Schedule A) or your **standard deduction** (see left margin)	40	-0-	
• People who check any box on line 39a or 39b or who can be claimed as a dependent, see instructions.	41	Subtract line 40 from line 38	41	40,429,983,529	90
	42	**Exemptions.** If line 38 is $155,650 or less, multiply $4,050 by the number on line 6d. Otherwise, see instructions	42	4,050	00
	43	**Taxable income.** Subtract line 42 from line 41. If line 42 is more than line 41, enter -0-.	43	⊖	
• All others:	44	Tax (see instructions). Check if any from: a ☐ Form(s) 8814 b ☐ Form 4972 c ☐	44	⊖	
Single or Married filing separately, $6,300	45	**Alternative minimum tax** (see instructions). Attach Form 6251	45	⊖	
	46	Excess advance premium tax credit repayment. Attach Form 8962	46	⊖	
Married filing jointly or Qualifying widow(er), $12,600	47	Add lines 44, 45, and 46 ▶	47	⊖	
	48	Foreign tax credit. Attach Form 1116 if required	48	⊖	
	49	Credit for child and dependent care expenses. Attach Form 2441	49	⊖	
Head of household, $9,300	50	Education credits from Form 8863, line 19	50	⊖	
	51	Retirement savings contributions credit. Attach Form 8880	51	⊖	
	52	Child tax credit. Attach Schedule 8812, if required. ...	52	⊖	
	53	Residential energy credits. Attach Form 5695	53	⊖	
	54	Other credits from Form: a ☐ 3800 b ☐ 8801 c ☐	54	⊖	
	55	Add lines 48 through 54. These are your **total credits**	55	⊖	
	56	Subtract line 55 from line 47. If line 55 is more than line 47, enter -0- ▶	56	⊖	
Other Taxes	57	Self-employment tax. Attach Schedule SE	57	⊖	
	58	Unreported social security and Medicare tax from Form: a ☐ 4137 b ☐ 8919	58	⊖	
	59	Additional tax on IRAs, other qualified retirement plans, etc. Attach Form 5329 if required	59	⊖	
	60a	Household employment taxes from Schedule H	60a	⊖	
	b	First-time homebuyer credit repayment. Attach Form 5405 if required	60b	⊖	
	61	Health care: individual responsibility (see instructions) Full-year coverage ☐	61	⊖	
	62	Taxes from: a ☐ Form 8959 b ☐ Form 8960 c ☐ Instructions; enter code(s)	62	⊖	
	63	Add lines 56 through 62. This is your **total tax** ▶	63	⊖	
Payments	64	Federal income tax withheld from Forms W-2 and 1099	64	⊖	
	65	2016 estimated tax payments and amount applied from 2015 return	65	⊖	
If you have a qualifying child, attach Schedule EIC.	66a	**Earned income credit (EIC)**	66a	⊖	
	b	Nontaxable combat pay election 66b			
	67	Additional child tax credit. Attach Schedule 8812	67	⊖	
	68	American opportunity credit from Form 8863, line 8 ...	68	⊖	
	69	Net premium tax credit. Attach Form 8962	69	⊖	
	70	Amount paid with request for extension to file	70	⊖	
	71	Excess social security and tier 1 RRTA tax withheld	71	⊖	
	72	Credit for federal tax on fuels. Attach Form 4136	72	⊖	
	73	Credits from Form: a ☐ 2439 b ☐ Reserved c ☐ 8885 d ☐	73	⊖	
	74	Add lines 64, 65, 66a, and 67 through 73. These are your **total payments** ▶	74	⊖	
Refund	75	If line 74 is more than line 63, subtract line 63 from line 74. This is the amount you **overpaid**	75	⊖	
	76a	Amount of line 75 you want **refunded to you.** If Form 8888 is attached, check here . ▶☑	76a	321,838,680	78
Direct deposit? See instructions.	b	Routing number ▶c Type: ☐ Checking ☐ Savings			
	d	Account number			
	77	Amount of line 75 you want applied to your 2017 estimated tax ▶ 77			
Amount You Owe	78	**Amount you owe.** Subtract line 74 from line 63. For details on how to pay, see instructions ▶	78	⊖	
	79	Estimated tax penalty (see instructions) 79			

Third Party Designee
Do you want to allow another person to discuss this return with the IRS (see instructions)? ☐ Yes. Complete below. ☐ No
Designee's name ▶   Phone no. ▶   Personal identification number (PIN) ▶

Sign Here
Under penalties of perjury, I declare that I have examined this return and accompanying schedules and statements, and to the best of my knowledge and belief, they are true, correct, and accurately list all amounts and sources of income I received during the tax year. Declaration of preparer (other than taxpayer) is based on all information of which preparer has any knowledge.

Joint return? See instructions. Keep a copy for your records.

Your signature: Bradley – J. [Franks]   Date: 9-14-17   Your occupation: Author / Self Emp   Daytime phone number: 605-432-7920

Spouse's signature. If a joint return, both must sign.   Date   Spouse's occupation   If the IRS sent you an Identity Protection PIN, enter it here (see inst.)

Paid Preparer Use Only
Print/Type preparer's name   Preparer's signature   Date   Check ☐ if self-employed   PTIN
Firm's name ▶   Firm's EIN ▶
Firm's address ▶   Phone no.

www.irs.gov/form1040   Form **1040** (2016)

Bradley - J.: [Franks] and Co-Author: Robert - C.: [Simpson]

Form **8888**	**Allocation of Refund (Including Savings Bond Purchases)**	OMB No. 1545-0074
Department of the Treasury Internal Revenue Service	▶ Information about Form 8888 and its instructions is at *www.irs.gov/form8888.* ▶ Attach to your income tax return.	**2016** Attachment Sequence No. **56**

Name(s) shown on return	Your social security number
Bradley - J : [Franks]	590·80·4016

Part I   Direct Deposit
Complete this part if you want us to directly deposit a portion of your refund to one or more accounts.

1a Amount to be deposited in first account (see instructions) **1a**

b Routing number ▶ c ☐ Checking ☐ Savings

d Account number

2a Amount to be deposited in second account **2a**

b Routing number ▶ c ☐ Checking ☐ Savings

d Account number

3a Amount to be deposited in third account **3a**

b Routing number ▶ c ☐ Checking ☐ Savings

d Account number

Part II   U.S. Series I Savings Bond Purchases
Complete this part if you want to buy paper bonds with a portion of your refund.

⚠️ CAUTION If a name is entered on line 5c or 6c below, co-ownership will be assumed unless the beneficiary box is checked. See instructions for more details.

4 Amount to be used for bond purchases for yourself (and your spouse, if filing jointly) **4**

5a Amount to be used to buy bonds for yourself, your spouse, **or** someone else **5a**
b Enter the owner's name (First then Last) for the bond registration

c If you would like to add a co-owner or beneficiary, enter the name here (First then Last). If beneficiary, also check here ▶ ☐

6a Amount to be used to buy bonds for yourself, your spouse, **or** someone else **6a**
b Enter the owner's name (First then Last) for the bond registration

c If you would like to add a co-owner or beneficiary, enter the name here (First then Last). If beneficiary, also check here ▶ ☐

Part III   Paper Check
Complete this part if you want a portion of your refund to be sent to you as a check.
7 Amount to be refunded by check **7** 321,838,680 78

Part IV   Total Allocation of Refund
8 Add lines 1a, 2a, 3a, 4, 5a, 6a, and 7. The total must equal the refund amount shown on your tax return **8** 321,838,680 78

For Paperwork Reduction Act Notice, see your tax return instructions.   Cat. No. 21858A   Form **8888** (2016)

259

Form **8888** | **Allocation of Refund (including Savings Bond Purchases)** | OMB No. 1545-0074

2016

Department of the Treasury
Internal Revenue Service

▶ Information about Form 8888 and its instructions is at *www.irs.gov/form8888.*
▶ Attach to your income tax return.

Attachment
Sequence No. **56**

Name(s) shown on return: Bradley - J · [Franks]

Your social security number: 590 · 80 · 4016

Part I **Direct Deposit**

Complete this part if you want us to directly deposit a portion of your refund to one or more accounts.

1a Amount to be deposited in first account (see instructions) **1a**

b Routing number ▶ c ☐ Checking ☐ Savings

d Account number

2a Amount to be deposited in second account **2a**

b Routing number ▶ c ☐ Checking ☐ Savings

d Account number

3a Amount to be deposited in third account **3a**

b Routing number ▶ c ☐ Checking ☐ Savings

d Account number

Part II **U.S. Series I Savings Bond Purchases**

Complete this part if you want to buy paper bonds with a portion of your refund.

⚠ CAUTION: *If a name is entered on line 5c or 6c below, co-ownership will be assumed unless the beneficiary box is checked. See instructions for more details.*

4 Amount to be used for bond purchases for yourself (and your spouse, if filing jointly) **4**

5a Amount to be used to buy bonds for yourself, your spouse, **or** someone else **5a**
b Enter the owner's name (First then Last) for the bond registration

c If you would like to add a co-owner or beneficiary, enter the name here (First then Last). If beneficiary, also check here ▶ ☐

6a Amount to be used to buy bonds for yourself, your spouse, **or** someone else **6a**
b Enter the owner's name (First then Last) for the bond registration

c If you would like to add a co-owner or beneficiary, enter the name here (First then Last). If beneficiary, also check here ▶ ☐

Part III **Paper Check**

Complete this part if you want a portion of your refund to be sent to you as a check.

7 Amount to be refunded by check **7** 321,838,680 78

Part IV **Total Allocation of Refund**

8 Add lines 1a, 2a, 3a, 4, 5a, 6a, and 7. The total must equal the refund amount shown on your tax
return **8** 321,838,680 78

For Paperwork Reduction Act Notice, see your tax return instructions. | Cat. No. 21858A | Form **8888** (2016)

260

IRS Department of the Treasury
Internal Revenue Service
Frivolous Return Prog., Stop 4450
OGDEN UT 84201-0021

BRADLEY J FRANKS
408 S LINCOLN ST
MILBANK SD 57252-2326

CUT OUT AND RETURN THE VOUCHER AT THE BOTTOM OF THIS PAGE IF YOU ARE MAKING A PAYMENT, EVEN IF YOU ALSO HAVE AN INQUIRY.

The IRS address must appear in the window.

1483000192

BODCD-WI

Use for payments

Letter Number: LTR3175C
Letter Date : 2017-09-05
Tax Period : 000000

390804016

INTERNAL REVENUE SERVICE
Frivolous Return Prog., Stop 4450
OGDEN UT 84201-0021

BRADLEY J FRANKS
408 S LINCOLN ST
MILBANK SD 57252-2326

390804016 LO FRAN 00 0 000000 670 0000000000

The Death of America

Sep. 05, 2017 LTR 3175C   0
390-80-4016 000000 00
Input Op: 1483385740 00017099

BRADLEY J FRANKS
_____ 408 S LINCOLN ST
MILBANK   SD 57252-2326

_____
_____

                    of $5,000.00

PENALTY IN ADDITION TO OTHER PENALTIES - The penalty imposed by
subsection (a) shall be in addition to any other penalty provided
by law.

     FOIA requests for Treasury Department records must meet the
following criteria before Treasury can take action:
     -   Must be in writing and signed by the person making the request;
     -   Must state that the request is being made pursuant to the FOIA;
     -   Must reasonably describe the records being requested;
     -   Must state the category of the requester for fee purposes
         (i.e. commercial, media, educational, scientific institutions,
         all other);
     -   Must contain an agreement to pay all fees that might be
         incurred;
     -   Must prove that the requester is entitled to receive the
         records;
     -   Must state whether the requester wants a copy of the records or
         only wants to inspect the records.

     If you have any questions, please write to us at the address
shown at the top of the first page of this letter. Or, you may call
us toll free at 866-883-0235. Whenever you write, please include
this letter and, in the spaces below, give us your telephone number
with the hours we can reach you. You may also wish to keep a copy of
this letter for your records.

Your Telephone Number (____)_____ Hours _____

262

1483000192
Sep. 05, 2017   LTR 3175C   0
390-80-4016   000000 00
Input Op: 1483385740 00017101

BRADLEY J FRANKS
408 S LINCOLN ST
MILBANK SD 57252-2326

PRIVACY ACT STATEMENT

Under the Privacy Act of 1974, we must tell you that our legal right to ask for information is Internal Revenue Code sections 6001, 6011, 6012(a) and their regulations. They say that you must furnish us with records or statements for any tax for which you are liable, including the withholding of taxes by your employer.

We ask for information to carry out the Internal Revenue laws of the United States, and you are required to give us this information. We may give the information to the Department of Justice for civil and criminal litigation, other federal agencies, states, cities, and the District of Columbia for use in administering their tax laws.

If you don't provide this information, or provide fraudulent information, the law provides that you may be charged penalties and, in certain cases, you may be subject to criminal prosecution. We may also have to disallow the exemptions, exclusions, credits, deductions, or adjustments shown on the tax return. This could make your tax higher or delay any refund. Interest may also be charged.

The Death of America

IRS Department of the Treasury
Internal Revenue Service

Frivolous Return Prog., Stop 4450   In reply refer to: 1483000192
OGDEN   UT   84201-0021   Sep. 05, 2017 LTR 3175C   0
                                           390-80-4016   000000 00
                                           Input Op: 1483385740 00017097
                                                                 BODC: WI

_____
_____ BRADLEY J FRANKS
         408 S LINCOLN ST
_____ MILBANK   SD 57252-2326

Dear Taxpayer:

    This is in reply to your correspondence received July 03, 2017.

    We have determined that the arguments you raised are frivolous and
have no basis in law. Federal courts have consistently ruled against
such arguments and imposed significant fines for taking such frivolous
positions.

    If you persist in sending frivolous correspondence, we will not
continue to respond to it. Our lack of response to further
correspondence does not in any way convey agreement or acceptance of
the arguments advanced. If you desire to comply with the law
concerning your tax liability, you are encouraged to seek advice from
a reputable tax practitioner or attorney.

    The claims presented in your correspondence do not relieve you
from your legal responsibilities to file federal tax returns and pay
taxes. We urge you to honor those legal duties.

    This letter advises you of the legal requirements for filing and
paying federal individual income tax returns and informs you of the
potential consequences of the position you have taken. Please observe
that the Internal Revenue Code sections listed below expressly
authorize IRS employees that act on behalf of the Secretary of the
Treasury to: 1.)examine taxpayer books, papers, records, or other data
which may be relevant or material; 2.) issue summonses in order to
gain possession of records so that determinations can be made of the
tax liability or for ascertaining the correctness of any return filed
by that person; and 3.) collect any such liability.

    There are some people who encourage others to violate our nation's
tax laws by arguing that there is no legal requirement for them to
file income tax returns or pay income taxes. These people base their
arguments on legal statements taken out of context and on frivolous
arguments that have been repeatedly rejected by federal courts.
People who rely on this kind of information can ultimately pay more in
taxes, interest and penalties than they would have paid simply by
filing correct tax returns.

    People who violate the tax laws also may be subject to federal
criminal prosecution and imprisonment. Information about the IRS's

264

                                                    1483000192
                                Sep. 05, 2017 LTR 3175C   0
                                590-80-4016   000000 00
                                Input Op: 1483385740 00017098

BRADLEY J FRANKS
408 S LINCOLN ST
MILBANK   SD   57252-2326

criminal enforcement program is available on the internet at
www.irs.gov. Once there, enter the IRS keyword: fraud.

     The IRS is working with the United States Department of Justice
and state taxing authorities to ensure that all taxpayers pay their
lawful share of taxes and to seek criminal indictments or civil
enforcement actions against people who promote or join in abusive and
fraudulent tax schemes.

     You can obtain IRS Publication 2105, Why do I Have to Pay Taxes?,
from our internet website at www.irs.gov/pub/irs-pdf/p2105.pdf. We
also refer you to a document entitled The Truth About Frivolous Tax
Arguments. It is also on our website at www.irs.gov/pub/irs-utl/
friv_tax.pdf. If you do not have internet access, you can obtain
copies of these documents from your local IRS office.

General Information on Filing Requirements and Authority to Collect
Tax

     Title 26, United States Code
          Section 6001 Notice or regulations requiring records,
          statements, and special returns
          Section 6011 General requirement of return, statement, or list
          Section 6012 Persons required to make returns of income
          Section 6109 Identifying numbers
          Section 6151 Time and place for paying tax shown on returns
          Section 6301 Collection Authority
          Section 6321 Lien for taxes
          Section 6331 Levy and distraint
          Section 7602 Examination of books and witnesses

INTERNAL REVENUE CODE SECTION 6702 (FRIVOLOUS INCOME TAX RETURN)
PROVIDES:

CIVIL PENALTY - If -
     (1) any individual files what purports to be a return of the tax
          imposed by subtitle A but which -
               (A) does not contain information on which the substantial
                    correctness of the self-assessment may be judged, or
               (B) contains information that on its face indicates that
                    the self-assessment is substantially incorrect; and
     (2) the conduct referred to in paragraph (1) is due to -
               (A) a position which is frivolous, or
               (B) a desire (which appears on the purported return) to
                    delay or impede the administration of Federal income
                    tax laws, then such individuals shall pay a penalty

1483000192
Sep. 05, 2017 LTR 3175C   0
390-80-4016   000000 00
Input Op: 1483385740 00017099

BRADLEY J FRANKS
408 S LINCOLN ST
MILBANK   SD   57252-2326

of $5,000.00

PENALTY IN ADDITION TO OTHER PENALTIES - The penalty imposed by
subsection (a) shall be in addition to any other penalty provided
by law.

    FOIA requests for Treasury Department records must meet the
following criteria before Treasury can take action:
  - Must be in writing and signed by the person making the request;
  - Must state that the request is being made pursuant to the FOIA;
  - Must reasonably describe the records being requested;
  - Must state the category of the requester for fee purposes
    (i.e. commercial, media, educational, scientific institutions,
    all other);
  - Must contain an agreement to pay all fees that might be
    incurred;
  - Must prove that the requester is entitled to receive the
    records;
  - Must state whether the requester wants a copy of the records or
    only wants to inspect the records.

    If you have any questions, please write to us at the address
shown at the top of the first page of this letter. Or, you may call
us toll free at 866-883-0235. Whenever you write, please include
this letter and, in the spaces below, give us your telephone number
with the hours we can reach you. You may also wish to keep a copy of
this letter for your records.

Your Telephone Number (___)_____ Hours _____

1483000192
Sep. 05, 2017   LTR 3175C   0
390-80-4016   000000 00
Input Op: 1483385740 00017100

BRADLEY J FRANKS
408 S LINCOLN ST
MILBANK   SD   57252-2326

Sincerely yours,

Christine L. Davis
Program Manager RICS/IVO

Enclosure(s):
Copy of this letter
Publication 1
Publication 2105

```
                                          1483000192
                       Sep. 05, 2017  LTR 3175C   0
                       390-80-4016  000000 00
                       Input Op:  1483385740 00017101
```

BRADLEY J FRANKS
408 S LINCOLN ST
MILBANK   SD   57252-2326

PRIVACY ACT STATEMENT

　　　Under the Privacy Act of 1974, we must tell you that our legal
right to ask for information is Internal Revenue Code sections 6001,
6011, 6012(a) and their regulations. They say that you must furnish
us with records or statements for any tax for which you are liable,
including the withholding of taxes by your employer.

We ask for information to carry out the Internal Revenue laws of
the United States, and you are required to give us this information.
We may give the information to the Department of Justice for civil
and criminal litigation, other federal agencies, states, cities, and
the District of Columbia for use in administering their tax laws.

If you don't provide this information, or provide fraudulent
information, the law provides that you may be charged penalties and,
in certain cases, you may be subject to criminal prosecution. We
may also have to disallow the exemptions, exclusions, credits,
deductions, or adjustments shown on the tax return. This could make
your tax higher or delay any refund. Interest may also be charged.

IRS Department of the Treasury
Internal Revenue Service

CCP-LU RICHARD A WALLIN
1550 AMERICAN BLVD EAST
SUITE 500 M/S 5128
BLOOMINGTON, MN 55425

9307 1107 5660 3959 6098 22

000933.805636.395530.17566 2 MB 0.423 1872

BRADLEY J FRANKS
408 S LINCOLN ST
MILBANK, SD 57252-2326

000933

The Death of America

IRS Department of the Treasury
Internal Revenue Service
CCP-LU RICHARD A WALLIN
1550 AMERICAN BLVD EAST
SUITE 500 M/S 5128
BLOOMINGTON, MN 55425

CERTIFIED MAIL

9307110756603959609822

Letter Date: 11/09/2017
Taxpayer Identification Number:
XXX-XX-4016
Person to Contact:
RICHARD A WALLIN
Contact Telephone Number:
(763) 347-7398
Employee Identification Number:
1000208166

BRADLEY J FRANKS
408 S LINCOLN ST
MILBANK, SD 57252-2326

000933

Notice of Federal Tax Lien Filing and Your Right to a Hearing Under IRC 6320

Dear BRADLEY J FRANKS

We filed a Notice of Federal Tax Lien on 11/09/2017 .

Type of Tax	Tax Period	Assessment Date	Amount on Lien
6702A	12/31/2016	05/29/2017	.00
6702A	12/31/2016	10/09/2017	55000.00

NOTE: Please contact the person whose name and telephone number appears on this notice to obtain the current amount you owe. Additional interest and penalties may be increasing the amount on the lien shown above.

A lien attaches to all property you currently own and to all property you may acquire in the future. It also may damage your credit rating and hinder your ability to obtain additional credit.

You have the right to a hearing with us to appeal this collection action and to discuss your payment method options. To explain the different collection appeal procedures available to you, we have enclosed Publication 1660, Collection Appeal Rights.

You must request your hearing by 12/18/2017 . Please complete the enclosed Form 12153, *Request for a Collection Due Process or Equivalent Hearing,* and mail it to:

Internal Revenue Service
1550 AMERICAN BLVD EAST
SUITE 500 M/S 5128
BLOOMINGTON, MN 55425

Letter 3172 (DO) rev. (3
Catalog No. 267671

270

Denial or revocation of United States passport

On December 4, 2015, as part of the Fixing America's Surface Transportation (FAST) Act, Congress enacted section 7345 of the Internal Revenue code, which requires the Internal Revenue Service to notify the State Department of taxpayers certified as owing a seriously delinquent tax debt. The FAST Act generally prohibits the State Department from issuing or renewing a passport to a taxpayer with seriously delinquent tax debt.

Seriously delinquent tax debt means an unpaid, legally enforceable federal tax debt of an individual totaling more than $50,000 for which, a Notice of Federal Tax lien has been filed and all administrative remedies under IRC § 6320 have lapsed or been exhausted, or a levy has been issued. If you are individually liable for tax debt (including penalties and interest) totaling more than $50,000 and you do not pay the amount you owe or make alternate arrangements to pay, or request a Collection Due Process hearing by 12/18/2017, we may notify the State Department that your tax debt is seriously delinquent. The State Department generally will not issue or renew a passport to you after we make this notification. If you currently have a valid passport, the State Department may revoke your passport or limit your ability to travel outside the United States. Additional information on passport certification is available at www.irs.gov/passports.

We will issue a Form 668(Z), *Certificate of Release of Notice of Federal Tax Lien* within 30 days:

- After you pay the full amount of your debt;
- We accept a bond guaranteeing payment of the amount owed; or
- A decision is made to adjust your account (i.e., during an Appeals hearing).

We have enclosed Publication 1450, *Instructions on How to Request a Certificate of Release of Federal Tax Lien.*

If you have any questions, please contact the person whose name and telephone number appear at the top of this letter.

· Sincerely,

Director, Specialty Collections

Enclosures:
Publication 594, *The Collection Process*
Publication 1450, *Instructions on Requesting a Certificate of Release of Federal Tax Lien*
Publication 1660, *Collection Appeal Rights*
Form 668 (Y) (C), *Notice of Federal Tax Lien*
Form 12153, *Request for a Collection Due Process Hearing*

Letter 3172 (DO) rev. (09-2016)
Catalog No. 267671

The Death of America

Form 668 (Y)(c)	1872	Department of the Treasury - Internal Revenue Service	
(Rev. February 2004)		**Notice of Federal Tax Lien**	

Area: SMALL BUSINESS/SELF EMPLOYED AREA #2 (800) 913-6050	Serial Number 284464217	For Optional Use by Recording Office

As provided by section 6321, 6322, and 6323 of the Internal Revenue Code, we are giving a notice that taxes (including interest and penalties) have been assessed against the following-named taxpayer. We have made a demand for payment of this liability, but it remains unpaid. Therefore, there is a lien in favor of the United States on all property and rights to property belonging to this taxpayer for the amount of these taxes, and additional penalties, interest, and costs that may accrue.

- This Notice of Federal Tax Lien has been filed as a matter of public record.
- IRS will continue to charge penalty and interest until you satisfy the amount you owe.
- Contact the Area Office Collection Function for information on the amount you must pay before we can release this lien.
- See the back of this page for an explanation of your Administrative Appeal rights.

Name of Taxpayer
BRADLEY J FRANKS

Residence
408 S LINCOLN ST
MILBANK, SD 57252-2326

000933

IMPORTANT RELEASE INFORMATION: For each assessment listed below, unless notice of the lien is refiled by the date given in column (e), this notice shall, on the day following such date, operate as a certificate of release as defined in IRC 6325(a).

Kind of Tax (a)	Tax Period Ending (b)	Identifying Number (c)	Date of Assessment (d)	Last Day for Refiling (e)	Unpaid Balance of Assessment (f)
6702A	12/31/2016	XXX-XX-4016	05/29/2017	06/28/2027	
6702A	12/31/2016	XXX-XX-4016	10/09/2017	11/08/2027	55000.00

Place of Filing		
Register of Deeds Grant County Milbank, SD 57252	Total	55000.00

This notice was prepared and signed at _____CHICAGO, IL_____ , on this,

the _31st_ day of _October_____ , ___2017__ .

Signature ~~Joan Flach~~ for RICHARD A WALLIN	Title REVENUE OFFICER 22-04-4772 (763) 347-7398

(**NOTE:** Certificate of officer authorized by law to take acknowledgment is not essential to the validity of Notice of Federal Tax Lien Rev. Rul. 71-466, 1971 - 2 C.B. 409)

Part 3 - Taxpayer's Copy

CAT. NO 60025X
Form **668 (Y)(c)** (Rev. 02-04)

Lien

This Notice of Federal Tax Lien gives public notice that the government has a lien on all your property (such as your house or car), all your rights to property (such as money owed to you) and to property you acquire after this lien is filed.

Your Administrative Appeal Rights

If you believe the IRS filed this Notice of Federal Tax Lien in error, you may appeal if any of the following conditions apply:

- You had paid all tax, penalty and interest before the lien was filed;

- IRS assessed tax after the date you filed a petition for bankruptcy;

- IRS mailed your notice of deficiency to the wrong address;

  You have already filed a timely petition with the Tax Court;

  The statute of limitations for collection ended before IRS filed the notice of lien.

Your appeal request must be in writing and contain the following:

- Your name, current address and SSN/EIN;

- Copy of this notice of lien, if available;

- The specific reason(s) why you think the IRS is in error;

- Proof that you paid the amount due (such as cancelled check);

- Proof that you filed a bankruptcy petition before this lien was filed.

Send your written request to the IRS, Attention: Technical Services Group Manager, in the office where this notice of lien was filed.

When This Lien Can Be Released

The IRS will issue a Certificate of Release of Federal Tax Lien within 30 days after:

- You pay the tax due, including penalties, interest, and any other additions under law, or IRS adjusts the amount due, or;

- The end of the time period during which we can collect the tax (usually 10 years).

Publication 1450, Request for Release of Federal Tax Lien, available at IRS offices, describes this process.

When a Lien against Property can be Removed

The IRS may remove the lien from a specific piece of property if any of the following conditions apply:

- You have other property subject to this lien that is worth at least two times the total of the tax you owe, including penalties and interest, plus the amount of any other debts you owe on the property (such as a mortgage);

- You give up ownership in the property and IRS receives the value of the government's interest in the property;

- IRS decides the government's interest in the property has no value when you give up ownership;

- The property in question is being sold; there is a dispute about who is entitled to the sale proceeds; and the proceeds are placed in escrow while the dispute is being resolved.

Publication 783, Instructions on How to Apply for a Certificate of Discharge of Property from a Federal Tax Lien, available at IRS offices, describes this process.

Gravamen

Este Aviso de Gravamen del Impuesto Federal da aviso público que el gobierno tiene un gravamen en todas sus propiedades (tal como su casa o carro), todos sus derechos a propiedad (tales como el dinero que le adeudan a usted) y la propiedad que adquiera después que se presentó éste gravamen.

Sus Derechos de Apelación Administrativos

Si usted cree que el IRS presentó éste Aviso de Gravamen del Impuesto Federal por error, usted puede apelar si cualquiera de las siguientes condiciones le aplican:

- Usted pagó todo el impuesto, multa, interés antes de que el gravamen fuera presentado;

- El IRS tasó el impuesto después del la fecha en que usted presentó una petición de quiebra;

- El IRS le envió por correo el aviso de deficiencia a una dirección incorrecta;

- Usted presentó a tiempo una petición ante la Corte de Impuesto;

- El IRS no presentó el aviso de gravamen dentro del término prescriptivo.

Su petición de apelación tiene que estar por escrito y debe incluir lo siguiente:

- Su nombre, dirección actual y SSN/EIN;

- Una copia de este aviso de gravamen, si está disponible;

- La razón (o razones) específica(s) por qué piensa que el IRS está erróneo;

- Prueba que pagó la cantidad adeudada (tal como un cheque cancelado);

- Prueba que presentó una petición de quiebra antes de que se presentara el gravamen.

Envíe su petición por escrito al IRS, Atención: "*Technical Services Group Manager*" (*Grupo de Gerente-Servicios Técnicos*) en la oficina dónde este aviso de gravamen fue presentado.

Cuándo Este Gravamen Se Puede Cancelar

El IRS emitirá un Certificado de Cancelación de Gravamen del Impuesto Federal dentro de 30 días después que:

- Usted paga el impuesto adeudado, incluyendo multas, intereses, y otras sumas adicionales según la ley, o el IRS ajusta la cantidad adeudada, o:

- Aceptemos una fianza garantizando el pago de su deuda;

- La expiración del término en que podemos cobrar el impuesto (usualmente 10 años).

La Publicación 1450, en inglés, "*Petición Para Cancelar el Gravamen del Impuesto-Federal*", describe este proceso y está disponible en las oficinas del IRS.

Cuándo un Gravamen en Contra de la Propiedad Puede Eliminarse

El IRS puede eliminar el gravamen de una propiedad específica si cualquiera de las siguientes condiciones aplica:

- Usted tiene otra propiedad sujeta a este gravamen cuyo valor es por lo menos dos veces el total del impuesto que usted adeuda, incluyendo intereses y multas, más la cantidad de cualquiera de las otras deudas que adeuda sobre la propiedad (tal como una hipoteca);

- Usted cede su interés en la propiedad y el IRS recibe el valor del interés del gobierno en la propiedad;

- El IRS decide que el interés del gobierno en la propiedad no tiene valor alguno cuando usted cedió su interés en la propiedad;

- La propiedad gravada será vendida; existe una controversia sobre quién tiene derecho al producto de la venta; y se depositan los fondos recibidos en la venta en una cuenta especial en lo que se resuelve la controversia.

La Publicación 783 en inglés, "*Instrucciones de Cómo Solicitar un Certificado de Relevo de la Propiedad de un Gravamen del Impuesto Federal*", describe éste proceso y está disponible en las oficinas del IRS.

Form **668 (Y) (c)** (Rev. 02-2004)

Instructions for Requesting a
Certificate of Release of Federal Tax Lien

IRS

Section 6325(a) of the Internal Revenue Code directs us to release a Federal tax lien within 30 days of when the liability is fully paid or becomes legally unenforceable or the IRS accepts a bond for payment of the liability. When all the liabilities shown on the Notice of Federal Tax Lien are satisfied, we will issue a Certificate of Release of Federal Tax Lien for filing in the same location where the notice of lien was filed. If we have not released the lien within 30 days, you can ask for a certificate of release.

Requesting a Copy of the Certificate

If it has been more than 30 days since you satisfied your tax liability and you have not received a copy of the Certificate of Release of Federal Tax Lien, you may call the Centralized Lien Operation to check the status of the certificate. If you prefer to write, your request should be mailed or faxed to the following address:

Internal Revenue Service
Centralized Lien Operation
P.O. Box 145595, Stop 8420G
Cincinnati, OH 45250-5595

Telephone Number: 800-913-6050
Outside the United States: 859-669-4811
Fax number: 855-390-3528

The copy of the certificate you receive will not show the official recording information. For a copy of the recorded certificate, you must contact the recording office where the Certificate of Release of Federal Tax Lien was filed.

Requesting a Certificate of Release

If the Federal tax lien has not been released, you can request a Certificate of Release of Federal Tax Lien. The request must be in writing and should be mailed to the Advisory Group servicing your area. Use Publication 4235, Collection Advisory Group Addresses, to determine the address to mail your request.

Your request must contain the following information:
• The date of your request
• The name and address of the taxpayer
• One copy of each Notice of Federal Tax Lien you want released
• Why the lien should be released
• A telephone number with the best time for us to call you should we need additional information

If you have paid the tax liability, enclose a copy of any of the following with your request:
• An Internal Revenue receipt
• A canceled check
• A record of payment by electronic fund transfer
• Any other acceptable proof of payment

We may need to research your account. We will provide a certificate of release once we have confirmed your liability is satisfied.

If you have an immediate or urgent need for a Certificate of Release of Federal Tax Lien, you can visit or telephone the local IRS office. A list of local offices, their available services, and their hours of operation may be found on our website www.irs.gov by searching "Local Contacts."

When visiting the IRS office, be prepared to show proof of payment or other documentation that demonstrates your liability has been satisfied. If there is an unpaid balance on your liability, you must pay the balance with a certified check, cashier's check, or acceptable money order before a certificate of release can be issued. For other forms of payment, the certificate of release will be issued within 30 days of the liability being satisfied.

To request a payoff or other information about your Notice of Federal Tax Lien, contact the Centralized Lien Operation as shown above. General information about Federal tax liens may be found at www.irs.gov by searching "liens."

Publication 1450 (Rev. 1-2016) Catalog Number 10665H Department of the Treasury **Internal Revenue Service** www.irs.gov

GฆO U.S. GOVERNMENT PRINTING OFFICE: 2017—747-091

Form **12153** (Rev. 12-2013)	**Request for a Collection Due Process or Equivalent Hearing**

Use this form to request a Collection Due Process (CDP) or equivalent hearing with the IRS Office of Appeals if you have been issued one of the following lien or levy notices:

- Notice of Federal Tax Lien Filing and Your Right to a Hearing under IRC 6320,
- Notice of Intent to Levy and Notice of Your Right to a Hearing,
- Notice of Jeopardy Levy and Right of Appeal,
- Notice of Levy on Your State Tax Refund,
- Notice of Levy and Notice of Your Right to a Hearing.

Complete this form and send it to the address shown on your lien or levy notice. Include a copy of your lien or levy notice to ensure proper handling of your request.

Call the phone number on the notice or 1-800-829-1040 if you are not sure about the correct address or if you want to fax your request.

You can find a section explaining the deadline for requesting a Collection Due Process hearing in this form's instructions. If you've missed the deadline for requesting a CDP hearing, you must check line 7 (Equivalent Hearing) to request an equivalent hearing.

1. Taxpayer Name: (Taxpayer 1) _____

   Taxpayer Identification Number _____

   Current Address _____

   City _____ State _____ Zip Code _____

2. Telephone Number and Best Time to Call During Normal Business Hours

   Home (___) ___ - _____   ☐ am. ☐ pm.
   Work (___) ___ - _____   ☐ am. ☐ pm.
   Cell (___) ___ - _____   ☐ am. ☐ pm.

3. Taxpayer Name: (Taxpayer 2) _____

   Taxpayer Identification Number _____

   Current Address
   (If Different from Address Above) City _____ State _____ Zip Code _____

4. Telephone Number and Best Time to Call During Normal Business Hours

   Home ( ) ___ - _____   ☐ am. ☐ pm.
   Work ( ) ___ - _____   ☐ am. ☐ pm.
   Cell ( ) ___ - _____   ☐ am. ☐ pm.

5. Tax Information as Shown on the Lien or Levy Notice (*If possible, attach a copy of the notice*)

Type of Tax (Income, Employment, Excise, etc. or Civil Penalty)	Tax Form Number (1040, 941, 720, etc)	Tax Period or Periods

The Death of America

Form **12153** (Rev. 12-2013)	**Request for a Collection Due Process or Equivalent Hearing**

6. Basis for Hearing Request (Both boxes can be checked if you have received both a lien and levy notice)

☐ Filed Notice of Federal Tax Lien   ☐ Proposed Levy or Actual Levy

7. Equivalent Hearing (See the instructions for more information on Equivalent Hearings)

☐ I would like an Equivalent Hearing - I would like a hearing equivalent to a CDP Hearing if my request for a CDP hearing does not meet the requirements for a timely CDP Hearing.

8. Check the most appropriate box for the reason you disagree with the filing of the lien or the levy. **See page 4 of this form for examples.** You can add more pages if you don't have enough space. If, during your CDP Hearing, you think you would like to discuss a Collection Alternative to the action proposed by the Collection function it is recommended you submit a completed Form 433A (Individual) and/or Form 433B (Business), as appropriate, with this form. See www.irs.gov for copies of the forms. Generally, the Office of Appeals will ask the Collection Function to review, verify and provide their opinion on any new information you submit. We will share their comments with you and give you the opportunity to respond.

Collection Alternative   ☐ Installment Agreement ☐ Offer in Compromise ☐ I Cannot Pay Balance

Lien   ☐ Subordination   ☐ Discharge   ☐ Withdrawal
Please explain:

My Spouse Is Responsible   ☐ Innocent Spouse Relief (Please attach Form 8857, *Request for Innocent Spouse Relief*, to your request.)

Other (*For examples, see page 4*)   ☐
Reason (*You must provide a reason for the dispute or your request for a CDP hearing will not be honored. Use as much space as you need to explain the reason for your request. Attach extra pages if necessary.*):

9. Signatures   I understand the CDP hearing and any subsequent judicial review will suspend the statutory period of limitations for collection action. I also understand my representative or I must sign and date this request before the IRS Office of Appeals can accept it. If you are signing as an officer of a company add your title (*president, secretary, etc.*) behind your signature.

SIGN HERE   Taxpayer 1's Signature   Date

Taxpayer 2's Signature (*if a joint request, both must sign*)   Date

☐ I request my CDP hearing be held with my authorized representative (*attach a copy of Form 2848*)

Authorized Representative's Signature | Authorized Representative's Name | Telephone Number

IRS Use Only
IRS Employee (Print) | Employee Telephone Number | IRS Received Date

Form **12153** (Rev. 12-2013)   Catalog Number 26685D   www.irs.gov   Department of the Treasury - Internal Revenue Service

276

Information You Need To Know When Requesting A Collection Due Process Hearing

What Is the Deadline for Requesting a Timely Collection Due Process (CDP) Hearing?

- Your request for a CDP hearing about a Federal Tax Lien filing must be postmarked by the date indicated in the *Notice of Federal Tax Lien Filing and Your Right to a Hearing under IRC 6320* (lien notice).

- Your request for a CDP hearing about a levy must be postmarked within 30 days after the date of the *Notice of Intent to Levy and Notice of Your Right to a Hearing* (levy notice) or Notice of Your Right to a Hearing After an Actual Levy.

Your timely request for a CDP hearing will prohibit levy action in most cases. A timely request for CDP hearing will also suspend the 10-year period we have, by law, to collect your taxes. Both the prohibition on levy and the suspension of the 10-year period will last until the determination the IRS Office of Appeals makes about your disagreement is final. The amount of time the suspension is in effect will be added to the time remaining in the 10-year period. For example, if the 10-year period is suspended for six months, the time left in the period we have to collect taxes will be extended by six months.

You can go to court to appeal the CDP determination the IRS Office of Appeals makes about your disagreement.

What Is an Equivalent Hearing?

If you still want a hearing with the IRS Office of Appeals after the deadline for requesting a timely CDP hearing has passed, you can use this form to request an equivalent hearing. You must check the Equivalent Hearing box on line 7 of the form to request an equivalent hearing. **An equivalent hearing request does not prohibit levy or suspend the 10-year period for collecting your taxes; also, you cannot go to court to appeal the IRS Office of Appeals' decision about your disagreement.** You must request an equivalent hearing within the following timeframe:

- Lien Notice—one year plus five business days from the filing date of the Notice of Federal Tax Lien.

- Levy Notice—one year from the date of the levy notice.

- Your request for a CDP levy hearing, whether timely or Equivalent, does not prohibit the Service from filing a Notice of Federal Tax Lien.

Where Should You File Your CDP or Equivalent Hearing Request?

File your request by mail at the address on your lien notice or levy notice. You may also fax your request. Call the telephone number on the lien or levy notice to ask for the fax number. **Do not send your CDP or equivalent hearing request directly to the IRS Office of Appeals, it must be sent to the address on the lien or levy notice. If you send your request directly to Appeals it may result in your request not being considered a timely request. Depending upon your issue the originating function may contact you in an attempt to resolve the issue(s) raised in your request prior to forwarding your request to Appeals.**

Where Can You Get Help?

You can call the telephone number on the lien or levy notice with your questions about requesting a hearing. The contact person listed on the notice or other representative can access your tax information and answer your questions.

In addition, you may qualify for representation by a low-income taxpayer clinic for free or nominal charge. Our Publication 4134, Low Income Taxpayer Clinic List, provides information on clinics in your area.

If you are experiencing economic harm, the Taxpayer Advocate Service (TAS) may be able to help you resolve your problems with the IRS. TAS cannot extend the time you have to request a CDP or equivalent hearing. See Publication 594, *The IRS Collection Process,* or visit www.irs.gov/advocate/index-html. You also can call 1-877-777-4778 for TAS assistance.

Note—The IRS Office of Appeals will not consider frivolous requests. You can find examples of frivolous reasons for requesting a hearing or disagreeing with a tax assessment in Publication 2105, *Why do I have to Pay Taxes?,* or at www.irs.gov by typing "frivolous" into the search engine.

You can get copies of tax forms, schedules, instructions, publications, and notices at www.irs.gov, at your local IRS office, or by calling toll-free *1-800-TAX-FORM (829-3676).*

Form **12153** (Rev. 12-2013)   Catalog Number 26685D   www.irs.gov   Department of the Treasury - **Internal Revenue Service**

Form 668-A(ICS)	Department of the Treasury – Internal Revenue Service
(January 2015)	**Notice of Levy**

DATE: **01/10/2018**

REPLY TO: Internal Revenue Service
         RICHARD A WALLIN
         1550 AMERICAN BLVD EAST
         STE 500 M/S 5128
         BLOOMINGTON, MN 55425

TO: **GREAT WESTERN BANK**
      302 S MAIN ST
      MILBANK, SD 57252

TELEPHONE NUMBER
OF IRS OFFICE: **(763)347-7398**

NAME AND ADDRESS OF TAXPAYER:
BRADLEY J FRANKS
408 S LINCOLN ST
MILBANK, SD 57252-2326088

IDENTIFYING NUMBER(S): **390-60-4016**

FRAN

Kind of Tax	Tax Period Ended	Unpaid Balance of Assessment	Statutory Additions	Total
CIVPEN	12/31/2016	$55,040.00	$969.88	$56,009.88

	Total Amount Due	
This levy won't attach funds in IRAs, Self-Employed Individuals' Retirement Plans, or any other Retirement Plans in your possession or control, unless it is signed in the block to the right. ===================== ⇒	Total Amount Due	$56,009.88

We figured the interest and late payment penalty to   **02/09/2018**

Although we have told you to pay the amount you owe, it is still not paid. This is your copy of a notice of levy we have sent to collect this unpaid amount. We will send other levies if we don't get enough with this one.

Banks, credit unions, savings and loans, and similar institutions described in section 408(n) of the Internal Revenue Code must hold your money for 21 calendar days before sending it to us. They must include the interest you earn during that time. Anyone else we send a levy to must turn over your money, property, credits, etc. that they have *(or are already obligated for)* when they would have paid you.

If you decide to pay the amount you owe now, please **bring** a guaranteed payment *(cash, cashier's check, certified check, or money order*)* to the nearest IRS office with this form, so we can tell the person who received this levy not to send us your money. Make checks and money orders payable to **United States Treasury.** If you mail your payment instead of bringing it to us, we may not have time to stop the person who received this levy from sending us your money.

If we have erroneously levied your bank account, we may reimburse you for the fees your bank charged you for handling the levy. You must file a claim with the IRS on Form 8546 within one year after the fees are charged.

If you have any questions, or want to arrange payment before other levies are issued, please call or write us. If you write to us, please include your telephone number and the best time to call. *Visit www.irs.gov to determine the closest IRS office that furnishes cash payment processing service.

Signature of Service Representative	Title
/S/ RICHARD A WALLIN	**REVENUE OFFICER**

Part 4 –   For Taxpayer

Form **668-A(ICS)** (1-2015)

Excerpts from the Internal Revenue Code
* * * * * * * * * *

Sec. 6331. LEVY AND DISTRAINT.

(b) Seizure and Sale of Property.–The term "levy" as used in this title includes the power of distraint and seizure by any means. Except as otherwise provided in subsection (e), a levy shall extend only to property possessed and obligations existing at the time thereof. In any case in which the Secretary may levy upon property or rights to property, he may seize and sell such property or rights to property (whether real or personal, tangible or intangible).

(c) Successive Seizures.–Whenever any property or right to property upon which levy has been made by virtue of subsection (a) is not sufficient to satisfy the claim of the United States for which levy is made, the Secretary may, thereafter, and as often as may be necessary, proceed to levy in like manner upon any other property liable to levy of the person against whom such claim exists, until the amount due from him, together with all expenses, is fully paid.

Sec. 6332. SURRENDER OF PROPERTY SUBJECT TO LEVY.

(a) Requirement.–Except as otherwise provided in this section, any person in possession of (or obligated with respect to) property or rights to property subject to levy upon which a levy has been made shall, upon demand of the Secretary, surrender such property or rights (or discharge such obligation) to the Secretary, except such part of the property or rights as is, at the time of such demand, subject to an attachment or execution under any judicial process.

(b) Special rule for Life Insurance and Endowment Contracts

(1) In general.–A levy on an organization with respect to a life insurance or endowment contract issued by such organization shall, without necessity for the surrender of the contract document, constitute a demand by the Secretary for payment of the amount described in paragraph (2) and the exercise of the right of the person against whom the tax is assessed to the advance of such amount. Such organization shall pay over such amount 90 days after service of notice of levy. Such notice shall include a certification by the Secretary that a copy of such notice has been mailed to the person against whom the tax is assessed at his last known address.

(2) Satisfaction of levy.–Such levy shall be deemed to be satisfied if such organization pays over to the Secretary the amount which the person against whom the tax is assessed could have had advanced to him by such organization on the date prescribed in paragraph (1) for the satisfaction of such levy, increased by the amount of any advance (including contractual interest thereon) made to such person on or after the date such person had actual notice or knowledge (within the meaning of section 6323 (i)(1)) of the existence of the lien with respect to which such levy is made, other than an advance (including contractual interest thereon) made automatically to maintain such contract in force under an agreement entered into before such organization had such notice or knowledge.

(3) Enforcement proceedings.–The satisfaction of a levy under paragraph (2) shall be without prejudice to any civil action for the enforcement of any lien imposed by this title with respect to such contract.

(c) Special Rule for Banks.–Any bank (as defined in section 408(n)) shall surrender (subject to an attachment or execution under judicial process) any deposits (including interest thereon) in such bank only after 21 days after service of levy.

(d) Enforcement of Levy.

(1) Extent of personal liability.–Any person who fails or refuses to surrender any property or rights to property, subject to levy, upon demand by the Secretary, shall be liable in his own person and estate to the United States in a sum equal to the value of the property or rights not so surrendered, but not exceeding the amount of the amount described in paragraph (2) and the exercise of the right of with respect to the collection of which such levy has been made, together with costs and interest on such sum at the underpayment rate established under section 6621 from the date of such levy (or, in the case of a levy described in section 6331 (d)(3), from the date such person would otherwise have been obligated to pay over such amounts to the taxpayer). Any amount (other than costs) recovered under this paragraph shall be credited against the tax liability for the collection of which such levy was made.

(2) Penalty for violation.–In addition to the personal liability imposed by paragraph (1), if any person required to surrender property or rights to property fails or refuses to surrender such property or rights to property without reasonable cause, such person shall be liable for a penalty equal to 50 percent of the amount recoverable under paragraph (1). No part of such penalty shall be credited against the tax liability for the collection of which such levy was made

(e) Effect of honoring levy.–Any person in possession of (or obligated with respect to) property or rights to property subject to levy upon which a levy has been made who, upon demand by the Secretary, surrenders such property or rights to property (or discharges such obligation) to the Secretary (or who pays a liability under subsection (d)(1)), shall be discharged from any obligation or liability to the delinquent taxpayer and any other person with respect to such property or rights to property arising from such surrender or payment.

Sec. 6333. PRODUCTION OF BOOKS.

If a levy has been made or is about to be made on any property, or right to property, any person having custody or control of any books or records, containing evidence or statements relating to the property or right to property subject to levy, shall, upon demand of the Secretary, exhibit such books or records to the Secretary

Sec. 6343. AUTHORITY TO RELEASE LEVY AND RETURN PROPERTY.

(a) Release of Levy and Notice of Release.

(1) In general.–Under regulations prescribed by the Secretary, the Secretary shall release the levy upon all, or part of, the property or rights to property levied upon and shall promptly notify the person upon whom such levy was made (if any) that such levy has been released if–

(A) the liability for which such levy was made is satisfied or becomes unenforceable by reason of lapse of time,

(B) release of such levy will facilitate the collection of such liability,

(C) the taxpayer has entered into an agreement under section 6159 to satisfy such liability by means of installment payments, unless such agreement provides otherwise,

(D) the Secretary has determined that such levy is creating an economic hardship due to the financial condition of the taxpayer, or

(E) the fair market value of the property exceeds such liability and release of the levy on a part of such property could be made without hindering the collection of such liability.

For purposes of subparagraph (C), the Secretary is not required to release such levy if such release would jeopardize the secured creditor status of the Secretary.

(2) Expedited determination on certain business property.–In the case of any tangible personal property essential in carrying on the trade or business of the taxpayer, the Secretary shall provide for an expedited determination under paragraph (1) if levy on such tangible personal property would prevent the taxpayer from carrying on such trade or business.

(3) Subsequent levy.–The release of levy on any property under paragraph (1) shall not prevent any subsequent levy on such property.

(b) Return of Property.–If the Secretary determines that property has been wrongfully levied upon, it shall be lawful for the Secretary to return-

(1) the specific property levied upon,

(2) an amount of money equal to the amount of money levied upon, or

(3) an amount of money equal to the amount of money received by the United States from a sale of such property.

Property may be returned at any time. An amount equal to the amount of money levied upon or received from such sale may be returned at any time before the expiration of 9 months from the date of such levy. For purposes of paragraph (3), if property is declared purchased by the United States at a sale pursuant to section 6335(e) (relating to manner and conditions of sale), the United States shall be treated as having received an amount of money equal to the minimum price determined pursuant to such section or (if larger) the amount received by the United States from the resale of such property.

(d) Return of Property in Certain Cases — If–

(1) any property has been levied upon, and

(2) the Secretary determines that—

(A) the levy on such property was premature or otherwise not in accordance with administrative procedures of the Secretary,

(B) the taxpayer has entered into an agreement under section 6159 to satisfy the tax liability for which the levy was imposed by means of installment payments, unless such agreement provides otherwise,

(C) the return of such property will facilitate the collection of the tax liability, or

(D) with the consent of the taxpayer or the National Taxpayer Advocate, the return of such property would be in the best interests of the taxpayer (as determined by the National Taxpayer Advocate) and the United States, the provisions of subsection (b) shall apply in the same manner as if such property had been wrongly levied upon, except that no interest shall be allowed under subsection (c).

* * * * * * * * * *

Applicable Sections of Internal Revenue Code

6321. LIEN FOR TAXES.
6322. PERIOD OF LIEN.
6325. RELEASE OF LIEN OR DISCHARGE OF PROPERTY.
6331. LEVY AND DISTRAINT.
6332. SURRENDER OF PROPERTY SUBJECT TO LEVY.
6333. PRODUCTION OF BOOKS.
6334. PROPERTY EXEMPT FROM LEVY.
6343. AUTHORITY TO RELEASE LEVY AND RETURN PROPERTY.
7426. CIVIL ACTIONS BY PERSONS OTHER THAN TAXPAYERS.
7429. REVIEW OF JEOPARDY LEVY OR ASSESSMENT PROCEDURES.

For more information about this notice, please call the phone number on the front of this form.

Form **668-A(ICS)** (1-2015)

279

Excerpts from the Internal Revenue Code
* * * * * * * * * * *

Sec. 6331. LEVY AND DISTRAINT.

(b) Seizure and Sale of Property.—The term "levy" as used in this title includes the power of distraint and seizure by any means. Except as otherwise provided in subsection (e), a levy shall extend only to property possessed and obligations existing at the time thereof. In any case in which the Secretary may levy upon property or rights to property, he may seize and sell such property or rights to property (whether real or personal, tangible or intangible).

(c) Successive Seizures.—Whenever any property or right to property upon which levy has been made by virtue of subsection (a) is not sufficient to satisfy the claim of the United States for which levy is made, the Secretary may, thereafter, and as often as may be necessary, proceed to levy in like manner upon any other property liable to levy of the person against whom such claim exists, until the amount due from him, together with all expenses, is fully paid.

Sec. 6332. SURRENDER OF PROPERTY SUBJECT TO LEVY.

(a) Requirement.—Except as otherwise provided in this section, any person in possession of (or obligated with respect to) property or rights to property subject to levy upon which a levy has been made shall, upon demand of the Secretary, surrender such property or rights (or discharge such obligation) to the Secretary, except such part of the property or rights as is, at the time of such demand, subject to an attachment or execution under any judicial process.

(b) Special rule for Life Insurance and Endowment Contracts

(1) In general.—A levy on an organization with respect to a life insurance or endowment contract issued by such organization shall, without necessity for the surrender of the contract document, constitute a demand by the Secretary for payment of the amount described in paragraph (2) and the exercise of the right of the person against whom the tax is assessed to the advance of such amount. Such organization shall pay over such amount 90 days after service of notice of levy. Such notice shall include a certification by the Secretary that a copy of such notice has been mailed to the person against whom the tax is assessed at his last known address.

(2) Satisfaction of levy.—Such levy shall be deemed to be satisfied if such organization pays over to the Secretary the amount which the person against whom the tax is assessed could have had advanced to him by such organization on the date prescribed in paragraph (1) for the satisfaction of such levy, increased by the amount of any advance (including contractual interest thereon) made to such person on or after the date such organization had actual notice or knowledge (within the meaning of section 6323 (i)(1)) of the existence of the lien with respect to which such levy is made, other than an advance (including contractual interest thereon) made automatically to maintain such contract in force under an agreement entered into before such organization had such notice or knowledge.

(3) Enforcement proceedings.—The satisfaction of a levy under paragraph (2) shall be without prejudice to any civil action for the enforcement of any lien imposed by this title with respect to such contract.

(c) Special Rule for Banks.—Any bank (as defined in section 408(n)) shall surrender (subject to an attachment or execution under judicial process) any deposits (including interest thereon) in such bank only after 21 days after service of levy.

(d) Enforcement of Levy.

(1) Extent of personal liability.—Any person who fails or refuses to surrender any property or rights to property, subject to levy, upon demand by the Secretary, shall be liable in his own person and estate to the United States in a sum equal to the value of the property or rights not so surrendered, but not exceeding the amount of taxes for the collection of which such levy has been made, together with costs and interest on such sum at the underpayment rate established under section 6621 from the date of such levy (or, in the case of a levy described in section 6331 (d)(3), from the date such person would otherwise have been obligated to pay over such amounts to the taxpayer). Any amount (other than costs) recovered under this paragraph shall be credited against the tax liability for the collection of which such levy was made.

(2) Penalty for violation.—In addition to the personal liability imposed by paragraph (1), if any person required to surrender property or rights to property fails or refuses to surrender such property or rights to property without reasonable cause, such person shall be liable for a penalty equal to 50 percent of the amount recoverable under paragraph (1). No part of such penalty shall be credited against the tax liability for the collection of which such levy was made.

(e) Effect of honoring levy.—Any person in possession of (or obligated with respect to) property or rights to property subject to levy upon which a levy has been made who, upon demand by the Secretary, surrenders such property or rights to property (or discharges such obligation) to the Secretary (or who pays a liability under subsection (d)(1)), shall be discharged from any obligation or liability to the delinquent taxpayer and any other person with respect to such property or rights to property arising from such surrender or payment.

Sec. 6333. PRODUCTION OF BOOKS.

If a levy has been made or is about to be made on any property, or right to property, any person having custody or control of any books or records, containing evidence or statements relating to the property or right to property subject to levy, shall, upon demand of the Secretary, exhibit such books or records to the Secretary.

Sec. 6343. AUTHORITY TO RELEASE LEVY AND RETURN PROPERTY.

(a) Release of Levy and Notice of Release.

(1) In general.—Under regulations prescribed by the Secretary, the Secretary shall release the levy upon all, or part of, the property or rights to property levied upon and shall promptly notify the person upon whom such levy was made (if any) that such levy has been released if—

(A) the liability for which such levy was made is satisfied or becomes unenforceable by reason of lapse of time,

(B) release of such levy will facilitate the collection of such liability,

(C) the taxpayer has entered into an agreement under section 6159 to satisfy such liability by means of installment payments, unless such agreement provides otherwise,

(D) the Secretary has determined that such levy is creating an economic hardship due to the financial condition of the taxpayer, or

(E) the fair market value of the property exceeds such liability and release of the levy on a part of such property could be made without hindering the collection of such liability.

For purposes of subparagraph (C), the Secretary is not required to release such levy if such release would jeopardize the secured creditor status of the Secretary.

(2) Expedited determination on certain business property.—In the case of any tangible personal property essential in carrying on the trade or business of the taxpayer, the Secretary shall provide for an expedited determination under paragraph (1) if levy on such tangible personal property would prevent the taxpayer from carrying on such trade or business.

(3) Subsequent levy.—The release of levy on any property under paragraph (1) shall not prevent any subsequent levy on such property.

(b) Return of Property.—If the Secretary determines that property has been wrongfully levied upon, it shall be lawful for the Secretary to return—

(1) the specific property levied upon,

(2) an amount of money equal to the amount of money levied upon, or

(3) an amount of money equal to the amount of money received by the United States from a sale of such property.

Property may be returned at any time. An amount equal to the amount of money levied upon or received from such sale may be returned at any time before the expiration of 9 months from the date of such levy. For purposes of paragraph (3), if property is declared purchased by the United States at a sale pursuant to section 6335(e) (relating to manner and conditions of sale), the United States shall be treated as having received an amount of money equal to the minimum price determined pursuant to such section or (if larger) the amount received by the United States from the resale of such property.

(d) Return of Property in Certain Cases.— If—

(1) any property has been levied upon, and

(2) the Secretary determines that—

(A) the levy on such property was premature or otherwise not in accordance with administrative procedures of the Secretary,

(B) the taxpayer has entered into an agreement under section 6159 to satisfy the tax liability for which the levy was imposed by means of installment payments, unless such agreement provides otherwise,

(C) the return of such property will facilitate the collection of the tax liability, or

(D) with the consent of the taxpayer or the National Taxpayer Advocate, the return of such property would be in the best interests of the taxpayer (as determined by the National Taxpayer Advocate) and the United States, the provisions of subsection (b) shall apply in the same manner as if such property had been wrongly levied upon, except that no interest shall be allowed under subsection (c).

* * * * * * * * * *

Applicable Sections of Internal Revenue Code

6321. LIEN FOR TAXES.
6322. PERIOD OF LIEN.
6325. RELEASE OF LIEN OR DISCHARGE OF PROPERTY.
6331. LEVY AND DISTRAINT.
6332. SURRENDER OF PROPERTY SUBJECT TO LEVY.
6333. PRODUCTION OF BOOKS.
6334. PROPERTY EXEMPT FROM LEVY.
6343. AUTHORITY TO RELEASE LEVY AND RETURN PROPERTY.
7426. CIVIL ACTIONS BY PERSONS OTHER THAN TAXPAYERS.
7429. REVIEW OF JEOPARDY LEVY OR ASSESSMENT PROCEDURES.

For more information about this notice, please call the phone number on the front of this form.

Form **668-A(ICS)** (1-2015)

Excerpts from the Internal Revenue Code

* * * * * * * * * * *

Sec. 6331. LEVY AND DISTRAINT.

(b) **Seizure and Sale of Property.**–The term "levy" as used in this title includes the power of distraint and seizure by any means. Except as otherwise provided in subsection (e), a levy shall extend only to property possessed and obligations existing at the time thereof. In any case in which the Secretary may levy upon property or rights to property, he may seize and sell such property or rights to property (whether real or personal, tangible or intangible).

(c) **Successive Seizures.**–Whenever any property or right to property upon which levy has been made by virtue of subsection (a) is not sufficient to satisfy the claim of the United States for which levy is made, the Secretary may, thereafter, and as often as may be necessary, proceed to levy in like manner upon any other property liable to levy of the person against whom such claim exists, until the amount due from him, together with all expenses, is fully paid.

Sec. 6332. SURRENDER OF PROPERTY SUBJECT TO LEVY.

(a) **Requirement** –Except as otherwise provided in this section, any person in possession of (or obligated with respect to) property or rights to property subject to levy upon which a levy has been made shall, upon demand of the Secretary, surrender such property or rights (or discharge such obligation) to the Secretary, except such part of the property or rights as is, at the time of such demand, subject to an attachment or execution under any judicial process.

(b) Special Rule for Life Insurance and Endowment Contracts

(1) In general.–A levy on an organization with respect to a life insurance or endowment contract issued by such organization shall, without necessity for the surrender of the contract document, constitute a demand by the Secretary for payment of the amount described in paragraph (2) and the exercise of the right of the person against whom the tax is assessed to the advance of such amount. Such organization shall pay over such amount 90 days after service of notice of levy. Such notice shall include a certification by the Secretary that a copy of such notice has been mailed to the person against whom the tax is assessed at his last known address.

(2) Satisfaction of levy.–Such levy shall be deemed to be satisfied if such organization pays over to the Secretary the amount which the person against whom the tax is assessed could have had advanced to him by such organization on the date prescribed in paragraph (1) for the satisfaction of such levy, increased by the amount of any advance (including contractual interest thereon) made to such person on or after the date such organization had actual notice or knowledge (within the meaning of section 6323 (i)(1)) of the existence of the lien with respect to which such levy is made, other than an advance (including contractual interest thereon) made automatically to maintain such contract in force under an agreement entered into before such organization had such notice or knowledge.

(3) Enforcement proceedings.–The satisfaction of a levy under paragraph (2) shall be without prejudice to any civil action for the enforcement of any lien imposed by this title with respect to such contract.

(c) Special Rule for Banks.–Any bank (as defined in section 408(n)) shall surrender (subject to an attachment or execution under judicial process) any deposits (including interest thereon) in such bank only after 21 days after service of levy.

(d) Enforcement of Levy.

(1) Extent of personal liability.–Any person who fails or refuses to surrender any property or rights to property, subject to levy, upon demand by the Secretary, shall be liable in his own person and estate to the United States in a sum equal to the value of the property or rights not so surrendered, but not exceeding the amount of taxes for the collection of which such levy has been made, together with costs and interest on such sum at the underpayment rate established under section 6621 from the date of such levy (or, in the case of a levy described in section 6331 (d)(3), from the date such person would otherwise have been obligated to pay over such amounts to the taxpayer). Any amount (other than costs) recovered under this paragraph shall be credited against the tax liability for the collection of which such levy was made.

(2) Penalty for violation.–In addition to the personal liability imposed by paragraph (1), if any person required to surrender property or rights to property fails or refuses to surrender such property or rights to property without reasonable cause, such person shall be liable for a penalty equal to 50 percent of the amount recoverable under paragraph (1). No part of such penalty shall be credited against the tax liability for the collection of which such levy was made.

(e) Effect of honoring levy.–Any person in possession of (or obligated with respect to) property or rights to property subject to levy upon which a levy has been made who, upon demand by the Secretary, surrenders such property or rights to property (or discharges such obligation) to the Secretary (or who pays a liability under subsection (d)(1)), shall be discharged from any obligation or liability to the delinquent taxpayer and any other person with respect to such property or rights to property arising from such surrender or payment.

Sec. 6333. PRODUCTION OF BOOKS.

If a levy has been made or is about to be made on any property, or right to property, any person having custody or control of any books or records, containing evidence or statements relating to the property or right to property subject to levy, shall, upon demand of the Secretary, exhibit such books or records to the Secretary.

Sec. 6343. AUTHORITY TO RELEASE LEVY AND RETURN PROPERTY.

(a) Release of Levy and Notice of Release.–

(1) In general.–Under regulations prescribed by the Secretary, the Secretary shall release the levy upon all, or part of, the property or rights to property levied upon and shall promptly notify the person upon whom such levy was made (if any) that such levy has been released if–

(A) the liability for which such levy was made is satisfied or becomes unenforceable by reason of lapse of time,

(B) release of such levy will facilitate the collection of such liability,

(C) the taxpayer has entered into an agreement under section 6159 to satisfy such liability by means of installment payments, unless such agreement provides otherwise,

(D) the Secretary has determined that such levy is creating an economic hardship due to the financial condition of the taxpayer, or

(E) the fair market value of the property exceeds such liability and release of the levy on a part of such property could be made without hindering the collection of such liability.

For purposes of subparagraph (C), the Secretary is not required to release such levy if such release would jeopardize the secured creditor status of the Secretary.

(2) Expedited determination on certain business property.–In the case of any tangible personal property essential to the trade or business of the taxpayer, the Secretary shall provide for an expedited determination under paragraph (1) if levy on such tangible personal property would prevent the taxpayer from carrying on such trade or business.

(3) Subsequent levy.–The release of levy on any property under paragraph (1) shall not prevent any subsequent levy on such property.

(b) Return of Property.–If the Secretary determines that property has been wrongfully levied upon, it shall be lawful for the Secretary to return–

(1) the specific property levied upon,

(2) an amount of money equal to the amount of money levied upon, or

(3) an amount of money equal to the amount of money received by the United States from a sale of such property.

Property may be returned at any time. An amount equal to the amount of money levied upon or received from such sale may be returned at any time before the expiration of 9 months from the date of such levy. For purposes of paragraph (3), if property is declared purchased by the United States at a sale pursuant to section 6335(e) (relating to manner and conditions of sale), the United States shall be treated as having received an amount of money equal to the minimum price determined pursuant to such section or (if larger) the amount received by the United States from the resale of such property.

(d) Return of Property in Certain Cases.— If–

(1) any property has been levied upon, and

(2) the Secretary determines that–

(A) the levy on such property was premature or otherwise not in accordance with administrative procedures of the Secretary,

(B) the taxpayer has entered into an agreement under section 6159 to satisfy the tax liability for which the levy was imposed by means of installment payments, unless such agreement provides otherwise,

(C) the return of such property will facilitate the collection of the tax liability, or

(D) with the consent of the taxpayer or the National Taxpayer Advocate, the return of such property would be in the best interests of the taxpayer (as determined by the National Taxpayer Advocate) and the United States, the provisions of subsection (b) shall apply in the same manner as if such property had been wrongly levied upon, except that no interest shall be allowed under subsection (c).

* * * * * * * * * *

Applicable Sections of Internal Revenue Code

6321. LIEN FOR TAXES.
6322. PERIOD OF LIEN.
6325. RELEASE OF LIEN OR DISCHARGE OF PROPERTY.
6331. LEVY AND DISTRAINT.
6332. SURRENDER OF PROPERTY SUBJECT TO LEVY.
6333. PRODUCTION OF BOOKS.
6334. PROPERTY EXEMPT FROM LEVY.
6343. AUTHORITY TO RELEASE LEVY AND RETURN PROPERTY.
7426. CIVIL ACTIONS BY PERSONS OTHER THAN TAXPAYERS.
7429. REVIEW OF JEOPARDY LEVY OR ASSESSMENT PROCEDURES.

For more information about this notice, please call the phone number on the front of this form.

Form **668-A(ICS)** (1-2015)

Form **668-A(ICS)**	Department of the Treasury – Internal Revenue Service
(January 2015)	**Notice of Levy**

DATE: **01/10/2018**

REPLY TO: **Internal Revenue Service**
RICHARD A WALLIN
1550 AMERICAN BLVD EAST
STE 500 M/S 5128
BLOOMINGTON, MN 55425

TO: **FIRST BANK & TRUST**
215 W 4TH AVE
MILBANK, SD 57252

TELEPHONE NUMBER
OF IRS OFFICE: **(763)347-7398**

NAME AND ADDRESS OF TAXPAYER:
BRADLEY J FRANKS
408 S LINCOLN ST
MILBANK, SD 57252-2326088

IDENTIFYING NUMBER(S): **390-80-4016**

FRAN

Kind of Tax	Tax Period Ended	Unpaid Balance of Assessment	Statutory Additions	Total
CIVPEN	12/31/2016	$55,040.00	$969.88	$56,009.88

This levy won't attach funds in IRAs, Self-Employed Individuals' Retirement Plans, or any other Retirement Plans in your possession or control, unless it is signed in the block to the right. =================== ⟹			Total Amount Due	$56,009.88

We figured the interest and late payment penalty to **02/09/2018**

Although we have told you to pay the amount you owe, it is still not paid. This is your copy of a notice of levy we have sent to collect this unpaid amount. We will send other levies if we don't get enough with this one.

Banks, credit unions, savings and loans, and similar institutions described in section 408(n) of the Internal Revenue Code must hold your money for 21 calendar days before sending it to us. They must include the interest you earn during that time. Anyone else we send a levy to must turn over your money, property, credits, etc. that they have *(or are already obligated for)* when they would have paid you.

If you decide to pay the amount you owe now, please **bring** a guaranteed payment *(cash, cashier's check, certified check, or money order*) to the nearest IRS office with this form, so we can tell the person who received this levy not to send us your money. Make checks and money orders payable to **United States Treasury**. If you mail your payment instead of bringing it to us, we may not have time to stop the person who received this levy from sending us your money.

If we have erroneously levied your bank account, we may reimburse you for the fees your bank charged you for handling the levy. You must file a claim with the IRS on Form 8546 within one year after the fees are charged.

If you have any questions, or want to arrange payment before other levies are issued, please call or write us. If you write to us, please include your telephone number and the best time to call. *Visit www.irs.gov to determine the closest IRS office that furnishes cash payment processing service.

Signature of Service Representative	Title
/S/ RICHARD A WALLIN	**REVENUE OFFICER**

Part 4 – For Taxpayer

Form **668-A(ICS)** (1-2015)

282

Excerpts from the Internal Revenue Code
* * * * * * * * * * *

Sec. 6331. LEVY AND DISTRAINT.

(b) Seizure and Sale of Property.–The term "levy" as used in this title includes the power of distraint and seizure by any means. Except as otherwise provided in subsection (e), a levy shall extend only to property possessed and obligations existing at the time thereof. In any case in which the Secretary may levy upon property or rights to property, he may seize and sell such property or rights to property (whether real or personal, tangible or intangible).

(c) Successive Seizures.–Whenever any property or right to property upon which levy has been made by virtue of subsection (a) is not sufficient to satisfy the claim of the United States for which levy is made, the Secretary may, thereafter, and as often as may be necessary, proceed to levy in like manner upon any other property liable to levy of the person against whom such claim exists, until the amount due from him, together with all expenses, is fully paid.

Sec. 6332. SURRENDER OF PROPERTY SUBJECT TO LEVY.

(a) Requirement.–Except as otherwise provided in this section, any person in possession of (or obligated with respect to) property or rights to property subject to levy upon which a levy has been made shall, upon demand of the Secretary, surrender such property or rights to property (or discharge such obligation) to the Secretary, except such part of the property or rights as is, at the time of such demand, subject to an attachment or execution under any judicial process.

(b) Special rule for Life Insurance and Endowment Contracts

(1) In general.–A levy on an organization with respect to a life insurance or endowment contract issued by such organization shall, without necessity for the surrender of the contract document, constitute a demand by the Secretary for payment of the amount described in paragraph (2) and the exercise of the right of the person against whom the tax is assessed to the advance of such amount. Such organization shall pay over such amount 90 days after service of notice of levy. Such notice shall include a certification by the Secretary that a copy of such notice has been mailed to the person against whom the tax is assessed at his last known address.

(2) Satisfaction of levy.–Such levy shall be deemed to be satisfied if such organization pays over to the Secretary the amount which the person against whom the tax is assessed could have had advanced to him by such organization on the date prescribed in paragraph (1) for the satisfaction of such levy, increased by the amount of any advance (including contractual interest thereon) made to such person on or after the date such organization had actual notice or knowledge (within the meaning of section 6323 (i)(1)) of the existence of the lien with respect to which such levy is made, other than an advance (including contractual interest thereon) made automatically to maintain such contract in force under an agreement entered into before such organization had such notice or knowledge.

(3) Enforcement proceedings.–The satisfaction of a levy under paragraph (2) shall be without prejudice to any civil action for the enforcement of any lien imposed by this title with respect to such contract.

(c) Special Rule for Banks.–Any bank (as defined in section 408(n)) shall surrender (subject to an attachment or execution under judicial process) any deposits (including interest thereon) in such bank only after 21 days after service of levy.

(d) Enforcement of Levy.

(1) Extent of personal liability.–Any person who fails or refuses to surrender any property or rights to property, subject to levy, upon demand by the Secretary, shall be liable in his own person and estate to the United States in a sum equal to the value of the property or rights not so surrendered, but not exceeding the amount of taxes for the collection of which such levy has been made, together with costs and interest on such sum at the underpayment rate established under section 6621 from the date of such levy (or, in the case of a levy described in section 6331 (d)(3), from the date such person would have been obligated to pay over such amounts to the taxpayer). Any amount (other than costs) recovered under this paragraph shall be credited against the tax liability for the collection of which such levy was made.

(2) Penalty for violation.–In addition to the personal liability imposed by paragraph (1), if any person required to surrender property or rights to property fails or refuses to surrender such property or rights to property without reasonable cause, such person shall be liable for a penalty equal to 50 percent of the amount recoverable under paragraph (1). No part of such penalty shall be credited against the tax liability for the collection of which such levy was made.

(e) Effect of honoring levy.–Any person in possession of or obligated with respect to) property or rights to property subject to levy upon which a levy has been made who, upon demand by the Secretary, surrenders such property or rights to property (or discharges such obligation) to the Secretary (or who pays a liability under subsection (d)(1)), shall be discharged from any obligation or liability to the delinquent taxpayer and any other person with respect to such property or rights to property arising from such surrender or payment.

Sec. 6333. PRODUCTION OF BOOKS.

If a levy has been made or is about to be made on any property, or right to property, any person having custody or control of any books or records, containing evidence or statements relating to the property or right to property subject to levy, shall, upon demand of the Secretary, exhibit such books or records to the Secretary.

Sec. 6343. AUTHORITY TO RELEASE LEVY AND RETURN PROPERTY.

(a) Release of Levy and Notice of Release.–

(1) In general.–Under regulations prescribed by the Secretary, the Secretary shall release the levy upon all, or part of, the property or rights to property levied upon and shall promptly notify the person upon whom such levy was made (if any) that such levy has been released if–

(A) the liability for which such levy was made is satisfied or becomes unenforceable by reason of lapse of time,

(B) release of such levy will facilitate the collection of such liability,

(C) the taxpayer has entered into an agreement under section 6159 to satisfy such liability by means of installment payments, unless such agreement provides otherwise,

(D) the Secretary has determined that such levy is creating an economic hardship due to the financial condition of the taxpayer, or

(E) the fair market value of the property exceeds such liability and release of the levy on a part of such property could be made without hindering the collection of such liability.

For purposes of subparagraph (C), the Secretary is not required to release such levy if such release would jeopardize the secured creditor status of the Secretary.

(2) Expedited determination on certain business property.–In the case of any tangible personal property essential in carrying on the trade or business of the taxpayer, the Secretary shall provide for an expedited determination under paragraph (1) if levy on such tangible personal property would prevent the taxpayer from carrying on such trade or business.

(3) Subsequent levy.–The release of levy on any property under paragraph (1) shall not prevent any subsequent levy on such property.

(b) Return of Property.–If the Secretary determines that property has been wrongfully levied upon, it shall be lawful for the Secretary to return–

(1) the specific property levied upon,

(2) an amount of money equal to the amount of money levied upon, or

(3) an amount of money equal to the amount of money received by the United States from a sale of such property.

Property may be returned at any time. An amount equal to the amount of money levied upon or received from such sale may be returned at any time before the expiration of 9 months from the date of such levy. For purposes of paragraph (3), if property is declared purchased by the United States at a sale pursuant to section 6335(e) (relating to manner and conditions of sale), the United States shall be treated as having received an amount of money equal to the minimum price determined pursuant to such section or (if larger) the amount received by the United States from the resale of such property.

(d) Return of Property in Certain Cases.— If—

(1) any property has been levied upon, and

(2) the Secretary determines that—

(A) the levy on such property was premature or otherwise not in accordance with administrative procedures of the Secretary,

(B) the taxpayer has entered into an agreement under section 6159 to satisfy tax liability for which the levy was imposed by means of installment payments, unless such agreement provides otherwise,

(C) the return of such property will facilitate the collection of the tax liability, or

(D) with the consent of the taxpayer or the National Taxpayer Advocate, the return of such property would be in the best interests of the taxpayer (as determined by the National Taxpayer Advocate) and the United States, the provisions of subsection (b) shall apply in the same manner as if such property had been wrongly levied upon, except that no interest shall be allowed under subsection (c).

* * * * * * * * *

Applicable Sections of Internal Revenue Code

6321. LIEN FOR TAXES.
6322. PERIOD OF LIEN.
6325. RELEASE OF LIEN OR DISCHARGE OF PROPERTY.
6331. LEVY AND DISTRAINT.
6332. SURRENDER OF PROPERTY SUBJECT TO LEVY.
6333. PRODUCTION OF BOOKS.
6334. PROPERTY EXEMPT FROM LEVY.
6343. AUTHORITY TO RELEASE LEVY AND RETURN PROPERTY.
7426. CIVIL ACTIONS BY PERSONS OTHER THAN TAXPAYERS.
7429. REVIEW OF JEOPARDY LEVY OR ASSESSMENT PROCEDURES.

For more information about this notice, please call the phone number on the front of this form.

Form **668-A(ICS)** (1-2015)

Internal Revenue Service
1973 North Rulon White Blvd.
M/S 4450
Ogden, UT 84201-0076

Department of the Treasury

Taxpayer Identification Number: 390-80-4016

Form: 1040 Tax Year(s): 201612

Date: February 23, 2017

Person to Contact: Mrs. Davis

BRADLEY J FRANKS
408 SOUTH LINCOLN STREET
MILBANK SD 57252

Employee Identification Number: 1000099771

Contact Telephone Number: 1-866-883-0235 (Toll Free)
Contact Hours: 7 A.M to 3:30 P.M MST Monday-Friday

Dear Taxpayer:

You recently filed a return or purported return claiming one or more frivolous positions. If not immediately corrected, the Internal Revenue Service will assess a $5,000 penalty against you. You can correct the problem and avoid the penalty if you submit a corrected return within 30 days of this letter to the address listed above.

If you continue to submit documents asserting frivolous positions, we will assess the $5,000 penalty each time you submit a frivolous return. If you file a joint return, we will assess the $5,000 penalty against both you and your spouse. Internal Revenue Code section 6702 provides the IRS with the authority to assess the penalty.

Why We Are Contacting You

Based on Section 6702, *Frivolous Tax Submissions*, we have determined the information you filed as a tax return, or purported tax return, on 1/21/2017 is frivolous and there is no basis in the law for your position.

Federal courts, including the Supreme Court of the United States, have considered positions such as yours and repeatedly rejected them as without merit. The enclosed Publication 2105, Why do I have to Pay Taxes?, includes examples of frivolous positions and arguments regarding the U.S. tax system under the heading "Don't Fall for These Arguments." Some of these examples include:

- Arguing that filing and paying taxes is voluntary.

Letter 3176(SC) (Rev. 4-2012)
Catalog Number 26860K

284

- Excluding salaries and/or wages from income based on the argument that the value of services is not taxable or that salaries and/or wages are not income.

- Arguing that the requirement to file a tax return violates Constitutional rights protecting taxpayers against self-incrimination.

- Submitting a claim for a refundable credit when there is no basis in law for the credit, such as a credit for reparations for slavery, or frivolous Forms 2439, 1099, or 4136 (fuel tax credit), or showing excessive withholding on your return.

- Submitting a document that purports to be a tax return but is not properly signed or contains an altered jurat (the written declaration that verifies that a return, declaration, statement or other document is made under penalties of perjury).

These are just some examples. For more information on positions identified as frivolous under section 6702, see Notice 2010-33, 2010-17 I.R.B., April 26, 2010, pp. 609-12, which can be found on the Internal Revenue Service's website at www.IRS.gov (See Notice 2010-33 at http://www.irs.gov/irb/2010-17_IRB/ar13.html). If you do not have a computer, you can access Notice 2010-33 in the Internal Revenue Bulletin (I.R.B.), which is the IRS's authoritative publication of rulings and statements of procedure. Consult a law library to obtain the I.R.B. You can find additional information in a publication titled The Truth About Frivolous Arguments, available on-line only at http://www.irs.gov/pub/irs-utl/friv_tax.pdf

As stated above, we are proposing to assess a $5,000 penalty against you for each frivolous tax return or purported tax return that you filed.

WHAT YOU NEED TO DO

To avoid the penalty, send us a corrected return for each taxable period in the heading of this letter within 30 days of the date of this letter. If you send us corrected returns, we will disregard the previous documents that you filed and not assess the frivolous tax return penalty for each corrected return filed.

Please attach this letter to your corrected return(s) and mail to the address shown at the top of this letter. We have enclosed a copy of this letter for your records and an envelope for your convenience.

WHAT IF YOU DO NOT SEND A CORRECTED RETURN?

If you do not file the corrected return(s) within 30 days of the date of this letter, or if you submit additional documents asserting a frivolous position, we will assess the $5,000 penalty for each frivolous tax return or purported return containing a frivolous position and send you a bill. If you filed a joint frivolous return, both you and your spouse will be assessed a $5,000 penalty. We will not respond to any future correspondence asserting any frivolous position.

Letter 3176(SC) (Rev. 4-2012)
Catalog Number 26860K

Notice	CP15
Tax Year	2016
Notice date	May 29, 2017
Social Security number	390-80-4016
To contact us	1-800-829-0922
Your Caller ID	813596
Page 1 of 2	18H

Department of the Treasury
Internal Revenue Service
Austin, TX 73301-0010

149182.610366.369556.2323 1 AB 0.403 538

BRADLEY J FRANKS
408 S LINCOLN ST
MILBANK SD 57252-2326

149182

Notice of Penalty Charge

666

You have been charged a penalty under Section 6702(a) of the Internal Revenue Code for Civil Penalty for Frivolous Tax Returns.

TAX STATEMENT

Prior Balance	$0.00
Penalty Assessment	$15,000.00
Interest	$0.00
Bad Check Penalty	$0.00
Balance Due	**$15,000.00**

BRADLEY J FRANKS
408 S LINCOLN ST
MILBANK SD 57252-2326

Notice	CP15
Notice date	May 29, 2017
Social Security number	390-80-4016

Payment

- Make your check or money order payable to the United States Treasury.
- Write your Social Security number (390-80-4016), the tax year (2016), and the form number (CVL PEN) on your payment and any correspondence.

Amount due by June 19, 2017 | **$15,000.00**

INTERNAL REVENUE SERVICE
AUSTIN, TX 73301-0010

390804016 LO FRAN 55 0 201612 670 00001500000

286

Notice	CP15
Tax Year	2016
Notice date	May 29, 2017
Social Security number	390-80-4016
Page 2 of 2	18H

We charged you a penalty under IRC section 6702(a) for filing a frivolous tax return. The penalty applies when a person files what purports to be a return but—

A.

1. fails to include information on which the substantial correctness of the self-assessment may be judged or
2. includes information that on its face indicates that the self-assessment is substantially incorrect and

B.

1. the penalty applies when the underlying conduct in relation to filing such return is based on a position that the Internal Revenue Service has identified as frivolous (see Notice 2007-30) or
2. the underlying conduct reflects a desire to delay or impede the administration of Federal tax laws.

The penalty is $5,000 for each person who files a frivolous tax return.

If you wish to contest the assertion of this penalty, you must fully pay the entire penalty and file a claim for refund with the IRS within three years from the time a return associated with the penalty was filed or two years from the date the penalty was paid, whichever period expires later.

If your refund claim is pending for six months or more and the IRS has not issued a notice of claim disallowance with regard to the claim, you may file suit in the United States District Court or United States Court of Federal Claims to contest the assertion of the penalty at any time. Once the IRS issues a notice of claim disallowance, however, you must file suit in the United States District Court or The United States Court of Federal Claims within two years of the date the IRS mails a notice of disallowance to you denying the refund claim.

IRS

Contact information

BRADLEY J FRANKS
408 S LINCOLN ST
MILBANK SD 57252-2326

Notice	CP15
Notice date	May 29, 2017
Social Security number	390-80-4016

If your address has changed, please call 1-800-829-0922 or visit www.irs.gov.
☐ Please check here if you've included any correspondence. Write your Social Security number (390-80-4016), the tax year (2016), and the form number (CVL PEN) on any correspondence.

Primary phone | Best time to call | ☐ a.m. ☐ p.m. Secondary phone | Best time to call | ☐ a.m. ☐ p.m.

INTERNAL REVENUE SERVICE
AUSTIN, TX 73301-0010

390804016 LO FRAN 55 0 201612

287

In addition, if we do not hear from you within the 30 day timeframe, we may issue a notice of deficiency for any taxes owed because of the frivolous submission or because of other items we may find during an examination. A notice of deficiency states the amount of additional tax and penalties you owe and explains your right to contest the deficiency by filing a petition with the United States Tax Court. The $5,000 frivolous filing penalty is not included on the notice of deficiency and cannot be contested in the Tax Court.

We have enclosed Publication 2105, Why Do I Have to Pay Taxes?, which provides basic information about the tax system. We also encourage you to seek advice from a competent tax professional or a tax attorney qualified to practice in your state.

Sincerely yours,

Christie L Davis

Program Manager
Return Integrity and Compliance Services

Enclosures:
Publication 2105
Copy of this letter
Envelope

Letter 3176(SC) (Rev. 4-2012)
Catalog Number 26860K

Notice	CP15
Tax Year	2016
Notice date	May 29, 2017
Social Security number	390-80-4016
Page 2 of 2	18H

We charged you a penalty under IRC section 6702(a) for filing a frivolous tax return. The penalty applies when a person files what purports to be a return but—

A.
1. fails to include information on which the substantial correctness of the self-assessment may be judged or
2. includes information that on its face indicates that the self-assessment is substantially incorrect and

B.
1. the penalty applies when the underlying conduct in relation to filing such return is based on a position that the Internal Revenue Service has identified as frivolous (see Notice 2007-30) or
2. the underlying conduct reflects a desire to delay or impede the administration of Federal tax laws.

The penalty is $5,000 for each person who files a frivolous tax return.

If you wish to contest the assertion of this penalty, you must fully pay the entire penalty and file a claim for refund with the IRS within three years from the time a return associated with the penalty was filed or two years from the date the penalty was paid, whichever period expires later.

If your refund claim is pending for six months or more and the IRS has not issued a notice of claim disallowance with regard to the claim, you may file suit in the United States District Court or United States Court of Federal Claims to contest the assertion of the penalty at any time. Once the IRS issues a notice of claim disallowance, however, you must file suit in the United States District Court or The United States Court of Federal Claims within two years of the date the IRS mails a notice of disallowance to you denying the refund claim.

IRS

Contact information

BRADLEY J FRANKS
408 S LINCOLN ST
MILBANK SD 57252-2326

Notice	CP15
Notice date	May 29, 2017
Social Security number	390-80-4016

If your address has changed, please call 1-800-829-0922 or visit www.irs.gov.

☐ Please check here if you've included any correspondence. Write your Social Security number (390-80-4016), the tax year (2016), and the form number (CVL PEN) on any correspondence.

Primary phone	Best time to call	Secondary phone	Best time to call
☐ a.m. ☐ p.m.		☐ a.m. ☐ p.m.	

INTERNAL REVENUE SERVICE
AUSTIN, TX 73301-0010

390804016 LO FRAN 55 0 201612

289

Notice	CP11
Tax Year	2016
Notice date	June 26, 2017
Social Security number	390-80-4016
To contact us	1-800-829-0922
Your Caller ID	813596
Page 1 of 4	89H

Department of the Treasury
Internal Revenue Service
Austin, TX 73301-0010

IRS

019901.620744.417131.3320 1 MB 0.423 701

BRADLEY J FRANKS
408 S LINCOLN ST
MILBANK SD 57252-2326

019901

Changes to your 2016 Form 1040

Amount due: $134,787,942.88

We found miscalculations on your 2016 Form 1040, which affect the following areas of your return:
- Tax Computation
- Standard Deduction
- Income

We changed your return to correct these errors. As a result, you owe $134,787,942.88.

Billing Summary

Tax you owed	$133,831,273.37
Payments you made	0.00
Interest charges	956,669.51
Amount due by July 3, 2017	$134,787,942.88

Continued on back...

IRS

Payment

BRADLEY J FRANKS
408 S LINCOLN ST
MILBANK SD 57252-2326

Notice	CP11
Notice date	June 26, 2017
Social Security number	390-80-4016

- Make your check or money order payable to the United States Treasury.
- Write your Social Security number (390-80-4016), the tax year (2016), and the form number (1040) on your payment and any correspondence.

Amount due by July 3, 2017	$134,787,942.88

INTERNAL REVENUE SERVICE
AUSTIN, TX 73301-0010

390804016 LO FRAN 30 0 201612 670 13478794288

290

Notice	CP11
Tax Year	2016
Notice date	June 26, 2017
Social Security number	390-80-4016
Page 2 of 4	89H

What you need to do immediately	Review this notice, and compare our changes to the information on your tax return.
	If you agree with the changes we made
	• Pay the amount due of $134,787,942.88 by July 3, 2017, to avoid additional penalty and interest charges.
	• Pay online or mail a check or money order with the attached payment stub. **You can pay online now at www.irs.gov/payments.**
	• If you contact us in writing within 60 days of the date of this notice, we will reverse the change we made to your account. However, if you are unable to provide us additional information that justifies the reversal and we believe the reversal is in error, we will forward your case for audit. This step gives you formal appeal rights, including the right to appeal our decision in court before you have to pay the additional tax. After we forward your case, the audit staff will contact you within 5 to 6 weeks to fully explain the audit process and your rights. If you do not contact us within the 60-day period, you will lose your right to appeal our decision before payment of tax.
	• If you do not contact us within 60 days, the change will not be reversed and you must pay the additional tax. You may then file a claim for refund. You must submit the claim within 3 years of the date you filed the tax return, or within 2 years of the date of your last payment for this tax.
	If you disagree with the amount due
	• Call us at 1-800-829-0922 to review your account with a representative. Be sure to have your account information available when you call.
	We'll assume you agree with the information in this notice if we don't hear from you.
Payment options	**Pay now electronically**
	We offer free payment options to securely pay your tax bill directly from your checking or savings account. When you pay online or with your mobile device, you can:
	• Receive instant confirmation of your payment
	• Schedule payments in advance
	• Reschedule or cancel a payment before the due date

019901

Payment options – continued

You can also pay by debit or credit card for a small fee. To see all of our payment options, visit www.irs.gov/payments.

Payment plans
If you can't pay the full amount you owe, pay as much as you can now and make arrangements to pay your remaining balance. Visit www.irs.gov/paymentplan for more information on installment agreements and online payment agreements. You can also call us at 1-800-829-0922 to discuss your options.

Offer in Compromise
An offer in compromise allows you to settle your tax debt for less than the full amount you owe. If we accept your offer, you can pay with either a lump sum cash payment plan or periodic payment plan. To see if you qualify, use the Offer in Compromise Pre-Qualifier tool on our website. For more information, visit www.irs.gov/offers.

Account balance and payment history
For information on how to obtain your current account balance or payment history, go to www.irs.gov/balancedue.

If you already paid your balance in full within the past 21 days or made payment arrangements, please disregard this notice.
If you think we made a mistake, call 1-800-829-0922 to review your account.

If we don't hear from you

- Pay $134,787,942.88 by July 3, 2017, to avoid penalty and interest charges.

Changes to your 2016 tax return

Information was changed because of the following:
- We changed the amount of total income on Line 22 of your Form 1040 because there was an error in the computation.
- We changed the amount claimed as standard deduction on line 40 of your Form 1040:
  - No amount was entered for the standard deduction, **or**
  - The amount entered for the standard deduction was incorrect for the filing status claimed on your return.
- We changed the refund amount on Line 76a or the amount you owe on Line 78 of your Form 1040 because the amount entered on your tax return was computed incorrectly.

Your tax calculations

Description	Your calculations	IRS calculations
Adjusted gross income, line 37	$8,074,743.00	$338,074,743.00
Taxable income, line 43	0.00	338,068,443.00
Total tax, line 63	$0.00	$133,831,273.37

Continued on back...

Notice	CP11
Tax Year	2016
Notice date	June 26, 2017
Social Security number	390-80-4016
Page 4 of 4	89H

Changes to your 2016 tax return — continued

Your payments and credits

Description	IRS calculations
Income tax withheld, line 64	$0.00
Estimated tax payments, line 65	0.00
Other credits, lines 66a, 67-73	0.00
Other payments	0.00
Total payments and credits	**$0.00**

Interest charges

We are required by law to charge interest when you do not pay your liability on time. Generally, we calculate interest from the due date of your return (regardless of extensions) until you pay the amount you owe in full, including accrued interest and any penalty charges. Interest on some penalties accrues from the date we notify you of the penalty until it is paid in full. Interest on other penalties, such as failure to file a tax return, starts from the due date or extended due date of the return. Interest rates are variable and may change quarterly. (Internal Revenue Code section 6601)

Description	Amount
Total interest	**$956,669.51**

The table below shows the rates used to calculate the interest on your unpaid amount due. For a detailed calculation of your interest, call 1-800-829-0922.

Period	Interest rate
Beginning April 1, 2016	4%

Additional information

- Visit www.irs.gov/cp11
- You may find the following publications helpful:
  - Publication 1, Your Rights as a Taxpayer
  - Publication 594, The Collection Process
- For tax forms, instructions, and publications, visit www.irs.gov or call 1-800-TAX-FORM (1-800-829-3676).
- Did you e-file your tax return? Electronically filed returns are less likely to have math errors resulting in notices such as this one. It's free to file your taxes electronically. Go to www.irs.gov/efile for information and instructions.
- Paying online is convenient, secure, and ensures timely receipt of your payment. To pay your taxes online or for more information, go to www.irs.gov/payments.
- You can contact us by mail at the address at the top of this notice. Be sure to include your social security number, the tax year, and the form number you are writing about.
- Keep this notice for your records.

If you need assistance, please don't hesitate to contact us.

Department of the Treasury
Internal Revenue Service
Austin, TX 73301-0030

9307 1107 5620 4205 9215 54

074872.626553.442459.3863 2 MB 0.423 1134

	WI
Notice	CP504
Tax Year	2016
Notice date	July 24, 2017
Social Security number	390-80-4016
To contact us	Phone 1-800-829-0922
Your Caller ID	813596
Page 1 of 4	

074872

BRADLEY J FRANKS
408 S LINCOLN ST
MILBANK SD 57252-2326

Notice of Intent to seize (levy) your property or rights to property

Amount due immediately: $15,092.33

This is a notice of intent to levy your state tax refund or other property. As we notified you before, our records show you have unpaid taxes for the tax year ending December 31, 2016 (Form CIVPEN). If you don't call us immediately to make payment arrangements or pay the amount due, we may levy your property or rights to property and apply it to the $15,092.33 you owe.

Billing Summary

Amount you owed	· $15,000.00
Interest charges	92.33
Amount due immediately	**$15,092.33**

Continued on back...

IRS

Payment

BRADLEY J FRANKS
408 S LINCOLN ST
MILBANK SD 57252-2326

Notice	CP504
Notice date	July 24, 2017
Social Security number	390-80-4016

- Make your check or money order payable to the United States Treasury.
- Write your Social Security number (390-80-4016), the tax year (2016), and the form number (CIVPEN) on your payment and any correspondence.

Amount due immediately	$15,092.33

INTERNAL REVENUE SERVICE
AUSTIN, TX 73301-0025

390804016 LO FRAN 55 0 201612 670 00001509233

	WI
Notice	CP504
Tax Year	2016
Notice date	July 24, 2017
Social Security number	390-80-4016
Page 2 of 4	

What you need to do immediately	**If you agree with the amount due and you're not working with an IRS representative**
	• Pay the amount due of $15,092.33 immediately or we may file Notice of Federal Tax Lien, the amount of interest will increase, and additional penalties may apply.
	• Pay online or mail a check or money order with the attached payment stub. **You can pay online now at www.irs.gov/payments.**
	If we notified you that we suspended enforced collection on your account because it would create a financial hardship (meaning you would be unable to pay basic reasonable living expenses if we levied) and your financial condition has not changed, you don't need to do anything.
	If you disagree with the amount due
	Call us at 1-800-829-0922 to review your account with a representative. Be sure to have your account information available when you call. We'll assume you agree with the information in this notice if we don't hear from you.
What you need to know	**Notice of Intent to Levy**
	This notice is your Notice of Intent to Levy (Internal Revenue Code Section 6331 (d).
	If you don't pay the amount due by August 3, 2017, we can levy your state tax refund or other property rights or rights to property. Property or rights to property includes:
	- Wages, real estate commissions, and other income
	- Bank accounts
	- Personal assets (e.g., your car and home)
	- Social security benefits
	Rights to request an appeal
	If you don't agree, you have the right to request an appeal under the Collection Appeals Program. Please call 1-800-829-0922 or send us a Collection Appeals Request (Form 9423) to the address at the top of the notice by August 3, 2017.

	WI
Notice	CP504
Tax Year	2016
Notice date	July 24, 2017
Social Security number	390-80-4016
Page 3 of 4	

)74872

What you need to know—continued

Denial or revocation of United States passport

On December 4, 2015, as part of the Fixing America's Surface Transportation (FAST) Act, Congress enacted section 7345 of the Internal Revenue Code, which requires the Internal Revenue Service to notify the State Department of taxpayers certified as owing a seriously delinquent tax debt. The FAST Act generally prohibits the State Department from issuing or renewing a passport to a taxpayer with seriously delinquent tax debt.

Seriously delinquent tax debt means an unpaid, legally enforceable federal tax debt of an individual totaling more than $50,000 for which, a Notice of Federal Tax lien has been filed and all administrative remedies under IRC § 6320 have lapsed or been exhausted, or a levy has been issued. If you are individually liable for tax debt (including penalties and interest) totaling more than $50,000 and you do not pay the amount you owe or make alternate arrangements to pay, we may notify the State Department that your tax debt is seriously delinquent. The State Department generally will not issue or renew a passport to you after we make this notification. If you currently have a valid passport, the State Department may revoke your passport or limit your ability to travel outside of the United States. Additional information on passport certification is available at www.irs.gov/passports.

Payment options

Pay now electronically

We offer free payment options to securely pay your tax bill directly from your checking account or savings account. When you pay online or from your mobile device, you can:
- Receive instant confirmation of your payment
- Schedule payments in advance
- Modify or cancel a payment before the due date

Payment plans

If you can't pay the full amount you owe, pay as much as you can now and make arrangements to pay your remaining balance. Visit www.irs.gov/paymentplan for more information on installment agreements and online payment agreements. You can also call us at 1-800-829-0922 to discuss your options.

Offer in Compromise

An offer in compromise allows you to settle your tax debt for less than the full amount you owe. If we accept your offer, you can pay with either a lump sum cash payment plan or periodic payment plan. To see if you qualify, use the Offer in Compromise Pre-Qualifier tool on our website. For more information, visit www.irs.gov/offers.

Account balance and payment history

For information on how to obtain your current account balance or payment history, go to www.irs.gov/balancedue.

If you've already paid your balance in full within the past 21 days or made payment arrangements, please disregard this notice.

If you think we made a mistake, call 1-800-829-0922 to review your account

Continued on back...

Notice	CP504
Tax Year	2016
Notice date	July 24, 2017
Social Security number	390-80-4016
Page 4 of 4	

If we don't hear from you

If you don't pay the amount due immediately or make payment arrangements, we can file a Notice of Federal Tax Lien on your property at any time or we may levy.

If we file a lien, it may be difficult to sell or borrow against your property. A tax lien will also appear on your credit report – which may harm your credit rating – and your creditors would also be publicly notified that the IRS has priority to seize your property.

Interest charges

We are required by law to charge interest when you do not pay your liability on time. Generally, we calculate interest from the due date of your return (regardless of extensions) until you pay the amount you owe in full, including accrued interest and any penalty charges. Interest on some penalties accrues from the date we notify you of the penalty until it is paid in full. Interest on other penalties, such as failure to file a tax return, starts from the due date or extended due date of the return. Interest rates are variable and may change quarterly. (Internal Revenue Code Section 6601)

Description	Amount
Total interest	**$92.33**

The table below shows the rates used to calculate the interest on your unpaid amount due. For a detailed calculation of your interest, call 1-800-829-0922.

Period	Interest Rate
October 1, 2016 through December 31, 2016	4%
January 1, 2017 through March 31, 2017	4%

Additional information

- Visit www.irs.gov/cp504
- You may find the following publications helpful:
  - Publication 1, Your Rights as a Taxpayer
- For tax forms, instructions, and publications, visit www.irs.gov or call 1-800-TAX-FORM (1-800-829-3676).
- Paying online is convenient, secure, and ensures timely receipt of your payment. To pay your taxes online or for more information, go to www.irs.gov/payments.
- Review the enclosed document: IRS Collection Process (Publication 594).
- You can contact us by mail at the following address. Be sure to include your social security number, the tax year, and the form number you are writing about.
  Internal Revenue Service
  Austin, TX 73301-0025
- Generally, we deal directly with taxpayers or their authorized representatives. However, occasionally we need to speak with other people, such as employees, employers, banks, or neighbors to gather or verify account information. If we contact a third party, the law prohibits us from sharing any more information than is necessary to obtain or verify what we need to know. You have the right to request a list of individuals we contact about your account.
- Keep this notice for your records

If you need assistance, please don't hesitate to contact us.

The **IRS** Collection Process

Publication 594

This publication provides a general description of the IRS collection process. The collection process is a series of actions that the IRS can take to collect the taxes you owe if you don't voluntarily pay them. The collection process will begin if you don't make your required payments in full and on time, after receiving your bill.

Please keep in mind that this publication is for information only, and may not account for every tax collection scenario. It's also not a technical analysis of tax law and does not include a detailed explanation of your rights. For an explanation of your rights, please see **Publication 1**, Your Rights as a Taxpayer.

If you have questions or need help

Please visit **http://www.irs.gov/Forms-&-Pubs** to find all the IRS tax forms and publications mentioned here, or to do a keyword search on any topic. You can visit **www.irsvideos.gov** to view informational videos on a variety of topics in this publication.

You can also visit your local IRS office, or call the number on your bill. If you don't have a bill, please call: 1-800-829-1040 (individuals) or 1-800-829-4933 (businesses). Before visiting your local IRS office, check the "Services Provided" and the hours of operation at **www.irs.gov/localcontacts**. Use the "Office Locator" link by entering your zip code to locate the nearest office which will give you the office address, hours of operation, and services provided.

Publication 594 (Rev. 1-2015) Catalog Number 46598B Department of the Treasury **Internal Revenue Service** www.irs.gov

Overview: Filing a tax return, billing, and collection

After you file your tax return and/or a final decision is made establishing your correct tax, we record the amount in our records. If you owe, we will send a bill for the amount due, including any penalties and interest. If you don't pay or make arrangements to pay, we can take actions to collect the debt. Our goal is to work with you to resolve your debt before we take collection actions. If your bill is for an individual shared responsibility payment as a result of the Affordable Care Act, the amount owed is not subject to the failure to pay penalty, levies or the filing of a Notice of Federal Tax Lien. However, interest will continue to accrue and the Service may offset federal tax refunds until the balance is paid in full.

➔ **General steps from billing to collection**
You file your tax return. Most returns are filed annually (by April 15th) or quarterly (businesses with employees).

1. **If you owe taxes, we will send you a bill.** This is your first bill for tax due. Based on your return, we will calculate how much tax you owe, plus any interest and penalties.

2. **If you don't pay your first bill, we will send you at least one more bill.** Remember, interest and penalties continue to accrue until you've paid your full amount due.

3. **If you still don't pay after you receive your final bill, we will begin collection actions.** Collection actions can range from applying your subsequent tax year refunds to tax due (until paid in full) to seizing your property and assets.

➔ **What you should do when you get an IRS bill**
If you agree with the information on the bill, pay the full amount before the due date. If you can't pay the full amount due, pay as much as you can and visit www.irs.gov/payments to consider our online payment options. Our online payment options include the Online Payment Agreement application which allows you to setup an installment agreement online. If you do not qualify for our online payment options, immediately contact us by calling the telephone number on your bill to explain your situation. You should have your financial information available, including your monthly income and expenses. Based on your ability to pay, we may provide you with alternate payment options such as setting up an installment agreement online.

If you disagree with the information on the bill, call the number on it, or visit your local IRS office. Be sure to have a copy of the bill and any tax returns, cancelled checks, or other records that will help us understand why you believe you're wrong. If we find that you're right, we will adjust your account and, if necessary, send a revised bill.

If you don't pay the amount due or tell us why you disagree with it, we may take collection actions.

If you are in bankruptcy, please notify us immediately. The bankruptcy may not eliminate your tax debt, but we may temporarily stop collection. Call the number on your bill or 1-800-973-0424. Have the following information available: the location of court, bankruptcy date, chapter and bankruptcy number.

➔ **Who to contact for help**
The Internal Revenue Service
Make IRS.gov your first stop for your tax needs. You can find answers with the Interactive Tax Assistant at IRS.gov/ITA. Please don't hesitate to contact us with any questions you may have. Call the number on your bill or 1-800-829-1040. You can find answers to your questions at IRS.gov or by visiting your local IRS office to speak with an IRS representative in person.

Taxpayer Advocate Service
The Taxpayer Advocate Service (TAS) is an independent organization within the Internal Revenue Service that helps taxpayers understand their rights and protects them under the Taxpayer Bill of Rights. The Taxpayer Bill of Rights describes 10 basic rights that all taxpayers have when dealing with the IRS. TAS helps taxpayers who are experiencing financial difficulties, facing an immediate threat of an adverse action, who have attempted but have been unable to resolve their problems with the IRS, and those who believe an IRS system or procedure is not working as it should. Their service is free. Your local advocate's number is in your local directory and www.taxpayeradvocate.irs.gov. You can also call us at 1-877-777-4778.

Low Income Taxpayer Clinics
Assistance can be obtained from individuals and organizations that are independent from the IRS. IRS Publication 4134, provides a listing of Low Income Taxpayer Clinic List (LITCs) and is available at www.irs.gov. Also, see the LITC page at www.taxpayeradvocate.irs.gov/litcmap. Assistance may also be available from a referral system operated by a state bar association, a state or local society of accountants or enrolled agents or another nonprofit tax professional organization. The decision to obtain assistance from any of these individuals and organizations will not result in the IRS giving preferential treatment in the handling of the issue, dispute or problem. You don't need to seek assistance to contact us. We will be pleased to deal with you directly and help you resolve your situation.

Ways to pay your taxes

To explore all of your payment options visit IRS.gov/payments. To minimize interest and penalties, we recommend paying your taxes in full. However, if you're unable to pay in full, you can request an Installment Agreement or Offer in Compromise. These payment plans allow you to pay your taxes in installments over time, to pay less than you owe, or both. It's also important to stay current on your payments for future taxes. This means making your estimated tax payments, withholding payments, or federal tax deposits as required by law.

➔ **Options for paying in full**
Electronic payments
We offer several electronic payment options. You can pay online, by phone or from your mobile device with the IRS2Go app. Go to IRS.gov/payments for the payment options, telephone numbers and easy secure ways to pay your taxes.

IRS Direct Pay
IRS Direct Pay is free and available at IRS.gov/DirectPay, where you can securely pay your taxes directly from your checking or savings accounts without any fees or pre-registration. Schedule payments up to 30 days in advance, and receive instant confirmation that you submitted your payment

Debit or credit card
You can pay your taxes by debit or credit card. Both paper and electronic filers can pay their taxes by phone or online through any of the authorized debit and credit card processors. Though the IRS does not charge a fee for this service, the card processors do. Go to IRS.gov/payments for authorized card processors and their phone numbers.

IRS2Go
To pay your federal taxes quickly on the go, use the IRS2Go mobile app. IRS2Go provides easy access to Direct Pay, offering you a free, secure way to pay directly from your checking or savings account. You can also make a debit or credit card payment through an approved payment processor for a fee. You can download IRS2Go from Google Play Store, the Apple App Store or Amazon Appstore, to pay your taxes anytime, anywhere.

Electronic Federal Tax Payment System
The Electronic Federal Tax Payment System is a free service that gives taxpayers a safe and convenient way to pay individual and business taxes by phone or online. To enroll or for more information, visit EFTPS.gov or call 800-555-4477.

The Death of America

or less in combined payroll taxes, penalty and interest for the current and prior calendar year, you can also use the Online Payment Agreement to request a payment agreement. To view an instructional video on the Online Payment Agreement application, visit **http://www.irsvideos.gov/Individual /PayingTaxes/OPA**.

- **By phone** Please call the number on your bill or 1-800-829-1040.
- **By mail** Please complete **Form 9465**, *Installment Agreement Request*. In addition to Form 9465, if you want to make your payments by payroll deduction, complete **Form 2159**, *Payroll Deduction Agreement*. If you owe more than $50,000, you will also need to complete **Form 433F**, *Collection Information Statement*. Mail your form to the address on your bill.
- **In person** at your local IRS office near you, please visit **www.irs .gov/localcontacts**.

If you request a payment plan, you can reduce the accrual of penalties and interest by making voluntary payments according to the proposed plan's terms until you're notified whether we've accepted your payment plan request. Our acceptance of your interim payments doesn't mean we've approved your request. We will notify you in writing once we've made our decision.

With an Installment Agreement, you can pay by direct debit, through payroll deductions, electronic funds transfer or check. There's a user fee for Installment Agreements. If you meet our low-income guidelines, you can pay a reduced user fee. For more information, see **Form 13844**, *Application for Reduced User Fee for Installment Agreements*. You do not need to submit the user fee for an installment agreement with the application. The fee can be taken from the initial payments made once the installment agreement is accepted.

To be eligible for an Installment Agreement, you must file all required tax returns. Prior to approving your Installment Agreement request, we may ask you to complete a Collection Information Statement (Form 433F, 433-A and/or Form 433-B) and provide proof of your financial status. Please have your financial information available if you apply over the phone or at an IRS office. For more information, see **Publication 1854**, *How to Complete a Collection Information Statement* (Form 433-A).

If we approve your request, we will still charge applicable interest and penalties until you pay the amount or balance due in full, and may file a Notice of Federal Tax Lien (see page 4). If we reject your Installment Agreement request, you may request that the Office of Appeals review your case. For more information, see **Publication 1660**, *Collection Appeal Rights*.

If you're unable to meet the terms of your approved Installment Agreement, please contact us immediately.

Apply for an Offer in Compromise

You may be eligible for an Offer in Compromise if you can't pay the amount you owe in full or through installments. By requesting an Offer in Compromise, you're asking to settle unpaid taxes for less than the full amount you owe. We may accept an Offer in Compromise if:

- We agree that your tax debt may not be accurate,
- You have insufficient assets and income to pay the amount due, or
- Because of your exceptional circumstances, paying the amount due would cause an economic hardship or would be unjust.

For an Offer in Compromise to be considered, you must pay an application fee and make an initial or periodic payment. However, low income taxpayers may qualify for a waiver of the application fee and initial or periodic payment. For more information, please see the Low Income Certification on **Form 656**, *Offer in Compromise*. This

form is contained in Form 656-B, *Offer in Compromise Booklet*.

You can use the Offer in Compromise Pre-Qualifier tool at **http://irs .treasury.gov/oic_pre_qualifier/** to explore the possibility that the Offer in Compromise program may be a realistic option to resolve your balance due. To apply for an Offer in Compromise, complete one of the following forms:

- **Form 656-L,** *Offer in Compromise (Doubt as to Liability)*
  Complete this if you think your tax debt isn't accurate.

- **Form 656,** *Offer in Compromise*
  Complete this if you're unable to pay the amount due, or have an economic hardship, or have another special circumstance that would cause paying the amount due to be unjust.

For more information, see **Form 656-B**, *Offer in Compromise Booklet* or visit **www.irs.gov/Individuals/Offer-in-Compromise-1**.

If you need more time to pay

Ask that we delay collection and report your account as currently not collectable

If you can't pay any of the amount due because payment would prevent you from meeting basic living expenses, you can request that we delay collection until you're able to pay. Prior to approving your request, we may ask you to complete a Collection Information Statement and provide proof of your financial status. Please remember that even if we delay collection, we will still charge applicable penalties and interest until you pay the full amount, and we may file a Notice of Federal Tax Lien (see page 4). We may also request updated financial information during this temporary delay to review your ability to pay.

How long we have to collect taxes

We can attempt to collect your taxes up to 10 years from the date they were assessed. However, there are ways this time period can be suspended. For example, by law, the time to collect may be suspended while:

- We're considering your request for an Installment Agreement or Offer in Compromise. If your request is rejected, we will suspend collection for another 30 days, and during any period the Appeals Office is considering your appeal request.
- You live outside the U.S. continuously for at least 6 months. Collection is suspended while you're outside the U.S.
- The tax periods we're collecting on are included in a bankruptcy with an automatic stay. We will suspend collection for the time period we can't collect because of the automatic stay, plus 6 months.
- You request a Collection Due Process hearing. Collection will be suspended from the date of your request until a Notice of Determination is issued or the Tax Court's decision is final.
- We're considering your request for Innocent Spouse Relief. Collection will be suspended from the date of your request until 90 days after a Notice of Determination is issued, or if you file a timely petition to the Tax Court, until 60 days after the Tax Court's final decision. If you appeal the Tax Court's decision to a U.S. Court of Appeals, the collection period will begin 60 days after the appeal is filed, unless a bond is posted.

How to appeal an IRS decision

You have the right to appeal most collection actions to the IRS Office of Appeals (Appeals). Appeals is separate from and independent of the IRS Collection office that initiates collection actions. Appeals ensures and protects its independence by adhering to a strict policy prohibiting certain communications with the IRS Collection office or other IRS offices, such as discussions regarding the strength or weakness of your case. When an IRS office is to be engaged in discussions, you will be invited you to

3

300

participate in the conference, or provided any written document to give you an opportunity to comment. Your main options for appeals are the following: Collection Due Process or Collection Appeals Program

Collection Due Process

The purpose of a Collection Due Process hearing is to have Appeals review collection actions that were taken or have been proposed. After Appeals has made their determination and you do not agree, you can go to court to appeal the Appeals' Collection Due Process determination. You can request a Collection Due Process hearing if you receive any of the following notices:

- Notice of Federal Tax Lien Filing and Your Right to a Hearing
- Final Notice—Notice of Intent to Levy and Notice of Your Right to a Hearing
- Notice of Jeopardy Levy and Right of Appeal
- Notice of Levy on Your State Tax Refund—Notice of Your Right to a Hearing
- Notice of Levy and of Your Right to a Hearing

To request a Collection Due Process hearing, complete **Form 12153**, *Request for a Collection Due Process* or Equivalent Hearing or a written request containing the same information as contained in Form 12153, and send it to the address on your notice. You must request a Collection Due Process hearing by the date indicated in the notice we send you (for proposed levies, that date is 30 days from the date of the letter). The request must be filed timely to preserve your right to judicial review of the determination issued in your Collection Due Process hearing. If your request for a Collection Due Process hearing is not timely, you can request an Equivalent Hearing within one year from the date of the notice, but you cannot go to court if you disagree with Appeals' decision.

During a Collection Due Process hearing, the 10-year period for collecting taxes is suspended and we are generally prohibited from seizing (levying) your property, if seizing your property is the subject of the hearing. We are permitted to seize your property during an Equivalent Hearing or a Collection Due Process hearing about filing of a Notice of Federal Tax Lien, but normally we will not seize property during these hearings. The 10-year period for collecting taxes is not suspended during an Equivalent Hearing.

You are entitled to only one Collection Due Process lien hearing and one levy hearing for each tax period or assessment. You are entitled to propose collection alternatives, such as entering into an installment agreement or an offer-in-compromise, for consideration by Appeals in the hearing. It may be necessary for you to submit financial information or tax returns to qualify for such collection alternatives.

All issues should be raised and all necessary supporting information presented to Appeals at the hearing. Your are prevented from raising issues during a judicial review that were not properly raised with Appeals in the Collection Due Process hearing. Your Appeals conference may be held by telephone, correspondence, or, if you qualify, in a face-to-face conference at the Appeals office closest to your home or place of business. You may be denied a face-to-face conference if you raise issues that are deemed frivolous or made with a desire solely to delay or impede collection. For a nonexclusive listing of issues identified by the IRS as frivolous, see "**The Truth About Frivolous Tax Arguments**" on **www.IRS.gov**.

Collection Appeals Program

Under the Collections Appeals Program, if you disagree with an IRS employee's decision regarding any levy, seizure, or Notice of Federal Tax Lien filing and want to appeal it, you can ask to have a conference with the employee's manager. If we seize your house, car, or other property in order to sell your interest in the property to apply the proceeds to your tax debt, you must make the request within 10 business days after the Notice of Seizure is given to you

or left at your home or business. There is no deadline to request a manager conference when a levy is served for other types of property (such as wages or bank accounts) or a levy or seizure or lien filing is proposed. The collection action may go forward if a conference is not requested within a reasonable time period.

If you then disagree with the manager's decision, you may request the IRS Office of Appeals review your case under the Collection Appeals Program as outlined in **Publication 1660**. If your case is assigned to a revenue officer, your request for Appeals consideration should be made within three (3) business days of the conference with the manager or collection actions may resume. You must submit your request for Appeals consideration in writing, preferably on **Form 9423**, *Collection Appeal Request*. If your case is not assigned to a Revenue Officer, you can appeal the manager's decision in writing or orally and your case will be forwarded to Appeals for review. Your request for Appeals consideration should be made within three (3) business days of the conference with the manager or collection actions may resume.

If you request a conference and are not contacted by a manager or his/her designee within two (2) business days of making the request, you may contact Collection again and request Appeals consideration. If you submit Form 9423, note the date of your request for a conference in Block 15 and indicate that you were not contacted by a manager. The Form 9423 should be received or postmarked within four (4) business days of your request for a conference as collection action may resume. Submit Form 9423 to the revenue officer involved in the lien, levy or seizure action.

If you file a Collection Appeals Request and do not agree with Appeals' decisions, you cannot proceed to court.

Instances in which you can pursue the Collection Appeals Program include, but aren't limited to:

- Before or after we file a Notice of Federal Tax Lien
- Before or after we seize ("levy") your property
- After we reject, terminate, or propose to terminate your Installment Agreement (a conference with the manager is recommended, but not required). Submit your written Installment Agreement Appeal request, preferably using **Form 9423**, *Collection Appeal Request*, within the timeframe listed in your notice.

For more information about the Collection Due Process and Collection Appeals Program, please see **Publication 1660**, Collection Appeal Rights or visit **http://www.irs.gov/Individuals /Appealing-a-Collection-Decision**.

If you don't pay on time: Understanding collection actions

There are several words and phrases particular to the collection process. Here, we've defined some of the most commonly used collection terms:

Federal tax lien: A legal claim against all your current and future property, such as a house or car, and rights to property, such as wages and bank accounts. The lien automatically comes into existence if you don't pay your amount due after receiving your first bill.

Notice of Federal Tax Lien: A public notice to creditors. It notifies them that there is a federal tax lien that attaches to all your current and future property and rights to property.

Levy: A legal seizure of property or rights to property to satisfy a tax debt. When property is seized ("levied"), it will be sold to help pay your tax debt. If wages or bank accounts are seized, the money will be applied to your tax debt.

4

The Death of America

Publication 594 **The IRS Collection Process**

Seizure: There is no legal difference between a seizure and a levy. Throughout this publication, we will use both terms interchangeably.

Notice of Intent to Levy and Notice of Your Right to a Hearing: Generally, before property is seized, we have to send you this notice. If you don't pay your overdue taxes, make other arrangements to satisfy the tax debt, or request a hearing within 30 days of the date of this notice, we may seize your property.

Summons: A summons legally compels you or a third party to meet with the IRS and provide information, documents or testimony.

Collection actions in detail

Federal tax lien: A legal claim against property

A lien is a legal claim against all your current and future property. When you don't pay your first bill for taxes due, a lien is created by law and attaches to your property. It applies to property (such as your home and car) and to any current and future rights you have to property.

Notice of Federal Tax Lien: Provides public notice to creditors that a lien exists

A Notice of Federal Tax Lien gives public notice to creditors. We file the Notice of Federal Tax Lien so we can establish the priority of our claim versus the claims of other creditors. The Notice of Federal Tax Lien is filed with local or state authorities, such as county recorder of deeds or the Secretary of State offices.

If a Notice of Federal Tax Lien is filed against you, it's often reported by consumer credit reporting agencies. This can have a negative effect on your credit rating and make it difficult for you to receive credit (such as a loan or credit card). Employers, landlords and others may also use this information and not favorably view the fact that a Notice of Federal Tax Lien has been filed against you. However by law, there will be no filing of the Notice of Federal Tax Lien or enforcement action taken to collect an individual shared responsibility payment associated with the Affordable Care Act.

What to do if a Notice of Federal Tax Lien is filed against you
You should pay the full amount you owe immediately. The Notice of Federal Tax Lien only shows your assessed balance as of the date of the notice. It doesn't show your payoff balance or include our charges for filing and releasing the lien. To find out the full amount you must pay to have the lien released, call 1-800-913-6050 or 859-669-4811 if you are calling from outside of the United States. If you have questions, call the number on your lien notice or 1-800-829-1040 or visit www.irs.gov/Businesses/Small -Businesses-&-Self-Employed/Understanding-a-Federal-Tax-Lien, or view instructional videos at http://www.irsvideos.gov/ Individual/IRSLiens.

How to appeal a Notice of Federal Tax Lien
Within five business days of the first filing of the Notice of Federal Tax Lien for a specific debt, we will send you a Notice of Federal Tax Lien Filing and Your Right to a Collection Due Process Hearing. You'll have until the date shown on the notice to request a Collection Due Process hearing with the Office of Appeals. Send your Collection Due Process hearing request to the address on the notice. For more information, see **Form 12153**, *Request for a Collection Due Process or Equivalent Hearing.*

After your Collection Due Process hearing, the Office of Appeals will issue a determination on whether the Notice of Federal Tax Lien should remain filed, or whether it should be withdrawn, released, discharged or subordinated. If you disagree with the determination, you have 30 days after it's made to seek a review in the U.S. Tax Court.

In addition to any Collection Due Process rights you may have, you may also appeal a proposed or actual filing of a Notice of Federal

Tax Lien under the Collection Appeals Program.

Reasons we will "release" a federal tax lien
A "release" of a federal tax lien means that we have cleared both the lien for your debt and the public Notice of Federal Tax Lien. We do this by filing a Certificate of Release of Federal Tax Lien with the same state and local authorities with whom we filed your Notice of Federal Tax Lien. We will release your lien if:

• Your debt is fully paid,
• Payment of your debt is guaranteed by a bond, or
• You have met the payment terms of an Offer in Compromise which the IRS has accepted, or
• The period for collection has ended. (In this case, the release is automatic.)

For more information, see **Publication 1450**, *Instructions on How to Request a Certificate of Release of Federal Tax Lien.*

Reasons we may "withdraw" a Notice of Federal Tax Lien
A "withdrawal" removes the Notice of Federal Tax Lien from public record. The withdrawal tells other creditors that we're abandoning our lien priority. This doesn't mean that the federal tax lien is released or that you're no longer liable for the amount due.

We may withdraw a Notice of Federal Tax Lien if:

• You've entered into an Installment Agreement to satisfy the tax liability, unless the Agreement provides otherwise. For certain types of taxes, we will routinely withdraw a Notice of Federal Tax Lien if you've entered into a direct debit installment agreement and meet certain other conditions,
• It will help you pay your taxes more quickly,
• We didn't follow IRS procedures,
• It was filed during a bankruptcy automatic stay period, or
• It's in your best interest and in the best interest of the government. For example, this could include when your debt has been satisfied and you request a withdrawal.

For more information, see **Form 12277**, *Application for Withdrawal of Filed Notice of Federal Tax Lien* or the instructional video at http://www.irsvideos.gov/Individual/IRSLiens /LienNoticeWithdrawal.

How to apply for a "discharge" of a federal tax lien from property
A "discharge" removes the lien from specific property. There are several circumstances under which the federal tax lien can be discharged. For example, we may issue a Certificate of Discharge if you're selling property and a Notice of Federal Tax Lien has been filed; you may be able to remove or discharge the lien from that property if the government receives its interest through the sale. For more information on whether you qualify for a discharge, see **Publication 783**, *Instructions on How to Apply for a Certificate of Discharge of Property from Federal Tax Lien.* To watch an instructional video about Publication 783, visit http://irsvideos.gov/ Individual/IRSLiens.

How to make the federal tax lien secondary to other creditors ("subordination")
A "subordination" is where a creditor is allowed to move ahead of the government's priority position. For example, if you're trying to refinance a mortgage on your home, but aren't able to because the federal tax lien has priority over the new mortgage, you may request that we subordinate our lien to the new mortgage. For more information on whether you qualify for a subordination, see **Publication 784**, *How to Prepare an Application for a Certificate of Subordination of Federal Tax Lien.* To watch an instructional video about Publication 784, visit http://irsvideos.gov/Individual /IRSLiens.

5

302

Publication 594 **The IRS Collection Process**

Appeal rights for withdrawal, discharge or subordination

If your application is denied you will receive **Form 9423**, *Collection Appeal Request* and Publication 1660, *Collection Appeal Rights*, with an explanation of why your application was denied. If we deny your request for a withdrawal, discharge, or subordination, you may appeal under the Collections Appeals Program.

Levy: A seizure of property

While a federal tax lien is a legal claim against your property, a levy is a legal seizure that actually takes your property (such as your house or car) or your rights to property (such as your income, bank account, or Social Security payments) to satisfy your tax debt.

We can't seize your property if you have a current or pending Installment Agreement, Offer in Compromise, or if we agree that you're unable to pay due to economic hardship, meaning seizing your property would result in your inability to meet basic, reasonable living expenses.

Reasons we may seize ("levy") your property or rights to property

If you don't pay your taxes (or make arrangements to settle your debt), we could seize and sell your property. We will not seize your property to collect an individual shared responsibility payment. We usually seize only after the following things have occurred.

* We assessed the tax and sent you a bill,
* You neglected or refused to pay the tax, and
* We sent you a Final Notice of Intent to Levy and Notice of Your Right to a Hearing at least 30 days before the seizure.

However, there are exceptions for when we don't have to offer you a hearing at least 30 days before seizing your property. These include situations when:

* The collection of the tax is in jeopardy,
* A levy is served to collect tax from a state tax refund,
* A levy is served to collect the tax debt of a federal contractor, or
* A Disqualified Employment Tax Levy (DETL) is served. A DETL is the seizure of unpaid employment taxes and can be served when a taxpayer previously requested a Collection Due Process appeal on employment taxes for other periods within the past 2 years.

If we serve a levy under one of these exceptions, we will send you a letter explaining the seizure and your appeal rights after the levy is issued.

What you should do if your property is seized ("levied")

If your property or federal payments are seized, call the number on your levy notice or 1-800-829-1040. If you're already working with an IRS employee, call him or her for assistance.

Examples of property we can seize ("levy")

* **Wages, salary, or commission held by someone else** If we seize your rights to wages, salary, commissions, or similar payments that are held by someone else, we will serve a levy once, not each time you're paid. The one levy continues until your debt is fully paid, other arrangements are made, or the collection period ends. Other payments you receive, such as dividends and payments on promissory notes, are also subject to seizure. However, the seizure only reaches the payments due or the right to future payments as of the date of the levy.
* **Your bank account** Seizure of the funds in your bank account will include funds available for withdrawal up to the amount of the seizure. After the levy is issued, the bank will hold the available funds and give you 21 days to resolve any disputes about who owns the account before sending us the money. After 21 days, the bank will send us your money, and any interest earned on that amount, unless you have resolved the issue in another way.

* **Your federal payments** As an alternative to the levy procedure used for other payments such as dividends and promissory notes, certain federal payments may be systemically seized through the Federal Payment Levy Program in order to pay your tax debt. Under this program, we can generally seize up to 15% of your federal payments (up to 100% of payments due to a vendor for goods or services sold or leased to the federal government). We will serve the levy once, not each time you are paid. The levy continues until your debt is fully paid, other arrangements are made, the collection period ends, or the IRS releases the levy. The federal payments that can be seized in this program include, but aren't limited to, federal retirement annuity income from the Office of Personnel Management, Social Security benefits under Title II of the Social Security Act (OASDI), and federal contractor/vendor payments.
* **Your house, car, or other property** If we seize your house or other property, we will sell your interest in the property and apply the proceeds (after the costs of the sale) to your tax debt. Prior to selling your property, we will calculate a minimum bid price. We will also provide you with a copy of the calculation and give you an opportunity to challenge the fair market value determination. We will then provide you with the notice of sale and announce the pending sale to the public, usually through local newspapers or flyers posted in public places. After giving public notice, we will generally wait 10 days before selling your property. Money from the sale pays for the cost of seizing and selling the property and, finally, your tax debt. If there's money left over from the sale after paying off your tax debt, we will tell you how to get a refund.

Property that can't be seized ("levied")

Certain property is exempt from seizure. For example, we can't seize the following: unemployment benefits, certain annuity and pension benefits, certain service-connected disability payments, workers compensation, certain public assistance payments, minimum weekly exempt income, assistance under the Job Training Partnership Act, and income for court-ordered child support payments.

We also can't seize necessary schoolbooks and clothing, undelivered mail, certain amounts worth of fuel, provisions, furniture, personal effects for a household, and certain amounts worth of books and tools for trade, business, or professions. There are also limitations on our ability to seize a primary residence and certain business assets.

Lastly, we can't seize your property unless we expect net proceeds to help pay off your tax debt.

How to appeal a proposed seizure ("levy")

You can request a Collection Due Process hearing within 30 days from the date of your Notice of Intent to Levy and Notice of Your Right to a Hearing. Send your request to the address on your notice. For more information, see **Form 12153**, *Request for a Collection Due Process or Equivalent Hearing*. At the conclusion of your hearing, the Office of Appeals will provide a determination. You'll have 30 days after the determination to challenge it in the U.S. Tax Court. If Collection Due Process rights aren't available for your case, you may have other appeal options, such as the Collection Appeals Program.

Reasons we "release" a levy

The Internal Revenue Code specifically provides that we must release a levy if we determine that:

* You paid the amount you owe,
* The period for collection ended prior to the levy being issued,
* It will help you pay your taxes,
* You enter into an Installment Agreement and the terms of the agreement don't allow for the levy to continue,

- The levy creates an economic hardship, meaning we've determined the levy prevents you from meeting basic, reasonable living expenses, or
- The value of the property is more than the amount owed and releasing the levy won't hinder our ability to collect the amount owed.

We will also release a levy if it was issued improperly. For example, we will release a levy if it was issued:

- Against property exempt from seizure,
- Prematurely,
- Before we sent you the required notice,
- While you were in bankruptcy and an automatic stay was in effect,
- Where the expenses of seizing and selling the levied property would be greater than the fair market value of the property,
- While an Installment Agreement request, Innocent Spouse Relief request, or Offer in Compromise was being considered or had been accepted and was in effect, or
- While the Office of Appeals or Tax Court was considering a collection due process case and the levy wasn't a Disqualified Employment Tax Levy to collect employment taxes, a state refund, a jeopardy levy, or to collect the tax debt of federal contractor.
- While the Office of Appeals or Tax Court is considering an appeal of the denial of innocent spouse relief.

Reasons we may return seized ("levied") property

We may return your property if;

- Its seizure was premature,
- Its seizure was in violation of the law,
- Returning the seized property will help our collection of your debt,
- You enter into an Installment Agreement to satisfy the liability for which the levy was made, unless the Agreement does not allow for the return of previously levied upon property.
- We didn't follow IRS procedures, or
- It's in your best interest and in the best interest of the government.

We may return property at any time if the property has not been sold. If we decided to return your property, but it's already sold, we will give you the money we received from the sale. You can file a request for return of seized money or money from the sale of seized proper, generally up to 9 months after the seizure.

How to recover seized ("levied") property that's been sold

To recover your real estate, you (and anyone with interest in the property) may recoup it within 180 days of the sale by paying the purchaser what they paid, plus interest at 20% annually.

If your property has been seized ("levied") to collect tax owed by someone else, you may appeal the seizure under the Collection Appeals Program or file a claim under Internal Revenue Code section 6343(b), generally within 9 months of the seizure, or you may file a suit under Internal Revenue Code section 7426 for the return of the wrongfully seized property, generally within 9 months of the seizure. You may also appeal the denial of the request to return the wrongfully seized property under the Collection Appeals Program. For more information, see **Publication 4528**, *Making an Administrative Wrongful Levy Claim under Internal Revenue Code section 6343(b).*

How to recover economic damages

If we wrongfully seized your property, we lost or misplaced your payment, or there was a direct debit Installment Agreement processing error and you incurred bank charges, we may reimburse you for charges you paid. For more information, see **Form 8546**, *Claim for Reimbursement of Bank Charges.* If your claim is denied,

you can sue the federal government for economic damages.

If we intentionally or negligently didn't follow Internal Revenue law while collecting your taxes, or you're not the taxpayer and we wrongfully seized your property, you may be entitled to recover economic damages. Mail your written administrative claim to the attention of the Advisory Group Manager for your area at the address listed in **Publication 4235**, *Collection Advisory Group Addresses.* If you've filed a claim and your claim is denied, you can sue the federal government, but not the IRS employee, for economic damages.

Summons: Used to secure information

If we're having trouble gathering information to determine or collect taxes you owe, we may serve a summons. A summons legally compels you or a third party to meet with an officer of the IRS and provide information, documents and/or testimony.

If you're responsible for a tax liability and we serve a summons on you, you may be required to:

- Testify,
- Bring books and records to prepare a tax return, and/or
- Produce documents to prepare a Collection Information Statement, Form 433-A or Form 433-B.

If you can't make your summons appointment, immediately call the number listed on your notice. If you don't call us and don't attend your appointment, we may sue you in federal district court to require you to comply with the summons.

If we serve a third-party summons to determine your tax liability, you'll receive a notice indicating that we're contacting a third party. Third parties can be financial institutions, record keepers, or people with information relevant to your case. We won't review their information or receive testimony until the end of the 23rd day after the notice was given. You also have the right to:

- Petition to reject ("quash") the summons before the end of the 20th day after the date of the notice, or
- Petition to intervene in a suit to enforce a summons to which the third party didn't comply.

If we issue a third-party summons to collect taxes you already owe, you won't receive notice or be able to petition to reject or intervene in a suit to enforce the summons.

Information for employers: Collection of employment tax

About employment taxes

Employment taxes are the amount you must withhold from your employees for their income tax and Social Security/Medicare tax (trust fund taxes) plus the amount of Social Security/Medicare tax you pay for each employee. Federal unemployment taxes are also considered employment taxes.

Employment taxes are incurred at the time you pay wages and generally paid in semi-weekly or monthly deposits. You must use electronic funds transfer to make all federal tax deposits, generally through the Electronic Federal Tax Payment System (EFTPS). See **Publication 966**, *Electronic Federal Tax Payment System: A Guide To Getting Started.*

What we will do if you don't pay your employment taxes:

- Assess a failure to deposit penalty, up to 15% of the amount not deposited in a timely manner.
- We may propose a Trust Fund Recovery Penalty assessment against the individuals responsible for failing to pay the trust fund taxes.

About trust fund taxes

Trust fund taxes are the income tax, Social Security tax, and Medicare tax (trust fund taxes) withheld from the employee's wages. They are called trust fund taxes because the employer holds these funds "in trust" for the government until it submits them in a federal tax deposit. Certain excise taxes are also considered trust fund taxes because they are collected and held in trust for the government until submitted in a federal tax deposit. For more information, see Publication 510, *Excise Taxes*.

To encourage prompt payment of withheld employment taxes and collected excise taxes, Congress has passed a law that provides for the Trust Fund Recovery Penalty.

For more information on employment taxes or trust fund taxes, see Publication 15, *Circular E, Employer's Tax Guide*.

Trust Fund Recovery Penalty

The Trust Fund Recovery Penalty is a penalty that is assessed personally against the individual or individuals who were responsible for paying the trust fund taxes, but who willfully did not do so. The amount of the penalty is equal to the amount of the unpaid trust fund taxes. For additional information, please see Notice 784, Could You be Personally Liable for Certain Unpaid Federal Taxes? or visit http://www.irs.gov/Businesses/Small-Businesses-&-Self -Employed/Employment-Taxes-and-the-Trust-Fund-Recovery -Penalty-TFRP.

If the Trust Fund Recovery Penalty is proposed against you, you'll receive a Letter 1153 and Form 2751, *Proposed Assessment of Trust Fund Recovery Penalty*.

If you agree with the penalty, sign and return Form 2751 within 60 days from the date of the letter. To avoid the assessment of the Trust Fund Recovery Penalty, you may also pay the trust fund taxes personally.

If you disagree with the penalty, you have 10 days from the date of the letter to let us know that you don't agree with the proposed assessment, have additional information to support your case, or want to try to resolve the matter informally. If you can't resolve the disagreement with us, you have 60 days from the date of the Letter 1153 to appeal with the Office of Appeals. For more information, see **Publication 5**, *Your Appeal Rights and How to Prepare a Protest if You Don't Agree*.

If you don't respond to the letter, we will assess the penalty amount against you personally and begin the collection process to collect it. We may assess this penalty against a responsible person regardless of whether the company is still in business.

Additional information

Innocent Spouse Relief

Generally, both you and your spouse are responsible, jointly and individually, for paying any tax, interest, or penalties on your joint return. If you believe your current or former spouse should be solely responsible for an incorrect item or an underpayment of tax on your joint tax return, you may be eligible for Innocent Spouse Relief. This could change the amount you owe, or you may be entitled to a refund. You must submit **Form 8857**, *Request for Innocent Spouse Relief*, no later than two years from the date of our first attempt to collect the outstanding debt, except for requests for equitable relief under Internal Revenue Code section 6015(f). For additional information, see **Publication 971**, *Innocent Spouse Relief*

Representation during the collection process

During the collection process, or an appeal before the IRS Office of Appeals you can be represented by yourself, an attorney, a certified public accountant, an enrolled agent, an immediate family member, or any person enrolled to practice before the IRS. If you're a business, full-time employees, general partners, or bona fide officers can also represent you.

To have your representative appear before us, contact us on your behalf, and/or receive your confidential material, file **Form 2848**, *Power of Attorney and Declaration of Representative*.

To authorize someone to receive or inspect confidential material, file **Form 8821**, *Tax Information Authorization*.

Sharing your tax information

During the collection process, we're authorized to share your tax information in some cases with city and state tax agencies, the Department of Justice, federal agencies, people you authorize to represent you, and certain foreign governments (under tax treaty provisions).

We may contact a third party

The law allows us to contact others (such as neighbors, banks, employers, or employees) to investigate your case. You have the right to request a list of third parties contacted about your case.

Past Due Tax Returns

File all tax returns that are due, regardless of whether or not you can pay in full. File a past due return at the same location where you would file an on-time return.

If you do not voluntarily file your individual income tax return you risk losing your refund and we may file a substitute return for you. This return might not give you credit for deductions and exemptions you may be entitled to receive. We may send you a Notice of Deficiency proposing a tax assessment. Filing a past due return after the Notice of Deficiency was sent does not extend the 90 day period for filing a petition to the United States Tax Court. However, the past due return will be considered in determining whether there will be a reduction in the amount of tax increase previously proposed in the Notice of Deficiency. If you do not file a petition in Tax Court and a tax increase has been determined, we will proceed with our proposed assessment as a substitute return. If the IRS files a substitute return, it is still in your best interest to file your own tax return to take advantage of any exemptions, credits and deductions you are entitled to receive. The IRS will generally adjust your account to reflect the correct figures.

8

Notice of Potential Third Party Contact

IRS

We are attempting to collect unpaid taxes from you. Generally, our practice is to deal directly with a taxpayer or a taxpayer's duly authorized representative. However, we sometimes talk with other persons when we need information that the taxpayer has been unable to provide, or to verify information we have received.

This notice is provided to tell you that we may contact other persons, such as a neighbor, bank, employer or employees, and will generally need to tell them limited information, such as your name. The law prohibits us from disclosing any more information than is necessary to obtain or verify the information we are seeking. Our need to contact other persons may continue as long as there is activity on this matter. If we contact other persons, you have the right to request a list of those contacted.

Department of the Treasury
Internal Revenue Service
Austin, TX 73301-0030

IRS

	Wi
Notice	CP503
Tax Year	2016
Notice date	July 24, 2017
Social Security number	390-80-4016
To contact us	Phone 1-800-829-0922
Your Caller ID	813596
Page 1 of 5	

001808.626555.442493.3865 2 AB 0.403 1339

BRADLEY J FRANKS
408 S LINCOLN ST
MILBANK SD 57252-2326

)01808

Second reminder: You have unpaid taxes for 2016
Amount due: $135,975,058.43

As we notified you before, our records show you have unpaid taxes for the tax year ended December 31, 2016 (Form 1040). If you don't pay $135,975,058.43 by August 3, 2017, the amount of interest will increase and additional penalties may apply.

If you already have an installment or payment agreement in place for this tax year, then continue with that agreement.

Billing Summary

Amount you owed	$134,787,942.88
Failure-to-pay penalty	669,156.37
Interest charges	517,959.18
Amount due by August 3, 2017	**$135,975,058.43**

Continued on back...

IRS

BRADLEY J FRANKS
408 S LINCOLN ST
MILBANK SD 57252-2326

Notice	CP503
Notice date	July 24, 2017
Social Security number	390-80-4016

Payment

- Make your check or money order payable to the United States Treasury.
- Write your Social Security number (390-80-4016), the tax year (2016), and the form number (1040) on your payment and any correspondence.

Amount due by
August 3, 2017

$135,975,058.43

INTERNAL REVENUE SERVICE
AUSTIN, TX 73301-0025

390804016 LO FRAN 30 0 201612 670 13597505843

307

	WI
Notice	CP503
Tax Year	2016
Notice date	July 24, 2017
Social Security number	390-80-4016
Page 2 of 5	

What you need to do immediately

If you agree with the amount due and you're not working with an IRS representative

- Pay the amount due of $135,975,058.43 by August 3, 2017, to avoid additional interest and applicable penalty charges.
- Pay online or mail a check or money order with the attached payment stub. **You can pay online now at www.irs.gov/payments**.

If we notified you that we suspended enforced collection on your account because it would create a financial hardship (meaning you would be unable to pay basic reasonable living expenses if we levied) and your financial condition has not changed, you don't need to do anything.

If you disagree with the amount due

Call us at 1-800-829-0922 to review your account with a representative. Be sure to have your account information available when you call.

We'll assume you agree with the information in this notice if we don't hear from you.

001808

Payment options

Pay now electronically

We offer free payment options to securely pay your tax bill directly from your checking or savings account. When you pay online or from your mobile device, you can:

- Receive instant confirmation of your payment
- Schedule payments in advance
- Modify or cancel a payment before the due date

You can also pay by debit or credit card for a small fee. To see all of our payment options, visit www.irs.gov/payments.

Payment plans

If you can't pay the full amount you owe, pay as much as you can now and make arrangements to pay your remaining balance. Visit www.irs.gov/paymentplan for more information on installment agreements and online payment agreements. You can also call us at 1-800-829-0922 to discuss your options.

Offer in Compromise

An offer in compromise allows you to settle your tax debt for less than the full amount you owe. If we accept your offer, you can pay with either a lump sum cash payment plan or periodic payment plan. To see if you qualify, use the Offer in Compromise Pre-Qualifier tool on our website. For more information, visit www.irs.gov/offers.

Account balance and payment history

For information on how to obtain your current account balance or payment history, go to www.irs.gov/balancedue.

If you already paid your balance in full within the past 21 days or made payment arrangements, please disregard this notice.

If you think we made a mistake, call 1-800-829-0922 to review your account.

If we don't hear from you

Pay $135,975,058.43 by August 3, 2017, to avoid additional interest and applicable penalty charges.

We may file a Notice of Federal Tax Lien against you. A tax lien generally attaches to all property you currently own and will attach to all property you acquire in the future. The Notice of Federal Tax Lien is a public record, and it can damage your credit or make it difficult for you to get credit (such as a loan or credit card).

Continued on back...

The Death of America

WI

Notice	CP503
Tax Year	2016
Notice date	July 24, 2017
Social Security number	390-80-4016

Page 4 of 5

Penalties

We are required by law to charge any applicable penalties.

Failure-to-pay

Description	Amount
Total failure-to-pay	**$669,156.37**

We assess a 1/2% monthly penalty for not paying the tax you owe by the due date. We base the monthly penalty for paying late on the net unpaid tax at the beginning of each penalty month following the payment due date for that tax. This penalty applies even if you filed the return on time.

We charge the penalty for each month or part of a month the payment is late; however, the penalty can't be more than 25% in total.
- The due date for payment of the tax shown on a return generally is the return due date, without regard to extensions.
- The due date for paying increases in tax is within 21 days of the date of our notice demanding payment (10 business days if the amount in the notice is $100,000 or more).

If we issue a Notice of Intent to Levy and you don't pay the balance due within 10 days of the date of the notice, the penalty for paying late increases to 1% per month.

For individuals who filed on time, the penalty decreases to 1/4% per month while an approved installment agreement with the IRS is in effect for payment of that tax. (Internal Revenue Code Section 6651)

For a detailed calculation of your penalty charges, call 1-800-829-0922.

Removal or reduction of penalties

We understand that circumstances—such as serious illness or injury, a family member's death, or loss of financial records due to natural disaster—may make it difficult for you to meet your taxpayer responsibility in a timely manner.

If you would like us to consider removing or reducing any of your penalty charges, please do the following:
- Identify which penalty charges you would like us to remove or reduce (e.g., 2005 late filing penalty).
- For each penalty charge, explain why you believe removal or reduction is appropriate.
- Sign your statement, and mail it to us along with any supporting documents.

We will review your statement and let you know whether we accept your explanation as reasonable cause to reduce or remove the penalty charge(s).

Notice	CP503
Tax Year	2016
Notice date	July 24, 2017
Social Security number	390-80-4016
	Page 5 of 5

Penalties—continued

Removal of penalties due to erroneous written advice from the IRS

If you were penalized based on written advice from the IRS, we will remove the penalty if you meet the following criteria:

- If you sent a written request to the IRS for written advice on a specific issue
- You gave us complete and accurate information
- You received written advice from us
- You reasonably relied on our written advice and were penalized based on that advice

To request removal of penalties based on erroneous written advice from us, submit a completed Claim for Refund and Request for Abatement (Form 843) to the IRS service center where you filed your tax return. For a copy of the form or to find your IRS service center, go to www.irs.gov or call 1-800-829-0922.

Interest charges

We are required by law to charge interest when you do not pay your liability on time. Generally, we calculate interest from the due date of your return (regardless of extensions) until you pay the amount you owe in full, including accrued interest and any penalty charges. Interest on some penalties accrues from the date we notify you of the penalty until it is paid in full. Interest on other penalties, such as failure to file a tax return, starts from the due date or extended due date of the return. Interest rates are variable and may change quarterly. (Internal Revenue Code Section 6601)

Description	Amount
Total interest	$517,959.18

The table below shows the rates used to calculate the interest on your unpaid amount due. For a detailed calculation of your interest, call 1-800-829-0922.

Period	Interest Rate
October 1, 2016 through December 31, 2016	4%
January 1, 2017 through March 31, 2017	4%

Additional information

- Visit www.irs.gov/cp503
- You may find the following publications helpful:
  - Publication 1, Your Rights as a Taxpayer
  - Publication 594, The Collection Process
- For tax forms, instructions, and publications, visit www.irs.gov or call 1-800-TAX-FORM (1-800-829-3676).
- Paying online is convenient, secure, and ensures timely receipt of your payment. To pay your taxes online or for more information, go to www.irs.gov/payments.
- You can contact us by mail at the following address. Be sure to include your social security number, the tax year, and the form number you are writing about.
  Internal Revenue Service
  Austin, TX 73301-0025
- Keep this notice for your records.

If you need assistance, please don't hesitate to contact us.

311

The Death of America

<table>
<tr><td>Form 9465
(Rev. February 2017)
Department of the Treasury
Internal Revenue Service</td><td>Installment Agreement Request
▶ Information about Form 9465 and its separate instructions is at www.irs.gov/form9465.
▶ If you are filing this form with your tax return, attach it to the front of the return.
▶ See separate instructions.</td><td>OMB No. 1545-0074</td></tr>
</table>

Tip: If you owe $50,000 or less, you may be able to establish an installment agreement online, even if you have not yet received a bill for your taxes. Go to IRS.gov to apply to pay online. **Caution:** *Don't file this form if you can pay your balance in full within 120 days. Instead, call 1-800-829-1040. Don't file if your business is still operating and owes employment or unemployment taxes. Instead, call the telephone number on your most recent notice. If you are in bankruptcy or we have accepted your offer-in-compromise, see* **Bankruptcy or offer-in-compromise,** *in the instructions.*

Part I

This request is for Form(s) (for example, Form 1040 or Form 941) ▶ _____ and for tax year(s) (for example, 2012 and 2013) ▶ _____

1a Your first name and initial | Last name | Your social security number

If a joint return, spouse's first name and initial | Last name | Spouse's social security number

Current address (number and street). If you have a P.O. box and no home delivery, enter your box number. | Apt. number

City, town or post office, state, and ZIP code. If a foreign address, also complete the spaces below (see instructions)

Foreign country name | Foreign province/state/county | Foreign postal code

1b If this address is new since you filed your last tax return, check here . . . . ▶ ☐

2 Name of your business (must be no longer operating) | Employer identification number (EIN)

3 Your home phone number   Best time for us to call | **4** Your work phone number   Ext.   Best time for us to call

5 Name of your bank or other financial institution: | **6** Your employer's name:

Address | Address

City, state, and ZIP code | City, state, and ZIP code

7 Enter the total amount you owe as shown on your tax return(s) (or notice(s)) . . . . | **7**

8 Enter the amount of any payment you are making with your tax return(s) (or notice(s)). See instructions | **8**

9 Subtract line 8 from line 7 and enter the result . . . . | **9**

10 Enter the amount you can pay each month. Make your payments as large as possible to limit interest and penalty charges. **The charges will continue until you pay in full. If no payment amount is listed on line 10, a payment will be determined for you by dividing the balance due by 72 months** . . | **10**

11 Divide the amount on line 9 by 72 and enter the result . . . . | **11**
 • If the amount on line 10 is less than the amount on line 11 and you are unable to increase your payment to the amount on line 11, complete and attach Form 433-F, Collection Information Statement.
 • If the amount on line 10 is equal to or greater than the amount on line 11 but the amount you owe is greater than $25,000 but not more than $50,000, you must complete either line 13 or 14, if you do not wish to complete Form 433-F.
 • If the amount on line 9 is greater than $50,000, complete and attach Form 433-F, Collection Information Statement.

12 Enter the date you want to make your payment each month. **Do not** enter a date later than the 28th ▶ _____

13 If you want to make your payments by direct debit from your checking account, see the instructions and fill in lines 13a and 13b. This is the most convenient way to make your payments and it will ensure that they are made on time.

▶ **a** Routing number ☐☐☐☐☐☐☐☐☐

▶ **b** Account number ☐☐☐☐☐☐☐☐☐☐☐☐☐☐☐☐☐

I authorize the U.S. Treasury and its designated Financial Agent to initiate a monthly ACH debit (electronic withdrawal) entry to the financial institution account indicated for payments of my Federal taxes owed, and the financial institution to debit the entry to this account. This authorization is to remain in full force and effect until I notify the U.S. Treasury Financial Agent to terminate the authorization. To revoke payment, I must contact the U.S. Treasury Financial Agent at **1-800-829-1040** no later than 14 business days prior to the payment (settlement) date. I also authorize the financial institutions involved in the processing of the electronic payments of taxes to receive confidential information necessary to answer inquiries and resolve issues related to the payments.

14 If you want to make your payments by payroll deduction, check this box and attach a completed Form 2159, Payroll Deduction Agreement . . . . ☐

Your signature | Date | Spouse's signature. If a joint return, **both** must sign. | Date

Bradley - J.: [Franks] and Co-Author: Robert - C.: [Simpson]

Form 9465 (Rev. 2-2017)   Page **2**

Part II   **Additional information.** Complete this part only if you have defaulted on an installment agreement within the past 12 months and the amount you owe is greater than $25,000 but not more $50,000 and the amount on line 10 is equal to or greater than the amount on line 11. If you owe more than $50,000, complete and attach Form 433-F, Collection Information Statement.

15   In which county is your primary residence? _____

16a   Marital status:
    ☐ Single. Skip question 16b and go to question 17.
    ☐ Married. Go to question 16b.
  b   Do you share household expenses with your spouse?
    ☐ Yes.
    ☐ No.

17   How many dependents will you be able to claim on this year's tax return? . . . . **17** | _____

18   How many people in your household are 65 or older? . . . . **18** | _____

19   How often are you paid?
    ☐ Once a week.
    ☐ Once every two weeks.
    ☐ Once a month.
    ☐ Twice a month.

20   What is your net income per pay period (take home pay)? . . . . **20** | $ _____

21   How often is your spouse paid?
    ☐ Once a week.
    ☐ Once every two weeks.
    ☐ Once a month.
    ☐ Twice a month.

22   What is your spouse's net income per pay period (take home pay)? . . . . **22** | $ _____

23   How many vehicles do you own? . . . . **23** | _____

24   How many car payments do you have each month? . . . . **24** | _____

25a   Do you have health insurance?
    ☐ Yes. Go to question 25b.
    ☐ No. Skip question 25b and go to question 26a.
  b   Are your premiums deducted from your paycheck?
    ☐ Yes. Skip question 25c and go to question 26a.
    ☐ No. Go to question 25c.
  c   How much are your monthly premiums? . . . . **25c** | $ _____

26a   Do you make court-ordered payments?
    ☐ Yes. Go to question 26b.
    ☐ No. Go to question 27.
  b   Are your court-ordered payments deducted from your paycheck?
    ☐ Yes. Go to question 27.
    ☐ No. Go to question 26c.
  c   How much are your court-ordered payments each month? . . . . **26c** | $ _____

27   Not including any court-ordered payments for child and dependent support, how much do you pay for child or dependent care each month? . . . . **27** | $ _____

Form **9465** (Rev. 2-2017)

♲ *Printed on recycled paper*   G⬤ U.S. GOVERNMENT PRINTING OFFICE: 2017—398-469/80663

313

Instructions for Form 9465

(Rev. February 2017)

Installment Agreement Request

Department of the Treasury
Internal Revenue Service

Section references are to the Internal Revenue Code unless otherwise noted.

What's New

Expanded use of form. You may use Form 9465 to request to add the liability for a new tax period to an existing installment agreement. You may also use this form to request an installment agreement for the individual shared responsibility payment.

Updated fee amounts. Beginning January 1, 2017, the fees for setting up an installment agreement are $225, $107 (if you make payments by direct deposit), $149 (if you set up an online payment agreement), or $31 (if you set up an online payment agreement and make payments by direct deposit). See *Payment methods* on page 2.

• There is an $89 fee to modify or reinstate an installment agreement.
• For low income taxpayers, the fee to set up an installment agreement is $43 or could be $31, if an online payment agreement is set up and the payments are made by direct debit.

Future Developments

For the latest developments related to Form 9465 and its instructions, such as legislation enacted after they were published, go to *IRS.gov/form9465*.

General Instructions

Purpose of Form

Use Form 9465 to request a monthly installment plan if you can't pay the full amount you owe shown on your tax return (or on a notice we sent you). Most installment agreements meet our streamlined installment agreement criteria. The maximum term for a streamlined agreement is 72 months. In certain circumstances, you can have longer to pay or your agreement can be approved for an amount that is less than the amount of tax you owe.

However, before requesting an installment agreement, you should consider other less costly alternatives, such as getting a bank loan or using available credit on a credit card. If you have any questions about this request, call 1-800-829-1040.

Use Form 9465 if you're an individual:
• Who owes income tax on Form 1040,
• Who is or may be responsible for a Trust Fund Recovery Penalty,
• Who owes employment taxes (for example, as reported on Forms 941, 943, or 940) related to a sole proprietor business that is no longer in operation, or
• Who owes an individual shared responsibility payment under the Affordable Care Act. See section 5000A.

Don't use Form 9465 if:
• You can pay the full amount you owe within 120 days (see *Can you pay in full within 120 days?*),
• You want to request an online payment agreement (see *Applying online for a payment agreement*), or
• Your business is still operating and owes employment or unemployment taxes. Instead, call the telephone number on your most recent notice to request an installment agreement.

Guaranteed installment agreement. You're eligible for a guaranteed installment agreement if the tax you owe isn't more than $10,000 and:
• During the past 5 tax years, you (and your spouse if filing a joint return) have timely filed all income tax returns and paid any income tax due, and haven't entered into an installment agreement for the payment of income tax;
• You agree to pay the full amount you owe within 3 years and to comply with the tax laws while the agreement is in effect; and
• You're financially unable to pay the liability in full when due.

Note. It is the practice of the Internal Revenue Service (IRS) to grant these installment agreements even if you can pay your liability in full if the tax you owe isn't more than $10,000 and you meet the other criteria.

Can you pay in full within 120 days? If you can pay the full amount you owe within 120 days, call 1-800-829-1040 to establish your request to pay in full. If you can do this, you can avoid paying the fee to set up an installment agreement. Instead of calling, you can apply online. To do that, go to IRS.gov and enter "Online Payment Agreement" in the "Search" box.

Applying online for a payment agreement. If your balance due isn't more than $50,000, you can apply online for a payment agreement instead of filing Form 9465. To do that, go to IRS.gov and enter "Online Payment Agreement" in the "Search" box or click on the link here for the *online payment agreement*. If you establish your installment agreement online, the user fee that you pay will be lower than it would be otherwise.

Bankruptcy or offer-in-compromise. If you're in bankruptcy or we have accepted your offer-in-compromise, don't file this form. Instead, call 1-800-829-1040 to get the number of your local IRS Insolvency function for bankruptcy or Technical Support function for offer-in-compromise.

How the Installment Agreement Works

We will usually let you know within 30 days after we receive your request whether it is approved or denied. However, if this request is for tax due on a return you filed after March 31, it may take us longer than 30 days to reply. If we approve your request, we will send you a

Mar 07, 2017　　　Cat. No. 58607N

notice detailing the terms of your agreement and requesting a user fee.

Installment agreement user fees. We charge an installment agreement user fee to set an installment plan. The amount of the user fee can vary depending on whether you set up an installment agreement online or agree to pay by direct debit. The fees are:
- $31, if you set up an online payment agreement and make your payments by direct debit;
- $107, if you don't set up an online payment agreement but make your payments by direct debit;
- $149, if you set up an online payment agreement but don't make your payments by direct debit; or
- $225, if you don't set up an online payment agreement and don't make your payments by direct debit.

Reduced installment agreement user fee. You may qualify to pay a reduced fee of $43 if your income is below a certain level. The IRS will let you know whether you qualify for the reduced fee. If the IRS doesn't say you qualify for the reduced fee, you can request the reduced fee using Form 13844, *Application For Reduced User Fee For Installment Agreements.* You can qualify for the $31 fee if you set up an online payment agreement and pay by direct debit.

There is also a reduced fee of $43 to modify or reinstate an installment agreement.

Other costs. You also will be charged interest and may be charged a late payment penalty on any tax not paid by its due date, even if your request to pay in installments is granted. Interest and any applicable penalties will be charged until the balance is paid in full. To limit interest and penalty charges, file your return on time and pay as much of the tax as possible with your return (or notice). All payments received will be applied to your account in the best interests of the United States.

By approving your request, we agree to let you pay the tax you owe in monthly installments instead of immediately paying the amount in full. In return, you agree to make your monthly payments on time. You also agree to meet all your future tax obligations. This means that you must have enough withholding or estimated tax payments so that your tax obligation for future years is paid in full when you timely file your return. Your request for an installment agreement will be denied if any required tax returns haven't been filed. Any refund you're due in a future year will be applied against the amount you owe. If your refund is applied to your balance, you're still required to make your regular monthly installment payment.

Payment methods. You can make your payments by check, money order, credit card, or one of the other payment methods shown next. The fee for setting up an installment agreement for each payment method is also shown. To be charged a lower fee you may want to set up an online payment agreement and/or agree to make your payments by direct debit.

Payment method	Applicable fee
Check, money order, or credit card	$225 ($149 with an online payment agreement)
Direct debit	$107 ($31 with an online payment agreement)
Payroll deduction installment agreement	$225

TIP *If the total amount you owe is not more than $50,000 (including any amounts you owe from prior years) and you request an installment agreement online, we may charge a lower fee. For more information, see* Applying online for a payment agreement, *earlier.*

For details on how to pay, see your tax return instructions, visit IRS.gov, or call 1-800-829-1040.

After we receive each payment, we will send you a notice showing the remaining amount you owe, and the due date and amount of your next payment. But if you choose to have your payments automatically withdrawn from your checking account, you won't receive a notice. Your bank statement is your record of payment. We will send you an annual statement showing the amount you owed at the beginning of the year, all payments made during the year, and the amount you owe at the end of the year.

If you don't make your payments on time or don't pay a balance due on a return you file later, you will be in default on your agreement and we may take enforcement actions, such as the filing of a Notice of Federal Tax Lien or an IRS levy action, to collect the entire amount you owe. To ensure that your payments are made timely, you should consider making them by direct debit. See the instructions for lines 13a and 13b.

Note. The shared responsibility payment (SRP) amount that you owe is the assessed payment for not having minimum essential health coverage for you and, if applicable, your dependents per section 5000A. The SRP amount that you owe isn't subject to penalties or to Notice of Federal Tax Lien or levy enforcement actions. However, interest will continue to accrue until you pay the total SRP balance due. We may apply your federal tax refunds to the SRP amount that you owe until it's paid in full.

Requests to modify or terminate an installment agreement. After an installment agreement is approved, you may submit a request to modify or terminate an installment agreement. You may modify your payment amount or due date by going to IRS.gov and entering "Online Payment Agreement" in the "Search" box. You may also call 1-800-829-1040 to modify or terminate your agreement. There is an $89 fee to modify the installment agreement. Low income taxpayers pay a $43 fee to modify an agreement.

An installment agreement may be terminated if you provide materially incomplete or inaccurate information in response to an IRS request for a financial update. For more information about what you need to do if your installment agreement is terminated, go to: www.irs.gov/individuals/understanding-your-cp523-notice.

A Notice of Federal Tax Lien (NFTL) may be filed to protect the government's interests until you pay in full. However, an NFTL generally isn't filed with a Guaranteed Installment Agreement or Streamlined Installment Agreement, but can be in certain situations.

We won't file an NFTL for the individual shared responsibility payment under the Affordable Care Act.

IRS collection process and taxpayer rights. For additional information on the IRS collection process and what to do if you cannot pay your taxes in full, see Pub. 594, The IRS Collection Process. You can find more information about the collection process, taxpayer rights and appealing a collection decision at this link, www.irs.gov/businesses/small-businesses-self-employed/collection-procedures-for-taxpayers-filing-and-or-paying-late.

Where To File

Attach Form 9465 to the front of your return and send it to the address shown in your tax return booklet. If you have already filed your return or you're filing this form in response to a notice, file Form 9465 by itself with the Internal Revenue Service Center using the address in the table below that applies to you.

For all taxpayers except those filing Form 1040 with Schedule(s) C, E, or F for any tax year for which this installment agreement is being requested

IF you live in . . .	THEN use this address . . .
Alaska, Arizona, Colorado, Connecticut, Delaware, District of Columbia, Hawaii, Idaho, Illinois, Maine, Maryland, Massachusetts, Montana, Nevada, New Hampshire, New Jersey, New Mexico, North Dakota, Oregon, Rhode Island, South Dakota, Tennessee, Utah, Vermont, Washington, Wisconsin, Wyoming	Department of the Treasury Internal Revenue Service 310 Lowell St. Stop 830 Andover, MA 01810
Alabama, Florida, Georgia, Kentucky, Louisiana, Mississippi, North Carolina, South Carolina, Texas, Virginia	Department of the Treasury Internal Revenue Service P.O. Box 47421 Stop 74 Doraville, GA 30362
Arkansas, California, Indiana, Iowa, Kansas, Michigan, Minnesota, Missouri, Nebraska, New York, Ohio, Oklahoma, Pennsylvania, West Virginia	Department of the Treasury Internal Revenue Service Stop P-4 5000 Kansas City, MO 64999-0250

For taxpayers filing Form 1040 with Schedule(s) C, E, or F for any tax year for which this installment agreement is being requested

IF you live in . . .	THEN use this address . . .
Connecticut, Maine, Massachusetts, New Hampshire, New York, Rhode Island, Vermont	Department of the Treasury Internal Revenue Service P.O. Box 480 Stop 660 Holtsville, NY 11742-0480
Alabama, Arkansas, Georgia, Illinois, Indiana, Iowa, Kansas, Kentucky, Louisiana, Michigan, Minnesota, Mississippi, Missouri, Nebraska, New Jersey, North Dakota, Ohio, Oklahoma, Pennsylvania, South Carolina, Tennessee, Texas, West Virginia, Wisconsin	Department of the Treasury Internal Revenue Service P.O. Box 69 Stop 811 Memphis, TN 38101-0069
Alaska, Arizona, California, Colorado, Hawaii, Idaho, Montana, Nevada, New Mexico, Oregon, Utah, Washington, Wyoming	Department of the Treasury Internal Revenue Service P.O. Box 9941 Stop 5500 Ogden, UT 84409
District of Columbia, Delaware, Florida, Maryland, North Carolina, South Carolina, Virginia	Department of the Treasury Internal Revenue Service Stop 4-N31.142 Philadelphia, PA 19255-0030

For all taxpayers living outside the 50 states, for any tax year for which the installment agreement is being requested

IF you live in . . .	THEN use this address . . .
A foreign country, American Samoa, Puerto Rico (or are excluding income under section 933), or use an APO or FPO address, or file Form 2555, 2555-EZ, or 4563, or are a dual-status alien	Department of the Treasury Internal Revenue Service 3651 South I-H 35 5501AUSC Austin, TX 78741

For all taxpayers who are bona fide residents of Guam, the U.S. Virgin Islands, or the Commonwealth of the Northern Mariana Islands, see Pub. 570, Tax Guide for Income From U.S. Possessions.

Specific Instructions

Part I

Line 1a

If you're making this request for a joint tax return, show the names and social security numbers (SSNs) in the same order as they appear on your tax return.

If you have a foreign address, enter the city name on the appropriate line. Do not enter any other information on that line, but also complete the spaces below that line. Do not abbreviate the country name. Follow the country's practice for entering the postal code and the name of the province, county, or state.

-3-

316

the sample check below, the account number is 20202086. Don't include the check number.

Note. We may have filed a Notice of Federal Tax Lien against your property. If so, you may be able to get the notice of lien withdrawn. To learn more about lien withdrawals and to see if you qualify, visit IRS.gov and enter "lien withdrawal" in the "Search" box.

TIP *The direct debit from your checking account won't be approved unless you (and your spouse if filing a joint return) sign Form 9465.*

Sample Check—Lines 13a and 13b

TIP *The routing and account numbers may be in different places on your check.*

Line 14

If you want to make your payments by payroll deduction, check the box on line 14 and attach a completed and signed Form 2159. Ask your employer to complete and sign the employer's portion of Form 2159.

CAUTION *If you choose to make your payments by payroll deduction, you won't be able to file Form 9465 electronically.*

Part II

If you have defaulted on an installment agreement within the last 12 months, and the amount you owe is greater than $25,000 but not more than $50,000, complete Part II on page 2 of Form 9465.

Privacy Act and Paperwork Reduction Act Notice. Our legal right to ask for the information on this form is sections 6001, 6011, 6012(a), 6109, and 6159 and their regulations. We will use the information to process your request for an installment agreement. The reason we need your name and social security number is to secure proper identification. We require this information to gain access to the tax information in our files and properly respond to your request. You aren't required to request an installment agreement. If you do request an installment agreement, you're required to provide the information requested on this form. Failure to provide this information may prevent processing your request; providing false information may subject you to fines or penalties.

You aren't required to provide the information requested on a form that is subject to the Paperwork Reduction Act unless the form displays a valid OMB control number. Books or records relating to a form or its instructions must be retained as long as their contents may become material in the administration of any Internal Revenue law. Generally, tax returns and return information are confidential, as required by section 6103. However, we may give this information to the Department of Justice for civil and criminal litigation, and to cities, states, the District of Columbia, and U.S. commonwealths and possessions to carry out their tax laws. We may also disclose this information to other countries under a tax treaty, to federal and state agencies to enforce federal nontax criminal laws, or to federal law enforcement and intelligence agencies to combat terrorism.

The average time and expenses required to complete and file this form will vary depending on individual circumstances. For the estimated averages, see the instructions for your income tax return.

If you have suggestions for making this form simpler, we would be happy to hear from you. See the instructions for your income tax return.

GPO U.S. GOVERNMENT PRINTING OFFICE: 2017—398-468/80664

IRS Department of the Treasury
Internal Revenue Service

IRS, STOP 6525
KANSAS CITY   MO   64999-0025

In reply refer to: 0135701196
Oct. 03, 2017   LTR 86C   0
390-80-4016 201612 30
                      00000215
BODC: WI

BRADLEY J FRANKS
408 S LINCOLN ST
MILBANK   SD   57252

022818

Taxpayer identification number: 390-80-4016
                Tax periods: Dec. 31, 2016

                              Dec. 31, 2016

                   Form: 1040

Dear Taxpayer:

Thank you for your correspondence of June 28, 2017.

We are sending your correspondence to our Michigan branch.

If you need forms, schedules, or publications, you can obtain them by
visiting the IRS website at www.irs.gov or by calling toll-free at
1-800-TAX-FORM (1-800-829-3676).

If you have questions, you can call us at 1-800-829-0922.

If you prefer, you can write to us at the address at the top of the
first page of this letter.

When you write, include a copy of this letter and provide in the
spaces below your telephone number with the hours we can reach you.
Keep a copy of this letter for your records.

Telephone number (   )_____   Hours_____

Thank you for your cooperation.

318

```
                                        0135701196
                    Oct. 03, 2017    LTR 86C    0
                    390-80-4016   201612 30
                                        00000216
```

BRADLEY J FRANKS
408 S LINCOLN ST
MILBANK   SD   57252

Sincerely yours,

Barbara Schaefer

Barbara Schaefer, Dept. Mgr.
Toll Free Dept. 1, Op 1

IRS Department of the Treasury
Internal Revenue Service
IRS, STOP 6525
KANSAS CITY MO 64999-0025

022818.795824.357535.16364 1 MB 0.423 530

BRADLEY J FRANKS
408 S LINCOLN ST
MILBANK SD 57252

022818

CUT OUT AND RETURN THE VOUCHER IMMEDIATELY BELOW IF YOU ONLY HAVE AN INQUIRY.
DO NOT USE IF YOU ARE MAKING A PAYMENT.

CUT OUT AND RETURN THE VOUCHER AT THE BOTTOM OF THIS PAGE IF YOU ARE MAKING A PAYMENT,
EVEN IF YOU ALSO HAVE AN INQUIRY.

The IRS address must appear in the window.　　　Use for inquiries only
　　　　　　　　　　　　0135701196　　　　　　　　　　　　　Letter Number:　LTR0086C
BODCD-WI　　　　　　　　　　　　　　　　　　　　　　　　　Letter Date　:　2017-10-03
　　　　　　　　　　　　　　　　　　　　　　　　　　　　　Tax Period　　:　201612

390804016

BRADLEY J FRANKS
408 S LINCOLN ST
MILBANK SD 57252

INTERNAL REVENUE SERVICE
IRS, STOP 6525
KANSAS CITY MO 64999-0025

390804016 LO FRAN 30 0 201612 670 00000000000

The IRS address must appear in the window.　　　Use for payments
　　　　　　　　　　　　0135701196　　　　　　　　　　　　Letter Number: LTR0086C
BODCD-WI　　　　　　　　　　　　　　　　　　　　　　　　Letter Date　: 2017-10-03
　　　　　　　　　　　　　　　　　　　　　　　　　　　　Tax Period　　: 201612

390804016

BRADLEY J FRANKS
408 S LINCOLN ST
MILBANK SD 57252

INTERNAL REVENUE SERVICE

KANSAS CITY MO 64999-0150

390804016 LO FRAN 30 0 201612 670 00000000000

320

Department of the Treasury
Internal Revenue Service
Austin, TX 73301-0010

IRS

Notice	CP15
Tax Year	2016
Notice date	October 9, 2017
Social Security number	390-80-4016
To contact us	1-800-829-0922
Your Caller ID	813596
Page 1 of 2	18H

148830.647626.4627.5763 1 AB 0.403 538

BRADLEY J FRANKS
408 S LINCOLN ST
MILBANK SD 57252-2326

148830

Notice of Penalty Charge

666

You have been charged a penalty under Section 6702(a) of the Internal Revenue Code for Civil Penalty for Frivolous Tax Returns.

TAX STATEMENT

Prior Balance	$15,000.00
Penalty Assessment	$40,000.00
Interest Charged	$220.22
Bad Check Penalty	$0.00
Balance Due	**$55,220.22**

IRS

BRADLEY J FRANKS
408 S LINCOLN ST
MILBANK SD 57252-2326

Notice	CP15
Notice date	October 9, 2017
Social Security number	390-80-4016

Payment

- Make your check or money order payable to the United States Treasury.
- Write your Social Security number (390-80-4016), the tax year (2016), and the form number (CVL PEN) on your payment and any correspondence.

Amount due by October 30, 2017	$55,220.22

INTERNAL REVENUE SERVICE
AUSTIN, TX 73301-0010

390804016 LO FRAN 55 0 201612 670 00005522022

321

Notice	CP15
Tax Year	2016
Notice date	October 9, 2017
Social Security number	390-80-4016
Page 2 of 2	18H

We charged you a penalty under IRC section 6702(a) for filing a frivolous tax return. The penalty applies when a person files what purports to be a return but—

A.
1. fails to include information on which the substantial correctness of the self-assessment may be judged or
2. includes information that on its face indicates that the self-assessment is substantially incorrect and

B.
1. the penalty applies when the underlying conduct in relation to filing such return is based on a position that the Internal Revenue Service has identified as frivolous (see Notice 2007-30) or
2. the underlying conduct reflects a desire to delay or impede the administration of Federal tax laws.

The penalty is $5,000 for each person who files a frivolous tax return.

If you wish to contest the assertion of this penalty, you must fully pay the entire penalty and file a claim for refund with the IRS within three years from the time a return associated with the penalty was filed or two years from the date the penalty was paid, whichever period expires later.

If your refund claim is pending for six months or more and the IRS has not issued a notice of claim disallowance with regard to the claim, you may file suit in the United States District Court or United States Court of Federal Claims to contest the assertion of the penalty at any time. Once the IRS issues a notice of claim disallowance, however, you must file suit in the United States District Court or The United States Court of Federal Claims within two years of the date the IRS mails a notice of disallowance to you denying the refund claim.

IRS

Contact information

BRADLEY J FRANKS
408 S LINCOLN ST
MILBANK SD 57252-2326

Notice	CP15
Notice date	October 9, 2017
Social Security number	390-80-4016

If your address has changed, please call 1-800-829-0922 or visit www.irs.gov.
☐ Please check here if you've included any correspondence. Write your Social Security number (390-80-4016), the tax year (2016), and the form number (CVL PEN) on any correspondence.

Primary phone | Best time to call | Secondary phone | Best time to call
☐ a.m. ☐ p.m. | | ☐ a.m. ☐ p.m.

INTERNAL REVENUE SERVICE
AUSTIN, TX 73301-0010

390804016 LO FRAN 55 0 201612

IRS Department of the Treasury
Internal Revenue Service

IRS, STOP 6525
KANSAS CITY MO 64999-0025

In reply refer to: 0138640000
Sep. 26, 2017 LTR 2644C KO
390-80-4016 201612 30
Input Op: 0109906473 00013909
                      BODC: WI

BRADLEY J FRANKS
408 S LINCOLN ST
MILBANK SD 57252-2326

022646

          Taxpayer Identification number: 390-80-4016
                    Tax periods: Dec. 31, 2016

                    Form: 1040

Dear Taxpayer:

We previously sent you a letter about your inquiry received
July 03, 2017. Although we try to respond quickly, we often need
additional time for research. We can't provide a complete response at
this time because:

We need more time to provide you with a complete response to your
inquiry.

While waiting to hear from us, if you have a balance, you can still
make payments to reduce your tax liability and interest charges. To
help us apply payments properly, make your check or money order
payable to the United States Treasury and provide on each payment:
   - Name
   - Address
   - Social security or employer identification number
   - Daytime telephone number
   - Tax year
   - Tax form

Please allow an additional 45 days for us to obtain the information
we need and let you know what action we're taking. You don't need to
do anything else right now.

If you have questions, you can call us toll free at
1-800-829-0922.

If you prefer, you can write to us at the address at the top of the
first page of this letter.

When you write, please include a copy of this letter and provide your
telephone number and the hours we can reach you in the spaces below.
Keep a copy of this letter for your records.

Your Telephone Number (___)_____ Hours _____

Thank you for your cooperation.

323

0138640000
Sep. 26, 2017 LTR 2644C KO
390-80-4016 201612 30
Input Op: 0109906473 00013910

BRADLEY J FRANKS
408 S LINCOLN ST
MILBANK   SD   57252-2326

Sincerely yours,

Selene Markowitz

Selene Markowitz, Operations Mgr.
Accounts Management Op 1

IRS Department of the Treasury
Internal Revenue Service

FRESNO   CA 93888-0025

In reply refer to: 1042000000
Aug. 10, 2017 LTR 2645C K0
390-80-4016   201612 30
Input Op: 1009960380 00027618
                              BODC: WI

BRADLEY J FRANKS
408 S LINCOLN ST
MILBANK   SD 57252-2326

026994

            Taxpayer identification number: 390-80-4016
                    Tax periods: Dec. 31, 2016

                         Form: 1040

Dear Taxpayer:

We received one of the following items from you or your authorized
third party on July 03, 2017.

- Correspondence
- Telephone inquiry
- Payment
- Form
- Response to our inquiry or notice
- Penalty abatement request
- Installment agreement
- Other

We're working on your account. However, we need an additional 45
days to send you a complete response on what action we are taking
on your account. We don't need any further information from you right
now.

If you have questions, you can call us toll free at
1-800-829-0922.

If you prefer, you can write to us at the address at the top of the
first page of this letter. However, you don't need to take any further
action at this time.

You can get any of the forms or publications mentioned in this letter
by calling 1-800-TAX-FORM (1-800-829-3676) or visiting our website at
www.irs.gov/formspubs.

When you write, include this letter and provide in the spaces below
your telephone number with the hours we can reach you. Keep a copy of
this letter for your records.

Telephone number (____)_____ Hours _____

Thank you for your cooperation.

```
                                          1042000000
                          Aug. 10, 2017  LTR 2645C  KO
                          390-80-4016  201612 30
                          Input Op:  1009960380 00027619
```

```
BRADLEY J FRANKS
408 S LINCOLN ST
MILBANK  SD  57252-2326
```

Sincerely yours,

Ursula S. Dean

URSULA DEAN
OPERATIONS MANAGER, OPERATIONS 2

IRS   Department of the Treasury
Internal Revenue Service
Ogden, UT 84201-0076

BRADLEY J FRANKS
408 SOUTH LINCOLN STREET
MILBANK SD 57252

The Death of America

| Form **1040** | Department of the Treasury—Internal Revenue Service (99)
 U.S. Individual Income Tax Return | **2016** | OMB No. 1545-0074 | IRS Use Only—Do not write or staple in this space. |

For the year Jan. 1–Dec. 31, 2016, or other tax year beginning **March 22,** , 20 **17** ending **June 21** , 20 **17**   See separate instructions.

Your first name and initial **Bradley J.**   Last name **Franks**   Your social security number

If a joint return, spouse's first name and initial   Last name   Spouse's social security number

Home address (number and street). If you have a P.O. box, see instructions. **% 408 S Lincoln St**   Apt. no.   ▲ Make sure the SSN(s) above and on line 6c are correct.

City, town or post office, state, and ZIP code. If you have a foreign address, also complete spaces below (see instructions). **Milbank, S.D.**

Foreign country name **United States**   Foreign province/state/county **Grant County**   Foreign postal code **57252**

Presidential Election Campaign — Check here if you, or your spouse if filing jointly, want $3 to go to this fund. Checking a box below will not change your tax or refund. ☐ You ☐ Spouse

Filing Status — 1 ☑ Single

Exemptions — 6a ☐ Yourself. Boxes checked on 6a and 6b **1**; No. of children on 6c who lived with you **0**; Dependents on 6c not entered above **8**; Add numbers on lines above ▶ **1**

Income
7	Wages, salaries, tips, etc. Attach Form(s) W-2	7	**0 0**
8a	Taxable interest. Attach Schedule B if required	8a	**396,333,53/32**
21	Other income. List type and amount **"Security Interest" on Principal**	21	**363,325.31**
22	Combine the amounts... This is your total income ▶	22	**392,968,666 63**
36	Add lines 23 through 35	36	**0 0**
37	Subtract line 36 from line 22. This is your adjusted gross income ▶	37	**392,968,666 63**

Form **1040** (2016)

328

Form 1040 (2016) — Page 2

Tax and Credits	38 Amount from line 37 (adjusted gross income)	38 3,992,968,666.63
	39a Check { You were born before January 2, 1952, Blind. } Total boxes / Spouse was born before January 2, 1952, Blind. } checked ▶ 39a	
	b If your spouse itemizes on a separate return or you were a dual-status alien, check here ▶ 39b	
Standard Deduction for—	40 Itemized deductions (from Schedule A) or your standard deduction (see left margin)	40 0 0
	41 Subtract line 40 from line 38	41 3,992,968,666.63
	42 Exemptions. If line 38 is $155,650 or less, multiply $4,050 by the number on line 6d. Otherwise, see instructions	42 4,050.00
	43 Taxable income. Subtract line 42 from line 41. If line 42 is more than line 41, enter -0-	43
	44 Tax (see instructions). Check if any from: a Form(s) 8814 b Form 4972 c	44
	45 Alternative minimum tax (see instructions). Attach Form 6251	45
	46 Excess advance premium tax credit repayment. Attach Form 8962	46
	47 Add lines 44, 45, and 46 ▶	47
	48 Foreign tax credit. Attach Form 1116 if required	48
	49 Credit for child and dependent care expenses. Attach Form 2441	49
	50 Education credits from Form 8863, line 19	50
	51 Retirement savings contributions credit. Attach Form 8880	51
	52 Child tax credit. Attach Schedule 8812, if required	52
	53 Residential energy credits. Attach Form 5695	53
	54 Other credits from Form: a 3800 b 8801 c	54
	55 Add lines 48 through 54. These are your total credits	55
	56 Subtract line 55 from line 47. If line 55 is more than line 47, enter -0- ▶	56
Other Taxes	57 Self-employment tax. Attach Schedule SE	57
	58 Unreported social security and Medicare tax from Form: a 4137 b 8919	58
	59 Additional tax on IRAs, other qualified retirement plans, etc. Attach Form 5329 if required	59
	60a Household employment taxes from Schedule H	60a
	b First-time homebuyer credit repayment. Attach Form 5405 if required	60b
	61 Health care: individual responsibility (see instructions) Full-year coverage	61
	62 Taxes from: a Form 8959 b Form 8960 c Instructions; enter code(s)	62
	63 Add lines 56 through 62. This is your total tax ▶	63
Payments	64 Federal income tax withheld from Forms W-2 and 1099	64
	65 2016 estimated tax payments and amount applied from 2015 return	65
	66a Earned income credit (EIC)	66a
	b Nontaxable combat pay election 66b	
	67 Additional child tax credit. Attach Schedule 8812	67
	68 American opportunity credit from Form 8863, line 8	68
	69 Net premium tax credit. Attach Form 8962	69
	70 Amount paid with request for extension to file	70
	71 Excess social security and tier 1 RRTA tax withheld	71
	72 Credit for federal tax on fuels. Attach Form 4136	72
	73 Credits from Form: a 2439 b Reserved c 8885 d	73
	74 Add lines 64, 65, 66a, and 67 through 73. These are your total payments ▶	74
Refund	75 If line 74 is more than line 63, subtract line 63 from line 74. This is the amount you overpaid	75
	76a Amount of line 75 you want refunded to you. If Form 8888 is attached, check here ▶	76a 3,965,325 31
	b Routing number ▶ Type: Checking Savings	
	d Account number	
	77 Amount of line 75 you want applied to your 2017 estimated tax ▶ 77	
Amount You Owe	78 Amount you owe. Subtract line 74 from line 63. For details on how to pay, see instructions ▶	78 0 0
	79 Estimated tax penalty (see instructions) 79	

Third Party Designee Do you want to allow another person to discuss this return with the IRS (see instructions)? Yes. Complete below. No

Designee's name ▶ Phone no. ▶ Personal identification number (PIN) ▶

Sign Here Under penalties of perjury, I declare that I have examined this return and accompanying schedules and statements, and to the best of my knowledge and belief, they are true, correct, and accurately list all amounts and sources of income I received during the tax year. Declaration of preparer (other than taxpayer) is based on all information of which preparer has any knowledge.

Your signature Bradley J. Frank Date 6-21-17 Your occupation Author / Self Emp. Daytime phone number 605-432-7920

Paid Preparer Use Only

www.irs.gov/form1040 — Form 1040 (2016)

The Death of America

Form **8888**	Allocation of Refund (Including Savings Bond Purchases)		OMB No. 1545-0074

8888

Department of the Treasury
Internal Revenue Service

► Information about Form 8888 and its instructions is at *www.irs.gov/form8888.*
► Attach to your income tax return.

2016

Attachment
Sequence No. **56**

Name(s) shown on return: Bradley J. Franks

Your social security number: 390-80-4016

Part I — Direct Deposit

Complete this part if you want us to directly deposit a portion of your refund to one or more accounts.

- 1a Amount to be deposited in first account (see instructions) **1a**
- b Routing number ► c ☐ Checking ☐ Savings
- d Account number
- 2a Amount to be deposited in second account **2a**
- b Routing number ► c ☐ Checking ☐ Savings
- d Account number
- 3a Amount to be deposited in third account **3a**
- b Routing number ► c ☐ Checking ☐ Savings
- d Account number

Part II — U.S. Series I Savings Bond Purchases

Complete this part if you want to buy paper bonds with a portion of your refund.

⚠ **CAUTION** If a name is entered on line 5c or 6c below, co-ownership will be assumed unless the beneficiary box is checked. See instructions for more details.

- 4 Amount to be used for bond purchases for yourself (and your spouse, if filing jointly) **4**
- 5a Amount to be used to buy bonds for yourself, your spouse, **or** someone else **5a**
- b Enter the owner's name (First then Last) for the bond registration
- c If you would like to add a co-owner or beneficiary, enter the name here (First then Last). If beneficiary, also check here ► ☐
- 6a Amount to be used to buy bonds for yourself, your spouse, **or** someone else **6a**
- b Enter the owner's name (First then Last) for the bond registration
- c If you would like to add a co-owner or beneficiary, enter the name here (First then Last). If beneficiary, also check here ► ☐

Part III — Paper Check

Complete this part if you want a portion of your refund to be sent to you as a check.

- 7 Amount to be refunded by check **7** 3963,325 31

Part IV — Total Allocation of Refund

- 8 Add lines 1a, 2a, 3a, 4, 5a, 6a, and 7. The total must equal the refund amount shown on your tax return **8** 3963,325 31

For Paperwork Reduction Act Notice, see your tax return instructions. Cat. No. 21858A Form **8888** (2016)

330

Bradley – J.: [Franks];

C/O: 408 South Lincoln Street;

Milbank, South Dakota; [57252].

Internal Revenue Service

1973 North Rulon White Blvd.

M/S 4450

Ogden, Utah 84201 – 0076

Date: March 12, 2017

RE: Response for Document Labeled; "Letter 3176(SC) (REV. 4-2012) Catalog number 26860K"

Attention: Mrs. Davis:

Please find enclosed a correction for the return filing for the months of October 21, 2016 through December 21, 2016. At 1% interest according to FDIC Rules and Laws you will find that these numbers are accurate for a "Security".

The second enclosure you will find the 1040 Tax return for the second quarter for the months of January 21, 2017 through March 21, 2017: at the same rate of Interest.

Please do not presume to assume that this is a "Frivolous Tax Submission" by your OPINION. Your Federal Courts, including the Supreme Court of the United States, try **FACTS _NOT_ OPINIONS.**

Sincerely,

Bradley - J. : [Franks]

Enclosures:

Corrected tax return

Copy of this letter

331

DEPARTMENT OF THE TREASURY
INTERNAL REVENUE SERVICE
WASHINGTON, DC 20224

SMALL BUSINESS/SELF-EMPLOYED DIVISION

Date: 10/05/2017

BRADLEY J FRANKS
408 S LINCOLN ST
MILBANK, SD 57252-2326088

Dear Mr. Franks:

We show that you have the following personal tax liability:

PENALTY/ TAX PERIOD	ASSESSED AMOUNT	ACCRUALS	TOTAL DUE
12/31/2016	$55,000.00	$231.90	$55,231.90

The accruals shown above have been calculated to 10/16/2017.

Your account has been assigned to me for resolution. To assist with this resolution, I am scheduling an appointment for you for Monday, October 16, 2017 at 9:30 AM. The location will be the Bloomington, Minnesota office at 1550 American Blvd E, Suite 500, Bloomington, MN 55425. You will need to bring the following documents with you to this meeting:

•   Collection Information Statement(s), both individual and for each business you operate (blanks are included).
•   Bank statements for the most recent twelve months for each bank account which you have signature authority (personal and business).
•   The last three statements from each credit card account you are able to negotiate.
•   The most recent statements from any investment account(s) in your control.
•   The most recent statement for any life insurance policy in you name or in the name of any company you control.
•   The most recent balance sheet(s) and profit and loss statement(s) for any and all companies you control.
•   The current accounts receivable ledger from all businesses you control.
•   The most recent loan statements for all loans secured by real property or vehicles in your possession.
•   Copies of the most recent federal income tax returns for you and companies you control.
•   Trust documents, articles of incorporation, and/or partnership agreements for all entities you control or for which you have controlling interest. This should include, but is

not limited to, all documents pertaining to the establishment and governance of these entities.

If the date I have scheduled for the meeting is not convenient, please call as soon as possible to arrange for a different time. However, the alternate time will have to be within one month of the currently scheduled date.

I am required to advise you that failure to comply with this request for a meeting, or provide the documents specified, may result in the contact of third parties and/or enforcement action without further notice to you. Such actions may include serving a summons; Filing a Federal Tax Lien; Levy against wages, bank accounts or account receivables; or seizure of real or personal property.

If you have any questions or need more information, please contact me at the address or the telephone number listed below:

Internal Revenue Service
1550 AMERICAN BLVD EAST
STE 500 M/S 5128
BLOOMINGTON, MN 55425

Phone#: (763)347-7398
Fax#: (888)221-7797

Sincerely,

RICHARD A WALLIN
REVENUE OFFICER
Employee ID#: 1000208166

Enclosures:
* Publication 1
* Publication 594
* Letter 3164
* Form 433A(2)
* Form 433B(2)

Department of the Treasury
Internal Revenue Service
1550 AMERICAN BLVD EAST
STE 500 M/S 5128
BLOOMINGTON, MN 55425

IRS

Date:
10/05/2017
Taxpayer ID number:
XXX-XX-4016
Person to contact:
RICHARD A WALLIN
Contact telephone number:
(763)347-7398
Contact fax number:

Bradley J. Franks
408 S. Lincoln St
Milbank, SD 57252-2326088

Employee ID number:
1000208166

We're attempting to collect taxes you owe. You should know about this from our previous contacts with you.

Generally, the IRS will deal directly with you or your duly authorized representative. However, we sometimes talk with other persons if we need information that you've been unable to provide, or to verify information we've received. If we do contact other persons, such as a neighbor, bank, employer, or employees, we'll generally need to tell them limited information, such as your name. The law prohibits us from disclosing any more information than is necessary to obtain or verify the information we're seeking. Our need to contact other persons may continue as long as there's activity in your case. If we do contact other persons, you have a right to request a list of those contacted.

In addition, the Taxpayer Bill of Rights describes ten basic rights that all taxpayers have when dealing with the IRS. To help you understand what these rights mean to you and how they apply visit our website IRS.gov.

If you have questions regarding this letter or want to request a list of persons we've contacted, please contact the person listed at the top of this letter. When you write, include the person to contact name and the employee ID number shown above.

Sincerely,

Richard A Wallin

RICHARD A WALLIN
REVENUE OFFICER

Letter 3164-B (Rev. 2-2017)
Catalog Number 73227V

334

Your Rights as a Taxpayer

IRS

Publication 1

This publication explains your rights as a taxpayer and the processes for examination, appeal, collection, and refunds. Also available in Spanish.

The Taxpayer Bill of Rights

1. The Right to Be Informed

Taxpayers have the right to know what they need to do to comply with the tax laws. They are entitled to clear explanations of the laws and IRS procedures in all tax forms, instructions, publications, notices, and correspondence. They have the right to be informed of IRS decisions about their tax accounts and to receive clear explanations of the outcomes.

2. The Right to Quality Service

Taxpayers have the right to receive prompt, courteous, and professional assistance in their dealings with the IRS, to be spoken to in a way they can easily understand, to receive clear and easily understandable communications from the IRS, and to speak to a supervisor about inadequate service.

3. The Right to Pay No More than the Correct Amount of Tax

Taxpayers have the right to pay only the amount of tax legally due, including interest and penalties, and to have the IRS apply all tax payments properly.

4. The Right to Challenge the IRS's Position and Be Heard

Taxpayers have the right to raise objections and provide additional documentation in response to formal IRS actions or proposed actions, to expect that the IRS will consider their timely objections and documentation promptly and fairly, and to receive a response if the IRS does not agree with their position.

5. The Right to Appeal an IRS Decision in an Independent Forum

Taxpayers are entitled to a fair and impartial administrative appeal of most IRS decisions, including many penalties, and have the right to receive a written response regarding the Office of Appeals' decision. Taxpayers generally have the right to take their cases to court.

6. The Right to Finality

Taxpayers have the right to know the maximum amount of time they have to challenge the IRS's position as well as the maximum amount of time the IRS has to audit a particular tax year or collect a tax debt. Taxpayers have the right to know when the IRS has finished an audit.

7. The Right to Privacy

Taxpayers have the right to expect that any IRS inquiry, examination, or enforcement action will comply with the law and be no more intrusive than necessary, and will respect all due process rights, including search and seizure protections and will provide, where applicable, a collection due process hearing.

8. The Right to Confidentiality

Taxpayers have the right to expect that any information they provide to the IRS will not be disclosed unless authorized by the taxpayer or by law. Taxpayers have the right to expect appropriate action will be taken against employees, return preparers, and others who wrongfully use or disclose taxpayer return information.

9. The Right to Retain Representation

Taxpayers have the right to retain an authorized representative of their choice to represent them in their dealings with the IRS. Taxpayers have the right to seek assistance from a Low Income Taxpayer Clinic if they cannot afford representation.

10. The Right to a Fair and Just Tax System

Taxpayers have the right to expect the tax system to consider facts and circumstances that might affect their underlying liabilities, ability to pay, or ability to provide information timely. Taxpayers have the right to receive assistance from the Taxpayer Advocate Service if they are experiencing financial difficulty or if the IRS has not resolved their tax issues properly and timely through its normal channels.

The IRS Mission Provide America's taxpayers top-quality service by helping them understand and meet their tax responsibilities and enforce the law with integrity and fairness to all.

Publication 1 (Rev. 12-2014) Catalog Number 64731W Department of the Treasury **Internal Revenue Service** www.irs.gov

335

Examinations, Appeals, Collections, and Refunds

Examinations (Audits)

We accept most taxpayers' returns as filed. If we inquire about your return or select it for examination, it does not suggest that you are dishonest. The inquiry or examination may or may not result in more tax. We may close your case without change; or, you may receive a refund.

The process of selecting a return for examination usually begins in one of two ways. First, we use computer programs to identify returns that may have incorrect amounts. These programs may be based on information returns, such as Forms 1099 and W-2, on studies of past examinations, or on certain issues identified by compliance projects. Second, we use information from outside sources that indicates that a return may have incorrect amounts. These sources may include newspapers, public records, and individuals. If we determine that the information is accurate and reliable, we may use it to select a return for examination.

Publication 556, Examination of Returns, Appeal Rights, and Claims for Refund, explains the rules and procedures that we follow in examinations. The following sections give an overview of how we conduct examinations.

By Mail

We handle many examinations and inquiries by mail. We will send you a letter with either a request for more information or a reason why we believe a change to your return may be needed. You can respond by mail or you can request a personal interview with an examiner. If you mail us the requested information or provide an explanation, we may or may not agree with you, and we will explain the reasons for any changes. Please do not hesitate to write to us about anything you do not understand.

By Interview

If we notify you that we will conduct your examination through a personal interview, or you request such an interview, you have the right to ask that the examination take place at a reasonable time and place that is convenient for both you and the IRS. If our examiner proposes any changes to your return, he or she will explain the reasons for the changes. If you do not agree with these changes, you can meet with the examiner's supervisor.

Repeat Examinations

If we examined your return for the same items in either of the 2 previous years and proposed no change to your tax liability, please contact us as soon as possible so we can see if we should discontinue the examination.

Appeals

If you do not agree with the examiner's proposed changes, you can appeal them to the Appeals Office of IRS. Most differences can be settled without expensive and time-consuming court trials. Your appeal rights are explained in detail in both Publication 5, Your Appeal Rights and How To Prepare a Protest If You Don't Agree, and Publication 556, Examination of Returns, Appeal Rights, and Claims for Refund.

If you do not wish to use the Appeals Office or disagree with its findings, you may be able to take your case to the U.S. Tax Court, U.S. Court of Federal Claims, or the U.S. District Court where you live. If you take your case to court, the IRS will have the burden of proving certain facts if you kept adequate records to show your tax liability, cooperated with the IRS, and meet certain other conditions. If the court agrees with you on most issues in your case and finds that our position was largely unjustified, you may be able to recover some of your administrative and litigation costs. You will not be eligible to recover these costs unless you tried to resolve your case administratively, including going through the appeals system, and you gave us the information necessary to resolve the case.

Collections

Publication 594, The IRS Collection Process, explains your rights and responsibilities regarding payment of federal taxes. It describes:

- What to do when you owe taxes. It describes what to do if you get a tax bill and what to do if you think your bill is wrong. It also covers making installment payments, delaying collection action, and submitting an offer in compromise.
- IRS collection actions. It covers liens, releasing a lien, levies, releasing a levy, seizures and sales, and release of property.

Your collection appeal rights are explained in detail in Publication 1660, Collection Appeal Rights.

Innocent Spouse Relief

Generally, both you and your spouse are each responsible for paying the full amount of tax, interest, and penalties due on your joint return. However, if you qualify for innocent spouse relief, you may be relieved of part or all of the joint liability. To request relief, you must file Form 8857, Request for Innocent Spouse Relief. For more information on innocent spouse relief, see Publication 971, Innocent Spouse Relief, and Form 8857.

Potential Third Party Contacts

Generally, the IRS will deal directly with you or your duly authorized representative.

However, we sometimes talk with other persons if we need information that you have been unable to provide, or to verify information we have received. If we do contact other persons, such as a neighbor, bank, employer, or employees, we will generally need to tell them limited information, such as your name. The law prohibits us from disclosing any more information than is necessary to obtain or verify the information we are seeking. Our need to contact other persons may continue as long as there is activity in your case. If we do contact other persons, you have a right to request a list of those contacted.

Refunds

You may file a claim for refund if you think you paid too much tax. You must generally file the claim within 3 years from the date you filed your original return or 2 years from the date you paid the tax, whichever is later. The law generally provides for interest on your refund if it is not paid within 45 days of the date you filed your return or claim for refund. Publication 556, Examination of Returns, Appeal Rights, and Claims for Refund, has more information on refunds.

If you were due a refund but you did not file a return, you generally must file your return within 3 years from the date the return was due (including extensions) to get that refund.

Taxpayer Advocate Service

TAS is an *independent* organization within the IRS that can help protect your taxpayer rights. We can offer you help if your tax problem is causing a hardship, or you've tried but haven't been able to resolve your problem with the IRS. If you qualify for our assistance, which is always free, we will do everything possible to help you. Visit *taxpayeradvocate.irs.gov* or call 1-877-777-4778.

Tax Information

The IRS provides the following sources for forms, publications, and additional information.

- *Tax Questions:* 1-800-829-1040 (1-800-829-4059 for TTY/TDD)
- *Forms and Publications:* 1-800-829-3676 (1-800-829-4059 for TTY/TDD)
- *Internet: www.irs.gov*
- *Small Business Ombudsman:* A small business entity can participate in the regulatory process and comment on enforcement actions of IRS by calling 1-888-REG-FAIR.
- *Treasury Inspector General for Tax Administration:* You can confidentially report misconduct, waste, fraud, or abuse by an IRS employee by calling 1-800-366-4484 (1-800-877-8339 for TTY/TDD). You can remain anonymous.

♲ *Printed on recycled paper*

GPO U.S. GPO: 2015-646-379

Form **433-A** (Rev. December 2012) Department of the Treasury Internal Revenue Service	**Collection Information Statement for Wage Earners and Self-Employed Individuals**

Wage Earners Complete Sections 1, 2, 3, 4, and 5 including the signature line on page 4. *Answer all questions or write N/A if the question is not applicable.*
Self-Employed Individuals Complete Sections 1, 3, 4, 5, 6 and 7 and the signature line on page 4. *Answer all questions or write N/A if the question is not applicable.*
For Additional Information, refer to Publication 1854, "How To Prepare a Collection Information Statement."
Include attachments if additional space is needed to respond completely to any question.

Name on Internal Revenue Service (IRS) Account	Social Security Number SSN on IRS Account	Employer Identification Number *EIN*

Section 1: Personal Information

1a Full Name of Taxpayer and Spouse *(if applicable)*	1c Home Phone ( )	1d Cell Phone ( )
1b Address *(Street, City, State, ZIP code) (County of Residence)*	1e Business Phone ( )	1f Business Cell Phone ( )
	2b Name, Age, and Relationship of dependent(s)	

2a Marital Status: ☐ Married ☐ Unmarried *(Single, Divorced, Widowed)*

	Social Security No. (SSN)	Date of Birth *(mmddyyyy)*	Driver's License Number and State
3a Taxpayer			
3b Spouse			

Section 2: Employment Information for Wage Earners

If you or your spouse have self-employment income instead of, or in addition to wage income, complete Business Information in Sections 6 and 7.

Taxpayer		Spouse	
4a Taxpayer's Employer Name		5a Spouse's Employer Name	
4b Address *(Street, City, State, and ZIP code)*		5b Address *(Street, City, State, and ZIP code)*	
4c Work Telephone Number ( )	4d Does employer allow contact at work ☐ Yes ☐ No	5c Work Telephone Number ( )	5d Does employer allow contact at work ☐ Yes ☐ No
4e How long with this employer (years) (months)	4f Occupation	5e How long with this employer (years) (months)	5f Occupation
4g Number of withholding allowances claimed on Form W-4	4h Pay Period: ☐ Weekly ☐ Bi-weekly ☐ Monthly ☐ Other	5g Number of withholding allowances claimed on Form W-4	5h Pay Period: ☐ Weekly ☐ Bi-weekly ☐ Monthly ☐ Other

Section 3: Other Financial Information *(Attach copies of applicable documentation)*

6 Are you a party to a lawsuit *(If yes, answer the following)*			☐ Yes ☐ No
☐ Plaintiff ☐ Defendant	Location of Filing	Represented by	Docket/Case No.
Amount of Suit $	Possible Completion Date *(mmddyyyy)*	Subject of Suit	

7 Have you ever filed bankruptcy *(If yes, answer the following)*				☐ Yes ☐ No
Date Filed *(mmddyyyy)*	Date Dismissed *(mmddyyyy)*	Date Discharged *(mmddyyyy)*	Petition No.	Location Filed

8 In the past 10 years, have you lived outside of the U.S for 6 months or longer *(If yes, answer the following)*	☐ Yes ☐ No
Dates lived abroad: from *(mmddyyyy)*	To *(mmddyyyy)*

9a Are you the beneficiary of a trust, estate, or life insurance policy *(If yes, answer the following)*		☐ Yes ☐ No
Place where recorded:		
Name of the trust, estate, or policy	Anticipated amount to be received $	When will the amount be received

9b Are you a trustee, fiduciary, or contributor of a trust		☐ Yes ☐ No
Name of the trust:	EIN:	

10 Do you have a safe deposit box (business or personal) *(If yes, answer the following)*		☐ Yes ☐ No
Location *(Name, address and box number(s))*	Contents	Value $

11 In the past 10 years, have you transferred any assets for less than their full value *(If yes, answer the following)*			☐ Yes ☐ No
List Asset(s)	Value at Time of Transfer $	Date Transferred *(mmddyyyy)*	To Whom or Where was it Transferred

Form 433-A (Rev. 12-2012)   Page **2**

Section 4: Personal Asset Information for All Individuals

12 **CASH ON HAND** Include cash that is not in a bank   **Total Cash on Hand** | $

PERSONAL BANK ACCOUNTS Include all checking, online and mobile *(e.g., PayPal)* accounts, money market accounts, savings accounts, and stored value cards *(e.g., payroll cards, government benefit cards, etc.)*.

Type of Account	Full Name & Address *(Street, City, State, ZIP code)* of Bank, Savings & Loan, Credit Union, or Financial Institution	Account Number	Account Balance As of _____ *mmddyyyy*
13a			$
13b			$
13c			$

13d Total Cash *(Add lines 13a through 13c, and amounts from any attachments)* | $

INVESTMENTS Include stocks, bonds, mutual funds, stock options, certificates of deposit, and retirement assets such as IRAs, Keogh, and 401(k) plans. Include all corporations, partnerships, limited liability companies, or other business entities in which you are an officer, director, owner, member, or otherwise have a financial interest.

Type of Investment or Financial Interest	Full Name & Address *(Street, City, State, ZIP code)* of Company	Current Value	Loan Balance *(if applicable)* As of _____ *mmddyyyy*	Equity Value minus Loan
14a				
	Phone	$	$	$
14b				
	Phone	$	$	$
14c				
	Phone	$	$	$

14d Total Equity *(Add lines 14a through 14c and amounts from any attachments)* | $

AVAILABLE CREDIT Include all lines of credit and bank issued credit cards. Full Name & Address *(Street, City, State, ZIP code)* of Credit Institution	Credit Limit	Amount Owed As of _____ *mmddyyyy*	Available Credit As of _____ *mmddyyyy*
15a			
Acct. No	$	$	$
15b			
Acct. No	$	$	$

15c Total Available Credit *(Add lines 15a, 15b and amounts from any attachments)* | $

16a **LIFE INSURANCE** Do you own or have any interest in any life insurance policies with cash value *(Term Life insurance does not have a cash value)*
☐ Yes   ☐ No   If yes, complete blocks 16b through 16f for each policy.

16b Name and Address of Insurance Company(ies):			
16c Policy Number(s)			
16d Owner of Policy			
16e Current Cash Value	$	$	$
16f Outstanding Loan Balance	$	$	$

16g Total Available Cash *(Subtract amounts on line 16f from line 16e and include amounts from any attachments)* | $

Form **433-A** (Rev. 12-2012)

Form 433-A (Rev. 12-2012)   Page **3**

REAL PROPERTY Include all real property owned or being purchased

	Purchase Date (mmddyyyy)	Current Fair Market Value (FMV)	Current Loan Balance	Amount of Monthly Payment	Date of Final Payment (mmddyyyy)	Equity FMV Minus Loan
17a Property Description		$	$	$		$
Location (Street, City, State, ZIP code) and County			Lender/Contract Holder Name, Address (Street, City, State, ZIP code), and Phone			
					Phone	
17b Property Description		$	$	$		$
Location (Street, City, State, ZIP code) and County			Lender/Contract Holder Name, Address (Street, City, State, ZIP code), and Phone			
					Phone	

17c Total Equity (Add lines 17a, 17b and amounts from any attachments) $

PERSONAL VEHICLES LEASED AND PURCHASED Include boats, RVs, motorcycles, all-terrain and off-road vehicles, trailers, etc.

Description (Year, Mileage, Make/Model, Tag Number, Vehicle Identification Number)	Purchase/ Lease Date (mmddyyyy)	Current Fair Market Value (FMV)	Current Loan Balance	Amount of Monthly Payment	Date of Final Payment (mmddyyyy)	Equity FMV Minus Loan
18a Year — Make/Model		$	$	$		$
Mileage — License/Tag Number	Lender/Lessor Name, Address (Street, City, State, ZIP code), and Phone					
Vehicle Identification Number					Phone	
18b Year — Make/Model		$	$	$		$
Mileage — License/Tag Number	Lender/Lessor Name, Address (Street, City, State, ZIP code), and Phone					
Vehicle Identification Number					Phone	

18c Total Equity (Add lines 18a, 18b and amounts from any attachments) $

PERSONAL ASSETS Include all furniture, personal effects, artwork, jewelry, collections (coins, guns, etc.), antiques or other assets. Include intangible assets such as licenses, domain names, patents, copyrights, mining claims, etc.

	Purchase/ Lease Date (mmddyyyy)	Current Fair Market Value (FMV)	Current Loan Balance	Amount of Monthly Payment	Date of Final Payment (mmddyyyy)	Equity FMV Minus Loan
19a Property Description		$	$	$		$
Location (Street, City, State, ZIP code) and County			Lender/Lessor Name, Address (Street, City, State, ZIP code), and Phone			
					Phone	
19b Property Description		$	$	$		$
Location (Street, City, State, ZIP code) and County			Lender/Lessor Name, Address (Street, City, State, ZIP code), and Phone			
					Phone	

19c Total Equity (Add lines 19a, 19b and amounts from any attachments) $

Form **433-A** (Rev. 12-2012)

The Death of America

Form 433-A (Rev. 12-2012)   Page **4**

If you are self-employed, sections 6 and 7 must be completed before continuing.

Section 5: Monthly Income and Expenses

Monthly Income/Expense Statement *(For additional information, refer to Publication 1854.)*

Total Income			Total Living Expenses		IRS USE ONLY
Source	Gross Monthly		Expense Items [6]	Actual Monthly	Allowable Expenses
20 Wages (Taxpayer) [1]	$		35 Food, Clothing and Misc. [7]	$	
21 Wages (Spouse) [1]	$		36 Housing and Utilities [8]	$	
22 Interest - Dividends	$		37 Vehicle Ownership Costs [9]	$	
23 Net Business Income [2]	$		38 Vehicle Operating Costs [10]	$	
24 Net Rental Income [3]	$		39 Public Transportation [11]	$	
25 Distributions (K-1, IRA, etc.) [4]	$		40 Health Insurance	$	
26 Pension (Taxpayer)	$		41 Out of Pocket Health Care Costs [12]	$	
27 Pension (Spouse)	$		42 Court Ordered Payments	$	
28 Social Security (Taxpayer)	$		43 Child/Dependent Care	$	
29 Social Security (Spouse)	$		44 Life Insurance	$	
30 Child Support	$		45 Current year taxes (Income/FICA) [13]	$	
31 Alimony	$		46 Secured Debts (Attach list)	$	
Other Income (Specify below) [5]			47 Delinquent State or Local Taxes	$	
32	$		48 Other Expenses (Attach list)	$	
33	$		49 Total Living Expenses (add lines 35-48)	$	
34 Total Income (add lines 20-33)	$		50 Net difference (Line 34 minus 49)	$	

1 **Wages, salaries, pensions, and social security:** Enter gross monthly wages and/or salaries. Do not deduct tax withholding or allotments taken out of pay, such as insurance payments, credit union deductions, car payments, etc. To calculate the gross monthly wages and/or salaries:

  If paid weekly - multiply weekly gross wages by 4.3. Example: $425.89 x 4.3 = $1,831.33

  If paid biweekly (every 2 weeks) - multiply biweekly gross wages by 2.17. Example: $972.45 x 2.17 = $2,110.22

  If paid semimonthly (twice each month) - multiply semimonthly gross wages by 2. Example: $856.23 x 2 = $1,712.46

2 **Net Income from Business:** Enter monthly net business income. This is the amount earned after ordinary and necessary monthly business expenses are paid. **This figure is the amount from page 6, line 89.** If the net business income is a loss, enter "0." Do not enter a negative number. If this amount is more or less than previous years, attach an explanation.

3 **Net Rental Income:** Enter monthly net rental income. This is the amount earned after ordinary and necessary monthly rental expenses are paid. Do not include deductions for depreciation or depletion. If the net rental income is a loss, enter "0." Do not enter a negative number.

4 **Distributions:** Enter the total distributions from partnerships and subchapter S corporations reported on Schedule K-1, and from limited liability companies reported on Form 1040, Schedule C, D or E. Enter total distributions from IRAs if not included under pension income.

5 **Other Income:** Include agricultural subsidies, unemployment compensation, gambling income, oil credits, rent subsidies, etc.

6 **Expenses not generally allowed:** We generally do not allow tuition for private schools, public or private college expenses, charitable contributions, voluntary retirement contributions or payments on unsecured debts. However, we may allow the expenses if proven that they are necessary for the health and welfare of the individual or family or for the production of income. See Publication 1854 for exceptions.

7 **Food, Clothing and Miscellaneous:** Total of food, clothing, housekeeping supplies, and personal care products for one month. The miscellaneous allowance is for expenses incurred that are not included in any other allowable living expense items. Examples are credit card payments, bank fees and charges, reading material, and school supplies.

8 **Housing and Utilities:** For principal residence: Total of rent or mortgage payment. Add the average monthly expenses for the following: property taxes, homeowner's or renter's insurance, maintenance, dues, fees, and utilities. Utilities include gas, electricity, water, fuel, oil, other fuels, trash collection, telephone, cell phone, cable television and internet services.

9 **Vehicle Ownership Costs:** Total of monthly lease or purchase/loan payments.

10 **Vehicle Operating Costs:** Total of maintenance, repairs, insurance, fuel, registrations, licenses, inspections, parking, and tolls for one month.

11 **Public Transportation:** Total of monthly fares for mass transit *(e.g., bus, train, ferry, taxi, etc.)*

12 **Out of Pocket Health Care Costs:** Monthly total of medical services, prescription drugs and medical supplies *(e.g., eyeglasses, hearing aids, etc.)*

13 **Current Year Taxes:** Include state and Federal taxes withheld from salary or wages, or paid as estimated taxes.

Certification: *Under penalties of perjury, I declare that to the best of my knowledge and belief this statement of assets, liabilities, and other information is true, correct, and complete.*

Taxpayer's Signature	Spouse's signature	Date

After we review the completed Form 433-A, you may be asked to provide verification for the assets, encumbrances, income and expenses reported. Documentation may include previously filed income tax returns, pay statements, self-employment records, bank and investment statements, loan statements, bills or statements for recurring expenses, etc.

IRS USE ONLY *(Notes)*

Form **433-A** (Rev. 12-2012)

340

Form 433-A (Rev. 12-2012) Page **5**

Sections 6 and 7 must be completed only if you are SELF-EMPLOYED.

Section 6: Business Information

51 Is the business a sole proprietorship *(filing Schedule C)* ☐ **Yes**, Continue with Sections 6 and 7. ☐ **No**, Complete Form 433-B.
All other business entities, including limited liability companies, partnerships or corporations, must complete Form 433-B.

52 Business Name & Address *(if different than 1b)*

53 Employer Identification Number | 54 Type of Business | 55 Is the business a Federal Contractor ☐ Yes ☐ No

56 Business Website (web address) | 57 Total Number of Employees | 58 Average Gross Monthly Payroll

59 Frequency of Tax Deposits | 60 Does the business engage in e-Commerce *(Internet sales)* If yes, complete *lines 61a and 61b* ☐ Yes ☐ No

PAYMENT PROCESSOR *(e.g., PayPal, Authorize.net, Google Checkout, etc.)* Name & Address *(Street, City, State, ZIP code)* | Payment Processor Account Number

61a

61b

CREDIT CARDS ACCEPTED BY THE BUSINESS

	Credit Card	Merchant Account Number	Issuing Bank Name & Address *(Street, City, State, ZIP code)*
62a			
62b			
62c			

63 **BUSINESS CASH ON HAND** Include cash that is not in a bank. | Total Cash on Hand $

BUSINESS BANK ACCOUNTS Include checking accounts, online and mobile *(e.g., PayPal)* accounts, money market accounts, savings accounts, and stored value cards *(e.g., payroll cards, government benefit cards, etc.)*. Report Personal Accounts in Section 4.

	Type of Account	Full Name & Address *(Street, City, State, ZIP code)* of Bank, Savings & Loan, Credit Union or Financial Institution.	Account Number	Account Balance As of _____ *mmddyyyy*
64a				$
64b				$

64c **Total Cash in Banks** *(Add lines 64a, 64b and amounts from any attachments)* | $

ACCOUNTS/NOTES RECEIVABLE Include e-payment accounts receivable and factoring companies, and any bartering or online auction accounts. *(List all contracts separately, including contracts awarded, but not started.)* **Include Federal, state and local government grants and contracts.**

	Accounts/Notes Receivable & Address *(Street, City, State, ZIP code)*	Status *(e.g., age, factored, other)*	Date Due *(mmddyyyy)*	Invoice Number or Government Grant or Contract Number	Amount Due
65a					$
65b					$
65c					$
65d					$
65e					$

65f **Total Outstanding Balance** *(Add lines 65a through 65e and amounts from any attachments)* | $

Form **433-A** (Rev. 12-2012)

Form 433-A (Rev. 12-2012)   Page **6**

BUSINESS ASSETS Include all tools, books, machinery, equipment, inventory or other assets used in trade or business. Include a list and show the value of all intangible assets such as licenses, patents, domain names, copyrights, trademarks, mining claims, etc.

	Purchase/ Lease Date (mmddyyyy)	Current Fair Market Value (FMV)	Current Loan Balance	Amount of Monthly Payment	Date of Final Payment (mmddyyyy)	**Equity** FMV Minus Loan
66a Property Description		$	$	$		$
Location *(Street, City, State, ZIP code)* and Country		Lender/Lessor/Landlord Name, Address *(Street, City, State, ZIP code)*, and Phone				
				Phone		
66b Property Description		$	$	$		$
Location *(Street, City, State, ZIP code)* and Country		Lender/Lessor/Landlord Name, Address *(Street, City, State, ZIP code)*, and Phone				
				Phone		

66c Total Equity *(Add lines 66a, 66b and amounts from any attachments)* $

Section 7 should be completed only if you are SELF-EMPLOYED

Section 7: Sole Proprietorship Information *(lines 67 through 87 should reconcile with business Profit and Loss Statement)*

Accounting Method Used: ☐ Cash   ☐ Accrual
Use the prior 3, 6, 9 or 12 month period to determine your typical business income and expenses.

Income and Expenses during the period *(mmddyyyy)* _____ to *(mmddyyyy)* _____
Provide a breakdown below of your average monthly income and expenses, based on the period of time used above.

Total Monthly Business Income		Total Monthly Business Expenses (Use attachments as needed)	
Source	Gross Monthly	Expense Items	Actual Monthly
67 Gross Receipts	$	77 Materials Purchased [1]	$
68 Gross Rental Income	$	78 Inventory Purchased [2]	$
69 Interest	$	79 Gross Wages & Salaries	$
70 Dividends	$	80 Rent	$
71 Cash Receipts not included in lines 67-70	$	81 Supplies [3]	$
Other Income (Specify below)		82 Utilities/Telephone [4]	$
72	$	83 Vehicle Gasoline/Oil	$
73	$	84 Repairs & Maintenance	$
74	$	85 Insurance	$
75	$	86 Current Taxes [5]	$
		87 Other Expenses, including installment payments (Specify)	$
76 Total Income (Add lines 67 through 75)	$	88 Total Expenses (Add lines 77 through 87)	$
		89 Net Business Income (Line 76 minus 88) [6]	$

Enter the monthly net income amount from line 89 on line 23, section 5. If line 89 is a loss, enter "0" on line 23, section 5.
Self-employed taxpayers must return to page 4 to sign the certification.

1 **Materials Purchased:** Materials are items directly related to the production of a product or service.

2 **Inventory Purchased:** Goods bought for resale.

3 **Supplies:** Supplies are items used in the business that are consumed or used up within one year. This could be the cost of books, office supplies, professional equipment, etc.

4 **Utilities/Telephone:** Utilities include gas, electricity, water, oil, other fuels, trash collection, telephone, cell phone and business internet.

5 **Current Taxes:** Real estate, excise, franchise, occupational, personal property, sales and employer's portion of employment taxes.

6 **Net Business Income:** Net profit from Form 1040, Schedule C may be used if duplicated deductions are eliminated (e.g., expenses for business use of home already included in housing and utility expenses on page 4). Deductions for depreciation and depletion on Schedule C are not cash expenses and must be added back to the net income figure. In addition, interest cannot be deducted if it is already included in any other installment payments allowed.

IRS USE ONLY *(Notes)*

Form **433-A** (Rev. 12-2012)

Form 433-B
(Rev. January 2008)
Department of the Treasury
Internal Revenue Service

Collection Information Statement for Businesses

Note: *Complete all entry spaces with the current data available or "N/A" (not applicable). Failure to complete all entry spaces may result in rejection of your request or significant delay in account resolution.* Include attachments if additional space is needed to respond completely to any question.

Section 1: Business Information

1a Business Name _____

1b Business Street Address _____
    Mailing Address _____
    City _____
    State _____ ZIP _____
1c County _____
1d Business Telephone (___) _____
1e Type of
    Business _____
1f Business
    Website _____

2a Employer Identification No. (EIN) _____
2b Type of Entity *(Check appropriate box below)*
  ☐ Partnership ☐ Corporation ☐ Other _____
  ☐ Limited Liability Company (LLC) classified as a corporation
  ☐ Other LLC – Include number of members _____
2c Date Incorporated/Established _____
                     mmddyyyy

3a Number of Employees _____
3b Monthly Gross Payroll _____
3c Frequency of Tax Deposits _____
3d Is the business enrolled in Electronic Federal
    Tax Payment System (EFTPS) ☐ Yes ☐ No

4 Does the business engage in e-Commerce (Internet sales) ☐ Yes ☐ No

Payment Processor (e.g., PayPal, Authorize.net, Google Checkout, etc.), Name and Address *(Street, City, State, ZIP code)*	Payment Processor Account Number
5a	
5b	

Credit cards accepted by the business

Type of Credit Card (e.g., Visa, MasterCard, etc.)	Merchant Account Number	Merchant Account Provider Name and Address *(Street, City, State, ZIP code)*
6a		Phone
6b		Phone
6c		Phone

Section 2: Business Personnel and Contacts

Partners, Officers, LLC Members, Major Shareholders, Etc.

7a Full Name _____
    Title _____
    Home Address _____
    City _____ State _____ ZIP _____
    Responsible for Depositing Payroll Taxes ☐ Yes ☐ No
Social Security Number _____
Home Telephone (___) _____
Work/Cell Phone (___) _____
Ownership Percentage & Shares or Interest _____

7b Full Name _____
    Title _____
    Home Address _____
    City _____ State _____ ZIP _____
    Responsible for Depositing Payroll Taxes ☐ Yes ☐ No
Social Security Number _____
Home Telephone (___) _____
Work/Cell Phone (___) _____
Ownership Percentage & Shares or Interest _____

7c Full Name _____
    Title _____
    Home Address _____
    City _____ State _____ ZIP _____
    Responsible for Depositing Payroll Taxes ☐ Yes ☐ No
Social Security Number _____
Home Telephone (___) _____
Work/Cell Phone (___) _____
Ownership Percentage & Shares or Interest _____

7d Full Name _____
    Title _____
    Home Address _____
    City _____ State _____ ZIP _____
    Responsible for Depositing Payroll Taxes ☐ Yes ☐ No
Social Security Number _____
Home Telephone (___) _____
Work/Cell Phone (___) _____
Ownership Percentage & Shares or Interest _____

The Death of America

Form 433-B (Rev. 1-2008)   Page **2**

| Section 3: Other Financial Information *(Attach copies of all applicable documentation.)* |

8   Does the business use a Payroll Service Provider or Reporting Agent *(If yes, answer the following)*   ☐ Yes ☐ No

Name and Address *(Street, City, State, ZIP code)*	Effective dates *(mmddyyyy)*

9   **Is the business a party to a lawsuit** *(If yes, answer the following)*   ☐ Yes ☐ No

	Location of Filing	Represented by	Docket/Case No.
☐ Plaintiff ☐ Defendant			

Amount of Suit	Possible Completion Date *(mmddyyyy)*	Subject of Suit
$		

10   **Has the business ever filed bankruptcy** *(If yes, answer the following)*   ☐ Yes ☐ No

Date Filed *(mmddyyyy)*	Date Dismissed or Discharged *(mmddyyyy)*	Petition No.	Location

11   Do any related parties (e.g., officers, partners, employees) have outstanding amounts owed to the business *(If yes, answer the following)*   ☐ Yes ☐ No

Name and Address *(Street, City, State, ZIP code)*	Date of Loan	Current Balance As of _____ *(mmddyyyy)*	Payment Date	Payment Amount
		$		$

12   Have any assets been transferred, in the last 10 years, from this business for less than full value *(If yes, answer the following)*   ☐ Yes ☐ No

List Asset	Value at Time of Transfer	Date Transferred *(mmddyyyy)*	To Whom or Where Transferred
	$		

13   **Does this business have other business affiliations (e.g., subsidiary or parent companies)** *(If yes, answer the following)*   ☐ Yes ☐ No

Related Business Name and Address *(Street, City, State, ZIP code)*	Related Business EIN:

14   Any increase/decrease in income anticipated *(If yes, answer the following)*   ☐ Yes ☐ No

Explain *(use attachment if needed)*	How much will it increase/decrease	When will it increase/decrease
	$	

| Section 4: Business Asset and Liability Information |

15   **Cash on Hand.** *Include cash that is not in the bank*   **Total Cash on Hand** $

Business Bank Accounts. Include online bank accounts, money market accounts, savings accounts, checking accounts, and stored value cards (e.g., payroll cards, government benefit cards, etc.)
List safe deposit boxes including location and contents.

	Type of Account	Full Name and Address *(Street, City, State, ZIP code)* of Bank, Savings & Loan, Credit Union or Financial Institution.	Account Number	Account Balance As of ___ *(mmddyyyy)*
16a				$
16b				$
16c				$

16d   **Total Cash in Banks** *(Add lines 16a through 16c and amounts from any attachments)* $

Form **433-B** (Rev. 1-2008)

344

Form 433-B (Rev. 1-2008)

Accounts/Notes Receivable. Include e-payment accounts receivable and factoring companies, and any bartering or online auction accounts. *(List all contracts separately, including contracts awarded, but not started.)*

17   **Is the business a Federal Government Contractor**   ☐ Yes ☐ No   *(Include Federal Government contracts below)*

Accounts/Notes Receivable & Address *(Street, City, State, ZIP code)*	Status *(e.g., age, factored, other)*	Date Due *(mmddyyyy)*	Invoice Number or Federal Government Contract Number	Amount Due
18a				
Contact Name: Phone:				$
18b				
Contact Name: Phone:				$
18c				
Contact Name: Phone:				$
18d				
Contact Name: Phone:				$
18e				
Contact Name: Phone:				$
18f Outstanding Balance *(Add lines 18a through 18e and amounts from any attachments)*				$

Investments. List all investment assets below. Include stocks, bonds, mutual funds, stock options, and certificates of deposit.

Name of Company & Address *(Street, City, State, ZIP code)*	Used as collateral on loan	Current Value	Loan Balance	Equity Value Minus Loan
19a	☐ Yes ☐ No			
Phone:		$	$	$
19b	☐ Yes ☐ No			
Phone:		$	$	$
19c Total Investments *(Add lines 19a, 19b, and amounts from any attachments)*				$

Available Credit. Include all lines of credit and credit cards. Full Name & Address *(Street, City, State, ZIP code)* of Credit Institution	Credit Limit	Amount Owed As of _____ mmddyyyy	Available Credit As of _____ mmddyyyy
20a			
Account No.	$	$	$
20b			
Account No.	$	$	$
20c Total Credit Available *(Add lines 20a, 20b, and amounts from any attachments)*			$

The Death of America

Real Property. Include all real property and land contracts the business owns/leases/rents.

	Purchase/Lease Date (mmddyyyy)	Current Fair Market Value (FMV)	Current Loan Balance	Amount of Monthly Payment	Date of Final Payment (mmddyyyy)	Equity FMV Minus Loan
21a Property Description		$	$	$		$
Location *(Street, City, State, ZIP code)* and County			Lender/Lessor/Landlord Name, Address *(Street, City, State, ZIP code)*, and Phone			
21b Property Description		$	$	$		$
Location *(Street, City, State, ZIP code)* and County			Lender/Lessor/Landlord Name, Address *(Street, City, State, ZIP code)*, and Phone			
21c Property Description		$	$	$		$
Location *(Street, City, State, ZIP code)* and County			Lender/Lessor/Landlord Name, Address *(Street, City, State, ZIP code)*, and Phone			
21d Property Description		$	$	$		$
Location *(Street, City, State, ZIP code)* and County			Lender/Lessor/Landlord Name, Address *(Street, City, State, ZIP code)*, and Phone			

21e Total Equity *(Add lines 21a through 21d and amounts from any attachments)* $

Vehicles, Leased and Purchased. Include boats, RVs, motorcycles, trailers, mobile homes, etc.

		Purchase/Lease Date (mmddyyyy)	Current Fair Market Value (FMV)	Current Loan Balance	Amount of Monthly Payment	Date of Final Payment (mmddyyyy)	Equity FMV Minus Loan
22a Year	Mileage		$	$	$		$
Make	Model	Lender/Lessor Name, Address, *(Street, City, State, ZIP code)* and Phone					
22b Year	Mileage		$	$	$		$
Make	Model	Lender/Lessor Name, Address, *(Street, City, State, ZIP code)* and Phone					
22c Year	Mileage		$	$	$		$
Make	Model	Lender/Lessor Name, Address, *(Street, City, State, ZIP code)* and Phone					
22d Year	Mileage		$	$	$		$
Make	Model	Lender/Lessor Name, Address, *(Street, City, State, ZIP code)* and Phone					

22e Total Equity *(Add lines 22a through 22d and amounts from any attachments)* $

Form **433-B** (Rev. 1-2008)

Form 433-B (Rev. 1-2008) Page 5

Business Equipment. Include all machinery, equipment, merchandise inventory, and/or other assets. Include Uniform Commercial Code (UCC) filings.

	Purchase/Lease Date (mmddyyyy)	Current Fair Market Value (FMV)	Current Loan Balance	Amount of Monthly Payment	Date of Final Payment (mmddyyyy)	Equity FMV Minus Loan
23a Asset Description		$	$	$		$
Location of asset (Street, City, State, ZIP code) and County			Lender/Lessor Name, Address, (Street, City, State, ZIP code) and Phone			
23b Asset Description		$	$	$		$
Location of asset (Street, City, State, ZIP code) and County			Lender/Lessor Name, Address, (Street, City, State, ZIP code) and Phone			
23c Asset Description		$	$	$		$
Location of asset (Street, City, State, ZIP code) and County			Lender/Lessor Name, Address, (Street, City, State, ZIP code) and Phone			
23d Asset Description		$	$	$		$
Location of asset (Street, City, State, ZIP code) and County			Lender/Lessor Name, Address, (Street, City, State, ZIP code) and Phone			

23e Total Equity (Add lines 23a through 23d and amounts from any attachments) $

Business Liabilities. Include notes and judgments below.

Business Liabilities	Secured/ Unsecured	Date Pledged (mmddyyyy)	Balance Owed	Date of Final Payment (mmddyyyy)	Payment Amount
24a Description:	☐ Secured ☐ Unsecured		$		$
Name / Street Address / City/State/ZIP code			Phone:		
24b Description:	☐ Secured ☐ Unsecured		$		$
Name / Street Address / City/State/ZIP code			Phone:		
24c Description:	☐ Secured ☐ Unsecured		$		$
Name / Street Address / City/State/ZIP code			Phone:		

24d Total Payments (Add lines 24a through 24c and amounts from any attachments) $

Form **433-B** (Rev. 1-2008)

Form 433-B (Rev. 1-2008)   Page **6**

Section 5: Monthly Income/Expense Statement for Business

Accounting Method Used: ☐ Cash ☐ Accrual

Income and Expenses during the period *(mmddyyyy)* _____ to *(mmddyyyy)* _____

	Total Monthly Business Income			Total Monthly Business Expenses	
	Source	Gross Monthly		Expense Items	Actual Monthly
25	Gross Receipts from Sales/Services	$	36	Materials Purchased[1]	$
26	Gross Rental Income	$	37	Inventory Purchased[2]	$
27	Interest Income	$	38	Gross Wages & Salaries	$
28	Dividends	$	39	Rent	$
29	Cash	$	40	Supplies[3]	$
	Other Income *(Specify below)*		41	Utilities/Telephone[4]	$
30		$	42	Vehicle Gasoline/Oil	$
31		$	43	Repairs & Maintenance	$
32		$	44	Insurance	$
33		$	45	Current Taxes[5]	$
34		$	46	Other Expenses *(Specify)*	$
35	**Total Income** *(Add lines 25 through 34)*	$	47	IRS Use Only Allowable Installment Payments	$
			48	**Total Expenses** *(Add lines 36 through 47)*	$

[1] **Materials Purchased:** Materials are items directly related to the production of a product or service.

[2] **Inventory Purchased:** Goods bought for resale.

[3] **Supplies:** Supplies are items used to conduct business and are consumed or used up within one year. This could be the cost of books, office supplies, professional equipment, etc.

[4] **Utilities/Telephone:** Utilities include gas, electricity, water, oil, other fuels, trash collection, telephone and cell phone.

[5] **Current Taxes:** Real estate, state, and local income tax, excise, franchise, occupational, personal property, sales and the employer's portion of employment taxes.

Certification: *Under penalties of perjury, I declare that to the best of my knowledge and belief this statement of assets, liabilities, and other information is true, correct, and complete.*

Signature	Title	Date

Print Name of Officer, Partner or LLC Member

Attachments Required: Copies of the following items for the last 3 months from the date this form is submitted (check all attached items):

☐ Banks and Investments - Statements for all money market, brokerage, checking/savings accounts, certificates of deposit, stocks/bonds.

☐ Assets - Statements from lenders on loans, monthly payments, payoffs, and balances, for all assets. Include copies of UCC financing statements and accountant's depreciation schedules.

☐ Expenses - Bills or statements for monthly recurring expenses of utilities, rent, insurance, property taxes, telephone and cell phone, insurance premiums, court orders requiring payments, other expenses.

☐ Other - credit card statements, profit and loss statements, all loan payoffs, etc.

☐ Copy of the last income tax return filed; Form 1120, 1120S, 1065, 1040, 990, etc.

Additional information or proof may be subsequently requested.

FINANCIAL ANALYSIS OF COLLECTION POTENTIAL FOR BUSINESSES		(IRS USE ONLY)
Cash Available (Lines 15, 16d, 18f, 19c, and 20c)	Total Cash	$
Distrainable Asset Summary (Lines 21e, 22e, and 23e)	Total Equity	$
Monthly Income Minus Expenses (Line 35 Minus Line 48)	Monthly Available Cash	$

Privacy Act: The information requested on this Form is covered under Privacy Acts and Paperwork Reduction Notices which have already been provided to the taxpayer.

Form **433-B** (Rev. 1-2008)

Internal Revenue Service
1973 North Rulon White Blvd.
M/S 4450
Ogden, UT 84201-0076

Department of the Treasury

Taxpayer Identification Number: 390-80-4016

Form: 1040 Tax Year(s): 201612

Date: February 23, 2017

Person to Contact: Mrs. Davis

BRADLEY J FRANKS
408 SOUTH LINCOLN STREET
MILBANK SD 57252

Employee Identification Number: 1000099771

Contact Telephone Number: 1-866-883-0235 (Toll Free)
Contact Hours: 7 A.M to 3:30 P.M MST Monday-Friday

Dear Taxpayer:

You recently filed a return or purported return claiming one or more frivolous positions. If not immediately corrected, the Internal Revenue Service will assess a $5,000 penalty against you. You can correct the problem and avoid the penalty if you submit a corrected return within 30 days of this letter to the address listed above.

If you continue to submit documents asserting frivolous positions, we will assess the $5,000 penalty each time you submit a frivolous return. If you file a joint return, we will assess the $5,000 penalty against both you and your spouse. Internal Revenue Code section 6702 provides the IRS with the authority to assess the penalty.

Why We Are Contacting You

Based on Section 6702, *Frivolous Tax Submissions*, we have determined the information you filed as a tax return, or purported tax return, on 1/21/2017 is frivolous and there is no basis in the law for your position.

Federal courts, including the Supreme Court of the United States, have considered positions such as yours and repeatedly rejected them as without merit. The enclosed Publication 2105, Why do I have to Pay Taxes?, includes examples of frivolous positions and arguments regarding the U.S. tax system under the heading "Don't Fall for These Arguments." Some of these examples include:

- Arguing that filing and paying taxes is voluntary.

- Excluding salaries and/or wages from income based on the argument that the value of

Letter 3176(SC) (Rev. 4-2012)
Catalog Number 26860K

services is not taxable or that salaries and/or wages are not income.

- Arguing that the requirement to file a tax return violates Constitutional rights protecting taxpayers against self-incrimination.

- Submitting a claim for a refundable credit when there is no basis in law for the credit, such as a credit for reparations for slavery, or frivolous Forms 2439, 1099, or 4136 (fuel tax credit), or showing excessive withholding on your return.

- Submitting a document that purports to be a tax return but is not properly signed or contains an altered jurat (the written declaration that verifies that a return, declaration, statement or other document is made under penalties of perjury).

These are just some examples. For more information on positions identified as frivolous under section 6702, see Notice 2010-33, 2010-17 I.R.B., April 26, 2010, pp. 609-12, which can be found on the Internal Revenue Service's website at www.IRS.gov (See Notice 2010-33 at http://www.irs.gov/irb/2010-17_IRB/ar13.html). If you do not have a computer, you can access Notice 2010-33 in the Internal Revenue Bulletin (I.R.B.), which is the IRS's authoritative publication of rulings and statements of procedure. Consult a law library to obtain the I.R.B. You can find additional information in a publication titled The Truth About Frivolous Arguments, available on-line only at http://www.irs.gov/pub/irs-utl/friv_tax.pdf

As stated above, we are proposing to assess a $5,000 penalty against you for each frivolous tax return or purported tax return that you filed.

WHAT YOU NEED TO DO

To avoid the penalty, send us a corrected return for each taxable period in the heading of this letter within 30 days of the date of this letter. If you send us corrected returns, we will disregard the previous documents that you filed and not assess the frivolous tax return penalty for each corrected return filed.

Please attach this letter to your corrected return(s) and mail to the address shown at the top of this letter. We have enclosed a copy of this letter for your records and an envelope for your convenience.

WHAT IF YOU DO NOT SEND A CORRECTED RETURN?

If you do not file the corrected return(s) within 30 days of the date of this letter, or if you submit additional documents asserting a frivolous position, we will assess the $5,000 penalty for each frivolous tax return or purported return containing a frivolous position and send you a bill. If you filed a joint frivolous return, both you and your spouse will be assessed a $5,000 penalty. We will not respond to any future correspondence asserting any frivolous position.

In addition, if we do not hear from you within the 30 day timeframe, we may issue a notice of deficiency for any taxes owed because of the frivolous submission or because of other items we

Letter 3176(SC) (Rev. 4-2012)
Catalog Number 26860K

may find during an examination. A notice of deficiency states the amount of additional tax and penalties you owe and explains your right to contest the deficiency by filing a petition with the United States Tax Court. The $5,000 frivolous filing penalty is not included on the notice of deficiency and cannot be contested in the Tax Court.

We have enclosed Publication 2105, Why Do I Have to Pay Taxes?, which provides basic information about the tax system. We also encourage you to seek advice from a competent tax professional or a tax attorney qualified to practice in your state.

Sincerely yours,

Program Manager
Return Integrity and Compliance Services

Enclosures:
Publication 2105
Copy of this letter
Envelope

Letter 3176(SC) (Rev. 4-2012)
Catalog Number 26860K

Form **1040**	Department of the Treasury—Internal Revenue Service (99) **U.S. Individual Income Tax Return**	20**16**	OMB No. 1545-0074	IRS Use Only—Do not write or staple in this space.

For the year Jan. 1–Dec. 31, 2016, or other tax year beginning **October 21**, 2016, ending **December 2, 2016** · · · See separate instructions.

Your first name and initial **Bradley J.** · Last name **Franks** · Your social security number **390 80 4016**

If a joint return, spouse's first name and initial · Last name · Spouse's social security number

Home address (number and street). If you have a P.O. box, see instructions. **C/O: 408 South Lincoln Street** · Apt. no.

City, town or post office, state, and ZIP code. **Milbank** **South Dakota**

Foreign country name **United States** · Foreign province/state/county **Grant County** · Foreign postal code **57252**

▲ Make sure the SSN(s) above and on line 6c are correct.

Presidential Election Campaign Check here if you, or your spouse if filing jointly, want $3 to go to this fund. Checking a box below will not change your tax or refund. ☐ You ☐ Spouse

Filing Status
Check only one box.
1. ☑ Single
2. ☐ Married filing jointly (even if only one had income)
3. ☐ Married filing separately. Enter spouse's SSN above and full name here. ▶
4. ☐ Head of household (with qualifying person). (See instructions.) If the qualifying person is a child but not your dependent, enter this child's name here. ▶
5. ☐ Qualifying widow(er) with dependent child

Exemptions
6a ☑ Yourself. If someone can claim you as a dependent, **do not** check box 6a . . .
b ☐ Spouse . . . .

Boxes checked on 6a and 6b **1**
No. of children on 6c who:
• lived with you **0**
• did not live with you due to divorce or separation (see instructions) **0**
Dependents on 6c not entered above **0**
Add numbers on lines above ▶ **1**

c Dependents:
(1) First name   Last name | (2) Dependent's social security number | (3) Dependent's relationship to you | (4) ✓ if child under age 17 qualifying for child tax credit (see instructions)

If more than four dependents, see instructions and check here ▶ ☐

d Total number of exemptions claimed . . . .

Income

Attach Form(s) W-2 here. Also attach Forms W-2G and 1099-R if tax was withheld.

If you did not get a W-2, see instructions.

7	Wages, salaries, tips, etc. Attach Form(s) W-2	7	⊖
8a	Taxable interest. Attach Schedule B if required	8a	388,524,195 00
b	Tax-exempt interest. Do not include on line 8a	8b	
9a	Ordinary dividends. Attach Schedule B if required	9a	⊖
b	Qualified dividends	9b	
10	Taxable refunds, credits, or offsets of state and local income taxes	10	⊖
11	Alimony received	11	⊖
12	Business income or (loss). Attach Schedule C or C-EZ	12	⊖
13	Capital gain or (loss). Attach Schedule D if required. If not required, check here ▶ ☐	13	⊖
14	Other gains or (losses). Attach Form 4797	14	⊖
15a	IRA distributions 15a	b Taxable amount	15b	⊖
16a	Pensions and annuities 16a	b Taxable amount	16b	⊖
17	Rental real estate, royalties, partnerships, S corporations, trusts, etc. Attach Schedule E	17	⊖
18	Farm income or (loss). Attach Schedule F	18	⊖
19	Unemployment compensation	19	⊖
20a	Social security benefits 20a	b Taxable amount	20b	⊖
21	Other income. List type and amount *"Security" Interest on Invvids*	21	38,852,419,500 00
22	Combine the amounts in the far right column for lines 7 through 21. This is your **total income** ▶	22	39,240,943,695 00

Adjusted Gross Income

23	Educator expenses	23	⊖
24	Certain business expenses of reservists, performing artists, and fee-basis government officials. Attach Form 2106 or 2106-EZ	24	⊖
25	Health savings account deduction. Attach Form 8889	25	⊖
26	Moving expenses. Attach Form 3903	26	⊖
27	Deductible part of self-employment tax. Attach Schedule SE	27	⊖
28	Self-employed SEP, SIMPLE, and qualified plans	28	⊖
29	Self-employed health insurance deduction	29	⊖
30	Penalty on early withdrawal of savings	30	⊖
31a	Alimony paid b Recipient's SSN ▶	31a	⊖
32	IRA deduction	32	⊖
33	Student loan interest deduction	33	⊖
34	Tuition and fees. Attach Form 8917	34	⊖
35	Domestic production activities deduction. Attach Form 8903	35	⊖
36	Add lines 23 through 35	36	⊖
37	Subtract line 36 from line 22. This is your **adjusted gross income** ▶	37	39,240,943,695 00

For Disclosure, Privacy Act, and Paperwork Reduction Act Notice, see separate instructions. Cat. No. 11320B Form **1040** (2016)

Form 1040 (2016)

Page **2**

Tax and Credits	38	Amount from line 37 (adjusted gross income)	38	39,240,943,695 00
	39a	Check { You were born before January 2, 1952, ☐ Blind. } Total boxes		
		if: { ☐ Spouse was born before January 2, 1952, ☐ Blind. } checked ► 39a		
	b	If your spouse itemizes on a separate return or you were a dual-status alien, check here ► 39b ☐		
Standard Deduction for—	40	**Itemized deductions** (from Schedule A) or your **standard deduction** (see left margin) . .	40	⊖
	41	Subtract line 40 from line 38	41	39,240,943,695 00
• People who check any box on line 39a or 39b or who can be claimed as a dependent, see instructions.	42	**Exemptions.** If line 38 is $155,650 or less, multiply $4,050 by the number on line 6d. Otherwise, see instructions	42	4,050 00
	43	**Taxable income.** Subtract line 42 from line 41. If line 42 is more than line 41, enter -0- . .	43	⊖
	44	**Tax** (see instructions). Check if any from: a ☐ Form(s) 8814 b ☐ Form 4972 c ☐ ____	44	⊖
	45	**Alternative minimum tax** (see instructions). Attach Form 6251	45	⊖
	46	Excess advance premium tax credit repayment. Attach Form 8962	46	⊖
• All others:	47	Add lines 44, 45, and 46 . . . . ►	47	⊖
Single or Married filing separately, $6,300	48	Foreign tax credit. Attach Form 1116 if required	48	⊖	
	49	Credit for child and dependent care expenses. Attach Form 2441	49	⊖	
Married filing jointly or Qualifying widow(er), $12,600	50	Education credits from Form 8863, line 19 . . .	50	⊖	
	51	Retirement savings contributions credit. Attach Form 8880	51	⊖	
	52	Child tax credit. Attach Schedule 8812, if required . . .	52	⊖	
Head of household, $9,300	53	Residential energy credits. Attach Form 5695 . . .	53	⊖	
	54	Other credits from Form: a ☐ 3800 b ☐ 8801 c ☐	54	⊖	
	55	Add lines 48 through 54. These are your **total credits**	55	⊖
	56	Subtract line 55 from line 47. If line 55 is more than line 47, enter -0- . . . ►	56	⊖
Other Taxes	57	Self-employment tax. Attach Schedule SE	57	⊖
	58	Unreported social security and Medicare tax from Form: a ☐ 4137 b ☐ 8919	58	⊖
	59	Additional tax on IRAs, other qualified retirement plans, etc. Attach Form 5329 if required . .	59	⊖
	60a	Household employment taxes from Schedule H	60a	⊖
	b	First-time homebuyer credit repayment. Attach Form 5405 if required	60b	⊖
	61	Health care: individual responsibility (see instructions) Full-year coverage ☐ . .	61	⊖
	62	Taxes from: a ☐ Form 8959 b ☐ Form 8960 c ☐ Instructions; enter code(s)	62	⊖
	63	Add lines 56 through 62. This is your **total tax** . . . . ►	63	⊖
Payments	64	Federal income tax withheld from Forms W-2 and 1099 . .	64	⊖	
	65	2016 estimated tax payments and amount applied from 2015 return	65	⊖	
If you have a qualifying child, attach Schedule EIC.	66a	**Earned income credit (EIC)**	66a	⊖	
	b	Nontaxable combat pay election 66b			
	67	Additional child tax credit. Attach Schedule 8812	67	⊖	
	68	American opportunity credit from Form 8863, line 8 . . .	68	⊖	
	69	Net premium tax credit. Attach Form 8962	69	⊖	
	70	Amount paid with request for extension to file	70	⊖	
	71	Excess social security and tier 1 RRTA tax withheld . . .	71	⊖	
	72	Credit for federal tax on fuels. Attach Form 4136 . . .	72	⊖	
	73	Credits from Form: a ☐ 2439 b ☐ Reserved c ☐ 8885 d ☐	73	⊖	
	74	Add lines 64, 65, 66a, and 67 through 73. These are your **total payments** . . . . ►	74	⊖
Refund	75	If line 74 is more than line 63, subtract line 63 from line 74. This is the amount you **overpaid**	75	⊖
	76a	Amount of line 75 you want **refunded to you.** If Form 8888 is attached, check here ► ☑	76a	388,524,195 00
Direct deposit? ► See instructions.	b	Routing number _____ ► c Type: ☐ Checking ☐ Savings		
	d	Account number _____		
	77	Amount of line 75 you want applied to your **2017 estimated tax** ► 77		
Amount You Owe	78	**Amount you owe.** Subtract line 74 from line 63. For details on how to pay, see instructions ►	78	⊖
	79	Estimated tax penalty (see instructions) 79		

Third Party Designee	Do you want to allow another person to discuss this return with the IRS (see instructions)? ☐ **Yes. Complete below.** ☐ No		
	Designee's name ►	Phone no. ►	Personal identification number (PIN) ►

Sign Here

Under penalties of perjury, I declare that I have examined this return and accompanying schedules and statements, and to the best of my knowledge and belief, they are true, correct, and accurately list all amounts and sources of income I received during the tax year. Declaration of preparer (other than taxpayer) is based on all information of which preparer has any knowledge.

Joint return? See instructions. Keep a copy for your records.

Your signature *Bradley - J.: Franks*	Date 1-21-17	Your occupation *Author / Self Employed*	Daytime phone number 605-432-7930
Spouse's signature. If a joint return, **both** must sign.	Date	Spouse's occupation	If the IRS sent you an Identity Protection PIN, enter it here (see inst.)

Paid Preparer Use Only

Print/Type preparer's name	Preparer's signature	Date	Check ☐ if self-employed	PTIN
Firm's name ►			Firm's EIN ►	
Firm's address ►			Phone no.	

www.irs.gov/form1040

Form **1040** (2016)

The Death of America

Form **8888**	**Allocation of Refund (Including Savings Bond Purchases)**	OMB No. 1545-0074

Form **8888**

Allocation of Refund (Including Savings Bond Purchases)

OMB No. 1545-0074

Department of the Treasury
Internal Revenue Service

► Information about Form 8888 and its instructions is at *www.irs.gov/form8888.*
► Attach to your income tax return.

2016
Attachment
Sequence No. 56

Name(s) shown on return: *Bradley - J. Franks*

Your social security number: 390·80·4016

Part I Direct Deposit
Complete this part if you want us to directly deposit a portion of your refund to one or more accounts.

1a Amount to be deposited in first account (see instructions) **1a**

b Routing number ► **c** ☐ Checking ☐ Savings

d Account number

2a Amount to be deposited in second account **2a**

b Routing number ► **c** ☐ Checking ☐ Savings

d Account number

3a Amount to be deposited in third account **3a**

b Routing number ► **c** ☐ Checking ☐ Savings

d Account number

Part II U.S. Series I Savings Bond Purchases
Complete this part if you want to buy paper bonds with a portion of your refund.

⚠ CAUTION: If a name is entered on line 5c or 6c below, co-ownership will be assumed unless the beneficiary box is checked. See instructions for more details.

4 Amount to be used for bond purchases for yourself (and your spouse, if filing jointly) **4**

5a Amount to be used to buy bonds for yourself, your spouse, or someone else **5a**
b Enter the owner's name (First then Last) for the bond registration

c If you would like to add a co-owner or beneficiary, enter the name here (First then Last). If beneficiary, also check here ► ☐

6a Amount to be used to buy bonds for yourself, your spouse, or someone else **6a**
b Enter the owner's name (First then Last) for the bond registration

c If you would like to add a co-owner or beneficiary, enter the name here (First then Last). If beneficiary, also check here ► ☐

Part III Paper Check
Complete this part if you want a portion of your refund to be sent to you as a check.

7 Amount to be refunded by check **7** 300,524,195 00

Part IV Total Allocation of Refund

8 Add lines 1a, 2a, 3a, 4, 5a, 6a, and 7. The total must equal the refund amount shown on your tax return **8** 300,524,195 00

For Paperwork Reduction Act Notice, see your tax return instructions. Cat. No. 21858A Form **8888** (2016)

354

Bradley - J.: [Franks] and Co-Author: Robert - C.: [Simpson]

Form 1040 Department of the Treasury—Internal Revenue Service (99)
U.S. Individual Income Tax Return **2016** OMB No. 1545-0074 | IRS Use Only—Do not write or staple in this space.

For the year Jan. 1–Dec. 31, 2016, or other tax year beginning Oct. 21, 2016, ending Dec. 21, 2016 | See separate instructions.

Your first name and initial: Bradley J. | Last name: Franks

Your social security number: 390-80-4016

Home address (number and street). If you have a P.O. box, see instructions. Apt. no.
c/o: 408 South Lincoln Street

City, town or post office, state, and ZIP code. Milbank South Dakota 57252

Foreign country name: United States | Foreign province/state/county: Grant County | Foreign postal code: 57252

Filing Status
1. ☑ Single

Exemptions
6a ☑ Yourself.

Boxes checked on 6a and 6b: 1

d Total number of exemptions claimed

Income

7	Wages, salaries, tips, etc. Attach Form(s) W-2	7	
8a	Taxable interest.	8a	485,655,243 75
21	Other income. List type and amount Security	21	38,852,419,500 00
22	Combine the amounts... total income ▶	22	39,338,074,743 75

Adjusted Gross Income

| 37 | Subtract line 36 from line 22. This is your adjusted gross income ▶ | 37 | 39,338,074,743 75 |

For Disclosure, Privacy Act, and Paperwork Reduction Act Notice, see separate instructions. Cat. No. 11320B Form **1040** (2016)

355

Form 1040 (2016)   Page **2**

Tax and Credits	38	Amount from line 37 (adjusted gross income)	38	39,338,074,743 75
	39a	Check if: ☐ You were born before January 2, 1952, ☐ Blind. ☐ Spouse was born before January 2, 1952, ☐ Blind. } Total boxes checked ▶ 39a		
	b	If your spouse itemizes on a separate return or you were a dual-status alien, check here ▶ 39b☐		
Standard Deduction for— • People who check any box on line 39a or 39b **or** who can be claimed as a dependent, see instructions. • All others: Single or Married filing separately, $6,300 Married filing jointly or Qualifying widow(er), $12,600 Head of household, $9,300	40	Itemized deductions (from Schedule A) or your **standard deduction** (see left margin)	40	0
	41	Subtract line 40 from line 38	41	39,338,074,743 75
	42	**Exemptions.** If line 38 is $155,650 or less, multiply $4,050 by the number on line 6d. Otherwise, see instructions	42	4,050 00
	43	**Taxable income.** Subtract line 42 from line 41. If line 42 is more than line 41, enter -0-	43	0
	44	Tax (see instructions). Check if any from: a ☐ Form(s) 8814 b ☐ Form 4972 c ☐	44	0
	45	Alternative minimum tax (see instructions). Attach Form 6251	45	0
	46	Excess advance premium tax credit repayment. Attach Form 8962	46	0
	47	Add lines 44, 45, and 46 ▶	47	0
	48	Foreign tax credit. Attach Form 1116 if required	48	0
	49	Credit for child and dependent care expenses. Attach Form 2441	49	0
	50	Education credits from Form 8863, line 19	50	0
	51	Retirement savings contributions credit. Attach Form 8880	51	0
	52	Child tax credit. Attach Schedule 8812, if required	52	0
	53	Residential energy credits. Attach Form 5695	53	0
	54	Other credits from Form: a ☐ 3800 b ☐ 8801 c ☐	54	0
	55	Add lines 48 through 54. These are your **total credits**	55	0
	56	Subtract line 55 from line 47. If line 55 is more than line 47, enter -0- ▶	56	0
Other Taxes	57	Self-employment tax. Attach Schedule SE	57	0
	58	Unreported social security and Medicare tax from Form: a ☐ 4137 b ☐ 8919	58	0
	59	Additional tax on IRAs, other qualified retirement plans, etc. Attach Form 5329 if required	59	0
	60a	Household employment taxes from Schedule H	60a	0
	b	First-time homebuyer credit repayment. Attach Form 5405 if required	60b	0
	61	Health care: individual responsibility (see instructions) Full-year coverage ☐	61	0
	62	Taxes from: a ☐ Form 8959 b ☐ Form 8960 c ☐ Instructions; enter code(s)	62	0
	63	Add lines 56 through 62. This is your **total tax** ▶	63	0
Payments If you have a qualifying child, attach Schedule EIC.	64	Federal income tax withheld from Forms W-2 and 1099	64	0
	65	2016 estimated tax payments and amount applied from 2015 return	65	0
	66a	**Earned income credit (EIC)**	66a	0
	b	Nontaxable combat pay election 66b		
	67	Additional child tax credit. Attach Schedule 8812	67	0
	68	American opportunity credit from Form 8863, line 8	68	0
	69	Net premium tax credit. Attach Form 8962	69	0
	70	Amount paid with request for extension to file	70	0
	71	Excess social security and tier 1 RRTA tax withheld	71	0
	72	Credit for federal tax on fuels. Attach Form 4136	72	0
	73	Credits from Form: a ☐ 2439 b ☐ Reserved c ☐ 8885 d ☐	73	
	74	Add lines 64, 65, 66a, and 67 through 73. These are your **total payments** ▶	74	0
Refund Direct deposit? See instructions.	75	If line 74 is more than line 63, subtract line 63 from line 74. This is the amount you **overpaid**	75	0
	76a	Amount of line 75 you want **refunded to you.** If Form 8888 is attached, check here ▶ ☑	76a	4,785,655,243 75
	b	Routing number ▶ c Type: ☐ Checking ☐ Savings		
	d	Account number ▶		
	77	Amount of line 75 you want **applied to your 2017 estimated tax** ▶ 77		
Amount You Owe	78	Amount you owe. Subtract line 74 from line 63. For details on how to pay, see instructions ▶	78	0
	79	Estimated tax penalty (see instructions) 79		
Third Party Designee		Do you want to allow another person to discuss this return with the IRS (see instructions)? ☐ **Yes. Complete below.** ☐ No		
		Designee's name ▶ Phone no. ▶ Personal identification number (PIN) ▶		

Sign Here Joint return? See instructions. Keep a copy for your records.

Under penalties of perjury, I declare that I have examined this return and accompanying schedules and statements, and to the best of my knowledge and belief, they are true, correct, and accurately list all amounts and sources of income I received during the tax year. Declaration of preparer (other than taxpayer) is based on all information of which preparer has any knowledge.

Your signature	Date	Your occupation	Daytime phone number
Bradley J Franks	1/21/17	Author / Self Emp.	605 432 7920
Spouse's signature. If a joint return, **both must sign.**	Date	Spouse's occupation	If the IRS sent you an Identity Protection PIN, enter it here (see inst.)

Paid Preparer Use Only

Print/Type preparer's name	Preparer's signature	Date	Check ☐ if self-employed	PTIN
Firm's name ▶			Firm's EIN ▶	
Firm's address ▶			Phone no.	

www.irs.gov/form1040   Form **1040** (2016)

Form **8888**	**Allocation of Refund (Including Savings Bond Purchases)**	OMB No. 1545-0074
Department of the Treasury Internal Revenue Service	▶ Information about Form 8888 and its instructions is at *www.irs.gov/form8888*. ▶ Attach to your income tax return.	20**16** Attachment Sequence No. **56**

Name(s) shown on return	Your social security number
Bradley J. Franks	390 - 80 - 4016

Part I Direct Deposit

Complete this part if you want us to directly deposit a portion of your refund to one or more accounts.

1a Amount to be deposited in first account (see instructions) **1a**

 b Routing number ▶ c ☐ Checking ☐ Savings

 d Account number

2a Amount to be deposited in second account **2a**

 b Routing number ▶ c ☐ Checking ☐ Savings

 d Account number

3a Amount to be deposited in third account **3a**

 b Routing number ▶ c ☐ Checking ☐ Savings

 d Account number

Part II U.S. Series I Savings Bond Purchases

Complete this part if you want to buy paper bonds with a portion of your refund.

⚠️ CAUTION *If a name is entered on line 5c or 6c below, co-ownership will be assumed unless the beneficiary box is checked. See instructions for more details.*

4 Amount to be used for bond purchases for yourself (and your spouse, if filing jointly) **4**

5a Amount to be used to buy bonds for yourself, your spouse, or someone else **5a**

 b Enter the owner's name (First then Last) for the bond registration

 c If you would like to add a co-owner or beneficiary, enter the name here (First then Last). If beneficiary, also check here ▶ ☐

6a Amount to be used to buy bonds for yourself, your spouse, or someone else **6a**

 b Enter the owner's name (First then Last) for the bond registration

 c If you would like to add a co-owner or beneficiary, enter the name here (First then Last). If beneficiary, also check here ▶ ☐

Part III Paper Check

Complete this part if you want a portion of your refund to be sent to you as a check.

7 Amount to be refunded by check **7** 485,655,243 75

Part IV Total Allocation of Refund

8 Add lines 1a, 2a, 3a, 4, 5a, 6a, and 7. The total must equal the refund amount shown on your tax return **8** 485,655,243 75

For Paperwork Reduction Act Notice, see your tax return instructions.	Cat. No. 21858A	Form **8888** (2016)

Form **1040**	Department of the Treasury—Internal Revenue Service (99)	**2016**	OMB No. 1545-0074	IRS Use Only—Do not write or staple in this space.

U.S. Individual Income Tax Return

For the year Jan. 1–Dec. 31, 2016, or other tax year beginning **Oct. 21** , 2016, ending **Dec. 21** , 20 **16**   See separate instructions.

Your first name and initial	Last name	Your social security number
Bradley J.	Franks	390-80-4016

If a joint return, spouse's first name and initial — Last name — Spouse's social security number

Home address (number and street). If you have a P.O. box, see instructions.   Apt. no.
%o: 408 South Lincoln Street

City, town or post office, state, and ZIP code. If you have a foreign address, also complete spaces below (see instructions).
Milbank, South Dakota 57252

▲ Make sure the SSN(s) above and on line 6c are correct.

Foreign country name	Foreign province/state/county	Foreign postal code
United States	Grant County	57252

Presidential Election Campaign
Check here if you, or your spouse if filing jointly, want $3 to go to this fund. Checking a box below will not change your tax or refund. ☐ You ☐ Spouse

Filing Status
Check only one box.

1. ☑ Single
2. ☐ Married filing jointly (even if only one had income)
3. ☐ Married filing separately. Enter spouse's SSN above and full name here. ▶
4. ☐ Head of household (with qualifying person). (See instructions.) If the qualifying person is a child but not your dependent, enter this child's name here. ▶
5. ☐ Qualifying widow(er) with dependent child

Exemptions

- 6a ☑ Yourself. If someone can claim you as a dependent, do not check box 6a . . . . .
- b ☐ Spouse . . . .

c Dependents:	(2) Dependent's social security number	(3) Dependent's relationship to you	(4) ✓ If child under age 17 qualifying for child tax credit (see instructions)
(1) First name Last name			☐
			☐
			☐
			☐

If more than four dependents, see instructions and check here ▶ ☐

d Total number of exemptions claimed . . . .

Boxes checked on 6a and 6b — **1**
No. of children on 6c who:
• lived with you
• did not live with you due to divorce or separation (see instructions)
Dependents on 6c not entered above
Add numbers on lines above ▶ **1**

Income

Attach Form(s) W-2 here. Also attach Forms W-2G and 1099-R if tax was withheld.

If you did not get a W-2, see instructions.

7	Wages, salaries, tips, etc. Attach Form(s) W-2	7	-0-
8a	Taxable interest. Attach Schedule B if required	8a	485,655,243 75
b	Tax-exempt interest. Do not include on line 8a . . .	8b	
9a	Ordinary dividends. Attach Schedule B if required	9a	-0-
b	Qualified dividends	9b	
10	Taxable refunds, credits, or offsets of state and local income taxes .	10	-0-
11	Alimony received	11	-0-
12	Business income or (loss). Attach Schedule C or C-EZ	12	-0-
13	Capital gain or (loss). Attach Schedule D if required. If not required, check here ▶ ☐	13	-0-
14	Other gains or (losses). Attach Form 4797	14	-0-
15a	IRA distributions . 15a	b Taxable amount . . .	15b	-0-
16a	Pensions and annuities 16a	b Taxable amount . . .	16b	-0-
17	Rental real estate, royalties, partnerships, S corporations, trusts, etc. Attach Schedule E	17	-0-
18	Farm income or (loss). Attach Schedule F	18	-0-
19	Unemployment compensation	19	-0-
20a	Social security benefits 20a	b Taxable amount . . .	20b	-0-
21	Other income. List type and amount *Lien* or *"Security"*	21	38,852,419,500 00
22	Combine the amounts in the far right column for lines 7 through 21. This is your **total income** ▶	22	39,338,074,743 75

Adjusted Gross Income

23	Educator expenses	23	-0-
24	Certain business expenses of reservists, performing artists, and fee-basis government officials. Attach Form 2106 or 2106-EZ	24	-0-
25	Health savings account deduction. Attach Form 8889 .	25	-0-
26	Moving expenses. Attach Form 3903	26	-0-
27	Deductible part of self-employment tax. Attach Schedule SE .	27	-0-
28	Self-employed SEP, SIMPLE, and qualified plans .	28	-0-
29	Self-employed health insurance deduction	29	-0-
30	Penalty on early withdrawal of savings	30	-0-
31a	Alimony paid b Recipient's SSN ▶	31a	-0-
32	IRA deduction	32	-0-
33	Student loan interest deduction	33	-0-
34	Tuition and fees. Attach Form 8917	34	-0-
35	Domestic production activities deduction. Attach Form 8903	35	-0-
36	Add lines 23 through 35	36	-0-
37	Subtract line 36 from line 22. This is your **adjusted gross income** . . . . . ▶	37	39,338,074,743 75

For Disclosure, Privacy Act, and Paperwork Reduction Act Notice, see separate instructions.   Cat. No. 11320B   Form **1040** (2016)

Form 1040 (2016)   Page **2**

Tax and Credits	38	Amount from line 37 (adjusted gross income)	38	39,330,074,743 75
	39a	Check { You were born before January 2, 1952, ☐ Blind. } Total boxes		
		if: { Spouse was born before January 2, 1952, ☐ Blind. } checked ▶ 39a		
	b	If your spouse itemizes on a separate return or you were a dual-status alien, check here ▶ 39b☐		
Standard Deduction for—	40	**Itemized deductions** (from Schedule A) or your **standard deduction** (see left margin) . .	40	-0-
• People who check any box on line 39a or 39b or who can be claimed as a dependent, see instructions.	41	Subtract line 40 from line 38	41	39,330,074,743 75
	42	**Exemptions.** If line 38 is $155,650 or less, multiply $4,050 by the number on line 6d. Otherwise, see instructions	42	4050 00
	43	**Taxable income.** Subtract line 42 from line 41. If line 42 is more than line 41, enter -0- . .	43	-0-
	44	**Tax** (see instructions). Check if any from: a ☐ Form(s) 8814 b ☐ Form 4972 c ☐	44	-0-
• All others:	45	Alternative minimum tax (see instructions). Attach Form 6251	45	-0-
Single or Married filing separately, $6,300	46	Excess advance premium tax credit repayment. Attach Form 8962	46	-0-
	47	Add lines 44, 45, and 46 . . . . ▶	47	-0-
Married filing jointly or Qualifying widow(er), $12,600	48	Foreign tax credit. Attach Form 1116 if required	48	-0-	
	49	Credit for child and dependent care expenses. Attach Form 2441	49	-0-	
	50	Education credits from Form 8863, line 19	50	-0-	
Head of household, $9,300	51	Retirement savings contributions credit. Attach Form 8880	51	-0-	
	52	Child tax credit. Attach Schedule 8812, if required . . .	52	-0-	
	53	Residential energy credits. Attach Form 5695	53	-0-	
	54	Other credits from Form: a ☐ 3800 b ☐ 8801 c ☐	54	-0-	
	55	Add lines 48 through 54. These are your **total credits**	55	-0-
	56	Subtract line 55 from line 47. If line 55 is more than line 47, enter -0- . . . ▶	56	-0-
Other Taxes	57	Self-employment tax. Attach Schedule SE	57	-0-
	58	Unreported social security and Medicare tax from Form: a ☐ 4137 b ☐ 8919	58	-0-
	59	Additional tax on IRAs, other qualified retirement plans, etc. Attach Form 5329 if required	59	-0-
	60a	Household employment taxes from Schedule H	60a	-0-
	b	First-time homebuyer credit repayment. Attach Form 5405 if required	60b	-0-
	61	Health care: individual responsibility (see instructions) Full-year coverage ☐ . . .	61	-0-
	62	Taxes from: a ☐ Form 8959 b ☐ Form 8960 c ☐ Instructions; enter code(s)	62	-0-
	63	Add lines 56 through 62. This is your **total tax** . . . . ▶	63	-0-
Payments	64	Federal income tax withheld from Forms W-2 and 1099 .	64	-0-	
	65	2016 estimated tax payments and amount applied from 2015 return	65	-0-	
If you have a qualifying child, attach Schedule EIC.	66a	**Earned income credit (EIC)**	66a	-0-	
	b	Nontaxable combat pay election	66b		
	67	Additional child tax credit. Attach Schedule 8812 ·	67	-0-	
	68	American opportunity credit from Form 8863, line 8 . . .	68	-0-	
	69	Net premium tax credit. Attach Form 8962	69	-0-	
	70	Amount paid with request for extension to file	70	-0-	
	71	Excess social security and tier 1 RRTA tax withheld . . .	71	-0-	
	72	Credit for federal tax on fuels. Attach Form 4136 . . .	72	-0-	
	73	Credits from Form: a ☐ 2439 b ☐ Reserved c ☐ 8885 d ☐	73	-0-	
	74	Add lines 64, 65, 66a, and 67 through 73. These are your **total payments** . . . ▶	74	-0-
Refund	75	If line 74 is more than line 63, subtract line 63 from line 74. This is the amount you **overpaid**	75	-0-
	76a	Amount of line 75 you want **refunded to you.** If Form 8888 is attached, check here . ▶☑	76a	485,655,243 75
Direct deposit? ▶	b	Routing number _____ ▶ c Type: ☐ Checking ☐ Savings		
See instructions. ▶	d	Account number _____		
	77	Amount of line 75 you want **applied to your 2017 estimated tax** ▶	77	
Amount You Owe	78	**Amount you owe.** Subtract line 74 from line 63. For details on how to pay, see instructions ▶	78	-0-
	79	Estimated tax penalty (see instructions)	79	

Third Party Designee Do you want to allow another person to discuss this return with the IRS (see instructions)? ☐ **Yes.** Complete below. ☐ **No**

Designee's name ▶ _____ Phone no. ▶ _____ Personal identification number (PIN) ▶ _____

Sign Here Under penalties of perjury, I declare that I have examined this return and accompanying schedules and statements, and to the best of my knowledge and belief, they are true, correct, and accurately list all amounts and sources of income I received during the tax year. Declaration of preparer (other than taxpayer) is based on all information of which preparer has any knowledge.

Joint return? See instructions. Keep a copy for your records.

Your signature *Bradley - J. Franks* Date 1-21-17 Your occupation Author / Self Emp Daytime phone number 605·432·7920

Spouse's signature. If a joint return, **both must sign.** Date Spouse's occupation If the IRS sent you an Identity Protection PIN, enter it here (see inst.) ☐☐☐☐☐☐

Paid Preparer Use Only

Print/Type preparer's name Preparer's signature Date Check ☐ if self-employed PTIN

Firm's name ▶ Firm's EIN ▶

Firm's address ▶ Phone no.

www.irs.gov/form1040 Form **1040** (2016)

359

Form **8888**	Allocation of Refund (Including Savings Bond Purchases)	OMB No. 1545-0074
Department of the Treasury Internal Revenue Service	▶ Information about Form 8888 and its instructions is at *www.irs.gov/form8888.* ▶ Attach to your income tax return.	**2016** Attachment Sequence No. **56**

Name(s) shown on return   *Bradley – J. Franks*

Your social security number   390 - 80 - 4016

Part I   **Direct Deposit**

Complete this part if you want us to directly deposit a portion of your refund to one or more accounts.

1a   Amount to be deposited in first account (see instructions) **1a**

   b   Routing number   ▶ c ☐ Checking   ☐ Savings

   d   Account number

2a   Amount to be deposited in second account **2a**

   b   Routing number   ▶ c ☐ Checking   ☐ Savings

   d   Account number

3a   Amount to be deposited in third account **3a**

   b   Routing number   ▶ c ☐ Checking   ☐ Savings

   d   Account number

Part II   **U.S. Series I Savings Bond Purchases**

Complete this part if you want to buy paper bonds with a portion of your refund.

⚠ CAUTION   If a name is entered on line 5c or 6c below, co-ownership will be assumed unless the beneficiary box is checked. See instructions for more details.

4   Amount to be used for bond purchases for yourself (and your spouse, if filing jointly) **4**

5a   Amount to be used to buy bonds for yourself, your spouse, or someone else **5a**

   b   Enter the owner's name (First then Last) for the bond registration

   c   If you would like to add a co-owner or beneficiary, enter the name here (First then Last). If beneficiary, also check here ▶ ☐

6a   Amount to be used to buy bonds for yourself, your spouse, or someone else **6a**

   b   Enter the owner's name (First then Last) for the bond registration

   c   If you would like to add a co-owner or beneficiary, enter the name here (First then Last). If beneficiary, also check here ▶ ☐

Part III   **Paper Check**

Complete this part if you want a portion of your refund to be sent to you as a check.

7   Amount to be refunded by check **7**   485,655,243 75

Part IV   **Total Allocation of Refund**

8   Add lines 1a, 2a, 3a, 4, 5a, 6a, and 7. The total must equal the refund amount shown on your tax return **8**   485,655,243 75

For Paperwork Reduction Act Notice, see your tax return instructions.   Cat. No. 21858A   Form **8888** (2016)

Form 1040 — Department of the Treasury—Internal Revenue Service (99)
U.S. Individual Income Tax Return **2016** OMB No. 1545-0074 | IRS Use Only—Do not write or staple in this space.

For the year Jan. 1–Dec. 31, 2016, or other tax year beginning **Jan. 21**, 2016 ending **March 21**, 20**17** | See separate instructions.

Your first name and initial: **Bradley J.** | Last name: **Franks** | Your social security number: **390 80 4016**

If a joint return, spouse's first name and initial | Last name | Spouse's social security number

Home address (number and street). If you have a P.O. box, see instructions. **C/o: 408 South Lincoln Street** | Apt. no. | ▲ Make sure the SSN(s) above and on line 6c are correct.

City, town or post office, state, and ZIP code. If you have a foreign address, also complete spaces below (see instructions). **Milbank, South Dakota** | Presidential Election Campaign — Check here if you, or your spouse if filing jointly, want $3 to go to this fund. Checking a box below will not change your tax or refund. ☐ You ☐ Spouse

Foreign country name **United States** | Foreign province/state/county **Grant County** | Foreign postal code **57252**

Filing Status — Check only one box.
1 ☑ Single
2 ☐ Married filing jointly (even if only one had income)
3 ☐ Married filing separately. Enter spouse's SSN above and full name here. ▶
4 ☐ Head of household (with qualifying person). (See instructions.) If the qualifying person is a child but not your dependent, enter this child's name here. ▶
5 ☐ Qualifying widow(er) with dependent child

Exemptions
6a ☑ Yourself. If someone can claim you as a dependent, do not check box 6a . . . . .
b ☐ Spouse
c Dependents:

(1) First name Last name	(2) Dependent's social security number	(3) Dependent's relationship to you	(4) ✓ if child under 17 qualifying for child tax credit (see instructions)
			☐
			☐
			☐
			☐

If more than four dependents, see instructions and check here ▶ ☐

d Total number of exemptions claimed . . . .

Boxes checked on 6a and 6b: **1**
No. of children on 6c who:
• lived with you: **0**
• did not live with you due to divorce or separation (see instructions): **0**
Dependents on 6c not entered above: **0**
Add numbers on lines above ▶ **1**

Income

Attach Form(s) W-2 here. Also attach Forms W-2G and 1099-R if tax was withheld.

If you did not get a W-2, see instructions.

7	Wages, salaries, tips, etc. Attach Form(s) W-2	7	0
8a	Taxable interest. Attach Schedule B if required	8a	392,408,436 95
b	Tax-exempt interest. Do not include on line 8a	8b	
9a	Ordinary dividends. Attach Schedule B if required	9a	0
b	Qualified dividends	9b	
10	Taxable refunds, credits, or offsets of state and local income taxes	10	0
11	Alimony received	11	0
12	Business income or (loss). Attach Schedule C or C-EZ	12	0
13	Capital gain or (loss). Attach Schedule D if required. If not required, check here ▶ ☐	13	0
14	Other gains or (losses). Attach Form 4797	14	0
15a	IRA distributions 15a	b Taxable amount	15b	0
16a	Pensions and annuities 16a	b Taxable amount	16b	0
17	Rental real estate, royalties, partnerships, S corporations, trusts, etc. Attach Schedule E	17	0
18	Farm income or (loss). Attach Schedule F	18	0
19	Unemployment compensation	19	0
20a	Social security benefits 20a	b Taxable amount	20b	0
21	Other income. List type and amount *"Security" Interest on Principal*	21	39,240,943,695 00
22	Combine the amounts in the far right column for lines 7 through 21. This is your total income ▶	22	39,633,353,131 95

Adjusted Gross Income

23	Educator expenses	23	0
24	Certain business expenses of reservists, performing artists, and fee-basis government officials. Attach Form 2106 or 2106-EZ	24	0
25	Health savings account deduction. Attach Form 8889	25	0
26	Moving expenses. Attach Form 3903	26	0
27	Deductible part of self-employment tax. Attach Schedule SE	27	0
28	Self-employed SEP, SIMPLE, and qualified plans	28	0
29	Self-employed health insurance deduction	29	0
30	Penalty on early withdrawal of savings	30	0
31a	Alimony paid b Recipient's SSN ▶	31a	0
32	IRA deduction	32	0
33	Student loan interest deduction	33	0
34	Tuition and fees. Attach Form 8917	34	0
35	Domestic production activities deduction. Attach Form 8903	35	0
36	Add lines 23 through 35	36	0
37	Subtract line 36 from line 22. This is your adjusted gross income ▶	37	39,633,353,131 95

For Disclosure, Privacy Act, and Paperwork Reduction Act Notice, see separate instructions. | Cat. No. 11320B | Form **1040** (2016)

361

Form 1040 (2016)								Page **2**

	38	Amount from line 37 (adjusted gross income)					38	39,633,353,131 95
Tax and Credits	39a	Check if: ☐ **You** were born before January 2, 1952, ☐ Blind. ☐ **Spouse** was born before January 2, 1952, ☐ Blind. Total boxes checked ▶ 39a						
	b	If your spouse itemizes on a separate return or you were a dual-status alien, check here ▶ 39b ☐						
Standard Deduction for—	40	Itemized deductions (from Schedule A) or your **standard deduction** (see left margin)					40	⊖
• People who check any box on line 39a or 39b **or** who can be claimed as a dependent, see instructions.	41	Subtract line 40 from line 38					41	39,633,353,131 95
	42	**Exemptions.** If line 38 is $155,650 or less, multiply $4,050 by the number on line 6d. Otherwise, see instructions					42	4,050 00
	43	**Taxable income.** Subtract line 42 from line 41. If line 42 is more than line 41, enter -0-					43	⊖
	44	**Tax** (see instructions). Check if any from: a ☐ Form(s) 8814 b ☐ Form 4972 c ☐					44	⊖
• All others:	45	**Alternative minimum tax** (see instructions). Attach Form 6251					45	⊖
Single or Married filing separately, $6,300	46	Excess advance premium tax credit repayment. Attach Form 8962					46	⊖
	47	Add lines 44, 45, and 46				▶	47	⊖
	48	Foreign tax credit. Attach Form 1116 if required		48	⊖			
Married filing jointly or Qualifying widow(er), $12,600	49	Credit for child and dependent care expenses. Attach Form 2441		49	⊖			
	50	Education credits from Form 8863, line 19		50	⊖			
	51	Retirement savings contributions credit. Attach Form 8880		51	⊖			
Head of household, $9,300	52	Child tax credit. Attach Schedule 8812, if required		52	⊖			
	53	Residential energy credits. Attach Form 5695		53	⊖			
	54	Other credits from Form: a ☐ 3800 b ☐ 8801 c ☐		54	⊖			
	55	Add lines 48 through 54. These are your **total credits**					55	⊖
	56	Subtract line 55 from line 47. If line 55 is more than line 47, enter -0-				▶	56	⊖
Other Taxes	57	Self-employment tax. Attach Schedule SE					57	⊖
	58	Unreported social security and Medicare tax from Form: a ☐ 4137 b ☐ 8919					58	⊖
	59	Additional tax on IRAs, other qualified retirement plans, etc. Attach Form 5329 if required					59	⊖
	60a	Household employment taxes from Schedule H					60a	⊖
	b	First-time homebuyer credit repayment. Attach Form 5405 if required					60b	⊖
	61	Health care: Individual responsibility (see instructions) Full-year coverage ☐					61	⊖
	62	Taxes from: a ☐ Form 8959 b ☐ Form 8960 c ☐ Instructions; enter code(s)					62	⊖
	63	Add lines 56 through 62. This is your **total tax**				▶	63	⊖
Payments	64	Federal income tax withheld from Forms W-2 and 1099		64	⊖			
If you have a qualifying child, attach Schedule EIC.	65	2016 estimated tax payments and amount applied from 2015 return		65	⊖			
	66a	**Earned income credit (EIC)**		66a	⊖			
	b	Nontaxable combat pay election	66b					
	67	Additional child tax credit. Attach Schedule 8812		67	⊖			
	68	American opportunity credit from Form 8863, line 8		68	⊖			
	69	Net premium tax credit. Attach Form 8962		69	⊖			
	70	Amount paid with request for extension to file		70	⊖			
	71	Excess social security and tier 1 RRTA tax withheld		71	⊖			
	72	Credit for federal tax on fuels. Attach Form 4136		72	⊖			
	73	Credits from Form: a ☐ 2439 b ☐ Reserved c ☐ 8885 d ☐		73	⊖			
	74	Add lines 64, 65, 66a, and 67 through 73. These are your **total payments**				▶	74	⊖
Refund	75	If line 74 is more than line 63, subtract line 63 from line 74. This is the amount you **overpaid**					75	⊖
Direct deposit? See instructions.	76a	Amount of line 75 you want **refunded to you.** If Form 8888 is attached, check here ▶ ☐					76a	342,409,436 95
	b	Routing number		▶ c Type: ☐ Checking ☐ Savings				
	d	Account number						
	77	Amount of line 75 you want **applied to your 2017 estimated tax** ▶	77					
Amount You Owe	78	**Amount you owe.** Subtract line 74 from line 63. For details on how to pay, see instructions ▶					78	⊖
	79	Estimated tax penalty (see instructions)		79				

Third Party Designee	Do you want to allow another person to discuss this return with the IRS (see instructions)? ☐ **Yes.** Complete below. ☐ **No** Designee's name ▶	Phone no. ▶	Personal identification number (PIN) ▶ ☐☐☐☐☐

Sign Here
Under penalties of perjury, I declare that I have examined this return and accompanying schedules and statements, and to the best of my knowledge and belief, they are true, correct, and accurately list all amounts and sources of income I received during the tax year. Declaration of preparer (other than taxpayer) is based on all information of which preparer has any knowledge.

Joint return? See instructions. Keep a copy for your records.

Your signature *Bradley - J. Franks*	Date 3·12·17	Your occupation Author / Self Emp.	Daytime phone number 605·432·7920
Spouse's signature. If a joint return, **both** must sign.	Date	Spouse's occupation	If the IRS sent you an Identity Protection PIN, enter it here (see inst.) ☐☐☐☐☐☐

Paid Preparer Use Only

Print/Type preparer's name	Preparer's signature		Date	Check ☐ if self-employed	PTIN
Firm's name ▶				Firm's EIN ▶	
Firm's address ▶				Phone no.	

www.irs.gov/form1040

Form **1040** (2016)

Form **8888**	Allocation of Refund (Including Savings Bond Purchases)	OMB No. 1545-0074
Department of the Treasury Internal Revenue Service	▶ Information about Form 8888 and its instructions is at *www.irs.gov/form8888.* ▶ Attach to your income tax return.	20**16** Attachment Sequence No. **56**

Name(s) shown on return	Your social security number
Bradley - J. : Franks	390 - 80 - 4016

Part I **Direct Deposit**

Complete this part if you want us to directly deposit a portion of your refund to one or more accounts.

1a Amount to be deposited in first account (see instructions) **1a**

b Routing number [   ] ▶c ☐ Checking ☐ Savings

d Account number [   ]

2a Amount to be deposited in second account **2a**

b Routing number [   ] ▶c ☐ Checking ☐ Savings

d Account number [   ]

3a Amount to be deposited in third account **3a**

b Routing number [   ] ▶c ☐ Checking ☐ Savings

d Account number [   ]

Part II **U.S. Series I Savings Bond Purchases**

Complete this part if you want to buy paper bonds with a portion of your refund.

⚠️ **CAUTION** If a name is entered on line 5c or 6c below, co-ownership will be assumed unless the beneficiary box is checked. See instructions for more details.

4 Amount to be used for bond purchases for yourself (and your spouse, if filing jointly) **4**

5a Amount to be used to buy bonds for yourself, your spouse, **or** someone else **5a**
b Enter the owner's name (First then Last) for the bond registration
[   ]

c If you would like to add a co-owner or beneficiary, enter the name here (First then Last). If beneficiary, also check here ▶ ☐
[   ]

6a Amount to be used to buy bonds for yourself, your spouse, **or** someone else **6a**
b Enter the owner's name (First then Last) for the bond registration
[   ]

c If you would like to add a co-owner or beneficiary, enter the name here (First then Last). If beneficiary, also check here ▶ ☐
[   ]

Part III **Paper Check**

Complete this part if you want a portion of your refund to be sent to you as a check.

7 Amount to be refunded by check **7** 392,409,436.95

Part IV **Total Allocation of Refund**

8 Add lines 1a, 2a, 3a, 4, 5a, 6a, and 7. The total must equal the refund amount shown on your tax return **8** 392,409,436.95

For Paperwork Reduction Act Notice, see your tax return instructions.   Cat. No. 21858A   Form **8888** (2016)

363

TAX COMPUTATIONS: 06/27/2017

The **Gross** amount of the **Security** for the Beneficiaries Bradley – J.; [Franks] and Robert – C.; [Simpson] is: $38,852,419,500.00 **USD.**

The **Interest percentage**, according to the F. D. I. C. Policy and Procedure, if the above stated amount were deposited into a bank account at 1% (every three months or quarterly) would be **$388,824,195.00 USD.** According to I. R. S. (by Law) this amount would be considered as **Taxable Income.**

The **Taxable Income** at the I. R. S. Percentage of 19.6% equates to $76,150,742.22 **USD.**

However, If you subtract $388,824,195.00 - $76,150,742.22 = $312,373,452.78 **USD** due for the months of October – December 2016 Refund for the Beneficiaries.

Furthermore, the Interest is carried over into the Months of January – March 2017.

The NEW **Gross** amount is: $39,240,943,695.00 **USD.**

The **Interest percentage** at 1% of the new Gross amount is: $392,409,436.95 **USD. Taxable Income.**

I. R. S. would receive at 19.6% a total of: $76,912,249.64 **USD.**

However, subtract $392,409,436.95 - $76,912,249.64 = **$315,497,187.31 USD** due for the months of January – March 2017 Refund for the Beneficiaries.

Adding the Interest from January – March to the NEW **Gross** amount is: $39,633,353,131.95 **USD.**

The months of March – June 2017:

The **Interest percentage** at 1% of the new Gross amount is: $396,333,531.3195 (rounded up = $396,333,531.32) **USD. Taxable Income.**

I. R. S. would receive at 19.6% a total of: $77,681,372.13782 (rounded up = $77,681,372.14) **USD. Taxable Income.**

Yet once again, we subtract $396,333,531.3195 - $77,681,372.13782 = $318,652,159.18078 (rounded off = $318,652,159.18) **USD** due for the Months of March – June 2017 Refund for the Beneficiaries.

In conclusion, if you add all of what the I. R. S. claims as **Taxable Income** at 19.6% for the three quarters = $230,744,363.99782 (Rounded up = $230,744,364.00) for I. R. S.

However, when you add up all of the **Interest rates TOTALS** at 1% of the Gross Amounts at the end of the three quarters and the subtraction of what the I. R. S. claims equals a **Refund Balance of:** $946,522,799.27 **USD** for the Beneficiaries. Payment is due upon receiving this notification.

Thank you for Attention.

Bradley - J.: [Franks] and Co-Author: Robert - C.: [Simpson]

TAX COMPUTATIONS: 06/27/2017

Summary of Tax Computations:

Gross Total Amount of "Security" (owned-by and owed-for the Beneficiaries) is: Date from <u>October 2016 – December 2016</u>: Principal: $ 38,852,419,500.00. USD

Interest Accrual for this (3 month quarter) at 1% is: $ 388,824,195.00. USD

Taxable Income by I.R.S. from the Interest Accrual at 19.6% is: $ 76,150,742.22. USD

The Total Amount of the Refund from I.R.S. is: $ 312,373,452.78. USD for the Beneficiaries.

Gross Total Amount of "Security" (owned-by and owed-for the Beneficiaries) is: Date from <u>January 2017 – March 2017</u>: New Principal with Interest carried-over: $ 39,240,943,695.00. USD

Interest Accrual for this (3 month quarter) at 1% is: $ 392,409,436.95. USD

Taxable Income by I.R.S. from the Interest Accrual at 19.6% is: $ 76,912,249.64. USD

The Total Amount of the Refund from I.R.S. is: $ 315,497,187.31. USD for the Beneficiaries.

Gross Total Amount of "Security" (owned-by and owed-for the Beneficiaries) is: Date from <u>April 2017 – June 2017</u>: New Principal with Interest carried-over: $ 39,633,353,131.95. USD

Interest Accrual for this (3 month quarter) at 1% is: $ 396,333,531.32. USD

Taxable Income by I.R.S. from the Interest Accrual at 19.6% is: $ 77,681,372.14. USD

The Total Amount of the Refund from I.R.S. is: $ 318,652,159.18. USD for the Beneficiaries.

Total Amount of Interest Accrual for (<u>9 Months – 3 quarters</u>) is: $ 1,177,567,163.27. USD

Total of Taxable Income by I.R.S. at 19.6% is: $ 230,744,364.00. USD

The Total Amount of the Refund from I.R.S. is: $ 946,522,799.27. USD for the Beneficiaries.

Amount Due upon receipt of this Document.

The Death of America

Form 1040 — Department of the Treasury—Internal Revenue Service (99)
U.S. Individual Income Tax Return **2016** OMB No. 1545-0074 — IRS Use Only—Do not write or staple in this space.

For the year Jan. 1–Dec. 31, 2016, or other tax year beginning *Sept. 2017*, 2016; ending *December*, 20 *17* — See separate instructions.

Your first name and initial: *Bradley J.* — Last name: *Franks*
Your social security number: *390 180 4016*

If a joint return, spouse's first name and initial — Last name
Spouse's social security number

Home address (number and street). If you have a P.O. box, see instructions. *½ 408 South Lincoln Street* — Apt. no.

City, town or post office, state, and ZIP code. *Milbank, South Dakota 57252*
Foreign country name *UNITED STATES Inc.* — Foreign province/state/county *S.D. (subsidiary)* — Foreign postal code *57252*

Filing Status — Check only one box.
1. ☑ Single
2. ☐ Married filing jointly (even if only one had income)
3. ☐ Married filing separately. Enter spouse's SSN above and full name here.
4. ☐ Head of household (with qualifying person). (See instructions.) If the qualifying person is a child but not your dependent, enter this child's name here.
5. ☐ Qualifying widow(er) with dependent child

Exemptions
6a ☑ Yourself. If someone can claim you as a dependent, do not check box 6a
b ☐ Spouse
c Dependents:
d Total number of exemptions claimed

Boxes checked on 6a and 6b: *1*
No. of children on 6c who: *2*
Dependents on 6c not entered above: *2*
Add numbers on lines above: *1*

Income
7 Wages, salaries, tips, etc. Attach Form(s) W-2 — 7 — *0*
8a Taxable interest. Attach Schedule B if required — 8a — *404,209,835 30*
8b Tax-exempt interest — 8b
9a Ordinary dividends — 9a — *0*
9b Qualified dividends — 9b
10 Taxable refunds — 10 — *0*
11 Alimony received — 11 — *0*
12 Business income or (loss) — 12 — *0*
13 Capital gain or (loss) — 13 — *0*
14 Other gains or (losses) — 14 — *0*
15a IRA distributions — 15b — *0*
16a Pensions and annuities — 16b — *0*
17 Rental real estate, royalties — 17 — *0*
18 Farm income or (loss) — 18 — *0*
19 Unemployment compensation — 19 — *0*
20a Social security benefits — 20b — *0*
21 Other income. List type and amount *Interest on principle "Security"* — 21 — *76,816,968 82*
22 Combine amounts for lines 7 through 21. Total income — 22 — *481,116,804 12*

Adjusted Gross Income
23 Educator expenses — 23
24 Certain business expenses — 24 — *0*
25 Health savings account deduction — 25 — *0*
26 Moving expenses — 26 — *0*
27 Deductible part of self-employment tax — 27 — *0*
28 Self-employed SEP, SIMPLE — 28 — *0*
29 Self-employed health insurance deduction — 29 — *0*
30 Penalty on early withdrawal of savings — 30 — *0*
31a Alimony paid — 31a — *0*
32 IRA deduction — 32 — *0*
33 Student loan interest deduction — 33 — *0*
34 Tuition and fees — 34 — *0*
35 Domestic production activities deduction — 35 — *0*
36 Add lines 23 through 35 — 36 — *0*
37 Subtract line 36 from line 22. This is your adjusted gross income — 37 — *481,116,804 12*

For Disclosure, Privacy Act, and Paperwork Reduction Act Notice, see separate instructions. Cat. No. 11320B Form **1040** (2016)

366

Form 1040 (2016)   Page **2**

	38	Amount from line 37 (adjusted gross income)	38	481116804 12

Tax and Credits

39a	Check if: ☐ You were born before January 2, 1952, ☐ Blind. / ☐ Spouse was born before January 2, 1952, ☐ Blind. } Total boxes checked ► 39a			
b	If your spouse itemizes on a separate return or you were a dual-status alien, check here► 39b ☐			

Standard Deduction for—
- People who check any box on line 39a or 39b or who can be claimed as a dependent, see instructions.
- All others:
Single or Married filing separately, $6,300
Married filing jointly or Qualifying widow(er), $12,600
Head of household, $9,300

40	Itemized deductions (from Schedule A) or your standard deduction (see left margin)	40	
41	Subtract line 40 from line 38	41	481116804 12
42	Exemptions. If line 38 is $155,650 or less, multiply $4,050 by the number on line 6d. Otherwise, see instructions	42	4050 —
43	Taxable income. Subtract line 42 from line 41. If line 42 is more than line 41, enter -0-	43	0
44	Tax (see instructions). Check if any from: a ☐ Form(s) 8814 b ☐ Form 4972 c ☐ ___	44	0
45	Alternative minimum tax (see instructions). Attach Form 6251	45	0
46	Excess advance premium tax credit repayment. Attach Form 8962	46	0
47	Add lines 44, 45, and 46 ►	47	0

48	Foreign tax credit. Attach Form 1116 if required	48	0	
49	Credit for child and dependent care expenses. Attach Form 2441	49	0	
50	Education credits from Form 8863, line 19	50	0	
51	Retirement savings contributions credit. Attach Form 8880	51	0	
52	Child tax credit. Attach Schedule 8812, if required	52	0	
53	Residential energy credits. Attach Form 5695	53	0	
54	Other credits from Form: a ☐ 3800 b ☐ 8801 c ☐ ___	54	0	
55	Add lines 48 through 54. These are your total credits		55	0
56	Subtract line 55 from line 47. If line 55 is more than line 47, enter -0- ►		56	0

Other Taxes

57	Self-employment tax. Attach Schedule SE		57	0
58	Unreported social security and Medicare tax from Form: a ☐ 4137 b ☐ 8919		58	0
59	Additional tax on IRAs, other qualified retirement plans, etc. Attach Form 5329 if required		59	0
60a	Household employment taxes from Schedule H		60a	0
b	First-time homebuyer credit repayment. Attach Form 5405 if required		60b	0
61	Health care: individual responsibility (see instructions) Full-year coverage ☐		61	0
62	Taxes from: a ☐ Form 8959 b ☐ Form 8960 c ☐ Instructions; enter code(s) ___		62	0
63	Add lines 56 through 62. This is your total tax ►		63	0

Payments

If you have a qualifying child, attach Schedule EIC.

64	Federal income tax withheld from Forms W-2 and 1099	64	7	
65	2016 estimated tax payments and amount applied from 2015 return	65	0	
66a	Earned income credit (EIC)	66a	0	
b	Nontaxable combat pay election	66b		
67	Additional child tax credit. Attach Schedule 8812	67	0	
68	American opportunity credit from Form 8863, line 8	68	0	
69	Net premium tax credit. Attach Form 8962	69	0	
70	Amount paid with request for extension to file	70	0	
71	Excess social security and tier 1 RRTA tax withheld	71	0	
72	Credit for federal tax on fuels. Attach Form 4136	72	0	
73	Credits from Form: a ☐ 2439 b ☐ Reserved c ☐ 8885 d ☐ ___	73	0	
74	Add lines 64, 65, 66a, and 67 through 73. These are your total payments ►		74	0

Refund

Direct deposit?
See instructions.

75	If line 74 is more than line 63, subtract line 63 from line 74. This is the amount you overpaid		75	0
76a	Amount of line 75 you want refunded to you. If Form 8888 is attached, check here ► ☐		76a	322472866 48
► b	Routing number ___ ► c Type: ☐ Checking ☐ Savings			
► d	Account number ___			
77	Amount of line 75 you want applied to your 2017 estimated tax ►	77		

Amount You Owe

78	Amount you owe. Subtract line 74 from line 63. For details on how to pay, see instructions ►		78	0
79	Estimated tax penalty (see instructions)	79		

Third Party Designee

Do you want to allow another person to discuss this return with the IRS (see instructions)? ☐ Yes. Complete below. ☐ No

Designee's name ►   Phone no. ►   Personal identification number (PIN) ►

Sign Here

Joint return? See instructions. Keep a copy for your records.

Under penalties of perjury, I declare that I have examined this return and accompanying schedules and statements, and to the best of my knowledge and belief, they are true, correct, and accurately list all amounts and sources of income I received during the tax year. Declaration of preparer (other than taxpayer) is based on all information of which preparer has any knowledge.

Your signature	Date 12/18/17	Your occupation Author / Self Emp	Daytime phone number 605-432-7920
Spouse's signature. If a joint return, both must sign.	Date	Spouse's occupation	If the IRS sent you an Identity Protection PIN, enter it here (see inst.)

Paid Preparer Use Only

Print/Type preparer's name	Preparer's signature	Date Check ☐ if self-employed PTIN
Firm's name ►		Firm's EIN ►
Firm's address ►		Phone no.

www.irs.gov/form1040   Form **1040** (2016)

The Death of America

Form **8888**	Allocation of Refund (Including Savings Bond Purchases)	OMB No. 1545-0074
Department of the Treasury Internal Revenue Service	▶ Information about Form 8888 and its instructions is at *www.irs.gov/form8888.* ▶ Attach to your income tax return.	20**16** Attachment Sequence No. **56**

Name(s) shown on return: Bradley J. Franks

Your social security number: 390-80-4016

Part I   Direct Deposit

Complete this part if you want us to directly deposit a portion of your refund to one or more accounts.

1a Amount to be deposited in first account (see instructions) . . . . | 1a |

b Routing number ▶ c ☐ Checking ☐ Savings

d Account number

2a Amount to be deposited in second account . . . . | 2a |

b Routing number ▶ c ☐ Checking ☐ Savings

d Account number

3a Amount to be deposited in third account . . . . | 3a |

b Routing number ▶ c ☐ Checking ☐ Savings

d Account number

Part II   U.S. Series I Savings Bond Purchases

Complete this part if you want to buy paper bonds with a portion of your refund.

⚠ CAUTION: If a name is entered on line 5c or 6c below, co-ownership will be assumed unless the beneficiary box is checked. See instructions for more details.

4 Amount to be used for bond purchases for yourself (and your spouse, if filing jointly) . . . . | 4 |

5a Amount to be used to buy bonds for yourself, your spouse, **or** someone else . . . . . . | 5a |
b Enter the owner's name (First then Last) for the bond registration

c If you would like to add a co-owner or beneficiary, enter the name here (First then Last). If beneficiary, also check here ▶ ☐

6a Amount to be used to buy bonds for yourself, your spouse, **or** someone else . . . . . . | 6a |
b Enter the owner's name (First then Last) for the bond registration

c If you would like to add a co-owner or beneficiary, enter the name here (First then Last). If beneficiary, also check here ▶ ☐

Part III   Paper Check

Complete this part if you want a portion of your refund to be sent to you as a check.

7 Amount to be refunded by check . . . . | 7 | 327482866 48 |

Part IV   Total Allocation of Refund

8 Add lines 1a, 2a, 3a, 4, 5a, 6a, and 7. The total must equal the refund amount shown on your tax return . . . . | 8 | 327482866 48 |

For Paperwork Reduction Act Notice, see your tax return instructions. Cat. No. 21858A Form **8888** (2016)

Form 1040 Department of the Treasury—Internal Revenue Service (99)
U.S. Individual Income Tax Return **2016** OMB No. 1545-0074 | IRS Use Only—Do not write or staple in this space.

For the year Jan. 1–Dec. 31, 2016, or other tax year beginning *Jan. 2018*, ending *March*, 20 *18* | See separate instructions.

Your first name and initial: *Bradley - J. -* Last name: *[Franks]*
Your social security number: 390 80 4016

Home address (number and street): *%: 408 South Lincoln Street*
City, town or post office, state, and ZIP code: *Milbank South Dakota; [57252]*
Foreign country name: *UNITED STATES INC.* *SD (subsidiary)* *57252*

Filing Status — 1 ☑ Single

Exemptions
6a ☑ Yourself. — Boxes checked on 6a and 6b: 1
d Total number of exemptions claimed: 1

Income
8a Taxable interest. Attach Schedule B if required — 8a: 408,342,833.65
21 Other income. List type and amount *Interest on Principle "Security"* — 21: 7,785,138.39
22 Combine the amounts — 22: 416,127,972.04

Adjusted Gross Income
36 Add lines 23 through 35: 0
37 Subtract line 36 from line 22. This is your adjusted gross income — 37: 416,127,972.84

For Disclosure, Privacy Act, and Paperwork Reduction Act Notice, see separate instructions. | Cat. No. 11320B | Form **1040** (2016)

The Death of America

		Form 1040 (2016)					Page **2**

Tax and Credits	38	Amount from line 37 (adjusted gross income)	**38**	416127972	04

	39a	Check if: ☐ You were born before January 2, 1952, ☐ Blind. / ☐ Spouse was born before January 2, 1952, ☐ Blind. } Total boxes checked ▶ 39a		
	b	If your spouse itemizes on a separate return or you were a dual-status alien, check here ▶ 39b ☐		

Standard Deduction for—	40	Itemized deductions (from Schedule A) or your **standard deduction** (see left margin) . .	**40**		
• People who check any box on line 39a or 39b or who can be claimed as a dependent, see instructions.	41	Subtract line 40 from line 38	**41**	416127972	04
	42	**Exemptions.** If line 38 is $155,650 or less, multiply $4,050 by the number on line 6d. Otherwise, see instructions	**42**	4050	0
	43	**Taxable income.** Subtract line 42 from line 41. If line 42 is more than line 41, enter -0- . .	**43**		
	44	**Tax** (see instructions). Check if any from: **a** ☐ Form(s) 8814 **b** ☐ Form 4972 **c** ☐ _____	**44**		
• All others:	45	**Alternative minimum tax** (see instructions). Attach Form 6251	**45**		
Single or Married filing separately, $6,300	46	Excess advance premium tax credit repayment. Attach Form 8962	**46**		
	47	Add lines 44, 45, and 46 . . . . ▶	**47**		
Married filing jointly or Qualifying widow(er), $12,600	48	Foreign tax credit. Attach Form 1116 if required	48		
	49	Credit for child and dependent care expenses. Attach Form 2441	49		
	50	Education credits from Form 8863, line 19	50		
Head of household, $9,300	51	Retirement savings contributions credit. Attach Form 8880	51		
	52	Child tax credit. Attach Schedule 8812, if required . . .	52		
	53	Residential energy credits. Attach Form 5695	53		
	54	Other credits from Form: **a** ☐ 3800 **b** ☐ 8801 **c** ☐ _____	54		
	55	Add lines 48 through 54. These are your **total credits**	**55**		
	56	Subtract line 55 from line 47. If line 55 is more than line 47, enter -0- . . . . . ▶	**56**		

Other Taxes	57	Self-employment tax. Attach Schedule SE	**57**		
	58	Unreported social security and Medicare tax from Form: **a** ☐ 4137 **b** ☐ 8919 . .	**58**		
	59	Additional tax on IRAs, other qualified retirement plans, etc. Attach Form 5329 if required . .	**59**		
	60a	Household employment taxes from Schedule H	**60a**		
	b	First-time homebuyer credit repayment. Attach Form 5405 if required	**60b**		
	61	Health care: individual responsibility (see instructions) Full-year coverage ☐ . . .	**61**		
	62	Taxes from: **a** ☐ Form 8959 **b** ☐ Form 8960 **c** ☐ Instructions; enter code(s)	**62**		
	63	Add lines 56 through 62. This is your **total tax** . . . . ▶	**63**		

Payments	64	Federal income tax withheld from Forms W-2 and 1099 .	64		
If you have a qualifying child, attach Schedule EIC.	65	2016 estimated tax payments and amount applied from 2015 return	65		
	66a	**Earned income credit (EIC)**	66a		
	b	Nontaxable combat pay election 66b			
	67	Additional child tax credit. Attach Schedule 8812	67		
	68	American opportunity credit from Form 8863, line 8 . . .	68		
	69	Net premium tax credit. Attach Form 8962	69		
	70	Amount paid with request for extension to file	70		
	71	Excess social security and tier 1 RRTA tax withheld	71		
	72	Credit for federal tax on fuels. Attach Form 4136 . . .	72		
	73	Credits from Form: **a** ☐ 2439 **b** ☐ Reserved **c** ☐ 8885 **d** ☐	73		
	74	Add lines 64, 65, 66a, and 67 through 73. These are your **total payments** . . . . . ▶	**74**		

Refund	75	If line 74 is more than line 63, subtract line 63 from line 74. This is the amount you **overpaid**	**75**		
Direct deposit? ▶ See instructions.	76a	Amount of line 75 you want **refunded to you.** If Form 8888 is attached, check here ▶ ☐	**76a**	400557695	26
	b	Routing number ▶ **c** Type: ☐ Checking ☐ Savings			
	d	Account number			
	77	Amount of line 75 you want **applied to your 2017 estimated tax** ▶ 77			

Amount You Owe	78	**Amount you owe.** Subtract line 74 from line 63. For details on how to pay, see instructions ▶	**78**		
	79	Estimated tax penalty (see instructions) 79			

Third Party Designee	Do you want to allow another person to discuss this return with the IRS (see instructions)? ☐ **Yes.** Complete below. ☐ **No**

Designee's name ▶   Phone no. ▶   Personal identification number (PIN) ▶ ☐☐☐☐☐

Sign Here

Under penalties of perjury, I declare that I have examined this return and accompanying schedules and statements, and to the best of my knowledge and belief, they are true, correct, and accurately list all amounts and sources of income I received during the tax year. Declaration of preparer (other than taxpayer) is based on all information of which preparer has any knowledge.

Joint return? See instructions. Keep a copy for your records.

Your signature	Date	Your occupation	Daytime phone number
Spouse's signature. If a joint return, **both** must sign.	Date	Spouse's occupation	If the IRS sent you an Identity Protection PIN, enter it here (see inst.) ☐☐☐☐☐☐

Paid Preparer Use Only

Print/Type preparer's name	Preparer's signature	Date	Check ☐ if self-employed	PTIN
Firm's name ▶			Firm's EIN ▶	
Firm's address ▶			Phone no.	

www.irs.gov/form1040   Form **1040** (2016)

Form **8888**	Allocation of Refund (Including Savings Bond Purchases)	OMB No. 1545-0074
Department of the Treasury Internal Revenue Service	▶ Information about Form 8888 and its instructions is at *www.irs.gov/form8888.* ▶ Attach to your income tax return.	20**16** Attachment Sequence No. **56**

Name(s) shown on return: Bradley - J.: [Franks]

Your social security number: 390-80-4016

Part I — Direct Deposit
Complete this part if you want us to directly deposit a portion of your refund to one or more accounts.

1a Amount to be deposited in first account (see instructions) **1a**

b Routing number ▶c ☐ Checking ☐ Savings

d Account number

2a Amount to be deposited in second account **2a**

b Routing number ▶c ☐ Checking ☐ Savings

d Account number

3a Amount to be deposited in third account **3a**

b Routing number ▶c ☐ Checking ☐ Savings

d Account number

Part II — U.S. Series I Savings Bond Purchases
Complete this part if you want to buy paper bonds with a portion of your refund.

⚠ **CAUTION** If a name is entered on line 5c or 6c below, co-ownership will be assumed unless the beneficiary box is checked. See instructions for more details.

4 Amount to be used for bond purchases for yourself (and your spouse, if filing jointly) **4**

5a Amount to be used to buy bonds for yourself, your spouse, **or** someone else **5a**
b Enter the owner's name (First then Last) for the bond registration

c If you would like to add a co-owner or beneficiary, enter the name here (First then Last). If beneficiary, also check here ▶ ☐

6a Amount to be used to buy bonds for yourself, your spouse, **or** someone else **6a**
b Enter the owner's name (First then Last) for the bond registration

c If you would like to add a co-owner or beneficiary, enter the name here (First then Last). If beneficiary, also check here ▶ ☐

Part III — Paper Check
Complete this part if you want a portion of your refund to be sent to you as a check.

7 Amount to be refunded by check **7** 400557695 26

Part IV — Total Allocation of Refund

8 Add lines 1a, 2a, 3a, 4, 5a, 6a, and 7. The total must equal the refund amount shown on your tax return **8** 400557695 26

For Paperwork Reduction Act Notice, see your tax return instructions. | Cat. No. 21858A | Form **8888** (2016)

The Death of America

Form **1040**	Department of the Treasury—Internal Revenue Service (99) U.S. Individual Income Tax Return	**2016**	OMB No. 1545-0074	IRS Use Only—Do not write or staple in this space.

For the year Jan. 1–Dec. 31, 2016, or other tax year beginning **Jan. 2018**, ending **March , 2018**   See separate instructions.

Your first name and initial: **Bradley – J.**   Last name: **[Franks]**

Your social security number: **390 100 4016**

If a joint return, spouse's first name and initial / Last name

Home address (number and street). If you have a P.O. box, see instructions. Apt. no.
c/o: 408 South Lincoln Street

City, town or post office, state, and ZIP code.
Milbank, South Dakota [57252]

Foreign country name: **United States Inc.**   Foreign province/state/county: **S.D. (subsidiary)**   Foreign postal code: **57252**

Filing Status
1. ☑ Single
2. ☐ Married filing jointly
3. ☐ Married filing separately
4. ☐ Head of household
5. ☐ Qualifying widow(er)

Exemptions
6a ☑ Yourself.
6b ☐ Spouse
Boxes checked on 6a and 6b: **1**
Add numbers on lines above ▶ **1**

Income

7	Wages, salaries, tips, etc.	7	0
8a	Taxable interest.	8a	408,342,833 65
8b	Tax-exempt interest.		
9a	Ordinary dividends.	9a	0
9b	Qualified dividends.		
10	Taxable refunds	10	0
11	Alimony received	11	0
12	Business income or (loss).	12	0
13	Capital gain or (loss).	13	0
14	Other gains or (losses).	14	0
15b	IRA distributions	15b	0
16b	Pensions and annuities	16b	0
17	Rental real estate, royalties, partnerships	17	0
18	Farm income or (loss).	18	0
19	Unemployment compensation	19	0
20b	Social security benefits	20b	0
21	Other income. List type and amount *Interest on Principle "Security"*	21	7,785,138 39
22	Combine the amounts... This is your total income ▶	22	416,127,972 04

Adjusted Gross Income

23	Educator expenses	23	0
24	Certain business expenses	24	0
25	Health savings account deduction	25	0
26	Moving expenses	26	0
27	Deductible part of self-employment tax	27	0
28	Self-employed SEP, SIMPLE	28	0
29	Self-employed health insurance deduction	29	0
30	Penalty on early withdrawal of savings	30	0
31a	Alimony paid	31a	0
32	IRA deduction	32	0
33	Student loan interest deduction	33	0
34	Tuition and fees	34	0
35	Domestic production activities deduction	35	0
36	Add lines 23 through 35	36	0
37	Subtract line 36 from line 22. This is your adjusted gross income ▶	37	416,127,972 04

For Disclosure, Privacy Act, and Paperwork Reduction Act Notice, see separate instructions.   Cat. No. 11320B   Form **1040** (2016)

372

The documentation and evidence presented in this chapter is complete as Facts not opinion. The undeclared FOREIGN-Agents of the Fictitious-Corporate-Government of the United-States have unlawfully declared WAR on Americans by their illegal-Actions and their lack of Actions. In addition, the I. R. S. (Internal Revenue Service) is trying any way they can to force me to "Break the Law" and place myself back under their sphere of control. Remember, the I. R. S. is not even a United-States-Corporate-Agency. The main-office is registered in Puerto Rico.

This author has more respect for the Mafia and Organized crime than I do for the Fictitious-United-States-Corporate-Government and its FOREIGN-AGENTS.

At least when the Mafia and Organized crime bosses make demands you know what would happen if you don't comply.

However, when the Fictitious-Corporate-Government makes demands they punish Americans who do good acts and who do wrong acts...it does not matter. Unfortunately, this is what Society calls "RULES and LAWS". If this is the case Society is greedy, selfish, arrogant, ignorant and insecure.

However, with the above information and documentation the Corporate-Government would have all Americans believe that they do not have any legal standing within their courts and they would be correct. However, they cannot produce any "CONTRACT" of "Performance" or enforce any type of Punishment against Innocent Americans that "exercise their RIGHTS".

Chapter 8:
BREACH OF CONTRACT

The idea that a State originated to serve any kind of social purpose is completely unhistorical. It originated in conquest and confiscation, that is to say, in and by criminal actions. It originated for the purpose of maintaining the division of society into an owning and exploiting class and a property-less class, that is, for a criminal purpose! No State known throughout history originated in any other manner, or for any other purpose!

The simple definition of what a contract is as follows: 'An agreement with specific terms between two or more persons or entities in which there is a promise to do something in return for a valuable benefit known as consideration". Unfortunately, the 'Legal' definition is at its basic definition and can involve a lot more variations, circumstances and complexities.

Within this chapter we will point out one specific 'Legal' contract made and entered into by two parties/entities…that contract is called the "Oath" or "Affirmation" or more formally called the "Oath of Office"! As Americans we all know or are aware that after every election all Politicians, Judges, Lawyers, Civil Servants and Bureaucrats are required by Federal Law to sign/autograph an "Oath of office" or "Affirmation" and is to be filed with the Secretary of State for that elected office or filed with the Secretary of State at the Federal level for those Federally elected Officials. However, STATE INCs. (Subsidiaries) may not keep the "Oath of Office" on file but they do have to file them in some sort of "Archives" for future reference.

The contract known as the "Oath" or "Affirmation" or formally known as the "Oath of Office" usually states as follows: "I, (insert name), do solemnly swear that I will support the Constitution of the United States and the Constitution and Laws of the State of (insert name of State); that I will bear true faith and allegiance to the same, and defend them against all enemies, foreign and domestic, and that I will faithfully and impartially discharge the duties of the Office of (insert Title of Office of elected official) according to the best of my ability, so help me God".

The newly elected official or incumbent affixes their signature/autograph on this contract before a Supreme Court Justice, Judge, Magistrate or Secretary of State, after verbally stating the "Oath of Office", dated, then filed with the appropriate office, usually the Secretary of State of the particular State or the Secretary of State at Federal Level for Congressmen, U. S. Senators and the Presidency accordingly. The "Oath of Office" is an example from one of the fifty (50) subsidiaries of the U. S. Corporate-Government. All other "Oaths of Office" may differ in form or language structure. However, they all state that they support the "Constitution" (Federal Document – a contract) and the individual Constitution of the particular State (another contract document); then continues to swear to defend these contracts from enemies, Foreign and Domestic. The "CONSTITUTION" also includes the 'Bill of Rights" …remember they are the first-ten 'Amendments'.

At this point, one needs to understand the "hierarchy" of who's who in the zoo, or rather who's on top, who's on the bottom…or who created whom!

1) The source of all rights came from a Supreme Creator, the Supreme Law Giver.

2) God (the Creator) created man, a Divine-Being, with a soul, flesh and blood and with spirit.

3) Man (We, the people) created and wrote the Constitution, as Thomas Jefferson Said, "to bind them down to the chains of the Constitution" being that they are supposedly 'public-servants'.

4) These so-called governments, State, County, City and national government (Federal U. S., Inc.) were, in actuality, created in artificial corporate capacities. Each State has its own Corporate Seal!

5) These so-called governments were created by and for the people with Christian Principles.

6) State constitutions, with powers and authorities were loosely defined and the Federal Constitution, with powers and authorities were

finitely enumerated. (With initial foundation being "The Declaration of Independence" – signed July 4, 1776 – where it was declared that "We hold these truths to be self-evident, that all men are created equal, that they are endowed by their Creator with certain unalienable Rights (sovereignty?), that among these are Life, Liberty and the Pursuit of Happiness…".

7) "That to secure these rights (from our Creator), Governments are instituted among Men, deriving their just powers from the consent of the governed". (Limited Powers!).

8) NOTE: These Rights were 1) Secured and, 2) They are un-a-lien-able. Which means, that your Rights cannot be surrendered or transferred (into privileges) without your consent, example, freedom of speech, of religion, right to keep and bear arms, to marry (without license), right to travel (without 'driver's license'), due process, equal protection of the laws, etc.

9) For the sole purpose of securing Life, Liberty, Pursuit of Happiness and property the people 'elected' men/women as Public/Civil-Servants to serve the people, in their respective capacities in the Legislative, Judicial and Executive branches in these so-called government-corporations.

10) The people did not in any manner, give-up, or surrender or vacate 'their' Rights or their sovereignty, always keeping and holding their 'power' over all of so-called government.

Note that 1 through 5 above create a 'Separation of Powers' Doctrine…on the Private side as against the Corporate Side! We the People, being flesh and blood / 'real' are separate from the artificial-corporate-entities, further supported by following cases for reference:

"But indeed, no private person has a right to complain, by suit in Court, on the ground of a breach of the Constitution. The Constitution, it is true, is a compact (contract), but he is not party to it. The States are party to it…" – Padelford, Fay & Co. vs. The Mayor and Alderman of the City of Savannah, Ga. 438 (1854).

"The people have succeeded to the rights of the King, the former sovereign of this State. They are not, therefore, bound by general words

376

in a statute restrictive of prerogative, without being expressly named. E.g., the Insolvent Law". – the People v. Herkimer, Gentleman, one, &c – 4 Cowen345; 1825 N. Y. Lexis 80.

The Supreme Court in the case of Wills vs. Michigan State Police, 105 L. Ed. 2D 45 (1989) …made it perfectly clear that (I) the Sovereign, [the people] cannot be named as merely a "person" or "any person"!

"All that government does and provides legitimately is in pursuit of its duty to provide protection for private rights, which duty is a debt owed to its creator, WE THE PEOPLE, (Wynhammer v. People, NY 378) … and the private unenfranchised individual; which debt and duty is never extinguished nor discharged, and is perpetual. No matter what the government/state provides us in manner of convenience and safety, the unenfranchised individual owes nothing to the government". – Hale vs. Henkel, 201 U.S. 43.

"It is not the function of our Government to keep the citizen from falling into error; it is the function of the citizen to keep the government from falling into error". – [U. S. Supreme Court in American Communications Association v. Douds, 339 U. S. 382, 442].

"If the state converts a liberty into a privilege the citizen can engage in the right with impunity". – Shuttlesworth v. Birmingham, 373 U. S. 262.

"The claim and exercise of a Constitutional right cannot be converted into a crime". Miller v. U.S., 230 F 2d 486, 489.

"Officers of the court have no immunity when violating a constitutional right, from liability, for they are deemed to know the law". – Owen v. Independence, 100 S. Ct. 1398.

By Law, if we can prove, and we can, that any Politician, Judge, Lawyer, (or any Political-Corporate-Whore) commits "Breach of Contract" or "Breach of Oath" any Law (I.E.; Statutes, Codes, Ordinances, Misdemeanors, or Federal Laws) are not enforceable against any American.

"Unlawful search and seizure. Your Rights must be interpreted in favor of the Citizen". – Byers v. U.S., 273 U.S. 28.

"This court is to protect against any encroachment of constitutionally secured liberty". – Boyd v. U.S., 116 U.S. 616.

"No state shall convert a liberty into a privilege; license it, and attach a fee to it." – Murdock v. Penn., 318 U.S. 105.

"Where rights secured by the Constitution are involved, there can be no rule (law) making legislation which would abrogate (abolish) them". – Miranda v. Arizona, 384 U.S. 436.

"An unconstitutional act is no law; it imposes no duties; affords not protection; it creates no office; it is illegal contemplation, as inoperative though it had never been passed". – Norton v. Shelby County, 118 U. S. 425.

"The Constitution of these United States is the supreme law of the land. Any law that is repugnant to the constitution is null and void of law". – Marbury v. Madison, 5 U. S. 137.

These cases are actual facts that have been adjudicated by Judges and Court Officers (under "Oath of Office" – a contract) in favor of the American [citizen], not the undeclared-Foreign-Fictitious-Political-Corporate-Whores.

With this being said, back to the 'Oath of Office':

The 'Oath of Office' is a "Legal-Lawful-Binding-Contract" entered into with Americans. What can America or an American do if they 'prove' "Breach of Contract" of the '" Oath of Office"? According to the Federal Ethics Committee (there are two – one for the House of Representatives and one for the Senate each has six (6) members); by the way, they too are under an "Oath of Office". A breach of 'Oath' (a contract) is an impeachable offense.

"Impeach"; "To proceed against a Public Officer, a criminal proceeding against a public officer, before a quasi-political court, instituted by a written accusation called "Articles of Impeachment" the formal written allegation of the causes for impeachment, answering the same purpose as an indictment." Black's Law Dict., 6th Ed., Pg. 753.

The Impeachment process does not include added charges that arise out of a "Breach of Office", such as: High-Treason, Organized Crime

Activities under the R.I.C.O. Laws (Racketeer Influenced and Corrupt Organizations Laws), Obstruction of Justice, Fraud upon the Court, Fraud from the Bench and Terrorism.

In addition to the above stated charges, Americans can also include: Insider Trading, Money Laundering, Civil Rights Violations and Torts. Here a Tort is; "A legal wrong committed upon the person or property independent of contract (but with a contract in place…it is even better!). It may be 1) A direct invasion of some legal right of the individual; 2) the infraction of some public duty by which special damage accrues to the individual".

Then there is Constitutional Tort: "Federal statute providing that every person who under color of any statute, ordinance, regulation, custom, or usage, of any state or territory, subjects, or causes to be subjected, any citizen of the United States or any other person within the jurisdiction thereof to the deprivation of any rights, privileges, or immunities secured by the Constitution and law, shall be held liable to the party injured in an action at law, suit in equity, *or other proper proceedings for redress. Black's Law Dict., 6th Ed., pg. 1489. Please note the 'italic-under-lined-statement': "or other proper proceedings for redress"; such as a Lien filed against a Subsidiary of the United-States-Corporate-Government-Subsidiary-State-of-California.

What might be "other proper proceeding for redress"? Why a Private International Administrative Remedy Process… Tort Claim! Where the 'tort-feasor' agrees to and with the monetary damages because he/she stipulates and agrees that he/she violate their 'Oath of Office' in regards to his/her dealings with you, the victim, outside of his/her jurisdiction!

Furthermore, If you, the reader was/were/ or are not aware, it is understood that if a Public/Civil Servant (Political-Corporate-Whore) is Sued three times or, liened three times (via a tort claim) and possible receives three complaint letters, he/she becomes a liability to the 'insurer', who underwrites their "Performance Bond", their bond is cancelled and the Public/Civil Servant (Political Corporate Whore) is Fired! Along with the importance of the "Oath of Office", if the Public/Civil Servant does not have a 'Performance Bond' on file, they do not and cannot fill the office of that position of their employment.

The following is a simple example of "Breach of Contract" by Public/Civil Servants of their "Oath" for the proof of a pattern for the R.I.C.O. Laws.

You are stopped by police (public/civil servant) for whatever violation. The Police Officer instructs you to produce a License, Registration and Proof of Insurance (which are also contracts).

However, we will use the "Speeding Violation" for our purpose in establishing and exposing a "Breach of Contract" of the "Oath of Office".

The Police Officer, (Public/Civil Servant) for the Corporate Government, uses a device that "measures your vehicle speed" by the use of "radar", a known cancer-causing machine. Now, realistically that machine can be "out of calibration" and can give a 'False-reading'. In addition, Police Officers are NOT professionals when it comes to using these machines. However, when the police give you the "ticket" (a.k.a. Bill of Attainder or Bill of Pain and Punishment) the information from the machine is applied as an 'opinion' to the ticket, not fact.

The reason the information applied to the ticket is an "opinion" is because the machine is not perfect and neither is the Public/Civil Servant. Furthermore, it is known as 'second hand information' which is not allowable in a court of law by their "Rule of Law". Courts by law, are supposed to try "Facts" not "Opinion". Remember, Public/Civil Servants, Bureaucrats, Politicians, Judges and Lawyers are under-contract of their own free-will and they cannot claim "ignorance of the Law" ...no excuse.

Note: Courts today are not 'Constitutional courts', due to the United States Bankruptcy, but are 'Administrative Tribunals'! These tribunals are now involved with Civil Right Violations in addition to these Foreign-Fictitious-Political-Corporate-Whores in violation of their "Oath of Office". (See: "The county court is no longer a constitutional court": Fehl vs. Jackson County, in re Will of Pittock, 102 OR. 159, 199 P., 2020 P. 216, 17 A.L.R. 218).

You are given the ticket and you have a choice: 1) Pay the fine and accept the inevitable punishments (yes more than one). 2) A court date for the opposition and denouncement of the ticket.

The second choice is where you establish a chain of evidence for "Breach of Contract" or 'Breach of Oath of Office' and all of the perpetrators that are involved. Starting with the Public/Civil Servant known as police.

The 'ticket' (in reality also known as a Bill of Attainder or Bill of Pain and Punishment) is turned into an instrument that will demand that you pay monies for an infraction/crime you may or may not have committed. As you stand before the Judge (in reality a Foreign Banker), he/she will call your name from the bench and establish you as a 'corporate-entity' under their venue {which turns out to be Maritime/Equity/Admiralty Jurisdiction} (their sphere of control); (meaning-look at the flag behind the Judge…is it red, white and blue? Or does it have a 'gold-fringe around it'?) (This is further evidence that you have been 'forced' into a "Foreign-Tribunal-Corporate-Court"; operated by Political-Corporate-Whores of a 'Foreign-Jurisdiction'). If by chance you try to correct the Judge and the court, by claiming yourself a "living-entity" the Judge and their Court will threaten you with "Contempt of Court". This is, by definition, an act of Terrorism and a "Breach of Contract". Furthermore, the Judge instructs the Court Stenographer (also under "Oath of Office" or Bailiff (Public/Civil Servant: Law Enforcement – also under the same "Oath of Office); "falsify-court-documents" by claiming that you are a "no-show". This is a blatant "Breach of Contract" or "Breach of Oath of Office" with accomplices and witnesses. Furthermore, you can establish "Fraud upon the Court" and "Fraud from the Bench." However, the least common denominator within this procedure is actually "Breach of Contract" and violation of the "Oath of Office", with witnesses. Although keep in mind they will become "hostile witnesses" …They do not like to be caught and will primarily do anything to protect the continuous deception, lie, deniability or whatever excuse just to protect themselves. These self-proclaimed professionals do NOT have license to "victimize anyone in any way shape or form and call it business".

Note: The public/civil servant (Governor, Motor Vehicle Director, Police Officer) have violated their "Oath of Office" in tricking you by misapplication of statutes to obtain a "driver license', as the Motor Vehicle Code only regulates 'commerce upon the highways', hauling people or freight for hire. The State(s) do not make available "Non-commercial Driver Licenses"! So by the police 'Officer' issuing a ticket/citation, he/she are in violation of their "Oath of Office", as you are not subject to the motor vehicle code as your right to travel in your conveyance without a license is a "Constitutional Right", as supported by The Bill of Rights and by Court cases, and the public/civil servant and/or police officer took an oath to uphold and protect the Constitution (a Federal Contract), that your Rights flowing from your Creator to the Constitutions (Federal/State) to state statutes must not be liened, (Unalienable!), in any manner.

From this point forward, we have established a chain of Evidence and Proof (Fact not Opinion) for the "Breach of Contract" (Breach of Oath of Office) and Organized Crime Activities under the R.I.C.O. Laws.

Another important example for the support of the "Breach of Contract" and "Violations of the "Oath of Office" is as follows: "...uphold, protect and defend the Constitution." (This is a Federal Contract) (the SUPREME LAW!). Then why have the Political-Corporate-Whores all violate Article I, Section X of the U.S. Constitution, U.S. Bankruptcy not withstanding? No State shall; ...make any Thing but gold and silver Coin a Tender in Payment of Debts..." However, in truth and Facts those same Political-Corporate-Whores have certainly breached this one and they continue to violate it every day... to your detriment!

In reality the UNITED STATES Corporate-Government INC. is forcing you as an American-Civilian to commit a "Felonious Crime". Through their Practices and Procedures, you are forced to accept their form of payment (U. S. D. Federal-Reserve-Notes) for whatever debts you incur. We all know that "Federal Reserve Notes" are nothing but paper and have no "real" equity involved. But they have to keep you in their "jurisdiction" because of the contract you signed as an infant...remember! Your foot Print! This includes the ignorance of your Birth-Parents...most of them did not know either.

If you were to ask any Political-Corporate-Whore (Politicians, Judges, Lawyers, Bureaucrats or Public/Civil-Servant) if the Laws apply to them, their answer is as follows: "We are not above the Law". If this statement is true made by those corporate personnel in all (50) Fifty States, then as Americans and a "society" it is our Duty to apply those

Laws they are not above, and have those Foreign-Fictitious-Political-Corporate-Whores held accountable for the crimes they have committed…such as Misapplication of Statutes, Fraud, Fraud by Scienter, and many others, because of the very fact they all have violated the very root of their contract…The "Oath of Office".

However, in reality ask yourself this question…What Court, within the (50) Fifty Corporate-States-INC. run by Foreign-Fictitious-Political-Corporate-Whores is going to adjudicate any crimes brought against anyone of them for "Breach of Oath of Office" or "Breach of Contract"?

The only charge we, as American Civilians, can apply against these Corrupt-Individuals has to start with "Breach of Contract". When that charge is proven (and NOT through their controlled courts) we can apply any other charges that may apply, since they lose 'immunity', 'authority', and 'jurisdiction' from prosecution. This is why these so-called professionals believe they are above the laws.

If any concerned-American writes a letter to their House Representative or Senator about any of these crimes committed against the Politicians or Judicial sector the response usually consists of a "computer-generated response" claiming "We cannot get involved". If you think about this response, you will realize that those responses create a connection and a chain of evidence for the continued "Breach of Contract" and "Organized Crime Activities" making them accomplices. Remember, the House of Representatives and the Senators are required "by Law" to take the "Oath or Affirmation" and will support the Constitution of the United States and the State they are seeking to represent. The "Oath or Affirmation" is a Federal Contract not just at State level. So when a Senator or U. S. Representative claims that they can't get involved in a situation because it is not in their "jurisdiction" they automatically become accomplices to the Organized Crime Activities…This is the connection for "Breach of Contract" and sets the pattern for R. I. C. O. Charges.

By Law, if we Americans civilians can prove, and we can, (the Foreign-Fictitious-Political-Corporate-Whores do not have a monopoly on intelligence); that there is a "Breach of Contract" or "Breach of Oath" any Law (i.e.; Statutes, Codes, Ordinances, Misdemeanors, or Federal Laws) are not enforceable against any American-Civilian. This means, any Individual Political-Corporate-Whore that is in violation of their "Oath of Office" or "Breach of Contract" loses any and all authority within that office or over you or any other American-Civilian.

How can any Judge adjudicate any case when they themselves know that they are in "Breach of Contract" of their "Oath of Office" and sitting on the bench as a criminal? Under these circumstances American-Civilians have an extremely difficult time in winning in any U. S. Court System within any of its (50) Fifty subsidiaries of the Foreign-United-States-Corporate-Government.

Most Americans, unfortunately, have become complacent and accept the illegal practices committed against them. However, as it stands the courts and Political officers have an abundant list of charges that they can apply against their victims hoping for any, if not all charges, will "stick". As Americans, in our defense, we can only apply one particular charge against them and show irrefutable-evidence of their guilt.

Any and all added charges can be applied when the "Breach of Contract" of the "Oath of Office" has been established. Here, we see a "Tortious (act), defined as; "...tortious is used throughout the Restatement, Second, Torts, to denote the fact that conduct whether of act or omission is of such a character as to subject the actor (the Political-Corporate-Whores both Federal and State and Public/civil servants) to liability, under the principles of the law of torts". Black's Law Dict. 6th Ed., pg. 1489.

What about our/your 'sovereignty, as bestowed by our Creator, and wherein all the American Court (that have ruled on the facts of the matter) has stated in general that "the American people are the sovereign authority"! This means that every 'Oath Taker' from the CEO of U.S., Inc. to Congressmen, Officers of Homeland Security, CIA, FBI, Governors, all State Officers, all County Officers, and all City/Municipal Officers, all of them, by and through their "Oath of Office" are to uphold, defend and protect... our collective and individual sovereignty...within our American form of so-called Corporate-Government.

However, they don't recognize our "Rights" through the Bill of Rights or the fact that in truth we, the People, are the "True-Government"; NOT THE UNDECLARED-FOREIGN-FICTITIOUS-POLITICAL-

CORPORATE-WHORES. In truth American-civilians have accepted the lie; they have bitten into the poisoned apple of 'progressive-democracy' also known as communism to come against and attack the American-Civilian People and labeling them as "sovereign-citizen-terrorists". This is an oxy-moron if there was ever one. Here again, they all have and are violating their 'Oath of Office' and have and are committing the crimes herein mentioned.

"It's easier to fool people than to convince them that they have been fooled." Mark Twain.

The "Police State", as developed here in America, prostituted by elected quasi-government 'Oath Takers', ignorant of the Rights and status of the people, or by design, to subjugate the people away from their rightful position to mere 'subjects' without recognition of "God-given Rights", sovereignty, property rights, all other Rights, enforced and protected in our supposed "Home of the Free and Land of the Brave", makes all of the "Oath Takers", as mentioned within this chapter…all CRIMINALS, IN VIOLATION OF THEIR OATH(S) by "Breach of Contract" and knowingly-guilty of High-Treason, Organized Crime Activities under the R.I.C.O. Laws (Racketeer Influenced and Corrupt Organizations Laws), Obstruction of Justice, followed by other multiple crimes against the Constitution and upon the people they are supposed to serve…Not their bank accounts.

So, ask yourself this question, why would you want to interact with them, or do any kind of business with them? All the while, yes, we as American-Civilians, have the right and a duty to hold the Politicians, Judges, Lawyers, Bureaucrats, and Public/Civil Servants (also known in plain English as: Political-Corporate-Whores) accountable for the Contracts that they Breach, but all of them are the 'criminal', they are the true "TERRORISTS"! As the Bible states, "Ye shall know them by their fruit"!

All (50) Fifty subsidiaries of the UNITED STATES Corporate-Government Inc. have applied a program known as P.E.R.S. (Public Employee Retirement System) or something of the equivalent for each individual State-subsidiary by their Charter or State Seal. The Corporate Public Employee is under a Monopoly and is a conflict of Interest against all accused (victims). They receive benefits in fines, fees, taxes, revenue and jail time served.

The Problem with an "Impeachment-Process" is an in-house matter in their "Quasi-Political" Chamber(s), where we can continue to observe them too continue the criminal acts. They, in reality will continue to claim "they are innocent and are just doing their jobs; nothing personal." This is one of the most misleading lies they can ever repeat for their supposed "defense".

But on the alternative, we might also consider that if any (Political-Corporate-Whore) Public/Civil Servant by and through the violation of their "Oath of Office", against any one 'American', wherein such criminal act(s) done is recognized as "High-Treason, Organized Crime Activities under the R.I.C.O. (Racketeer Influenced and Corrupt Organizations Laws), Obstruction of Justice", crime(s) against their Constitution and otherwise to be discovered, then the one so injured can, other than a law-suit or utilizing a 'Tort Claim', can 'NOTICE' that Officer/Department, Office, etc., by certified mail that"…in violation of his/her "Oath of Office", as detailed by the Private Man/Tort Claimant of the deprivation of any rights, privileges, or immunities secured by the Constitution and law and crimes committed, i.e.; High Treason, Organized Crime Activities under the R.I.C.O. Laws (Racketeer Influenced and Corrupt Organizations Laws), and Obstruction of Justice, demands that you and your office, superiors and otherwise cease and desist from further dealings, contact, communication(s) or otherwise with me or to me, otherwise, if you do, each of you, whomever, agree that any such contract or communication with or to me, you agree to pay my fee of $25,000.00 U.S.D. per contact/communication per capita/head/officer, waiver of tort not with-standing and with all Rights Reserved and Preserved".

This chapter gives you the reader something to think about, as your Creator/God-given Rights, as recognized in the Declaration of Independence, Bill of Rights and the United States Constitution, are yours; they ARE valuable! If not accepted, protected, and exercised…then one day soon you may wake-up and find they have been taken from you, though illegally, none the less… taken… and history may have to be repeated in taking them back, if at all possible, at that time. So, it is imperative to take action now before it gets worse.

Furthermore, the Government, as it stands at this time in our history, is nothing more than a Nom Deguerre (a fictitious "entity"). In truth which government exists? Is it the Government "for the People by the People"? Or is it a Corporate-Government run by "Policy and Procedure" where we American Civilians have no chance of defending ourselves from blatant lies brought or levied against us?

There is a way to go after these self-proclaimed "professionals" by using the same laws they claim they are "not above".

"We the People" can hold their feet to the fire by Filing-Charges of "Breach of Contract" or by placing a 'Lien' against those perpetrators for all injuries incurred. This is the one-charge that is provable, precise, and they will have to answer the charges. However, this type of case cannot be "heard" or "Tried" within the United States Corporate Government as all Judges, Lawyers and Court Bureaucrats are part of the crimes being committed against all American civilians. This type of case can be filed with the International Hague Courts under the heading "Crimes against Humanity", as a 'Class Action Suit' with added charges of acts of "WAR CRIMES against AMERICAN CIVILIANS".

As a Corporation, The United States (a corporate government) has and continues to commit heinous crimes through their "judicial-process" against American Civilians. The "judicial officers" claim that they process and Try "Facts" on all cases and that all cases are completely different. This is the first notable "perjury" (LIE) the Officers of the Courts tell their victims. First of all, the "subject-matter may be different" in each individual case, the presentation before their court system is the same…they operate under Admiralty/Equity/Maritime Jurisdiction.

The UNITED STATES INC. Court system, as now operated, is UN-Constitutional. Supreme Court Judges and most Court Judges do not take the constitutionally "required" Oath of Office. These judges commit high crimes and misdemeanors, HIGH-TREASON, R. I. C. O. (Organized Crime Practices), Violation of Sherman Anti-Trust Act (they are a MONOPOLY). Biased, Prejudiced, Union Bar Attorney Judge operates under the law known only to Attorneys and Judges. The Judges and all the court officers that do not swear an "Oath of Office" are not only in "Breach of Contract" but can be brought up on added charges of "Impersonating a Government Official".

The "Court Officers" are already in violation and "Breach of Contract" (under the Oath of Office) within their first-case. This is how… 1. NO-full disclosures, 2. Of "Bondage" Contract, 3. of "Birth Certificate", 4. Of "Social Security", 5. Of "Driver's License". These contracts alone disqualify any and all Judges and Attorneys from representing any case in their "judicial system'. Their attitude is this: "Please, come into our Babylonian Court. We want your Labor, Liberty, Property, and Authority over you. We want more fines, taxes, fees, revenue; or we will put you in jail".

Furthermore, to which "Contract" does the Politicians, Judges, Attorneys or any Bureaucrat take the "Oath of Office" for? We all know that there are at least 2 Constitutions that were written in 1700's 1. Is used for the development of the government "For the People and by the people". The other was to keep American-Civilians ignorant and confused just so they can "screw-everybody-over" within their 'authority or jurisdiction' to help fatten their bank accounts or defend the "King's-Money".

We are going to start off with the one-contract that everyone seems to be in agreement with…the "CONSTITUTION" …it is a "CONTRACT" – a majority of the Politicians, Judges and Attorneys agree that "the Constitution is a contract" …more-over we will point out the "Oath/Affirmation" of Office before any politician can assume the Office, he/she was elected for. This includes Judges, Attorneys, Police, basically any and all Public-Officials – City, County, State and Federal, Incs.

A contract is a two-way street…just like trust. We trust those we elect into office to do the right thing and not concentrate on their personal pocket books or Re-election funds or false-persecution, prosecution, false-statements in general, or false-swearing etc., etc.… by BREACH OF CONTRACT.

The "CONSTITUTION" and the ten (10) Amendments: (the Amendments also known as the Bill of Rights are part of the "Constitution") … a "CONTRACT".

But everyone is looking for the so-called "silver-bullet" or "sword" to put a stop to the Criminal actions against American Civilians from those that "claim" superior knowledge...because of a higher education?... "Polly-Parrot" strikes again. This is why "LADY-JUSTICE" is blind-folded...and yet carries a scale to weigh the FACTS and TRUTH against "untruth". What we mean by "Polly-Parrot" is that the Undeclared-Foreign-Fictitious-Corporate-Impersonators that claim they are United-States-Corporate-Government-Agents with authority to do what they want anytime they want is nothing but a repeat of what they were instructed to say to try and convince their victims that they are in the right.

However, let's start with the definition of the word "Contract". The definition is extensive and can be found in "Black's Law Dictionary".

The Definition of the words "Contract Law" is as follows: "The body of law that governs oral and written agreements associated with exchange of goods and services, money, and properties. It includes topics such as the nature of contractual obligations, limitation of actions, freedom of contract, privity of contract, termination of contract, and covers also agency relationships, commercial paper, and contracts of employment".

The "Oath of Office" or Affirmation of Office is one that is an Oral and Written Contract for Americans. The Oath of Office is as follows: "I, (Official states name here), having been elected to the office of (insert office-title), (District, Division and State), do solemnly swear that I will defend the Constitution of the United States and the Constitution and Laws of the State of (insert name of State), and that I will faithfully and impartially discharge the duties of said office to the best of my ability".

The "Oath of Office" is subscribed, sworn and autographed before a District Judge, Secretary of State, or State Attorney General who act as witness for this contract then they too autograph the "Oath of Office/Affirmation as a 'Witness'.

Remember, these 'people' are supposedly "Highly-Educated" and graduates of prestigious Colleges or Universities. This is why I call them "Polly-Parrots" because they are not learning something new under Law or Political Sciences (which is just a joke) ... they are just repeating the same old information and not adding any new thoughts or approaches for any of the problems facing American-Civilians or U. S. Citizens. In other words, they keep compounding the same mistakes over and over...not unlike the Medical field, Physics, Astral Physics or even Computer Science where those fields are making new discoveries and actually finding something new on a daily basis whether it is good, bad or indifferent.

However, back to our discussion about "Breach of Contract" otherwise known as the "golden-key".

Let's say you as the reader of this article are under many contracts…and you are! The first contract your parents autograph is your "Birth-Certificate". However, you also as a first-born-infant sign as well… your "foot-print" with a number attached to be used by the Corporate Government to be levied in and used through their Banking system.

The next contract you and your parents Autograph is the "Social Security" (aka. Tax Identification Number) which in reality is a "Corporate" number that identifies you 'personally' used for employment purposes, yet another number. In this example, you have been attached to a 9-digit number for the Social Security for work "Privileges".

The next contract you autograph for is the "Driver's License or Identification card". The driver' license is, if you noticed, all in capital letters making you into a mini-corporation known as a Nom Daguerre (a fiction); with yet another set of numbers. My point in using the above contracts is this…if we, as American-Civilians, have to abide by or conform with or even accept this type of business practice (these contracts are established by the Uniform Commercial Codes…and are another form of contract including, oral, written or implied etc. etc.) then so does the Senate, Judicial and Executive branch and employees of the Government. But if you have noticed the Government Officials have considered themselves above the law through their actions and claim they can do anything they want legally or not.

However, the "magic-key happens to be "BREACH OF CONTRACT". This applies to ALL bureaucrats and their so-called security-departments including all of the police force across our nation.

Let's use "FRAUD UPON THE COURT" as a prime example…because most American-Civilians do not seem to understand how the courts work or how a (banker) Judge adjudicates or come to the decisions they do on any case in front of them. In addition, most of the cases that are adjudicated by the court officer or judge is by "opinion" not fact. By the way, all court officers…from the judges, lawyers, stenographer, and bailiffs/sheriffs are under "contract". They are under a "sworn oath of office" …once again by the "Constitution". Now there seems to be some misunderstanding about the Constitution…It does not apply to individual Americans…but it does set limitations to what the Corporate-Government, Inc. can do to Americans. With that said, the one contract that was added to the Constitution is called the first Ten Amendments as we know them as our Civil Rights and is commonly referred to as "The Bill of Rights". NOT A BILL OF PRIVILEDGES!

If the Courts or any of its officers or any Politician under a sworn oath or Affirmation of Office violate your "Rights" that particular Court District, City, County, State or Federal Agency loses all jurisdiction, control and authority of the case under "Breach of Contract". Remember, the Oath of Office is a contract.

I contacted the State of South Dakota, State Attorney General, Marty Jackley and his staff and asked his department a simple generic question… "Are any contracts (such as: Verbal, Implied, written, treaties, compacts, etc. etc.) enforceable if either party Breaches the contract or covenant"? The second part that question is as follows: Would this apply for-living "persons" as well as Business and Corporations alike"?

First let me say that I am withholding the actual name of the individual from the State Attorney General's Office (which was an attorney) that gave this ludicrous-insidious answer…"The question you asked is a legal question. You will have to ask an attorney" …lol! To my surprise I thought I was speaking to an Attorney, I mean he claimed to be an Attorney with the State Attorney General's Office. This is a prime-example of "Polly-Parrot".

However, this is my interpretation, my answer or opinion, as far as my understanding about 'Breach of Contract" …All contracts become "null and void" and unenforceable if either party Breaches it. This means you cannot be punished for a crime or breach if you can prove that any Agency/Government Agent is in breach. We may not win monetary-compensation through their controlled courts…but we will win the point of argument or contention. In easy terms, the corporate government loses what little "authority" and "jurisdiction" they think they have over us. This is why the Court Officers use "Threats, Duress, and Coercion, Collusion, Subterfuge and Subjugation" against their victims.

For example, your car insurance, life insurance, or any type of insurance or contract you autograph will become "null and void" if you stop paying the premiums, Right? The same thing works for the Politicians and all Government Officials...but they do not want you to know this...after all they believe they are doing a "good job" ... which amounts to being just Bull-Shit!

The court system itself is geared to separate you from your hard-earned money that does not belong to you and split it between the court officers...the judge being the chief officer; and in some cases, the judge is acting as a banker representing those who are "embezzling and extorting" monies from innocent individual victims.

The key with "Fraud upon the Court" is the simplicity of the matter when you have identified that the opposing party has "purchased-injustice" by buying out the officers of the court. The "Attorney of Record" ...the one you pay exorbitant fees for to represent you..."works in concert" and is instrumental in the "Law and Motion Waltz" ultimately withholding critical "Material Evidence" from being admitted on your behalf.

"Please note: Fraud Upon the Court is fraud which is directed at the judicial machinery itself. It is not fraud between parties or documents, false statements or perjury".

Fraud upon the Court is commonly associated with "Extrinsic Fraud". It deals directly in withholding information by "Omissions". It is a specific form of fraud that allows the "Attorney of Record" (your attorney) to use "Attorney Client Privilege", "Excusable Negligence", "Plausible Deniability", and "Omission" for critical facts that would allow the aggrieved party no-means the establishment for a "Cause of Action". Furthermore, extrinsic fraud is typically accompanied by "Demurrers, Motion for Summary Judgement" and other means of avoiding "Discovery" that regards the "Gravamen of the Complaint". The result for the solution for the aggrieved party is usually a "Declaratory Judgement" without relief which is a proven means in accordance with the "Evidence Code".

The courts like to use this excuse when you lose…"Sorry! No Hard Feelings…but Business is Business". When a person enters the court and/or the court system they go through a wide-range of emotions. You have to remember, although it is difficult at the time, to keep your emotions in check…because the matter is not an emotional one…just strictly "business". You have to remove the emotional-ties and emotional-entanglements. You have to strictly adhere with the "Law and Motion Waltz" (which is nothing but a dog and pony show at a three-ring circus). However, we now know that we can turn-the-tables back on them so-to-speak. These self-proclaimed professionals within the court system will use any tactic and/or distraction to play on your emotions for the distraction away from the shear simplicity of a "Declaratory Judgement" in your behalf. Keeping your Gravamen of the Complaint in simplicity and related with the Controversy in question will help you establish a Cause of Action.

A Law and Motion Waltz, is a dog and pony show that is usually headed up by YOUR "Attorney of Record" (which in truth does not exist) for your benefit to make you think and believe he/she is doing a great job and is on your side. Here is the simple truth within this matter…when the courts suspect that you believe that they are fraudulent, the courts will set a "Trial" date and do what is called a "Law and Motion Dump". In reality, your attorney of record, whether he/she is the lead person or just following the judge's-instructions is working in concert, with the court and is putting a on a circus-show for "POMP and CIRCUMSTANCE". The Prosecution and/or the Defense Attorney would do the same under Pomp and Circumstance.

Your Attorney of Record was given the ability to act and speak on your behalf (by you!…A Contract! You autographed it.) Furthermore, you do not have a direct-voice within their court. This is the means that allows blood-money to be dissipated through the court wherein the officers of the court end up with a majority if not all of the blood-money and the party that committed the initial-fraud gets off by allowing the officers of the court to take what they want from the blood-money. Remember all Officers of the Court are working in concert. This means

ANY attorney you hire will most likely and certainly participate in Fraud upon the Court or the other officers of the court will ultimately report them to the State Bar for some sort of reason. Furthermore, and this is usually what happens, if the judge is "on the take" your attorney will ultimately side with the court and take a bribe as well. This is called... "Legal-Malpractice". This terminology is known as a misnomer and an OXY-MORON. The definition of "Legal" and "Malpractice" is defined within Black's law Dictionary. However, the terminology cannot be found-together for the definition. There is no such word within Black's law dictionary as "Legal-Malpractice". Both of these words are opposites (and no they do not attract). There is actually no-such word found in Black's Law Dictionary...individually yes...but not as two words placed together or as a compound-noun. The word "Legal-Malpractice" does not exist. If this is the case then Doctors, Physicians, Surgeons or even Nurses cannot be held responsible for their "Malpractice". The reason is because you "hold them blameless" for any mistake they make. However, through example we know that his is not entirely the truth.

In any event, if your attorney is not engaged against you then the reality of the situation is that the opposing counsel or attorney is engaged in "Malicious Prosecution". This is an attorney that uses their authority over a litigant directly engaged in actions that are directly targeted to hold the litigant in actions that would be the same as "Vexatious Litigation". One of the ways the attorneys like to cover-up their fraud is to commit more fraud in the hopes that they will place you in default. One reason is because the cycle becomes more pronounced and they fear that their "Bar-Card" (not a license) is at stake...This also includes the Judges "Bar-Card". However, be aware these so-called professionals will resort to "Entrapment" too cause more damages against you and your "case".

Furthermore, to inform you of how crooked this particular part of the government is...this is what they do to confuse you even more...they "Fabricate-Evidence" for the benefit on their illegal-actions over a long period of time with extensive litigations to hide any and all "Omissions." The court system is set up to deny the 'Facts' in the case that are clearly within your possession, withholding critical information through Omission and ultimately unleashing fraudulent and fabricated evidence during the trial; and the judge will simply admit this at the trial.

The "Omission of Evidence" during a trial is a fraud, not to mention the fact it is against the "Evidence Codes". As they conduct this fraud, they are careful not to present direct evidence that is fraudulent based on wanton Omission. However, they do not fabricate the evidence until the "Trial". Wherein the Material Misrepresentations and Inconsistent Declarations are made to focus on the efforts away from the wanton omissions. Now by their laws the "Statute of Frauds" and "Errors and Omissions" come into play.

But here is the explanation of "Plausible Deniability". The fact is when lawyers are engaged in "Fraud upon the Court" they are looking for a means of creating a "hook" that will cause your case to ultimately lose by omission of critical evidence. In this manner, your attorney has Plausible Deniability that the omission ever existed. Unfortunately, you have to prove that your attorney actually took direct "Acts" to hide the omissions from being produced/introduced into evidence. (However, by "Breach of Contract" we can.). By the time you figure out that you have been "Screwed" over by your own attorney, he/she is long gone from the case, the judge has dismissed him/her from the case because you stopped "paying" them, ran out of "money" or unable to continue to pay them. In self-defense, your attorney can and will directly state that there is a lack of evidence for the proof that they have omitted any facts intentionally. Furthermore, the opposing attorney and judge will cite that the issue was never raised by opposing counsel and therefore your attorney did not have any need to bring the matter into evidence or into the case. Therefore, Plausible Deniability is the key to finding this Omission and all the circumstances that relate to it.

Both Attorneys and the Officers of the court that are against their clients ultimately leave the clients without any admissible evidence, the matter is set for "Pre-Trial" where no further evidence is admissible and the client's own counsel admits to the court that they "informally" accept the evidence on behalf of their client. However, the client will no longer be able to communicate with his/her counsel about any of the evidence he/she accepted. The client is set for "TRIAL" with no means of admitting evidence for the pending trial and his/her own counsel has ultimately requested to be removed from the case. By these actions, there is no-chance of even having a "fair-trial" and the matter is not merely being able to admit evidence or object to any of the "Fraudulent-Evidence" that the opposing counsel will unleash on the court at the "Trial". The judge ultimately accepts any and all fraudulent evidence by the favored party and denies the defense against fraudulent "Allegations". Leaving the result that the judge does not need to "rule" on the merits of the case but rather on the "Admission and Objection" for the "Facts in Evidence", that will be used as the deciding factor of the case.

These are the "Basic Principles" that involve "Facts in Evidence, Conclusive Presumption, Material Misrepresentation and Plausible Deniability". There is a loop-hole: the loop-hole that directly causes most all Fraud upon the Court Cases to look alike is based on the attorney that relies on the basic principles of "Attorney Client Privilege, Excusable Neglect, and Plausible Deniability".

Within the Evidence Codes there is a presumption of what a "Reasonable Person" would infer from "Circumstantial Evidence". (Your attorney failed to explain any of this to you). In reviewing your case, it becomes obvious that all of the court officers "Work in Concert" to create a cloud of litigation that allows their opinion for "Plausible Deniability".

Within the Evidence Codes there is a presumption of what a "Reasonable Person" would infer from "Circumstantial Evidence". (Your attorney failed to explain any of this to you). In reviewing your case, it becomes obvious that all of the court officers "Work in Concert" to create a cloud of litigation that allows their opinion for "Plausible Deniability".

Furthermore, to make matters even worse and confusing the Court Officers "Mirror your claims to confuse the issue". When you state a claim, it will most likely be turned into a claim against you in order to confuse the issue. Unfortunately, this is a very common practice in Fraud upon the Court case. By them making outrageous claims against you it confuses the issue and it allows them to diffuse your claims you made against them. If you claim "Money Laundering" and "Embezzlement", they will make the same claims against you but with a twist…they will pile more outrageous charges against you, even if they do not have any evidence to back it up. Eventually you will have a claim for "Defamation of Character", Liable and Slander in a following-case because their claims are clearly unfounded and filed with malicious intent.

What most American Civilians or U. S. Citizens do not seem to understand is where is all the money coming from? Well, here it is in a nut-shell, it's called "Blood-Money" that fuels this particular type of Fraud upon the Court. It requires the opposing litigants who actually commit the Initial Fraud, Deceit, Material Misrepresentation, Inconsistent Declarations, Money Laundering, I. R. S. Fraud, Embezzlement, etc. etc. etc. against you has "Blood-Money" and that they cannot keep it unless the attorneys and the court are complicit (in total agreement) and working in concert to conceal the "Omissions", "Inconsistent Declarations and Material Misrepresentations". These will ultimately result in providing a "Plausible" story that will only be revealed within the "Trial".

The reality of hiring your own counsel will prove for "Fraudulent Evidence". Your own counsel will be directly involved in making sure that none of the evidence "you provide and are in possession of" that would prove your innocence is never provided for the court. Furthermore, your own counsel will informally advise the court that he/she accepted evidenced from the Opposing Counsel...however, that evidence will never be provided for you and that the so-called evidence against you cannot be contested. The Judge only needs to inform you that you should not have dismissed your counsel and that your prior counsel accepted the evidence on your behalf; even if your counsel quit or asked to be removed from your case.

The idea of the court system, the judges and the court officers, as it stands, is to have all of them working against you. This is called "Working in Concert". Any attempt for you to claim "conspiracy" is directly dismissed by the court. Any attempt for you to "admit-evidence" is directly dismissed by the court. Any attempt for you to expose the "Fraudulent-Evidence" that was presented as a (subterfuge tactic) as an ambush during the "trial" is directly accepted by the court without any qualification. By the "Judicial-Reality", the matter is set-up by the court and all of the officers within that court, to directly rule against you after the "trial" without objection. During the trial the court does not need to evaluate any "Cause of Action" against them since the "Fraudulent-Evidence" was accepted against you without objection. "How can you defend yourself against "Perjury" without evidence"? The judge does not need to rule on the case, all the court did was admit and deny "Material-Evidence".

The court officers working in concert create a "cloud of litigation" in order to hide the Fraud upon the Court. This is known as "Creating a Cloud of Litigation". They attempt to hide the fact that most, if not all, of what is happening is an attempt to hide a "Wanton Omission". They do this to create the "impression" that justice is being served within this "extensive-litigation" that is intended to give you the impression that your attorney is actually doing something to further your cause or case. "Believe it or not"! This is the farthest from the truth or facts.

In truth "your own counsel is harming your case". During this "Cloud of Litigation" your counsel is "instructed" either by the Judge or by the "Opposing Counsel" too "skew" the evidence, which proves your innocence, by hiding your evidence and not objecting to the fraudulent material misrepresentation brought against you. Your attorney will put on a show of "Pomp and Circumstance" much like a circus-parade before the main-event or show. What your attorney is doing at this time against you is called "sandbagging". Your counsel is merely following the instructions of opposing counsel and the court in compliance with any and all requests through "Law and Motion". In reality both counsel, are merely giving the impression that they are working hard and charging massive fees for the compliance with any and all requests that the court and opposing counsel are demanding. Your counsel will explain or inform you that your "account" is daunting and the requests are massive. Your counsel will further explain and inform you, that the ""Cloud of Litigation" will cause lots of problems for them and take up most of their time in the attempt for your defense". Your Counsel will then inform you that they need to be relieved as your counsel, unless you produce as much "payment" as possible and "bill your account" without creating a suspicion that they are merely depleting your resources prior to setting you up for the "Pretrial Dump". In truth, through their actions, your counsel is merely depleting your resource, making sure that none of your evidence is properly admitted for the court and also allows the opposing counsel to admit evidence that is completely fabricated. The reality of this is that both-counsels, (your counsel and the opposing counsel) are committing "Legal-Malpractice" and the court is complacent and complicit with the allowance of the parties to do so.

The "Blood-Money" that rightfully and ultimately belonging to you is being used against you and all of the "Officers of the Court" directly benefit at your expense. Your own counsel is doing most of the harm for your case as your attorney of record. They do the most harm since anything they do – on your behalf – will ultimately result in that action being recorded by the court as "your direct statement".

We have discussed both counsels (your counsel and the opposing counsel) but have not addressed the "Ring-Leader of the Circus" …the impersonating Judge (Banker). I understand that in life there is no-such thing as "absolutes". However, it is "absolutely" ridiculous to believe that the Judge (which is the ring-leader of this circus) is not on the take or even leading the "feeding-frenzy". Any "Reasonable-Person" that sees or even notices, just a glimpse of the depravity or subterfuge and sheer wicked behavior that results from this complete and utter debauchery of the "legal-system" would surely know that, by definition, this is "Fraud". The Judge has to sit through-a-complete two-years of this "Cloud of Litigation" that your counsel and the opposing counsel have created. The Judge has to maintain a great deal of avoidance in order to maintain "Plausible Deniability". The judge has to maintain as much distance from the matter or "subject-matter" as possible as the "feeding-frenzy" attacks the "struggling-swimmer". Keep in mind that both counsels (yours and the opposing) will gladly throw themselves at the "mercy" of the courts…lol! (What mercy?), in order to protect the judge. In turn the Judge will protect the attorneys if the matter is brought before the court or before the "State-Bar". When the Judge is involved in "Fraud upon the Court" they will focus the efforts on your counsel too lead the direction of the fraud. Many cases that involve "Fraud upon the Court" will have many counsel or attorneys that will represent your interests. They will come at you one after the other, those that take the case, but will intentionally cause more damage than they ANSWER. Because of this, the "Declaratory Judgement" without relief will allow your case to move forward for the resolution of the "Basic-Issue". If you attempt to find an "HONEST" counsel or attorney it will NOT prove fruitful. If you decide to be the "Pro-se-Litigant" the Judge will dismiss any and all pleadings you have strictly on the basis that you are not represented by "counsel of record" (which in truth does not exist). In addition, you as the moving-party do-not have a voice in their court. In this way the Judge is trying to "FORCE-YOU" to hire an attorney or counsel that they can coerce, threaten or use subterfuge into engage in their fraud.

Most of the cases that deal with "Fraud upon the Court" take advantage of the "lower-income" bracket of American-Civilians. It's like a school of sharks hunting for injured fish for an "easy-target". If you prove that you are NOT an easy target, they will leave you alone. However, remember they have been in this practice for some-time and this is not their first-feeding-frenzy. The reality is this, more than likely there is a "Class-Action" Lawsuit, in the works, if you are successful and it is not just you that would be suing them if this was exposed. It would be in their best interest to negotiate and NOT be exposed. If you know of any other victims that have been targets in their past endeavors it will help in providing substance and weight for your "Cause of Action" against the "feeding-frenzy" ...they are out there and you will find them. There are many cases where the "Feeding-frenzy" was exposed and the matter turns into a "Class-Action-Suit".

The goal of your counsel and the opposing counsel is to deplete your funds and resources before a trial. This is how the court-system-works by their ultimate-goal, (1). Your counsel stacks your evidence against you, (2). They deplete your funds, (3). They set your case for "Pre-Trial", (4). Then "Withdraw" as your counsel of record, (5). Then leave you penniless and Defenseless and Devoid of "Material-Evidence" before the "TRIAL" is set. Now here is the stinger, your counsel will, with most certainty, be generously compensated by the opposing counsel and the Judge for devastating your case at which time your counsel will "defame" you before the court and tell the court that you owe them a "balance that is unpaid". The Judge (the banker) and the court will, undoubtedly, view you and your case with "Contempt" before the trial is set. Every-one of your counsels, (that you have hired and involved within your-case) have completely devastated your case and is directly compensated from "Blood-Money" ...the funds that were stolen from you by the "Opposition".

The "Law and Motion Dump" defines a specific-procedure that results during the "Law and motion Waltz" when you discover that your counsel is leading the "Fraud upon the Court" against you. Your "counsel of record" knows full-well that they are liable for "Legal-Malpractice" if you should discover that they are acting against your interests. At this point, the "feeding-frenzy" is simply waiting for the matter to go before the "Pretrial". This allows your counsel to petition the court and withdraw

400

on the basis that you are not willing to pay "exorbitant" fees for the continuation of their representation of the misrepresentation for your case for the "TRIAL" that they set-up. If your counsel is not willing to help you during the case, why would they be any better during a trial?

With so much information being brought against you and your case, "finding a resolution" may not be simple. In reality, you have to understand how to identify and understand the "Gravamen of the Complaint", "Establish a Cause of Action" and prepare a "Declaratory-Judgement".

An "Appeal" is not appropriate since the case is not riddled with technical-errors but rather with "Intentional-Fraud". In "Fraud upon the Court" the matter is much more related to "Extrinsic-Fraud" and your petition would directly bring the action back in on the findings for the "material-facts". The "Statute of Frauds" defines that in the event of "fraud" the Statute of Limitations, "Collateral Estoppel" and "Res Judicata" do-not apply. The subject-matter or the "MATTER" can be re-dressed and/or addressed within a "new-petition" well after the normal "Statutes of Limitations" are long expired. The finding of the "Omissions" that were adamantly and intentionally withheld due for fraud becomes the way to bring back the "Subject-matter" or "Matter" back in on a new petition.

If you are an "injured-fish" you would never be able to define an "Architectural-Blueprint" that could and would resolve your case. The "architectural-blueprint" in your case is called the "Factual and Procedural History" and the "Memorandum and Points of Authorities". However, trying to find an "honest" counsel that will help in the exposure of a Judge, Prominent Businessmen and their Corrupt Counsels will be futile. After all, there are Judges and Counsels that have been arrested, disbarred and held in prison for NOT playing the game (lose term) that a majority of the courts are playing. I agree - none of this is a game. However, they need to be stopped and exposed once and for all.

If you choose to take the chance to represent your-self within a case through their courts, you need to at-least find a counselor that will agree with a "Limited-Scope of Representation" with a viable option for a "Declaratory-Judgement". If your counselor is willing to guide you as a "Pro se Litigant" They will help you create your "architectural plan" by

"Establishing Your Cause of Action" for the exposure of the "Omission" through a "Declaratory Judgement" or through a "Motion for Summary of Judgement"; that is related directly with the "Gravamen of the Complaint". If you come before a judge that is "corrupt", your counsel – no matter how honest – you may think they are will have no-choice but to "Throw you under a bus" in other words "sandbag" you. If you have a truly-honest-counsel they will not take the case directly as an "Attorney of Record" and will help guide your case through solving the "Gravamen". It would literally be "political-suicide" for a counselor or an attorney that has a State-Bar (not a license) too take on a litigant, if you are able to gain a "Declaratory-Judgement" that regards your "Gravamen", you will have re-solved approximately 80% of your case. At this time the "honest-Attorney" will be safe to take the "SIMPLE" part of the case. They will look at your "Factual and Procedural History" and help in making improvements. However, if the so-called "Honest-Attorney" merely looks at the "Factual and Procedural History" and tells you that it will not work, never explains to you why, and/or does not provide an alternate route, then beware. All that the counselor wants to do is to play the "Law and Motion Waltz" and throw you under the bus or once again "Sandbag you" and your case.

As you approach this problem, based on the aforementioned circumstances, you find yourself in a situation similar to the one "David" found himself in when he faced an expert-warrior "Goliath" with an undefeated mighty army behind him. However, the "Omission" and the "Gravamen of the Complaint" becomes your "Stone" that ultimately defeated Goliath. You need a "Declaratory Judgement" on your very issue and you will be home-free and your case becomes 80% resolved. However, you may have to resolve the gravamen on your own because you will be unable to find an Honest Counsel that will take on the case. Beware of those that claim that they are "Honest Counsels" and merely does the "Law and Motion Waltz". If you act as your own counsel known as a "Pro Se Litigant" (Oh! By the way…most judges will scoff and add their personal slur against you because you, in reality, know more about your case (Gravamen) than a counsel does) and you understand the art of "Negotiation", you can most likely resolve the "Gravamen". You will have to maintain an offensive strategy through a barrage of litigation thrown against you by multiple sources attempting to create a cloud of litigation that ultimately is intended to discourage you and distract the court from the Omission and the gravamen that you are attempting to resolve. Furthermore, if there is a possibility of a class action lawsuit, it may be prudent to couple up with another "victim" that was the prior subject or current subject for the courts feeding frenzy. Remember this is not the first time for a feeding frenzy. Once the "sharks get a taste for blood they seem to be compelled to repeat the process" whenever another struggling swimmer comes within their cites. You have to be able to prove that you have the direct ability for the litigation for the gravamen and the "Sharks" will take you seriously.

The last step within this part of the article consists of a "Declaratory Judgement". In truth your case is a "blind intersection" because you cannot see the solution due to the "Errors and Omissions" created by your counsel. However, a "Limited Scope of Representation" is a possible solution for moving forward. The only way for you to recover from "Fraud upon the Court", if you are the "Pro Se Litigant" is to get a "Declaratory Judgement" that relate with your "Gravamen of the Complaint". In many cases you can bring "Facts in Evidence" from your discovery through "Errors and Omissions".

This article appears in the 'American's Bulletin' Volume 44 Issue 09/10 to show just how "Unprofessional", "Opportunistic", and "Nasty" the Court and their Officers are in reality. However, there is one other way to get this part of the government off your-back. Remember, every Judge, Attorney (counsel), Bailiff/Sheriff, Stenographer…ALL Court Officers are supposed to have an "Oath of Office" or "Affirmation". ANY "Breach of Contract", which includes and is not, limited to "CIVIL RIGHT" violations – remember the "Bill of Rights" are part of the "Constitution" which is a "CONTRACT" with Americans – these individuals, including the Politicians and any and ALL Corporate Government employees loose the "protection of the government" such as the loss of "Immunity from subject matter", "Immunity from prosecution", Charges-levied against them "Under Breach of Contract", "Authority" and "Jurisdiction" that they think they have against you. In other words, these so-called highly-educated professionals loose what domination they have over you through illegal-practices against you and through "Breach of Contract".

In conclusion, if All American-Civilians were to file a "Notice" or "Put them on Notice" against these Highly-Educated(?) Professional Individuals you may want to consider adding "Breach of Contract" within you Gravamen (Complaint). After all the "Bill of Rights" is/are-our Laws that will put them in check once and for all and are part of the "Constitution-Contract" sworn, autographed and witnessed by those that were elected.

As a Corporation, THE/The/the United States (a corporate government) has and will continue to commit heinous crimes through their "judicial process" against Americans Native/Nationals/Citizens/Civilians. The "judicial process" claims that they process and Try "Facts" on all cases and that all cases are completely different. This is the first notable "Perjury" the Officers of the Courts tell their victims. First of all, the "subject-matter may be different" in each individual case, but the presentation and the 'Rules' they apply before their court system is the same…they operate under Admiralty/Equity/Maritime Jurisdiction (in other words they want the money). In truth it is their burden to produce any and all Contracts against the opposition within the 'subject-matter'.

The UNITED-STATES-CORPORATE-GOVERNMENT, INC. Court system, as now operated, is UN-Constitutional. Supreme Court Judges and most Court Judges do not take the constitutionally "required" Oath of Office. These judges commit high crimes and misdemeanors, HIGH-TREASON, R. I. C. O. (Organized Crime Practices), Violation of Sherman Anti-Trust Act (they are a MONOPOLY). Biased, Prejudiced, Union Bar Attorney Judge operates under the law known only to Attorneys and Judges (that work in unison with all of the Banks and Financial Institutions) all for what they think is the "glory" of the all-mighty U. S. D. which still is nothing more than a fraud.

The "Court Officers" are already in violation and "Breach of Contract" (by their 'Oath of Office') in their first case. This is how… 1. They offer NO-full disclosures, 2. They tie you into a "Bondage" Contract, 3. Without your knowledge they use your "Birth-Certificate", 4. The "Social-Security" card-number and 5. The "Driver's-License" number. These contracts alone disqualify any and all Judges and Attorneys from representing any case in their "judicial system'. These contracts are commonly referred to as "IMPLIED CONTRACTS" or "Hidden Contracts" and are not enforceable if you can prove they have committed "Breach of Contract"; which is easily done…just not within their 'Courts'. Their attitude is: "Please, come into our Babylonian Court. We want your Labor, Liberty, Property, and Authority over you. We want more fines, taxes, fees, revenue; or we will put you in jail".

Furthermore, to which "Contract" does the Politicians, Judges, Attorneys or any Bureaucrat take the "Oath of Office" for? We all know that there are at least 2 Constitutions that were written in 1700's 1. Was for the development of the government "For the People and by the people" Or 2. The second one that makes everyone into a "Corporate-Entity" through Fraud, Deceit, Trickery, Out Right Lies, Threat, Duress, Coercion?

We, as American-Civilians, can stop this practice by going after those perpetrators with one-single-charge… "Breach of Contract" and hold them responsible for other criminal activities they believe they are "immune from".

The only court that we may be able to proceed with and be heard would be through the International Hague Courts; through a CLASS-ACTION-SUIT. The main reason why is-not only to prove "Breach of Contract" but to charge THE/The/the UNITED STATES INC. with International War Crimes against American-Civilians and Crimes against Humanity; through the use of Threat, Duress, Coercion and Fraud…just to name a few charges.

The second point for a charge of "Breach of Contract" against these impersonating-self-proclaimed-professionals is the fact that the courts like to use something that is Unconstitutional called 'Administrative-Court-System' or 'Administrative-Hearing''.

Now here is the problem with using this type system. All legitimate corporations that are in business and have established a D. B. A. (doing business as) within the State Inc. follow their own set of rules known as Policy and Procedures. When an employee commits some sort of wrong or negligence within the company, they have what is known as an 'Administrative Hearing'. The internal Investigation makes a decision to terminate or not terminate that employee. It does not matter how large the

Corporation is or how small…as an employee you can be terminated for ANY reason, even if it proves to be false.

However, the Corporate Government Inc., especially the socialists tore everything about the idea of a Democracy apart. They were more than taxing one party to the cheers of another in denial of equal protection. It was about creating administrative agencies (1) delegating them to create rules with the force of law as if passed by Congress sanctioned by the people; (2) the creation of administrative courts that defeated the Tripartite (Executive, Legislative and Judicial Branches) government structure usurping all power into the hand of the executive branch, as if this were a dictatorship run by the great hoard of unelected officials. This type of illegal procedure has been conducted for over 81 years (eighty-one years).

Administrative Law Courts are a fiefdom. They have long been corrupt and traditionally rule in favor of their agencies, making it extremely costly for anyone to even try to defend themselves. If anyone were to attempt to defend themselves, they would have the burden of the costs of an Administration proceeding and appeal to an Article III court judge (Oath of Office – Contract or the lack there of… Breach of Contract), then they must appeal to the Court of Appeals, and finally plea to the Supreme Court. Here you will see that there is a chain of evidence and witnesses for a "Breach of Contract" Class-Action-Law-Suit. In truth the cost of such cases are well into the millions of dollars, and then good luck in getting any form of justice.

Furthermore, Administrative Law Courts cannot sentence you to prison, but they can (illegally) fine you into bankruptcy. So the lack of a "criminal prosecution" meant the judges did not have to be lawyers. They could be anyone; brother, sister, brother-in-law etc. etc. who is looking for a job where he/she just rules in favor of the agency not to be bothered with law. Unless the victim has a pile of money, there is no real-chance that they can afford to defend themselves. This is why the agencies cut deals with the "big houses" (courts and banks) and prosecute the small upstarts who lack the funds to defend themselves.

In reality, the Corporate-Government decided that the Administrative Law Courts are really reminiscent of the notorious extrajudicial proceedings of the Star Chamber operated by King James I.

The court of Chancery set up outside the King's Bench (so there were no trials by jury), had the same purpose, to circumvent the law. This is where our Fifth Amendment 'Rights' came into being.

The third and final part of the evidence for your Gravamen (Complaint) is that the U. S. Corporate Government Inc. through its "Officials" (elected or not) and all of its subsidiaries (all fifty (50) of them) force you personally into committing a "felonious crime" on a daily basis…this is how they do it:

The Constitution states that all government shall pay for services with gold and/or silver. But yet gives the "government" the right to make coin for the realm…so to speak. However, the Corporate-Government Inc. has decided that it is illegal for anyone to own gold or horde it. So they decided to create a "fictional" monetary system under the Banking system. Instead of individuals paying substance for substance they decided to create a debt-society. For example, if you were to examine a U. S. D. (United States Dollar – such as it is) you will notice across the top of the bill it states "FEDERAL RESERVE NOTE". This paper money actually has no benefit for American-Civilians. In truth you are paying a debt you incur with a debt that they are supplying you with. Furthermore, 'Federal Reserve Notes' you are using are not yours they belong to the "Corporate Government, Inc." and they can come in and take or confiscate any or all of those notes. Why do you think that the National Deficit is so high? We American Civilians cannot pay off a debt with debt.

This is the third piece of evidence to be used against the Judicial Government. Any Corporate Government office or Official that makes a claim you owe them money to their Agency is a fraud. How can you be forced to pay money if you do not have any?

For example, I will explain it this way…We all know who Warren Buffet is and we all know who Donald Trump is…They have made a lot of "MONEY" however, they are no different than you or I... How you ask? They are not "Solvent". They are using the same "debt for debt" bullshit-conscript that everyone else is using.

When the Courts order a victim to pay for restitution, remuneration or damages, those same courts are in control of the Banking System to the point that you will receive nothing or very little if anything…because they absorb it all under trickery, lies and deceit. It's no wonder why that there is "No-Justice" …you cannot buy it, because it does not exist under the debt for debt fraud.

The difference between Trump and Buffet and other members of the Billionaire Boys club and American-Civilians who work on a daily basis for a weekly paycheck, is that they understand how to levy debt against debt. In reality, neither gentlemen actually own anything. They are just as destitute and poor as All American-Civilians; and yes, the so-called UNITED STATES Government, Inc. can come and confiscate any and all of their assets under any guise they choose.

Fraud upon the Court is where the Judge (Banker) (who is NOT the "Court") does NOT support or uphold the Judicial Machinery of the Court. The Court is an unbiased, but methodical "creature" which is governed by the Rule of Law…that is, the Rules of Civil Procedure, the Rules of Criminal Procedure, and the Rules of Evidence, all which is overseen by Constitutional Law. The Court can only be effective, fair and "just" if it is allowed to function as the laws proscribe. The sad fact is that in most Courts, if not all, across the country, from Federal Courts down to local District Courts, have judges who are violating their oath of office and are not properly following these rules, (as most attorney's do not as well, and are usually grossly ignorant of the rules and both judges and attorneys are playing a revised legal-game with their own created rules) and THIS is a Fraud upon the Court, immediately removing jurisdiction from that Court, and vitiates (makes ineffective – invalidates) every decision from that point on. Any judge who does such a thing is under mandatory, nondiscretionary duty to recuse themselves from the case, and this rarely happens unless someone can force them to do so with the evidence of violations of procedure and threat of losing half their pensions for life which is what can take place. In any case, it is illegal, and EVERY case which has had fraud involved can be re-opened AT ANY TIME, because there are no-statutes of limitations on fraud.

You may be asking yourself who is an "Officer of the Court?" The answer: a judged is an officer of the court as well as all attorneys. A state is a state judicial officer, paid by the federal government to act impartially and lawfully. State and Federal attorneys fall into the same general category and must meet the same requirements. A judge is not the court. People vs. Zajic 88 Ill. App. 3d. 477, 410 N. E. 2d. 626 (1980).

The definition for "fraud on the court" is as follows: Whenever any officer of the court commits fraud during a proceeding in the court, they become engaged in "fraud upon the court": Bulloch vs. United States, 763 F. 2d. 1115, 1121 (10th Cir. 1985), the court stated "Fraud upon the court is fraud which is directed to the judicial machinery itself and is not fraud between the parties of fraudulent documents, false statements or perjury ... It is where the court or a member is corrupted or influenced or influence is attempted or where the judge has not performed their judicial function --- thus where the impartial functions of the court have been directly corrupted".

"Fraud upon the court" has been defined by the 7th Circuit Court of Appeals to "embrace that species of fraud which does, or attempts to, defile the court itself, or is a fraud perpetrated by officers of the court so that the judicial machinery cannot perform in the usual manner its impartial task of adjudging cases that are presented for adjudication". Kenner vs. C. I. R., 387 F. 3d 689 (1968); 7 Moore's Federal Practice, 2d ed., pg. 512, Â¶, 60.23. The 7th Circuit further stated "a decision produced by fraud upon the court is not in essence a decision at all, and never becomes final".

What effect does "fraud upon the court" have upon any court proceeding?

"Fraud upon the court" makes void the orders and judgements of that court. It is also clear and well-settled Illinois law that any attempt to commit "fraud upon the court" vitiates the entire proceeding. The People of the State of Illinois vs. Fred E. Sterling, 357 Ill.354; 192 N. E. 229 (1934) ("The maximum that fraud vitiates every transaction into which it enters applies to judgements as well as to contracts and other transactions".); Allen F. Moore vs. Stanley F. Sievers, 336 Ill. 316; 168 N. E. 259 (1929) ("The maximum that fraud vitiates every transaction into which it enters ..."); In re Village of Willowbrook, 37 Ill. App. 2d. 393 (1962) ("It is axiomatic that fraud vitiates everything".); Dunham vs. Dunham, 57 Ill. App. 475 (1984), affirmed 162 Ill. 589 (1986); Skelly Oil Co. vs. Universal Oil Products Co., 338 Ill. App. 79, 86 N. E. 2d. 875,

883-4 (1949); Thomas Stasel vs. The American Home Security Corporation, 362 Ill. 350; 199 N. E. 798 (1935).

Under Illinois and Federal Law, when any officer of the court has committed "fraud upon the court", the orders and judgement of that court are void, of no legal force of effect.

One of the Remedies for "Breach of Contract" is the 'Disqualification of Judges', Deposed, Deported and the loss of their Pensions. Of course, this would also apply to all Foreign-Agents that are undeclared and call themselves Civil-Servants.

How do we American Civilians accomplish this?

Federal law requires the automatic disqualification of a Federal judge under certain circumstances.

In 1994, the U. S. Supreme Court held that "Disqualification is required if an objective observer would entertain reasonable questions about the judge's impartiality. If a judge's attitude or state of mind leads a detached observer to conclude that a fair and impartial hearing is unlikely, the judge must be disqualified". [Emphasis added]. Liteky vs. U. S., 114 S. Ct. 1147, 1162 (1994). Courts have repeatedly held that positive proof of the partiality of a judge is not a requirement, only the appearance of partiality. Liljeberg vs. Health Services Acquisition Corp., 486 U. S. 847, 108 S. Ct. 2194 (1988) (what matters is not the reality of bias or prejudice but its appearance); United States vs. Balistrieri, 779 F. 2d. 1191 (7th Cir. 1985) (Section 455(a) "is directed against the appearance of partiality, whether or not the judge is actually biased".) (Section 455(a) of the Judicial Code, 28 U. S. C. § 455(a), is not intended to protect litigants from actual bias in their judge but rather to promote public confidence in the impartiality of the judicial process".).

That Court also stated that Section 455(a) "requires a judge to recuse themselves in any proceeding in which their impartiality might reasonably be questioned". Taylor vs. O'Grady, 88 F. 2d. 1189 (7th Cir. 1989). In the case of Pfizer Inc. vs. Lord, 456 F. 2d. 532 (8th Cir. 1972), the court stated that "It is important that the litigant not only actually receive justice, but that they believe that they have received justice". The Supreme Court has ruled and has reaffirmed the principle that "justice must satisfy the appearance of justice", Levine vs. United States, 362 U. S. 610, 80 S. Ct.

1038 (1960), citing Offutt vs. United States, 348 U. S. 11, 14, 75 S. Ct. 11, 13 (1954). A judge receiving a bribe from an interested party over which they are presiding over, does not give the appearance of justice.

"Recusal under Section 455 is self-executing; a party need not file affidavits in support of recusal and the judge is obligated to recuse themselves sua sponte under the stated circumstances." Taylor vs. O'Grady, 888 F. 2d 1189 (7th Cir. 1989).

Further, the judge has a legal duty to disqualify himself even if there is no motion asking for his disqualification. The Seventh Circuit Court of Appeals further stated that "We think that this language [455(a)] imposes a duty on the judge to act sua sponte, even if no motion or affidavit is filed". Balistrieri, at 1202.

Judges do not have discretion not to disqualify themselves. By law, they are bound to follow the law. Should a judge not disqualify themselves as required by law, then the judge has given another example of their "appearance of partiality" which, possibly, further disqualifies the judge. Should another judge not accept the disqualification of the judge, then the second judge has evidenced an "appearance of partiality" and has possibly disqualified himself/herself. None of the orders issued by any judge who has been disqualified by law would appear to be valid. It would appear that they are void as a matter of law, and are of no legal force or effect.

Should a judge not disqualify themselves, the judge is violation of the Due Process Clause of the U. S. Constitution. United States vs. Sciuto, 521 F.2d 842, 845 (7th Cir. 1996) ("The right to a tribunal free from bias or prejudice is based, not on section 144, but on the Due Process Clause.").

Should a judge issue any order after he has been disqualified by law, and if the party has been denied of any of his / her property, then the judge may have been engaged in the Federal Crime of "interference with interstate commerce". The judge has acted in the judge's personal capacity and not in the judge's judicial capacity. It has been said that this judge, acting in this manner, has no more lawful authority than someone's next-door neighbor (provided that he is not a judge). However, some judges may not follow the law.

If you were a non-represented litigant, and should the court not follow the law as to non-represented litigants, then the judge has expressed an "appearance of partiality" and, under the law, it would seem that he/she has disqualified him/herself.

However, since not all judges keep up to date in the law, and since not all judges follow the law, it is possible that a judge may not know the ruling of the U. S. Supreme Court and the other courts on this subject. Notice that it states "disqualification is required" and that a judge "must be disqualified" under certain circumstances.

The Supreme Court has also held that if a judge wars against the Constitution, or if he acts without jurisdiction, he has engaged in treason to the Constitution. If a judge acts after he has been automatically disqualified by law, then he is acting without jurisdiction, and that suggest that he is then engaging in criminal acts of treason, and may be engaged in extortion and the interference with interstate commerce.

Courts have repeatedly ruled that judges have no immunity for their criminal acts. Since both treason and the interference with interstate commerce are criminal acts, no judge has immunity to engage in such acts.

However, this also applies those who have taken and "Oath of Office" such as the Politicians – who claim they have no 'authority to get involved with (other) STATE BUSINESS or (other) COURT PROCEEDINGS. This is misinformation they are giving you, remember they took an oath to support and defend the "CONSTITUTION" of the United States from 'Foreign and Domestic'. If they refuse to help or guide you they now become by definition 'accomplices after the fact'. It is like when a bank robber or bank robbers go into a bank and rob it…the get-away driver is NOT in the bank but in a parking lot…Why then, does the Driver receive MORE years as opposed to those who actually robbed the Bank? This question is not trying to mix apple and oranges, but to prove a point…and I do believe I made it.

Unlike The United-States-Corporate-Government (Major), the United-States-of-America (Minor) allows corporations organized under its auspices to be "citizens", a fact that has led to no end of Fraud and Criminality. All "U. S. Citizens" have only "Civil Rights" – that is, privileges – granted by "the United-States-Corporate-Congress". This separate national entity initially operated its business affairs as "United States of America, Inc." – a corporation chartered in Delaware, under By-Laws published as the Constitution of the United States of America. Note the differences in capitalization and the use of the preposition "of" in place of "for" which distinguishes this version of "Constitution" as a separate legal document from the original equity contract known as The Constitution for the United States of America. The undeclared-Impersonating-Corporate-Agents of the United-States-of-America (Minor) also popularized "The Pledge of Allegiance" as a means of providing tacit public notice and securing assumed consent for its actions without, however, fully disclosing its nature and intentions or the process of usurpation against "The United States of America" (Major) it engaged in.

Observe the actual words of the "Pledge of Allegiance": "I (secures a claim of individual consent) pledge (this is an ancient feudal act) allegiance (form of Contract) to the United States of America (which version is only indicated by the lack of capitalization on the word "the") and to the Republic (original-organic-states'-corporate-government) for which it stands, one nation, under God, indivisible, with liberty and justice for all".

In reality there hasn't been "one nation" since 1871. There have been two nations operating under two separate administrative protocols and two national trusts, but it has been the subversive objective of Congress to join both into one entity and operate it as an oligarchy, just as the Congress currently operates the United-States-of-America, Inc. (Minor) as an oligarchy.

The Pledge of Allegiance – an innocuous-appearing mantra endlessly repeated in public schools and public meetings across America is a VERBAL CONTRACT secretly obligating the victims to accept representation of their Republic by "the United-States-of-America" which failed to properly identify itself or seek open consent and which merely claimed to "stand for" the American Republic.

The Pledge of Allegiance is and undisclosed entrapment into contract ceding authority to represent the individual inhabitants and the American Republic to "the United-States-of-America" similar to what

413

happens when an unwary individual hires an attorney/lawyer to "represent" them and "stand for" them in a court.

The representative gains a largely-unaccountable-controlling-interest in the affairs of their actual employer who is relegated to the status of a ward of the Corporate-Subsidiary-State, incompetent, or dependent.

As a result of this semantic-deceit and duplicity, no-valid new contract between the organic American states and the United-States-of-America, Inc. (Minor) was ever established. The "Constitution of the United States of America" remains a document peculiar to the United States of America, Inc. (Minor), not to be confused with the original equity contract known as The Constitution for the United States of America.

At the beginning of the last century there were two completely separate versions of "United-States-of-America" operating and two kinds of "US (C)itzens" and two "Constitutions" and the "US Congress" was acting in two roles in conflict of interest. The original Constitution known as "The Constitution for the United States of America" and the By-Laws of the newly formed federal corporation known as "the Constitution of the United States of America" formed under the auspices of the United States of America (Minor). All this semantic deceit was and is extremely complex and deliberately designed to defraud and confuse.

One last note for the reader's observation and enlightenment:

There are many types of contracts that the United-States-Corporate-Government enforces upon the Americans whether they are legal or NOT and whether the parties honor those contracts or NOT. They use hidden and obscure clauses along with implied contracts that appear so beneficial for you as the beneficiary that you become confused and muddled. However, this is how the Corporate-Government, Inc. likes to do business. We will attempt to explain what a contract is, in laymen's-terms, and then explain how the Political-Corporate-Whores are in Breach of those contracts just to line their pockets and Bank accounts at American-Civilian's expense.

The following is the **legal** definition for the word 'CONTRACT' as defined from Black's Law Dictionary, 6th Edition, page; 322:

Contract. An agreement between two or more persons which creates an obligation to do or not to do a particular thing. As defined in Restatement, Second, Contracts § 3: "A contract is a promise or a set of promises for the breach of which the law gives a remedy, or the performance of which the law in some way recognizes as a duty". A legal relationship consisting of the rights and duties of the contracting parties; a promise or set of promises constituting an agreement between the parties that gives each a legal duty to the other and also the right to seek a remedy for the breach of those duties. Its essentials are competent parties, subject matter, a legal consideration, mutuality of agreement, and mutuality of obligation. **Lamoureux v. Burrillville Racing Ass'n, 91 R.I. 94, 161 A.2d 213, 215**.

Under U. C. C. (Uniform Commercial Codes), term refers to total legal obligation which results from parties' agreement as affected by the Code. Section 1-201(11). As to sales, "contract" and "agreement" are limited to those relating to present or future sales of goods, and "contract for sale" includes both a present sale of goods and a contract to sell goods at a future time. **U.C.C. § 2-106(1)**.

The writing which contains the agreement of parties, with the terms and conditions, and which serves as a proof of the obligation.

Contracts may be classified on several different methods, according to the element in them which is brought into prominence. The usual classifications are as follows:

Blanket contract; Certain and Hazardous; Commutative and Independent; Conditional Contract; Consensual and real; Constructive contract; Cost-plus contract; Divisible and indivisible; Entire and severable; Entire contract clause; Exclusive contract; Executed and executory; Express and implied; Gratuitous and onerous; Investment contract; Joint and several; Mutual interest, mixed, etc.; Open end contract; Output contract; Parol contract; Personal contract; Pre-contract; Principal and accessory contract; Quasi contract; Record, specialty, simple; Requirements contract; Shipment contract; Special contract; Subcontract; Tying contract; Unconscionable contract; Unenforceable contract; Unilateral and bilateral; Usurious contract; Voidable contract; Void contract; Written contract.

There are several other types of contracts and they are as follows: Adhesion contract; Agreement; Aleatory contract; Alteration of contract; Bilateral contract; Bottom hole contract; Breach of contract; Collateral contract; Compact; Constructive contract; Contingency contract; Entire output contract; Executory contract; Formal contract; Futures contract; Impairing the obligation of contracts, Indemnity; Innominate contracts; Installment contract; Integrated contract; Investment contract; Letter contract; Letter of intent; Literal contract; Marketing contract; Novation; Oral contract; Parol evidence rule; Privity (Privity of contract); Procurement contract; Quasi contract; Requirement contract; Severable contract; Simulated contract; Specialty; and Liberty of contract.

You will notice that there is no-such **contract** that compels or orders any American-Civilian to "PERFORM" any or all of these contracts. In other words, there is no-such "PERFORMANCE CONTRACT".

Chapter 9:
SUMMARY OF THE FACTS

1983 - Robert – Charles: [Simpson] begins construction of his home located in California State, County of Riverside, in an unincorporated area called Thousand Palms. We used our **own** labor, time and finances under what was known at that time as; "Owner-Builder".

Robert and I went to the "Building and Safety"; located in Indio, seeking information concerned with which if any "Laws" we would or could be in violation of if we build our home "without" permits (known to some as extortion-money). An Inspector by the name of "McLeod" (last name only) stated, "None. However, the County will not allow the electric company to hook up the electricity". (At the time the Electric Company was Imperial Irrigation Water and Power. A county owned and controlled business). McLeod further explained that "It was our Right to build our home as Owner-Builder". In reality we did not mind if we were not allowed an electrical hook-up, because we decided to go with an alternative electrical source (i. e. generator, wind power and solar power).

We then asked about Size-variances. Was there a 'minimum' square footage? McLeod stated, "Yes! A minimum of 750 square feet. However, there is no maximum for the square footage." Robert and I asked one-more question about Height-variance. The answer McLeod stated was that "there is no height-variance." McLeod then physically wrote down (pen to paper) the measurements that we were able to build by, they were/are as follows: "10' from the back property-line; 5' on each side of the property-line; and 27 ½' from the center of the Street". However, we went 29' from the center of the street.

The County Supervisor for the Fourth District Riverside County, at the time, was Al McCandles.

After time went by, a new administration was elected into the County Supervisor's Office. That is when our problems really began. Out of Malicious Intent, Hatred, Spite and Jealousy, the new administration moved against us for following the above stated "information" that was given to us by 'McLeod'.

1989 – Robert obtained the finances to pay-off the balance of the mortgage and was instructed by an Attorney by the name of Stephen L. Fingal **NOT** to "Record the Variance with Riverside County".

This was the same year I decided to see if I could make a difference in helping Americans for injustices, I witnessed by Campaigning for County Supervisor and Campaigning against an Incumbent who was extremely crooked, prejudiced and corrupt…and proved it.

1990 – 1992 – Robert and I continued to build our home without interruption. However, Robert decided to Campaign for Congress in 1991 against Al McCandles but did not pass the Primaries.

1993 – I once again decided to Campaign for County Supervisor for Riverside County Fourth District and Campaign for Change on massive scale. But once again I was defeated by the powers that be that are in control of Riverside County and the State of California legally or illegally.

1994 – I started a business that was set up to help the customers of the "Electric-Companies" from information I received during the Campaign. The Billing process of the electric companies across the nation are sending out fraudulent bills by claiming that they are "measuring the consumption" between $300.00+ and $700.00+ dollars-worth of electricity per month, just for residential zones alone.

1995 – 1996 - Robert and I continued to expose the electric companies and reported this crime too Senator Barbara Levy Boxer; Assemblyman James F. Battin; Public Utility Commissioner of California Josiah Nepier; Federal Energy Regulatory Commission; which turned out to be Bill Richardson appointed by the Clinton Administration before becoming Governor of New Mexico; Internal Revenue Service; Riverside County Supervisor Roy Wilson and all of the Mayors and City Counsels surrounding Palm Springs. We also reported and interviewed by the "Desert Sun" August 21, 1996 written by: Cecelia Chan. We were also guests on talk-radio programs (Ron Fortner, Art Bell and Chuck Harder) explaining how the electric companies were defrauding their customers. In the interim of all of this, the Electric Companies finally admitted that

"Yes they can speed-up or slow-down the meter. But trust us we would never commit fraud".

1997 – 2001 – I came to the decision to ask Supervisor Roy Wilson "what laws would I be breaking if I staged a Peaceful Protest" against the Electric Companies? Mr. Wilson's reply was as follows, "None. It is within your rights as an American to protest a 'peaceful-protest' against illegal acts against Americans".

So, on **August 04, 1997** I climbed a "Utility-Pole" **NOT** the 'Power-Pole', that belonged to Robert – C. Simpson and sat on the cross-piece where the Phone-Line and Television Cable connect for their services. Robert was arrested and charged with "Theft Utility Services" for Twenty-Years and "Obtain Utility W/out Paying". I was charged with "Theft Utility Services" for Twenty-Years; "Obtain Utility W/out Paying"; "Resisting Arrest"; "Trespass/Refuse to leave land"; and "Obstruction of Justice".

On **March 24, 1998** - Robert and I were found "Guilty" on certain counts. However, the jury at the time found and declared us "*NOT GUILTY*". The judge at the time 'refused' the verdict and instructed the jury to "re-deliberate the case and come to a DIFFERENT verdict or they would be sequestered for as long as it took to change their decision".

On **May 1, 1998** - Robert and I were once again 'ordered' for Report and Sentencing before the court. We were terrified that were going to be sentenced for up to 25 years in prison for a crime that according to the County of Riverside never took place. But as luck would have it, all we received was 15 days of community-service with a Jewish Owned and Jewish Mafia Controlled business called "The Palm Spring Desert Air Museum" and "restitution" for crimes that were not committed.

In **1999 – 2000** - we resided within our home continuing the construction hoping that this would be the end of the punishment for exposing a crime against Americans.

In **2001** – Governor Gray Davis demanded 9 Billion U. S. Dollars refund for the "Power Overcharges", in an article from the "Desert Sun" dated: June 21, 2001; written by H. Josef Herbert.

In **December 2, 2001** came the downfall of Enron. We were known as the "outside-source". The subsidiary in Texas was the focal point of Money-Laundering for the State of California for their Retirement, Pension Funds and 'Slush Funds' for all of the Employees of the Subsidiary-Corporate-Government of California and the 'Politicians'. When California, realized the truth in what we reported as a crime, they withdrew all of the 'finances' it invested within Enron, which helped in the cause of the Collapse of the Texas based subsidiary. In reality, the State of California was Laundering-Money for their selfish greed and got caught.

Robert and I were "Ordered" by Senator Barbara Levy Boxer through all of the County Agents/Employees, Police, and the Court system to "Get out of California or you will die". The exact quote was "We want their home gone, his son gone, and Robert gone and not necessarily in that order".

Our home was demolished and the land sold for "Back-Taxes"; with an added charge of $265,000 dollars for the demolition; of which they applied through a Lien. Our taxes were paid up until 1998, and yes we still have that "Original" documentation; Tax-receipts, that the courts and all known an unknown perpetrators refused to 'notice' as evidence.

According to the Laws of California and their Tax-Laws a person has 5 years to catch up their property taxes. Furthermore, before any person can pay their "current" Property-Taxes they have to pay for the arrears-taxes (taxes they are behind on). Our property-taxes were current as of 1998, with the documentation (receipts from the tax assessor's office).

However, we were forced to become homeless and traveled until 2002.

The following information is taken directly from "Your Day In Court" Using Common Law With Common Sense"; Published through Lulu Publishing Company in 2011; Authors; Bradley J. Franks and Robert – C. Simpson.

In **2002 – 2006** - I applied for a career as a 'Correction Officer' in Torrance County, New Mexico. However, what we did not realize, until it was almost too late, was that Bill Richardson (appointed to be in charge of the Federal Energy Regulatory Commission by the Clinton Administration) became the Governor of New Mexico, at this time.

I purchased a 5-acre parcel of property with permanent-mobile-home with add-ons, septic system and a private-well. The entire mortgage was complete and paid-off on November 4, 2005.

Robert decided to help protect the residential structure by building a 'Pole-Building-Structure" around the existing-trailer for protection from hail and other weather conditions; including screened-in-porches. We contacted a State Building Code Enforcement Officer by the name of Fema Aragon. We asked if there were any "permits" required for a "Pole-Building" in the State of New Mexico. His reply was "No. For a Pole-Building there are no-permits required".

In **March 21, 2006** - I decided to try and Campaign one more time to help Americans that were in need of help from those Crooked Corrupt Bureaucrats/Employees/Agents/Officers/Elected or Appointed Officials that were in the practice of using T. D. C. (Threat, Duress and Coercion). I Campaigned for Magistrate of Torrance County against the "Incumbent; Steve Jones 'also known as Larry Jones'". Unfortunately, some of the "polling-sites were closed" or the "Democrats did not vote"; either way I was not elected and furthermore, the Secretary of State of New Mexico did not "Sanction" the election during that time at the County level.

In **May 21, 2007** - I received a "criminal complaint", (that any reasonable-intelligent-individual would observe that was "false" upon its face). The charges were as follows: "1 count of Solid Waste, 1 count of Public Nuisance, 1 count Development Review Permit, 1 count of Abandonment of Dangerous Containers." The description is as follows: "1 accumulation of trash, C&D materials and appliances on the property; 2 the addition to the mobile home on the property with no land use permit; 3 you notified back in May 2007 as to the need of the clean-up of the property and to obtain a land use permit were given time to do so". The complaint was autographed by <u>Richard A. Ledbetter.</u>

The agent/officer who autographed the "complaint" also claimed he was the "prosecution" and "decision-maker" of this case, in other words he appointed himself as judge, jury and executioner. He was nothing but an Imposter.

I was ordered by a "Criminal Summons" for the appearance on August 2, 2007, in Estancia, County of TORRANCE, STATE of New Mexico; for the pleadings; with a threat of "jail time if I did not show up".

Through my ignorance of what the County and the Court were doing, at the time, I plead "Not Guilty".

As of **August 2, 2007** - the courts ordered "to appoint a Public Defender". (OMG! Here we go again).

Now, I autographed the documents using Upper and lower casing letters of my given name and used the U. C. C. 1 – 207 for the reserve of my rights. However, I was threatened with a $3,000.00 USD fine and/or both a jail sentence of 1,088 days.

The first decision I made was that Mr. Steve Jones or Larry Jones was, in reality "Disqualified" as the judge for this case, because I campaigned against him for the Office of Magistrate and would reflect a conflict of interest. Therefore, he had to "Recuse" himself for conflicting interests. So as of August 16, 2007; Steve Jones or Larry Jones "Recused himself".

Now as I understand how the courts in New Mexico work, is if an elected Magistrate cannot adjudicate/try a case, that case is passed on to the higher State Courts and State Judges; which would be a mistake as well. However, I hired an Attorney by the name of Charles E. Knoblauch, for defense. This was a real stupid mistake on my part; but I can claim ignorance and you will understand later within this chapter and other chapters following why it was a "stupid-mistake".

The faxed-documents that were sent to me in September 17, 2007 was for information that I was ordered to supply for Sgt. R. A. Ledbetter who agreed to "dismiss" the case if I were to comply with the following conditions and provide the following information: "i. Warranty deed or Real Estate Contract. ii. State Building Permit. iii. State Solid Waste Permit. iv. Pay $200 application fee. v. Development Plans; and then arrange for an inspector to come out to the property and approve the structure in question".

It continued with the "Removal of all junk materials, C&D materials and trash from the property" and ended with Bring the property taxes up to date." I, as the author and the individual in question, can produce THE evidence to show just how stupid and "ignorant" these Bureaucrats really were and are.

Unfortunately, I did not understand what was in store for me. I did know that under Civil Rights, I had the Right for Privacy"; which includes, "Right to privacy, Papers and Self".

As of **September 17, 2007**, Charles E. Knoblauch and staff "quit" this case, even after paying their required fee; that also included "a letter sent for Complaint to the 'Bar Association' for not completing the contract for representation". Therefore, a "Motion" was sent or the courts for the withdraw as Counsel"; because counsel was not "representing" the client.

As of **October 12, 2007** - I was sent "Notices to Appear" or be arrested for the "Review of Hearing". The "Notice of Review of Hearing" was changed for November 16, 2007 before Thomas G. Pestak (another elected magistrate in and for another county). I was ordered to appear once again before a Magistrate for a "Review Hearing" on November 16, 2007 or I would be arrested and jailed.

However, people explained to me at the time, that if there was a "conflict" between a "Magistrate" that the case would have to be presented to the higher courts (State Courts). , It doesn't mean I would win necessarily, it just means that, according to the law and my Civil Rights, I would be heard; or so I thought. (LOL).

On **November 28, 2007** - I was accompanied with two (2) witnesses to the court in Estancia for a "Jury Trial". If I did not show up, once again, I was threatened with being arrested.

I showed up with "witness" which were "locked in a room" and kept away from me and no "Legal Representation" during a "Jury selection" on the same day. This included the same "Threat" that if I did not show up, I would arrested and imprisoned.

On the same date, I was arrested for what they charged me with for "Public Drunk". Here is the reality of this charge: 1. there is "no such law or charge in the State of New Mexico of "<u>Public Drunk</u>"; 2. I was not drunk; as they claim; 3. I had no witnesses at this conference; and 4. I had no-legal counsel present for any advice guidance or any "Legal Representation". I was transported to "Torrance County Detention Facility"/Correction Corporation of America and processed and held for 7 days within the Segregation Unit, then transferred to Cibola County Jail for the remainder of the "kidnapping". The "Bond" was set for "$10,000.00 Cash only" for my release.

However, it did not matter. I was arrested and put in jail for 30 days for a charge that does not exist in law or on the books called "Public Drunk" in the State of New Mexico. After being released I was advised and instructed to leave the state of New Mexico or I would be once again "Killed" for the exposure of what these Evil, Hateful and Deceitful Bureaucrats wit Malicious Intent were doing to other American Victims.

So, for my self-preservation I left and moved to Minnesota. I again sought a career in Corrections in Appleton, Minnesota within "Prairie Hills Correction Facility"/Correction Corporation of America until they closed that prison down in 2010.

I realized that if I did not do something to notify "Americans", "U. S. Citizens" or the "Public in General" the Corporate State of California and the Corporate State of New Mexico would "win" and "invent more lies to pad their claims against me". So, I wrote "Your Day In Court Using Common Law With Common Sense"; Published in 2011 through Lulu publishing; the Authors Bradley J. Franks and Robert C. Simpson. This book contains all of the "information" that I saved and added as "evidence" against the Corporate State of New Mexico and its subsidiary "Torrance County". The second book "! AT GUN POINT... Whistleblower's point of view" Published through Author House in 2012; Authors Bradley – J. Franks and Robert C. Simpson was what took place in the Corporate State of California and its subsidiary "Riverside County".

These books were and are our chance and opportunity to prove to the "General Public" that they are and will be not alone and that there were/are other "Americans" and "U. S. Citizens" that were/are being "abused" by the so-called "Public-Servants".

I went back through all of the information within the books examining the documents, records, and other information I received and was astounded when I came to the realization that the Corporate

Government of the U. S. and its Subsidiaries: The Corporate State of California and the sub-subsidiary "Riverside County" and the Corporate State of New Mexico and the sub-subsidiary "Torrance County" had one thing in common… "BREACH OF CONTRACT!"

Remember, the "Government" was and is set up under three distinct parts: Executive Branch; Legislative Branch and the Judicial Branch". The <u>Executive Branch</u> is for the "Elected" President and his Administration/Cabinet and the "<u>Contract</u>" they have to sign and swear for is/are the "<u>Constitution</u>"; which by the way include the "<u>First Ten Amendments</u>" known as "the <u>Bill of Rights</u>". The <u>Legislative Branch</u> is for those "individuals" who are elected into Office of Senate or Congress and their Office Staff; and well we all understand how the Senate and House of Congress work…lol. However, they too have to sign and swear by the same "<u>Constitution</u>" and "<u>Bill of Rights</u>" that the President and his Administration has to uphold. The final part of the "Government" is the <u>Judicial Branch</u>. This is the branch of Government that tries and hears cases that supposedly makes "sound" Legal decisions that affect all of the **people** as a whole. The Judges, from the Supreme Court all the way down to the lowest of Traffic Courts and **ALL** Court Officers are under <u>THE</u> <u>SAME</u> "Contract" that the Executive and Legislative Branch have to uphold. However, the Courts were given a mandate to lie, deny and deceive under "maritime and admiralty courts".

But I digress a little, since this chapter is for the history of our Actions and their Reactions.

On **September 3, 2015** - Robert – C.: [Simpson] and Bradley – J.: [Franks] file a "Lien" against the Corporate State of California, INC. and the main perpetrators within the action.

On **December 3, 2015** - we sent the "Corporate" government of California presentments consisting of the following: "**Lien-Documents; Declaration Letter – Oath Purgatory; Affidavits – Plain Statement of Facts; Our Affidavit; U. C. C. 1; Affidavit; U. C. C. 4; Private Security Agreement; Commercial-Affidavit Statement; True-Bill and Accounting; and Pre-Invoice**".

These presentments were received and autographed through acceptance via certified/registered mail. They were given thirty-days (30-days) with a five-day (5-day) grace period for the "response/rebuttal".

The response was Nihil Dicit – Total Silence, Acceptance and Agreement.

On **January 14, 2016** we sent a presentment; a Second-Notice: **"Affidavit and Notice of [De]fault and Opportunity-to-Cure"** with an allowance of Twenty-days (20-days) with a five-day (5-day) grace period for the "response/rebuttal".

Presentments were received and autographed through acceptance via certified/registered mail.

The response was Nihil Dicit – Total Silence, Acceptance and Agreement.

On **February 10, 2016** we sent a presentment; a Third-Notice: **"Affidavit and Notice of [De]fault and Demand-for-Cure"** with an allowance of Ten-days (10-days) with a five-day (5-day) grace period for the "response/rebuttal".

Presentments were received and autographed through acceptance via certified/registered mail.

The response was Nihil Dicit – Total Silence, Acceptance and Agreement.

On **February 29, 2016** - we sent a presentment; a Final-Notice: **"Affidavit and Notice of [De]fault and Demand-for Cure"** with an allowance of Three-days (3-days) with a five-day (5-days) grace period for the "response/rebuttal".

Presentments were received and autographed through acceptance via certified/registered mail.

The response was Nihil Dicit – Total Silence, Acceptance and Agreement.

On **March 18, 2016** the presentment we sent was a: **"Notice for violation of Oath of Office 'Breach of Contract' – Demand for Cease and Desist – Notice for Lien – Lis Pendens by Necessity – Subrogation**

of Autograph/Signature/Authority – Notice for the Suspension of the Charter for the State of California" with an allowance of Thirty-days (30-days) with a Five-day (5-days) grace period for the "response/rebuttal".

Presentments were received and autographed through acceptance via certified/registered mail.

The response was Nihil Dicit – Total Silence, Acceptance and Agreement.

On **April 29, 2016** the presentment that we sent was a Final-Notice: "**Affidavit and Notice of [De]fault and Demand-for-Cure**" with an allowance of Three-days (3-Days) with a Five-day (5-days) grace period for the "response/rebuttal".

Presentments were received and autographed through acceptance via certified/registered mail.

The response was Nihil Dicit – Total Silence, Acceptance and Agreement.

On **May 20, 2016** - the presentment we sent was a "**Notice and Entry of [De]fault by Affidavit**" with an allowance of Three-days (3-days); Seventy-two-hours (72 Hours) for the "response/rebuttal".

Presentments were received and autographed through acceptance via certified/registered mail.

The response was Nihil Dicit – Total Silence, Acceptance and Agreement.

"The above-stated presentments met with autograph acceptance through via certified/registered-mail and the time for "response/rebuttal" have/has expired and **Res Judicata** has occurred against the Lien-Debtors. The [De]fault will be recorded as Public-Record".

"The Lien-Debtors; and All known and unknown Individuals/Agencies/Agents within this action; autograph/signatures were set by accommodation as per U. C. C. 3 – 415 by the lien-claimants because the lien-debtors are adversaries of the lien claimants, who-caused and injury to-the Lien Claimants' "Birth-Right" of Liberty and

Sovereignty. When the Lien-Debtors were confronted-with the claim, they said nothing. **NIHIL DICIT**"!

"This Lien place-on the Lien-Debtors is not a friendly transaction whereby the Lien-Debtors were willing to-enter into an agreement with lien claimants' quid pro quo, by consent. This lien arose in this manner because no-other remedy for the compensation of the injury is available for the Lien Claimants and the Lien Claimants have/has the right to-use applicable law".

Now I know that this confusing and you are probably asking yourself "Why would these people file a Lien against California and the perpetrators involved in the State of New York"? The answer is simple – New York is the Business-Hub for all the U. S. Corporate Government and the International Community as well.

The "**PUBLIC-NOTICE: NOTICE OF LIEN DEFAULT**" was placed within the "ROLL CALL" (news-paper) in Washington D. C. The first publication was August 3, 2016; Vol: 62; No. 8. The second publication was September 7, 2016; Vol: 62; No. 10. The third publication was September 14, 2016; Vol: 62; No. 14.

The "**FINAL-NOTICE: FORM UCC – Ad**" was placed within the "ROLL CALL" (news-paper) in September 21, 2016; Vol: 62; No.18.

In **October 21, 2016** - the Lien against California and the Lien-Debtors became a "**Lien Surety or Lien Security**" through their acts of "Breach of Contract", Negligence and NIHIL DICIT, not to mention the fact that they accepted all presentments through and with their silence.

You are probably asking yourself why we would place the "Public Notice" in the Roll Call (News-paper). This is another no-brainer for the answer…the United States Corporate Government is located in Washington D. C. It is the Corporate-Head for all of the 50 States, which are in reality, subsidiaries of the Corporate Government or equal to the Main Head-Office of a Multi-Billion-Dollar-Corporation.

Now that time has "Legally" expired for a "response/rebuttal" and the Presentments met with "silence" through "NIHIL DICIT" and the perpetrators remained silent even through the "Legal-Publication" through a very legal "Public-Notice", I had to carry this out one step farther. I asked a Bank if I had to "report" the Interest to the Internal Revenue Service, their reply was "yes, you do"! Accountants and Lawyers also confirmed that I would have to report the Interest as Income to the I. R. S.

As of October – December of 2016 - as one of the Beneficiaries of the "Lien Security, I "voluntarily-file" a "1040 U. S. Individual Income Tax Return", just for the "Interest" that the "Principle" has been and still is "accruing"; in accordance with the F. D. I. C. "Policy and Procedure" and in accordance with the I. R. S. "Policy and Procedure".

Because the "Principle" is such a large amount, as the beneficiary of a "Lien-Security", it is my choice to "Voluntarily" report the "Income/Interest" quarterly (every three months) not once a year.

I am not an Accountant, Banker, I. R. S. Agent or Lawyer, so if I have made a mistake on filing these documents or used the wrong form – so be it! This is why the word "Service" is part of the Corporate Name in I. R. S.

However, I sent the forms to the Department of the Treasury Internal Revenue Service in Fresno, California. But received a "Response/Threat" from Internal Revenue Service from Ogden, Utah; Dated: February 23, 2017; and "with an Autograph". But their "opinion" consisted of a statement that the "Documents" I sent were *Frivolous Tax Submissions*" and they further threatened with an "assessment Penalty of $5,000.00 Dollars". The I. R. S. continues to claim that the "frivolous filing penalty is not included on the notice of deficiency and cannot be contested in the Tax Court" …. Who are they kidding?

On March of 2017 - I re-sent the "corrected forms" per their request and included a second set of 1040 Tax Returns for the Months of January through March 2017; with an added statement: "Please do not presume to assume that this is a "Frivolous Tax Submission" by your OPINION. Your Federal Courts, including the Supreme Court of the United States, try **FACTS <u>NOT</u> OPINIONS**".

The Department of the Treasury Internal Revenue Service in Austin, Texas sent me a "Response/Threat" for what they claim as a "Penalty Assessment" of "15,000.00 Dollars".

Furthermore, the I. R. S. in Austin, Texas sent me an "Amount Due" for Taxes: (please note: I am not going to state what the amount is but I will say that the amount is an eleven-digit amount {$000,000,000.00}). Remember, any communication from the I. R. S. is invalid because it is NOT a REAL BILL or DEMAND.

Now you can realize just how frustrated I became when I read this letter. However, after a couple of days I realized that the I. R. S. (a branch of the Federal Government and a Subsidiary of the Head-Office Washington D. C.) in reality "VALIDATED" our "LIEN SECURITY" against the Corporate State Government of California.

On **August 10, 2017** - I received another I. R. S. Correspondence form Fresno, California. This correspondence was signed as well. However, it turned out to be another "Threat/Response"; "We're working on your account. However, we need an additional 45 days to send you a complete response on what action we are taking on your account. We don't need any further information from you right now". This is the last correspondence. But to set one thing straight…I do not have an "Account with I. R S. It does not belong to me but to them", otherwise they would not be able to do anything without my approval for that "ACCOUNT" or yours for that matter.

All throughout these above incidents, the Corporate-Subsidiary-State of California and the Foreign-Agents (Civil-Servants) and their Courts and the Court Officers refused and still refuse the evidence from their own Agencies. This in itself is an Act of High Treason, Sedition, and BREACH of CONTRACT.

Chapter 10:
THE AUTHOR'S LAST WORDS, FACTS AND EVIDENCE FOR THE ALLEGATIONS

Now comes the best part of doing this book when we as authors can explain in our own way what we went through starting in 1983. In addition, these books are NOT fiction. They are exact accounts of our lives taken and written about from 1983 to the current date of this Publication. This would make them Autobiographies written by those that lived through the criminal acts committed against American-Civilians that exercised their Rights under the Bill of Rights but was met with animosity, hatred, jealousy, and thievery, under the guise of "we are just doing our jobs".

The one thing that terrorizes the Imposter/Agents and THE United-States-Corporate-Government and the (50) Subsidiaries are FACTS from the victims and EVIDENCE/documentation of their opinionated documents. Remember they believe that they have jurisdiction, authority, and that they are immune from any and all prosecution from any wrong doing...this is nothing but another lie.

As we have stated before in this book and in "! At Gun Point...Whistle Blower's Point of View" in 1994 we Robert – C.: [Simpson] and Bradley – J.: [Franks] exposed a crime of fleecing (Billing Fraud) from the Electric Companies Billing Process and Money Laundering that the Fictitious-Corporate-Subsidiary-of-the-State-of-California and its Fictitious-Imposter-Undeclared-[so-called]-Government-Agents that were laundering monies through Enron of Texas for their so-called Retirements and Pensions.

We were, at the time, under the impression that these Imposter-Civil-Servants were hired to help guide American-Civilians that needed guidance and information without being victimized, punished, raped and stolen from not to mention the fact fed false information, miscommunications, and out-right-lies just so their Fictitious-Corporation can make a quick-illegal dollar. "ANY attack on an American, is an attack on all Americans", this includes Foreign and Domestic Enemies. (Note: emphasis added to make a point).

It appears that not even the President of the united-States of America is immune to the illegal acts of this Corporate-Government and its Insidious Acts against Americans. Our enemies are not Mexico, Venezuela, South America, Russia, China or even North Korea. Our enemy is within The-United-States-of-America-Fictitious-Corporate-Government and all of its Imposter-Agents that claim "We are just doing our jobs"; this is a piss-poor excuse for committing crimes against humanity, lies, deceit, trickery and Organized Criminal Practices under R. I. C. O. (Racketeer Influenced and Corrupt Organizations) laws, for what? The protection of THE United-States-Corporate-America? Or The Bankers that are under the impression they own America and American-Civilians?

The one thing the Corporate-Government-Imposters/Agents and all of the Subsidiaries that are in office have in common is under what is called a contract (Oath of Office) declared as well as undeclared are telling American-Civilians is "Trust us". Even the News Media claims "all we are doing is reporting the news". These excuses are the most Heinous-Lies that have been perpetrated against all of us. THE-United-States-Corporate-Government, as it is, has lost the American trust even the News Media has now been categorized as 'Entertainment'.

As it stands and as American-Civilians, we do not owe THE-United-States-Corporate-Government or any of it Subsidiaries (50 of them) or any of their Corporate-Agencies any kind of Allegiance or Pledge. After all, they are "FORCING" us to break their 'Federal-Laws" by using their form of 'Conscript'…meaning we cannot pay debt for debt and be clear and solvent. If you examine the 'Bills' you will notice the phrase "IN GOD WE TRUST". However, the new 'Bills' should read "WE SCREW THEM ALL", because they do. The United-States-Corporate-Government keeps its indentured-servants insolvent by using 'conscript', 'lies', 'deceit' and 'trickery'. Remember "DEBT for DEBT". How can an American-Civilian be 'solvent' under these conditions?

We used the opinionated-case-history, the opinionated-accusations, and the opinionated-evidence/documentation from the Imposters and their Agencies and THE United-States-Corporate-Fictitious-Subsidiary-Government-of-California and other Corporate-Agencies as proof and evidence against them for their criminal activities which are nothing but opinions and out-right lies that were and are still being used against us, personally! (Special note: We fully understand that we are NOT the only victims that the Corporate-Government and its Fictitious-Subsidiaries have raped, violated, or falsely accused. We just want American-Civilians to wake-up and fight-back for their RIGHTS).

However unfortunately, most American-citizens are lazy, ignorant, complacent and indentured. These are a few of the reasons why other Countries Hate the Corporate-Government. Because of the ignorance of what is truly happening in their lives.

In the particular-cases that affected us we wanted to let the American-Civilians know that they are not alone or singled-out for punishment for crimes that they did NOT commit, unless there was a 'Corpus Delicti' (a body or hard evidence). Everything else is nothing but a money-making scheme for the Court System, Judges (bankers), lawyers, and the Politicians. This is not business this is STRONG-ARMED-ROBBERY by those who are IMPOSTERS, LIARS and THIEVES with opinions without a Corpus Delicti or CONTRACT.

Society and its so-called laws can be completely wrong. Those that fight against the so-called-normalcy can be put in their place with enough evidence and FACTS. Unfortunately, the term 'Society' is a joke. It is a term THE-United-States-Corporation-uses to control the people.

We were accused and arrested after a "peaceful protest" That I did in 1997 when we proved that the Electric Companies through their Billing Process have been 'fleecing their clients/customers'. Imperial Irrigation Water and Power claimed we "Stole electricity for Twenty (20) years". This was and still is a complete lie. The math just does not add up. From 1983 to 1997 is NOT twenty years but "SEVENTEEN (17) YEARS".

We were released out on our 'own recognizance' after 48 hours. We continued to expose and prove that the Electric Companies in the Subsidiary-State-of-California was and are still committing fraud against their customers/clients. The Court system/agency in the Fictitious-County-of-Riverside and in conjunction with the Fictitious-Subsidiary-State-of-California, Inc. and ALL of the Perpetrators falsely accused and found us "Guilty" of Twenty-(20)-years of "Utility Theft" for a home that according to the Fictitious-Corporate-County-of-Riverside and the Fictitious-State-of-California, Inc. "Did not exist". The Judge/ (Banker) at the time ordered the Defense Attorney and Public Defender to "SIT DOWN and SHUT UP". None of the evidence was presented into their controlled court that would prove our innocence.

The bottom line of this accusation and illegal Court Proceeding (Jury-Trial) (if one could that a proceeding) was to "SILENCE" and Stop us from continuation of the exposure of the Electric Companies from Committing Fraud against their Public Clients/Customers. At the time we did not realize that what we exposed caused the 'Collapse of Enron' because the Fictitious-Subsidiary-State-of-California invested monies into this Subsidiary-Corporate-State-of-Texas based Corporation for expanding Pensions and Retirement Funds for the State-Imposter-Agents for the Fictitious-Subsidiary-State-of-California. When the Fictitious-State-of-California found out what we exposed they immediately pulled the money out of Enron that led to its collapse. This would be considered Money-Laundering for the illegal-benefit of the Fictitious-State-of-California and its Imposter-Agents.

However, their punishment did not stop there! We were ordered out of our home 'AT GUN POINT' and told to "leave the State and our home" on the threat of 'LIFE-THREATENING AND GRAVE BODILY HARM' and "not to come back"! Our home was subjected to what they called an "ADMINISTRATIVE HEARING" which we all know is in "Direct violation of the CONSTITUTION both STATE AND FEDERAL" and "Violation of Civil Rights".

But the most important point of this situation that we were subject to is…BREACH OF CONTRACT. Everything they did to us and against us was in violation of their Fictitious-Subsidiary-State-of-California, Inc.-Constitution and the original ORGANIC Constitution of the united State of America. With the lack of help from the Corporate-Federal-Government, Inc. they became Accessories after the fact, of a crime that has been and continues to be ignored and covered-up.

The reason why they told us that they were "destroying" our home was because we did NOT pay Taxes in the 1990s. We realized that this was another 'LIE' and another Charge of "FRAUD UPON THE COURT".

In reality, we did nothing wrong but to exercise our "CIVIL-RIGHTS" and "REPORT A CRIME BEING COMMITTED" by a crooked Fictitious-State and its Imposter-Agents.

Now because of the lack of these Imposter-Agents that did not and will not do their duty, we decided to place a LIEN against the Fictitious-Subsidiary-State-Government-of-California and all of its Imposter-Agents out of necessity not law. The lien was filed in the Fictitious-Subsidiary-Corporate-Government-of-New-York-State. The reasoning behind this decision is this; most if not all MONIES pass through the MAIN BRANCHES of the BANKS in New York, making it the Financial-hub of the Corporate-United-States-of-America, Inc. The last step for the LIEN process was to inform the Public of this Lien. Since the Fictitious-State-of-California and its Imposter-Agents refused to recognize or answer any of the Allegations set forth in the Lien under the "CONTRACT-LIEN", they accepted all of it as Truth and Fact and under subrogation they lose all of their Immunities, authority, jurisdiction, and rights. In reality these so-called "professionals", (agents for a fictitious-government) have committed a heinous crime against humanity and attacked American-Civilians for no-reason, but to protect their debt for debt money.

The last and final step for our lien was to inform the "public" about this situation. We tried to place a "Public-Notice" in the News Media in the Fictitious-State-of-California but were/was told "NO-WAY"! After recovering from this set-back, we decided that the MAIN-CORPORATION-of-THE-UNITED-STATES-of-America, Inc. was the best way to let them know-by their law that they were in [de]fault. We paid for a column in the "ROLLCALL NEWS PAPER" based in Washington D. C. For ninety (90) days we waited for any response whether it is positive or negative...no-response came forth. With this action or lack of action they lost all Immunities, Authority, Jurisdiction, and Rights not to mention STATUS AND STANDING within their "controlled-COURTS". After all these so-called Foreign-Agents become nothing but pests just like "RATS" or "ROACHES". Chapter 6 within this book contains the Lien Documents and the "lack of responses".

After a time, I decided to do some checking by contacting the F. D. I. C. (Federal Deposit Insurance Corporation) which was established in 1933. I simply asked that "if any Corporation is in BREACH OF CONTRACT and that Corporation refused to answer Charges/Allegations after the legal-time limit can an American-Civilian charge Interest on the Principal? And at what amount can be charged"? The Corporate-Agent of the F. D. I. C. explained that the individual Banks were in charge of setting their Interest Rates. I contacted a few different banks which explained that "most banks only pay interest on Savings Accounts. The minimum amount that the Banks pay out on Interest is .15%". However, remember all banks set their own amount for Interest Rates.

I used a 1% Interest Rate to figure the amount of Interest on the Principal of the Lien Documentation and reported it to the I. R. S. (Internal Revenue Service) after contacting them and asking what form would I have to use for reporting the "Interest as Income". Their only reply was "We cannot give you legal-advice".

So, I took it upon myself and used the "1040 Form" to report the "Interest-Rate as Income" by their Laws. Chapter 7 within this book contains the documentation and the responses and the "threats" that I received from the I. R. S. and yet I have no Contract of Performance from them. The I. R. S. claimed that "my paperwork" (which is on their contracts and printed paper) was "Frivolous and that I had no-Status or Standing". So in reality, the I. R. S. has set out to punish us for, yet again, exercising our RIGHTS.

NOTE: The following is a "PUBLIC-ANNOUNCEMENT" for all those Subsidiary-Corporate-Governments, Inc. (all 50 of them) that with the belief that all American-Civilians are a Corporation, Incorporated or are made into Businesses and are forced into participating in their form of "Organized-Crime-Practices" that forces the American-Civilian to pay FEES, PENALTIES or FINES by using their "Debt for Debt-Policy".

DECLARATION OF INTENTIONS:

I, Bradley – Jefferson: [Franks], an American live-born-individual, hereby: Rescind, Reject, Revoke, Cancel, Suspend-Indefinitely any and all Federal/Federal INC.; Federal-State/State INC.; County/County INC.; City/City INC.; Municipality/Municipality Inc.; contracts that they believe they have over my individual-live-personage.

I, Bradley – Jefferson: [Franks] also hereby, Rescind, Revoke, Cancel, and Suspend-Indefinitely any and ALL Signatures/Autographs affixed on any "Contracts" that have been produced by said above-perpetrators for the reasons of "LACK OF FULL-DISCLOSURE", "BREACH OF CONTRACT", and "FRAUDULENT-CLAIMS" this includes and is not limited to "Implied Contracts".

As an American-Civilian, I, Bradley – Jefferson: [Franks] have the RIGHT (by the "CONSTITUTION" which 'sets limits' for what the Fictitious-United-States-Corporate-Government can do legally and by the "Bill Of Rights as they do apply to American-Civilians directly) for any contract for my "LIFE, LIBERTY, and PURSUIT OF HAPPINESS" without interference, negligence, force, coercion, blackmail, threats or any other Organized-Criminal-Practices brought-against or applied-against me through what the Government, Inc. calls "license, permits, fees or demands".

Any deviation of this "Public-Announcement" from any FEDERAL, Inc., STATE, Inc., COUNTY, Inc. or CITY, Inc. ADMINISTRATION will be considered an ACT OF WAR and will be subject to Penalties and Fines for "BREACH OF CONTRACT" under the guise of "DOING-BUSINESS".

All of the above is TRUE and CORRECT! So, help me GOD!

By my-own electronic-autograph: Bradley - Jefferson: [Franks];

Date: February 12, 2018.

PLEASE-NOTE: For those readers who want to get out of the Yoke of Slavery, being-Indentured, or having to comply with the United-State-Corporate-Government, Inc. use this document for your intentions. You can make changes as necessary that suits your individual-needs.

Now, there is a way to go after these Imposter-Fictitious/Agents and the Fictitious-Agencies of these Fictitious-Subsidiary-Corporate-Governments (all 50 of them) that commit their illegal-acts against American-Civilians that do not have legal-justification, jurisdiction, the RIGHT, Status and Standing, Authority, and Credibility or the correct-contracts signed/autographed by all parties concerned.

All of these Agencies use "Subjugation", "Trickery", "Deceit" and "Threats" to get American-Civilians within their sphere of control.

The consequences for these Corporate-Imposter-Agents and the Fictitious-Corporate-Agencies and the Fictitious-Corporate-Subsidiaries of the Parent-Corporate-United-States-Government will be forcibly Depose[d], Deport[ed] and the loss of their Pensions for life for their wrongs that they commit against any American-Civilian.

One last note about the Electric Companies that are engaged in committing fraud against its customers/clients; All electric companies in the United-States-Fictitious-Government has what is called a BOND or INSURANCE for protection of their equipment that may be or was damaged by situations like Tornados, Blizzards, or Powerful Storms in other words 'Acts of God'. However, there are no-laws to force them into getting a BOND or INSURANCE, but the electric companies pass on the cost to their clients/customers; even when the customers/clients have no-electricity for some time. Their bills will be the same as if they were receiving electricity…this is known as fraud by definition.

For those individual readers of these books or for those undeclared-Fictitious-Agents aka Civil-Servants claim that we are talking without credibility or Conspiracies you would be dead-wrong. All one needs to do is to observe the evidence throughout the books we have written and using their so-called opinionated-evidence. The Court system does not use FACTS only opinions to separate American-Civilians from the Monies we are forced to use through threat, duress, and coercion.

It is our intention to help any Country that hates or greatly dislikes the United-States-Corporate-Government or its Subsidiaries for the destruction for what they are doing by exposing Organized-Criminal Practices under the R. I. C. O. Laws.

These four (4) books that we have written; (Title: Your Day In Court, Using Common Law with Common Sense; Title: ! AT GUN

POINT… Whistle Blowers' Point of View; Title: BREACH OF CONTRACT, What the Government Does NOT want you to know; and this last book) are actual non-fiction/autobiographies that has FACTS and EVIDENCE presented for your observation. We realize that THE-FICTITIOUS-CORPORATE-GOVERNMENT-of-THE-UNITED-STATES-of-AMERICA punishes any and all American-Civilians that exercise their Rights through the use of Opinions, Lies, and False Documentation. We wrote these books in honor of ALL AMERICAN-CIVILIANS who feel that they are the only victims from these Civil-Servant-Imposters and the crooked-Corporate-Government.

We are not by any means Para-Military, Military, or even Civil-Servants (imposters) to take orders from their so-called "Chain of Command". We are NOT at War with any Nation! Just with a Corporate-Government that seems to be under the illusion that they own everything.

Sometimes, American-Civilians have to do what is RIGHT and DAMN the CONSEQUENCES.

This is the end of our FACTS and EVIDENCE and the end of our quest to expose the crimes against us and All American-Civilians. We hope with all this information Americans will fight back and say "NO-MORE". It is difficult to have respect for a Corporate-Government or its Civil-Servants (Imposters) that have no-respect for themselves except for they steal through Cheating, Lying and Stealing through Threat, Duress, Coercion and Color of Law. If American-Civilians started going after these Civil-Servant-Imposters and depose them, deport them and take their Pensions then maybe, just maybe, these imposters will start listening and changes will be made within the Government.

Denialism has become the Norm for people who cannot see with their eyes, hear with their ears or read what is in front of them.

We sincerely hope that these books will illuminate, educate and enlighten ALL American-Civilians for all of our plights and challenges against these HATEFUL, SPITEFUL, and JEALOUS People.

THE END!

www.ingramcontent.com/pod-product-compliance
Lightning Source LLC
Chambersburg PA
CBHW042248040426
42335CB00043B/2869